Ford Super Duty Pick-ups and Excursion Automotive Repair Manual

by Larry Warren and John H Haynes

Member of the Guild of Motoring Writers

Models covered:

Ford Super Duty F-250 and F-350 1999 through 2010
Ford Excursion 2000 through 2005
Does not include F-450 or F-550 models

(36060-10U22-2)

ABCDE
FGHIJ
KLMNO

3

AUTOMOTIVE
PARTS &
ACCESSORIES
ASSOCIATION MEMBER

Haynes Publishing Group
Sparkford Nr Yeovil
Somerset BA22 7JJ England

Haynes North America, Inc
859 Lawrence Drive
Newbury Park
California 91320 USA
www.haynes.com

Acknowledgements

Wiring diagrams provided exclusively for Haynes North America, Inc. by Valley Forge Technical Information Services. Technical writers who contributed to this project include Bob Henderson, Mike Stubblefield, Robert Maddox and John Wegmann.

A book in the Haynes Automotive Repair Manual Series

Printed in Malaysia

ISBN-13: 978-1-56392-856-7
ISBN-10: 1-56392-856-6

Library of Congress Control Number: 2010932179

Contents

Introductory pages

About this manual 0-5
Introduction 0-5
Vehicle identification numbers 0-6
Buying parts 0-8
Maintenance techniques, tools and working facilities 0-8
Jacking and towing 0-14
Booster battery (jump) starting 0-15
Automotive chemicals and lubricants 0-16
Conversion factors 0-17
Safety first! 0-18
Fraction/decimal/millimeter equivalents 0-19
Troubleshooting 0-20

Chapter 1
Tune-up and routine maintenance 1-1

Chapter 2 Part A
Gasoline engines 2A-1

Chapter 2 Part B
Diesel engines 2B-1

Chapter 2 Part C
General engine overhaul procedures 2C-1

Chapter 3
Cooling, heating and air conditioning systems 3-1

Chapter 4 Part A
Fuel and exhaust systems - gasoline engines 4A-1

Chapter 4 Part B
Fuel and exhaust systems - diesel engine 4B-1

Chapter 5
Engine electrical systems 5-1

Chapter 6
Emissions and engine control systems 6-1

Chapter 7 Part A
Manual transaxle 7A-1

Chapter 7 Part B
Automatic transaxle 7B-1

Chapter 7 Part C
Transfer case 7C-1

Chapter 8
Clutch and driveline 8-1

Chapter 9
Brakes 9-1

Chapter 10
Suspension and steering systems 10-1

Chapter 11
Body 11-1

Chapter 12
Chassis electrical system 12-1

Wiring diagrams 12-17

Index IND-1

Haynes photographer, mechanic and author with a 2001 Excursion

About this manual

Its purpose

The purpose of this manual is to help you get the best value from your vehicle. It can do so in several ways. It can help you decide what work must be done, even if you choose to have it done by a dealer service department or a repair shop; it provides information and procedures for routine maintenance and servicing; and it offers diagnostic and repair procedures to follow when trouble occurs.

We hope you use the manual to tackle the work yourself. For many simpler jobs, doing it yourself may be quicker than arranging an appointment to get the vehicle into a shop and making the trips to leave it and pick it up. More importantly, a lot of money can be saved by avoiding the expense the shop must pass on to you to cover its labor and overhead

costs. An added benefit is the sense of satisfaction and accomplishment that you feel after doing the job yourself.

Using the manual

The manual is divided into Chapters. Each Chapter is divided into numbered Sections, which are headed in bold type between horizontal lines. Each Section consists of consecutively numbered paragraphs.

At the beginning of each numbered Section you will be referred to any illustrations which apply to the procedures in that Section. The reference numbers used in illustration captions pinpoint the pertinent Section and the Step within that Section. That is, illustration 3.2 means the illustration refers to Section 3 and Step (or paragraph) 2 within that

Section.

Procedures, once described in the text, are not normally repeated. When it's necessary to refer to another Chapter, the reference will be given as Chapter and Section number. Cross references given without use of the word "Chapter" apply to Sections and/or paragraphs in the same Chapter. For example, "see Section 8" means in the same Chapter.

References to the left or right side of the vehicle assume you are sitting in the driver's seat, facing forward.

Even though we have prepared this manual with extreme care, neither the publisher nor the author can accept responsibility for any errors in, or omissions from, the information given.

NOTE

A **Note** provides information necessary to properly complete a procedure or information which will make the procedure easier to understand.

CAUTION

A **Caution** provides a special procedure or special steps which must be taken while completing the procedure where the Caution is found. Not heeding a Caution can result in damage to the assembly being worked on.

WARNING

A **Warning** provides a special procedure or special steps which must be taken while completing the procedure where the Warning is found. Not heeding a Warning can result in personal injury.

Introduction

These models are available in pick-up and four-door sport utility body styles.

Available engines are 5.4L V8 and 6.8L V10 gasoline models as well as 6.0L, 6.4L and 7.3L turbo diesel V8s. All models are equipped with the On Board Diagnostic Second-Generation (OBD-II) computerized engine management system that controls virtually every aspect of engine operation. OBD-II monitors emissions system components for signs of degradation and engine operation for any malfunction that could affect emissions,

turning on the CHECK ENGINE light if any faults are detected.

Chassis layout is conventional, with the engine mounted at the front and the power being transmitted through a 5- or 6-speed manual or 4-speed automatic transmission and a driveshaft to the solid rear axle. On 4WD models, a transfer case transmits power to a front differential by way of a driveshaft and then to the front wheels through the axles.

Suspension is independent twin I-beam with coil springs in the front on 2WD models

or semi-elliptical leaf springs (2004 and earlier models) or coil springs (2005 and later models) with solid front axle on 4WD models. The rear suspension features semi-elliptical leaf springs. All models use hydraulic shock absorbers at each corner.

The brakes are disc-type on all four wheels, with an Anti-Lock Brake System (ABS) standard on most models.

The power-assisted recirculating ball-type steering gear is mounted on the chassis frame rail to the left of the engine.

Vehicle identification numbers

Modifications are a continuing and unpublicized process in vehicle manufacturing. Since spare parts lists and manuals are compiled on a numerical basis, the individual vehicle numbers are necessary to correctly identify the component required.

The VIN is visible through the windshield on the driver's side

Vehicle Identification Number (VIN)

This very important identification number is stamped on a plate attached to the dashboard inside the windshield on the driver's side of the vehicle (see illustration). The VIN also appears on the Vehicle Certificate of Title and Registration. It contains information such as where and when the vehicle was manufactured, the model year and the body style.

VIN engine and model year codes

Two particularly important pieces of information found in the VIN are the engine code and the model year code. Counting from the left, the engine code letter designation is the 8th digit and the model year code letter designation is the 10th digit.

On the models covered by this manual the engine codes are:

5	5.4L V8 gasoline
L	5.4L V8 gasoline
P	6.0L V8 turbo diesel
R	6.4L 4V V8 diesel
S	6.8L V10 gasoline
Y	6.8L V10 gasoline
V	6.8L V10 gasoline (3 valve)
F	7.3L V8 turbo diesel

On the models covered by this manual the model year codes are:

X	1999
Y	2000
1	2001
2	2002
3	2003
4	2004
5	2005
6	2006
7	2007
8	2008
9	2009
A	2010

Vehicle Certification Label

The Vehicle Certification Label is attached to the driver's side door pillar (see illustration). Information on this label includes the name of the manufacturer, the month and year of production, as well as information on the options with which it is equipped. This label is especially useful for matching the color and type of paint for repair work.

Engine identification number

Labels containing the engine code, engine number and build date can be found on the valve cover (see illustration). The engine number is also stamped onto a machined pad on the external surface of the engine block.

The vehicle certification label is affixed to the driver's side door pillar

The engine identification label is affixed to the valve cover

The manual transmission identification label is affixed to the side of the transmission case

The automatic transmission identification tag (arrow) is located on the left (driver's) side of the case

Manual transmission identification number

The manual transmission ID number is on a label affixed to the side of the case **(see illustration)**.

Automatic transmission identification number

The automatic transmission ID number is on a label affixed to the left side of the case **(see illustration)**.

Transfer case identification number

The transfer case ID number is stamped on a tag which is fastened to the rear cover **(see illustration)**.

Differential identification number

The differential ID number is stamped on a tag which is bolted to the differential cover **(see illustration)**.

Vehicle Emissions Control Information label

This label is found in the engine compartment. See Chapter 6 for more information on this label.

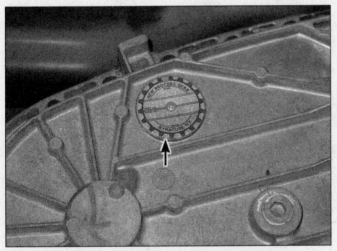

The transfer case identification tag location (arrow)

The differential identification tag is bolted to the differential cover

Buying parts

Replacement parts are available from many sources, which generally fall into one of two categories - authorized dealer parts departments and independent retail auto parts stores. Our advice concerning these parts is as follows:

Retail auto parts stores: Good auto parts stores will stock frequently needed components which wear out relatively fast, such as clutch components, exhaust systems, brake parts, tune-up parts, etc. These stores often supply new or reconditioned parts on an exchange basis, which can save a considerable amount of money. Discount auto parts stores are often very good places to buy materials and parts needed for general vehicle maintenance such as oil, grease, filters, spark plugs, belts, touch-up paint, bulbs, etc. They also usually sell tools and general accessories, have convenient hours, charge lower prices and can often be found not far from home.

Authorized dealer parts department: This is the best source for parts which are unique to the vehicle and not generally available elsewhere (such as major engine parts, transmission parts, trim pieces, etc.).

Warranty information: If the vehicle is still covered under warranty, be sure that any replacement parts purchased - regardless of the source - do not invalidate the warranty!

To be sure of obtaining the correct parts, have engine and chassis numbers available and, if possible, take the old parts along for positive identification.

Maintenance techniques, tools and working facilities

Maintenance techniques

There are a number of techniques involved in maintenance and repair that will be referred to throughout this manual. Application of these techniques will enable the home mechanic to be more efficient, better organized and capable of performing the various tasks properly, which will ensure that the repair job is thorough and complete.

Fasteners

Fasteners are nuts, bolts, studs and screws used to hold two or more parts together. There are a few things to keep in mind when working with fasteners. Almost all of them use a locking device of some type, either a lockwasher, locknut, locking tab or thread adhesive. All threaded fasteners should be clean and straight, with undamaged threads and undamaged corners on the hex head where the wrench fits. Develop the habit of replacing all damaged nuts and bolts with new ones. Special locknuts with nylon or fiber inserts can only be used once. If they are removed, they lose their locking ability and must be replaced with new ones.

Rusted nuts and bolts should be treated with a penetrating fluid to ease removal and prevent breakage. Some mechanics use turpentine in a spout-type oil can, which works quite well. After applying the rust penetrant, let it work for a few minutes before trying to loosen the nut or bolt. Badly rusted fasteners may have to be chiseled or sawed off or removed with a special nut breaker, available at tool stores.

If a bolt or stud breaks off in an assembly, it can be drilled and removed with a special tool commonly available for this purpose. Most automotive machine shops can perform this task, as well as other repair procedures, such as the repair of threaded holes that have been stripped out.

Flat washers and lockwashers, when removed from an assembly, should always be replaced exactly as removed. Replace any damaged washers with new ones. Never use a lockwasher on any soft metal surface (such as aluminum), thin sheet metal or plastic.

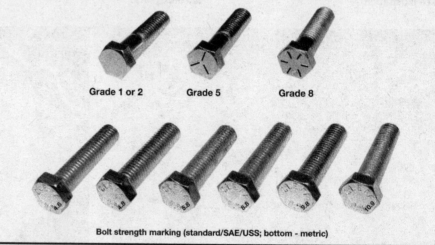

Grade 1 or 2   Grade 5   Grade 8

Bolt strength marking (standard/SAE/USS; bottom - metric)

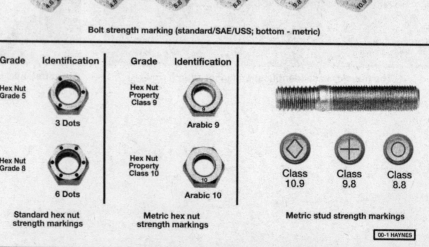

Grade	Identification
Hex Nut Grade 5	3 Dots
Hex Nut Grade 8	6 Dots

Standard hex nut strength markings

Grade	Identification
Hex Nut Property Class 9	Arabic 9
Hex Nut Property Class 10	Arabic 10

Metric hex nut strength markings

Class 10.9   Class 9.8   Class 8.8

Metric stud strength markings

00-1 HAYNES

Fastener sizes

For a number of reasons, automobile manufacturers are making wider and wider use of metric fasteners. Therefore, it is important to be able to tell the difference between standard (sometimes called U.S. or SAE) and metric hardware, since they cannot be interchanged.

All bolts, whether standard or metric, are sized according to diameter, thread pitch and length. For example, a standard 1/2 - 13 x 1 bolt is 1/2 inch in diameter, has 13 threads per inch and is 1 inch long. An M12 - 1.75 x 25 metric bolt is 12 mm in diameter, has a thread pitch of 1.75 mm (the distance between threads) and is 25 mm long. The two bolts are nearly identical, and easily confused, but they are not interchangeable.

In addition to the differences in diameter, thread pitch and length, metric and standard bolts can also be distinguished by examining the bolt heads. To begin with, the distance across the flats on a standard bolt head is measured in inches, while the same dimension on a metric bolt is sized in millimeters (the same is true for nuts). As a result, a standard wrench should not be used on a metric bolt and a metric wrench should not be used on a standard bolt. Also, most standard bolts have slashes radiating out from the center of the head to denote the grade or strength of the bolt, which is an indication of the amount of torque that can be applied to it. The greater the number of slashes, the greater the strength of the bolt. Grades 0 through 5 are commonly used on automobiles. Metric bolts have a property class (grade) number, rather than a slash, molded into their heads to indicate bolt strength. In this case, the higher the number, the stronger the bolt. Property class numbers 8.8, 9.8 and 10.9 are commonly used on automobiles.

Strength markings can also be used to distinguish standard hex nuts from metric hex nuts. Many standard nuts have dots stamped into one side, while metric nuts are marked with a number. The greater the number of dots, or the higher the number, the greater the strength of the nut.

Metric studs are also marked on their ends according to property class (grade). Larger studs are numbered (the same as metric bolts), while smaller studs carry a geometric code to denote grade.

It should be noted that many fasteners, especially Grades 0 through 2, have no distinguishing marks on them. When such is the case, the only way to determine whether it is standard or metric is to measure the thread pitch or compare it to a known fastener of the same size.

Standard fasteners are often referred to as SAE, as opposed to metric. However, it should be noted that SAE technically refers to a non-metric fine thread fastener only. Coarse thread non-metric fasteners are referred to as USS sizes.

Since fasteners of the same size (both standard and metric) may have different strength ratings, be sure to reinstall any bolts,

Metric thread sizes	Ft-lbs	Nm
M-6	6 to 9	9 to 12
M-8	14 to 21	19 to 28
M-10	28 to 40	38 to 54
M-12	50 to 71	68 to 96
M-14	80 to 140	109 to 154

Pipe thread sizes		
1/8	5 to 8	7 to 10
1/4	12 to 18	17 to 24
3/8	22 to 33	30 to 44
1/2	25 to 35	34 to 47

U.S. thread sizes		
1/4 - 20	6 to 9	9 to 12
5/16 - 18	12 to 18	17 to 24
5/16 - 24	14 to 20	19 to 27
3/8 - 16	22 to 32	30 to 43
3/8 - 24	27 to 38	37 to 51
7/16 - 14	40 to 55	55 to 74
7/16 - 20	40 to 60	55 to 81
1/2 - 13	55 to 80	75 to 108

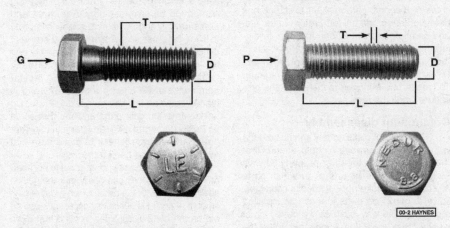

Standard (SAE and USS) bolt dimensions/grade marks

G   Grade marks (bolt strength)
L   Length (in inches)
T   Thread pitch (number of threads per inch)
D   Nominal diameter (in inches)

Metric bolt dimensions/grade marks

P   Property class (bolt strength)
L   Length (in millimeters)
T   Thread pitch (distance between threads in millimeters)
D   Diameter

studs or nuts removed from your vehicle in their original locations. Also, when replacing a fastener with a new one, make sure that the new one has a strength rating equal to or greater than the original.

Tightening sequences and procedures

Most threaded fasteners should be tightened to a specific torque value (torque is the twisting force applied to a threaded component such as a nut or bolt). Overtightening the fastener can weaken it and cause it to break, while undertightening can cause it to eventually come loose. Bolts, screws and studs, depending on the material they are made of and their thread diameters, have specific torque values, many of which are noted in the Specifications at the beginning of each Chapter. Be sure to follow the torque recommendations closely. For fasteners not assigned a specific torque, a general torque value chart is presented here as a guide. These torque values are for dry (unlubricated) fasteners threaded into steel or cast iron (not aluminum). As was previously mentioned, the size and grade of a fastener determine the amount of torque that can safely be applied to it. The figures listed here are approximate for Grade 2 and Grade 3 fasteners. Higher grades can tolerate higher torque values.

Fasteners laid out in a pattern, such as cylinder head bolts, oil pan bolts, differential cover bolts, etc., must be loosened or tightened in sequence to avoid warping the com-

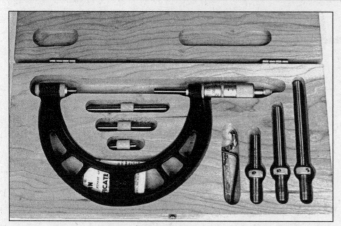

Micrometer set

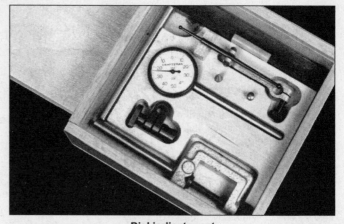

Dial indicator set

ponent. This sequence will normally be shown in the appropriate Chapter. If a specific pattern is not given, the following procedures can be used to prevent warping.

Initially, the bolts or nuts should be assembled finger-tight only. Next, they should be tightened one full turn each, in a criss-cross or diagonal pattern. After each one has been tightened one full turn, return to the first one and tighten them all one-half turn, following the same pattern. Finally, tighten each of them one-quarter turn at a time until each fastener has been tightened to the proper torque. To loosen and remove the fasteners, the procedure would be reversed.

Component disassembly

Component disassembly should be done with care and purpose to help ensure that the parts go back together properly. Always keep track of the sequence in which parts are removed. Make note of special characteristics or marks on parts that can be installed more than one way, such as a grooved thrust washer on a shaft. It is a good idea to lay the disassembled parts out on a clean surface in the order that they were removed. It may also be helpful to make sketches or take instant photos of components before removal.

When removing fasteners from a component, keep track of their locations. Sometimes threading a bolt back in a part, or putting the washers and nut back on a stud, can prevent mix-ups later. If nuts and bolts cannot be returned to their original locations, they should be kept in a compartmented box or a series of small boxes. A cupcake or muffin tin is ideal for this purpose, since each cavity can hold the bolts and nuts from a particular area (i.e. oil pan bolts, valve cover bolts, engine mount bolts, etc.). A pan of this type is especially helpful when working on assemblies with very small parts, such as the carburetor, alternator, valve train or interior dash and trim pieces. The cavities can be marked with paint or tape to identify the contents.

Whenever wiring looms, harnesses or connectors are separated, it is a good idea to identify the two halves with numbered pieces of masking tape so they can be easily reconnected.

Gasket sealing surfaces

Throughout any vehicle, gaskets are used to seal the mating surfaces between two parts and keep lubricants, fluids, vacuum or pressure contained in an assembly.

Many times these gaskets are coated with a liquid or paste-type gasket sealing compound before assembly. Age, heat and pressure can sometimes cause the two parts to stick together so tightly that they are very difficult to separate. Often, the assembly can be loosened by striking it with a soft-face hammer near the mating surfaces. A regular hammer can be used if a block of wood is placed between the hammer and the part. Do not hammer on cast parts or parts that could be easily damaged. With any particularly stubborn part, always recheck to make sure that every fastener has been removed.

Avoid using a screwdriver or bar to pry apart an assembly, as they can easily mar the gasket sealing surfaces of the parts, which must remain smooth. If prying is absolutely necessary, use an old broom handle, but keep in mind that extra clean up will be necessary if the wood splinters.

After the parts are separated, the old gasket must be carefully scraped off and the gasket surfaces cleaned. Stubborn gasket material can be soaked with rust penetrant or treated with a special chemical to soften it so it can be easily scraped off. **Caution:** *Never use gasket removal solutions or caustic chemicals on plastic or other composite components.* A scraper can be fashioned from a piece of copper tubing by flattening and sharpening one end. Copper is recommended because it is usually softer than the surfaces to be scraped, which reduces the chance of gouging the part. Some gaskets can be removed with a wire brush, but regardless of the method used, the mating surfaces must be left clean and smooth. If for some reason the gasket surface is gouged, then a gasket sealer thick enough to fill scratches will have to be used during reassembly of the components. For most applications, a non-drying (or semi-drying) gasket sealer should be used.

Hose removal tips

Warning: *If the vehicle is equipped with air conditioning, do not disconnect any of the A/C*

hoses without first having the system depressurized by a dealer service department or a service station.

Hose removal precautions closely parallel gasket removal precautions. Avoid scratching or gouging the surface that the hose mates against or the connection may leak. This is especially true for radiator hoses. Because of various chemical reactions, the rubber in hoses can bond itself to the metal spigot that the hose fits over. To remove a hose, first loosen the hose clamps that secure it to the spigot. Then, with slip-joint pliers, grab the hose at the clamp and rotate it around the spigot. Work it back and forth until it is completely free, then pull it off. Silicone or other lubricants will ease removal if they can be applied between the hose and the outside of the spigot. Apply the same lubricant to the inside of the hose and the outside of the spigot to simplify installation.

As a last resort (and if the hose is to be replaced with a new one anyway), the rubber can be slit with a knife and the hose peeled from the spigot. If this must be done, be careful that the metal connection is not damaged.

If a hose clamp is broken or damaged, do not reuse it. Wire-type clamps usually weaken with age, so it is a good idea to replace them with screw-type clamps whenever a hose is removed.

Tools

A selection of good tools is a basic requirement for anyone who plans to maintain and repair his or her own vehicle. For the owner who has few tools, the initial investment might seem high, but when compared to the spiraling costs of professional auto maintenance and repair, it is a wise one.

To help the owner decide which tools are needed to perform the tasks detailed in this manual, the following tool lists are offered: *Maintenance and minor repair, Repair/overhaul* and *Special.*

The newcomer to practical mechanics should start off with the *maintenance and minor repair* tool kit, which is adequate for the simpler jobs performed on a vehicle. Then, as confidence and experience grow, the owner can tackle more difficult tasks, buying additional tools as they are needed. Eventually the

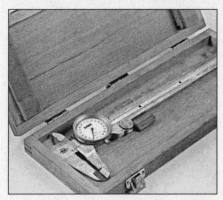

Dial caliper

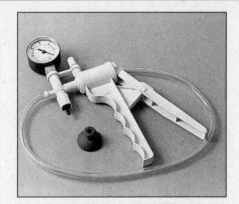

Hand-operated vacuum pump

Timing light

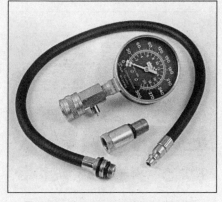

Compression gauge with spark plug hole adapter

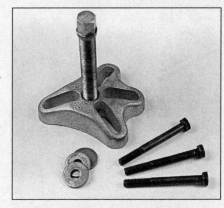

Damper/steering wheel puller

General purpose puller

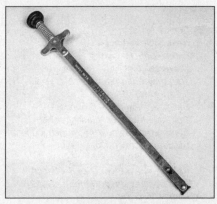

Hydraulic lifter removal tool

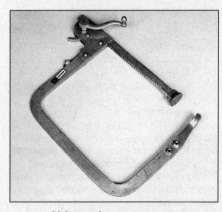

Valve spring compressor

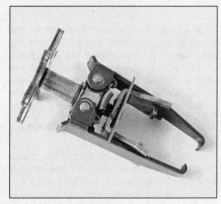

Valve spring compressor

Ridge reamer

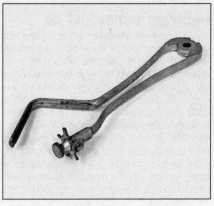

Piston ring groove cleaning tool

Ring removal/installation tool

Ring compressor

Cylinder hone

Brake hold-down spring tool

Torque angle gauge

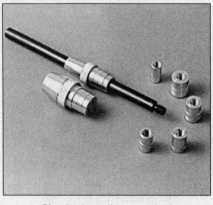

Clutch plate alignment tool

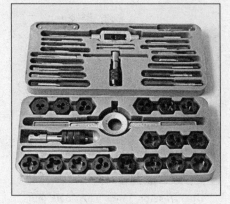

Tap and die set

basic kit will be expanded into the *repair and overhaul* tool set. Over a period of time, the experienced do-it-yourselfer will assemble a tool set complete enough for most repair and overhaul procedures and will add tools from the special category when it is felt that the expense is justified by the frequency of use.

Maintenance and minor repair tool kit

The tools in this list should be considered the minimum required for performance of routine maintenance, servicing and minor repair work. We recommend the purchase of combination wrenches (box-end and open-end combined in one wrench). While more expensive than open end wrenches, they offer the advantages of both types of wrench.

Combination wrench set (1/4-inch to 1 inch or 6 mm to 19 mm)
Adjustable wrench, 8 inch
Spark plug wrench with rubber insert
Spark plug gap adjusting tool
Feeler gauge set
Brake bleeder wrench
Standard screwdriver (5/16-inch x 6 inch)
Phillips screwdriver (No. 2 x 6 inch)
Combination pliers - 6 inch
Hacksaw and assortment of blades
Tire pressure gauge
Grease gun
Oil can

Fine emery cloth
Wire brush
Battery post and cable cleaning tool
Oil filter wrench
Funnel (medium size)
Safety goggles
Jackstands (2)
Drain pan

Note: *If basic tune-ups are going to be part of routine maintenance, it will be necessary to purchase a good quality stroboscopic timing light and combination tachometer/dwell meter. Although they are included in the list of special tools, it is mentioned here because they are absolutely necessary for tuning most vehicles properly.*

Repair and overhaul tool set

These tools are essential for anyone who plans to perform major repairs and are in addition to those in the maintenance and minor repair tool kit. Included is a comprehensive set of sockets which, though expensive, are invaluable because of their versatility, especially when various extensions and drives are available. We recommend the 1/2-inch drive over the 3/8-inch drive. Although the larger drive is bulky and more expensive, it has the capacity of accepting a very wide range of large sockets. Ideally, however, the mechanic should have a 3/8-inch drive set and a 1/2-inch drive set.

Socket set(s)
Reversible ratchet
Extension - 10 inch
Universal joint
Torque wrench (same size drive as sockets)
Ball peen hammer - 8 ounce
Soft-face hammer (plastic/rubber)
Standard screwdriver (1/4-inch x 6 inch)
Standard screwdriver (stubby - 5/16-inch)
Phillips screwdriver (No. 3 x 8 inch)
Phillips screwdriver (stubby - No. 2)
Pliers - vise grip
Pliers - lineman's
Pliers - needle nose
Pliers - snap-ring (internal and external)
Cold chisel - 1/2-inch
Scribe
Scraper (made from flattened copper tubing)
Centerpunch
Pin punches (1/16, 1/8, 3/16-inch)
Steel rule/straightedge - 12 inch
Allen wrench set (1/8 to 3/8-inch or 4 mm to 10 mm)
A selection of files
Wire brush (large)
Jackstands (second set)
Jack (scissor or hydraulic type)

Note: *Another tool which is often useful is an electric drill with a chuck capacity of 3/8-inch and a set of good quality drill bits.*

Special tools

The tools in this list include those which are not used regularly, are expensive to buy, or which need to be used in accordance with their manufacturer's instructions. Unless these tools will be used frequently, it is not very economical to purchase many of them. A consideration would be to split the cost and use between yourself and a friend or friends. In addition, most of these tools can be obtained from a tool rental shop on a temporary basis.

This list primarily contains only those tools and instruments widely available to the public, and not those special tools produced by the vehicle manufacturer for distribution to dealer service departments. Occasionally, references to the manufacturer's special tools are included in the text of this manual. Generally, an alternative method of doing the job without the special tool is offered. However, sometimes there is no alternative to their use. Where this is the case, and the tool cannot be purchased or borrowed, the work should be turned over to the dealer service department or an automotive repair shop.

> *Valve spring compressor*
> *Piston ring groove cleaning tool*
> *Piston ring compressor*
> *Piston ring installation tool*
> *Cylinder compression gauge*
> *Cylinder ridge reamer*
> *Cylinder surfacing hone*
> *Cylinder bore gauge*
> *Micrometers and/or dial calipers*
> *Hydraulic lifter removal tool*
> *Balljoint separator*
> *Universal-type puller*
> *Impact screwdriver*
> *Dial indicator set*
> *Stroboscopic timing light (inductive pick-up)*
> *Hand operated vacuum/pressure pump*
> *Tachometer/dwell meter*
> *Universal electrical multimeter*
> *Cable hoist*
> *Brake spring removal and installation tools*
> *Floor jack*

Buying tools

For the do-it-yourselfer who is just starting to get involved in vehicle maintenance and repair, there are a number of options available when purchasing tools. If maintenance and minor repair is the extent of the work to be done, the purchase of individual tools is satisfactory. If, on the other hand, extensive work is planned, it would be a good idea to purchase a modest tool set from one of the large retail chain stores. A set can usually be bought at a substantial savings over the individual tool prices, and they often come with a tool box. As additional tools are needed, add-on sets, individual tools and a larger tool box can be purchased to expand the tool selection. Building a tool set gradually allows the cost of the tools to be spread over a longer period of time and gives the mechanic the freedom to choose only those tools that will actually be used.

Tool stores will often be the only source of some of the special tools that are needed, but regardless of where tools are bought, try to avoid cheap ones, especially when buying screwdrivers and sockets, because they won't last very long. The expense involved in replacing cheap tools will eventually be greater than the initial cost of quality tools.

Care and maintenance of tools

Good tools are expensive, so it makes sense to treat them with respect. Keep them clean and in usable condition and store them properly when not in use. Always wipe off any dirt, grease or metal chips before putting them away. Never leave tools lying around in the work area. Upon completion of a job, always check closely under the hood for tools that may have been left there so they won't get lost during a test drive.

Some tools, such as screwdrivers, pliers, wrenches and sockets, can be hung on a panel mounted on the garage or workshop wall, while others should be kept in a tool box or tray. Measuring instruments, gauges, meters, etc. must be carefully stored where they cannot be damaged by weather or impact from other tools.

When tools are used with care and stored properly, they will last a very long time. Even with the best of care, though, tools will wear out if used frequently. When a tool is damaged or worn out, replace it. Subsequent jobs will be safer and more enjoyable if you do.

How to repair damaged threads

Sometimes, the internal threads of a nut or bolt hole can become stripped, usually from overtightening. Stripping threads is an all-too-common occurrence, especially when working with aluminum parts, because aluminum is so soft that it easily strips out.

Usually, external or internal threads are only partially stripped. After they've been cleaned up with a tap or die, they'll still work. Sometimes, however, threads are badly damaged. When this happens, you've got three choices:

1) *Drill and tap the hole to the next suitable oversize and install a larger diameter bolt, screw or stud.*
2) *Drill and tap the hole to accept a threaded plug, then drill and tap the plug to the original screw size. You can also buy a plug already threaded to the original size. Then you simply drill a hole to the specified size, then run the threaded plug into the hole with a bolt and jam nut. Once the plug is fully seated, remove the jam nut and bolt.*
3) *The third method uses a patented thread repair kit like Heli-Coil or Slimsert. These easy-to-use kits are designed to repair damaged threads in straight-through holes and blind holes. Both are available as kits which can handle a variety of sizes and thread patterns. Drill the hole, then tap it with the special included tap. Install the Heli-Coil and the hole is back to its original diameter and thread pitch.*

Regardless of which method you use, be sure to proceed calmly and carefully. A little impatience or carelessness during one of these relatively simple procedures can ruin your whole day's work and cost you a bundle if you wreck an expensive part.

Working facilities

Not to be overlooked when discussing tools is the workshop. If anything more than routine maintenance is to be carried out, some sort of suitable work area is essential.

It is understood, and appreciated, that many home mechanics do not have a good workshop or garage available, and end up removing an engine or doing major repairs outside. It is recommended, however, that the overhaul or repair be completed under the cover of a roof.

A clean, flat workbench or table of comfortable working height is an absolute necessity. The workbench should be equipped with a vise that has a jaw opening of at least four inches.

As mentioned previously, some clean, dry storage space is also required for tools, as well as the lubricants, fluids, cleaning solvents, etc. which soon become necessary.

Sometimes waste oil and fluids, drained from the engine or cooling system during normal maintenance or repairs, present a disposal problem. To avoid pouring them on the ground or into a sewage system, pour the used fluids into large containers, seal them with caps and take them to an authorized disposal site or recycling center. Plastic jugs, such as old antifreeze containers, are ideal for this purpose.

Always keep a supply of old newspapers and clean rags available. Old towels are excellent for mopping up spills. Many mechanics use rolls of paper towels for most work because they are readily available and disposable. To help keep the area under the vehicle clean, a large cardboard box can be cut open and flattened to protect the garage or shop floor.

Whenever working over a painted surface, such as when leaning over a fender to service something under the hood, always cover it with an old blanket or bedspread to protect the finish. Vinyl covered pads, made especially for this purpose, are available at auto parts stores.

Jacking and towing

Jacking

Warning: *The jack supplied with the vehicle should only be used for changing a tire or placing jackstands under the frame. Never work under the vehicle or start the engine while this jack is being used as the only means of support.*

The vehicle should be on level ground. Place the shift lever in Park, if you have an automatic, or Reverse if you have a manual transmission. Block the wheel diagonally opposite the wheel being changed. Set the parking brake.

Remove the spare tire and jack from stowage. Remove the wheel cover and trim ring (if so equipped) with the tapered end of the lug nut wrench by inserting and twisting the handle and then prying against the back of the wheel cover. Loosen the wheel lug nuts

about 1/4-to-1/2 turn each.

Place the jack under the vehicle in the indicated position **(see illustrations)**. Turn the jack handle clockwise until the tire clears the ground. Remove the lug nuts and pull the wheel off. Replace it with the spare.

Install the lug nuts with the beveled edges facing in. Tighten them snugly. Don't attempt to tighten them completely until the vehicle is lowered or it could slip off the jack. Turn the jack handle counterclockwise to lower the vehicle. Remove the jack and tighten the lug nuts in a diagonal pattern.

Install the cover and be sure it's snapped into place all the way around.

Stow the tire, jack and wrench. Unblock the wheels.

Towing

We recommend these vehicles (except

four-wheel drive models) be towed from the rear, with the rear wheels off the ground. Vehicles with four-wheel drive must only be towed with all four wheels off the ground.

Equipment specifically designed for towing should be used. It must be attached to the main structural members of the vehicle, not the bumpers or brackets.

Safety is a major consideration when towing and all applicable state and local laws must be obeyed. A safety chain must be used at all times.

The parking brake must be released and the transmission must be in Neutral. The steering must be unlocked (ignition switch in the Off position). Remember that power steering and power brakes won't work with the engine off.

Left (driver's side) front jacking location - 4WD models (the jack head must engage the notch in the differential housing)

Right (passenger's side) front jacking location - 4WD models

Front jacking locations - 2WD models

Rear jacking location - all models

Booster battery (jump) starting

Observe these precautions when using a booster battery to start a vehicle:

a) *Before connecting the booster battery, make sure the ignition switch is in the Off position.*
b) *Turn off the lights, heater and other electrical loads.*
c) *Your eyes should be shielded. Safety goggles are a good idea.*
d) *Make sure the booster battery is the same voltage as the dead one in the vehicle.*
e) *The two vehicles MUST NOT TOUCH each other!*
f) *Make sure the transaxle is in Neutral (manual) or Park (automatic).*
g) *If the booster battery is not a maintenance-free type, remove the vent caps and lay a cloth over the vent holes.*

Connect the red jumper cable to the positive (+) terminals of each battery **(see illustration)**.

Connect one end of the black jumper cable to the negative (-) terminal of the booster battery. The other end of this cable should be connected to a good ground on the vehicle to be started, such as a bolt or bracket on the body.

Start the engine using the booster battery, then, with the engine running at idle speed, disconnect the jumper cables in the reverse order of connection.

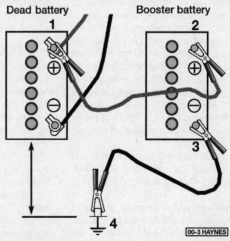

Make the booster battery cable connections in the numerical order shown (note that the negative cable of the booster battery is NOT attached to the negative terminal of the dead battery)

Automotive chemicals and lubricants

A number of automotive chemicals and lubricants are available for use during vehicle maintenance and repair. They include a wide variety of products ranging from cleaning solvents and degreasers to lubricants and protective sprays for rubber, plastic and vinyl.

Cleaners

Carburetor cleaner and choke cleaner is a strong solvent for gum, varnish and carbon. Most carburetor cleaners leave a dry-type lubricant film which will not harden or gum up. Because of this film it is not recommended for use on electrical components.

Brake system cleaner is used to remove brake dust, grease and brake fluid from the brake system, where clean surfaces are absolutely necessary. It leaves no residue and often eliminates brake squeal caused by contaminants.

Electrical cleaner removes oxidation, corrosion and carbon deposits from electrical contacts, restoring full current flow. It can also be used to clean spark plugs, carburetor jets, voltage regulators and other parts where an oil-free surface is desired.

Demoisturants remove water and moisture from electrical components such as alternators, voltage regulators, electrical connectors and fuse blocks. They are non-conductive and non-corrosive.

Degreasers are heavy-duty solvents used to remove grease from the outside of the engine and from chassis components. They can be sprayed or brushed on and, depending on the type, are rinsed off either with water or solvent.

Lubricants

Motor oil is the lubricant formulated for use in engines. It normally contains a wide variety of additives to prevent corrosion and reduce foaming and wear. Motor oil comes in various weights (viscosity ratings) from 0 to 50. The recommended weight of the oil depends on the season, temperature and the demands on the engine. Light oil is used in cold climates and under light load conditions. Heavy oil is used in hot climates and where high loads are encountered. Multi-viscosity oils are designed to have characteristics of both light and heavy oils and are available in a number of weights from 0W-20 to 20W-50.

Gear oil is designed to be used in differentials, manual transmissions and other areas where high-temperature lubrication is required.

Chassis and wheel bearing grease is a heavy grease used where increased loads and friction are encountered, such as for wheel bearings, balljoints, tie-rod ends and universal joints.

High-temperature wheel bearing grease is designed to withstand the extreme temperatures encountered by wheel bearings in disc brake equipped vehicles. It usually contains molybdenum disulfide (moly), which is a dry-type lubricant.

White grease is a heavy grease for metal-to-metal applications where water is a problem. White grease stays soft under both low and high temperatures (usually from -100 to +190-degrees F), and will not wash off or dilute in the presence of water.

Assembly lube is a special extreme pressure lubricant, usually containing moly, used to lubricate high-load parts (such as main and rod bearings and cam lobes) for initial start-up of a new engine. The assembly lube lubricates the parts without being squeezed out or washed away until the engine oiling system begins to function.

Silicone lubricants are used to protect rubber, plastic, vinyl and nylon parts.

Graphite lubricants are used where oils cannot be used due to contamination problems, such as in locks. The dry graphite will lubricate metal parts while remaining uncontaminated by dirt, water, oil or acids. It is electrically conductive and will not foul electrical contacts in locks such as the ignition switch.

Moly penetrants loosen and lubricate frozen, rusted and corroded fasteners and prevent future rusting or freezing.

Heat-sink grease is a special electrically non-conductive grease that is used for mounting electronic ignition modules where it is essential that heat is transferred away from the module.

Sealants

RTV sealant is one of the most widely used gasket compounds. Made from silicone, RTV is air curing, it seals, bonds, waterproofs, fills surface irregularities, remains flexible, doesn't shrink, is relatively easy to remove, and is used as a supplementary sealer with almost all low and medium temperature gaskets.

Anaerobic sealant is much like RTV in that it can be used either to seal gaskets or to form gaskets by itself. It remains flexible, is solvent resistant and fills surface imperfections. The difference between an anaerobic sealant and an RTV-type sealant is in the curing. RTV cures when exposed to air, while an anaerobic sealant cures only in the absence of air. This means that an anaerobic sealant cures only after the assembly of parts, sealing them together.

Thread and pipe sealant is used for sealing hydraulic and pneumatic fittings and vacuum lines. It is usually made from a Teflon compound, and comes in a spray, a paint-on liquid and as a wrap-around tape.

Chemicals

Anti-seize compound prevents seizing, galling, cold welding, rust and corrosion in fasteners. High-temperature ant-seize, usually made with copper and graphite lubricants, is used for exhaust system and exhaust manifold bolts.

Anaerobic locking compounds are used to keep fasteners from vibrating or working loose and cure only after installation, in the absence of air. Medium strength locking compound is used for small nuts, bolts and screws that may be removed later. High-strength locking compound is for large nuts, bolts and studs which aren't removed on a regular basis.

Oil additives range from viscosity index improvers to chemical treatments that claim to reduce internal engine friction. It should be noted that most oil manufacturers caution against using additives with their oils.

Gas additives perform several functions, depending on their chemical makeup. They usually contain solvents that help dissolve gum and varnish that build up on carburetor, fuel injection and intake parts. They also serve to break down carbon deposits that form on the inside surfaces of the combustion chambers. Some additives contain upper cylinder lubricants for valves and piston rings, and others contain chemicals to remove condensation from the gas tank.

Miscellaneous

Brake fluid is specially formulated hydraulic fluid that can withstand the heat and pressure encountered in brake systems. Care must be taken so this fluid does not come in contact with painted surfaces or plastics. An opened container should always be resealed to prevent contamination by water or dirt.

Weatherstrip adhesive is used to bond weatherstripping around doors, windows and trunk lids. It is sometimes used to attach trim pieces.

Undercoating is a petroleum-based, tar-like substance that is designed to protect metal surfaces on the underside of the vehicle from corrosion. It also acts as a sound-deadening agent by insulating the bottom of the vehicle.

Waxes and polishes are used to help protect painted and plated surfaces from the weather. Different types of paint may require the use of different types of wax and polish. Some polishes utilize a chemical or abrasive cleaner to help remove the top layer of oxidized (dull) paint on older vehicles. In recent years many non-wax polishes that contain a wide variety of chemicals such as polymers and silicones have been introduced. These non-wax polishes are usually easier to apply and last longer than conventional waxes and polishes.

Conversion factors

Length (distance)

Inches (in)	X	25.4	= Millimeters (mm)	X 0.0394	= Inches (in)
Feet (ft)	X	0.305	= Meters (m)	X 3.281	= Feet (ft)
Miles	X	1.609	= Kilometers (km)	X 0.621	= Miles

Volume (capacity)

Cubic inches (cu in; in³)	X	16.387	= Cubic centimeters (cc; cm³)	X 0.061	= Cubic inches (cu in; in³)
Imperial pints (Imp pt)	X	0.568	= Liters (l)	X 1.76	= Imperial pints (Imp pt)
Imperial quarts (Imp qt)	X	1.137	= Liters (l)	X 0.88	= Imperial quarts (Imp qt)
Imperial quarts (Imp qt)	X	1.201	= US quarts (US qt)	X 0.833	= Imperial quarts (Imp qt)
US quarts (US qt)	X	0.946	= Liters (l)	X 1.057	= US quarts (US qt)
Imperial gallons (Imp gal)	X	4.546	= Liters (l)	X 0.22	= Imperial gallons (Imp gal)
Imperial gallons (Imp gal)	X	1.201	= US gallons (US gal)	X 0.833	= Imperial gallons (Imp gal)
US gallons (US gal)	X	3.785	= Liters (l)	X 0.264	= US gallons (US gal)

Mass (weight)

Ounces (oz)	X	28.35	= Grams (g)	X 0.035	= Ounces (oz)
Pounds (lb)	X	0.454	= Kilograms (kg)	X 2.205	= Pounds (lb)

Force

Ounces-force (ozf; oz)	X	0.278	= Newtons (N)	X 3.6	= Ounces-force (ozf; oz)
Pounds-force (lbf; lb)	X	4.448	= Newtons (N)	X 0.225	= Pounds-force (lbf; lb)
Newtons (N)	X	0.1	= Kilograms-force (kgf; kg)	X 9.81	= Newtons (N)

Pressure

Pounds-force per square inch (psi; lbf/in²; lb/in²)	X	0.070	= Kilograms-force per square centimeter (kgf/cm²; kg/cm²)	X 14.223	= Pounds-force per square inch (psi; lbf/in²; lb/in²)
Pounds-force per square inch (psi; lbf/in²; lb/in²)	X	0.068	= Atmospheres (atm)	X 14.696	= Pounds-force per square inch (psi; lbf/in²; lb/in²)
Pounds-force per square inch (psi; lbf/in²; lb/in²)	X	0.069	= Bars	X 14.5	= Pounds-force per square inch (psi; lbf/in²; lb/in²)
Pounds-force per square inch (psi; lbf/in²; lb/in²)	X	6.895	= Kilopascals (kPa)	X 0.145	= Pounds-force per square inch (psi; lbf/in²; lb/in²)
Kilopascals (kPa)	X	0.01	= Kilograms-force per square centimeter (kgf/cm²; kg/cm²)	X 98.1	= Kilopascals (kPa)

Torque (moment of force)

Pounds-force inches (lbf in; lb in)	X	1.152	= Kilograms-force centimeter (kgf cm; kg cm)	X 0.868	= Pounds-force inches (lbf in; lb in)
Pounds-force inches (lbf in; lb in)	X	0.113	= Newton meters (Nm)	X 8.85	= Pounds-force inches (lbf in; lb in)
Pounds-force inches (lbf in; lb in)	X	0.083	= Pounds-force feet (lbf ft; lb ft)	X 12	= Pounds-force inches (lbf in; lb in)
Pounds-force feet (lbf ft; lb ft)	X	0.138	= Kilograms-force meters (kgf m; kg m)	X 7.233	= Pounds-force feet (lbf ft; lb ft)
Pounds-force feet (lbf ft; lb ft)	X	1.356	= Newton meters (Nm)	X 0.738	= Pounds-force feet (lbf ft; lb ft)
Newton meters (Nm)	X	0.102	= Kilograms-force meters (kgf m; kg m)	X 9.804	= Newton meters (Nm)

Vacuum

Inches mercury (in. Hg)	X	3.377	= Kilopascals (kPa)	X 0.2961	= Inches mercury
Inches mercury (in. Hg)	X	25.4	= Millimeters mercury (mm Hg)	X 0.0394	= Inches mercury

Power

Horsepower (hp)	X	745.7	= Watts (W)	X 0.0013	= Horsepower (hp)

Velocity (speed)

Miles per hour (miles/hr; mph)	X	1.609	= Kilometers per hour (km/hr; kph)	X 0.621	= Miles per hour (miles/hr; mph)

Fuel consumption*

Miles per gallon, Imperial (mpg)	X	0.354	= Kilometers per liter (km/l)	X 2.825	= Miles per gallon, Imperial (mpg)
Miles per gallon, US (mpg)	X	0.425	= Kilometers per liter (km/l)	X 2.352	= Miles per gallon, US (mpg)

Temperature

Degrees Fahrenheit = (°C x 1.8) + 32

Degrees Celsius (Degrees Centigrade; °C) = (°F - 32) x 0.56

*It is common practice to convert from miles per gallon (mpg) to liters/100 kilometers (l/100km), where mpg (Imperial) x l/100 km = 282 and mpg (US) x l/100 km = 235

Safety first!

Regardless of how enthusiastic you may be about getting on with the job at hand, take the time to ensure that your safety is not jeopardized. A moment's lack of attention can result in an accident, as can failure to observe certain simple safety precautions. The possibility of an accident will always exist, and the following points should not be considered a comprehensive list of all dangers. Rather, they are intended to make you aware of the risks and to encourage a safety conscious approach to all work you carry out on your vehicle.

Essential DOs and DON'Ts

DON'T rely on a jack when working under the vehicle. Always use approved jackstands to support the weight of the vehicle and place them under the recommended lift or support points.

DON'T attempt to loosen extremely tight fasteners (i.e. wheel lug nuts) while the vehicle is on a jack - it may fall.

DON'T start the engine without first making sure that the transmission is in Neutral (or Park where applicable) and the parking brake is set.

DON'T remove the radiator cap from a hot cooling system - let it cool or cover it with a cloth and release the pressure gradually.

DON'T attempt to drain the engine oil until you are sure it has cooled to the point that it will not burn you.

DON'T touch any part of the engine or exhaust system until it has cooled sufficiently to avoid burns.

DON'T siphon toxic liquids such as gasoline, antifreeze and brake fluid by mouth, or allow them to remain on your skin.

DON'T inhale brake lining dust - it is potentially hazardous (see *Asbestos* below).

DON'T allow spilled oil or grease to remain on the floor - wipe it up before someone slips on it.

DON'T use loose fitting wrenches or other tools which may slip and cause injury.

DON'T push on wrenches when loosening or tightening nuts or bolts. Always try to pull the wrench toward you. If the situation calls for pushing the wrench away, push with an open hand to avoid scraped knuckles if the wrench should slip.

DON'T attempt to lift a heavy component alone - get someone to help you.

DON'T *rush or take unsafe shortcuts to finish a job.*

DON'T allow children or animals in or around the vehicle while you are working on it.

DO wear eye protection when using power tools such as a drill, sander, bench grinder, etc. and when working under a vehicle.

DO keep loose clothing and long hair well out of the way of moving parts.

DO make sure that any hoist used has a safe working load rating adequate for the job.

DO get someone to check on you periodically when working alone on a vehicle.

DO carry out work in a logical sequence and make sure that everything is correctly assembled and tightened.

DO keep chemicals and fluids tightly capped and out of the reach of children and pets.

DO remember that your vehicle's safety affects that of yourself and others. If in doubt on any point, get professional advice.

Steering, suspension and brakes

These systems are essential to driving safety, so make sure you have a qualified shop or individual check your work. Also, compressed suspension springs can cause injury if released suddenly - be sure to use a spring compressor.

Airbags

Airbags are explosive devices that can **CAUSE** injury if they deploy while you're working on the vehicle. Follow the manufacturer's instructions to disable the airbag whenever you're working in the vicinity of airbag components.

Asbestos

Certain friction, insulating, sealing, and other products - such as brake linings, brake bands, clutch linings, torque converters, gaskets, etc. - may contain asbestos or other hazardous friction material. Extreme care must be taken to avoid inhalation of dust from such products, since it is hazardous to health. If in doubt, assume that they do contain asbestos.

Fire

Remember at all times that gasoline is highly flammable. Never smoke or have any kind of open flame around when working on a vehicle. But the risk does not end there. A spark caused by an electrical short circuit, by two metal surfaces contacting each other, or even by static electricity built up in your body under certain conditions, can ignite gasoline vapors, which in a confined space are highly explosive. Do not, under any circumstances, use gasoline for cleaning parts. Use an approved safety solvent.

Always disconnect the battery ground (-) cable at the battery before working on any part of the fuel system or electrical system. Never risk spilling fuel on a hot engine or exhaust component. It is strongly recommended that a fire extinguisher suitable for use on fuel and electrical fires be kept handy in the garage or workshop at all times. Never try to extinguish a fuel or electrical fire with water.

Fumes

Certain fumes are highly toxic and can quickly cause unconsciousness and even death if inhaled to any extent. Gasoline vapor falls into this category, as do the vapors from some cleaning solvents. Any draining or pouring of such volatile fluids should be done in a well ventilated area.

When using cleaning fluids and solvents, read the instructions on the container carefully. Never use materials from unmarked containers.

Never run the engine in an enclosed space, such as a garage. Exhaust fumes contain carbon monoxide, which is extremely poisonous. If you need to run the engine, always do so in the open air, or at least have the rear of the vehicle outside the work area.

The battery

Never create a spark or allow a bare light bulb near a battery. They normally give off a certain amount of hydrogen gas, which is highly explosive.

Always disconnect the battery ground (-) cable at the battery before working on the fuel or electrical systems.

If possible, loosen the filler caps or cover when charging the battery from an external source (this does not apply to sealed or maintenance-free batteries). Do not charge at an excessive rate or the battery may burst.

Take care when adding water to a non maintenance-free battery and when carrying a battery. The electrolyte, even when diluted, is very corrosive and should not be allowed to contact clothing or skin.

Always wear eye protection when cleaning the battery to prevent the caustic deposits from entering your eyes.

Household current

When using an electric power tool, inspection light, etc., which operates on household current, always make sure that the tool is correctly connected to its plug and that, where necessary, it is properly grounded. Do not use such items in damp conditions and, again, do not create a spark or apply excessive heat in the vicinity of fuel or fuel vapor.

Secondary ignition system voltage

A severe electric shock can result from touching certain parts of the ignition system (such as the spark plug wires) when the engine is running or being cranked, particularly if components are damp or the insulation is defective. In the case of an electronic ignition system, the secondary system voltage is much higher and could prove fatal.

Hydrofluoric acid

This extremely corrosive acid is formed when certain types of synthetic rubber, found in some O-rings, oil seals, fuel hoses, etc. are exposed to temperatures above 750-degrees F (400-degrees C). The rubber changes into a charred or sticky substance containing the acid. *Once formed, the acid remains dangerous for years. If it gets onto the skin, it may be necessary to amputate the limb concerned.*

When dealing with a vehicle which has suffered a fire, or with components salvaged from such a vehicle, wear protective gloves and discard them after use.

DECIMALS to MILLIMETERS

Decimal	mm	Decimal	mm
0.001	0.0254	0.500	12.7000
0.002	0.0508	0.510	12.9540
0.003	0.0762	0.520	13.2080
0.004	0.1016	0.530	13.4620
0.005	0.1270	0.540	13.7160
0.006	0.1524	0.550	13.9700
0.007	0.1778	0.560	14.2240
0.008	0.2032	0.570	14.4780
0.009	0.2286	0.580	14.7320
		0.590	14.9860
0.010	0.2540		
0.020	0.5080		
0.030	0.7620		
0.040	1.0160	0.600	15.2400
0.050	1.2700	0.610	15.4940
0.060	1.5240	0.620	15.7480
0.070	1.7780	0.630	16.0020
0.080	2.0320	0.640	16.2560
0.090	2.2860	0.650	16.5100
		0.660	16.7640
0.100	2.5400	0.670	17.0180
0.110	2.7940	0.680	17.2720
0.120	3.0480	0.690	17.5260
0.130	3.3020		
0.140	3.5560		
0.150	3.8100	0.700	17.7800
0.160	4.0640	0.710	18.0340
0.170	4.3180	0.720	18.2880
0.180	4.5720	0.730	18.5420
0.190	4.8260	0.740	18.7960
0.200	5.0800	0.750	19.0500
0.210	5.3340	0.760	19.3040
0.220	5.5880	0.770	19.5580
0.230	5.8420	0.780	19.8120
0.240	6.0960	0.790	20.0660
0.250	6.3500		
0.260	6.6040		
0.270	6.8580	0.800	20.3200
0.280	7.1120	0.810	20.5740
0.290	7.3660	0.820	20.8280
		0.830	21.0820
0.300	7.6200	0.840	21.3360
0.310	7.8740	0.850	21.5900
0.320	8.1280	0.860	21.8440
0.330	8.3820	0.870	22.0980
0.340	8.6360	0.880	22.3520
0.350	8.8900	0.890	22.6060
0.360	9.1440		
0.370	9.3980		
0.380	9.6520		
0.390	9.9060	0.900	22.8600
0.400	10.1600	0.910	23.1140
0.410	10.4140	0.920	23.3680
0.420	10.6680	0.930	23.6220
0.430	10.9220	0.940	23.8760
0.440	11.1760	0.950	24.1300
0.450	11.4300	0.960	24.3840
0.460	11.6840	0.970	24.6380
0.470	11.9380	0.980	24.8920
0.480	12.1920	0.990	25.1460
0.490	12.4460	1.000	25.4000

FRACTIONS to DECIMALS to MILLIMETERS

Fraction	Decimal	mm	Fraction	Decimal	mm
1/64	0.0156	0.3969	33/64	0.5156	13.0969
1/32	0.0312	0.7938	17/32	0.5312	13.4938
3/64	0.0469	1.1906	35/64	0.5469	13.8906
1/16	0.0625	1.5875	9/16	0.5625	14.2875
5/64	0.0781	1.9844	37/64	0.5781	14.6844
3/32	0.0938	2.3812	19/32	0.5938	15.0812
7/64	0.1094	2.7781	39/64	0.6094	15.4781
1/8	0.1250	3.1750	5/8	0.6250	15.8750
9/64	0.1406	3.5719	41/64	0.6406	16.2719
5/32	0.1562	3.9688	21/32	0.6562	16.6688
11/64	0.1719	4.3656	43/64	0.6719	17.0656
3/16	0.1875	4.7625	11/16	0.6875	17.4625
13/64	0.2031	5.1594	45/64	0.7031	17.8594
7/32	0.2188	5.5562	23/32	0.7188	18.2562
15/64	0.2344	5.9531	47/64	0.7344	18.6531
1/4	0.2500	6.3500	3/4	0.7500	19.0500
17/64	0.2656	6.7469	49/64	0.7656	19.4469
9/32	0.2812	7.1438	25/32	0.7812	19.8438
19/64	0.2969	7.5406	51/64	0.7969	20.2406
5/16	0.3125	7.9375	13/16	0.8125	20.6375
21/64	0.3281	8.3344	53/64	0.8281	21.0344
11/32	0.3438	8.7312	27/32	0.8438	21.4312
23/64	0.3594	9.1281	55/64	0.8594	21.8281
3/8	0.3750	9.5250	7/8	0.8750	22.2250
25/64	0.3906	9.9219	57/64	0.8906	22.6219
13/32	0.4062	10.3188	29/32	0.9062	23.0188
27/64	0.4219	10.7156	59/64	0.9219	23.4156
7/16	0.4375	11.1125	15/16	0.9375	23.8125
29/64	0.4531	11.5094	61/64	0.9531	24.2094
15/32	0.4688	11.9062	31/32	0.9688	24.6062
31/64	0.4844	12.3031	63/64	0.9844	25.0031
1/2	0.5000	12.7000	1	1.0000	25.4000

Troubleshooting

Contents

Symptom	Section

Engine

Alternator light fails to come on when key is turned on 13
Alternator light stays on 12
Battery will not hold a charge 11
CHECK ENGINE light .... See Chapter 6
Engine backfires 18
Engine diesels (continues to run) after being turned off 21
Engine hard to start when cold 4
Engine hard to start when hot 5
Engine lacks power 17
Engine 'lopes' while idling or idles erratically 8
Engine misses at idle speed 9
Engine misses throughout driving speed range 14
Engine rotates but will not start 2
Engine stalls 16
Engine starts but stops immediately 7
Engine surges while holding accelerator steady 19
Engine will not rotate when attempting to start 1
Excessive fuel consumption 24
Excessively high idle speed 10
Excessive oil consumption 23
Fuel odor 25
Hesitation or stumble during acceleration 15
Low oil pressure 22
Miscellaneous engine noises 26
Pinging or knocking engine sounds when engine
    is under load 20
Starter motor noisy or engages roughly 6
Starter motor operates without turning engine 3

Cooling system

Abnormal coolant loss 31
Corrosion 33
External coolant leakage 29
Internal coolant leakage 30
Overcooling 28
Overheating 27
Poor coolant circulation 32

Clutch

Clutch pedal stays on floor when disengaged 39
Clutch slips (engine speed increases with no increase
    in vehicle speed) 35
Fails to release (pedal pressed to the floor - shift lever
    does not move freely in and out of Reverse) 34
Grabbing (chattering) as clutch is engaged 36
Squeal or rumble with clutch fully disengaged
    (pedal depressed) 38
Squeal or rumble with clutch fully engaged
    (pedal released) 37

Manual transmission

Difficulty in engaging gears 44

Symptom	Section

Noisy in all gears 41
Noisy in Neutral with engine running 40
Noisy in one particular gear 42
Oil leakage 45
Slips out of high gear 43

Automatic transmission

Fluid leakage 49
General shift mechanism problems 46
Transmission slips, shifts rough, is noisy or has no drive
    in forward or reverse gears 48
Transmission will not downshift with accelerator pedal
    pressed to the floor 47

Transfer case

Lubricant leaks from the vent or output shaft seals 53
Noisy or jumps out of four-wheel drive Low range 52
Transfer case is difficult to shift into the desired range 50
Transfer case noisy in all gears 51

Driveshaft

Knock or clunk when the transmission is under initial
    load (just after transmission is put into gear) 55
Metallic grinding sound consistent with vehicle speed 56
Oil leak at front of driveshaft 54
Vibration 57

Axles

Noise 58
Oil leakage 60
Vibration 59

Brakes

Brake pedal feels spongy when depressed 64
Brake pedal pulsates during brake application 67
Excessive brake pedal travel 63
Excessive effort required to stop vehicle 65
Noise (high-pitched squeal with the brakes applied) 62
Pedal travels to the floor with little resistance 66
Vehicle pulls to one side during braking 61

Suspension and steering systems

Excessive pitching and/or rolling around corners or
    during braking 70
Excessive play in steering 72
Excessive tire wear (not specific to one area) 74
Excessive tire wear on inside edge 76
Excessive tire wear on outside edge 75
Excessively stiff steering 71
Lack of power assistance 73
Shimmy, shake or vibration 69
Tire tread worn in one place 77
Vehicle pulls to one side 68

Engine

1   Engine will not rotate when attempting to start

1   Battery terminal connections loose or corroded. Check the cable terminals at the battery; tighten cable clamp and/or clean off corrosion as necessary (see Chapter 1).

2   Battery discharged or faulty. If the cable ends are clean and tight on the battery posts, turn the key to the On position and switch on the headlights or windshield wipers. If they won't run, the battery is discharged.

3   Automatic transmission not engaged in park (P) or Neutral (N).

4   Broken, loose or disconnected wires in the starting circuit. Inspect all wires and connectors at the battery, starter solenoid and ignition switch (on steering column).

5   Starter motor pinion jammed in drive-plate ring gear. Remove starter (Chapter 5) and inspect pinion and driveplate (Chapter 2).
6   Starter solenoid faulty (Chapter 5).
7   Starter motor faulty (Chapter 5).
8   Clutch pedal neutral start switch faulty.
9   Ignition switch faulty (Chapter 12).
10   Engine seized. Try to turn the crankshaft with a large socket and breaker bar on the pulley bolt.
11   Starter relay faulty (Chapter 5).
12   Air in the fuel system (diesel) (Chapter 4).

2   Engine rotates but will not start

1   Fuel tank empty.
2   Battery discharged (engine rotates slowly).
3   Battery terminal connections loose or corroded.
4   Fuel not reaching fuel injectors. Check for clogged fuel filter or lines and defective fuel pump. Also make sure the tank vent lines aren't clogged (Chapter 4).
5   Low cylinder compression. Check as described in Chapter 2.
6   Water in fuel. Drain tank and fill with new fuel.
7   Defective ignition coil(s) (Chapter 5).
8   Dirty or clogged fuel injector(s) (Chapter 4).
9   Wet or damaged ignition components (Chapters 1 and 5).
10   Worn, faulty or incorrectly gapped spark plugs (Chapter 1).
11   Broken, loose or disconnected wires in the starting circuit (see previous Section).
12   Broken, loose or disconnected wires at the ignition coil or faulty coil (Chapter 5).
13   Timing chain failure or wear affecting valve timing (Chapter 2).
14   Fuel injection or engine control systems failure (Chapters 4 and 6).
15   Defective MAF sensor (Chapter 6)
16   Glow plug system malfunctioning (diesel engine) (Chapter 4B).

3   Starter motor operates without turning engine

1   Starter pinion sticking. Remove the starter (Chapter 5) and inspect.
2   Starter pinion or driveplate teeth worn or broken. Remove the inspection cover and inspect.

4   Engine hard to start when cold

1   Battery discharged or low. Check as described in Chapter 1.
2   Fuel not reaching the fuel injectors. Check the fuel filter, lines and fuel pump (Chapters 1 and 4).

3   Defective spark plugs (Chapter 1).
4   Defective engine coolant temperature sensor (Chapter 6).
5   Fuel injection or engine control systems malfunction (Chapters 4 and 6).
6   Glow plug system malfunctioning (diesel engine) (Chapter 4B).

5   Engine hard to start when hot

1   Air filter dirty (Chapter 1).
2   Bad engine ground connection.
3   Fuel injection or engine control systems malfunction (Chapters 4 and 6).

6   Starter motor noisy or engages roughly

1   Pinion or driveplate teeth worn or broken. Remove the inspection cover on the left side of the engine and inspect.
2   Starter motor mounting bolts loose or missing.

7   Engine starts but stops immediately

1   Loose or damaged wire harness connections at distributor, coil or alternator.
2   Intake manifold vacuum leaks. Make sure all mounting bolts/nuts are tight and all vacuum hoses connected to the manifold are attached properly and in good condition.
3   Insufficient fuel pressure (see Chapter 4).
4   Fuel injection or engine control systems malfunction (Chapters 4 and 6).

8   Engine 'lopes' while idling or idles erratically

1   Vacuum leaks. Check mounting bolts at the intake manifold for tightness. Make sure that all vacuum hoses are connected and in good condition. Use a stethoscope or a length of fuel hose held against your ear to listen for vacuum leaks while the engine is running. A hissing sound will be heard. A soapy water solution will also detect leaks. Check the intake manifold gasket surfaces.
2   Leaking EGR valve or plugged PCV valve (see Chapters 1 and 6).
3   Air filter clogged (Chapter 1).
4   Fuel pump not delivering sufficient fuel (Chapter 4).
5   Leaking head gasket. Perform a cylinder compression check (Chapter 2).
6   Timing chain(s) worn (Chapter 2).
7   Camshaft lobes worn (Chapter 2).
8   Valves burned or otherwise leaking (Chapter 2).
9   Ignition system not operating properly (Chapters 1 and 5).

10   Fuel injection or engine control systems malfunction (Chapters 4 and 6).

9   Engine misses at idle speed

1   Spark plugs faulty or not gapped properly (Chapter 1).
2   Faulty spark plug wires (Chapter 1).
3   Wet or damaged ignition components (Chapter 5).
4   Short circuits in ignition, coil or spark plug wires.
5   Sticking or faulty emissions systems (see Chapter 6).
6   Clogged fuel filter and/or foreign matter in fuel. Remove the fuel filter (Chapter 1) and inspect.
7   Vacuum leaks at intake manifold or hose connections. Check as described in Section
8   Low or uneven cylinder compression. Check as described in Chapter 2.
9   Fuel injection or engine control systems malfunction (Chapters 4 and 6).

10   Excessively high idle speed

1   Sticking throttle linkage (Chapter 4).
2   Vacuum leaks at intake manifold or hose connections. Check as described in Section 8.
3   Fuel injection or engine control systems malfunction (Chapters 4 and 6).

11   Battery will not hold a charge

1   Alternator drivebelt defective or not adjusted properly (Chapter 1).
2   Battery cables loose or corroded (Chapter 1).
3   Alternator not charging properly (Chapter 5).
4   Loose, broken or faulty wires in the charging circuit (Chapter 5).
5   Short circuit causing a continuous drain on the battery.
6   Battery defective internally.

12   Alternator light stays on

1   Fault in alternator or charging circuit (Chapter 5).
2   Alternator drivebelt defective or not properly adjusted (Chapter 1).

13   Alternator light fails to come on when key is turned on

1   Faulty bulb (Chapter 12).
2   Defective alternator (Chapter 5).
3   Fault in the printed circuit, dash wiring or bulb holder (Chapter 12).

14 Engine misses throughout driving speed range

1 Fuel filter clogged and/or impurities in the fuel system. Check fuel filter (Chapter 1) or clean system (Chapter 4).
2 Faulty or incorrectly gapped spark plugs (Chapter 1).
3 Defective spark plug wires (Chapter 1).
4 Emissions system components faulty (Chapter 6).
5 Low or uneven cylinder compression pressures. Check as described in Chapter 2.
6 Weak or faulty ignition coil(s) (Chapter 5).
7 Weak or faulty ignition system (Chapter 5).
8 Vacuum leaks at intake manifold or vacuum hoses (see Section 8).
9 Dirty or clogged fuel injector(s) (Chapter 4).
10 Leaky EGR valve (Chapter 6).
11 Fuel injection or engine control systems malfunction (Chapters 4 and 6).

15 Hesitation or stumble during acceleration

1 Ignition system not operating properly (Chapter 5).
2 Dirty or clogged fuel injector(s) (Chapter 4).
3 Low fuel pressure. Check for proper operation of the fuel pump and for restrictions in the fuel filter and lines (Chapter 4).
4 Fuel injection or engine control systems malfunction (Chapters 4 and 6).

16 Engine stalls

1 Idle speed incorrect (Chapter 4).
2 Fuel filter clogged and/or water and impurities in the fuel system (Chapter 1).
3 Damaged or wet distributor cap and wires.
4 Emissions system components faulty (Chapter 6).
5 Faulty or incorrectly gapped spark plugs (Chapter 1). Also check the spark plug wires (Chapter 1).
6 Vacuum leak at the intake manifold or vacuum hoses. Check as described in Section 8.
7 Fuel injection or engine control systems malfunction (Chapters 4 and 6).

17 Engine lacks power

1 Faulty or incorrectly gapped spark plugs (Chapter 1).
2 Air filter dirty (Chapter 1).
3 Faulty ignition coil(s) (Chapter 5).
4 Brakes binding (Chapters 1 and 9).

5 Automatic transmission fluid level incorrect, causing slippage (Chapter 1).
6 Fuel filter clogged and/or impurities in the fuel system (Chapters 1 and 4).
7 EGR system not functioning properly (Chapter 6).
8 Use of sub-standard fuel. Fill tank with proper octane fuel.
9 Low or uneven cylinder compression pressures. Check as described in Chapter 2.
10 Vacuum leak at intake manifold or vacuum hoses (check as described in Section 8).
11 Dirty or clogged fuel injector(s) (Chapters 1 and 4).
12 Fuel injection or engine control systems malfunction (Chapters 4 and 6).
13 Restricted exhaust system (Chapter 4).

18 Engine backfires

1 EGR system not functioning properly (Chapter 6).
2 Damaged valve springs or sticking valves (Chapter 2).
3 Vacuum leak at the intake manifold or vacuum hoses (see Section 8).

19 Engine surges while holding accelerator steady

1 Vacuum leak at the intake manifold or vacuum hoses (see Section 8).
2 Restricted air filter (Chapter 1).
3 Fuel pump or pressure regulator defective (Chapter 4).
4 Fuel injection or engine control systems malfunction (Chapters 4 and 6).

20 Pinging or knocking engine sounds when engine is under load

1 Incorrect grade of fuel. Fill tank with fuel of the proper octane rating.
2 Carbon build-up in combustion chambers. Remove cylinder head(s) and clean combustion chambers (Chapter 2).
3 Incorrect spark plugs (Chapter 1).
4 Fuel injection or engine control systems malfunction (Chapters 4 and 6).
5 Restricted exhaust system (Chapter 4).

21 Engine diesels (continues to run) after being turned off

1 Idle speed too high (Chapter 4).
2 Incorrect spark plug heat range (Chapter 1).
3 Vacuum leak at the intake manifold or vacuum hoses (see Section 8).
4 Carbon build-up in combustion chambers. Remove the cylinder head(s) and clean

the combustion chambers (Chapter 2).
5 Valves sticking (Chapter 2).
6 EGR system not operating properly (Chapter 6).
7 Fuel injection or engine control systems malfunction (Chapters 4 and 6).
8 Check for causes of overheating (Section 27).

22 Low oil pressure

1 Improper grade of oil.
2 Oil pump worn or damaged (Chapter 2).
3 Engine overheating (refer to Section 27).
4 Clogged oil filter (Chapter 1).
5 Clogged oil strainer (Chapter 2).
6 Oil pressure gauge not working properly (Chapter 2).

23 Excessive oil consumption

1 Loose oil drain plug.
2 Loose bolts or damaged oil pan gasket (Chapter 2).
3 Loose bolts or damaged front cover gasket (Chapter 2).
4 Front or rear crankshaft oil seal leaking (Chapter 2).
5 Loose bolts or damaged valve cover gasket (Chapter 2).
6 Loose oil filter (Chapter 1).
7 Loose or damaged oil pressure switch (Chapter 2).
8 Pistons and cylinders excessively worn (Chapter 2).
9 Piston rings not installed correctly on pistons (Chapter 2).
10 Worn or damaged piston rings (Chapter 2).
11 Intake and/or exhaust valve oil seals worn or damaged (Chapter 2).
12 Worn or damaged valves/guides (Chapter 2).
13 Faulty or incorrect PCV valve allowing too much crankcase airflow.

24 Excessive fuel consumption

1 Dirty or clogged air filter element (Chapter 1).
2 Incorrect idle speed (Chapter 4).
3 Low tire pressure or incorrect tire size (Chapter 10).
4 Inspect for binding brakes (see Chapter 9).
5 Fuel leakage. Check all connections, lines and components in the fuel system (Chapter 4).
6 Dirty or clogged fuel injectors (Chapter 4).
7 Fuel injection or engine control systems malfunction (Chapters 4 and 6).
8 Thermostat stuck open or not installed.
9 Improperly operating transmission.

25 Fuel odor

1   Fuel leakage. Check all connections, lines and components in the fuel system (Chapter 4).
2   Fuel tank overfilled. Fill only to automatic shut-off.
3   Charcoal canister filter in Evaporative Emissions Control system clogged (Chapter 1).
4   Vapor leaks from Evaporative Emissions Control system lines (Chapter 6).

26 Miscellaneous engine noises

1   A strong dull noise that becomes more rapid as the engine accelerates indicates worn or damaged crankshaft bearings or an unevenly worn crankshaft. To pinpoint the trouble spot, remove the spark plug wire from one plug at a time and crank the engine over. If the noise stops, the cylinder with the removed plug wire indicates the problem area. Replace the bearing and/or service or replace the crankshaft (Chapter 2).
2   A similar (yet slightly higher pitched) noise to the crankshaft knocking described in the previous paragraph, that becomes more rapid as the engine accelerates, indicates worn or damaged connecting rod bearings (Chapter 2). The procedure for locating the problem cylinder is the same as described in Paragraph 1.
3   An overlapping metallic noise that increases in intensity as the engine speed increases, yet diminishes as the engine warms up indicates abnormal piston and cylinder wear (Chapter 2). To locate the problem cylinder, use the procedure described in Paragraph 1.
4   A rapid clicking noise that becomes faster as the engine accelerates indicates a worn piston pin or piston pin hole. This sound will happen each time the piston hits the highest and lowest points in the stroke (Chapter 2). The procedure for locating the problem piston is described in Paragraph 1.
5   A metallic clicking noise coming from the water pump indicates worn or damaged water pump bearings or pump. Replace the water pump with a new one (Chapter 3).
6   A rapid tapping sound or clicking sound that becomes faster as the engine speed increases indicates "valve tapping." This can be identified by holding one end of a section of hose to your ear and placing the other end at different spots along the valve cover. The point where the sound is loudest indicates the problem valve. If the pushrod and rocker arm components are in good shape, you likely have a collapsed valve lifter. Changing the engine oil and adding a high viscosity oil treatment will sometimes cure a stuck lifter problem. If the problem persists, the lifters, pushrods and rocker arms must be removed for inspection (see Chapter 2).
7   A steady metallic rattling or rapping sound coming from the area of the timing chain cover indicates a worn, damaged or out-of-adjustment timing chain. Service or replace the chain and related components (Chapter 2).

Cooling system

27 Overheating

1   Insufficient coolant in system (Chapter 1).
2   Drivebelt defective or not adjusted properly (Chapter 1).
3   Radiator core blocked or radiator grille dirty and restricted (Chapter 3).
4   Thermostat faulty (Chapter 3).
5   Cooling fan not functioning properly (Chapter 3).
6   Expansion tank cap not maintaining proper pressure. Have cap pressure tested by a gas station or repair shop.
7   Defective water pump (Chapter 3).
8   Improper grade of engine oil.
9   Inaccurate temperature gauge (Chapter 12).
10   Blown cylinder head gasket (Chapter 2).

28 Overcooling

1   Thermostat faulty (Chapter 3).
2   Inaccurate temperature gauge (Chapter 12).

29 External coolant leakage

1   Deteriorated or damaged hoses. Loose clamps at hose connections (Chapter 1).
2   Water pump seals defective. If this is the case, water will drip from the weep hole in the water pump body (Chapter 3).
3   Leakage from radiator core or header tank. This will require the radiator to be professionally repaired (see Chapter 3 for removal procedures).
4   Leakage from the coolant reservoir or degas bottle.
5   Engine drain plugs or water jacket freeze plugs leaking (see Chapters 1 and 2).
6   Leak from coolant temperature switch (Chapter 3).
7   Leak from damaged gaskets or small cracks (Chapter 2).
8   Leak from oil cooler or oil cooler adapter housing (Chapter 3).

30 Internal coolant leakage

Note: *Internal coolant leaks can usually be detected by examining the oil. Check the dipstick and inside the rocker arm cover for water deposits and an oil consistency like that of a milkshake.*

1   Leaking cylinder head gasket. Have the system pressure tested or remove the cylinder head (Chapter 2) and inspect.
2   Cracked cylinder bore or cylinder head. Dismantle engine and inspect (Chapter 2).
3   Loose cylinder head bolts (tighten as described in Chapter 2).
4   Leakage from internal coolant pipe/hose (gasoline engines) (accessible only with intake manifold removed (Chapter 2A).

31 Abnormal coolant loss

1   Overfilling system (Chapter 1).
2   Coolant boiling away due to overheating (see causes in Section 27).
3   Internal or external leakage (see Sections 29 and 30).
4   Faulty expansion tank cap. Have the cap pressure tested.
5   Cooling system being pressurized by engine compression. This could be due to a cracked head or block or leaking head gasket(s). Have the system tested for the presence of combustion gas in the coolant at a shop.

32 Poor coolant circulation

1   Inoperative water pump. A quick test is to pinch the top radiator hose closed with your hand while the engine is idling, then release it. You may be able to feel a surge of coolant if the pump is working properly (Chapter 3).
2   Restriction in cooling system. Drain, flush and refill the system (Chapter 1). If necessary, remove the radiator (Chapter 3) and have it reverse flushed or professionally cleaned.
3   Loose water pump drivebelt (Chapter 1).
4   Thermostat sticking (Chapter 3).
5   Insufficient coolant (Chapter 1).

33 Corrosion

1   Excessive impurities in the water. Soft, clean water is recommended. Distilled or rainwater is satisfactory.
2   Insufficient antifreeze solution (refer to Chapter 1 for the proper ratio of water to antifreeze).
3   Infrequent flushing and draining of system. Regular flushing of the cooling system should be carried out at the specified intervals as described in Chapter 1.

Clutch

34 Fails to release (pedal pressed to the floor - shift lever does not move freely in and out of Reverse)

1   Leak in the clutch hydraulic system. Check the master cylinder, release cylinder and lines (Chapter 8).
2   Clutch plate warped or damaged (Chapter 8).

35 Clutch slips (engine speed increases with no increase in vehicle speed)

1 Clutch plate oil soaked or lining worn. Remove clutch (Chapter 8) and inspect.
2 Clutch plate not seated. It may take 30 or 40 normal starts for a new one to seat.
3 Pressure plate worn (Chapter 8).

36 Grabbing (chattering) as clutch is engaged

1 Oil on clutch plate lining. Remove (Chapter 8) and inspect. Correct any leakage source.
2 Worn or loose engine or transmission mounts. These units move slightly when the clutch is released. Inspect the mounts and bolts (Chapter 2).
3 Worn splines on clutch plate hub. Remove the clutch components (Chapter 8) and inspect.
4 Warped pressure plate or flywheel. Remove the clutch components and inspect.

37 Squeal or rumble with clutch fully engaged (pedal released)

1 Release bearing binding on transmission bearing retainer. Remove clutch components (Chapter 8) and check bearing. Remove any burrs or nicks; clean and relubricate bearing retainer before installing.

38 Squeal or rumble with clutch fully disengaged (pedal depressed)

1 Worn, defective or broken release bearing (Chapter 8).
2 Worn or broken pressure plate springs (or diaphragm fingers) (Chapter 8).

39 Clutch pedal stays on floor when disengaged

1 Linkage or release bearing binding. Inspect the linkage or remove the clutch components as necessary.
2 Make sure proper pedal stop (bumper) is installed.

Manual transmission

Note: *All the following references are in Chapter 7A, unless noted.*

40 Noisy in Neutral with engine running

1 Input shaft bearing worn.
2 Damaged main drive gear bearing.

3 Worn countershaft bearings.
4 Worn or damaged countershaft endplay shims.

41 Noisy in all gears

1 Any of the above causes, and/or:
2 Insufficient lubricant (see the checking procedures in Chapter 1).

42 Noisy in one particular gear

1 Worn, damaged or chipped gear teeth for that particular gear.
2 Worn or damaged synchronizer for that particular gear.

43 Slips out of high gear

1 Transmission loose on clutch housing.
2 Dirt between the transmission case and engine or misalignment of the transmission.

44 Difficulty in engaging gears

1 Clutch not releasing completely (see clutch adjustment in Chapter 1).
2 Loose, damaged or out-of-adjustment shift linkage. Make a thorough inspection, replacing parts as necessary.

45 Oil leakage

1 Excessive amount of lubricant in the transmission (see Chapter 1 for correct checking procedures). Drain lubricant as required.
2 Transmission oil seal or vehicle speed sensor O-ring in need of replacement.

Automatic transmission

Note: *Due to the complexity of the automatic transmission, it's difficult for the home mechanic to properly diagnose and service this component. For problems other than the following, the vehicle should be taken to a dealer service department or a transmission shop.*

46 General shift mechanism problems

1 Common problems which may be attributed to a misadjusted shift cable are:
a) *Engine starting in gears other than Park or Neutral.*
b) *Indicator on shifter pointing to a gear other than the one actually being selected.*
c) *Vehicle moves when in Park.*
2 Refer to Chapter 7 to check the transmission range (TR) sensor adjustment.

47 Transmission will not downshift with accelerator pedal pressed to the floor

Since these transmissions are electronically controlled, your dealer or a professional shop with the proper equipment will have to diagnose the probable cause.

48 Transmission slips, shifts rough, is noisy or has no drive in forward or reverse gears

1 There are many probable causes for the above problems, but the home mechanic should be concerned with only one possibility - fluid level.
2 Before taking the vehicle to a repair shop, check the level and condition of the fluid as described in Chapter 1. Correct fluid level as necessary or change the fluid and filter if needed. If the problem persists, have a professional diagnose the problem.

49 Fluid leakage

1 Automatic transmission fluid is a deep red color. Fluid leaks should not be confused with engine oil, which can easily be blown by airflow to the transmission.
2 To pinpoint a leak, first remove all built-up dirt and grime from around the transmission. Degreasing agents and/or steam cleaning will achieve this. With the underside clean, drive the vehicle at low speeds so air flow will not blow the leak far from its source. Raise the vehicle and determine where the leak is coming from. Common areas of leakage are:
a) *Pan: Tighten the mounting bolts and/or replace the pan gasket as necessary (see Chapter 7).*
b) *Filler pipe: Replace the rubber seal where the pipe enters the transmission case.*
c) *Transmission oil lines: Tighten the connectors where the lines enter the transmission case and/or replace the lines.*
d) *Vent pipe: Transmission overfilled and/or water in fluid (see checking procedures, Chapter 1).*
e) *Speedometer connector: Replace the O-ring where the speedometer sensor enters the transmission case (Chapter 7).*

Transfer case

50 Transfer case is difficult to shift into the desired range

1 Speed may be too great to permit engagement. Stop the vehicle and shift into the desired range.
2 Shift linkage loose, bent or binding on a

manual shift transfer case. Check the linkage for damage or wear and replace or lubricate as necessary (Chapter 7).

3   Defective circuit and or range switch on electric shift transfer case (Chapter 7).

4   If the vehicle has been driven on a paved surface for some time, the driveline torque can make shifting difficult. Stop and shift into two-wheel drive on paved or hard surfaces.

5   Insufficient or incorrect grade of lubricant. Drain and refill the transfer case with the specified lubricant (Chapter 1).

6   Worn or damaged internal components. Disassembly and overhaul of the transfer case may be necessary (Chapter 7).

51   Transfer case noisy in all gears

Insufficient or incorrect grade of lubricant. Drain and refill (Chapter 1).

52   Noisy or jumps out of four-wheel drive Low range

1   Transfer case not fully engaged. Stop the vehicle, shift into Neutral and then engage 4L.

2   Shift linkage loose, worn or binding. Tighten, repair or lubricate linkage as necessary.

3   Shift fork cracked, inserts worn or fork binding on the rail. See your dealer for a new or rebuilt unit.

53   Lubricant leaks from the vent or output shaft seals

1   Transfer case is overfilled. Drain to the proper level (Chapter 1).

2   Vent is clogged or jammed closed. Clear or replace the vent.

3   Output shaft seal incorrectly installed or damaged. Replace the seal and check contact surfaces for nicks and scoring.

Driveshaft

54   Oil leak at seal end of driveshaft

Defective transmission or transfer case oil seal. See Chapter 7 for replacement procedures. While this is done, check the splined yoke for burrs or a rough condition which may be damaging the seal. Burrs can be removed with crocus cloth or a fine whetstone.

55   Knock or clunk when the transmission is under initial load (just after transmission is put into gear)

1   Loose or disconnected rear suspension components. Check all mounting bolts, nuts

and bushings (see Chapter 10).

2   Loose driveshaft bolts. Inspect all bolts and nuts and tighten them to the specified torque.

3   Worn or damaged universal joint bearings. Check for wear (see Chapter 8).

56   Metallic grinding sound consistent with vehicle speed.

Pronounced wear in the universal joint bearings. Check as described in Chapter 8.

57   Vibration

Note: *Before assuming that the driveshaft is at fault, make sure the tires are perfectly balanced and perform the following test.*

1   Install a tachometer inside the vehicle to monitor engine speed as the vehicle is driven. Drive the vehicle and note the engine speed at which the vibration (roughness) is most pronounced. Now shift the transmission to a different gear and bring the engine speed to the same point.

2   If the vibration occurs at the same engine speed (rpm) regardless of which gear the transmission is in, the driveshaft is NOT at fault since the driveshaft speed varies.

3   If the vibration decreases or is eliminated when the transmission is in a different gear at the same engine speed, refer to the following probable causes.

4   Bent or dented driveshaft. Inspect and replace as necessary (see Chapter 8).

5   Undercoating or built-up dirt, etc. on the driveshaft. Clean the shaft thoroughly and recheck.

6   Worn universal joint bearings. Remove and inspect (see Chapter 8).

7   Driveshaft and/or companion flange out of balance. Check for missing weights on the shaft. Remove the driveshaft (see Chapter 8) and reinstall 180-degrees from original position, then retest. Have the driveshaft professionally balanced if the problem persists.

Axles

58   Noise

1   Road noise. No corrective procedures available.

2   Tire noise. Inspect tires and check tire pressures (Chapter 1).

3   Rear wheel bearings loose, worn or damaged (Chapter 8).

59   Vibration

See probable causes under *Driveshaft*. Proceed under the guidelines listed for the driveshaft. If the problem persists, check the rear wheel bearings by raising the rear of the

vehicle and spinning the rear wheels by hand. Listen for evidence of rough (noisy) bearings. Remove and inspect (see Chapter 8).

60   Oil leakage

1   Pinion seal damaged (see Chapter 8).

2   Axleshaft oil seals damaged (see Chapter 8).

3   Differential inspection cover leaking. Tighten the bolts or replace the gasket as required (see Chapters 1 and 8).

Brakes

Note: *Before assuming that a brake problem exists, make sure that the tires are in good condition and inflated properly (see Chapter 1), that the front end alignment is correct and that the vehicle is not loaded with weight in an unequal manner.*

61   Vehicle pulls to one side during braking

1   Defective, damaged or oil-contaminated disc brake pads on one side. Inspect as described in Chapter 9.

2   Excessive wear of brake pad material or disc on one side. Inspect and correct as necessary.

3   Loose or disconnected front suspension components. Inspect and tighten all bolts to the specified torque (Chapter 10).

4   Defective brake caliper assembly. (Chapter 9).

62   Noise (high-pitched squeal with the brakes applied)

1   Disc brake pads worn out. The noise comes from the wear sensor rubbing against the disc (does not apply to all vehicles) or the actual pad backing plate itself if the material is completely worn away. Replace the pads with new ones immediately (Chapter 9). If the pad material has worn completely away, the brake discs should be inspected for damage as described in Chapter 9.

2   Linings contaminated with dirt or grease. Replace pads or shoes.

3   Incorrect linings. Replace with correct linings.

63   Excessive brake pedal travel

1   Partial brake system failure. Inspect the entire system (Chapter 9) and correct as required.

2   Insufficient fluid in the master cylinder. Check (Chapter 1), add fluid and bleed the system if necessary (Chapter 9).

3   Problem with the anti-lock brake system (Chapter 9).

64   Brake pedal feels spongy when depressed

1   Air in the hydraulic lines. Bleed the brake system (Chapter 9).
2   Faulty flexible hoses. Inspect all system hoses and lines. Replace parts as necessary.
3   Master cylinder mounting bolts/nuts loose.
4   Master cylinder defective (Chapter 9).
5   Problem with the anti-lock brake system (Chapter 9).

65   Excessive effort required to stop vehicle

1   Power brake booster not operating properly (Chapter 9).
2   Excessively worn pads. Inspect and replace if necessary (Chapter 9).
3   One or more caliper pistons seized or sticking (Chapter 9).
4   Brake pads contaminated with oil or grease. Inspect and replace as required (Chapter 9).
5   New pads installed and not yet seated. It will take a while for the new material to seat against the disc.
6   Problem with the anti-lock brake system (Chapter 9).

66   Pedal travels to the floor with little resistance

1   Little or no fluid in the master cylinder reservoir caused by leaking wheel cylinder(s), leaking caliper piston(s), loose, damaged or disconnected brake lines. Inspect the entire system and correct as necessary.
2   Worn master cylinder seals (Chapter 9).
3   Problem with the anti-lock brake system (Chapter 9).

67   Brake pedal pulsates during brake application

1   Caliper improperly installed. Remove and inspect (Chapter 9).
2   Disc defective. Remove (Chapter 9) and check for excessive lateral runout and parallelism. Have the disc resurfaced or replace it with a new one.

Suspension and steering systems

68   Vehicle pulls to one side

1   Tire pressures uneven (Chapter 1).
2   Defective tire (Chapter 1).
3   Excessive wear in suspension or steering components (Chapter 10).
4   Front end in need of alignment.
5   Front brakes dragging. Inspect the brakes as described in Chapters 1 and 9.

69   Shimmy, shake or vibration

1   Tire or wheel out-of-balance or out-of-round. Have professionally balanced.
2   Loose, worn or out-of-adjustment front wheel bearings (Chapter 1).
3   Shock absorbers and/or suspension components worn or damaged (Chapter 10).

70   Excessive pitching and/or rolling around corners or during braking

1   Defective shock absorbers. Replace as a set (Chapter 10).
2   Broken or weak springs and/or suspension components. Inspect as described in Chapter 10.

71   Excessively stiff steering

1   Lack of fluid in power steering fluid reservoir (Chapter 1).
2   Incorrect tire pressures (Chapter 1).
3   Lack of lubrication at steering joints (see Chapter 1).
4   Front end out of alignment.
5   Lack of power assistance (see Section 73).

72   Excessive play in steering

1   Loose front wheel bearings (Chapter 1).
2   Excessive wear in suspension or steering components (Chapter 10).
3   Steering gearbox damaged or out of adjustment (Chapter 10).

73   Lack of power assistance

1   Steering pump drivebelt faulty or not adjusted properly (Chapter 1).
2   Fluid level low (Chapter 1).
3   Hoses or lines restricted. Inspect and replace parts as necessary.
4   Air in power steering system. Bleed the system (Chapter 10).

74   Excessive tire wear (not specific to one area)

1   Incorrect tire pressures (Chapter 1).
2   Tires out-of-balance. Have professionally balanced.
3   Wheels damaged. Inspect and replace as necessary.
4   Suspension or steering components excessively worn (Chapter 10).

75   Excessive tire wear on outside edge

1   Inflation pressures incorrect (Chapter 1).
2   Excessive speed in turns.
3   Front end alignment incorrect. Have professionally aligned.
4   Suspension arm bent or twisted (Chapter 10).

76   Excessive tire wear on inside edge

1   Inflation pressures incorrect (Chapter 1).
2   Front end alignment incorrect (toe-out). Have professionally aligned.
3   Loose or damaged steering components (Chapter 10).

77   Tire tread worn in one place

1   Tires out-of-balance.
2   Damaged or buckled wheel. Inspect and replace if necessary.
3   Defective tire (Chapter 1).

Chapter 1
Tune-up and routine maintenance

Contents

	Section
Air filter check and replacement	25
Automatic transmission fluid and filter change	27
Automatic transmission fluid level check	7
Battery check, maintenance and charging	11
Brake check	21
Brake fluid change	29
Chassis lubrication	10
Cooling system check	17
Cooling system servicing (draining, flushing and refilling)	26
Differential lubricant change	36
Differential lubricant level check	24
Drivebelt check and replacement	30
Engine oil and filter change	9
Exhaust system check	14
Fluid level checks	4
Front wheel bearing check, repack and adjustment (2WD models)	28
Fuel filter replacement	19
Fuel filter/water separator draining	8

	Section
Fuel system check	18
Ignition coil check and replacement	33
Introduction	2
Maintenance schedule	1
Manual transmission lubricant change	34
Manual transmission lubricant level check	22
Positive Crankcase Ventilation (PCV) valve check	31
Power steering fluid level check	6
Seat belt check	15
Spark plug check and replacement	32
Steering and suspension check	20
Tire and tire pressure checks	5
Tire rotation	13
Transfer case lubricant change (4WD models)	35
Transfer case lubricant level check (4WD models)	23
Tune-up general information	3
Underhood hose check and replacement	16
Windshield wiper blade inspection and replacement	12

Specifications

Note: *Listed here are manufacturer recommendations at the time this manual was written. Manufacturers occasionally upgrade their fluid and lubricant specifications, so check with your local auto parts store for current recommendations.*

Recommended lubricants and fluids

Engine oil
  Type
    Gasoline engines .... API "certified for gasoline engines"
    Diesel engines .... API grade CH-4/SH or CH-4/SJ
  Viscosity
    Gasoline engines 5W-20
    Diesel engine
      Above 30-degrees F 15W-40
      -10-degrees to 30-degrees F 10W-30
      Consistently below -10-degrees F 0W-30
Power steering fluid .... MERCON automatic transmission fluid
Brake fluid .... DOT 3 heavy duty brake fluid
Automatic transmission fluid
  4-speed .... MERCON automatic transmission fluid.
  5-speed .... MERCON SP automatic transmission fluid.
  Caution: *Do not use MERCON V or dual-usage MERCON/MERCON V automatic transmission fluid. Do not mix types*
Manual transmission lubricant .... MERCON V automatic transmission fluid
Transfer case lubricant .... MERCON automatic transmission fluid

Recommended lubricants and fluids (continued)

Coolant

1999 through 2002	50/50 mixture of ethylene glycol-based coolant and distilled or demineralized water. Use the same type as originally equipped.
2003 through 2004	Motorcraft Premium Gold coolant VC-7-A or equivalent. (In Oregon use VC-7-B or equivalent).
2005 and later	Motorcraft Premium Gold coolant VC-7-A or equivalent. (In Oregon, California and New Mexico use VC-7-B or equivalent).
Front wheel bearing grease	NLGI No. 2 lithium base grease containing polyethylene and molybdenum disulfide
Chassis grease	NLGI No. 2 lithium base grease containing polyethylene and molybdenum disulfide

Differential lubricant

Front axle	SAE 75W-90 QL synthetic gear lubricant
Rear axle	
Ford 10.50 inch axles	SAE 75W-140 GL synthetic gear lubricant*
Dana 80 axles	SAE 75W-90 QL synthetic gear lubricant*
Dana 135 axles	SAE 80W-90 QL synthetic gear lubricant*

For Traction-Lok axles (limited slip) add friction modifier (Ford part no. C8AZ-19B546-A, or equivalent) when oil is changed

Capacities*

Engine oil (with filter change)

Gasoline engines	6 quarts
Diesel engines	15 quarts
Automatic transmission (capacity with torque converter drained)	17.7 quarts

Note: *The best way to determine the amount of fluid to add during a routine fluid change is to measure the amount drained. It is important not to overfill the transmission. After draining the transmission, begin the refilling procedure by initially adding 6-1/2 quarts, then adding 1/2-pint at a time until the level is correct on the dipstick.*

Manual transmission

Five-speed	3.4 quarts
Six-speed	5.8 quarts

Cooling system

Gasoline engines	
Without rear heating	26 to 29 quarts
With rear heating	28 to 31 quarts
Diesel engine	
Without rear heating	31 to 33 quarts
With rear heating	35 quarts

All capacities approximate. Add as necessary to bring to the appropriate level.

5.4L V8 ENGINE
1-3-7-2-6-5-4-8

36059-1-specs.C HAYNES

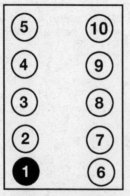

6.8L V10 ENGINE
1-6-5-10-2-7-3-8-4-9

36059-1-specs.C HAYNES

DIESEL ENGINE
1-2-7-3-4-5-6-8

36060-1-specs.C HAYNES

Cylinder location diagrams

Brakes

Disc brake pad thickness (minimum)...	1/16-inch
Parking brake shoe lining thickness (minimum)	1/32-inch above rivet heads

Ignition system

Spark plug

    Type

1999 through 2002...	Motorcraft AWS-22E or equivalent

      2003 and later

5.4L models...	Motorcraft AWSF-22W or equivalent
6.8L models...	Motorcraft AWSF-22E or equivalent
2005 through 2007..	PZT-2F
2008 and later...	HJFS-24FP or equivalent

    Gap

1999 through 2004..	0.054 inch
2005 through 2007..	Non-adjustable
2008 and later...	0.039 to 0.043 inch
Ignition timing	10-degrees BTDC (base timing - not adjustable)

Firing order

    Gasoline engines

V8	1-3-7-2-6-5-4-8
V10	1-6-5-10-2-7-3-8-4-9
Diesel engines...	1-2-7-3-4-5-6-8

Fuel system

Idle speed..	Not adjustable

Torque specifications

Ft-lbs (unless otherwise indicated)

Note: *One foot-pound (ft-lb) of torque is equivalent to 12 inch-pounds (in-lbs) of torque. Torque values below approximately 15 foot-pounds are expressed in inch-pounds, because most foot-pound torque wrenches are not accurate at these smaller values.*

Automatic transmission

Fluid pan bolts..	132 in-lbs

    Torque converter drain plug

2001 and earlier models	18 to 20
2002 and later models	108 in-lbs

Front hub adjusting nut (2WD models)

Step 1...	21
Step 2...	Back off 1/2-turn
Step 3...	18 in-lbs
Oil filter cap, 6.0L engines	18

Spark plugs

1999 through 2004..	132 in-lbs
2005 through 2007..	25

    2008

Early build (black coil boot)...................................	25
Late build (brown coil boot)...................................	106 in-lbs
2009 and later	106 in-lbs

Wheel lug nuts*

1999 and 2000 models	148
2001 and 2002 models...	155
2003 and later models...	165

* The manufacturer recommends that wheel lug nuts be retightened 100 miles after being installed. On dual-rear wheels, the lug nuts should have a second retightening at 500 miles.

Typical engine compartment components (7.3L diesel engine shown)

1	Brake master cylinder reservoir	7	Engine drivebelt
2	Engine compartment fuse box	8	Engine coolant expansion tank
3	Air filter housing	9	Windshield washer fluid reservoir
4	Battery	10	Engine oil dipstick
5	Power steering fluid reservoir	11	Engine oil filler cap
6	Upper radiator hose	12	Automatic transmission fluid dipstick

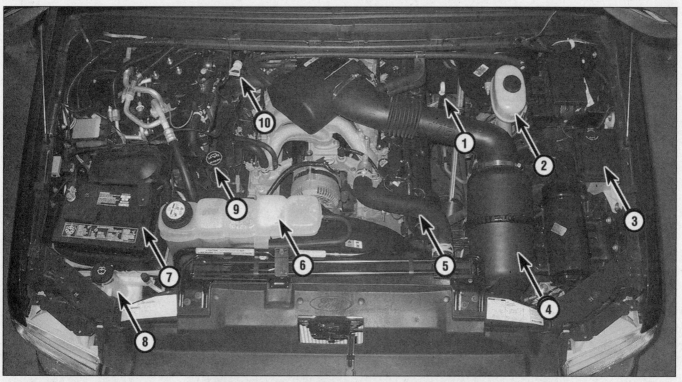

Typical engine compartment components (gasoline engine)

1 Engine oil dipstick
2 Brake master cylinder reservoir
3 Power steering fluid reservoir
4 Air filter housing

5 Upper radiator hose
6 Coolant expansion tank
7 Battery

8 Windshield washer fluid reservoir
9 Engine oil filler cap
10 Automatic transmission fluid dipstick

Typical rear underside components

1 Fuel tank
2 Exhaust pipe

3 Differential cover
4 Rear shock absorber

5 Leaf spring
6 Parking brake cable

7 Rear disc brake caliper

Typical engine underside components (7.3L diesel 4WD shown)

1 Lower radiator hose	*5 Front axle housing*	*9 Automatic transmission drain plug*
2 Lower radiator hose	*6 Oil filter*	*10 Steering damper*
3 Radiator drain	*7 Engine oil drain plug*	*11 Front disc brake caliper*
4 Steering linkage grease fitting	*8 Exhaust pipe*	

1 Ford Super Duty F-250/350 and Excursion Maintenance schedule

The following maintenance intervals are based on the assumption that the vehicle owner will be doing the maintenance or service work, as opposed to having a dealer service department or other repair shop do the work. Although the time/mileage intervals are loosely based on factory recommendations, most have been shortened to ensure, for example, that such items as lubricants and fluids are checked/changed at intervals that promote maximum engine/driveline service life. Also, subject to the preference of the individual owner interested in keeping his or her vehicle in peak condition at all times, and with the vehicle's ultimate resale in mind, many of the maintenance procedures may be performed more often than recommended in the following schedule. We encourage such owner initiative.

When the vehicle is new it should be serviced initially by a factory authorized dealer service department to protect the factory warranty. In many cases the initial maintenance check is done at no cost to the owner (check with your dealer service department for more information).

Owner's Manual and VECI label information

Your vehicle owner's manual was written for your year and model and contains very specific information on component locations, specifications, fuse ratings, part numbers, etc. The Owner's Manual is an important resource for the do-it-yourselfer to have; if one was not supplied with your vehicle, it can generally be ordered from a dealer parts department.

Among other important information, the Vehicle Emissions Control Information (VECI) label contains specifications and procedures for applicable tune-up adjustments (if applicable) and, in some instances, spark plug replacement (see Chapter 6 for more information on the VECI label). The information on this label is the exact maintenance data recommended by the manufacturer. This data often varies by intended altitude, local emissions regulations, month of manufacture, etc.

This Chapter contains procedural details, safety information and more ambitious maintenance intervals than you might find in manufacturer's literature. However, you may find procedures or specifications in your Owner's Manual or VECI label can be considered correct, since it is specific to your particular vehicle.

Every 250 miles or weekly, whichever comes first

Check the engine oil level (Section 4)
Check the engine coolant level (Section 4)
Check the windshield washer fluid level (Section 4)
Check the brake and the clutch fluid level (Section 4)
Check the tires and tire pressures (Section 5)
On diesel models, check the air filter restriction gauge (Section 25)

Every 3000 miles or 3 months, whichever comes first

All items listed above, plus:
Check the power steering fluid level (Section 6)
Check the automatic transmission fluid level (Section 7)
Check and drain if necessary, the diesel engine fuel/water separator (Section 8)
Change the engine oil and oil filter (Section 9)
Lubricate the chassis (Section 10)
Check the engine drivebelt (Section 30)

Every 6000 miles or 6 months, whichever comes first

All items listed above, plus:
Check and service the battery (Section 11)
Inspect and replace, if necessary, the windshield wiper blades (Section 12)
Rotate the tires (Section 13)
Inspect the exhaust system (Section 14)
Check the seat belt operation (Section 15)

Every 15,000 miles or 12 months, whichever comes first

All items listed above, plus:
Inspect and replace, if necessary, all underhood hoses (Section 16)
Inspect the cooling system (Section 17)
Check the fuel system (Section 18)
Replace the fuel filter (Section 19)
Inspect the steering and suspension components (Section 20)
Inspect the brakes (Section 21)
Check the manual transmission lubricant level (Section 22)
Check the transfer case lubricant level (Section 23)
Check the differential lubricant level (Section 24)

Every 30,000 miles or 24 months, whichever comes first

Replace the air filter (Section 25)*
Service the cooling system (drain, flush and refill) (Section 26)
Change the automatic transmission fluid and filter (Section 27)**
Inspect and repack the front wheel bearings (2WD models) (Section 28)
Change the brake fluid (Section 29)

Every 60,000 miles or 48 months, whichever comes first

Check the engine drivebelt (Section 30)
Check the PCV valve (Section 31)
Replace the spark plugs (Section 32)
Inspect and replace, if necessary, the ignition coils (Section 33)
Change the manual transmission lubricant (Section 34)
Change the transfer case lubricant (Section 35)
Change the differential lubricant (Section 36)

* Replace more often if is the vehicle is driven in dusty areas
** If the vehicle is operated in continuous stop-and-go driving or in mountainous areas, change at 15,000 miles

2   Introduction

This Chapter is designed to help the home mechanic maintain the Ford Super Duty F-250/F-350 and the Ford Excursion with the goals of maximum performance, economy, safety and reliability in mind.

Included is a master maintenance schedule, followed by procedures dealing specifically with each item on the schedule. Visual checks, adjustments, component replacement and other helpful items are included. Refer to the **accompanying illustrations** of the engine compartment and the underside of the vehicle for the locations of various components.

Servicing the vehicle, in accordance with the mileage/time maintenance schedule and the step-by-step procedures will result in a planned maintenance program that should produce a long and reliable service life. Keep in mind that it is a comprehensive plan, so maintaining some items but not others at the specified intervals will not produce the same results.

As you service the vehicle, you will discover that many of the procedures can - and should - be grouped together because of the nature of the particular procedure you're performing or because of the close proximity of two otherwise unrelated components to one another.

For example, if the vehicle is raised for chassis lubrication, you should inspect the exhaust, suspension, steering and fuel systems while you're under the vehicle. When you're rotating the tires, it makes good sense to check the brakes since the wheels are already removed. Finally, let's suppose you have to borrow or rent a torque wrench. Even if you only need it to tighten the spark plugs, you might as well check the torque of as many critical fasteners as time allows.

The first step in this maintenance program is to prepare yourself before the actual work begins. Read through all the procedures you're planning to do, then gather up all the parts and tools needed. If it looks like you might run into problems during a particular job, seek advice from a mechanic or an experienced do-it-yourselfer.

3   Tune-up general information

The term tune-up is used in this manual to represent a combination of individual operations rather than one specific procedure.

If, from the time the vehicle is new, the routine maintenance schedule is followed closely and frequent checks are made of fluid levels and high wear items, as suggested throughout this manual, the engine will be kept in relatively good running condition and the need for additional work will be minimized.

More likely than not, however, there will be times when the engine is running poorly due to lack of regular maintenance. This is even more likely if a used vehicle, which has not received regular and frequent maintenance checks, is purchased. In such cases, an engine tune-up will be needed outside of the regular routine maintenance intervals.

The first step in any tune-up or diagnostic procedure to help correct a poor running engine is a cylinder compression check. A compression check (see Chapter 2) will help determine the condition of internal engine components and should be used as a guide for tune-up and repair procedures. If, for instance, a compression check indicates serious internal engine wear, a conventional tune-up will not improve the performance of the engine and would be a waste of time and money. Because of its importance, the compression check should be done by someone with the right equipment and the knowledge to use it properly.

The following procedures are those most often needed to bring a generally poor running engine back into a proper state of tune.

Minor tune-up

Check all engine related fluids (Section 4)
Clean, inspect and test the battery
*   (Section 11)*
Check all underhood hoses (Section 16)
Check the cooling system (Section 17)
Check the fuel system (Section 18)
Check the air filter (Section 25)

Major tune-up

All items listed under Minor tune-up, plus . . .

Replace the fuel filter (Section 19)
Replace the air filter (Section 25)
Check the drivebelt (Section 30)
Replace the PCV valve (Section 31)
Replace the spark plugs (Section 32)
Check the charging system (Chapter 5)

4   Fluid level checks (every 250 miles or weekly)

1   Fluids are an essential part of the lubrication, cooling, brake and windshield washer systems. Because the fluids gradually become depleted and/or contaminated during normal operation of the vehicle, they must be periodically replenished. See *Recommended lubricants and fluids* at the beginning of this Chap-

4.2 The oil dipstick is located on the side of the engine

ter before adding fluid to any of the following components. **Note:** *The vehicle must be on level ground when fluid levels are checked.*

Engine oil

Refer to illustrations 4.2, 4.4 and 4.6

2   The oil level is checked with a dipstick, which is located on the side of the engine **(see illustration)**. The dipstick extends through a metal tube down into the oil pan.

3   The oil level should be checked before the vehicle has been driven, or about 5 minutes after the engine has been shut off. If the oil is checked immediately after driving the vehicle, some of the oil will remain in the upper part of the engine, resulting in an inaccurate reading on the dipstick. On diesel engines wait at least 20 minutes after the engine is shut off before checking the oil level because it takes longer for the greater quality of oil in the upper part to drain into the oil pan.

4   Pull the dipstick out of the tube and wipe all the oil from the end with a clean rag or paper towel. Insert the clean dipstick all the way back into the tube and pull it out again. Note the oil at the end of the dipstick. At its highest point, the level on gasoline engines should be between the MIN and MAX marks on the dipstick **(see illustration)**. On diesel engines the level should be between the ADD and OPERATING RANGE marks on the dipstick.

4.4 The oil level should be at or near the MAX area on the dipstick - if it isn't, add enough oil to bring the level to near the MAX mark

4.6 The oil filler cap is located on the valve cover - note that on this model it is marked with the engine oil type

4.9 The coolant expansion tank is located at the front of the engine compartment, behind the radiator - keep the level near the MAX mark - DO NOT remove the cap until the engine has cooled completely

4.15a The brake fluid level should be kept between the MIN and MAX marks on the translucent plastic reservoir

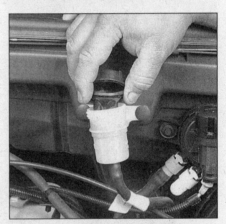

4.15b The clutch fluid reservoir is mounted on the firewall - add fluid until it reaches the FULL line

5   On gasoline engines it takes one quart of oil to raise the level from the MIN mark to the MAX mark on the dipstick. Do not allow the level to drop below the MIN mark or oil starvation may cause engine damage. Conversely, overfilling the engine (adding oil above the MAX mark) may cause oil fouled spark plugs, oil leaks or oil seal failures. On diesel engines it takes two quarts of oil to raise the level from the ADD to the OPERATING RANGE mark on the dipstick. Maintaining the oil level above the OPERATING RANGE mark can cause excessive oil consumption.

6   To add oil, remove the filler cap from the valve cover (see illustration). After adding oil, wait a few minutes to allow the level to stabilize, then pull out the dipstick and check the level again. Add more oil if required. Install the filler cap and tighten it by hand only.

7   Checking the oil level is an important preventive maintenance step. A consistently low oil level indicates oil leakage through damaged seals, defective gaskets or past worn rings or valve guides. If the oil looks milky in color or has water droplets in it, the cylinder head gasket(s) may be blown or the head(s) or block may be cracked. The engine should be checked immediately. The condition of the oil should also be checked. Whenever you check the oil level, slide your thumb and index finger up the dipstick before wiping off the oil. If you see small dirt or metal particles clinging to the dipstick, the oil should be changed (see Section 9).

Engine coolant

Refer to illustration 4.9

Warning: *Do not allow antifreeze to come in contact with your skin or painted surfaces of the vehicle. Flush contaminated areas immediately with plenty of water. Don't store new coolant or leave old coolant lying around where it's accessible to children or pets - they're attracted by its sweet smell. Ingestion of even a small amount of coolant can be fatal! Wipe up garage floor and drip pan spills*

immediately. Keep antifreeze containers covered and repair cooling system leaks as soon as they're noticed.

8   All vehicles covered by this manual are equipped with a pressurized coolant recovery system. A plastic expansion tank located at the front of the engine compartment is connected by a hose to the radiator. As the engine heats up during operation, the expanding coolant fills the tank.

9   The coolant level in the tank should be checked regularly. **Warning:** *Do not remove the expansion tank cap to check the coolant level when the engine is warm!* The level in the tank varies with the temperature of the engine. When the engine is cold, the coolant level should be at or slightly above the FULL COLD mark on the reservoir. Once the engine has warmed up, the level should be at or near the FULL HOT mark. If it isn't, allow the engine to cool, then remove the cap from the tank and add a 50/50 mixture of ethylene glycol based antifreeze and water (see illustration).

10   Drive the vehicle and recheck the coolant level. Don't use rust inhibitors or additives. If only a small amount of coolant is required to bring the system up to the proper level, water can be used. However, repeated additions of water will dilute the antifreeze and water solution. In order to maintain the proper ratio of antifreeze and water, always top up the coolant level with the correct mixture. An empty plastic milk jug or bleach bottle makes an excellent container for mixing coolant.

11   If the coolant level drops consistently, there may be a leak in the system. Inspect the radiator, hoses, filler cap, drain plugs and water pump (see Section 17). If no leaks are noted, have the expansion tank cap pressure tested by a service station.

12   If you have to remove the expansion tank cap wait until the engine has cooled completely, then wrap a thick cloth around the cap and unscrew it slowly, stopping if you hear a hissing noise. If coolant or steam escapes, let

the engine cool down longer, then remove the cap.

13   Check the condition of the coolant as well. It should be relatively clear. If it's brown or rust colored, the system should be drained, flushed and refilled. Even if the coolant appears to be normal, the corrosion inhibitors wear out, so it must be replaced at the specified intervals.

Brake and clutch fluid

Refer to illustrations 4.15a and 4.15b

14   The brake master cylinder is mounted on the front of the power booster unit in the engine compartment. The hydraulic clutch master cylinder used on manual transmission vehicles is located next to the brake master cylinder.

15   To check the fluid level of the brake and clutch master cylinders, simply look at the MAX and MIN marks on the reservoir (see illustrations). The level should be within the specified distance from the maximum fill line.

16   If the level is low, wipe the top of the reservoir cover with a clean rag to prevent contamination of the brake system before lifting the cover.

4.22 The windshield washer reservoir (arrow) is located at the right front corner of the engine compartment next to the battery

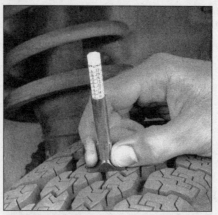

5.2 Use a tire tread depth indicator to monitor tire wear - they are available at auto parts stores and service stations and cost very little

17   Add only the specified brake fluid to the brake and clutch reservoirs (refer to *Recommended lubricants and fluids* at the front of this Chapter or to your owner's manual). Mixing different types of brake fluid can damage the system. Fill the brake master cylinder reservoir only to the MAX line. **Warning:** *Use caution when filling either reservoir - brake fluid can harm your eyes and damage painted surfaces. Do not use brake fluid that is more than one*

year old or has been left open. Brake fluid absorbs moisture from the air. Excess moisture can cause a dangerous loss of braking.
18   While the reservoir cap is removed, inspect the master cylinder reservoir for contamination. If deposits, dirt particles or water droplets are present, the system should be drained and refilled.
19   After filling the reservoir to the proper level,

make sure the lid is properly seated to prevent fluid leakage and/or system pressure loss.
20   The fluid in the brake master cylinder will drop slightly as the brake pads at each wheel wear down during normal operation. If either master cylinder requires repeated replenishing to keep it at the proper level, this is an indication of leakage in the brake or clutch system, which should be corrected immediately. If the brake system shows an indication of leakage check all brake lines and connections, along with the calipers, wheel cylinders and booster (see Section 21 for more information). If the hydraulic clutch system shows an indication of leakage check all clutch lines and connections, along with the clutch release cylinder (see Chapter 8 for more information).
21   If, upon checking the brake or clutch master cylinder fluid level, you discover one or both reservoirs empty or nearly empty, the systems should be bled (see Chapter 9).

Windshield washer fluid

Refer to illustration 4.22
22   Fluid for the windshield washer system is stored in a plastic reservoir located at the right front of the engine compartment **(see illustration)**.
23   In milder climates, plain water can be used in the reservoir, but it should be kept no more than 2/3 full to allow for expansion if the water freezes. In colder climates, use windshield washer system antifreeze, available at any auto parts store, to lower the freezing point of the fluid. Mix the antifreeze with water in accordance with the manufacturer's directions on the container. **Caution:** *Do not use cooling system antifreeze - it will damage the vehicle's paint.*

5   Tire and tire pressure checks (every 250 miles or weekly)

Refer to illustrations 5.2, 5.3, 5.4a, 5.4b and 5.8
1   Periodic inspection of the tires may spare you the inconvenience of being stranded with a flat tire. It can also provide you with vital information regarding possible problems in the steering and suspension systems before major damage occurs.
2   The original tires on this vehicle are equipped with 1/2-inch wide bands that will appear when tread depth reaches 1/16-inch, at which point they can be considered worn out. Tread wear can be monitored with a simple, inexpensive device known as a tread depth indicator **(see illustration)**.
3   Note any abnormal tread wear **(see illustration)**. Tread pattern irregularities such as cupping, flat spots and more wear on one side than the other are indications of front end alignment and/or balance problems. If any of these conditions are noted, take the vehicle to a tire shop or service station to correct the problem.
4   Look closely for cuts, punctures and embedded nails or tacks. Sometimes a tire

CUPPING

Cupping may be caused by:

- Underinflation and/or mechanical irregularities such as out-of-balance condition of wheel and/or tire, and bent or damaged wheel.
- Loose or worn steering tie-rod or steering idler arm.
- Loose, damaged or worn front suspension parts.

UNDERINFLATION

INCORRECT TOE-IN OR EXTREME CAMBER

OVERINFLATION

FEATHERING DUE TO MISALIGNMENT

5.3 This chart will help you determine the condition of the tires, the probable cause(s) of abnormal wear and the corrective action necessary

5.4a If a tire loses air on a steady basis, check the valve stem core first to make sure it's snug (special inexpensive wrenches are commonly available at auto parts stores)

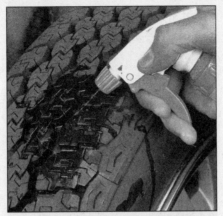

5.4b If the valve stem core is tight, raise the corner of the vehicle with the low tire and spray a soapy water solution onto the tread as the tire is turned slowly - leaks will cause small bubbles to appear

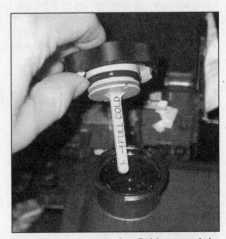

5.8 To extend the life of the tires, check the air pressure at least once a week with an accurate gauge (don't forget the spare!)

will hold air pressure for a short time or leak down very slowly after a nail has embedded itself in the tread. If a slow leak persists, check the valve stem core to make sure it is tight **(see illustration)**. Examine the tread for an object that may have embedded itself in the tire or for a "plug" that may have begun to leak (radial tire punctures are repaired with a plug that is installed in a puncture). If a puncture is suspected, it can be easily verified by spraying a solution of soapy water onto the puncture area **(see illustration)**. The soapy solution will bubble if there is a leak. Unless the puncture is unusually large, a tire shop or service station can usually repair the tire.

5   Carefully inspect the inner sidewall of each tire for evidence of brake fluid leakage. If you see any, inspect the brakes immediately.

6   Correct air pressure adds miles to the life span of the tires, improves mileage and enhances overall ride quality. Tire pressure cannot be accurately estimated by looking at a tire, especially if it's a radial. A tire pressure gauge is essential. Keep an accurate gauge in the glove compartment. The pressure gauges attached to the nozzles of air hoses at gas stations are often inaccurate.

7   Always check tire pressure when the tires are cold. Cold, in this case, means the vehicle has not been driven over a mile in the three hours preceding a tire pressure check. A pressure rise of four to eight pounds is not uncommon once the tires are warm.

8   Unscrew the valve cap protruding from the wheel or hubcap and push the gauge firmly onto the valve stem **(see illustration)**. Note the reading on the gauge and compare the figure to the recommended tire pressure shown on the tire placard on the driver's side door. Be sure to reinstall the valve cap to keep dirt and moisture out of the valve stem mechanism. Check all four tires and, if necessary, add enough air to bring them up to the recommended pressure.

9   Don't forget to keep the spare tire inflated to the specified pressure (refer to the pressure molded into the tire sidewall).

6   Power steering fluid level check (every 3000 miles or 3 months)

Refer to illustrations 6.3a and 6.3b

1   Check the power steering fluid level periodically to avoid steering system problems, such as damage to the pump. **Caution:** *DO NOT hold the steering wheel against either stop (extreme left or right turn) for more than five seconds. If you do, the power steering pump could be damaged.*

2   The fluid reservoir for the power steering pump is mounted at the left front corner of the engine on diesel models, or on the left inner fender panel on gasoline models. On later gasoline and diesel models, the power steering reservoir is located at the left side of the radiator.

3   The fluid level can be checked by removing the dipstick **(see illustration)**.

4   The fluid level should be kept between the MIN and MAX marks on the dipstick.

5   Add small amounts of fluid until the level is correct. **Caution:** *Do not overfill the reservoir. If too much fluid is added, remove the excess with a clean syringe or suction pump.*

6   If the reservoir requires frequent fluid additions, all power steering hoses, hose connections, the power steering pump and the steering gear assembly should be carefully checked for leaks.

7   Automatic transmission fluid level check (every 3000 miles or 3 months)

Refer to illustrations 7.4a, 7.4b and 7.6

1   The automatic transmission fluid level should be carefully maintained. Low fluid level can lead to slipping or loss of drive, while overfilling can cause foaming and loss of fluid. Either condition can cause transmission damage.

2   Since transmission fluid expands as it heats up, the fluid level should be checked

when the transmission is warm (at normal operating temperature). If the vehicle has just been driven over 20 miles (32 km), the transmission can be considered warm. **Caution:** *If the vehicle has just been driven for a long time at high speed or in city traffic in hot weather, or if it has been pulling a trailer, an accurate fluid level reading cannot be obtained. Allow the transmission to cool down for about 30 minutes.* You can also check the transmission fluid level when the transmission is cold. If the vehicle has not been driven for over five hours and the fluid is about room temperature (70 to 95-degrees F), the transmission is cold. However, the fluid level is normally checked with the transmission warm to ensure accurate results.

3   Immediately after driving the vehicle, park it on a level surface, set the parking brake and start the engine. While the engine is idling, depress the brake pedal and move the selector lever through all the gear ranges, beginning and ending in Park.

6.3a The power steering fluid reservoir is located along the left side of the engine compartment on gasoline models - remove the cap and check the fluid level on the dipstick

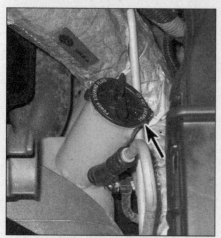

6.3b On 7.3L diesel-engine models, the power steering fluid reservoir is located on the pump itself - remove the cap (arrow) to check the dipstick

7.4a The automatic transmission fluid dipstick is located on the passenger's side of the engine on gasoline powered vehicles

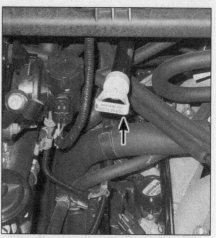

7.4b On diesel powered vehicles the automatic transmission fluid dipstick is located near the passenger's side firewall in the engine compartment

4   Locate the automatic transmission dipstick tube in the engine compartment **(see illustrations)**.

5   With the engine still idling, pull the dipstick from the tube, wipe it off with a clean rag, push it all the way back into the tube and withdraw it again, then note the fluid level.

6   If the transmission is cold, the level should be in the room temperature range on the dipstick (between the two holes); if it's warm, the fluid level should be in the operating temperature range (in the cross-hatched area) **(see illustration)**. If the level is low, add the specified automatic transmission fluid through the dipstick tube - use a funnel to prevent spills.

7   Add just enough of the recommended fluid to fill the transmission to the proper level. It takes about one pint to raise the level from the low mark to the high mark when the fluid is hot, so add the fluid a little at a time and keep checking the level until it's correct.

8   The condition of the fluid should also be checked along with the level. If the fluid is black or a dark reddish-brown color, or if it smells burned, it should be changed (see Section 27). If you are in doubt about its con-

dition, purchase some new fluid and compare the two for color and smell.

8   Fuel filter/water separator draining (every 3000 miles or 3 months)

Warning: *Diesel fuel isn't as volatile as gasoline, but it is flammable, so take extra precautions when you work on any part of the fuel system. Don't smoke or allow open flames or bare light bulbs near the work area. Don't work in a garage or other enclosed space where there is a gas-type appliance (such as a water heater or clothes dryer). Finally, when you perform any work on the fuel system, wear safety glasses, latex gloves and have a Class B type fire extinguisher on hand. If you spill any diesel fuel on your skin, rinse it off immediately with soap and water.*

1   The diesel engine fuel filter incorporates a water separator that removes and traps water in the fuel. The water must be drained from the filter at the specified interval or when the "Water In Fuel" light is on (indicating at least 100 cc of water has collected).

2   Place a small container under the filter drain tube (diesel fuel can damage asphalt paving). Make sure the rubber drain tube is open and hangs free so it can drain easily.

3   With the engine off, turn the lever on the filter clockwise and allow the accumulated water to drain out, then close the valve by turning the lever counterclockwise.

4   Remove the container and dispose of the fuel/water mixture properly.

9   Engine oil and filter change (every 3000 miles or 3 months)

Refer to illustrations 9.2, 9.7, 9.12 and 9.15

1   Frequent oil changes are the most important preventive maintenance procedures

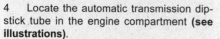

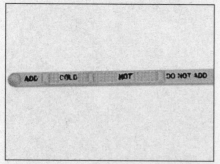

7.6 Check the fluid with the transmission at normal operating temperature - the level should be kept in the HOT range in the cross-hatched area (don't add fluid if the level is anywhere in the cross-hatched area)

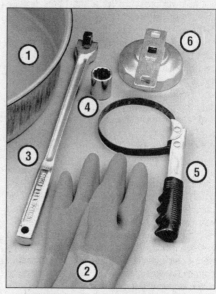

9.2 These tools are required when changing the engine oil and filter

1   **Drain pan** - *It should be fairly shallow in depth, but wide to prevent spills*

2   **Rubber gloves** - *When removing the drain plug and filter, you will get oil on your hands (the gloves will prevent burns)*

3   **Breaker bar** - *Sometimes the oil drain plug is tight, and a long breaker bar is needed to loosen it*

4   **Socket** - *To be used with the breaker bar or a ratchet (must be the correct size to fit the drain plug - six-point preferred)*

5   **Filter wrench** - *This is a metal band-type wrench, which requires clearance around the filter to be effective*

6   **Filter wrench** - *This type fits on the bottom of the filter and can be turned with a ratchet or breaker bar (different-size wrenches are available for different types of filters)*

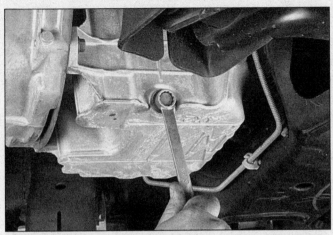

9.7 Use a proper size wrench or socket to remove the oil drain plug and avoid rounding it off

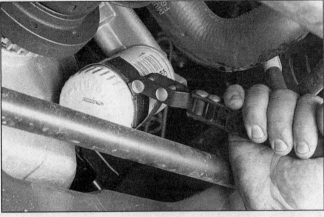

9.12 The oil filter is usually on very tight and will require a special oil filter wrench to remove it - DO NOT use the wrench to tighten the new filter

that can be done by the home mechanic. As engine oil ages, it becomes diluted and contaminated, which leads to premature engine wear.

2   Make sure that you have all the necessary tools before you begin this procedure (see illustration). You should also have plenty of rags or newspapers handy for mopping up oil spills.

3   Access to the oil drain plug and filter will be improved if the vehicle can be lifted on a hoist, driven onto ramps or supported by jackstands. **Warning:** *Do not work under a vehicle supported only by a jack - always use jackstands!*

4   If you haven't changed the oil on this vehicle before, get under it and locate the oil drain plug and the oil filter. The exhaust components will be warm as you work, so note how they are routed to avoid touching them when you are under the vehicle.

5   Start the engine and allow it to reach normal operating temperature - oil and sludge will flow out more easily when warm. If new oil, a filter or tools are needed, use the vehicle to go get them and warm up the engine/oil at the same time. Park on a level surface and shut off the engine when it's warmed up. Remove the oil filler cap from the valve cover.

6   Raise the vehicle and support it on jackstands. Make sure it is safely supported! **Note:** *On 6.0L diesel engines, always perform the oil filter replacement before draining the oil from the crankcase. The oil filter housing on these engines drains into the oil pan when it is serviced.*

7   Being careful not to touch the hot exhaust components, position a drain pan under the plug in the bottom of the engine, then remove the plug (see illustration). It's a good idea to wear a rubber glove while unscrewing the plug the final few turns to avoid being scalded by hot oil.

8   It may be necessary to move the drain pan slightly as oil flow slows to a trickle. Inspect the old oil for the presence of metal particles.

9   After all the oil has drained, wipe off the drain plug with a clean rag. Any small metal particles clinging to the plug would immediately contaminate the new oil.

10   Clean the area around the drain plug opening, reinstall the plug and tighten it securely, but don't strip the threads.

11   Move the drain pan into position under the oil filter.

All engines except 6.0L and 6.4L diesel engines

12   Loosen the oil filter by turning it counter-clockwise with a filter wrench (see illustration). Any standard filter wrench will work.

13   Once the filter is loose, use your hands to unscrew it from the block. Just as the filter is detached from the block, immediately tilt the open end up to prevent the oil inside the filter from spilling out.

14   Using a clean rag, wipe off the mounting surface on the block. Also, make sure that none of the old gasket remains stuck to the mounting surface. It can be removed with a scraper if necessary.

15   Compare the old filter with the new one to make sure they are the same type. Smear some engine oil on the rubber gasket of the new filter and screw it into place (see illustration). Overtightening the filter will damage the gasket, so don't use a filter wrench. Most filter manufacturers recommend tightening the filter by hand only. Normally they should be tightened 3/4-turn (on diesel models 1-1/4 to 2-turns) after the gasket contacts the block, but be sure to follow the directions on the filter or container.

6.0L and 6.4L diesel engines

Refer to illustration 9.16

16   The oil filter is located on top of the engine (see illustration). Instead of the spin-on style filter used on gasoline engines, 6.0L diesels use a cartridge filter.

17   Place rags around the filter housing to catch spillage.

18   Loosen the cap from the housing using a large wrench, socket or an oil filter wrench, then unscrew the cap approximately two

9.15 Lubricate the oil filter gasket with clean engine oil before installing the filter on the engine

turns. This opens a valve and allows oil from inside the housing to drain into the engine.

19   When the housing is drained, remove the cap along with the filter.

20   Remove the old oil filter from the lid and dispose of it properly.

9.16 The oil filter on 6.0L diesel engines is in the larger of the two housings on top of the engine. Place rags around the housing to catch any spillage before you open it

21   Snap the new filter onto the lid.
22   Check the cap's O-ring to make sure it's in good condition. If it's damaged it must be replaced. Apply a little clean oil to the O-ring to ensure that it won't catch as it's being tightened.
23   Screw the cap onto the housing and tighten it to the torque listed in this Chapter's Specifications.
24   Wipe up any spilled oil.

All engines

25   Remove all tools and materials from under the vehicle, being careful not to spill the oil in the drain pan, then lower the vehicle.
26   Add new oil to the engine through the oil filler cap. Use a funnel to prevent oil from spilling onto the top of the engine. Pour four quarts of fresh oil into the engine. **Note:** *On diesel engines add 13 quarts.* Wait a few minutes to allow the oil to drain into the pan, then check the level on the dipstick (see Section 4 if necessary). If the oil level is in the OK range, install the filler cap.
27   Start the engine and run it for about a minute. While the engine is running, look under the vehicle and check for leaks at the oil pan drain plug and around the oil filter. If either one is leaking, stop the engine and tighten the plug or filter slightly.
28   Wait a few minutes, then recheck the level on the dipstick. Add oil as necessary to bring the level into the OK range.
29   During the first few trips after an oil change, make it a point to check frequently for leaks and proper oil level.
30   The old oil drained from the engine cannot be reused in its present state and should be disposed of. Check with your local auto parts store, disposal facility or environmental agency to see if they will accept the oil for recycling. After the oil has cooled it can be drained into a container (capped plastic jugs, topped bottles, milk cartons, etc.) for transport to one of these disposal sites. Don't dispose of the oil by pouring it on the ground or down a drain!

10   Chassis lubrication (every 3000 miles or 3 months)

Refer to illustrations 10.1 and 10.6

1   Refer to *Recommended lubricants and fluids* at the front of this Chapter to obtain the necessary grease, etc. You will also need a grease gun **(see illustration)**. Occasionally plugs will be installed rather than grease fittings. If so, grease fittings will have to be purchased and installed.
2   Look under the vehicle for grease fittings or plugs on the steering, suspension, and driveline components. They are normally found on the balljoints, tie-rod ends and universal joints. If there are plugs, remove them and install grease fittings, which will thread into the component. An automotive parts store will be able to supply the correct fittings. Straight, as well as angled, fittings are available.

10.1 Materials required for chassis and body lubrication

1   **Engine oil** - *Light engine oil in a can like this can be used for door and hood hinges*
2   **Graphite spray** - *Used to lubricate lock cylinders*
3   **Grease** - *Grease, in a variety of types and weights, is available for use in a grease gun. Check the Specifications for your requirements*
4   **Grease gun** - *A common grease gun, shown here with a detachable hose and nozzle, is needed for chassis lubrication. After use, clean it thoroughly!*

3   For easier access under the vehicle, raise it with a jack and place jackstands under the frame. Make sure it is safely supported by the stands. If the wheels are to be removed at this interval for tire rotation or brake inspection, loosen the lug nuts slightly while the vehicle is still on the ground.
4   Before beginning, force a little grease out of the nozzle to remove any dirt from the end of the gun. Wipe the nozzle clean with a rag.
5   With the grease gun and plenty of clean rags, crawl under the vehicle and begin lubricating the components.
6   Wipe the balljoint grease fitting clean and push the nozzle firmly over it. Squeeze the trigger on the grease gun to force grease into the component. The balljoints should be lubricated until the rubber seal is firm to the touch **(see illustration)**. Do not pump too much grease into the fittings as it could rupture the seal. For all other suspension and steering components, continue pumping grease into the fitting until it oozes out of the joint between the two components. If it escapes around the grease gun nozzle, the fitting is clogged or the nozzle is not completely seated on the fitting. Resecure the gun nozzle to the fitting and try again. If necessary, replace the fitting with a new one.
7   Wipe the excess grease from the components and the grease fitting. Repeat the procedure for the remaining fittings.

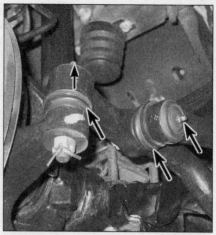

10.6 On the steering joints, pump grease into the fittings until the rubber seals are firm to the touch

8   On models equipped with an automatic transmission, lubricate the shift linkage with a little clean engine oil.
9   On 4WD models, lubricate the transfer case shift mechanism contact surfaces with clean engine oil.
10   Lubricate the driveshaft slip-joints. **Note:** *It may be necessary to disassemble the driveshaft to lubricate the slip joint* (see Chapter 8).
11   Lubricate conventional universal joints until grease can be seen coming out of the contact points.
12   While you are under the vehicle, clean and lubricate the parking brake cable along with the cable guides and levers. This can be done by smearing some chassis grease onto the cable and its related parts with your fingers.
13   Open the hood and smear a little chassis grease on the hood latch mechanism. Have an assistant pull the hood release lever from inside the vehicle as you lubricate the cable at the latch.
14   Lubricate all the hinges (door, hood, etc.) with engine oil to keep them in proper working order.
15   The key lock cylinders can be lubricated with spray-on graphite or silicone lubricant, which is available at auto parts stores.
16   Lubricate the door weatherstripping with silicone spray. This will reduce chafing and retard wear.

11   Battery check, maintenance and charging (every 6000 miles or 6 months)

Refer to illustrations 11.1, 11.6a, 11.6b, 11.7a and 11.7b

Warning: *Certain precautions must be followed when checking and servicing the battery. Hydrogen gas, which is highly flammable, is always present in the battery cells, so keep lighted tobacco and all other open flames and*

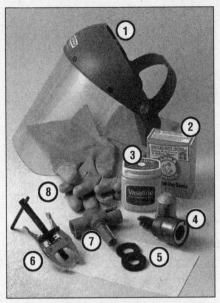

11.1 Tools and materials required for battery maintenance

1 *Face shield/safety goggles* - *When removing corrosion with a brush, the acidic particles can easily fly up into your eyes*
2 *Baking soda* - *A solution of baking soda and water can be used to neutralize corrosion*
3 *Petroleum jelly* - *A layer of this on the battery posts will help prevent corrosion*
4 *Battery post/cable cleaner* - *This wire brush cleaning tool will remove all traces of corrosion from the battery posts and cable clamps*
5 *Treated felt washers* - *Placing one of these on each post, directly under the cable clamps, will help prevent corrosion*
6 *Puller* - *Sometimes the cable clamps are very difficult to pull off the posts, even after the nut/bolt has been completely loosened. This tool pulls the clamp straight up and off the post without damage*
7 *Battery post/cable cleaner* - *Here is another cleaning tool which is a slightly different version of Number 4 above, but it does the same thing*
8 *Rubber gloves* - *Another safety item to consider when servicing the battery; remember that's acid inside the battery!*

sparks away from the battery. The electrolyte inside the battery is actually diluted sulfuric acid, which will cause injury if splashed on your skin or in your eyes. It will also ruin clothes and painted surfaces. When removing the battery cables, always detach the negative cable first and hook it up last!

1 A routine preventive maintenance program for the battery in your vehicle is the only way to ensure quick and reliable starts. But before performing any battery maintenance,

11.6a Battery terminal corrosion usually appears as light, fluffy powder

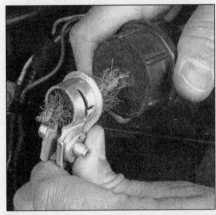

11.7a When cleaning the cable clamps, all corrosion must be removed (the inside of the clamp is tapered to match the taper on the post, so don't remove too much material)

make sure that you have the proper equipment necessary to work safely around the battery **(see illustration)**.
2 There are also several precautions that should be taken whenever battery maintenance is performed. Before servicing the battery, always turn the engine and all accessories off and disconnect the cables from the negative terminal of the battery (see Chapter 5, Section 1).
3 The battery produces hydrogen gas, which is both flammable and explosive. Never create a spark, smoke or light a match around the battery. Always charge the battery in a ventilated area.
4 Electrolyte contains poisonous and corrosive sulfuric acid. Do not allow it to get in your eyes, on your skin or your clothes. Never ingest it. Wear protective safety glasses when working near the battery. Keep children away from the battery.
5 Note the external condition of the battery. If the positive terminal and cable clamp on your vehicle's battery is equipped with a rubber protector, make sure that it's not torn or damaged. It should completely cover the

11.6b Removing the cable from a battery post with a wrench - sometimes special battery pliers are required for this procedure if corrosion has caused deterioration of the nut hex (always remove the ground cable first and hook it up last!)

11.7b Regardless of the type of tool used on the battery posts, a clean, shiny surface should be the result

terminal. Look for any corroded or loose connections, cracks in the case or cover or loose hold-down clamps. Also check the entire length of each cable for cracks and frayed conductors.
6 If corrosion, which looks like white, fluffy deposits **(see illustration)** is evident, particularly around the terminals, the battery should be removed for cleaning. Loosen the cable clamp bolts with a wrench, being careful to remove the ground cable first, and slide them off the terminals **(see illustration)**. Then disconnect the hold-down clamp bolt and nut, remove the clamp and lift the battery from the engine compartment.
7 Clean the cable clamps thoroughly with a battery brush or a terminal cleaner and a solution of warm water and baking soda **(see illustration)**. Wash the terminals and the top of the battery case with the same solution but make sure that the solution doesn't get into the battery. When cleaning the cables, terminals and battery top, wear safety goggles and rubber gloves to prevent any solution from

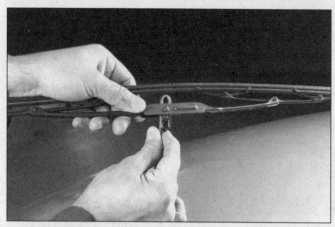

12.4 Press on the release tab and push the blade assembly down out of the hook in the arm

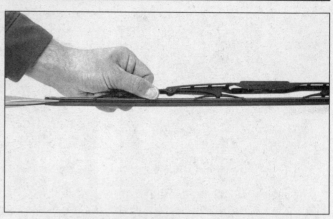

12.5 Use needle-nose pliers to compress the rubber element, then slide the element out - slide the new element in and lock the blade assembly fingers into the notches of the wiper element

coming in contact with your eyes or hands. Wear old clothes too - even diluted, sulfuric acid splashed onto clothes will burn holes in them. If the terminals have been extensively corroded, clean them up with a terminal cleaner **(see illustration)**. Thoroughly wash all cleaned areas with plain water.

8   Make sure that the battery tray is in good condition and the hold-down clamp bolts are tight. If the battery is removed from the tray, make sure no parts remain in the bottom of the tray when the battery is reinstalled. When reinstalling the hold-down clamp bolts, do not overtighten them.

9   Information on removing and installing the battery can be found in Chapter 5. Information on jump starting can be found at the front of this manual. For more detailed battery checking procedures, refer to the *Haynes Automotive Electrical Manual*.

Cleaning

10   Corrosion on the hold-down components, battery case and surrounding areas can be removed with a solution of water and baking soda. Thoroughly rinse all cleaned areas with plain water.

11   Any metal parts of the vehicle damaged by corrosion should be covered with a zinc-based primer, then painted.

Charging

Warning: *When batteries are being charged, hydrogen gas, which is very explosive and flammable, is produced. Do not smoke or allow open flames near a charging or a recently charged battery. Wear eye protection when near the battery during charging. Also, make sure the charger is unplugged before connecting or disconnecting the battery from the charger.*

12   Slow-rate charging is the best way to restore a battery that's discharged to the point where it will not start the engine. It's also a good way to maintain the battery charge in a vehicle that's only driven a few miles between starts. Maintaining the battery charge is particularly important in the winter when the battery must work harder to start the engine and

electrical accessories that drain the battery are in greater use.

13   It's best to use a one or two-amp battery charger (sometimes called a "trickle" charger). They are the safest and put the least strain on the battery. They are also the least expensive. For a faster charge, you can use a higher amperage charger, but don't use one rated more than 1/10th the amp/hour rating of the battery. Rapid boost charges that claim to restore the power of the battery in one to two hours are hardest on the battery and can damage batteries not in good condition. This type of charging should only be used in emergency situations.

14   The average time necessary to charge a battery should be listed in the instructions that come with the charger. As a general rule, a trickle charger will charge a battery in 12 to 16 hours.

12   Windshield wiper blade inspection and replacement (every 6000 miles or 6 months)

Refer to illustrations 12.4 and 12.5

1   The windshield wiper and blade assembly should be inspected periodically for damage, loose components and cracked or worn blade elements.

2   Road film can build up on the wiper blades and affect their efficiency, so they should be washed regularly with a mild detergent solution.

3   If the wiper blade elements are cracked, worn or warped, or no longer clean adequately, they should be replaced with new ones.

4   Lift the arm assembly away from the glass for clearance, press on the release lever, then slide the wiper blade assembly out of the hook in the end of the arm **(see illustration)**.

5   Use needle-nose pliers to compress the blade element, then slide the element out of the frame and discard it **(see illustration)**.

6   Installation is the reverse of removal.

13   Tire rotation (every 6000 miles or 6 months)

Refer to illustration 13.2

1   The tires should be rotated at the specified intervals and whenever uneven wear is noticed. Since the vehicle will be raised and the tires removed anyway, check the brakes also (see Section 21).

2   Radial tires must be rotated in a specific pattern **(see illustration)**. If your vehicle has a compact spare tire, don't include it in the rotation pattern.

3   Refer to the information in *Jacking and towing* at the front of this manual for the proper procedure to follow when raising the vehicle and changing a tire. If the brakes must be checked, don't apply the parking brake as stated.

4   The vehicle must be raised on a hoist or supported on jackstands to get all four wheels off the ground. Make sure the vehicle is safely supported!

5   After the rotation procedure is finished, check and adjust the tire pressures as neces-

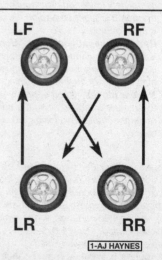

13.2 The recommended tire rotation pattern for these vehicles

14.2a Check the connections for exhaust leaks - also check that the clamp retaining nuts are securely tightened

14.2b Check the exhaust system hangers for damage and cracks

sary and be sure to check the lug nut tightness.

---

14   Exhaust system check (every 6000 miles or 6 months)

Refer to illustrations 14.2a and 14.2b

1   With the engine cold (at least three hours after the vehicle has been driven), check the complete exhaust system from the engine to the end of the tailpipe. Ideally, the inspection should be done with the vehicle on a hoist to permit unrestricted access. If a hoist isn't available, raise the vehicle and support it securely on jackstands.

2   Check the exhaust pipes and connections for evidence of leaks, severe corrosion and damage. Make sure that all brackets and hangers are in good condition and tight **(see illustrations)**.

3   At the same time, inspect the underside of the body for holes, corrosion, open seams, etc. which may allow exhaust gases to enter the passenger compartment. Seal all body openings with silicone or body putty.

4   Rattles and other noises can often be traced to the exhaust system, especially the mounts and hangers. Try to move the pipes, muffler and catalytic converter. If the components can come in contact with the body or suspension parts, secure the exhaust system with new mounts.

5   Check the running condition of the engine by inspecting inside the end of the tailpipe. The exhaust deposits here are an indication of engine state-of-tune. If the pipe is black and sooty or coated with white deposits, the engine may need a tune-up, including a thorough fuel system inspection and adjustment.

---

15   Seat belt check (every 6000 miles or 6 months)

1   Check seat belts, buckles, latch plates and guide loops for obvious damage and signs of wear.

2   See if the seat belt reminder light comes on when the key is turned to the Run or Start position. A chime should also sound.

3   The seat belts are designed to lock up during a sudden stop or impact, yet allow free movement during normal driving. Make sure the retractors return the belt against your chest while driving and rewind the belt fully when the buckle is unlatched.

4   If any of the above checks reveal problems with the seat belt system, replace parts as necessary.

---

16   Underhood hose check and replacement (every 15,000 miles or 12 months)

Warning: *Replacement of air conditioning hoses must be left to a dealer service department or air conditioning shop that has the equipment to depressurize the system safely. Never remove air conditioning components or hoses until the system has been depressurized.*

General

1   High temperatures under the hood can cause deterioration of the rubber and plastic hoses used for engine, accessory and emission systems operation. Periodic inspection should be made for cracks, loose clamps, material hardening and leaks.

2   Information specific to the cooling system hoses can be found in Section 17.

3   Most (but not all) hoses are secured to the fittings with clamps. Where clamps are used, check to be sure they haven't lost their tension, allowing the hose to leak. If clamps aren't used, make sure the hose has not expanded and/or hardened where it slips over the fitting, allowing it to leak.

PCV system hose

4   To reduce hydrocarbon emissions, crankcase blow-by gas is vented through the PCV valve in the rocker arm cover to the intake manifold via a rubber hose on most models. The blow-by gases mix with incoming air in the intake manifold before being burned in the combustion chambers.

5   Check the PCV hose for cracks, leaks and other damage. Disconnect it from the valve cover and the intake manifold and check the inside for obstructions. If it's clogged, clean it out with solvent.

Vacuum hoses

6   It's quite common for vacuum hoses, especially those in the emissions system, to be color coded or identified by colored stripes molded into them. Various systems require hoses with different wall thickness, collapse resistance and temperature resistance. When replacing hoses, be sure the new ones are made of the same material.

7   Often the only effective way to check a hose is to remove it completely from the vehicle. If more than one hose is removed, be sure to label the hoses and fittings to ensure correct installation.

8   When checking vacuum hoses, be sure to include any plastic T-fittings in the check. Inspect the fittings for cracks and the hose where it fits over each fitting for distortion, which could cause leakage.

9   A small piece of vacuum hose (1/4-inch inside diameter) can be used as a stethoscope to detect vacuum leaks. Hold one end of the hose to your ear and probe around vacuum hoses and fittings, listening for the "hissing" sound characteristic of a vacuum leak. **Warning:** *When probing with the vacuum hose stethoscope, be careful not to come into contact with moving engine components such as drivebelts, the cooling fan, etc.*

Fuel hose

Warning: *Gasoline and diesel fuels are flammable, so take extra precautions when you work on any part of the fuel system. Don't smoke or allow open flames or bare light bulbs near the work area, and don't work in a garage where a gas-type appliance (such as a water heater or clothes dryer) is present. Since fuel is carcinogenic, wear latex gloves when there's a possibility of being exposed to fuel, and, if you spill any fuel on your skin, rinse it off immediately with soap and water. Mop up any spills immediately and do not store fuel-soaked rags where they could ignite. The fuel system is under constant pressure, so, if any fuel lines are to be disconnected, the fuel pressure in the system must be relieved first (see Chapter 4 for more information). When you perform any kind of work on the fuel system, wear safety glasses and have a Class B type fire extinguisher on hand.*

10   The fuel lines are usually under pressure, so if any fuel lines are to be disconnected be prepared to catch spilled fuel. **Warning:** *Your vehicle is equipped with fuel injection and you must relieve the fuel system pressure before servicing the fuel lines. Refer to Chapter 4 for the fuel system pressure relief procedure.*

11   Check all flexible fuel lines for deteriora-

tion and chafing. Check especially for cracks in areas where the hose bends and just before fittings, such as where a hose attaches to the fuel pump, fuel filter and fuel injection unit.

12   When replacing a hose, use only hose that is specifically designed for your fuel injection system.

13   Spring-type clamps are sometimes used on fuel return or vapor lines. These clamps often lose their tension over a period of time, and can be "sprung" during removal. Replace all spring-type clamps with screw clamps whenever a hose is replaced. Some fuel lines use spring-lock type couplings, which require a special tool to disconnect. See Chapter 4 for more information on this type of couplings.

Check for a chafed area that could fail prematurely.

Check for a soft area indicating the hose has deteriorated inside.

Overtightening the clamp on a hardened hose will damage the hose and cause a leak.

Check each hose for swelling and oil-soaked ends. Cracks and breaks can be located by squeezing the hose.

17.4a Hoses, like drivebelts, have a habit of failing at the worst possible time - to prevent the inconvenience of a blown radiator or heater hose, inspect them carefully as shown here

Metal lines

14   Sections of metal line are often used for fuel line between the fuel pump and the fuel injection unit. Check carefully to make sure the line isn't bent, crimped or cracked.

15   If a section of metal fuel line must be replaced, use seamless steel tubing only, since copper and aluminum tubing do not have the strength necessary to withstand vibration caused by the engine.

16   Check the metal brake lines where they enter the master cylinder and brake proportioning unit (if used) for cracks in the lines and loose fittings. Any sign of brake fluid leakage calls for an immediate thorough inspection of the brake system.

17   Cooling system check (every 15,000 miles or 12 months)

Refer to illustrations 17.4a and 17.4b

1   Many major engine failures can be attributed to a faulty cooling system. The cooling system also plays an important role in prolonging transmission life because it cools the fluid.

2   The engine should be cold for the cooling system check, so perform the following procedure before the vehicle is driven for the day or after it has been shut off for at least three hours.

3   Remove the cap from the expansion tank. Clean the cap thoroughly, inside and out, with clean water. Also clean the filler neck on the expansion tank. The presence of rust or corrosion in the filler neck means the coolant should be changed (see Section 26). The coolant inside the radiator should be relatively clean and transparent. If it's rust colored, drain the system and refill it with new coolant.

4   Carefully check the radiator hoses and the smaller diameter heater hoses **(see illustration)**. Inspect each coolant hose along its entire length, replacing any hose which is cracked, swollen or deteriorated. Cracks will

17.4b A leak in the gasoline engine heater hose means the intake manifold will have to be removed for hose replacement - coolant coming out the back of the engine is the symptom

show up better if the hose is squeezed. Pay close attention to hose clamps that secure the hoses to cooling system components. Hose clamps can pinch and puncture hoses, resulting in coolant leaks. Some hoses are hidden from view so sometimes you'll have to trace a coolant leak. For example, on gasoline engines the heater hose connects to the water pump under the intake manifold. If it leaks, coolant will run down the rear of the engine **(see illustration)**.

5   Make sure that all hose connections are tight. A leak in the cooling system will usually show up as white or rust colored deposits on the area adjoining the leak. If wire-type clamps are used on the hoses, it may be a good idea to replace them with screw-type clamps.

6   Clean the front of the radiator and air conditioning condenser with compressed air, if available, or a soft brush. Remove all bugs, leaves, etc. embedded in the radiator fins. Be extremely careful not to damage the cooling fins or cut your fingers on them.

7   If the coolant level has been dropping consistently and no leaks are detectable, have the radiator cap and cooling system pressure checked at a service station.

18   Fuel system check (every 15,000 miles or 12 months)

Warning: *Gasoline and diesel fuels are flammable, so take extra precautions when you work on any part of the fuel system. Don't smoke or allow open flames or bare light bulbs near the work area, and don't work in a garage where a gas-type appliance (such as a water heater or clothes dryer) is present. Since fuel is carcinogenic, wear latex gloves when there's a possibility of being exposed to fuel, and, if you spill any fuel on your skin, rinse it off immediately with soap and water. Mop up any spills immediately and do not store fuel-soaked rags where they could ignite. When you perform any kind of work on the fuel system, wear safety glasses and have a Class B type fire extinguisher on hand. The fuel system is under constant pressure, so, before any lines are disconnected, the fuel system pressure must be relieved (see Chapter 4).*

1   If you smell gasoline while driving or after the vehicle has been sitting in the sun, inspect the fuel system immediately.

2   Remove the fuel filler cap and inspect it for damage and corrosion. The gasket should have an unbroken sealing imprint. If the gasket is damaged or corroded, install a new cap.

3   Inspect the fuel feed and return lines for cracks. Make sure that the connections between the fuel lines and the fuel injection system and between the fuel lines and the in-line fuel filter are tight. **Warning:** *Your vehicle is fuel injected, so you must relieve the fuel system pressure before servicing fuel system components. The fuel system pressure relief procedure is outlined in Chapter 4.*

19.3a Detach the safety clips from the inlet and outlet ports of the fuel filter

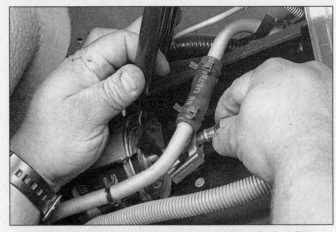

19.3b Install the fuel line disconnect tool onto the fuel filter port, then push the disconnect tool into the coupling until the fuel line releases itself

4   Since some components of the fuel system - the fuel tank and part of the fuel feed and return lines, for example - are underneath the vehicle, they can be inspected more easily with the vehicle raised on a hoist. If that's not possible, raise the vehicle and support it on jackstands.

5   With the vehicle raised and safely supported, inspect the gas tank and filler neck for punctures, cracks and other damage. The connection between the filler neck and the tank is particularly critical. Sometimes a rubber filler neck will leak because of loose clamps or deteriorated rubber. Inspect all fuel tank mounting brackets and straps to be sure that the tank is securely attached to the vehicle. **Warning:** *Do not, under any circumstances, try to repair a fuel tank (except rubber components). A welding torch or any open flame can easily cause fuel vapors inside the tank to explode.*

6   Carefully check all rubber hoses and metal lines leading away from the fuel tank. Check for loose connections, deteriorated hoses, crimped lines and other damage. Repair or replace damaged sections as necessary (see Chapter 4).

---

19   Fuel filter replacement (every 15,000 miles or 12 months)

Warning: *Gasoline and diesel fuels are flammable, so take extra precautions when you work on any part of the fuel system. Don't smoke or allow open flames or bare light bulbs near the work area, and don't work in a garage where a gas-type appliance (such as a water heater or clothes dryer) is present. Since fuel is carcinogenic, wear latex gloves when there's a possibility of being exposed to fuel, and, if you spill any fuel on your skin, rinse it off immediately with soap and water. Mop up any spills immediately and do not store fuel-soaked rags where they could ignite. When you perform any kind of work on the fuel system, wear safety glasses and have a Class B type fire extinguisher on hand.*

Gasoline engine

Refer to illustration 19.3a and 19.3b

1   The fuel filter on gasoline engines is mounted under the vehicle on the inside of the left frame rail.

2   Inspect the hose fittings at both ends of the filter to see if they're clean. If more than a light coating of dust is present, clean the fittings before proceeding.

3   Relieve the fuel system pressure (see Chapter 4). Removal of the fuel lines from the fuel filter is a two-stage procedure. First, detach any safety clips from the inlet and outlet lines. Second, install the special fuel line disconnect tool onto the fuel filter inlet port, then push the disconnect tool into the fuel line coupling until it releases itself from the fuel filter **(see illustrations)**. Repeat this procedure on the outlet port. **Note:** *See Chapter 4 for more information on spring-lock couplings.*

4   After both couplings have been released, grasp the fuel hoses, one at a time, and pull them straight off the filter. Be prepared for fuel spillage.

5   After the hoses have been detached, check the clips for damage and distortion. If they were damaged in any way during removal, new ones must be used when the hoses are reattached to the new filter (if new

clips are packaged with the filter, be sure to use them in place of the originals).

6   Remove the fuel filter from the mounting clamp, while noting the direction the fuel filter is installed.

7   On models with limited clearance, it may be necessary to unbolt the mounting bracket from the frame rail and remove it along with the filter, then separate the filter from the bracket.

8   Install the new filter in the same direction. Carefully push each hose onto the filter until it's seated against the collar on the fitting, then install the clips. Make sure the clips are securely attached to the hose fittings - if they come off, the hoses could back off the filter and a fire could result!

9   Start the engine and check for fuel leaks.

Diesel engines

Refer to illustration 19.13a, 19.13b, 19.14 and 19.15

10   The fuel filter on diesel engines is mounted on top of the engine.

11   Remove the engine cover (if equipped).

12   Relieve the fuel system pressure (see Chapter 4B).

13   Unscrew the filter housing cover **(see illustrations)**.

19.13a Remove the 7.3L diesel fuel filter cover by turning it counterclockwise

19.13b The secondary fuel filter housing on 6.0L diesel engines is the smaller of the two on top of the engine. The larger housing contains the oil filter

19.14 Lift the filter out of the housing

19.15 Make sure the housing is clean before installing the new filter

19.21 The primary (larger mesh) fuel filter on 6.0L diesel engines is in the fuel conditioning module. Unscrew the cap from the rear of the module to remove the filter

14   Lift the filter and O-ring out of the housing **(see illustration)**.

15   Use a syringe or poultry baster to draw out any residual fuel from the housing. Clean out the housing before installing the new filter **(see illustration)**.

16   Coat the O-ring with clean diesel fuel and install it onto the filter element.

17   Lower the new filter into place, making sure to seat the O-ring.

18   Install the cover and tighten it slowly so the filter element can soak up fuel. Once the cap contacts the housing surface, tighten it fully.

19   Start the engine and check for fuel leaks.

6.0L models - primary filter

Refer to illustration 19.21

Note: *There is no recommended replacement interval for this filter. It should be replaced any time there is concern about poor or contaminated fuel or there is simply high vehicle mileage.*

20   6.0L diesel models use a primary (10 micron) filter before the main (4 micron) engine-mounted filter. This filter is part of the fuel conditioning module that is bolted to the frame of the vehicle. For additional information on the fuel conditioning module, refer to

Chapter 4B.

21   Raise the vehicle and support it securely on jackstands. Locate the fuel conditioning module forward of the fuel tank on the left frame rail **(see illustration)**.

22   Relieve the fuel system pressure (refer to Chapter 4B).

23   Place a drain pan and rags under the fuel conditioning module.

24   Unscrew the cover from the rear side of the module. On some vehicles it is easier to first remove the fuel conditioning module (refer to Chapter 5).

25   Remove the fuel filter cartridge and dispose of it properly.

26   Inspect the O-ring and replace it if necessary.

27   Installation is the reverse of removal.

28   Start the engine and check for fuel leaks before driving the vehicle.

20   Steering and suspension check (every 15,000 miles or 12 months)

Refer to illustrations 20.6, 20.9a, 20.9b, 20.9c and 20.11

Note: *The steering linkage and suspension components should be checked peri-*

odically. Worn or damaged suspension and steering linkage components can result in excessive and abnormal tire wear, poor ride quality and vehicle handling and reduced fuel economy. For detailed illustrations of the steering and suspension components, refer to Chapter 10.

Shock absorber check

1   Park the vehicle on level ground, turn the engine off and set the parking brake. Check the tire pressures.

2   Push down at one corner of the vehicle, then release it while noting the movement of the body. It should stop moving and come to rest in a level position within one or two bounces.

3   If the vehicle continues to move up-and-down or if it fails to return to its original position, a worn or weak shock absorber is probably the reason.

4   Repeat the above check at each of the three remaining corners of the vehicle.

5   Raise the vehicle and support it securely on jackstands.

6   Check the shock absorbers for evidence of fluid leakage **(see illustration)**. A light film of fluid is no cause for concern. Make sure that any fluid noted is from the shocks and not from some other source. If leakage is noted,

20.6 Check the shocks for leakage at the indicated area (arrow)

20.9a Inspect the steering and suspension components for torn grease seals (arrows)

20.9b Check the stabilizer bar and link bushings for deterioration at the front and the rear of the vehicle

replace the shocks as a set.

7   Check the shocks to be sure that they are securely mounted and undamaged. Check the upper mounts for damage and wear. If damage or wear is noted, replace the shocks as a set (front or rear).

8   If the shocks must be replaced, refer to Chapter 10 for the procedure.

Steering and suspension check

9   Visually inspect the steering and suspension components for damage and distortion. Look for damaged seals, boots and bushings and leaks of any kind (see illustrations).

10   Clean the lower end of the steering knuckle. Have an assistant grasp the lower edge of the tire and move the wheel in-and-out while you look for movement at the steering knuckle-to-control arm balljoint. If there is 1/32-inch or more movement the suspension balljoint(s) must be replaced.

11   Grasp each front tire at the front and rear edges, push in at the front, pull out at the rear and feel for play in the steering system com-

ponents. If any freeplay is noted, check the tie-rod ends for looseness (see illustration).

12   Additional steering and suspension system information and illustrations can be found in Chapter 10.

---

21   Brake check (every 15,000 miles or 12 months)

Warning: *The dust created by the brake system is harmful to your health. Never blow it out with compressed air and don't inhale any of it. An approved filtering mask should be worn when working on the brakes. Do not, under any circumstances, use petroleum-based solvents to clean brake parts. Use brake system cleaner only! Try to use non-asbestos replacement parts whenever possible.*
Note: *For detailed photographs of the brake system, refer to Chapter 9.*

1   In addition to the specified intervals, the brakes should be inspected every time the wheels are removed or whenever a defect is suspected.

2   Any of the following symptoms could indicate a potential brake system defect: The vehicle pulls to one side when the brake pedal is depressed; the brakes make squealing or dragging noises when applied; brake pedal travel is excessive; the pedal pulsates; brake fluid leaks, usually onto the inside of the tire or wheel.

3   Loosen the wheel lug nuts.

4   Raise the vehicle and place it securely on jackstands.

5   Remove the wheels (see *Jacking and towing* at the front of this book, or your owner's manual, if necessary).

Disc brakes

Refer to illustrations 21.6 and 21.11

6   There are two pads (an outer and an inner) in each caliper. The pads are visible through inspection holes in each caliper (see illustration).

7   Check the pad thickness by looking at each end of the caliper and through the inspection hole in the caliper body. If the lining material is less than the thickness listed in this

20.11 With the steering wheel locked and the vehicle raised, grasp the front tire as shown and try to move it back-and-forth - if any play is noted, check the tie-rod ends for looseness

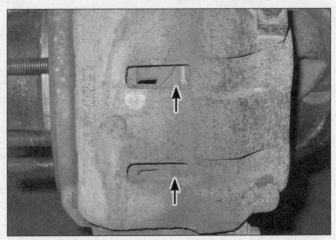

21.6 You will find an inspection hole(s) like this in each caliper - placing a ruler across the hole should enable you to determine the thickness of remaining pad material for the inner and outer pads

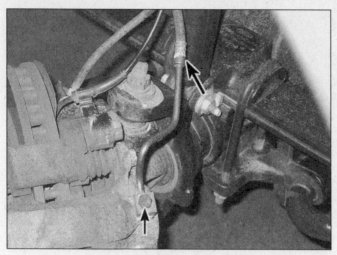

21.11 Check along the brake hoses and at each fitting for deterioration and cracks

22.2 The manual transmission fill plug and drain plug are located on the side of the transmission case

Chapter's Specifications, replace the pads. **Note:** *Keep in mind that the lining material is riveted or bonded to a metal backing plate and the metal portion is not included in this measurement.*

8   If it is difficult to determine the exact thickness of the remaining pad material by the above method, or if you are at all concerned about the condition of the pads, remove the caliper(s), then remove the pads from the calipers for further inspection (refer to Chapter 9).

9   Once the pads are removed from the calipers, clean them with brake cleaner and re-measure them with a ruler or a vernier caliper.

10   Measure the disc thickness with a micrometer to make sure that it still has service life remaining. If any disc is thinner than the specified minimum thickness, replace it (see Chapter 9). Even if the disc has service life remaining, check its condition. Look for scoring, gouging and burned spots. If these conditions exist, remove the disc and have it resurfaced (see Chapter 9).

11   Before installing the wheels, check all brake lines and hoses for damage, wear, deformation, cracks, corrosion, leakage, bends and twists, particularly in the vicinity of the rubber hoses at the calipers **(see illustration)**. Check the clamps for tightness and the connections for leakage. Make sure that all hoses and lines are clear of sharp edges, moving parts and the exhaust system. If any of the above conditions are noted, repair, reroute or replace the lines and/or fittings as necessary (see Chapter 9).

Brake booster check

12   Sit in the driver's seat and perform the following sequence of tests.

13   With the brake fully depressed, start the engine - the pedal should move down a little when the engine starts.

14   With the engine running, depress the brake pedal several times - the travel distance should not change.

15   Depress the brake, stop the engine and hold the pedal in for about 30 seconds - the pedal should neither sink nor rise.

16   Restart the engine, run it for about a minute and turn it off. Then firmly depress the brake several times - the pedal travel should decrease with each application.

17   If your brakes do not operate as described, the brake booster has failed. Refer to Chapter 9 for the replacement procedure.

Parking brake

18   One method of checking the parking brake is to park the vehicle on a steep hill with the parking brake set and the transmission in Neutral (stay in the vehicle for this check!). If the parking brake cannot prevent the vehicle from rolling, it's in need of adjustment (see Chapter 9).

22   Manual transmission lubricant level check (every 15,000 miles or 12 months)

Refer to illustration 22.2

1   The manual transmission has a filler plug which must be removed to check the lubricant level. If the vehicle is raised to gain access to the plug, be sure to support it safely on jackstands - DO NOT crawl under a vehicle which is supported only by a jack! Be sure the vehicle is level or the check may be inaccurate.

2   Using a wrench, unscrew the plug from the transmission **(see illustration)** and use a finger to reach inside the housing to determine the lubricant level. The level should be at or near the bottom of the plug hole.

3   If it isn't, add the recommended lubricant through the plug hole with a pump or squeeze bottle.

4   Install and tighten the plug and check for leaks after the first few miles of driving.

23   Transfer case lubricant level check (4WD models) (every 15,000 miles or 12 months)

Refer to illustration 23.1

1   The lubricant level is checked by removing a plug from the side of the case **(see illustration)**. If the vehicle is raised to gain access to the plug, be sure to support it safely on jackstands - DO NOT crawl under the vehicle when it's supported only by a jack!

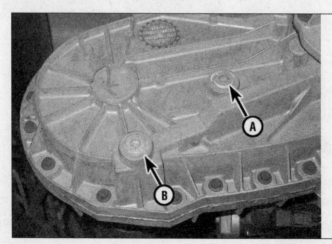

23.1 The transfer case fill plug (A) and drain plug (B) are located on the rear of the transfer case

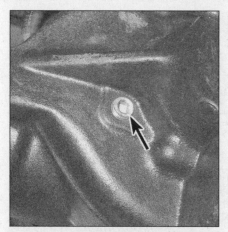

24.2a Some check/fill plugs (arrow) are located at the front of the differential housing

24.2b On other models the check/ fill plug is on the differential cover - use a 3/8-inch drive ratchet or breaker bar and an extension to remove it

2   With the engine and transfer case cold, remove the plug. If lubricant immediately starts leaking out, thread the plug back into the case - the level is correct. If it doesn't, completely remove the plug and reach inside the hole with your little finger. The level should be even with the bottom of the plug hole.

3   If more lubricant is needed, use a syringe or small pump to add it through the opening.

4   Thread the plug back into the case and tighten it securely. Drive the vehicle, then check for leaks around the plug.

24   Differential lubricant level check (every 15,000 miles or 12 months)

Refer to illustrations 24.2a, 24.2b and 24.2c

1   The differential has a check/fill plug which must be removed to check the lubricant level. If the vehicle is raised to gain access to the plug, be sure to support it safely on jackstands - DO NOT crawl under the vehicle when it's supported only by the jack!

2   Remove the check/fill plug from the dif-

ferential **(see illustrations)**.

3   Use your little finger as a dipstick to make sure the lubricant level is even with the bottom of the plug hole. If not, use a syringe to add the recommended lubricant until it just starts to run out of the opening. On some models a tag is located in the area of the plug which gives information regarding lubricant type, particularly on models equipped with a Traction Lok differential.

4   Install the plug and tighten it securely.

25   Air filter check and replacement (every 30,000 miles or 24 months)

Gasoline engines

Refer to illustration 25.1

1   The air filter is located inside a housing at the left (driver's) side of the engine compartment. To remove the air filter, disconnect the mass air flow electrical connector, release the clamp that secures the two halves of the air cleaner housing together, then separate the cover halves and remove the air filter ele-

ment **(see illustration)**. On models with the MAF sensor located in the air intake tube, disconnect the sensor electrical connector before changing the air filter.

2   Inspect the outer surface of the filter element. If it is dirty, replace it. If it is only moderately dusty, it can be reused by blowing it clean from the back to the front surface with compressed air. Because it is a pleated paper type filter, it cannot be washed or oiled. If it cannot be cleaned satisfactorily with compressed air, discard and replace it. While the cover is off, be careful not to drop anything down into the housing. **Caution:** *Never drive the vehicle with the air cleaner removed. Excessive engine wear could result and backfiring could even cause a fire under the hood.*

3   Wipe out the inside of the air cleaner housing.

4   Place the new filter into the air cleaner housing, making sure it seats properly.

5   Installation of the housing is the reverse of removal.

Diesel engines

Refer to illustration 25.6, 25.7a and 25.7b

6   Since an uninterrupted air supply is cru-

24.2c Use your finger as a dipstick to check the lubricant level

25.1 After separating the housing halves, withdraw the air filter element

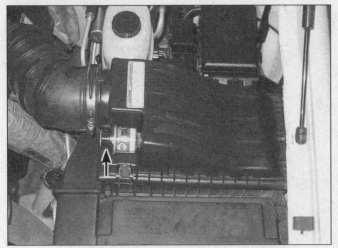

25.6 Check the diesel engine air restriction gauge
and change the filter element if necessary

25.7a Loosen the hose clamp screw and detach the air hose, then
release the two air cleaner cover clips on 7.3L engine

25.7b Rotate the cover up and lift the air filter element
from the housing

25.12 On 6.0L diesel engines, release these four air filter
clamps - 6.4L similar (two clamps)

cial to the operation of a diesel engine, these models have an air filter restriction gauge mounted on the intake side of the air cleaner housing to monitor the condition of the air filter element. The air filter restriction gauge should be checked periodically to determine if dirt in the element is restricting the air flow. Regardless of mileage, replace the filter with a new one if the gauge is at the "Change Filter" mark **(see illustration)**.

7.3L engines

7   To replace the filter, detach the air intake hose, then release the two clips that secure the air cleaner housing cover and remove the air filter element **(see illustrations)**.

8   Wipe out the inside of the air cleaner housing.

9   Place the new filter into the air cleaner housing, making sure it seats properly.

10   Installation of the housing is the reverse of removal.

11   After replacing the filter element, reset the air restriction gauge by pressing the button on the end.

6.0L engines

Refer to illustrations 25.12, 25.13 and 25.14.

12   This engine uses a PowerCore-type air filter. Release the two clamps at each end of the intake duct/air filter **(see illustration)**.

13   Carefully disengage the tabs on the rear cover from the slots in the air filter/duct **(see illustration)**. Separate the two pieces and push the rear cover back so it is held out of the way under the coolant reservoir.

25.13 The 6.0L air filter element uses slots that engage with tabs to secure it; use care when releasing them. These pins engage holes in the air filter support

1   Air filter slots
2   Air filter support pins

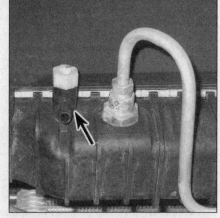

25.14 The rear and the front filter ends must be pulled away after releasing the tabs from the slots in order to lift the 6.0L diesel air filter straight up from its base

1   *Rear air filter cover with tabs*
2   *Front air filter cover with tabs*
3   *Air filter support*

26.4 The radiator drain fitting is located at the lower corner of the radiator (arrow)

26.5 The block drain plugs (arrow) are generally located about one to two inches above the oil pan - there is one on each side of the engine block

14   Carefully disengage the tabs on the front cover from the slots in the air filter/duct. Separate the two pieces and lift the air filter off of its base **(see illustration)**.

15   Installation is the reverse of removal. Be sure that all of the tabs and slots are properly engaged so that there will be no air leaks. The four clamps must also be securely fastened.

26   Cooling system servicing (draining, flushing and refilling) (every 30,000 miles or 24 months)

Refer to illustrations 26.4 and 26.5
Warning: *Do not allow antifreeze to come in contact with your skin or painted surfaces of the vehicle. Rinse off spills immediately with plenty of water. Antifreeze is highly toxic if ingested. Never leave antifreeze lying around in an open container or in puddles on the floor; children and pets are attracted by it's sweet smell and may drink it. Check with local* authorities about disposing of used antifreeze. *Many communities have collection centers which will see that antifreeze is disposed of safely.*

1   Periodically, the cooling system should be drained, flushed and refilled to replenish the antifreeze mixture and prevent formation of rust and corrosion, which can impair the performance of the cooling system and cause engine damage. When the cooling system is serviced, all hoses and the expansion tank cap should be checked and replaced if necessary.

Draining

2   Apply the parking brake and block the wheels. If the vehicle has just been driven, wait several hours to allow the engine to cool down before beginning this procedure.

3   Once the engine is completely cool, remove the expansion tank cap.

4   Move a large container under the radiator drain to catch the coolant. Attach a 3/8-inch diameter hose to the drain fitting to direct the coolant into the container, then open the drain fitting (a pair of pliers may be required to turn it) **(see illustration)**.

5   After the coolant stops flowing out of the radiator, move the container under the engine block drain plugs and allow the coolant in the block to drain **(see illustration)**.

6   While the coolant is draining, check the condition of the radiator hoses, heater hoses and clamps (refer to Section 17 if necessary). Replace any damaged clamps or hoses.

7   Reinstall the block drain plugs and tighten them securely.

Flushing

Refer to illustration 26.10

8   Once the system has completely drained, remove the thermostat housing from the engine (see Chapter 3), then reinstall the housing without the thermostat. This will allow the system to be thoroughly flushed.

9   Disconnect the upper hose from the radiator.

10   Place a garden hose in the upper radiator inlet and flush the system until the water runs clear at the upper radiator hose **(see illustration)**.

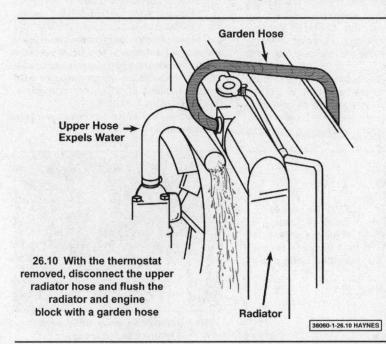

Garden Hose

Upper Hose Expels Water

26.10 With the thermostat removed, disconnect the upper radiator hose and flush the radiator and engine block with a garden hose

Radiator

36060-1-26.10 HAYNES

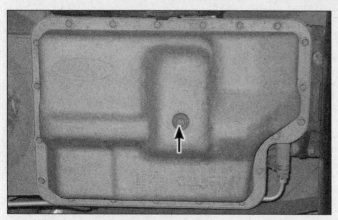

27.5 Remove the drain plug (arrow) and allow the fluid to drain

27.9 Carefully rotate the filter as you pull straight down to remove it

11   Severe cases of radiator contamination or clogging will require removing the radiator (see Chapter 3) and reverse flushing it. This involves inserting the hose in the bottom radiator outlet to allow the clean water to run against the normal flow, draining out through the top. A radiator repair shop should be consulted if further cleaning or repair is necessary.

12   When the coolant is regularly drained and the system refilled with the correct coolant mixture there should be no need to employ chemical cleaners or descalers.

Refilling

13   Close and tighten the radiator drain.

14   Place the heater temperature control in the maximum heat position.

15   Slowly add new coolant (a 50/50 mixture of water and antifreeze) to the expansion tank until the level is between the MIN and MAX marks.

16   Leave the expansion tank cap off and run the engine in a well-ventilated area until the thermostat opens (coolant will begin flowing through the radiator and the upper radiator hose will become hot).

17   Turn the engine off and let it cool. Add more coolant mixture to bring the level between the MIN and MAX marks on the expansion tank.

18   Squeeze the upper radiator hose to expel air, then add more coolant mixture if necessary. Replace the expansion tank cap.

19   Start the engine, allow it to reach normal operating temperature and check for leaks. Also, set the heater and blower controls to

the maximum setting and check to see that the heater output from the air ducts is warm. This is a good indication that all air has been purged from the cooling system.

---

27   Automatic transmission fluid and filter change (every 30,000 miles or 24 months)

Refer to illustrations 27.5, 27.9, 27.11, 27.12, and 27.13

1   At the specified intervals, the transmission fluid should be drained and replaced. Since the fluid will remain hot long after driving, perform this procedure only after the engine has cooled down completely.

2   Before beginning work, purchase the transmission fluid specified in *Recommended lubricants and fluids* at the front of this Chapter, a new torque converter drain plug, a new filter and, if necessary, a new gasket. Never reuse the old filter! **Note:** *The gasket is reusable as long as it isn't damaged.* **Note:** *On later models with Torqshift transmission, the transmission fluid filter is located remotely from the transmission on a bracket under the bellhousing. Remove the mounting bracket to access the filter.*

3   Other tools necessary for this job include jackstands to support the vehicle in a raised position, a drain pan capable of holding at least ten quarts, newspapers and clean rags.

4   Raise the vehicle and support it securely

on jackstands.

5   With the drain pan in place, remove the plug and allow the fluid to run into the pan **(see illustration)**. **Note:** *If your fluid pan isn't equipped with a drain plug, loosen all of the pan bolts, then remove the front and side bolts. Carefully pry the rear of the pan down and allow the fluid to drain. Now remove the rear pan bolts and detach the pan, being careful not to spill the remaining fluid.*

6   Remove the bolts and carefully pry the transmission pan loose with a screwdriver. Don't damage the pan or transmission gasket surfaces or leaks could develop.

7   Carefully clean the gasket surface of the transmission to remove all traces of the old gasket and sealant.

8   Clean the transmission pan with solvent and dry it thoroughly.

9   Remove the old filter from the transmission **(see illustration)**. If the filter seal did not come out with the filter, remove it from the transmission being careful not to gouge the seal bore in any way.

10   Install a new seal and filter.

11   Make sure the gasket surface on the transmission pan is clean, then install a new gasket **(see illustration)**. Put the pan in place against the transmission and install the bolts. Working around the pan, tighten each bolt a little at a time until the final torque figure listed in this Chapter's Specifications is reached. Don't overtighten the bolts!

12   Remove the torque converter cover **(see illustration)**.

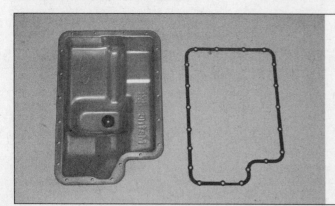

27.11 Be sure to clean all traces of the old gasket from the pan before installing a new one

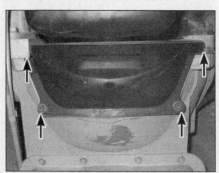

27.12 Remove the bolts and detach the torque converter cover

27.13 Remove the torque converter drain plug (arrow) and drain the fluid

13 Remove the drain plug and allow the fluid in the torque converter to drain out **(see illustration)**.

14 After the fluid has drained completely, install the new drain plug. Some models may have an inline fuel filter in the transmission cooler line. Replace this filter with a new one whenever the fluid is changed.

15 Lower the vehicle and add 6-1/2 quarts of automatic transmission fluid through the filler tube (see Section 7).

16 With the transmission in Park and the parking brake set, run the engine at a fast idle, but don't race it.

17 Move the gear selector through each range and back to Park. Check the fluid level. Add fluid if needed to reach the correct level. **Caution:** Add fluid 1/2-pint at a time to avoid overfilling the transmission.

18 Check under the vehicle for leaks during the first few trips.

28 Front wheel bearing check, repack and adjustment (2WD models) (every 30,000 miles or 24 months)

Check and repack

Refer to illustrations 28.1, 28.3, 28.6, 28.7, 28.10, 28.11, 28.15 and 28.19

1 In most cases the front wheel bearings

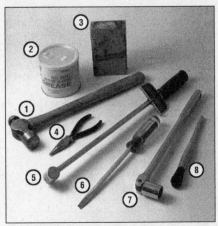

28.1 Tools and materials needed for front wheel bearing maintenance

1 **Hammer** - *A common hammer will do just fine*

2 **Grease** - *High-temperature grease that is formulated specially for front wheel bearings should be used*

3 **Wood block** - *If you have a scrap piece of 2x4, it can be used to drive the new seal into the hub*

4 **Needle-nose pliers** - *Used to straighten and remove the cotter pin in the spindle*

5 **Torque wrench** - *Used for pre-loading the bearing before adjustment*

6 **Screwdriver** - *Used to remove the seal from the hub (a long screwdriver is preferred)*

7 **Socket/breaker bar** - *Needed to loosen the nut on the spindle if it's extremely tight*

8 **Brush** - *Together with some clean solvent, this will be used to remove old grease from the hub and spindle*

will not need servicing until the brake pads are changed. However, the bearings should be checked whenever the front of the vehicle is raised for any reason. Several items, including a torque wrench and special grease, are required for this procedure **(see illustration)**.

28.3 To check the wheel bearings, move the tire in and out as shown above - if there's any noticeable freeplay, the bearings should be checked and then repacked with grease (or replaced if necessary)

2 With the vehicle securely supported on jackstands, spin each wheel and check for noise, rolling resistance and freeplay.

3 Grasp the top of each tire with one hand and the bottom with the other **(see illustration)**. Move the wheel in-and-out on the spindle. If there's any noticeable movement, the bearings should be checked and then repacked with grease or replaced if necessary.

4 Remove the wheel.

5 Remove the brake caliper (see Chapter 9) and hang it out of the way on a piece of wire.

6 Dislodge the dust cap from the hub/disc assembly using a screwdriver or hammer and chisel **(see illustration)**.

7 Straighten the bent ends of the cotter pin, then pull the cotter pin out of the nut lock **(see illustration)**. Discard the cotter pin and use a new one during reassembly.

8 Remove the nut lock, nut and washer from the end of the spindle.

9 Pull the hub/disc assembly out slightly, then push it back into its original position. This should force the outer bearing off the spindle enough so it can be removed.

10 Pull the disc assembly off the spindle **(see illustration)**.

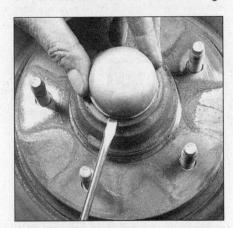

28.6 Dislodge the dust cap by working around the outer circumference with a screwdriver or a hammer and chisel

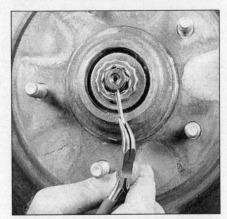

28.7 Remove the cotter pin and discard it - use a new one when the disc assembly is reinstalled

28.10 After the washer and outer wheel bearing have been dislodged, pull the disc off the spindle

28.11 Use a seal puller or large screwdriver to remove the inner grease seal - note the seal installed position

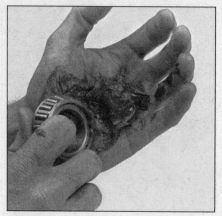

28.15 Work the grease completely into the bearing rollers

28.19 Gently tap the grease seal into place

11   Use a screwdriver or a seal puller tool to pry the seal out of the rear of the hub **(see illustration)**. Note how the seal is installed.
12   Remove the inner wheel bearing from the hub.
13   Use solvent to remove all traces of the old grease from the bearings, hub and spindle. A small brush may prove helpful; however make sure no bristles from the brush embed themselves inside the bearing rollers. Allow the parts to air dry.
14   Carefully inspect the bearings for cracks, heat discoloration, worn rollers, etc. Check the bearing races inside the hub for wear and damage. If the bearing races are defective, the hubs should be taken to a machine shop with the facilities to remove the old races and press new ones in. Note that the bearings and races come as matched sets and old bearings should never be installed on new races.
15   Use high-temperature front wheel bearing grease to pack the bearings. Work the grease completely into the bearings, forcing it between the rollers, cone and cage from the larger diameter side **(see illustration)**.
16   Apply a thin coat of grease to the spindle at the outer bearing seat, inner bearing seat, shoulder and seal seat.
17   Put a small quantity of grease inboard of each bearing race inside the hub.
18   Place the grease-packed inner bearing into the rear of the hub and put a little more grease outboard of the bearing.
19   Place a new seal over the inner bearing and tap the seal evenly into place until it's flush with the hub **(see illustration)**.
20   Carefully place the hub assembly onto the spindle and push the grease-packed outer bearing into position.

Adjustment

21   Install the washer and spindle nut. Tighten the nut only slightly (no more than 12 ft-lbs of torque).
22   Spin the hub in a forward direction while tightening the spindle nut to the Step 1 torque torque listed in this Chapter's Specifications.
23   Loosen the spindle nut 1/2-turn, then

tighten the nut to the Step 3 torque listed in this Chapter's Specifications. Install the nut lock and a new cotter pin through the hole in the spindle and the slots in the nut lock. If the slots in the nut lock don't line up with the hole in the spindle, reposition the nut lock until they do.
24   Check that the hub/disc assembly spins freely with no noticeable freeplay. If freeplay exists repeat Steps 22 and 23 until proper adjustment is obtained.
25   Bend the ends of the cotter pin until they're flat against the nut. Cut off any extra length which could interfere with the dust cap.
26   Install the dust cap, lightly tapping it into place with a hammer.
27   Install the brake caliper mount, pads and caliper in the reverse order of removal (see Chapter 9).
28   Install the wheel on the hub and tighten the lug nuts.
29   Lower the vehicle and tighten the lug nuts to the torque listed in this Chapter's Specifications.

29   Brake fluid change (every 30,000 miles or 24 months)

Warning: *Brake fluid can harm your eyes and damage painted surfaces, so use extreme caution when handling or pouring it. Do not use brake fluid that has been standing open or is more than one year old. Brake fluid absorbs moisture from the air. Excess moisture can cause a dangerous loss of braking effectiveness.*
1   At the specified intervals, the brake fluid should be drained and replaced. Since the brake fluid may drip or splash when pouring it, place plenty of rags around the master cylinder to protect any surrounding painted surfaces.
2   Before beginning work, purchase the specified brake fluid (see *Recommended lubricants and fluids* at the beginning of this Chapter).
3   Remove the cap from the master cylinder reservoir.

4   Using a hand suction pump or similar device, withdraw the fluid from the master cylinder reservoir.
5   Add new fluid to the master cylinder until it rises to the base of the filler neck.
6   Bleed the brake system as described in Chapter 9 at all four brakes until new and uncontaminated fluid is expelled from the bleeder screw. Be sure to maintain the fluid level in the master cylinder as you perform the bleeding process. If you allow the master cylinder to run dry, air will enter the system.
7   Refill the master cylinder with fluid and check the operation of the brakes. The pedal should feel solid when depressed, with no sponginess. **Warning:** *Do not operate the vehicle if you are in doubt about the effectiveness of the brake system.*

30   Drivebelt check (every 3000 miles or 3 months) and replacement (every 60,000 miles or 48 months)

1   The drivebelt is located at the front of the engine and plays an important role in the overall operation of the vehicle and its components. Due to its function and material make-up, the drivebelt is prone to failure after a period of time and should be inspected and adjusted periodically to prevent major engine damage.
2   The vehicles covered by this manual are equipped with a single self-adjusting serpentine drivebelt, which is used to drive all of the accessory components such as the alternator, power steering pump, water pump and air conditioning compressor.

Inspection

Refer to illustrations 30.4 and 30.5
3   With the engine off, open the hood and locate the drivebelt at the front of the engine. Using your fingers (and a flashlight, if necessary), move along the belts checking for cracks and separation of the belt plies. Also check for fraying and glazing, which gives the belt a shiny appearance. Both sides of each belt should be inspected, which means you

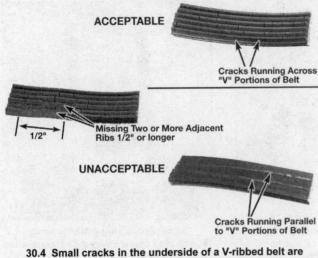

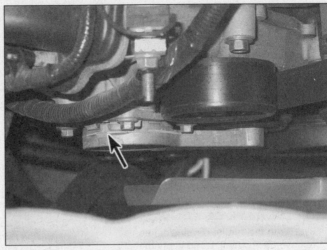

30.4 Small cracks in the underside of a V-ribbed belt are acceptable - lengthwise cracks, or missing pieces that cause the belt to make noise, are cause for replacement

30.5 Belt wear indicator marks (arrow) are located on the side of the tensioner body - when the belt reaches the maximum wear mark it must be replaced

will have to twist the belt to check the underside.

4   Check the ribs on the underside of the belt. They should all be the same depth, with none of the surface uneven **(see illustration)**.

5   The tension of the belt is automatically adjusted by the belt tensioner and does not require any adjustments. Drivebelt wear can be checked visually by inspecting the wear indicator marks located on the side of the tensioner body. Locate the belt tensioner at the front of the engine on the right (passenger) side, adjacent to the lower crankshaft pulley, then find the tensioner operating marks **(see illustration)**. If the indicator mark is outside the operating range, the belt should be replaced.

Replacement

Refer to illustrations 30.6 and 30.18

Gasoline engines

6   To replace the belt, rotate the tensioner to relieve the tension on the belt **(see illustration)**. Some models have a square hole in the tensioner arm that will accept a 1/2 inch drive breaker bar. On other models, place a wrench on the tensioner pulley bolt.

Diesel engines

Warning: *Wait until the engine is completely cool before beginning this procedure.*

7   Drain the cooling system (see Section 26).

7.3L engine

8   Remove the upper radiator hose (see Chapter 3).

6.0L engine

9   Remove the cooling fan and fan clutch (see Chapter 3). **Note:** *On some models, it may be necessary to cut the shroud for removal. Carefully slice the upper and lower sections along the molded-in line on each side,*

at the indentations, using a sharp razor knife. After the upper and lower shrouds have been separated, drill two small holes on each side (four total) and install self-tapping screws to secure the shroud together during installation.

6.4L engine

10   Disconnect the coolant hose-to-fuel cooler at the power steering reservoir.

11   Remove the power steering reservoir from the upper shroud.

12   Remove the cooling fan upper shroud and the right side intercooler duct.

13   On models with an electric vacuum pump:

   a) *Disconnect the vacuum solenoid and the retainers from the upper fan shroud.*

   b) *Disconnect the vacuum hose at the right battery.*

   c) *Disconnect the vacuum hose at the coolant expansion tank (see Chapter 3).*

14   Remove the four bolts and separate the upper cooling shroud from the lower cooling shroud.

15   Rotate the engine cooling fan until the unevenly spaced blades allow for drivebelt tensioner access.

All diesel engines

16   To replace the belt, rotate the tensioner to relieve the tension on the belt **(see illustration 30.6)**. Some models have a square hole in the tensioner arm that will accept a 1/2 inch drive breaker bar. On other models, place a wrench on the tensioner pulley bolt.

All engines

17   Remove the belt from the auxiliary components and carefully release the tensioner.

18   Route the new belt over the various pulleys, again rotating the tensioner to allow the belt to be installed, then release the belt tensioner. Make sure the belt fits properly into the pulley grooves - it must be completely engaged. **Note:** *Most models have a drivebelt routing decal on the upper radiator panel to help during drivebelt installation* **(see illustration)**.

30.6 Rotate the tensioner arm to relieve belt tension

30.18 The routing schematic for the serpentine belt is usually found on the fan shroud

31.2 With the engine running at idle, remove the PCV valve and verify that vacuum can be felt at the end of the valve

31 Positive Crankcase Ventilation (PCV) valve check (every 60,000 miles or 48 months)

Refer to illustration 31.2

Note 1: *To maintain efficient operation of the PCV system, clean the hoses and check the PCV valve at the intervals recommended in the maintenance schedule. For additional information on the PCV system, refer to Chapter 6.*

Note 2: *This Section applies to models with gasoline engines only.*

1   The PCV valve on all gasoline engines covered by this manual is located in the valve cover.

2   Start the engine and allow it to idle, then disconnect the PCV valve from the valve cover and feel for vacuum at the end of the valve **(see illustration)**. If vacuum is felt, the PCV valve/system is working properly (see Chapter 6 for additional PCV system information).

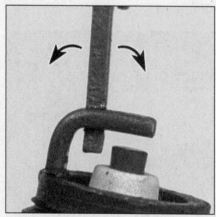

32.5b To change the gap, bend the side electrode only, as indicated by the arrows, and be very careful not to crack or chip the porcelain insulator surrounding the center electrode

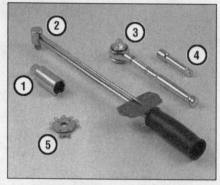

32.2 Tools required for changing spark plugs

1   *Spark plug socket* - This will have special padding inside to protect the spark plug's porcelain insulator

2   *Torque wrench* - Although not mandatory, using this tool is the best way to ensure the plugs are tightened properly

3   *Ratchet* - Standard hand tool to fit the spark plug socket

4   *Extension* - Depending on model and accessories, you may need special extensions and universal joints to reach one or more of the plugs

5   *Spark plug gap gauge* - This gauge for checking the gap comes in a variety of styles. Make sure the gap for your engine is included

3   If no vacuum is felt, remove the valve and check for vacuum at the hose. If vacuum is present at the hose but not at the valve, replace the valve. If no vacuum is felt at the hose, check for a plugged or cracked hose between the PCV valve and the intake plenum.

4   Check the rubber grommet in the valve cover for cracks and distortion. If it's damaged, replace it.

5   If the valve is clogged, the hose is also probably plugged. Remove the hose between the valve and the intake manifold and clean it with solvent.

6   After cleaning the hose, inspect it for damage, wear and deterioration. Make sure it fits snugly on the fittings.

7   If necessary, install a new PCV valve.

32 Spark plug check and replacement (every 60,000 miles or 48 months)

Refer to illustrations 32.2, 32.5a, 32.5b, 32.6, 32.10a and 32.10b

Caution: *Ford has issued a Technical Service Bulletin (TSB 08-7-6) stating that attempting to remove the spark plugs is likely to result in the extended electrode of the plug breaking off in the cylinder head. This TSB pertains to 4.6L three-valve engines built before 11/30/07, and 5.4L and 6.8L three-valve engines built before 10/9/07. Engine build date can be found on*

32.5a Spark plug manufacturers recommend using a wire-type gauge when checking the gap - if the wire does not slide between the electrodes with a slight drag, adjustment is required

a label affixed to the left valve cover. We highly recommend entrusting this procedure to a Ford dealer service department or other qualified technician equipped with the necessary special tools. If you do decide to attempt spark plug replacement, we recommend that you obtain the Ford TSB (it can be obtained via internet search) and follow the procedure exactly.

1   On these vehicles the spark plugs are located at the top of the engine.

2   In most cases, the tools necessary for spark plug replacement include a spark plug socket which fits onto a ratchet (spark plug sockets are padded inside to prevent damage to the porcelain insulators on the new plugs), various extensions and a gap gauge to check and adjust the gaps on the new plugs **(see illustration)**. A torque wrench should be used to tighten the new plugs.

3   The best approach when replacing the spark plugs is to purchase the new ones in advance, adjust them to the proper gap and replace the plugs one at a time. When buying the new spark plugs, be sure to obtain the correct plug type for your particular engine. This information can be found in the Specifications Section at the beginning of this Chapter, on the Emission Control Information label located under the hood or in the factory owner's manual. If differences exist between the plug specified on the emissions label, Specifications Section or in the owner's manual, assume that the emissions label is correct.

4   Allow the engine to cool completely before attempting to remove any of the plugs. These engines are equipped with aluminum cylinder heads, which can be damaged if the spark plugs are removed when the engine is hot. While you are waiting for the engine to cool, check the new plugs for defects and adjust the gaps.

5   The gap is checked by inserting the proper thickness gauge between the electrodes at the tip of the plug **(see illustration)**.

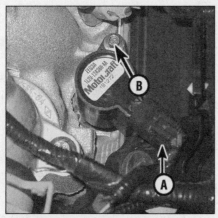

32.6 The ignition coils must be removed to access the spark plugs - disconnect the electrical connector (A) and remove the coil retaining screw (B) - pull straight up and out to remove the coil

32.10a Apply a thin film of anti-seize compound to the spark plug threads to prevent damage to the cylinder head

32.10b A length of rubber hose will save time and prevent damaged threads when installing the spark plugs

The gap between the electrodes should be the same as the one specified on the Emissions Control Information label. The wire should just slide between the electrodes with a slight amount of drag. If the gap is incorrect, use the adjuster on the gauge body to bend the curved side electrode slightly until the specified gap is obtained **(see illustration)**. If the side electrode is not exactly over the center electrode, bend it with the adjuster until it is. Check for cracks in the porcelain insulator (if any are found, the plug should not be used).

6   These engines are equipped with individual ignition coils which must be removed first to access the spark plugs **(see illustration)**.

7   If compressed air is available, use it to blow any dirt or foreign material away from the spark plug hole. The idea here is to eliminate the possibility of debris falling into the cylinder as the spark plug is removed.

8   Place the spark plug socket over the plug and remove it from the engine by turning it in a counterclockwise direction.

9   Compare the spark plug to those shown in the photos located on the inside back cover to get an indication of the general running condition of the engine.

10   Apply a small amount of anti-seize compound to the spark plug threads **(see illustration)**. Install one of the new plugs into the hole until you can no longer turn it with your fingers, then tighten it with a torque wrench (if available) or the ratchet. It is a good idea to slip a short length of rubber hose over the end of the plug to use as a tool to thread it into place **(see illustration)**. The hose will grip the plug well enough to turn it, but will start to slip if the plug begins to cross-thread in the hole - this will prevent damaged threads and the accompanying repair costs.

11   Before pushing the ignition coil onto the end of the plug, inspect it following the procedures outlined in Section 33.

12   Repeat the procedure for the remaining spark plugs.

33 Ignition coil check and replacement (every 60,000 miles or 48 months)

1   Clean the coils with a dampened cloth and dry them thoroughly.

2   Inspect each coil for cracks, damage and carbon tracking. Make sure the coil fits securely onto the spark plug. If damage exists, replace the coil **(see illustration 32.6)**.

34 Manual transmission lubricant change (every 60,000 miles or 48 months)

1   Raise the vehicle and support it securely on jackstands.

2   Move a drain pan, rags, newspapers and wrenches under the transmission.

3   Remove the transmission drain plug at the bottom of the case and allow the lubricant to drain into the pan **(see illustration 22.2)**.

4   After the lubricant has drained completely, reinstall the plug and tighten it securely.

5   Remove the fill plug from the side of the transmission case. Using a hand pump, syringe or funnel, fill the transmission with the specified lubricant until it is level with the lower edge of the filler hole. Reinstall the fill plug and tighten it securely.

6   Lower the vehicle.

7   Drive the vehicle for a short distance, then check the drain and fill plugs for leakage.

35 Transfer case lubricant change (4WD models) (every 60,000 miles or 48 months)

1   Drive the vehicle for at least 15 minutes to warm the lubricant in the case. Perform this

warm-up procedure with 4WD engaged, if possible.

2   Raise the vehicle and support it securely on jackstands.

3   Remove the drain plug from the lower part of the case and allow the old lubricant to drain completely **(see illustration 23.1)**.

4   After the lubricant has drained completely, reinstall the plug and tighten it securely.

5   Remove the filler plug from the case.

6   Fill the case with the specified lubricant until it is level with the lower edge of the filler hole.

7   Install the filler plug and tighten it securely.

8   Drive the vehicle for a short distance, then check the drain and fill plugs for leakage.

36 Differential lubricant change (every 30,000 miles or 24 months)

Drain

Refer to illustration 36.6, 36.8, 36.11a and 36.11b

1   This procedure should be performed after the vehicle has been driven so the lubricant will be warm and therefore flow out of the differential more easily.

2   Raise the vehicle and support it securely on jackstands.

3   The easiest way to drain the differential(s) is to remove the lubricant through the filler plug hole with a suction pump. If the differential cover gasket is leaking, it will be necessary to remove the cover to drain the lubricant (which will also allow you to inspect the differential).

Changing the lubricant with a suction pump

4   Remove the filler plug from the differential (see Section 24).

5   Insert the flexible hose.

36.6 This is the easiest way to remove the differential lubricant - work the end of the hose to the bottom of the differential housing and draw out the old lubricant with a suction pump

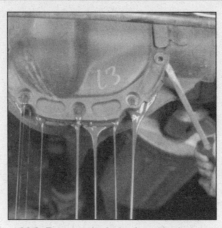

36.8 Remove the bolts from the lower edge of the cover then loosen the top bolts and let the lubricant drain

36.11a If you drain the differential by removing the cover, apply a thin film of RTV sealant to the differential cover just before installation

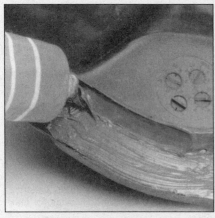

36.11b Apply a bead of RTV sealant around the inside edge of the cover inboard of the bolt holes

6   Work the hose down to the bottom of the differential housing and pump the lubricant out **(see illustration)**.

Changing rear differential lubricant by removing the cover

7   Move a drain pan, rags, newspapers and wrenches under the vehicle.

8   Remove the bolts on the lower half of the cover. Loosen the bolts on the upper half and use them to loosely retain the cover. Allow the oil to drain into the pan, then completely remove the cover **(see illustration)**.

9   Using a lint-free rag, clean the inside of the cover and the accessible areas of the differential housing. As this is done, check for chipped gears and metal particles in the lubricant, indicating that the differential should be more thoroughly inspected and/or repaired.

10   Thoroughly clean the gasket mating surfaces of the differential housing and the cover plate. Use a gasket scraper or putty knife to remove all traces of the old gasket.

11   Apply a thin layer of RTV sealant to the cover flange, then press a new gasket into position on the cover **(see illustrations)**. Make sure the bolt holes align properly.

Refill

12   Use a hand pump, syringe or funnel to fill the differential housing with the specified lubricant until it's level with the bottom of the filler plug hole.

13   Install the fill plug and tighten it securely.

Service record

Date	Mileage	Work performed

Service record

Date	Mileage	Work performed

Chapter 2 Part A
Gasoline engines

Contents

	Section
Balance shaft (V10 engine) - removal and installation	7
Camshafts - removal, inspection and installation	9
CHECK ENGINE light	See Chapter 6
Crankshaft oil seals - replacement	17
Crankshaft pulley - removal and installation	5
Cylinder heads - removal and installation	13
Engine mounts - check and replacement	18
Exhaust manifolds - removal and installation	12
Flywheel/driveplate - removal and installation	16
General information	1
Intake manifold - removal and installation	11

	Section
Oil pan - removal and installation	14
Oil pump - removal and installation	15
Repair operations possible with the engine in the vehicle	2
Rocker arms and valve lash adjusters - removal, inspection and installation	8
Timing chain cover, timing chains, tensioners and sprockets - removal, inspection and installation	6
Top Dead Center (TDC) for number one piston - locating	3
Valve covers - removal and installation	4
Valve springs, retainers and seals - removal and installation	10

Specifications

General

Displacement
V8	5.4 liters (329 cubic inches)
V10	6.8 liters (415 cubic inches)

Bore and stroke
V8	3.554 X 4.168 inches
V10	3.554 X 4.168 inches

Cylinder numbers (front to rear)
V8
Right side	1-2-3-4
Left (driver's) side	5-6-7-8

V10
Right side	1-2-3-4-5
Left (driver's) side	6-7-8-9-10

Firing order
V8	1-3-7-2-6-5-4-8
V10	1-6-5-10-2-7-3-8-4-9

5.4L V8 ENGINE

1-3-7-2-6-5-4-8

Camshaft

Lobe lift
V8
1999 through 2002
Exhaust left side	0.260 inch
Exhaust right side	0.259 inch
Intake	0.259 inch

2003 through 2004
Exhaust	0.295 inch
Intake	0.280 inch

2005 and later	0.217 inch

V10
1999 through 2002
Exhaust	0.260 inch
Intake	0.259 inch

2003 through 2004	0.259 inch

2005 and later
Exhaust	0.217 inch
Intake	0.216 inch

6.8L V10 ENGINE

1-6-5-10-2-7-3-8-4-9

36060-2A-specs HAYNES

Cylinder numbering and firing order; both engines are equipped with coil-over-plug assemblies in which an ignition coil is mounted on top of each spark plug

Camshaft (continued)

Allowable lobe lift loss	
1999 through 2002...	0.004 inch
2003 through 2004...	0
2005 and later...	0.005 inch
Endplay	
V8	
1999 through 2004...	0.001 to 0.007 inch
2005 and later...	0.0003 to 0.007 inch
V10	
1999 through 2004...	0.001 to 0.007 inch
2005 through 2007...	0.001 to 0.002 inch
2008 and later...	0.001 to 0.007 inch
Journal diameter	
1999 through 2004...	1.060 to 1.062 inches
2005 and later...	1.126 to 1.127 inches
Bearing inside diameter	
1999 through 2004...	1.062 to 1.063 inches
2005 and later...	1.128 to 1.129 inches
Journal-to-bearing (oil) clearance	
Standard..	0.001 to 0.003 inch
Service limit...	0.005 inch

Torque specifications

Ft-lbs (unless otherwise indicated)

Note: *One foot-pound (ft-lb) of torque is equivalent to 12 inch-pounds (in-lbs) of torque. Torque values below approximately 15 foot-pounds are expressed in inch-pounds, because most foot-pound torque wrenches are not accurate at these smaller values.*

Balance shaft caps (V10 only)................................	89 in-lbs*
Camshaft caps-to-cylinder head............................	89 in-lbs*
Camshaft sprocket bolts	
V8	
1999 through 2004	
M10 (center) bolt	
Step 1..	30
Step 2..	Tighten an additional 90 degrees
M12 bolt..	90
2005 and later (camshaft phaser bolt)	
Step 1..	30
Step 2..	Tighten an additional 90 degrees
V10	
1999 through 2002...................................	41 to 55
2003 and later	
Step 1..	30
Step 2..	Tighten an additional 90 degrees
Crankshaft pulley bolt	
Step 1...	66
Step 2...	Loosen completely
Step 3...	37
Step 4...	Tighten an additional 90 degrees
Crankshaft rear oil seal retainer-to-block bolts	
1999 through 2002	
Step 1...	89 in-lbs
Step 2...	Tighten an additional 90 degrees
2003 and 2004...	89 in-lbs
2005 through 2007	
Step 1...	89 in-lbs
Step 2...	Tighten an additional 60 degrees
2008 and later...	89 in-lbs
Cylinder head bolts*	
Step 1...	30
Step 2...	Tighten an additional 90 degrees
Step 3...	Tighten an additional 90 degrees
Drivebelt idler and tensioner bolts	18
Engine mounts	
Engine mount-to-crossmember nuts	
1999 through 2004...................................	66
2005 through 2007...................................	76
2008 and later	
Left side...	48
Right side	85

Engine mount-to-engine mount bolts

1999 through 2004	59
2005 through 2007	46
2008 and later (throughbolt)	258
Exhaust manifold-to-cylinder head nuts*	18
Flywheel/driveplate bolts*	59

Intake manifold-to-cylinder head bolts*

1999 through 2004	
Step 1	89 in-lbs
Step 2	18
2005 and later	
Step 1	18 in-lbs
Step 2	89 in-lbs
Oil cooler-to-filter adapter nut	42
Oil filter adapter bolts	18

Oil pan-to-engine block bolts*

Step 1	18 in-lbs
Step 2	15
Step 3	Tighten an additional 60 degrees
Oil pump pick-up tube-to-main bearing cap nut (1999 through 2002)	15 to 22
Oil pump pick-up tube-to-oil pump bolts	89 in-lbs
Oil pump-to-engine block bolts	89 in-lbs

Timing chain cover bolts*

1999 though 2003	
Bolts 1 through 5	18
Bolts 6 through 15	35
2004 and later	
Step 1	15
Step 2	Tighten an additional 60 degrees

Timing chain cover-to oil pan bolts*

Step 1	18 in-lbs
Step 2	15
Step 3	
1999 through 2004	Tighten an additional 90 degrees
2005 and later	Tighten an additional 60 degrees
Timing chain guides	89 in-lbs
Timing chain tensioners	18
Valve cover bolts*	89 in-lbs

* Replace bolts with new ones whenever they are removed.

1 General information

This Part of Chapter 2 is devoted to in-vehicle repair procedures for the Single Overhead Cam (SOHC) 5.4L V8 and 6.8L V10 engines. Both engines share the same modular design: a chain-driven single overhead camshaft for each cylinder head, aluminum heads and an iron block. Except for an additional cylinder on each bank, the V10 engine design is virtually identical in design to the V8 engine. The bore and stroke of the V10 is the same as the V8. The only significant difference, besides the two extra cylinders, is a balance shaft on the left cylinder head, adjacent to the camshaft.

Beginning in 2005, both V8 and V10 engines have a new design using three valves per cylinder rather than the previous two. In addition, the 2005 and 2006 5.4L V8 is equipped with a variable camshaft timing system operated by the PCM.

The following repair procedures were written as if the engine were still in the vehicle. If the engine has been removed from the vehicle and mounted on a stand, many of the steps outlined in this Part of Chapter 2 will not apply. The Specifications included in this Part of Chapter 2 apply only to the procedures contained in this Part. Part C of Chapter 2 contains the Specifications necessary for other procedures. Information about engine removal and installation, and engine block and cylinder head overhaul is also in Part C.

2 Repair operations possible with the engine in the vehicle

Many major repair operations can be accomplished without removing the engine from the vehicle.

If possible, clean the engine compartment and the exterior of the engine with some type of pressure washer before any work is started. It will make the job easier and help keep dirt out of the internal areas of the engine.

If vacuum, exhaust, oil or coolant leaks develop, indicating a need for gasket or seal replacement, the repairs can generally be made with the engine in the vehicle. The intake and exhaust manifold gaskets, timing cover gasket, oil pan gasket, crankshaft oil seals and cylinder head gaskets are all accessible with the engine in place.

Exterior engine components, such as the intake and exhaust manifolds, the oil pan, the water pump, the starter motor, the alternator and the fuel system components can be removed for repair with the engine in place.

Since the cylinder heads can be removed without pulling the engine, valve component servicing can also be accomplished with the engine in the vehicle. Replacement of the timing chain and sprockets and oil pump is also possible with the engine in the vehicle.

In extreme cases caused by a lack of necessary equipment, repair or replacement of piston rings, pistons, connecting rods and rod bearings is also possible with the engine in the vehicle. However, this practice is not recommended because of the cleaning and preparation work that must be done to the components involved.

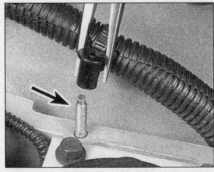

4.2 Disconnect the PVC valve hoses (center arrow) from the valve cover; to remove the valve cover, loosen the bolts around the perimeter of the cover (the bolts aren't removable; they stay with the valve cover when it comes off) (V8 engine)

4.7 Detach the wiring harness from each valve cover stud by pulling it straight up

3   Top Dead Center (TDC) for number one piston - locating

1   Top Dead Center (TDC) is the highest point in the cylinder that each piston reaches as it travels up-and-down when the crankshaft turns. Each piston reaches TDC on the compression stroke and again on the exhaust stroke, but TDC generally refers to piston position on the compression stroke.

2   Positioning the number one piston at TDC is an essential part of many procedures such as timing chain replacement.

3   Before beginning this procedure, be sure to disable the ignition system by disconnecting the electrical connector from the ignition coil at each spark plug (see Chapter 5).

4   Remove the spark plugs (see Chapter 1) and install a compression gauge in the number one cylinder (see the cylinder identification diagrams at the beginning of this Chapter).

5   In order to bring any piston to TDC, the crankshaft must be turned using one of the following methods. When looking at the front of the engine, normal crankshaft rotation is clockwise. **Warning:** *Before beginning this procedure, be sure to place the transmission in Park.*

 a) *The preferred method is to turn the crankshaft with a large socket and breaker bar attached to the pulley bolt threaded into the front of the crankshaft. Turn the bolt in a clockwise direction.*

 b) *A remote starter switch, which may save some time, can also be used. Attach the switch leads to the small ignition switch terminal and the positive (red) battery cable terminal on the starter solenoid (mounted near the battery). Once the piston is close to TDC, use a socket and breaker bar as described above.*

 c) *If an assistant is available to turn the ignition switch to the START position in short bursts, you can get the piston close to TDC without a remote starter switch. Use a socket and breaker bar as described in Paragraph a) to complete the procedure.*

6   Turn the crankshaft clockwise until you see compression building up on the gauge - you are on the compression stroke for that cylinder. If you did not see compression build up, continue with one more complete revolution to achieve TDC for the number one cylinder.

7   Remove the compression gauge. Through the number one cylinder spark plug hole insert a wooden dowel or plastic rod and slowly push it down until it reaches the top surface of the piston crown. **Caution:** *Don't insert a metal or sharp object into the spark plug hole as the piston crown may be damaged.*

8   With the dowel or rod in place on top of the piston crown, slowly rotate the crankshaft clockwise until the dowel or rod is pushed upward, stops, and then starts to move back down. At this point, rotate the crankshaft slightly counterclockwise until the dowel or rod has reached its uppermost travel. At this point the number one piston is at the TDC position.

9   After the number one piston has been positioned at TDC on the compression stroke, TDC for the next cylinder can be located by turning the crankshaft another 90-degrees (5.4L V8 engine) or 72 degrees (6.8L V10 engine) (refer to the firing order in this Chapter's Specifications).

4   Valve covers - removal and installation

V8 engine
Left valve cover
1999 through 2004 models
Refer to illustrations 4.2, 4.7 and 4.15

1   Remove the air cleaner and the air intake duct (see Chapter 4).

2   Disconnect the PCV valve from the valve cover **(see illustration)**.

3   Remove the exhaust manifold-to-EGR valve tube, if equipped.

4   Disconnect the electrical connectors from the left cylinder bank fuel injectors (see Chapter 4).

5   Disconnect the electrical connectors from the left cylinder bank ignition coils (see Chapter 5).

6   Disconnect the fuel pressure regulator vacuum hose (see Chapter 4).

7   Detach the fuel injection harness from the valve cover studs **(see illustration)**.

2005 and later models

8   Remove the air cleaner duct.

9   Remove the left ignition coils (refer to Chapter 5).

10   Remove the dipstick tube.

11   Disconnect and remove the PCV tube.

12   Disconnect any interfering wiring and hoses such as the brake booster hose and the variable camshaft timing solenoid connectors.

All models

13   Unscrew the valve cover bolts **(see illustration 4.2)** and remove the valve cover. **Note:** *The valve cover bolts are not removable; they stay with the valve cover.*

14   Remove the old valve cover gasket and any gasket material that's stuck to the head.

15   Apply RTV sealant to the mating joints between the timing cover and the cylinder head **(see illustration)**, then install the valve cover and gasket. **Note:** *Install the cover within*

4.15 Apply a dab of RTV sealant to the mating joints between the timing cover and the cylinder head before installing the valve cover

4.36 Disconnect the crankcase ventilation hose from the left valve cover, then remove the air cleaner housing and the air intake duct (the crankcase ventilation hose is not removable from the air intake duct) (V10 engine)

five minutes of applying the RTV sealant.

16   Working from the center of the valve cover out toward the ends, tighten the valve cover bolts in a criss-cross fashion, gradually and evenly, to the torque listed in this Chapter's Specifications.

17   Installation is otherwise the reverse of removal.

Right valve cover

1999 through 2004 models

18   Disconnect the vacuum canister vacuum hose and set it aside (see Chapter 6).

19   Remove the nuts from the EVAP canister purge valve bracket and remove the EVAP canister purge valve, the bracket and the heater coolant hose and set them aside (see Chapter 6).

20   Disconnect the PCV ventilation tube from the valve cover.

21   Remove the three screws from the accumulator bracket.

22   Unscrew the evaporator core cover screws and remove the evaporator core cover (Chapter 3).

23   Disconnect the electrical connectors from the right cylinder bank ignition coils (Chapter 5).

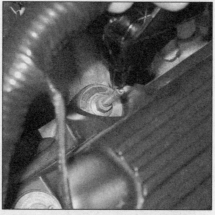

4.40 To detach the fuel injector wiring harness from the valve cover studs, pull each connector straight up

24   Disconnect the electrical connectors from the right cylinder bank fuel injectors (Chapter 4).

25   Release the harness routing clips from the valve cover studs **(see illustration 4.7)** and from the air conditioning compressor-to-condenser hose. Lift the fuel charging wiring harness off the valve cover studs and set it aside.

2005 and later models

26   If there is a transmission filler tube that interferes, remove it.

27   Remove the control solenoid for the right variable camshaft timing system.

28   Remove the right ignition coils (refer to Chapter 5).

29   Remove the evaporative emissions purge valve (refer to Chapter 6).

30   Disconnect any interfering hoses and wiring.

All models

31   Unscrew the valve cover bolts **(see illustration 4.2)** and remove the valve cover. **Note:** *The valve cover bolts are not removable; they stay with the valve cover.*

32   Remove the old valve cover gasket and any gasket material that's stuck to the head.

33   Apply RTV sealant to the mating joints between the timing cover and the cylinder head **(see illustration 4.15)**, then install the valve

cover and gasket. **Note:** *Install the cover within five minutes of applying the RTV sealant.*

34   Working from the center of the valve cover out toward the ends, tighten the valve cover bolts in a criss-cross fashion, gradually and evenly, to the torque listed in this Chapter's Specifications.

35   Installation is otherwise the reverse of removal.

V10 engine

Left valve cover

Refer to illustrations 4.36, 4.40, 4.47 and 4.48

1999 through 2004 models

36   Disconnect the crankcase ventilation hose from the valve cover **(see illustration)** and then remove the air cleaner and the air intake duct (see Chapter 4).

37   Disconnect the electrical connectors from the left cylinder bank fuel injectors (see Chapter 4).

38   Disconnect the electrical connectors from the left cylinder bank ignition coils (see Chapter 5).

39   Disconnect the fuel pressure regulator vacuum hose (see Chapter 4).

40   Detach the fuel injection wiring harness from the valve cover studs **(see illustration)**.

2005 and later models

41   Remove the air inlet duct.

42   Remove the left ignition coils (refer to Chapter 5).

43   Remove the dipstick.

44   Remove the two mounting bolts from the degas bottle (coolant reservoir). Move the bottle aside.

45   Disconnect and remove the PCV tube.

46   Disconnect the wiring harness retainers from the valve cover. Also disconnect any other interfering wiring or hoses.

All models

47   Unscrew the valve cover bolts **(see illustration)** and remove the valve cover. **Note:** *The valve cover bolts are not removable; they stay with the valve cover.*

48   Remove the old valve cover gasket **(see illustration)** and any gasket material that's stuck to the head.

4.47 To remove the valve cover from a V10 engine, unscrew these bolts (the bolts aren't removable; they stay with the valve cover when it comes off) (V10 engine)

4.48 Remove the old valve cover gasket

49   Apply RTV sealant to the mating joints between the timing cover and the cylinder head **(see illustration 4.15)** and install the valve cover and gasket. **Note:** *Install the cover within five minutes of applying the RTV sealant.*

50   Working from the center of the valve cover out toward the ends, tighten the valve cover bolts in a criss-cross fashion, gradually and evenly, to the torque listed in this Chapter's Specifications.

51   Installation is otherwise the reverse of removal.

Right valve cover

1999 through 2004 models

Refer to illustrations 4.53, 4.57a, 4.57b, 4.59 and 4.60

52   Drain the cooling system (see Chapter 1).

53   Disconnect the crankcase ventilation tube from the valve cover **(see illustration)**.

54   Disconnect the electrical connectors from the right cylinder bank fuel injectors (see Chapter 4).

55   Disconnect the electrical connectors from the right cylinder bank ignition coils (see Chapter 5).

56   Remove the alternator (see Chapter 5).

57   Install an engine support fixture **(see illustrations)**.

58   Raise the vehicle and support it securely on jackstands.

59   Remove the right engine mount nuts **(see illustration)**.

60   Disconnect the front heater hose **(see illustration)**.

61   Disconnect the vapor management valve vacuum hose and the vacuum canister vacuum harness.

62   Detach the fuel injection harness from the valve cover studs **(see illustration 4.30)** and then set it aside.

63   Raise the engine just enough to access the lower valve cover bolts.

2005 and later models

64   Remove the right ignition coils (refer to

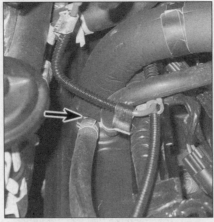

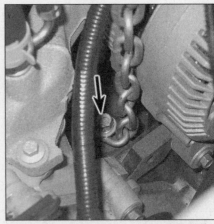

4.53 Disconnect the crankcase ventilation tube (arrow) from the right valve cover (V10 engine)

4.57a Attach a lifting chain to the block with a bolt . . .

4.57b . . . then install an engine support fixture and attach the chain to the fixture

Chapter 5).

65   On automatic transmission vehicles, remove the transmission filler tube.

66   Remove the alternator (see Chapter 5).

67   Remove the throttle body air inlet ducting.

68   Remove the fan shroud (see Chapter 3).

69   Install an engine support fixture **(see illustration 4.57a and 4.57b)**.

70   Loosen but do not remove the transmission mount nuts and the left engine mount nuts.

71   Remove the three right engine mount nuts.

72   Disconnect the catalytic converters from the exhaust manifolds.

4.59 To detach the right engine mount from the frame, remove these two nuts (arrows)

4.60 Loosen the hose clamp and disconnect the heater hose (arrow); plug the hose to prevent coolant from dripping on the engine

5.4 With an assistant holding the crankshaft at the flywheel/
driveplate end, unscrew the crankshaft pulley bolt

5.5 Remove the crankshaft pulley with a puller that bolts
to the crankshaft pulley hub

73   Remove the tubes from the evaporative emissions purge valve and the PCV valve along with any other interfering wiring or hoses.
74   Raise the engine enough for access to all of the bolts.

All models
75   Unscrew the valve cover bolts **(see illustration 4.47)** and remove the valve cover **Note:** *The valve cover bolts are not removable; they stay with the valve cover.*
76   Remove the old valve cover gasket **(see illustration 4.48)** and any gasket material that's stuck to the head.
77   Apply RTV sealant to the mating joints between the timing cover and the cylinder head **(see illustration 4.15)**, then install the valve cover and gasket. **Note:** *Install the cover within five minutes of applying the RTV sealant.*
78   Working from the center of the valve

cover out toward the ends, tighten the valve cover bolts in a criss-cross fashion, gradually and evenly, to the torque listed in this Chapter's Specifications.
79   Installation is otherwise the reverse of removal.

5   Crankshaft pulley - removal and installation

Removal
Refer to illustrations 5.4 and 5.5
1   Remove the engine cooling fan and fan shroud (see Chapter 3).
2   Remove the accessory drivebelt (see Chapter 1).
3   Remove the flywheel/driveplate inspection cover (see Chapter 7) and have an assistant wedge a large prybar or screwdriver into the starter ring gear teeth to prevent the crankshaft from turning.
4   Remove the large center bolt from the crankshaft pulley **(see illustration)**.
5   Using a suitable puller, detach the crankshaft pulley **(see illustration)**. Leave the Woodruff key in place in the crankshaft keyway. **Caution:** *Don't use a puller with jaws that grip the outer edge of the crankshaft pulley. The puller must be the type shown in the illustration that utilizes bolts to apply force to the crankshaft pulley hub only.*

Installation
Refer to illustration 5.6
6   Lubricate the oil seal contact surface of the crankshaft pulley hub **(see illustration)** with multi-purpose grease or clean engine oil. Apply a dab of RTV sealant to the front end of the keyway in the crankshaft pulley before installation.
7   Install the crankshaft pulley on the end of the crankshaft. The keyway in the crankshaft pulley must be aligned with the Woodruff key in the crankshaft. If the crankshaft pulley can-

not be seated by hand, slip the large washer over the bolt, install the bolt and tighten it to pull the crankshaft pulley into place. Now loosen the bolt one full turn, then tighten the bolt to the torque listed in this Chapter's Specifications.
8   The remaining installation steps are the reverse of removal.
9   Check the oil level. Run the engine and check for oil leaks.

6   Timing chain cover, timing chains, tensioners and sprockets - removal, inspection and installation

Removal
Refer to illustrations 6.9, 6.15, 6.17, 6.18, 6.19a, 6.19b, 6.20a, 6.20b, 6.22, 6.27a, 6.27b, 6.27c and 6.27d
Caution: *The timing system is complex. Severe engine damage will occur if you make any mistakes. Do not attempt this procedure unless you are highly experienced with this type of repair. If you are at all unsure of your abilities, consult an expert. Double-check all your work and be sure everything is correct before you attempt to start the engine.*
Caution: *Once the timing chain(s) have been removed, DO NOT ROTATE the crankshaft or the camshafts, or the valves and/or pistons will be damaged. Special tools are necessary to prevent the camshafts from moving when the timing chain is removed. Read through the entire procedure and obtain the necessary tools before proceeding.*
Note: *Because these engines are an interference design, there will be damage to the valves and/or pistons if a chain has broken, and this will require removal of the cylinder head(s).*
1   Position the number one cylinder on TDC (see Section 3), then remove the spark plugs (see Chapter 1). Disconnect the negative bat-

5.6 Inspect the crankshaft pulley for signs of damage or excessive wear

1   *Oil seal surface*
2   *Woodruff keyway*

6.9 Unscrew the bolts and remove the drivebelt tensioner and the idler pulley from the timing chain cover

6.15 Separate the timing chain cover from the engine, using a soft-faced hammer if necessary to break the gasket seal

tery cable (see Chapter 5, Section 1).

2   Remove the engine cooling fan (refer to Chapter 3). On 1999 through 2004 models, the radiator must also be removed.

3   Remove the valve covers (refer to Section 4).

4   Remove the drivebelt(s).

5   Drain the engine oil (refer to Chapter 1).

6   Remove the crankshaft pulley (refer to Section 5).

7   On 1999 through 2004 models, remove the water pump (refer to Chapter 3). On 2005 and later models, remove the water pump pulley.

8   Remove the bolts from the power steering pump, move the pump aside and secure it so it will not move.

9   Remove the drivebelt tensioner and idler pulleys **(see illustration)**.

10   Disconnect the camshaft position sensor wiring on 1999 through 2004 models. On 2005 and later models, the sensors themselves must be removed (refer to Chapter 6).

11   Disconnect the crankshaft position sen-

sor wiring on 1999 through 2004 models. On 2005 and later models, the sensor itself must be removed (refer to Chapter 6).

12   On 2005 and later models, unbolt the air conditioning compressor and set it aside. Do not loosen or disconnect the refrigerant fittings/hoses.

13   There are several wiring harnesses and brackets attached to the front cover that vary from year to year. Make sure to disconnect all interfering wiring, etc.

14   Remove the wiring harness retaining nuts and set the wiring harness aside.

15   Remove the timing chain cover bolts in the reverse order of the tightening sequence **(see illustration 6.44)** and remove the cover **(see illustration)**. If it's stuck, tap it gently with a soft-face hammer to break the gasket bond. **Caution:** *DO NOT use excessive force or you may crack the cover. If the cover is difficult to remove, make sure all of the bolts have been removed.*

16   Remove the timing chain cover gasket and dowel pins.

17   There are two long timing chains connecting the crankshaft to the camshafts **(see illustration)**.

18   Remove the crankshaft position sensor toothed-wheel by sliding it off the end of the crankshaft nose. Note the word "REAR" stamped on the wheel **(see illustration)**; when you reinstall the wheel, make sure it's facing in the correct direction.

1999 through 2004 2-valve engines

19   On V10 engines, remove the balance shaft (see Section 7). On all two-valve engines, install the camshaft and crankshaft retaining tools **(see illustrations)**. The camshaft holding tools lock the camshafts in position to prevent any movement of the cams in either direction - caused by valve spring pressure - when the timing chains are removed. **Caution:** *The camshafts MUST be retained exactly at TDC. If the valve timing is off when the timing chain(s) are reinstalled, severe engine damage could result.* The crankshaft holding tool locks the crankshaft into place to

6.17 Both the V8 and the V10 engines have two long timing chains and two tensioners

6.18 The toothed wheel for the crankshaft sensor must be installed with the word "REAR" facing toward the crankshaft timing chain sprockets

6.19a Use this crankshaft positioning tool to lock the crank in place while the timing chains are removed; the side hole fits over the dowel on the right side of the engine

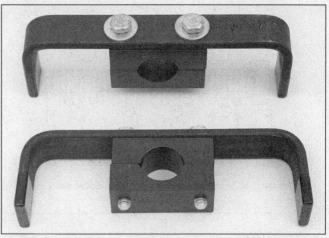

6.19b Lock each camshaft in the TDC position with a camshaft holding tool, which bolts onto the camshaft between the second and third (from the front) camshaft retaining caps; the "legs" fit against the valve cover mounting surface on the cylinder head

prevent it from turning, which would allow the pistons to hit the valves.

20 Remove the right side timing chain tensioner **(see illustrations)**.

21 Remove the right timing chain from the crankshaft and camshaft sprockets, by slipping the chain off the camshaft sprocket and pulling the crankshaft sprocket off with the chain.

22 Remove the stationary guide **(see illustration)**.

23 Remove the left side timing chain tensioner. Lift the chain off the camshaft sprocket and remove the chain along with the crankshaft sprocket.

24 Remove the left side stationary guide.

25 If the camshaft sprockets are to be replaced, remove the camshaft sprocket bolt and large washer from the camshafts, then pull the camshaft sprockets off. Use a two-bolt puller to remove the camshaft sprockets. **Note:** *Note the location and direction of any spacers on the crankshaft or camshafts, but do not remove the spacers unless necessary.*

6.20a To remove the right timing chain tensioner, remove the two bolts from the tensioner . . .

2005 and later 3-valve models

Note: *The three-valve engines use a different method of securing the camshafts in position because they use phasers rather than simple sprockets.*

26 Rotate the engine until the crankshaft keyway is at the 12 o'clock position. The exhaust cam lobe must be coming up on the exhaust stroke and the intake lobes must be in about the 10 o'clock position. If it's not in

6.20b . . . and then detach the guide assembly from the dowel at the opposite end (the left tensioner is removed the same way)

6.22 To remove the stationary chain guide, remove these bolts from the mounting plate

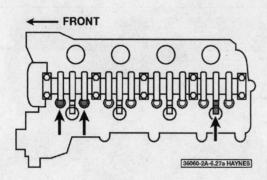

6.27a On 5.4L V8 engines, remove these rocker arms from the left head

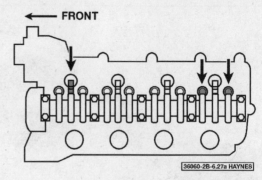

6.27b On 5.4L V8 engines, remove these rocker arms from the right head

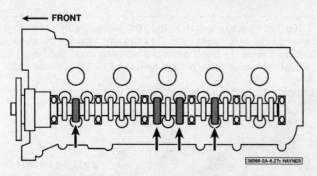

6.27c On 6.8L V10 engines, remove these rocker arms from the left head

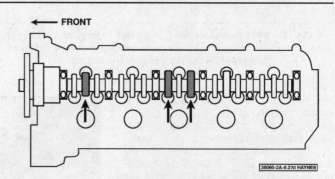

6.27d On 6.8L V10 engines, remove these rocker arms from the right head

this position, rotate the crankshaft one full turn until it is correct.

27   Use a special tool **(see illustrations 8.3a and 8.3b)** to remove the camshaft rocker arms shown **(see illustrations)**. *Caution: Be careful to avoid dropping the valve keepers into the cylinders during this operation.*

28   Rotate the crankshaft clockwise one-half turn so the keyway is at the 6 o'clock position. *Caution: Once you have set the crankshaft at this position, do not move it. Don't try to turn it farther than this or damage will result.*

29   Unbolt and remove the timing chain tensioners. The timing chain tensioner arms can also be removed at this time. **Note:** *Inspect the tensioner sealing beads for wear and damage. If there are any unusual signs, replace them.*

30   Remove the timing chain guides.

31   *Caution: Only use hand tools when working on the phasers. They are fragile; any lifting or prying on them will cause damage.* **Note:** *The manufacturer recommends that you use a special tool to hold the camshaft phasers while you loosen the phaser bolts. If you can't get access to this tool, a rubber strap-type wrench will work instead.* Hold the phasers and remove the mounting bolts. Carefully lift the phasers from the ends of the camshafts.

Inspection

Refer to illustrations 6.33a and 6.33b

32   Inspect the individual sprocket teeth and keyways for wear and damage. Check the chain for cracked plates and pitted or worn roll-ers. Check the wear surface of the chain guides for wear and damage. Replace any excessively worn or defective parts with new ones. *Caution: If excessive plastic material is missing from the chain guides, the oil pan should be removed and cleaned of all debris (see Section 14). Check the oil pick-up tube and screen. Replace the assembly if it is clogged.*

33   Check the primary tensioners for proper operation:

a) *Release the plunger lock* **(see illustration)** *and make sure the piston moves freely.*

b) *Submerge the tensioner in a can of oil or solvent, remove from the fluid and depress the plunger to make sure the oil feed hole is not plugged* **(see illustration)**. **Note:** *Also inspect the oil feed hole in the engine block to be certain it's not plugged.*

Installation

Caution: Before starting the engine, carefully rotate the crankshaft by hand through at least two full revolutions (use a socket and breaker bar on the crankshaft pulley center bolt). If you feel any resistance, STOP! There is something wrong - most likely, valves are contacting the pistons. You must find the problem before proceeding. Check your work and see if any updated repair information is available.

1999 through 2004 engines

Refer to illustrations 6.35, 6.39a, 6.39b and 6.40

34   Install the stationary chain guides, for both sides, and tighten the bolts to the torque listed in this Chapter's Specifications.

35   If removed, install the inner crankshaft sprocket (for the left timing chain) on the crankshaft with the shoulder of the sprocket facing forward. When the two sprockets are correctly installed, the shoulders on the hubs face each other, creating a space between the two sprockets **(see illustration)**. For now, only install the inner (left chain) crankshaft sprocket, with its shoulder forward.

36   The two timing chains should each have two bright or colored links. The links separate the chain in two equal halves. If no colored links are present, lay the chain down, make a paint mark on a link, then count links and make another paint mark halfway around the chain. Reinstall both stationary chain guides. **Note:** *The longer bolts are the ones that hold the guide to the cylinder head - the shorter ones go to the engine block.*

37   Loosen the camshaft holding tools just enough to permit minor movement of the camshafts for alignment. Using a camshaft positioning tool, available at most auto parts stores, or a two-pin spanner that catches two of the camshaft sprocket holes, turn the left camshaft until the timing mark on the sprocket is at 12 o'clock (viewed from the front of the engine). Turn the right sprocket until its mark is at 11 o'clock, then retighten both camshaft holding tools.

38   Install the inner crankshaft sprocket with the shoulder facing out, if not already done **(see illustration 6.35)**.

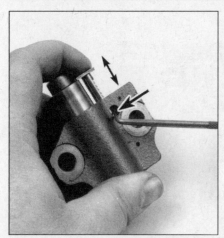

6.33a To fully retract the primary tensioner, release the plunger lock and push the plunger into the tensioner body

6.33b Check the tensioner oil feed hole to be sure it's not plugged by debris

6.35 When both crankshaft sprockets are installed, they should align like this, with the shoulder of the sprocket for the left timing chain facing forward, and the sprocket for the right chain with its shoulder facing toward the other sprocket

39　Install the left timing chain, aligning the bright link with the dimple on the camshaft sprocket (see illustration 6.39b). Loop the timing chain under the crankshaft sprocket and align the bright link with the alignment mark on the crankshaft sprocket. The timing marks on the crankshaft sprocket should be in the 6 o'clock position (see illustration). Note: *The slack side of the chain (towards the water pump) must be below the dowel pin on the block.* Install the crankshaft sprocket for the right timing chain with its shoulder facing in (see illustration 6.35). Install the right timing chain as described above, with the bright link aligned with the alignment mark on the crankshaft sprocket (see illustration) but with its slack side (the bottom run of the chain) *above* the dowel on the block. Note: *If necessary to achieve exact alignment of the chains and sprockets, move the camshaft sprockets slightly by loosening the holding tools.*

40　The installation procedure for the timing chain tensioners and guides is the same for both chains, so either side can be done first. Before assembling the tensioner with the chain guide, compress the tensioner and lock it in this position with a straightened paper clip, Allen wrench or drill bit (see illustration).

41　Remove the slack from the chain by hand, install the moveable guide assembly to the engine block, then install the tensioner in the retracted position. Tighten the bolts to the torque listed in this Chapter's Specifications. Repeat for the other chain.

42　Remove the paper clip and apply pressure against the tensioner chain guide so the tensioner fully extends against the chain guide and all slack is removed from the chain.

43　Recheck all the timing marks to make sure they are still in alignment (see illustration 6.39a).

44　Remove the camshaft and crankshaft positioning tools.

2005 and later 3-valve models

Refer to illustrations 6.54, 6.57, 6.58 and 6.60

45　While holding the camshaft phasers, tighten the phaser bolts to the torque listed in

this Chapter's Specifications

46　Rotate the engine counterclockwise so that the crankshaft keyway is at the 11 o'clock position and install the crankshaft holding tool.

47　Check that the timing chain marks are visible. The right-hand camshaft phaser timing mark should point at 12 o'clock, and the left-hand phaser's mark should point to roughly 11 o'clock.

48　Install the first crankshaft sprocket with the flange faces forward.

49　Install both timing chain guides.

50　Put the left/inner timing chain over the crankshaft sprocket. Align the single marked link with the mark on the crankshaft sprocket. The mark should be in the 6 o'clock position.

51　Put the upper end of the chain over the camshaft sprocket, keeping the upper half

6.39a Align the bright link at the lower end of the chain with the timing mark on the crankshaft sprocket (it should be at 6 o'clock) then bolt the camshaft sprocket to the camshaft - both chains are correctly aligned in this photo

6.39b When installing the timing chain, align one of the bright links in the timing chain with the dimple on the camshaft sprocket

6.40 Lock the timing chain tensioner in the fully retracted position by placing a paper clip into the hole in the tensioner body

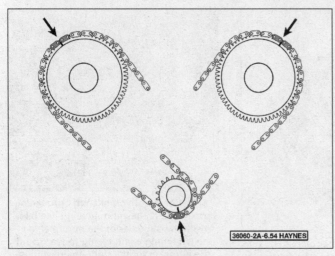

6.54 Crankshaft and camshaft TDC timing marks for V8 and V10 engines

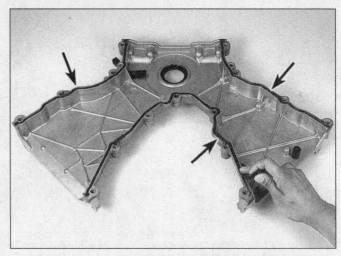

6.57 Install three new gaskets into the grooves in the back of the timing chain cover

of the chain below the tension arm dowel. Align the mark on the dowel between the two marked chain links.

52   Install the left timing chain tensioner and arm using the dowel. The left tensioner arm has a small raised spot near the dowel hole. Tighten the bolts to the torques listed in this Chapter's Specifications.

53   The procedure for the right timing chain is the same, however the lower part of the timing chain must be positioned above the timing chain dowel during installation.

54   Verify that the sprockets and chains are set correctly with the single marked links aligned with the marks on the crankshaft sprockets and the double marked links straddling the marks on the camshaft sprockets **(see illustration)**. Rotate the engine clockwise until the crankshaft keyway is at 6 o'clock. Install the balance shaft (see Section 7), then install the rocker arms.

All models

55   Slowly rotate the crankshaft in the normal direction of rotation (clockwise) at least two revolutions and again bring the engine to TDC. If you feel any resistance, stop and find out why. Check all alignment marks to verify that everything is properly assembled.

56   Clean the mating surfaces of the timing chain cover, engine block and cylinder heads to remove all traces of old gasket material, oil and dirt. Final cleaning should be with lacquer thinner or acetone. **Warning:** *Be careful when cleaning any of the aluminum components. Use of a metal scraper could cause scratches or gouges that could lead to an oil leak later.*

57   Install three new gaskets to the backside of the timing chain cover **(see illustration)**.

58   Apply a 1/8-inch bead of RTV sealant to the junctions of the oil pan-to-engine block and the cylinder head-to-engine block **(see illustration)**. Apply a small dab of RTV where the timing chain cover and engine block meet at the valve cover surface.

59   Lubricate the timing chains and the lip of the crankshaft front oil seal with clean engine oil.

60   Install the timing chain cover on the engine within five minutes of applying the RTV sealant. Position the bottom/front edge of the timing chain cover flush with the front edge of the oil pan and "tilt" the top of the cover into place against the engine. Do not press the cover straight in against the engine or the sealant may be scraped off the front of the oil pan and cause a leak. Tighten the timing chain cover-to-engine block bolts in the recommended sequence **(see illustration)** to the torque listed in this Chapter's Specifications. Tighten the oil pan-to-timing chain cover bolts to the specified torque as well.

61   Install a new crankshaft front oil seal (see Section 17).

62   The remainder of installation is the reverse of removal.

63   Add the correct type and quantity of engine oil and coolant (see Chapter 1).

64   Run the engine and check for leaks.

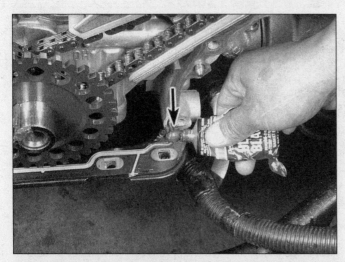

6.58 Apply a small bead of RTV sealant to the mating junctions of the oil pan-to-engine block and cylinder head-to-engine block

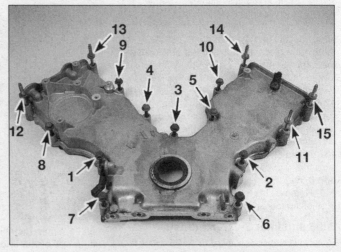

6.60 Timing chain cover bolt tightening sequence

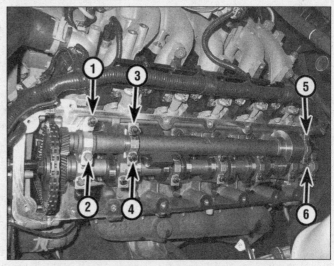

7.3 Verify that the timing mark on the balance shaft drive gear on the camshaft (lower arrow) is aligned with the index mark (upper arrow) on the balance shaft driven gear (the index mark is just a thin line on the balance shaft; after removing the balance shaft, it's a good idea to mark the tooth adjacent to the index mark with chalk or paint, which will be easier to see when reinstalling the balance shaft)

7.6 Balance shaft bearing cap bolt tightening sequence

7 Balance shaft (V10 engine) - removal and installation

Refer to illustrations 7.3 and 7.6

1   Position the number one cylinder on TDC (see Section 3). Disconnect the negative battery cable (see Chapter 5, Section 1).
2   Remove the left valve cover (see Section 4).
3   Verify that the timing mark on the balance shaft drive gear (on the camshaft) is aligned with the index mark on the balance shaft driven gear **(see illustration)**. **Note:** *The index mark on the balance shaft driven gear is difficult to see when the balance shaft is installed, so after removing the balance shaft, it's a good idea to mark the gear tooth next to the index mark with chalk or paint.*
4   Clearly mark the balance shaft bearing caps, then remove the bearing cap bolts in the reverse order of the tightening sequence **(see illustration 7.6)**.

5   Make sure that the timing mark on the camshaft and the index mark on the balance shaft are correctly aligned **(see illustration 7.3)**.
6   Install the bearing cap bolts in the same location from which each was removed, then tighten the bearing caps bolts in the indicated sequence **(see illustration)** to the torque listed in this Chapter's Specifications.
7   Installation is otherwise the reverse of removal.

8 Rocker arms and valve lash adjusters - removal, inspection and installation

Note: *There are two ways to remove the rocker arms and lash adjusters on these engines. The first method, which is recommended by the manufacturer, allows removal of the camshaft roller followers without remov-*

ing the camshafts by using two special tools: a valve spring spacer and a valve spring compressor which are made specifically for these engines and are available at some auto parts stores (or can be ordered from specialty tool dealers). The valve spring compressor uses the camshaft as a pivot point and, with a ratchet or bar attached, pushes down on the spring to release tension on the cam follower. The spring spacer keeps the spring from collapsing too far and hitting the valve stem seal. The second method requires the removal of the camshaft (see Section 9) to remove the cam followers. Either method will work, but the first one is much easier.

Removal

Refer to illustrations 8.3a, 8.3b and 8.4

1   Remove the valve cover(s) (see Section 4).
2   Because of the interference design of these modular engines, the pistons must be positioned off TDC before compressing the valve springs to remove the rocker arms or lash adjusters. For whatever cylinder you are removing the rocker arms from, remove the spark plug and insert a wooden dowel or plastic rod (hold onto it) to see how far the piston is from the top of its travel. If necessary, turn the crankshaft until the pen indicates the pistons are down at least an inch or two from TDC.
3   Install a valve spring compressor and compress the spring enough to remove the rocker arm **(see illustrations)**. The rocker arms and hydraulic lash adjusters MUST be reinstalled with the same camshaft lobe that they were removed from. Label and store all components to avoid confusion during reassembly. **Caution:** *A valve spring spacer should be inserted into the coils of the spring before compressing it. If the spacer isn't in place between one of the valve spring coils, the spring can be compressed too far and the valve seal may be damaged.*
4   Remove the hydraulic lash adjuster

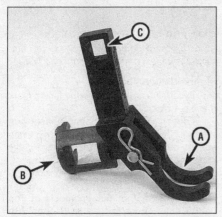

8.3a The special valve spring compressor hooks under the camshaft at (A), pushes on the valve spring retainer at (B), and is operated by a 1/2-inch drive breaker bar placed at (C)

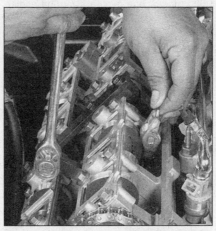

8.3b Compress the valve spring until you can slip the rocker arm out - keep the rocker arms and lash adjusters matched to their original locations

8.4 Pull the lash adjuster straight up and out of the cylinder head

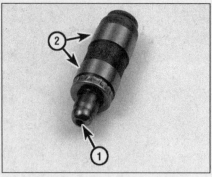

8.5 Inspect the lash adjuster for signs of excessive wear or damage, such as pitting, scoring or signs of overheating (bluing or discoloration), where the tip contacts the camshaft follower (1) and the side surfaces that contact the lifter bore in the cylinder head (2)

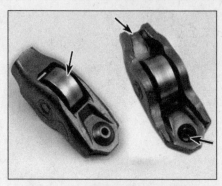

8.7 Check the roller surface of the rocker arms and the areas where the valve stem and lash adjuster contact the rocker

(see illustration). If there are many miles on the vehicle, the adjusters may have become varnished and difficult to remove. Apply a little penetrating oil around the lash adjuster to help loosen the varnish. **Note:** *Keep the rocker arm and lash adjuster for each valve together in a marked plastic sandwich bag.*

Inspection

Refer to illustrations 8.5 and 8.7

5   Inspect each adjuster carefully for signs of wear or damage. The areas of possible wear are the ball tip that contacts the cam follower and the sides of the adjuster that contact the bore in the cylinder head **(see illustration)**. Since the lash adjusters can become clogged as mileage increases, we recommend replacing them if you're concerned about their condition or if the engine is exhibiting valve "tapping" noises.

6   A thin wire or paper clip can be placed in the oil hole to move the plunger and make sure it's not stuck. **Note:** *The lash adjuster must have no more than 1/16-inch of total plunger travel.* It's recommended that if replacement of any of the adjusters is necessary, that the entire set be replaced. This will avoid the need to repeat the repair procedure as the others require replacement in the future.

7   Inspect the rocker arms for signs of wear

or damage. The areas of wear are the ball socket that contacts the lash adjuster and the roller where the follower contacts the camshaft **(see illustration)**.

Installation

8   Before installing the lash adjusters, bleed as much air as possible out of them. Stand the adjusters upright in a container of oil. Use a thin wire or paper clip to work the plunger up and down. This "primes" the adjuster and removes most of the air. Leave the adjusters in the oil until ready to install.

9   Lubricate the valve stem tip, rocker arm, and lash adjuster bore with clean engine oil.

10   Install the lash adjusters and, with the valve spring depressed as in Step 3, install each rocker arm.

11   The remainder of installation is the reverse of the removal procedure.

12   When re-starting the engine after replacing the adjusters, the adjusters will normally make some "tapping" noises, until all the air is bled from the lash adjusters. After the engine is warmed-up, raise the speed from idle to 3,000 rpm for one minute. Stop the engine

9.3 Check camshaft endplay with a dial indicator mounted on the front of each cylinder head

and let it cool down. All of the noise should be gone when it is restarted.

9   Camshafts - removal, inspection and installation

Removal

Refer to illustration 9.3

1   Disconnect the cable from the negative battery terminal. Remove the valve covers (see Section 4).

2   If you're removing the camshaft from the left cylinder head on a V10 engine, remove the balance shaft (see Section 7).

3   Measure the thrust clearance (endplay) of the camshaft(s) with a dial indicator **(see illustration)**. If the clearance is greater than the value listed in this Chapter's Specifications, replace the camshaft and/or the cylinder head.

1999 through 2004 2-valve engines

4   Remove the timing chains, camshaft sprockets and spacers (see Section 6). **Caution:** *Don't mix up the sprockets, which are marked "LB" (left bank) and "RB" (right bank). The sprockets must go back on the appropriate camshaft.*

2005 and later 3-valve models

Note: *If you're going to remove both camshafts, you must remove the right one first.*

Right-side camshaft

5   Rotate the crankshaft so the timing mark is at the 1 o'clock position.

6   Loosen the right camshaft phaser bolt one turn. **Caution:** *Only use hand tools when working on the phasers. They are fragile; any lifting or prying on them will cause damage.*

7   Remove the right camshaft position sensor (refer to Chapter 6).

8   Make sure that the engine is at Top Dead Center (refer to Section 6, Step 26). The exhaust cam lobe for cylinder number one must be coming up on the exhaust stroke and the intake lobes must be in about the 10 o'clock position. If it's not in this position, rotate the crankshaft one full turn until it is correct.

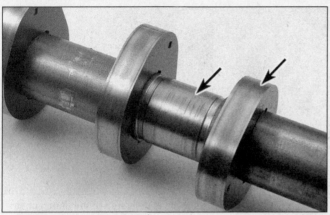

9.22a Areas to look for excessive wear or damage on the camshafts are the bearing surfaces and the camshaft lobes

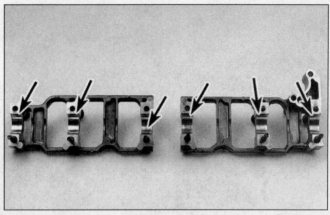

9.22b Inspect the bearing surfaces of the camshaft bearing caps for signs of excessive wear, damage or overheating

9.23a Measuring the camshaft bearing journal diameter

9.23b Measure the height of the camshaft lobe . . .

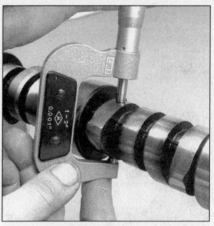

9.23c . . . measure the diameter of the base circle, then subtract the diameter of the base circle from the lobe height to obtain the lobe lift specification

9   Use a special tool to remove the camshaft rocker arms (see Section 8).

Left-side camshaft

10   Remove the left valve cover (refer to Section 4). Check that the left camshaft is in the correct position set in Step 8. The camshaft exhaust lobe for the number five cylinder must be coming up on the exhaust valve stroke. The intake valve lobes must be in about the 9 o'clock position. If it's not in this position, rotate the crankshaft one full turn until it is correct.

11   Loosen the left camshaft phaser bolt one turn. **Caution:** *Only use hand tools when working on the phasers. They are fragile; any lifting or prying on them will cause damage.*

12   Remove the left camshaft position sensor (refer to Chapter 6). On V10 models, remove the balance shaft (refer to Section 7).

13   Use a special tool to remove the camshaft rocker arms (see Section 8).

Both camshafts

14   Remove the right valve cover (refer to Section 4). Rotate the crankshaft one-half turn so the timing mark is in the 7 o'clock position. **Caution:** *Don't try to turn it farther than this or damage will result.*

15   A special tool is available from the manufacturer and some specialty tool suppliers that can be inserted down into the timing chain cover to wedge and lock the timing chain(s) into position. Insert the special tool into the timing chain on the side being worked on. Make sure that the timing chain cannot be moved. **Caution:** *At no time can the tool be removed until the procedure is completed and both of the chains are reinstalled on their sprockets.*

16   Paint an alignment mark on the timing chain and the sprocket so they can be reinstalled in exactly the same orientation.

All models

17   Remove the camshaft cap bolts in the reverse order of the tightening sequence **(see illustrations 9.29a and 9.29b)**.

18   Mark the camshaft bearing caps to indicate their positions. Don't mix up the caps for the left and right cylinder heads.

19   On 2005 and later models, separate the phaser from the camshaft. Leave the sprocket/phaser assembly in place. Remove the caps and lift the camshaft off the cylinder head. You may have to tap lightly under the camshaft caps to jar them loose. Don't mix up the camshafts or any of the components. They must

all go back on the same positions, and on the same cylinder head they were removed from. **Note:** *It's IMPORTANT to loosen the bearing cap bolts only 1/4-turn at a time, following the reverse of the tightening sequence* **(see illustrations 9.29a and 9.29b)**, *until they can be removed by hand.*

20   Repeat this procedure for removal of the camshaft from the other cylinder head.

Inspection

Refer to illustrations 9.22a, 9.22b, 9.23a, 9.23b, 9.23c, 9.24a, 9.24b and 9.26

21   Wipe off the camshafts with a clean shop rag.

22   Visually examine the cam lobes and bearing journals for score marks, pitting, galling and evidence of overheating (blue, discolored areas). Look for flaking of the hardened surface of each lobe **(see illustrations)**.

23   Using a micrometer, measure the diameter of each camshaft journal and the lift of each camshaft lobe **(see illustrations)**. Compare your measurements with the Specifications listed at the front of this Chapter, and if the diameter of any one of these is less than specified, replace the camshaft.

9.24a Lay a strip of Plastigage on each of the camshaft journals

9.24b Compare the width of the crushed Plastigage to the scale on the envelope to determine the oil clearance

9.26 Oil is delivered to the timing chain tensioner by a feed tube and reservoir in the cylinder head
1   Tensioner oil feed tube
2   Reservoir

9.29a Camshaft cap tightening sequence (V8 engine)

9.29b Camshaft cap tightening sequence (2004 and earlier V10 engines)

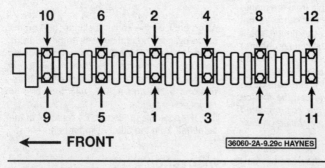

9.29c Camshaft cap tightening sequence - 2005 and later V10 engines

FRONT

24   Check the oil clearance for each camshaft journal as follows:

a) Clean the bearing surfaces and the camshaft journals with lacquer thinner or acetone.
b) Carefully lay the camshaft(s) in place in the cylinder head. Don't install the rocker arms or lash adjusters and don't use any lubrication.
c) Lay a strip of Plastigage on each journal (see illustration).
d) Install the camshaft bearing caps.
e) Tighten the cap bolts, a little at a time, to the torque listed in this Chapter's Specifications. Note: Don't turn the camshaft while the Plastigage is in place.

f) Remove the bolts and detach the caps.
g) Compare the width of the crushed Plastigage (at its widest point) to the scale on the Plastigage envelope (see illustration).
h) If the clearance is greater than specified, and the diameter of any journal is less than specified, replace the camshaft. If the journal diameters are within specifications but the oil clearance is too great, the cylinder head is worn and must be replaced.

25   Scrape off the Plastigage with your fingernail or the edge of a credit card - don't scratch or nick the journals or bearing surfaces.

26   Finally, be sure to check the timing chain tensioner oil feed tube and reservoir before installing the cam caps (see illustration). It must be absolutely clean and free of all obstructions or it will affect the operation of the timing chain tensioner.

Installation

Refer to illustrations 9.29a, 9.29b and 9.29c

27   If the lash adjusters and/or camshaft followers have been removed, install them in their original locations (see Section 8).
28   Apply or camshaft installation lube to the camshaft lobes and bearing journals, then install the camshaft(s).
29   Install the camshaft caps in the correct locations, and loosely install all the bolts. Align the camshaft sprockets before tightening the cap bolts (see Section 6). Following the correct bolt-tightening sequence (see illustrations), tighten the bolts in 1/4-turn increments to the torque listed in this Chapter's Specifications.
30   On 1999 through 2004 2-valve engines, reinstall the camshaft positioning and retaining tools (see Section 6) to set the camshafts at TDC before reinstalling the timing chain(s).
31   On 1999 through 2004 models, install the timing chain cover (refer to Section 6).

On 2005 and later models, remove the timing chain locking tool(s) after the chains are installed. Be sure to verify that the marks you made on the timing chains and the sprockets are aligned.

32   The remainder of installation is the reverse of the removal procedure.

10   Valve springs, retainers and seals - removal and installation

Broken valve springs and/or defective valve stem seals can be replaced without removing the cylinder heads. There is a method described in Section 8, using a tool recommended by the manufacturer, which accomplishes the removal of the valve springs and seals without the removal of the camshafts. The alternative method uses a more commonly available tool, but will require the removal of the camshaft (see Section 9) in order to remove the valve spring. Either method will achieve the same results, but it is much easier using the manufacturer's recommended procedure, if the correct tools can be located.

In either repair procedure, a compressed air source is normally required to perform this operation, so read through this Section carefully and rent or buy the tools before beginning the job.

Removal

Refer to illustration 10.4

1   Remove the valve cover (see Section 4).
2   Remove the spark plug from the cylinder with the defective component. If all of the valve stem seals are being replaced, remove all the spark plugs.
3   Turn the crankshaft until the piston in the affected cylinder is at Top Dead Center (TDC) on the compression stroke (see Section 3). If you're replacing all of the valve stem seals, begin with cylinder number one and work on the valves for one cylinder at a time. Move from cylinder-to-cylinder following the firing

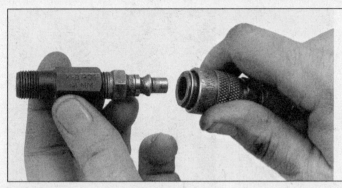

10.4 This is the air hose adapter that threads into the spark plug hole - they're commonly available from auto parts stores

order sequence (see this Chapter's Specifications).
4   Thread an air hose adapter into the spark plug hole **(see illustration)** and connect an air hose from a compressed air source to it. Most auto parts stores can supply the air hose adapter. **Note:** *Many cylinder compression gauges utilize a screw-in fitting that may work with your air hose quick-disconnect fitting.*
5   Apply compressed air to the cylinder. **Warning:** *The piston may be forced down by compressed air, causing the crankshaft to turn suddenly. If the wrench used when positioning the number one piston at TDC is still attached to the bolt in the crankshaft nose, it could cause damage or injury when the crankshaft moves.*
6   The valves should be held in place by the air pressure.
7   Stuff shop rags into the cylinder head holes above and below the valves to prevent parts and tools from falling into the engine.

Method using special tools

8   Install a valve spring spacer, available at most auto parts stores. **Caution:** *If the spacer isn't in place between one of the spring coils, the spring can be compressed too far, possibly damaging the valve seal.*
9   Compress the spring and remove the rocker arm (see Section 8). Rocker arms and hydraulic lash adjusters MUST be reinstalled with the same camshaft lobe that

they were removed from. Label and store all components to avoid confusion during reassembly.
10   Keeping the spring compressed, remove the keepers with small needle-nose pliers or a magnet **(see illustration 10.13)**. Remove the spring retainer and valve spring. Remove the valve stem seal **(see illustration 10.15)**. If air pressure fails to hold the valve in the closed position during this operation, the valve face and/or seat is probably damaged. If so, the cylinder head will have to be removed for additional repair operations.

Alternative procedure

Refer to illustrations 10.12, 10.13 and 10.15

11   Remove the camshaft(s) (see Section 9).
12   Install the commonly available clamp-type valve spring compressor **(see illustration)**.
13   Compress the spring and remove the keepers with small needle-nose pliers or a magnet **(see illustration)**.
14   Remove the spring retainer and valve spring.
15   Remove the stem seal **(see illustration)**. If air pressure fails to hold the valve in the closed position during this operation, the valve face and/or seat is probably damaged. If so, the cylinder head will have to be removed for additional repair operations.

10.12 Installation of a valve spring compressor more commonly available at local automotive parts stores (the camshaft must be removed for the use of this type of valve spring compressor)

10.13 Once the spring is compressed, remove the keepers with needle-nose pliers or a magnet, as shown here

10.15 Use pliers to firmly grasp the old seal and pull it off the valve guide

10.20a The valve stem seals combine a seal with the valve spring seat

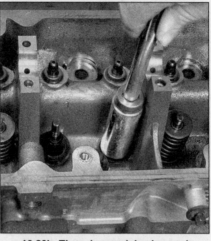

10.20b There is special valve seal installation tool available, but a deep socket that fits over the seal can be used to gently tap the seal into place

10.22 Apply a small dab of grease to each keeper as shown here before installation - it'll hold them in place on the valve stem as the spring is released

Installation

Refer to illustrations 10.20a, 10.20b and 10.22

16   Wrap a rubber band or tape around the top of the valve stem so the valve won't fall into the cylinder, then release the air pressure.

17   Inspect the valve stem for damage. Rotate the valve in the guide and check the end for eccentric movement, which would indicate that the valve is bent.

18   Move the valve up-and-down in the guide and make sure it doesn't bind. If the valve stem binds, either the valve is bent or the guide is damaged. In either case, the cylinder head will have to be removed for repair.

19   Reapply air pressure to the cylinder to retain the valve in the closed position, then remove the tape or rubber band from the valve stem.

20   Lubricate the valve stem with engine oil and install a new seal **(see illustration)**. There is a special tool for the installation of the valve seal. If the tool isn't available, a socket that will fit over the seal and is deep enough to make contact with the seat **(see illustration)**, can be used to carefully tap the new seal into place. **Caution:** *The valve seal used on these engines is a combination seal and spring seat. Never place a valve spring directly against the aluminum cylinder head (without a seal/spring seat) - the hardened spring would damage the cylinder head.*

21   Make sure the garter spring on the seal is still in place, and install the spring in position over the valve.

22   Install the valve spring retainer. Compress the valve spring and carefully position the keepers in the groove. Apply a small dab of grease to the inside of each keeper to hold it in place if necessary **(see illustration)**.

23   Remove the pressure from the spring tool and make sure the keepers are seated.

24   Disconnect the air hose and remove the adapter from the spark plug hole.

25   If the camshaft(s) were removed, reinstall them at this time (see Section 9).

26   Install the spark plug(s) and ignition coil(s).

27   The remaining installation steps are the

reverse of removal.

28   Start and run the engine, then check for oil leaks and unusual sounds coming from the valve cover area.

11   Intake manifold - removal and installation

Note: *The intake manifold on some models is designed as a two piece unit. The lower section of the intake manifold can only be accessed after the intake manifold has been removed from the engine. The lower section of the intake manifold contains the intake manifold tuning valve. Refer to Chapter 4 for additional information. On later models, the manifold comes off as a one-piece assembly.*

V8 engine

Removal

Upper intake manifold

1   Relieve the fuel system pressure (see Chapter 4). Disconnect the cable from the negative battery terminal (see Chapter 5, Section 1).

2   Drain the cooling system (see Chapter 1).

3   Remove the air cleaner housing and air intake duct (see Chapter 4).

4   Disconnect the upper radiator hose from the thermostat housing.

5   Remove the accessory drivebelt (see Chapter 1).

6   Remove the alternator (see Chapter 5).

7   Remove the accelerator cable splash shield, disconnect the accelerator cable, the cruise control cable (if equipped) and the throttle return spring, then remove the accelerator cable bracket bolts and set the accelerator cable bracket aside (see Chapter 4).

8   Disconnect the Throttle Position (TP) sensor electrical connector (see Chapter 6).

9   Detach the Idle Air Control (IAC) fresh air tube from its retaining clip and then remove it (see Chapter 6).

10   Disconnect the EVAP canister purge valve vacuum hose from the throttle body adapter (see Chapter 6).

11   Disconnect the brake booster vacuum hose and the main vacuum harness from the throttle body adapter.

1999 through 2004 two-valve models

12   Disconnect the IAC electrical connector (see Chapter 6).

13   On vehicles with an EGR system, disconnect the upper fitting from the exhaust manifold-to-EGR tube, loosen the lower fitting and then put the tube aside. Remove the bolts from the differential pressure feedback EGR system bracket and then put the bracket aside. Disconnect the EGR vacuum regulator solenoid connections. Disconnect the EGR valve vacuum hose (see Chapter 6).

14   Remove the four throttle body adapter bolts, remove the throttle body adapter, then remove and discard the throttle body gasket (see Chapter 4).

15   Disconnect the electrical connectors from all eight ignition coils (see Chapter 5). On 2003 through 2004 models, it will be necessary to remove the coils entirely.

16   Disconnect the fuel pressure regulator vacuum hose (see Chapter 4).

17   Disconnect the clamp and remove the heater hose (see Chapter 3).

18   Remove the thermostat (see Chapter 3).

2005 and later three-valve models

19   Disconnect the heater hose from the bypass tube. Disconnect the fuel rail pressure/temperature sensor wiring and hose. Disconnect the electrical connectors from the PCV intake fitting, the Throttle Position sensor, the acceleration control, and the CMP sensors. Tag and disconnect the hoses and electrical connectors at the IMRC valves on the front of the intake manifold.

20   Disconnect the wiring from the charge motion control valve. Disconnect the vacuum tube from the retainer and the bracket.

21   Disconnect the wiring from the cylinder head temperature harness and both knock

sensors. Disconnect the engine wiring harness from the stud and push it aside. Remove the three bolts and the coolant crossover assembly from between the cylinder heads.

All models

22   Loosen the upper intake manifold bolts in 1/4-turn increments, following the reverse order of the tightening sequence **(see illustration 11.36)**, until they can be removed by hand.

23   Lift the upper intake manifold from the cylinder heads. The manifold may be stuck to the cylinder heads and force may be required to break the gasket seal. A prybar can be used to pry up the manifold, but make sure all bolts and nuts have been removed first! **Caution:** *Don't pry between the engine block and manifold or the cylinder heads, or damage to the gasket sealing surface may occur, leading to vacuum and oil leaks. Pry only at the manifold protrusion.*

24   Remove the old intake manifold gaskets.

Lower intake manifold (1999 models)

25   Remove the bolts that attach the upper and lower intake manifolds, following the reverse order of the tightening sequence **(see illustration 11.30)**. Remove the old gasket.

26   If you are going to remove or replace the Intake Manifold Tuning Valve, which is bolted to the lower intake manifold, refer to Chapter 4.

Installation

Lower intake manifold (1999 models)

Refer to illustration 11.30

27   Remove all traces of old gasket material from the mating surfaces of the two manifolds. **Caution:** *Do NOT use metal scrapers, wire brushes, grinding discs or other types of abrasive tools to clean off the gasket surfaces. These tools can cause scratches and gouges that will result in air leaks.*

28   If you removed the Intake Manifold Tuning Valve, install it (see Chapter 4).

29   Be sure to install a new gasket between the upper and lower intake manifolds.

30   Tighten the bolts, in two stages, to the torque listed in this Chapter's Specifications, following the correct tightening sequence **(see illustration)**.

Upper intake manifold

Refer to illustration 11.36

31   Clean the gasket mating surfaces with lacquer thinner or acetone. If there's old sealant or oil on the mating surfaces when the intake manifold is installed, oil or vacuum leaks may develop. **Caution:** *The mating surfaces of the intake manifold and the cylinder heads must be perfectly clean. Gasket removal solvents in aerosol cans are available at most auto parts stores and may be helpful when removing old gasket material that's stuck to the cylinder heads and intake manifold. Since the cylinder heads are aluminum and the intake manifold is aluminum or plastic, aggressive scraping can cause damage! Be sure to follow directions printed on the container, and use only a plastic-tipped scraper, not a metal one.*

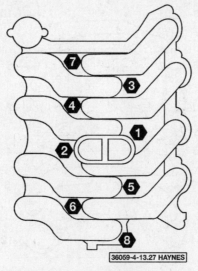

11.30 **Upper intake manifold-to-lower intake manifold bolt tightening sequence**

32   When working on the cylinder heads and engine block, cover the open engine areas with shop rags to keep debris out of the engine. Use a vacuum cleaner to remove any gasket material that falls into the intake ports in the cylinder heads.

33   Use a tap of the correct size to chase the threads in the bolt holes, then use compressed air (if available) to remove the debris from the holes. **Warning:** *Wear safety glasses or a face shield to protect your eyes when using compressed air!* Remove excessive carbon deposits and corrosion from the exhaust and coolant passages in the cylinder heads and intake manifold. **Note:** *If the vehicle has many miles on it, replace the water pump hose (normally hidden by the intake manifold) before replacing the manifold (see Chapter 3).*

34   Install the gaskets on the cylinder heads. Make sure all alignment tabs, intake port openings, coolant passage holes and bolt holes are aligned correctly. The gasket that goes on the cylinder head will have projecting plastic pins to align it with holes in the cylinder head.

35   Carefully set the intake manifold in place. Don't disturb the gaskets and don't move the manifold fore-and-aft after it contacts the gaskets on the engine block.

36   Install the intake manifold bolts and, following the recommended tightening sequence **(see illustration)**, tighten them to the torque listed in this Chapter's Specifications.

37   The remainder of installation is the reverse of removal. Start the engine and check carefully for air, oil and coolant leaks.

V10 engine

Removal

Upper intake manifold

38   Relieve the fuel system pressure (see Chapter 4). Disconnect the cable from the negative battery terminal.

39   Drain the cooling system (see Chapter 1).

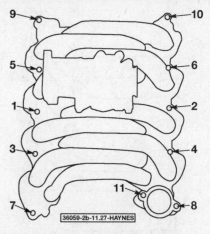

11.36 **Intake manifold bolt tightening sequence (V8 engine)**

40   Remove the air intake duct (see Chapter 4).

41   Disconnect the coolant outlet hose from the thermostat housing (see Chapter 3).

42   Disconnect the PCV vacuum hose(s).

1999 through 2002 2-valve models

43   Remove the accelerator cable splash shield. Disconnect the accelerator cable, the cruise control cable (if equipped) and the throttle return spring, then remove the accelerator cable bracket bolts and set the accelerator cable bracket aside (see Chapter 4).

44   Disconnect the brake booster vacuum hose (see Chapter 6).

45   Disconnect the engine sensor control wiring harness vacuum line (see Chapter 6).

46   Remove the capacitor and set it aside. Disconnect any other vacuum lines or wiring connected to the intake manifold.

47   Disconnect the electrical connectors from all five right bank fuel injectors (see Chapter 4).

48   Disconnect the electrical connectors from all five right bank ignition coils (see Chapter 5).

49   Disconnect the Idle Air Control (IAC) motor electrical connector and the bypass hose (see Chapter 6).

50   Disconnect the heater hose. Disconnect the coolant temperature sending unit wiring (see Chapter 5). Disconnect the cylinder head temperature sensor wiring (see Chapter 6). Disconnect the fuel supply and return lines (see Chapter 4).

51   Disconnect the Throttle Position (TP) sensor connector (see Chapter 6).

52   On vehicles with an EGR system, disconnect the EGR transducer electrical connector, disconnect the EGR transducer vacuum lines, remove the EGR transducer bracket, disconnect the upper EGR valve-to-exhaust manifold tube fitting, loosen the lower fitting and then set the EGR valve tube aside. Disconnect the EGR valve vacuum line (see Chapter 6).

53   On vehicles with an EGR system, disconnect the EGR vacuum regulator solenoid electrical and vacuum harness (see Chapter 6).

54   Remove the four throttle body adapter bolts, remove the throttle body adapter and then remove and discard the throttle body gasket (see Chapter 4).

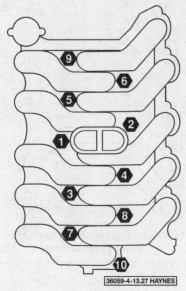

11.83 Upper intake-to-lower intake manifold bolt tightening sequence (V10 engine)

55   On vehicles with an EGR system, remove the two EGR vacuum regulator solenoid bracket bolts and then remove the EGR vacuum regulator solenoid bracket (see Chapter 6).

56   Disconnect the electrical connectors from all five left bank fuel injectors (see Chapter 4).

57   Disconnect the electrical connectors from all five left bank ignition coils (see Chapter 5).

58   Remove the alternator (see Chapter 5).

59   Remove the ignition coils (see Chapter 5).

60   Disconnect the fuel pressure regulator vacuum line and the fuel supply and return lines (see Chapter 4).

61   Remove the capacitor retaining bolt, remove the capacitor and then set it aside.

62   Remove the thermostat housing (see Chapter 3).

2003 through 2004 2-valve models

63   Disconnect the fuel line couplings (see Chapter 3).

64   Disconnect the cable from the negative battery terminal.

65   Remove the alternator (see Chapter 5).

66   Remove the accelerator cable splash shield. Disconnect the accelerator cable, the cruise control cable (if equipped) and the throttle return spring, then remove the accelerator cable bracket bolts and set the accelerator cable bracket aside (see Chapter 4).

67   Disconnect the PCV hose along with its vacuum hoses and the coolant hose.

68   Disconnect the idle air control wiring and the bypass hose

69   Disconnect fuel injection wiring connectors.

70   Remove the ignition coils (see Chapter 5).

71   Disconnect the vacuum line from the fuel pressure regulator.

2005 and later 3-valve models

72   Disconnect the fuel line couplings (see

Chapter 3).

73   Disconnect the interfering heater hose.

74   Disconnect all interfering wiring connectors including all 10 fuel injection connectors.

75   Disconnect the PCV tube from the intake manifold.

76   Remove the EVAP tube using the quick-connect couplings (see Chapter 5).

77   Disconnect the brake booster vacuum hose and the PCV coolant hoses. Remove the two bolts and the coolant crossover assembly from between the cylinder heads.

All models

78   Loosen the upper intake manifold bolts in 1/4-turn increments, following the reverse order of the tightening sequence **(see illustration 11.77)**, then remove the upper and lower intake manifolds as a single assembly.

79   Remove the intake manifold gaskets.

80   Remove the fuel rail assembly from the intake manifold (see Chapter 4).

Lower intake manifold

81   Working in 1/4-turn increments, loosen the 10 bolts that attach the upper and lower intake manifolds, following the reverse order of the tightening sequence **(see illustration 11.83)** and then separate the upper and lower manifolds.

Installation

Lower intake manifold

Refer to illustration 11.83

82   Clean off the mating surfaces of the two manifolds. **Caution:** *Do NOT use metal scrapers, wire brushes, grinding discs or other types of abrasive tools to clean off the mating surfaces. These tools can cause scratches and gouges that will result in air leaks.*

83   Tighten the bolts that attach the upper and lower intake manifolds, in two stages, to the torque listed in this Chapter's Specifications, following the correct tightening sequence **(see illustration)**.

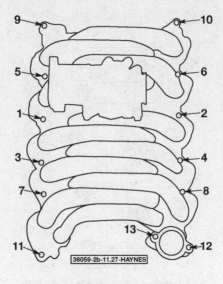

11.89 Intake manifold bolt tightening sequence (V10 engine)

Upper intake manifold

Refer to illustration 11.89

84   Clean the gasket mating surfaces of the upper intake manifold and the cylinder heads with lacquer thinner or acetone. If there's old sealant or oil on the mating surfaces when the intake manifold is installed, oil or vacuum leaks may develop. **Caution:** *The mating surfaces of the intake manifold and the cylinder heads must be perfectly clean. Gasket removal solvents in aerosol cans are available at most auto parts stores and may be helpful when removing old gasket material that's stuck to the cylinder heads and intake manifold. Since the cylinder heads are aluminum and the intake manifold is aluminum or plastic, aggressive scraping can cause damage! Be sure to follow directions printed on the container, and use only a plastic-tipped scraper, not a metal one.*

85   When working on the cylinder heads and engine block, cover the open engine areas with shop rags to keep debris out of the engine. Use a vacuum cleaner to remove any gasket material that falls into the intake ports in the cylinder heads.

86   Use a tap of the correct size to chase the threads in the bolt holes, then use compressed air (if available) to remove the debris from the holes. **Warning:** *Wear safety glasses or a face shield to protect your eyes when using compressed air!* Remove excessive carbon deposits and corrosion from the exhaust and coolant passages in the cylinder heads and intake manifold. **Note:** *If the vehicle has many miles on it, replace the water pump hose (normally hidden by the intake manifold) before replacing the manifold (see Chapter 3).*

87   Install the gaskets on the cylinder heads. Make sure all alignment tabs, intake port openings, coolant passage holes and bolt holes are aligned correctly. The gasket that goes on the cylinder head will have projecting plastic pins to align it with holes in the cylinder head.

88   Carefully set the intake manifold in place. Don't disturb the gaskets and don't move the manifold fore-and-aft after it contacts the gaskets on the engine block.

89   Install the intake manifold bolts and, following the recommended tightening sequence **(see illustration)**, tighten them to the torque listed in this Chapter's Specifications.

90   The remainder of installation is the reverse of removal. Refill the cooling system as described in Chapter 1.

91   Start the engine and check carefully for air, oil and coolant leaks.

12   Exhaust manifolds - removal and installation

Refer to illustrations 12.1, 12.22a, 12.22b, 12.22c and 12.22d

1999 through 2002 models

1   If you're going to remove the left exhaust manifold on a vehicle equipped with an EGR system, disconnect the EGR valve tube fitting **(see illustration)** from the exhaust manifold,

then disconnect the tube from the manifold (see Chapter 6).

2   If you're going to remove the left exhaust manifold on a V10 engine, remove the air intake duct (see Chapter 4).

3   Raise the vehicle and place it securely on jackstands. On V8 models, remove the left or right front wheel. If you're going to remove the right exhaust manifold on a V10 model, remove the right front wheel.

4   On V8 models, remove the left or right front inner fenderwell (see Chapter 11). If you're going to remove the right exhaust manifold on a V10 model, remove the right front inner fenderwell (see Chapter 11).

2003 through 2004 2-valve models

5   Raise the vehicle and support it securely on jackstands.

6   If you're working on a 4X4 vehicle, remove the appropriate wheel well opening molding.

7   Remove the front fender inner splash shields.

8   On models with 6.8L engines, remove the air filter outlet tube for access to the left manifold.

9   On 2003 models with 6.8L engines, disconnect the EGR tube from the left manifold.

2005 and later 3-valve models

10   Remove the air filter housing and interfering ducts. **Note:** *This is not required for right-side manifolds on 6.8L engines.*

11   On 4X4 models with 5.4L engines, remove the front driveshaft (see Chapter 8).

12   If you're removing a right-side manifold,

remove the starter (see Chapter 5).

13   On 6.8L models remove the transmission filler tube for access to the right-side manifold.

14   For left-side manifold replacement on 6.8L models, unbolt the coolant degas reservoir and set it out of the way.

15   Remove the front fender inner splash shields.

All models

16   Working under the vehicle, apply penetrating oil to the exhaust pipe-to-exhaust manifold studs and nuts and to the exhaust manifold nuts and studs. They're usually corroded or rusty.

17   Remove the exhaust pipe-to-exhaust manifold nuts.

18   Remove the eight exhaust manifold nuts (V8 models) or 10 nuts (V10 models) and then remove the exhaust manifold and the old exhaust manifold gaskets.

19   Clean off all old gasket material from the cylinder head and from the exhaust manifold. The exhaust manifold and cylinder head mating surfaces must be clean before the exhaust manifolds are reinstalled. Use a gasket scraper to remove all carbon deposits.

20   Inspect the exhaust manifold for cracks. If a manifold is cracked, it must be replaced or repaired. Depending on the size and location of the crack, an automotive machine shop might be able to repair a cracked manifold by welding it. Sometimes, though, the welding might cost more than a new manifold. If a manifold has gotten hot enough to crack, it

12.1 Disconnect the EGR tube (arrow) from the left exhaust manifold (V8 engine)

might very well be warped as well as cracked. Take the manifold to an automotive machine shop and get an estimate for any needed repairs, and then compare the estimate to the cost of a new manifold.

21   Make sure that the threads of the exhaust manifold studs are clean and undamaged. If they're damaged, clean them up with a thread chaser or replace them. To replace damaged exhaust manifold studs, "double-nut" them.

22   Install new gaskets, place the exhaust manifold in position and then, working in the specified sequence **(see illustrations)**, tighten the exhaust manifold nuts to the torque listed in this Chapter's Specifications.

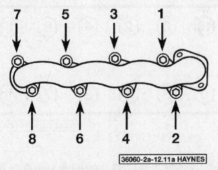

12.22a Left exhaust manifold nut tightening sequence (V8 engine)

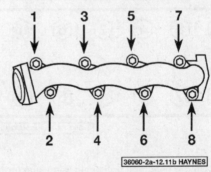

12.22b Right exhaust manifold nut tightening sequence (V8 engine)

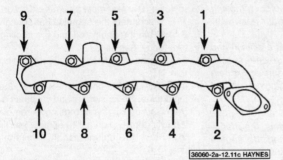

12.22c Left exhaust manifold tightening sequence (V10 engine)

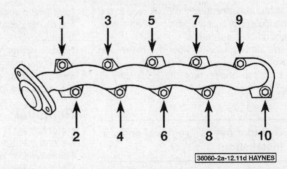

12.22d Right exhaust manifold tightening sequence (V10 engine)

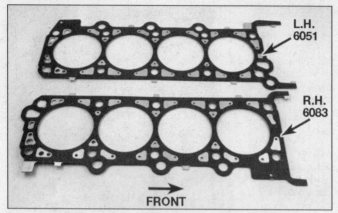

13.16 Examine the left and right cylinder head gaskets very carefully and you will find that they're slightly different and therefore cannot be interchanged (typical V8 head gaskets shown, V10 head gaskets similar)

13.17 Position the gaskets on the correct cylinder banks, then push them down over the alignment dowels

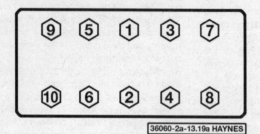

13.19a Cylinder head bolt tightening sequence for the left cylinder head (V8 engine)

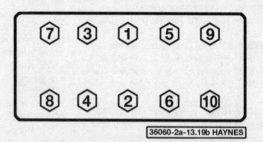

13.19b Cylinder head bolt tightening sequence for the right cylinder head (V8 engine)

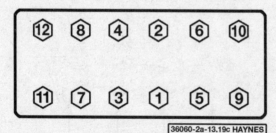

13.19c Cylinder head bolt tightening sequence for the left cylinder head (V10 engine)

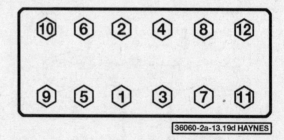

13.19d Cylinder head bolt tightening sequence for the right cylinder head (V10 engine)

23   When reconnecting the EGR tube to the left manifold, use a slight amount of anti-seize compound on the threads.

24   Installation is otherwise the reverse of removal.

25   Start the engine and check for exhaust leaks.

13 Cylinder heads - removal and installation

Caution: *The engine must be completely cool when the cylinder heads are removed. Failure*

to allow the engine to cool off before removing the heads could result in cylinder head warpage.

Note: *Cylinder head removal is a difficult and time-consuming job requiring several special tools. Read through the procedure and obtain the necessary tools before beginning.*

Removal

Note: *On 2003 and later models, the manufacturer recommends removing the engine before performing the following steps (refer to Chapter 2 Part C). It is recommended that the flywheel be removed and the engine mounted on a stand. This would also be a good time to*

install a new rear main seal (see Section 17).

1   Disconnect the negative battery cable.

2   Drain the engine oil and the cooling system (see Chapter 1).

3   Remove the valve covers (see Section 4).

4   Remove the timing chain cover, the timing chains, the tensioners and the chain guides (see Section 6). If you're going to remove the left cylinder head on a V10 engine, you'll need to remove the balance shaft, too (see Section 7).

5   Remove the intake manifold (see Section 11).

6   Remove the exhaust manifolds (see

13.19e Mark each cylinder head bolt with a paint stripe if you don't have a torque-angle adapter

Section 12). **Note:** *On some configurations it is easier to simply disconnect the exhaust manifolds from the exhaust pipes and leave them connected to the cylinder heads during removal.*

7 If you're only removing the cylinder heads to replace the head gaskets, the cylinder heads can be removed with the camshafts, rocker arms and lash adjusters in place. **Caution:** *Use the required camshaft holding fixtures to lock the camshafts and leave the tools in place.*

8 If you're planning to overhaul the cylinder heads, remove the rocker arms (see Section 8) and the camshafts (see Section 9).

9 Following the reverse of the tightening sequence **(see illustration 13.19a, 13.19b, 13.19c or 13.19d)**, use a breaker bar to remove the cylinder head bolts. Loosen the bolts in sequence 1/4-turn at a time.

10 Use a pry bar at the corners of the cylinder head-to-engine block mating surface to break the cylinder head gasket seal. Do not pry between the cylinder head and engine block in the gasket sealing area.

11 Lift the cylinder head(s) off the engine. If resistance is felt, place a wood block against the end and strike the wood block with a hammer. **Caution:** *The cylinder heads are aluminum - store them on wood blocks to prevent damage to the gasket sealing surfaces.*

12 Before removing the cylinder head gaskets, note which gasket goes on which side (they are different and cannot be interchanged).

Installation

Refer to illustrations 13.16, 13.17, 13.19a, 13.19b, 13.19c, 13.19d and 13.19e

Caution: *New cylinder head bolts must be used for reassembly. Failure to use new bolts may result in cylinder head gasket leakage and engine damage.*

13 The mating surfaces of the cylinder heads and engine block must be perfectly clean when the cylinder heads are installed. Use a gasket scraper to remove all traces of carbon and old gasket material, then clean the mating surfaces with lacquer thinner or acetone. If there's oil on the mating surfaces when the cylinder heads are installed, the gaskets may not seal correctly and leaks may develop.

When working on the engine block, cover the open areas of the engine with shop rags to keep debris out during repair and reassembly. Use a vacuum cleaner to remove any debris that falls into the cylinders. **Caution:** *Do not use abrasive wheels or sharp metal scrapers on the heads or block surface; use a plastic scraper and chemical gasket remover, or the head gasket surfaces could have future leaks.*

14 Inspect the engine block and cylinder head mating surfaces for nicks, deep scratches and other damage.

15 Use a tap of the correct size to chase the threads in the cylinder head bolt holes. Dirt, corrosion, sealant and damaged threads will affect torque readings.

16 Make sure the new gaskets are installed on the correct cylinder banks **(see illustration)**. They are not interchangeable.

17 Position the new gasket(s) over the alignment dowels **(see illustration)** in the engine block.

18 If the cylinder heads are being installed with the camshafts in place, make sure the camshafts are back in their original TDC positions (see Sections 6 and 9) before placing the cylinder heads on the engine block. **Caution:** *If the camshafts aren't in the position described, damage may result to either the pistons and/or valve train parts.*

19 Carefully position the cylinder heads on the engine block without disturbing the gaskets. Install NEW cylinder head bolts (the cylinder head bolts are torque-to-yield design and cannot be reused). Following the recommended sequence **(see illustrations)**, tighten the cylinder head bolts, in three steps, to the torque listed in this Chapter's Specifications. **Note:** *The method used for the cylinder head bolt tightening procedure is referred to as "torque-angle" or "torque-to-yield" method. Follow the procedure exactly. Tighten the bolts in the first step using a torque wrench, then use a breaker bar and a special torque-angle adapter (available at most auto parts stores) to tighten the bolts the required angle. If the adapter is not available, mark each bolt with a paint stripe to aid in the torque angle process* **(see illustration)**.

20 The remainder of installation is the reverse of removal.

21 Refill the cooling system and change

the engine oil and filter (see Chapter 1), then start the engine and check carefully for oil and coolant leaks.

14 Oil pan - removal and installation

Removal

1 Disconnect the negative battery cable from the battery.

2 Drain the engine oil and remove the oil filter (see Chapter 1).

3 Drain the engine coolant (see Chapter 1) and then remove the upper radiator hose (see Chapter 3).

4 Remove the air cleaner and the air intake duct (see Chapter 4).

5 Remove the engine cooling fan and shroud (see Chapter 3).

6 Remove the alternator (see Chapter 5).

7 Remove the throttle body from the intake manifold (see Chapter 4). Remove any other components from the top of the engine that would interfere with raising the engine as far as possible.

8 Raise the vehicle and place it securely on jackstands.

9 Disconnect the exhaust "Y-pipe" from the exhaust manifold flanges and from the exhaust pipe flange in front of the catalytic converter and remove it (see Chapter 4).

10 On automatic transmission models, detach any transmission cooler line brackets that are located near the oil pan and set the cooler lines aside.

11 Remove the flywheel/driveplate inspection cover from the transmission bellhousing.

12 Remove the driveshaft (see Chapter 8). On 4WD models, disconnect the rear end of the front driveshaft from the transfer case (see Chapter 8).

13 Remove the nuts from the front engine mounts (see Section 18) and remove the nuts from the transmission mount (see Chapter 7).

14 Attach an engine hoist to the engine and carefully raise it up as high as possible without the intake manifold touching the cowl. **Caution:** *Raise the engine slowly while observing the location of the intake manifold. Do not allow the manifold to contact the vehicle or the manifold might be damaged.*

15 **Note:** *On 2003 and later models the rear of the transmission must also be raised for access.* After the engine is securely supported, unbolt the rear transmission mount from the crossmember (refer to Chapter 7 Part B). Remove any sensors that could be damaged on automatic transmissions and plug the openings to prevent contamination. Position a block of wood on a jack and raise the rear of the transmission. **Caution:** *Do not place the jack under any part of the transmission that could be dented or otherwise damaged.*

16 Remove the oil pan mounting bolts in the reverse order of the tightening sequence **(see illustration 14.22a or 14.22b)**. Carefully separate the oil pan from the engine block. Don't pry between the engine block and oil

14.20 Apply a bead of RTV sealant at the junctions of the timing chain cover-to-engine block and the rear seal retainer-to-engine block (shown) before installing the oil pan

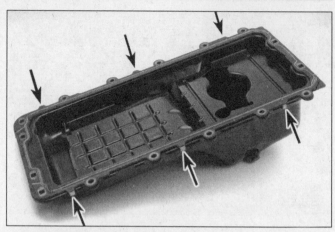

14.21 Place the gasket on the oil pan - the locating tabs on each side of the gasket will keep the gasket aligned during installation

pan or damage to the sealing surfaces may result and oil leaks could develop. Instead, dislodge the oil pan with a large rubber mallet or a wood block and a hammer. **Note:** *The oil pan gasket is reusable if care is taken in oil pan removal.*

17　You can't remove the oil pan yet because of interference from the oil pump pick-up tube. With the oil pan resting on the crossmember, remove the pick-up tube bolts **(see illustration 15.3)** and allow the pick-up tube to fall into the pan. Now you can remove the pan.

Installation

Refer to illustrations 14.20, 14.21, 14.22a and 14.22b

18　Use a gasket scraper or putty knife to remove all traces of old gasket material and sealant from the pan and engine block. **Caution:** *Be careful not to gouge the oil pan or block, or oil leaks could develop later.*

19　Clean the mating surfaces with lacquer thinner or acetone. Make sure the bolt holes in the engine block are clean.

20　Apply a bead of RTV sealant to the four corner seams where the rear seal retainer meets the engine block, and the front cover meets the engine block **(see illustration)**.

21　Install a new gasket on the oil pan flange **(see illustration)**. Place the pick-up tube in the pan.

22　Raise the pan into position on the crossmember and attach the pick-up tube. Tighten the bolts to the torque listed in this Chapter's Specifications. Carefully position the oil pan against the engine block and install the bolts finger tight. Make sure the gaskets haven't shifted, then tighten the bolts in the indicated sequence **(see illustrations)** to the torque listed in this Chapter's Specifications.

23　The remaining steps are the reverse of removal. **Caution:** *Don't forget to refill the engine with oil before starting it* (see Chapter 1).

24　Start the engine and check carefully for oil leaks at the oil pan. Drive the vehicle and check again.

15　Oil pump - removal and installation

Note: *The oil pump is available as a complete replacement unit only. No service parts or repair specifications are available from the manufacturer.*

Removal

Refer to illustrations 15.3 and 15.5

1　Raise the vehicle and support it securely on jackstands.

2　Drain the engine oil (see Chapter 1).

3　Unbolt and lower the oil pan as described in Section 14. It's not necessary to completely remove the oil pan. Remove the two bolts that attach the oil pump pick-up tube to the oil pump **(see illustration)**.

4　Remove the timing chain cover, the timing chains, the chain guides and the crankshaft timing chain sprockets (see Section 6).

5　Remove the four oil pump mounting bolts **(see illustration)** and separate the pump from the engine block.

Installation

Refer to illustration 15.6

6　Inspect the O-ring gasket on the pick-up tube **(see illustration)**. If it's damaged, replace it.

7　Install the oil pump to the engine and tighten the bolts to the torque listed in this Chapter's Specifications. **Note:** *Prime the oil pump prior to installation. Pour clean oil into the pick-up port and turn the pump by hand.*

8　The remainder of installation is the reverse of the removal procedure.

9　Fill the engine with the correct type and quantity of oil. Start the engine and check for leaks.

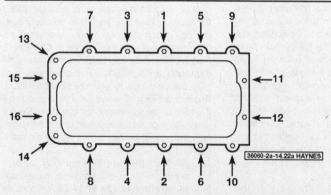

14.22a Oil pan bolt tightening sequence (V8 engine)

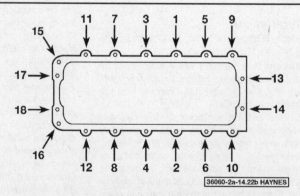

14.22b Oil pan bolt tightening sequence (V10 engine)

15.3 Remove the two bolts retaining the pick-up
tube to the oil pump

15.5 Remove the four oil pump mounting bolts (arrows)
and detach the oil pump from the engine block

16 Flywheel/driveplate - removal and installation

Removal

Refer to illustration 16.4

1 Disconnect the cable from the negative battery terminal.

2 Raise the vehicle and support it securely on jackstands.

3 Remove the transmission (see Chapter 7).

4 Look for factory paint marks that indicate flywheel/driveplate-to-crankshaft alignment. If they aren't there, scribe or paint marks on the flywheel/driveplate and crank-shaft to ensure correct alignment during reassembly **(see illustration)**.

5 Remove the bolts that secure the fly-wheel/driveplate to the crankshaft. Insert a screwdriver or punch through one of the holes in the driveplate to keep the crankshaft from turning while loosening the bolts.

6 Remove the flywheel/driveplate from the crank-shaft. Be sure to support it while removing the last bolt. **Warning:** *The teeth on the*

flywheel/driveplate may be sharp. Be sure to hold it with gloves or rags. After the flywheel/driveplate is removed, there is a sheetmetal cover plate located between the engine block and the flywheel/driveplate. It's not necessary to remove the cover plate unless you're going to remove the crankshaft rear oil seal retainer (see Section 17).

Installation

Refer to illustration 16.8

7 Clean and inspect the mating surfaces of the flywheel/driveplate and the crankshaft. And be sure to inspect the crankshaft rear oil seal. If the rear seal is leaking, replace it before reinstalling the driveplate (see Section 17).

8 If the reinforcement plate was removed, be sure to install it as shown **(see illustration)**, so it is correctly positioned for the starter installation.

9 Check for cracked, broken or missing ring gear teeth. If any of these conditions are found, replace the flywheel/driveplate.

10 Install the flywheel/driveplate, aligning the marks made during removal. Note that

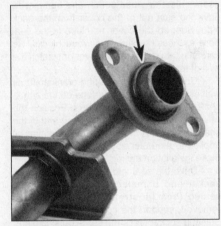

15.6 Before bolting the pick-up tube back into the oil pump, inspect the O-ring (arrow) and replace it if necessary

some engines have an alignment dowel or staggered bolt holes to ensure correct installation. Before installing the bolts, apply Teflon thread sealant to the threads.

11 Prevent the flywheel/driveplate from

16.4 Make an alignment mark, if there is not already one on the driveplate, to ensure proper reassembly

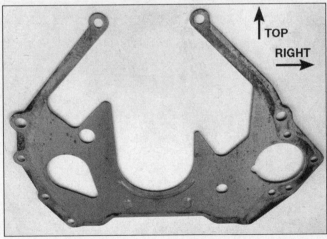

16.8 If the reinforcement plate is removed for any reason, make sure that it's installed correctly

turning as you tighten the bolts to the torque listed in this Chapter's Specifications.

12   The remainder of installation is the reverse of the removal procedure.

---

17   Crankshaft oil seals - replacement

Front seal

Refer to illustrations 17.4 and 17.6

1   Remove the drivebelt (Chapter 1).
2   Remove the engine cooling fan and shroud assembly (Chapter 3).
3   Remove the crankshaft pulley (see Section 5).
4   Carefully remove the seal from the cover with a seal removal tool **(see illustration)**. If a seal removal tool is not available, carefully use a screwdriver. If the timing cover is removed, use a chisel or small punch and hammer to drive the seal out of the cover from the back side. Support the cover as close to the seal bore as possible with two wood blocks. Be careful not to damage the cover or scratch the wall of the seal bore.
5   Check the seal bore and crankshaft, as well as the seal contact surface on the crankshaft pulley for nicks and burrs. Position the new seal in the bore with the open end of the seal facing IN. A small amount of engine oil applied to the outer edge of the new seal will make installation easier.
6   Drive the seal into the bore with a large socket and hammer until it's completely seated **(see illustration)**. If the cover is removed, support the cover on wood blocks. Select a socket that's the same outside diameter as the seal (a section of pipe can be used if a socket isn't available).
7   Lubricate the lip of the seal with clean engine oil and install the crankshaft pulley on the end of the crankshaft. The keyway in the crankshaft pulley bore must be aligned with the Woodruff key in the crankshaft nose.
Note: *Before reinstalling the crankshaft pulley, apply a small dab of RTV sealant to the*

17.4 Using a special seal removal tool or screwdriver, remove the crankshaft front oil seal, being very careful not to scratch the crankshaft during seal removal

front end of the crankshaft key groove.
8   If the crankshaft pulley can't be seated by hand, tap it into place with a soft-face hammer, or install the bolt and washer and tighten it to press the crankshaft pulley into place.
9   Tighten the crankshaft pulley bolt to the torque listed in this Chapter's Specifications.
10   Install the drivebelt.
11   Install the remaining parts removed for access to the seal.
12   Start the engine and check for leaks.

Rear seal

Refer to illustrations 17.15, 17.16, 17.17 and 17.18

13   Disconnect the cable from the negative battery terminal. Raise the vehicle and support it securely on jackstands. Refer to Chapter 7 and remove the transmission.
14   Remove the flywheel/driveplate (see Section 16), then remove the reinforcement plate from the engine.
15   Remove the bolts, detach the seal retainer **(see illustration)** and clean off all the

17.6 There is special tool for installing the front oil seal into the timing chain cover, but if the tool is unavailable a large socket or section of tubing (the same diameter as the seal) can be used to drive the seal into place

old gasket and/or sealant material from both the engine block and the seal retainer.
16   Support the seal and retainer assembly on wood blocks and drive the old seal out from the back side with a punch and hammer **(see illustration)**.
17   Drive the new seal into the retainer with a wood block **(see illustration)**.
18   Clean the crankshaft and seal bore with lacquer thinner or acetone. Check the seal contact surface on the crankshaft very carefully for scratches or nicks that could damage the new seal lip and cause oil leaks **(see illustration)**. If the crankshaft is damaged, the only alternative is a new or different crankshaft.
19   Lubricate the crankshaft seal journal and the lip of the new seal with engine oil.
20   Place a 1/16-inch wide bead of anaerobic sealant on either the engine block or the seal retainer.
21   Install the oil seal retainer by slowly and carefully pushing the seal onto the crankshaft.

17.15 Remove the eight bolts (arrows) and separate the seal retainer from the engine block

17.16 Support the seal retainer on two wood blocks and drive out the old seal with a blunt punch and hammer

17.17 Support the seal retainer and drive the new seal into the housing with a wood block (be careful not to cock the seal in the bore while installing)

17.18 Inspect the seal contact surface on the crankshaft for signs of excessive wear or grooves

The seal lip is stiff, so work it onto the crankshaft with a smooth object such as the end of a socket extension as you push the retainer against the engine block.

22 Install and tighten the retainer bolts to the torque listed in this Chapter's Specifications.

23 Reinstall the engine rear cover plate (see illustration 16.8). Make sure that it fits over all positioning dowels and that the hole for the starter motor is on the correct side.

24 Install the flywheel/driveplate (see Section 16).

25 Install the transmission (see Chapter 7).

26 Check the oil level and add if necessary, run the engine and check for oil leaks.

18 Engine mounts - check and replacement

Check

1 Engine mounts seldom require attention, but broken or deteriorated mounts should be replaced immediately or the added strain placed on the driveline components may cause damage or wear.

2 During the check, the engine must be raised slightly to remove the weight from the mounts.

3 Raise the vehicle and support it securely on jackstands, then position a jack under the engine oil pan. Place a large wood block between the jack head and the oil pan, then carefully raise the engine just enough to take the weight off the mounts.

4 Inspect the mounts to see if the rubber is cracked, hardened or separated from the metal plates. Sometimes the rubber will split right down the center.

5 Check for relative movement between the mount plates and the engine or frame (use a large screwdriver or pry bar to attempt to move the mounts). If movement is noted,

18.13 To detach an engine mount from the crossmember, remove these two big nuts (left arrows); to detach a mount from the engine block, remove all four mounting bolts (right arrows indicate rear bolts, front bolts not visible in this photo) (left mount shown, right mount identical)

lower the engine and tighten the mount fasteners.

6 Rubber preservative should be applied to the mounts to slow deterioration.

Replacement

Refer to illustration 18.13

Note: Because the mount replacement procedure involves a great deal of disassembly, it's a good idea to replace BOTH mounts, even if only one mount actually needs to be replaced.

7 Remove the air cleaner and the air intake duct (see Chapter 4).

8 Remove the engine cooling fan and shroud (see Chapter 3).

9 Remove the alternator (see Chapter 5).

10 Remove the throttle body from the intake manifold (see Chapter 4).

11 Raise the vehicle and place it securely on jackstands.

12 If you're going to replace the right mount, remove the starter motor (see Chapter 5).

13 Remove the mount-to-crossmember nuts (see illustration) and remove the nuts that attach the transmission mount to the

transmission crossmember (see Chapter 7). Note: Even if you're only planning to replace one mount, you must remove the mount-to-crossmember nuts from both mounts in order to raise the engine.

14 Attach an engine hoist to the engine and carefully raise the engine until it's supported, i.e. the weight of the engine is no longer on the mounts.

15 Remove the four mount-to-engine block bolts (see illustration 18.13).

16 Raise the engine as high as necessary in order to pull out the mount(s). Basically, you need to raise the engine high enough so that the two studs protruding downward from each mount can be removed from their respective holes in the crossmember. Do NOT raise the engine so high that the intake manifold touches the cowl. Caution: Raise the engine slowly while observing the location of the intake manifold. Do not allow the intake manifold to contact the cowl, which might damage the manifold.

17 Installation is the reverse of removal. Tighten the bolts and nuts to the torque listed in this Chapter's Specifications

Notes

Chapter 2 Part B
Diesel engines

Contents

	Section			Section
Camshaft and tappets - inspection, removal		Flywheel/driveplate - removal and installation		10
and installation	See Chapter 2C	General information		1
Crankshaft front oil seal - replacement	9	Intake manifold, 6.0L and 6.4L engines - removal and installation		6
Crankshaft pulley - removal and installation	8	Intake manifold covers, 7.3L engine - removal and installation		5
Crankshaft rear oil seal - replacement	11	Oil pan - removal and installation	See Chapter 2C	
Cylinder heads - removal and installation	See Chapter 2C	Oil pump - removal and installation		12
Engine front cover - removal and installation	See Chapter 2C	Repair operations possible with the engine in the vehicle		2
Engine mounts - check and replacement	See Chapter 2A	Rocker arms and pushrods - removal and installation		4
Exhaust manifolds - removal and installation	7	Valve covers - removal and installation		3

Specifications

General

Displacement
  1999 through 2003 .... 7.3L (444 cu. in.)
  2003 through 2007 .... 6.0L (365 cu. in.)
  2008 and later .... 6.4L (390 cu. in.)
Cylinder numbering
  Left cylinder bank (front to rear) 2-4-6-8
  Right cylinder bank (front to rear) 1-3-5-7
Firing order 1-2-7-3-4-5-6-8

Exhaust manifold

Allowable warpage
  Between exhaust ports .... 0.010 inch
  Everywhere else .... 0.005 inch

Torque Specifications

Ft-lbs (unless otherwise indicated)

Note: *One foot-pound (ft-lb) of torque is equivalent to 12 inch-pounds (in-lbs) of torque. Torque values below approximately 15 foot-pounds are expressed in inch-pounds, because most foot-pound torque wrenches are not accurate at these smaller values.*

Crankshaft pulley fastener(s)
  7.3L engines 212
  6.4L and 6.0L engines
    Step 1 50
    Step 2 .... Tighten an additional 90 degrees
Crankshaft rear oil seal retainer bolts, 7.3L engines .... 180 in-lbs
Exhaust manifold bolts
  7.3L engines 45
  6.4L engines
    Step1 18
    Step 2 18
  6.0L engines 28
Exhaust manifold-to-turbo inlet fasteners 20
Flywheel/driveplate bolts
  7.3L engines 89
  6.4L and 6.0L engines
    Step 1 .... 44 in-lbs
    Step 2 69
Intake manifold cover bolts, 7.3L engines 18
Intake manifold bolt
  6.4L engines
    Step1 .... Hand-tight
    Step 2 .... 96 in-lbs
  6.0L engines
    Step 1, bolts 9 through 16 only .... 96 in-lbs
    Step 2, all bolts .... 96 in-lbs

36060-1-specs.C HAYNES

Cylinder numbering diagram

Torque Specifications (continued)   Ft-lbs (unless otherwise indicated)

Note: *One foot-pound (ft-lb) of torque is equivalent to 12 inch-pounds (in-lbs) of torque. Torque values below approximately 15 foot-pounds are expressed in inch-pounds, because most foot-pound torque wrenches are not accurate at these smaller values.*

Oil pump bolts	
7.3L engines...	18
6.0L engines...	71 in-lbs
Oil pump housing bolts, 6.4L engines	
Long bolts...	23
Short bolts..	16
Rocker arm bolts, 7.3L engines...	20
Rocker arm fulcrum plate, 6.0L engines................................	23
Valve cover bolts	
7.3L engines...	96 in-lbs
6.4L engines...	80 in-lbs
6.0L engines...	71 in-lbs

1   General information

This part of Chapter 2 is devoted to in-vehicle repair procedures for the V8 diesel engines. For information regarding engine removal and installation and engine overhaul, see Part C of this Chapter. The specifications included in this part of Chapter 2 apply only to the procedures included here. You'll find more specifications in Part C.

Most of the repair procedures included in this Part are based on the assumption that the engine is still installed in the engine compartment. If you're going to refer to any of these procedures after the engine has been removed from the engine compartment, many of the steps included here will not apply.

2   Repair operations possible with the engine in the vehicle

Some major repairs are possible with the engine installed in the engine compartment.

Clean the engine compartment and the exterior of the engine with some type of pressure washer before doing any work. A clean engine makes the job easier and helps to keep dirt out of the internal areas of the engine.

Depending on the procedure, it might be a good idea to remove the hood to improve access to the engine (see Chapter 11).

Oil and coolant leaks usually indicate a need for a new gasket or seal. Most of these repairs can be made with the engine installed. The intake and exhaust manifold gaskets, engine front cover gasket and crankshaft oil seals are accessible without removing the engine.

Some exterior engine components can be removed with the engine in place. They include:

The valve covers (see Section 3)
The rocker arms and pushrods (see Section 4)
The intake manifold covers (see Section 5)
The exhaust manifolds (see Section 6)
The crankshaft pulley (see Section 7)

The crankshaft front oil seal (see Section 8)
The flywheel/driveplate (see Section 9)
The crankshaft rear oil seal (see Section 10)
The oil pump (see Section 11)
The water pump (see Chapter 3)
The turbocharger and the fuel injection components (see Chapter 4B)
The starter motor and the alternator (see Chapter 5)
The transmission (see Chapter 7)

However, the removal of other components - such as the cylinder heads, the front cover, the camshaft and lifters, and the oil pan - are far easier and safer to do with the engine removed. The removal and installation procedures for those components are in Chapter 2C. But even the procedures in this Chapter sometimes require extensive removal of other components. So read through a procedure before deciding whether you want to tackle it. Pay particularly close attention to any fuel system components that have to be removed before certain components in this Chapter can be removed.

3.3a If you're going to remove the right valve cover, detach these two heater hose routing clips from the valve cover bolts by pulling them straight up (remember where they go for reassembly) - 7.3L engine

3.3b Unplug the large electrical connector for the fuel injectors and glow plugs (left injector/glow plug connector shown, right connector similar) - 7.3L engine

3.4 To unplug the electrical connector for the engine control sensor circuit, remove this bolt

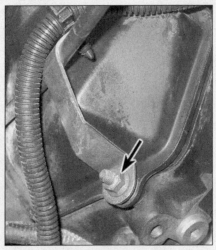

3.5a To remove a valve cover, remove these ten bolts and nuts (arrows indicate nine bolts/nuts, rear valve cover bolt not visible) (left valve cover shown, right valve cover similar) (breather box removed for clarity) - 7.3L engine

3.5b If you're removing the right valve cover, note that the engine oil dipstick tube bracket is attached to the front valve cover stud (7.3L engine)

3 Valve covers - removal and installation

Refer to illustrations 3.3a, 3.3b, 3.4, 3.5a, 3.5b, 3.6a, 3.6b and 3.6c

1 Disconnect the cables from the negative terminals of the batteries (see Chapter 5, Section 1).

7.3L engines

2 Remove the large duct between the intercooler and the turbocharger (see Chapter 4B).

3 If you're removing the right valve cover, disengage the heater hoses from their routing clips and then remove the clips **(see illustration)**. Disengage the fuel injector/glow plug nine-pin electrical connector and then unplug the connector **(see illustration)**.

4 Disconnect the engine control sensor wiring connector **(see illustration)**.

5 Remove the 10 valve cover bolts and nuts **(see illustration)**, then remove the valve cover. If you're removing the right valve cover, note that the engine oil dipstick tube bracket is attached to the front valve cover stud **(see illustration)**.

6 Disconnect the electrical connectors

from the glow plugs and the fuel injectors **(see illustrations)**, unplug the glow plug/injector harness connector at the valve cover gasket **(see illustration)**, then remove the valve cover gasket.

7 Installation is the reverse of removal.

6.0L and 6.4L engines

8 Remove the air cleaner assembly and the outlet duct (refer to Chapter 4B).

9 Pull out the vent tube(s) from the valve cover.

10 Disconnect the fuel injector wiring con-

nectors and the ignition coils.

11 Remove the wiring harness support bracket. Lift the wiring assembly from the valve cover. On 6.4L engines, disconnect the electrical connectors at the firewall end of the PCM, then set the harness aside.

3.6a Disconnect the electrical connectors from the glow plugs (front two glow plug connectors shown, other two connectors not visible in this photo) (7.3L engine)

3.6b Release the locking wire retainers and disconnect the electrical connectors (arrows) from the fuel injectors (front two injector connectors shown, other two connectors not visible in this photo) (7.3L engine)

3.6c Unplug the injector/glow plug harness electrical connector, then remove the valve cover gasket (7.3L engine)

Right valve cover

12   Remove the alternator (refer to Chapter 5).

13   Drain the coolant (refer to Chapter 3). Disconnect the front heater hose. Disconnect the right motor mount so the engine can be raised slightly (refer to Chapter 2A).

14   Disconnect the interfering hoses and wiring components from the valve cover. On 6.4L engines, unbolt and set aside the glow-plug module.

15   Install an over-engine support fixture, support it securely between the fenders and use it to raise the engine on the right side.

Both valve covers

16   Remove the valve cover bolts and remove the valve cover from the engine. **Note:** *The valve cover bolts are captive with the valve cover; don't try to remove them.*

17   Clean the sealing surfaces of the cylinder head and the valve cover. **Caution:** *Be extremely careful to avoid scratching either sealing surface. Don't use steel scrapers or abrasive discs on these parts. The manufacturer recommends plastic scraping tools. Specialty chemicals are also acceptable for cleaning these parts.*

18   Installation is the reverse of removal.

19   Apply a small amount of silicone sealer to the two joints where the front cover meets the engine block.

20   Tighten the valve cover bolts to the torque listed in this Chapter's Specifications and in the proper sequence **(see illustration)**.

4   Rocker arms and pushrods - removal, inspection and installation

Note: *The procedure shown is for the 7.3L engine. The 6.0L engine uses similar components with the addition of a valve bridge that is operated by the rocker arm.*

Removal

Refer to illustrations 4.2 and 4.3

1   Remove the valve covers (see Section 3).

2   Mark the rocker arms to ensure that they will be reinstalled in the same location.

4.2 To remove the rocker arm assemblies for each cylinder, remove these four bolts (fuel injector removed for clarity, but it's not necessary to remove the fuel injectors to remove the rocker arms) (7.3L engine)

Remove the rocker arm bolts from each cylinder head **(see illustration)** and then remove the rocker arms.

3   Mark the pushrods to ensure that they will be reinstalled in the same location. Remove the pushrods **(see illustration)**. Keep the pushrod and rocker arm assembly for each cylinder together to ensure that they will be installed together. Do not mix up the pushrods and rocker arms.

Inspection

Refer to illustrations 4.4, 4.5 and 4.10

4   On the workbench, remove the snap retaining clip from the rocker arm **(see illustration)**, then disengage the rocker arm pedestal and the rocker arm.

5   Remove the steel ball **(see illustration)** from the rocker arm. **Caution:** *Be careful not to lose the steel ball.* Keep each disassembled rocker arm assembly together to ensure that the same parts are reassembled. Do not mix up the rocker arm parts.

6   Inspect each rocker arm for wear, cracks and other damage, especially at the friction surfaces where the pushrods and the valve

4.3 To remove the pushrods, pull them straight out

stems contact the rocker arm tips. If a rocker arm is worn or damaged, replace it.

7   Inspect each steel ball for galling, scoring and excessive wear. Replace any damaged steel balls.

8   Inspect the pushrods for cracks and excessive wear at the ends. Roll each pushrod across a piece of plate glass to see if it is bent (if it wobbles, it is bent). Replace any damaged or worn pushrods.

9   Place the steel ball in the rocker arm cup and lubricate it with clean engine oil.

10   Place the rocker arm pedestal on the steel ball and the rocker arm **(see illustration)**.

11   Snap the retaining clip over the rocker arm pedestal groove **(see illustration 4.4)**. On 6.4L engines, use new clips during assembly.

Installation

12   Lubricate the pushrod ends with engine oil, then install the pushrods, *copper end up.*

13   Install the rocker arms and bolts and tighten them to the torque listed in this Chapter's Specifications. **Caution:** *To prevent bent valves when installing the rocker arms, rotate the engine until the pushrods for each cylinder are at their lowest point.*

14   Install the valve covers.

4.4 To disassemble a rocker arm assembly, remove this snap retaining clip (arrow)

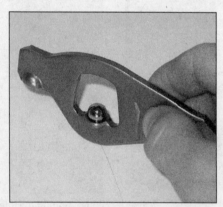

4.5 Remove the steel ball from each rocker arm

4.10 This is how the rocker arm and pedestal should look when they're reassembled; if they're not correctly reassembled, the retaining clip won't snap back into place

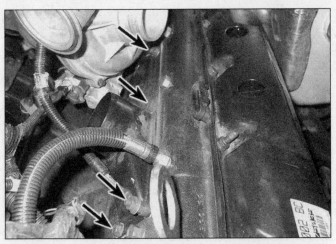

5.2a To remove either intake manifold cover on a 7.3L engine, remove all eight bolts and/or nuts (arrows; not all bolts visible); be sure to reattach any ground wires, such as the manifold air heater ground on the left cover . . .

5.2b . . . or any brackets, such as the fuel line bracket on the right cover (turbocharger removed for clarity in this photo, but turbocharger removal is not necessary to remove either intake manifold cover)

5 Intake manifold covers - removal and installation

Refer to illustrations 5.2a and 5.2b

1   Remove the turbocharger manifold and remove the intake manifold hose, or hoses, depending on whether you're going to remove one or both of the intake manifold covers (see Chapter 4B).

2   Remove the intake manifold cover bolts and/or nuts **(see illustrations)** and remove the intake manifold cover. Remove and discard the old gasket.

3   Using a new gasket, install the intake manifold cover and tighten the cover bolts and/or nuts to the torque listed in this Chapter's Specifications.

4   Installation is otherwise the reverse of removal.

6 Intake manifold, 6.0L and 6.4L engines – removal and installation

Removal

1   Disconnect the cable from the negative battery terminal. If the vehicle is equipped with an auxiliary battery, remove it (refer to Chapter 5).

2   Remove the cooling fan and fan stator (refer to Chapter 3). This procedure involves removing the drivebelt. If your vehicle has two alternators, remove the extra drivebelts belt tensioners and idler pulleys.

3   Remove the alternator(s). If your vehicle has two alternators, remove the auxiliary alternator mounting bracket as well (refer to Chapter 5).

4   Drain the coolant and remove the coolant reservoir (refer to Chapter 3). On 6.4L engines, remove the clamps securing the power steering hoses to the intake manifold,

then unbolt and set aside the power steering pump (see Chapter 10).

5   Remove the upper radiator hose.

6   Remove the turbocharger-to-intercooler duct (refer to Chapter 4B).

7   Remove the turbocharger and its mount (refer to Chapter 4B).

8   Remove the intercooler duct from the intake manifold (refer to Chapter 4B).

9   Remove the two bolts from the heater coolant tube at the front of the manifold. Move it aside.

10   Disconnect the manifold absolute pressure (MAP) sensor, the engine oil pressure (EOP) sensor, the exhaust gas recirculation (EGR) valve connector, the engine oil temperature (EOT) sensor, the engine coolant temperature (ECT) sensor, the intake air temperature (IAT2) sensor and, if equipped, the exhaust pressure (EP) sensor.

11   Disconnect the coolant vent hose and move it aside.

12   Remove the fuel injection control module.

13   Remove the fuel injection pressure regulator heat shield, pull back the heat wrap and disconnect the wiring connectors beneath it.

14   Disconnect the wiring from all eight fuel injectors, pull back the wiring harnesses and set them aside.

15   Disconnect the fuel lines from the fuel filter. The sealing washers must be replaced with new ones upon reassembly. Remove the fuel filter (refer to Chapter 4B).

16   Remove the oil filter (refer to Chapter 1). Unbolt the oil filter housing and remove it.

17   Remove the mounting bolt and the oil filter return tube.

18   Remove the steel fuel line from the top of the intake manifold, and on 6.4L engines, the bolts securing the fuel rails.

19   Disconnect the EGR coolant hose. To do so, pull the EGR cooler clamp forward, twist it so that the flat edge aligns with the line on the supply housing, and then slide the hose to the rear.

20   Loosen the fasteners on both sides of the turbocharger pipe.

21   Loosen the V-clamp on the EGR cooler line. The V-clamp will stay with the turbocharger pipe on removal.

22   Remove the intake manifold bolts. Lift the manifold off the engine.

Installation

Refer to illustration 6.26

23   Thoroughly clean all sealing surfaces prior to installation.

24   Be sure to install the new intake manifold gaskets with the tabs up and toward the middle of the engine. Also install a new O-ring at the front module.

25   Use a little grease to hold the EGR gasket in place during assembly. Set the EGR cooler V-clamp loosely on the turbocharger pipe.

26   Install the manifold and tighten the bolts in two steps to the torque listed in this Chapter's Specifications. Follow the correct tightening sequence **(see illustration)**. Step 1 involves tightening bolts 9 through 16 only. Step 2 involves tightening of all of the

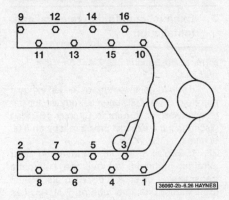

6.26 6.0L and 6.4L diesel engine intake manifold bolt tightening sequence

7.2 If you're removing the right exhaust manifold, unscrew this fitting and disconnect the exhaust back pressure sensor line - 7.3L engine

7.4 To disconnect the turbocharger inlet from the exhaust manifold, remove these nuts and bolts (right manifold shown, left manifold similar)

7.5a To detach the exhaust manifold from the cylinder head, remove these eight bolts (front bolt not visible in this photo) - 7.3L engine

7.5b Exhaust manifold bolt locations on a 6.0L diesel engine

bolts (including re-tightening of bolts 9 through 16 to the same torque as in Step 1).

27   The remainder of installation is the reverse of removal. Be certain to install new sealing washers on the fuel and oil line banjo fittings.

7   Exhaust manifolds - removal and installation

Refer to illustrations 7.2, 7.4, 7.5a, 7.5b and 7.9

1   If you're going to remove the left exhaust manifold on a 7.3L engine, remove the air cleaner assembly (refer to Chapter 4B). Also disconnect the exhaust pressure tube on 6.0L engines.

2   If you're going to remove the right exhaust manifold, remove the automatic transmission dipstick tube. Also disconnect the exhaust pressure tube on 7.3L engines **(see illustration)**.

3   Raise the vehicle and place it securely on jackstands.

4   Remove the two nuts and two bolts **(see illustration)** that attach the turbocharger exhaust inlet pipe to the exhaust manifold.

5   Remove the eight exhaust manifold bolts **(see illustration)** and remove the exhaust manifold.

6   Clean off the exhaust manifold and cylinder head mating surfaces.

7   Using a straightedge and a feeler gauge, check the flatness of the exhaust manifold and

compare your measurements to the allowable warpage listed in this Chapter's Specifications.

8   Install the exhaust manifold and tighten the manifold bolts to the torque listed in this Chapter's Specifications.

9   Reattach the turbocharger exhaust inlet pipe to the exhaust manifold and tighten the nuts and bolts to the torque listed in this Chapter's Specifications, starting from the center and working out towards the ends **(see illus-**

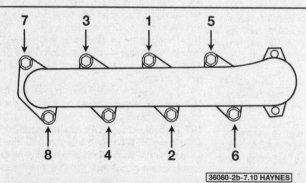

7.9 Start the bolt in hole #1 first, then install the others. Tighten them in this sequence

8.7a Use a chain wrench to hold the crankshaft pulley while you loosen the pulley bolt (it's a good idea to wrap a piece of old drivebelt around the pulley to prevent damage)

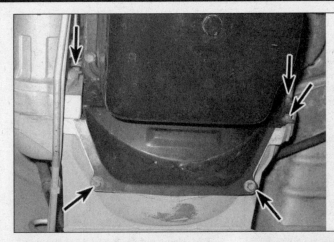

8.7b To remove the flywheel/ driveplate access cover, remove these bolts (automatic transmission shown)

8.7c Hold the flywheel or driveplate with a special flywheel/driveplate holding tool . . .

8.7d . . . or use a prybar wedged between the ring gear teeth and the bellhousing

tration). The #1 hole on these manifolds is slightly smaller than the rest. Start the first bolt in this hole so that all the rest will start easily.

10   Installation is otherwise the reverse of removal.

8   Crankshaft pulley - removal and installation

Refer to illustrations 8.7a, 8.7b, 8.7c, 8.7d, 8.8a, 8.8b, 8.9, 8.10 and 8.11

1   Disconnect the cable from the negative battery terminal.

2   Remove the accessory drivebelt (refer to Chapter 1).

3   On vehicles with 7.3L engines, remove the radiator (refer to Chapter 3).

4   Raise the vehicle and support it securely on jackstands.

5   On vehicles with 6.0L engines, remove the cooling fan stator for clearance (refer to Chapter 3). On 6.4L engines, remove the entire fan and the right-hand hose from the charge-air cooler.

6   On models with 6.0L and 6.4L engines and two alternators, remove the drivebelt and the auxiliary alternator pulley.

7   Remove the crankshaft pulley bolt(s). A chain wrench can be used to hold the pulley. If you don't have a chain wrench, remove the flywheel driveplate access cover. Use a special flywheel holding tool or wedge a large prybar between the flywheel teeth and the transmission bellhousing **(see illustrations)**.

8   A crankshaft pulley puller is not required

on 6.0L or 6.4L engines. On 7.3L engines, remove the crankshaft pulley with a puller **(see illustration)**. **Caution:** *Don't use a puller with jaws that grip the outer edge of the crankshaft pulley. The puller must be the type that utilizes bolts to apply force to the pulley hub. Don't lose the key* **(see illustration)**.

9   On 7.3L engines, inspect the crankshaft pulley wear ring **(see illustration)** for galling, scoring and other damage. If the wear ring is excessively worn or damaged, replace it.

8.8a Remove the crankshaft pulley with a puller

8.8b After removing the crankshaft pulley, retrieve the key and store it in a plastic bag until you're ready to install the pulley

8.9 Inspect the crankshaft pulley wear ring for galling, scoring and any other damage

8.10 Use a small three-jaw puller to remove the crankshaft damper wear ring

8.11 Use a big socket to drive the new crankshaft damper wear ring into place on the pulley hub

9.2 Use a seal removal tool to pry out the old crankshaft front seal

10   Use a puller to remove the crankshaft pulley wear ring **(see illustration)**.

11   Use a big socket to install the new crankshaft pulley wear ring **(see illustration)**. The socket must be large enough to clear the pulley hub, but small enough to push down on the edge of the wear ring.

12   On 7.3L engines, install the key in the slot in the nose of the crankshaft and install the pulley and washer using a pulley installation tool if possible. On 6.0L engines, simply place the pulley on the crankshaft snout and immediately bolt it in place.

13   Tighten the bolt(s) to the torque listed in this Chapter's Specification. On 6.0L engines tighten the bolts in a criss-cross pattern. **Note:** *On 6.0L and 6.4L engines it is mandatory to replace the crankshaft pulley bolts with lightly-oiled new ones any time they are removed.*

14   The remainder of installation is the reverse of removal.

9   Crankshaft front oil seal - replacement

Refer to illustrations 9.2 and 9.4

1   Remove the crankshaft pulley (see Section 7).

2   Using a seal removal tool, carefully remove the old crank seal **(see illustration)**.

3   Coat the new seal with multi-purpose grease.

4   Using a seal driver or a big socket, drive the new seal into place **(see illustration)**.

5   Installation is otherwise the reverse of removal.

10   Flywheel/driveplate - removal and installation

Refer to illustration 10.3

1   Remove the transmission (see Chapter 7).

2   Remove the bolts (and spacers, if equipped) and remove the flywheel or driveplate from the crankshaft flange.

3   Install the flywheel or driveplate, install the flywheel or driveplate bolts (and, spacers, if equipped) and tighten the bolts to the torque listed in this Chapter's Specifications. On 6.0L engines follow the correct tightening sequence **(see illustration)**. On 6.4L engines, follow a criss-cross pattern and tighten the bolts in several stages to the torque listed in this Chapter's Specifications.

4   Install the transmission (see Chapter 7).

11   Crankshaft rear oil seal - replacement

7.3L engines

Caution: *The rear seal should be removed, and MUST be installed, with the Rear Crank*

9.4 Use a big socket with an outside diameter slightly smaller than the outside diameter of the seal to drive the new seal into place

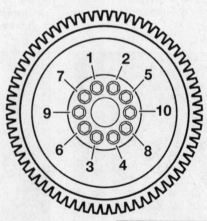

36060 2b-10.3 HAYNES

10.3 6.0L diesel flywheel bolt tightening sequence

Service Set (special tool No. T94T-6701-AH). This set is quite expensive, but if you try to install a new rear seal without it, the new seal might not be perfectly centered, which will allow oil to leak past the seal and will ruin the seal, and the CRANKSHAFT, very quickly. So if you don't have access to the special tool set, do not attempt the following procedure.

Removal

1   Remove the transmission (see Chapter 7).
2   Remove the flywheel or driveplate (see Section 10).
3   Carefully remove the rear cover. Make sure you don't damage or lose the dowel pins. (It's a good idea to store the dowel pins in a plastic bag until you're ready to reassemble everything.)
4   Remove the crankshaft rear oil seal retainer bolts and remove the oil seal retainer.
5   Separate the retainer and the old seal and then remove any traces of sealant from the retainer.
6   Remove the wear sleeve from the crankshaft.

Installation

7   Apply a coat of RTV silicone sealant (F5TZ-19G204-AB, or a suitable equivalent which meets Ford specification NAVSTR SLR) to the seal retainer and attach the new rear seal to the retainer. Install the wear sleeve in the rear oil seal (the wear sleeve and oil seal are installed as a single assembly).
8   Using the special installation tools, install the wear sleeve, rear oil seal and seal retainer on the crankshaft.
9   When the seal is fully seated, install the five seal retainer bolts and tighten them to the torque listed in this Chapter's Specifications.
10   Installation is otherwise the reverse of removal.

6.0L engines

11   Remove the flywheel/driveplate (refer to Section 10).
12   Remove the flywheel front adapter. **Caution:** *Be very careful to avoid damage to the dowel pin while removing the adapter. Also, don't remove the crankshaft rear flange bolts. The flange can't be reinstalled without resulting in vibration and engine damage.*
13   Drive several sheet metal screws into the seal and pry it out using a claw hammer or a similar tool.
14   Lubricate the outer edge of the new seal only with soapy water and install it using a large socket and a hammer.
15   The rest of the installation is he reverse of removal.

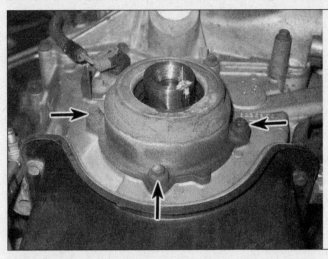

12.3 To detach the oil pump housing from the front cover, remove these four bolts (upper bolt not visible)

6.4L engines

16   Remove the flywheel/driveplate (see Section 10).
17   Remove the flywheel front adapter. **Caution:** *Be very careful to avoid damage to the dowel pin while removing the adapter.*
18   Drive several sheet metal screws into the seal and pry it out using a claw hammer or a similar tool.
19   If you're working on an engine equipped with an original seal, remove the wear ring from the engine using a wear ring removal tool.
20   Clean the crankshaft and seal bore in the retainer thoroughly.
21   Find the metal face of the wear ring. **Note:** *The crankshaft rear seal and wear ring are of a one-piece design and must be installed as an assembly.* Lubricate the lip of the new seal with soap and water.
22   Posistion the new seal on the crankshaft. Use a special tool and install the seal.
23   The remainder of installation is the reverse of removal.

---

12   Oil pump - removal and installation

7.3 engines

Removal

Refer to illustration 12.3

1   Remove the accessory drivebelt (see Chapter 1).
2   Remove the crankshaft pulley (see Section 7).
3   Remove the oil pump housing bolts **(see illustration)** and remove the pump housing from the front cover.
4   Remove the oil pump housing O-ring.

5   Remove the oil pump drive gear from the crankshaft.

Installation

6   Insert the oil pump drive gear into the oil pump. When installing the drive gear, make sure that the words OUT or DAMPER face away from the engine (toward the crankshaft pulley).
7   Install a new O-ring.
8   Install the oil pump on the front cover and tighten the bolts to the torque listed in this Chapter's Specifications.
9   Install the crankshaft pulley (see Section 7).
10   Install the accessory drivebelt (see Chapter 1).

6.0L and 6.4L engines

11   Remove the crankshaft front oil seal (refer to Section 8).
12   Remove the five oil pump cover bolts and lift off the cover. On 6.4L engines, there is one long bolt, five nuts and four short bolts. Mark the locations for the four short bolts.
13   Carefully clean the front surfaces of the gears and then make match marks with dabs of paint or a punch so they can be installed in the same orientation. The marks serve to indicate which sides face forward.
14   Remove the gerotors.
15   Inspect all components for wear and damage. Replace any components that are faulty.
16   Install the gerotors with the correct sides facing forward. Pack lithium grease generously around them.
17   Replace the O-ring in the oil pump cover and install it. Tighten the bolts to the torque listed in this Chapter's Specifications.
18   The remainder of installation is the reverse of removal.

Notes

Chapter 2 Part C
General engine overhaul procedures

Contents

	Section
Camshaft and lifters (diesel engine) - inspection, removal and installation	12
CHECK ENGINE light	See Chapter 6
Crankshaft - removal and installation	14
Cylinder compression check	3
Cylinder heads (diesel engines) - removal and installation	9
Engine - removal and installation	7
Engine front cover (diesel engines) - removal and installation	11
Engine overhaul - disassembly sequence	8

	Section
Engine overhaul - reassembly sequence	15
Engine rebuilding alternatives	5
Engine removal - methods and precautions	6
General information - engine overhaul	1
Initial start-up and break-in after overhaul	16
Oil pan (diesel engines) - removal and installation	10
Oil pressure check	2
Pistons and connecting rods - removal and installation	13
Vacuum gauge diagnostic checks (gasoline engines)	4

Specifications

General

Displacement

V8 gasoline engine	330 cubic inches (5.4L)
V10 gasoline engine	415 cubic inches (6.8L)
1999 through 2003 diesel engine	444 cubic inches (7.3L)
2003 through 2007 diesel engine	365 cubic inches (6.0L)
2008 and later diesel engine	390 cubic inches (6.4L)

Bore and stroke

Gasoline engines	3.55 x 4.17 inches
7.3L diesel engine	4.11 x 4.18 inches
6.4L diesel engine	3.87 x 4.13 inches
6.0L diesel engine	3.74 x 4.13 inches

Oil pressure

5.4L engine

1999 through 2003, at 2000 rpm	40 to 60 psi
2004 and later, at 2000 rpm	40 to 75 psi

6.8L engine

1999 through 2002, at 2000 rpm	40 to 60 psi
2003	
At 650 rpm	18 psi
At 4000 rpm	100 psi
2004 and later, at 2000 rpm	40 to 75 psi

7.3L engine

At idle	10 psi
At 3300 rpm	40 to 70 psi

6.0L engine

2003	10 to 40 psi
2004 and later 6.0L and 2008 and later 6.4L engines	
At 700 rpm	12 psi
At 1200 rpm	24 psi
At 1800 rpm	45 psi

Torque specifications

Ft-lbs (unless otherwise indicated)

Note: *One foot-pound (ft-lb) of torque is equivalent to 12 inch-pounds (in-lbs) of torque. Torque values below approximately 15 foot-pounds are expressed in inch-pounds, because most foot-pound torque wrenches are not accurate at these smaller values.*

Camshaft thrust plate bolts
  7.3L diesel engine 18
  6.4L and 6.0L diesel engines 23
Connecting rod bearing cap bolts
  Gasoline engines
    Step 1 32
    Step 2 .... Tighten an additional 115 degrees
  7.3L diesel engine
    Step 1 53
    Step 2 80
  6.4L and 6.0L diesel engines
    Step 1 33
    Step 2 50
Cylinder head bolts (refer to Section 9 for sequences)
  7.3L diesel engine
    Step 1 (use first tightening sequence) 65
    Step 2 (use first tightening sequence) 85
    Step 3 (use second tightening sequence) 95
  6.4L diesel engine
    Step 1, bolts 1 through 10 70
    Step 2, bolts 1 through 10 .... Loosen
    Step 3, bolts 1 through 10 115
    Step 4, bolts 1 through 10 .... Tighten an additional 90 degrees
    Step 5, bolts 1 through 10 .... Tighten an additional 90 degrees
    Step 6, bolts 11 through 15 18
    Step 7, bolts 11 through 15 23
  6.0L diesel engine
    Step 1, bolts 1 through 10 65
    Step 2, bolts 1, 3, 5, 7, 9 85
    Step 3, bolts 1 through 10 .... Tighten an additional 90 degrees
    Step 4 .... Repeat Step 3
    Step 5 .... Repeat Step 3
    Step 6, bolts 11 through 15 18
    Step 7, bolts 11 through 15 23
Front cover bolts
  7.3L diesel engine 15
  6.4L diesel engine 23
  6.0L diesel engine 18
Lifter retainer bolts
  7.3L diesel engine .... 180 in-lbs
  6.0L diesel engine 10
Main bearing bolts (refer to Section 14 for sequences)
  Gasoline engines
    Vertical bolts
      Step 1 30
      Step 2 .... Tighten an additional 90 degrees
    Side bolts
      Step 1 22
      Step 2 .... Tighten an additional 90 degrees
  7.3L diesel engine
    Step 1 76
    Step 2 96
  6.0L diesel engine
    20 inner bolts
      Step 1 90
      Step 2 120
      Step 3 170
    8 outer bolts 23
  6.4L diesel engine, lower crankcase-to-block
    Step 1 110
    Step 2 130
    Step 3 170
Oil pan bolts
  7.3L diesel engine 18
  6.4L diesel engine .... 115 in-lbs
  6.0L diesel engine .... 120 in-lbs
Oil pump pickup tube fasteners
  7.3L diesel engine 18
  6.4L diesel engine .... 115 in-lbs
  6.0L diesel engine .... 120 in-lbs

1 General information - engine overhaul

Refer to illustrations 1.1, 1.2, 1.3, 1.4, 1.5 and 1.6

Included in this portion of Chapter 2 are general information and diagnostic testing procedures for determining the overall mechanical condition of your engine.

The information ranges from advice concerning preparation for an overhaul and the purchase of replacement parts and/or components to detailed, step-by-step procedures covering removal and installation.

The following Sections have been written to help you determine whether your engine needs to be overhauled and how to remove and install it once you've determined it needs to be rebuilt. For information concerning in-vehicle engine repair, see Chapter 2A or 2B.

The Specifications included in this Part are general in nature and include only those necessary for testing the oil pressure and checking the engine compression. Refer to Chapter 2A or 2B for additional engine Specifications.

It's not always easy to determine when, or if, an engine should be completely overhauled, because a number of factors must be considered.

High mileage is not necessarily an indication that an overhaul is needed, while low mileage doesn't preclude the need for an overhaul. Frequency of servicing is probably the most important consideration. An engine that's had regular and frequent oil and filter changes, as well as other required maintenance, will most likely give many thousands of miles of reliable service. Conversely, a neglected engine may require an overhaul very early in its service life.

Excessive oil consumption is an indication that piston rings, valve seals and/or valve guides are in need of attention. Make sure that oil leaks aren't responsible before deciding that the rings and/or guides are bad. Perform a cylinder compression check to determine the extent of the work required (see Section 3). Also check the vacuum readings under various conditions (see Section 4).

Check the oil pressure with a gauge installed in place of the oil pressure sending unit and compare it to this Chapter's Specifications (see Section 2). If it's extremely low, the bearings and/or oil pump are probably worn out.

Loss of power, rough running, knocking or metallic engine noises, excessive valve train noise and high fuel consumption rates may also point to the need for an overhaul, especially if they're all present at the same time. If a complete tune-up doesn't remedy the situation, major mechanical work is the only solution.

An engine overhaul involves restoring the internal parts to the specifications of a new engine. During an overhaul, the piston rings are replaced and the cylinder walls are reconditioned (rebored and/or honed) **(see illustrations 1.1 and 1.2)**. If a rebore is done by an automotive machine shop, new oversize pistons will also be installed. The main bearings, connecting rod bearings and camshaft bearings are generally replaced with new ones and, if necessary, the crankshaft may be reground to restore the journals **(see illustration 1.3)**. Generally, the valves are serviced as well, since they're usually in

1.1 An engine block being bored. An engine rebuilder will use special machinery to recondition the cylinder bores

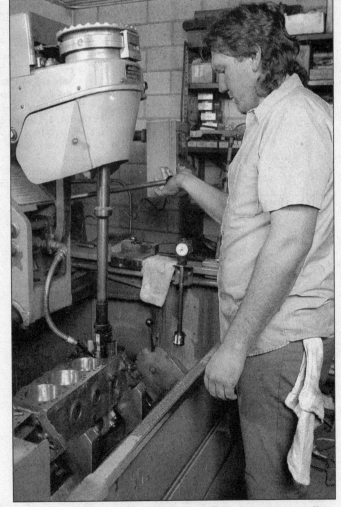

1.2 If the cylinders are bored, the machine shop will normally hone the engine on a machine like this

1.3 A crankshaft having a main bearing journal ground

1.4 A machinist checks for a bent connecting rod, using specialized equipment

less-than-perfect condition at this point. While the engine is being overhauled, other components, such as the starter and alternator, can be rebuilt as well. The end result should be a like new engine that will give many trouble free miles. **Note:** *Critical cooling system com-*

ponents such as the hoses, drivebelts, thermostat and water pump should be replaced with new parts when an engine is overhauled. The radiator should be checked carefully to ensure that it isn't clogged or leaking (see Chapter 3). If you purchase a rebuilt engine or short block, some rebuilders will not warranty their engines unless the radiator has been professionally flushed. Also, we don't recommend overhauling the oil pump - always install a new one when an engine is rebuilt.

Overhauling the internal components on today's engines is a difficult and time-consuming task which requires a significant amount of specialty tools and is best left to a professional engine rebuilder **(see illustrations 1.4, 1.5 and 1.6)**. A competent engine rebuilder will handle the inspection of your old parts and offer advice concerning the reconditioning or replacement of the original engine, never purchase parts or have machine work done on other components until the block has been thoroughly inspected by a professional machine shop. As a general rule, time is the primary cost of an overhaul, especially since the vehicle may be tied up for a minimum of two weeks or more. Be aware that

some engine builders only have the capability to rebuild the engine you bring them while other rebuilders have a large inventory of rebuilt exchange engines in stock. Also be aware that many machine shops could take as much as two weeks time to completely rebuild your engine depending on shop workload. Sometimes it makes more sense to simply exchange your engine for another engine that's already rebuilt to save time.

2   Oil pressure check

Refer to illustrations 2.2a and 2.2b

1   Low engine oil pressure can be a sign of an engine in need of rebuilding. A "low oil pressure" indicator (often called an "idiot light") is not a test of the oiling system. Such indicators only come on when the oil pressure is dangerously low. Even a factory oil pressure gauge in the instrument panel is only a relative indication, although much better for driver information than a warning light. A better test is with a mechanical (not electrical) oil pressure gauge.

2   Locate the oil pressure indicator sending

1.5 A bore gauge being used to check a main bearing bore

1.6 Uneven piston wear like this indicates a bent connecting rod

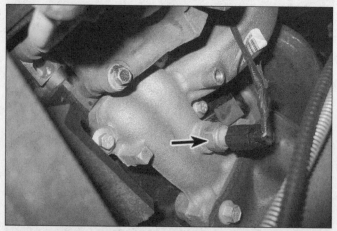

2.2a On gasoline engines, the oil pressure sending unit is located on the left side of the engine block, in front of the left engine mount (V10 engine shown, V8 engine similar)

2.2b On 7.3L diesel engines, the oil pressure sending unit is located on top of the oil reservoir for the high-pressure oil system reservoir (the reservoir itself is pressurized by the engine oil pump, not by the high-pressure oil pump)

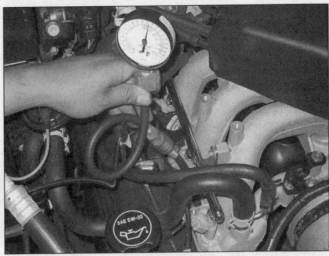

3.6 Use a compression gauge with a threaded fitting for the spark plug hole, not the type that requires hand pressure to maintain the seal (V10 engine shown)

unit on the engine block:

a) *On gasoline engines, the oil pressure sending unit is located on the left side of the engine block, in front of the left engine mount* **(see illustration)**.

b) *On diesel engines, the oil pressure sending unit is located on top of the oil reservoir for the high-pressure oil system, at the front of the engine (the oil reservoir for the high-pressure oil system is not itself part of the high-pressure system; it's at the same pressure as the rest of the engine lubrication system)* **(see illustration)**.

3   Unscrew and remove the oil pressure sending unit and then screw in the hose for your oil pressure gauge. If necessary, install an adapter fitting. Use Teflon tape or thread sealant on the threads of the adapter and/or the fitting on the end of your gauge's hose.

4   Connect an accurate tachometer to the engine, according to the tachometer manufacturer's instructions.

5   Check the oil pressure with the engine running (normal operating temperature) at the specified engine speed, and compare it to this Chapter's Specifications. If it's extremely low, the bearings and/or oil pump are probably worn out.

3   Cylinder compression check

Gasoline engines

Refer to illustration 3.6

1   A compression check will tell you what mechanical condition the upper end of your engine (pistons, rings, valves, head gaskets) is in. Specifically, it can tell you if the compression is down due to leakage caused by worn piston rings, defective valves and seats or a blown head gasket. **Note:** *The engine must be at normal operating temperature and the*

battery must be fully charged for this check.

2   Begin by cleaning the area around the spark plugs before you remove them (compressed air should be used, if available). The idea is to prevent dirt from getting into the cylinders as the compression check is being done.

3   Remove all of the spark plugs from the engine (see Chapter 1).

4   Block the throttle wide open.

5   Disable the ignition system by disconnecting the primary (low voltage) electrical connectors from the ignition coils (see Chapter 5). The fuel pump circuit should also be disabled (see Chapter 4A).

6   Install a compression gauge in the spark plug hole **(see illustration)**.

7   Crank the engine over at least seven compression strokes and watch the gauge. The compression should build up quickly in a healthy engine. Low compression on the first stroke, followed by gradually increasing pressure on successive strokes, indicates worn piston rings. A low compression reading on the first stroke, which doesn't build up during successive strokes, indicates leaking valves or a blown head gasket (a cracked head could also be the cause). Deposits on the undersides of the valve heads can also cause low compression. Record the highest gauge reading obtained.

8   Repeat the procedure for the remaining cylinders and compare the results to this Chapter's Specifications.

9   Add some engine oil (about three squirts from a plunger-type oil can) to each cylinder, through the spark plug hole, and repeat the test.

10   If the compression increases after the oil is added, the piston rings are definitely worn. If the compression doesn't increase significantly, the leakage is occurring at the valves or head gasket. Leakage past the valves may be caused by burned valve seats and/or faces or warped, cracked or bent valves.

11   If two adjacent cylinders have equally low compression, there's a strong possibility that the head gasket between them is blown. The appearance of coolant in the combustion chambers or the crankcase would verify this condition.

12   If one cylinder is slightly lower than the others, and the engine has a slightly rough idle, a worn lobe on the camshaft could be the cause.

13   If the compression is unusually high, the combustion chambers are probably coated with carbon deposits. If that's the case, the cylinder head(s) should be removed and decarbonized.

14   If compression is way down or varies greatly between cylinders, it would be a good idea to have a leak-down test performed by an automotive repair shop. This test will pinpoint exactly where the leakage is occurring and how severe it is.

Diesel engine

15   Because of the special tools needed to check compression on a diesel engine, this procedure is beyond the scope of the home mechanic. Have the compression checked by a dealer service department or other qualified repair shop with the right tools.

4   Vacuum gauge diagnostic checks (gasoline engines)

Refer to illustrations 4.4 and 4.6

1   A vacuum gauge provides inexpensive but valuable information about what is going on in the engine. You can check for worn rings or cylinder walls, leaking head or intake manifold gaskets, incorrect carburetor adjustments, restricted exhaust, stuck or burned valves, weak valve springs, improper ignition or valve timing and ignition problems.

2   Unfortunately, vacuum gauge readings

are easy to misinterpret, so they should be used in conjunction with other tests to confirm the diagnosis.

3   Both the absolute readings and the rate of needle movement are important for accurate interpretation. Most gauges measure vacuum in inches of mercury (in-Hg). The following references to vacuum assume the diagnosis is being performed at sea level. As elevation increases (or atmospheric pressure decreases), the reading will decrease. For every 1,000 foot increase in elevation above approximately 2000 feet, the gauge readings will decrease about one inch of mercury.

4   Connect the vacuum gauge directly to the intake manifold vacuum, not to ported (throttle body) vacuum **(see illustration)**. Be sure no hoses are left disconnected during the test or false readings will result.

5   Before you begin the test, allow the engine to warm up completely. Block the wheels and set the parking brake. With the transmission in Park, start the engine and allow it to run at normal idle speed. **Warning:** *Keep your hands and the vacuum gauge clear of the fans.*

6   Read the vacuum gauge; an average, healthy engine should normally produce about 17 to 22 in-Hg with a fairly steady needle **(see illustration)**. Refer to the following vacuum gauge readings and what they indicate about the engine's condition:

7   A low steady reading usually indicates a leaking gasket between the intake manifold and cylinder head(s) or throttle body, a leaky vacuum hose, late ignition timing or incorrect camshaft timing. Check ignition timing with a timing light and eliminate all other possible causes, utilizing the tests provided in this Chapter before you remove the timing chain cover to check the timing marks.

8   If the reading is three to eight inches below normal and it fluctuates at that low reading, suspect an intake manifold gasket leak at an intake port or a faulty fuel injector.

9   If the needle has regular drops of about two-to-four inches at a steady rate, the valves are probably leaking. Perform a compression check or leak-down test to confirm this.

10   An irregular drop or down-flick of the needle can be caused by a sticking valve or an ignition misfire. Perform a compression check or leak-down test and read the spark plugs.

11   A rapid vibration of about four in-Hg vibration at idle combined with exhaust smoke indicates worn valve guides. Perform a leak-down test to confirm this. If the rapid vibration occurs with an increase in engine speed, check for a leaking intake manifold gasket or head gasket, weak valve springs, burned valves or ignition misfire.

12   A slight fluctuation, say one inch up and down, may mean ignition problems. Check all the usual tune-up items and, if necessary, run the engine on an ignition analyzer.

13   If there is a large fluctuation, perform a compression or leak-down test to look for a weak or dead cylinder or a blown head gasket.

4.4 A simple vacuum gauge can be handy in diagnosing engine condition and performance (V10 engine shown, V8 similar)

14   If the needle moves slowly through a wide range, check for a clogged PCV system, incorrect idle fuel mixture, carburetor/throttle body or intake manifold gasket leaks.

15   Check for a slow return after revving the engine by quickly snapping the throttle open until the engine reaches about 2,500 rpm and let it shut. Normally the reading should drop to near zero, rise above normal idle reading (about 5 in-Hg over) and then return to the previous idle reading. If the vacuum returns slowly and doesn't peak when the throttle is snapped shut, the rings may be worn. If there is a long delay, look for a restricted exhaust system (often the muffler or catalytic converter). An easy way to check this is to temporarily disconnect the exhaust ahead of the suspected part and redo the test.

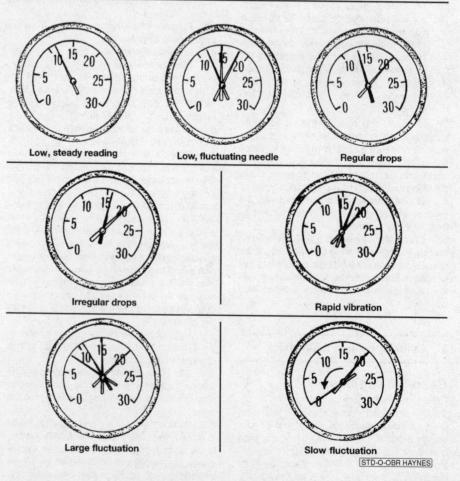

Low, steady reading   Low, fluctuating needle   Regular drops

Irregular drops   Rapid vibration

Large fluctuation   Slow fluctuation

STD-O-OBR HAYNES

4.6 Typical vacuum gauge readings

6.1 After tightly wrapping water-vulnerable components, use a spray cleaner on everything, with particular concentration on the greasiest areas, usually around the valve cover and lower edges of the block. If one section dries out, apply more cleaner

6.2 Depending on how dirty the engine is, let the cleaner soak in according to the directions and then hose off the grime and cleaner. Get the rinse water down into every area you can get at; then dry important components with a hair dryer or paper towels

5   Engine rebuilding alternatives

The do-it-yourselfer is faced with a number of options when purchasing a rebuilt engine. The major considerations are cost, warranty, parts availability and the time required for the rebuilder to complete the project. The decision to replace the engine block, piston/connecting rod assemblies and crankshaft depends on the final inspection results of your engine. Only then can you make a cost effective decision whether to have your engine overhauled or simply purchase an exchange engine for your vehicle.

Some of the rebuilding alternatives include:

Individual parts - If the inspection procedures reveal that the engine block and most engine components are in reusable condition, purchasing individual parts and having a rebuilder rebuild your engine may be the most economical alternative. The block, crankshaft and piston/connecting rod assemblies should all be inspected carefully by a machine shop first.

Short block - A short block consists of an engine block with a crankshaft and piston/ connecting rod assemblies already installed. All new bearings are incorporated and all clearances will be correct. The existing camshafts, valve train components, cylinder head and external parts can be bolted to the short block with little or no machine shop work necessary.

Long block - A long block consists of a short block plus an oil pump, oil pan, cylinder head, valve cover, camshaft and valve train components, timing sprockets and chain or gears and timing cover. All components are installed with new bearings, seals and gaskets incorporated throughout. The installation of manifolds and external parts is all that's necessary.

Low mileage used engines - Some companies now offer low mileage used engines which is a very cost effective way to get your vehicle up and running again. These engines often come from vehicles which have been totaled in accidents or come from other countries which have a higher vehicle turnover rate. A low mileage used engine also usually has a warranty similar to the newly remanufactured engines.

Give careful thought to which alternative is best for you and discuss the situation with local automotive machine shops, auto parts dealers and experienced rebuilders before ordering or purchasing replacement parts.

6   Engine removal - methods and precautions

Refer to illustrations 6.1, 6.2, 6.3, 6.4 and 6.5

If you've decided that an engine must be removed for overhaul or major repair work, several preliminary steps should be taken. Read all removal and installation procedures carefully prior to committing to this job. Some engines are removed by lowering to the floor and then raising the vehicle sufficiently to slide it out; this will require a vehicle hoist.

Locating a suitable place to work is extremely important. Adequate work space, along with storage space for the vehicle, will be needed. If a shop or garage isn't available, at the very least a flat, level, clean work surface made of concrete or asphalt is required. Cleaning the engine compartment and engine before beginning the removal procedure will help keep tools clean and organized **(see illustrations 6.1 and 6.2)**.

An engine hoist or A-frame will also be necessary. Make sure the equipment is rated in excess of the combined weight of the engine and transmission. Safety is of primary importance, considering the potential hazards involved in lifting the engine out of the vehicle.

If you're a novice at engine removal, get at least one helper. One person cannot easily do all the things you need to do to lift a big heavy engine out of the engine compartment. Also helpful is to seek advice and assistance from someone who's experienced in engine removal.

Plan the operation ahead of time. Arrange for or obtain all of the tools and

6.3 Get an engine hoist that's strong enough to easily lift your engine in and out of the engine compartment (the V10 and the diesel engine are particularly heavy, so make sure that you obtain a heavy-duty hoist if you're planning to lift either of these engines out of the engine compartment); an adapter, like the one shown here, can be used to change the angle of the engine as it's being removed or installed

6.4 Get an engine stand sturdy enough to firmly support the engine while you're working on it. Stay away from three-wheeled models: they have a tendency to tip over more easily, so get a four-wheeled unit. The V10 and the diesel engine are particularly heavy, so make sure that you obtain a heavy-duty stand capable of supporting one of these engines

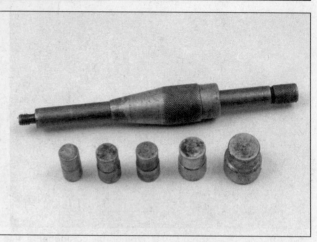

6.5 A clutch alignment tool is necessary if you plan to install a rebuilt engine mated to a manual transmission

equipment you'll need prior to beginning the job **(see illustrations 6.3, 6.4 and 6.5)**. Some of the equipment necessary to perform engine removal and installation safely and with relative ease are (in addition to an engine hoist) a heavy duty floor jack, complete sets of wrenches and sockets as described in the front of this manual, wooden blocks, plenty of rags and cleaning solvent for mopping up spilled oil, coolant and fuel. If the hoist must be rented, make sure that you arrange for it in advance and have everything disconnected and/or removed before bringing the hoist home. This will save you money and time.

Plan for the vehicle to be out of use for quite a while. A machine shop can do the work that is beyond the scope of the home mechanic. Machine shops often have a busy schedule, so before removing the engine, consult the shop for an estimate of how long it will take to rebuild or repair the components that may need work.

7   Engine - removal and installation

Refer to illustrations 7.6, 7.9, 7.10, 7.16a, 7.16b, 7.16c, 7.17 and 7.26

Warning 1: *DO NOT use a cheap engine hoist designed for lifting four-cylinder engines. Obtain a heavy-duty hoist designed for lifting heavy engines. And always be extremely careful when removing and installing the engine. Serious injury can result from careless actions.*

Warning 2: *Gasoline and diesel fuel are flammable, so take extra precautions when you work on any part of the fuel system. Don't smoke or allow open flames or bare light bulbs*

near the work area, and don't work in a garage where a gas-type appliance (such as a water heater or a clothes dryer) is present. Since fuel is carcinogenic, wear latex gloves when there's a possibility of being exposed to fuel, and, if you spill any fuel on your skin, rinse it off immediately with soap and water. Mop up any spills immediately and do not store fuel-soaked rags where they could ignite. The fuel system is under constant pressure, so, if any fuel lines are to be disconnected, the fuel pressure in the system must be relieved first (see Chapter 4 for more information). When you perform any kind of work on the fuel system, wear safety glasses and have a Class B type fire extinguisher on hand.

Warning 3: *The air conditioning system is under high pressure, and refrigerant is expensive. Have a dealer service department or an automotive air conditioning shop discharge the system before beginning this procedure.*

1   On vehicles with air conditioning, have the air conditioning system discharged.

2   Relieve the fuel system pressure (see Chapter 4).

3   Remove the battery(ies) (see Chapter 5).

4   Remove the hood (see Chapter 11) and cover the fenders and cowl. Special pads are available to protect the fenders, but an old bedspread or blanket will also work.

5   Remove the air cleaner assembly and the air intake duct (see Chapter 4).

6   Label all vacuum lines, emissions system hoses, wiring harness electrical connectors and ground straps to ensure correct reinstallation, then disconnect them. Pieces of masking tape with numbers or letters written on them work well **(see illustration)**. So does colored electrical tape. If there's any possibility of confusion, make a sketch of the engine compartment and clearly label the lines, hoses and wires. You can also use a camera to take photos of connectors, grounds, harness routing, etc.

7   Disconnect the fuel lines running from the engine to the chassis (see Chapter 4). Plug or cap all open fittings/lines.

8   On gasoline models, disconnect the throttle cable from the throttle linkage on the throttle body and remove the throttle body (see Chap-

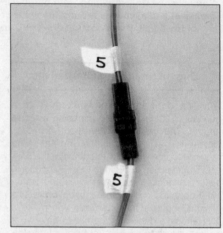

7.6 Label both ends of each wire and hose before disconnecting it - do the same for vacuum hoses

ter 4A). Remove the fuel rail and the injectors (see Chapter 4A). Remove the intake manifold (see Chapter 2A). Also remove all fuel and/or emission control components that might be damaged during engine removal (see Chapters 4 and 6).

9   On diesel models, remove the ducts between the intercooler and the turbocharger and between the turbocharger and the intake manifold covers, remove the turbocharger manifold, then remove the turbocharger and the turbocharger pedestal (see Chapter 4B). Disconnect the fuel lines from the cylinder heads **(see illustration)**. Also disconnect the electrical connector from the high-pressure oil system sensor, then disconnect the high-pressure oil hose from each head (see Chapter 4B). Remove the glow plug relay and relay bracket (see Chapter 4B). Remove the fuel filter/water separator (see Chapter 4B).

10   Clearly label and disconnect all coolant and heater hoses **(see illustration)**. Remove the cooling fan, shroud and radiator (see Chapter 3).

11   Remove the accessory drivebelt(s) (see Chapter 1) and remove the alternator (see Chapter 5).

12   On vehicles with air conditioning, remove the condenser and the compressor (see

7.9 On 7.3L diesel engines, disconnect the fuel line fitting from each cylinder head; (left cylinder head fuel line fitting shown; right cylinder head fuel line fitting similar)

7.10 Disconnect all heater and coolant hoses from the engine; this heater hose is connected to the right cylinder head on 7.3L diesel engines

Chapter 3). Look carefully at the air conditioning system plumbing. If some section(s) of the plumbing - particularly any section consisting of rigid metal lines - looks like it's going to impede engine removal and installation, detach it from the engine and/or vehicle and set it aside. Secure it with wire if necessary to make sure that it won't be damaged by the engine when the engine is lifted out of the engine compartment.

13 On diesel engines, remove the intercooler (see Chapter 4B). On some models equipped with an automatic transmission, there is an *external* oil cooler, which is located below the space occupied by an intercooler on diesel models. This auxiliary cooler, which is installed in addition to the regular oil cooler that's integrated into the radiator, must also be removed (see Chapter 7B).

14 Remove the grille (see Chapter 11) and the upper radiator crossmember, which is secured by three bolts on each end. Removing the grille and the upper radiator crossmember gives you more room when maneuvering the engine forward to clear the cowl, and it lowers the minimum height which the bottom of the engine must clear when it's hoisted out of the engine compartment.

15 Remove the power steering pump from its mounting bracket (see Chapter 10) and secure it with wire so that it won't interfere with engine removal. On diesel engines, you'll have to remove the power steering pump pulley before you can unbolt the pump from its mounting bracket.

16 If you're going to be replacing the block, now is a good time to remove all large brackets such as the alternator, air conditioning compressor and power steering pump brackets **(see illustrations)**.

17 Raise the vehicle and place it securely on jackstands **(see illustration)**. **Note:** *On 4WD models, and on models with large tires, this step may not be necessary, because some models already have sufficient ground clear-*

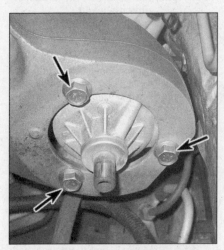

7.16a To remove the 7.3L engine alternator bracket, remove these three bolts from the power steering pump . . .

7.16b . . . and these four bolts from the cylinder head and the block (diesel engine)

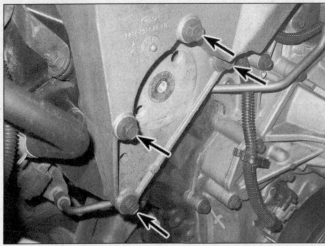

7.16c To detach the compressor mounting bracket from the 7.3L engine, remove these bolts (diesel engine)

7.17 Place sturdy jackstands under the frame of the vehicle and set them both at uniform height

7.26 Use long high-strength bolts to hold the engine block on the engine stand - make sure they are tight before resting all the weight on the stand

ance to allow disconnection of the exhaust system, the engine mounts, etc. from underneath the vehicle. Raising these vehicles any higher might even make engine removal more difficult because it might position the vehicle too high to lift the engine out of the engine compartment with a hoist.

18   Drain the engine oil and remove the oil filter (see Chapter 1). Detach the engine oil dipstick tube bracket and remove the engine oil dipstick tube.

19   Drain the cooling system (see Chapter 1).

20   Remove the part of the exhaust system that's routed underneath the engine, between the exhaust manifolds and the downstream catalytic converter (see Chapter 4). It's not absolutely necessary to remove the exhaust manifolds in order to remove the engine, but removing the manifolds will shave a little weight off the engine.

21   Remove the starter motor (see Chapter 5).

22   If you're working on a model with a manual transmission, remove the transmission (see Chapter 7A). If equipped with an automatic transmission, unbolt the torque converter from the driveplate. Also remove the transmission-to-engine bolts accessible from under the vehicle.

23   Lower the vehicle. Locate the lifting brackets on the engine. Roll a heavy-duty hoist into position and then attach it to the lifting brackets with a couple pieces of heavy-duty chain. Take up the slack in the sling or chain, but don't lift the engine. **Warning:** *DO NOT use a cheap hoist designed to lift four-cylinder engines. Obtain a heavy-duty lift designed for lifting heavy engines. And DO NOT place any part of your body under the engine when it's supported only by a hoist or other lifting device.*

24   On automatic transmission models, sup-

port the transmission with a jack (preferably one made for this purpose), then remove the remaining transmission-to-engine bolts.

25   Remove the engine mount fasteners (see Chapter 2A). Recheck to be sure nothing is still connecting the engine to the transmission or vehicle. Disconnect anything still remaining. Raise the engine slightly and inspect it thoroughly once more to make sure that *nothing* is still attached, then slowly lift the engine out of the engine compartment. Check carefully to make sure nothing is hanging up.

26   Remove the flywheel/driveplate (see Chapter 2A or 2B) and then mount the engine on an engine stand **(see illustration)**.

27   Inspect the engine and transmission mounts (see Chapter 2A and Chapter 7A). If they're worn or damaged, replace them.

Installation

28   Install the flywheel/driveplate (see Chapter 2A or 2B).

29   If you're working on a vehicle with manual transmission, install the clutch and pressure plate (see Chapter 8). Now is a good time to install a new clutch.

30   Carefully lower the engine into the engine compartment and then reattach it to the engine mounts.

31   If you're working on a manual transmission model, install the transmission (see Chapter 7A). If you're working on a vehicle with an automatic transmission, guide the torque converter into the crankshaft following the procedure outlined in Chapter 7B. Install the transmission-to-engine bolts and tighten them securely. **Caution:** *DO NOT use the bolts to force the transmission and engine together!* If you're working on a model with an automatic transmission, tighten the torque-converter-to-driveplate bolts to the torque listed in the Chapter 7B Specifications.

32   Reinstall the remaining components in the reverse order of removal.

33   Add coolant, oil and transmission fluid as needed.

34   Run the engine and check for leaks and proper operation of all accessories, then install the hood and test drive the vehicle.

35   Have the air conditioning system recharged and leak tested, if it was discharged.

8   Engine overhaul - disassembly sequence

1   It's much easier to remove the external components if it's mounted on a portable engine stand. A stand can often be rented quite cheaply from an equipment rental yard. Before the engine is mounted on a stand, the flywheel/driveplate should be removed from the engine.

2   If a stand isn't available, it's possible to remove the external engine components with it blocked up on the floor. Be extra careful not to tip or drop the engine when working without a stand.

3   If you're going to obtain a rebuilt engine, all external components must come off first, to be transferred to the replacement engine. These components include:

> *Clutch and flywheel (models with manual transmission)*
> *Driveplate (models with automatic transmission)*
> *Emissions-related components*
> *Engine front cover (diesel engine)*
> *Engine mounts and mount brackets*
> *Engine rear cover (spacer plate between flywheel/driveplate and engine block)*
> *Fuel injection components*
> *Ignition coils*
> *Intake/exhaust manifolds*
> *Oil filter*
> *Spark plug wires and spark plugs*
> *Thermostat and housing assembly*
> *Water pump*

Note: *When removing the external components from the engine, pay close attention to details that may be helpful or important during installation. Note the installed position of gaskets, seals, spacers, pins, brackets, washers, bolts and other small items.*

4   If you're going to obtain a short block (assembled engine block, crankshaft, pistons and connecting rods), then remove the timing belt, cylinder head, oil pan, oil pump pick-up tube, oil pump and water pump from your engine so that you can turn in your old short block to the rebuilder as a core. See *Engine rebuilding alternatives* for additional information regarding the different possibilities to be considered.

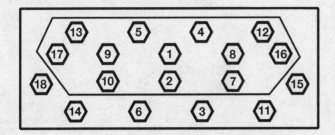

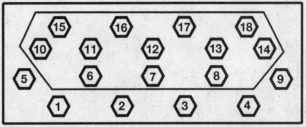

9.12a Cylinder head bolt tightening sequences (left diagram, first sequence; right diagram, second sequence) - 7.3L engine

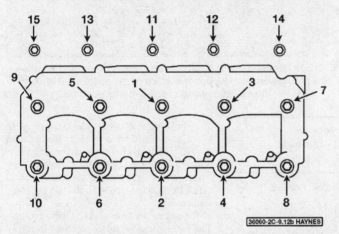

9.12b 6.0L and 6.4L diesel cylinder head bolt tightening sequence

9.13 6.0L diesel high pressure oil rail bolt tightening sequence

9 Cylinder heads (diesel engine) - removal and installations

Refer to illustrations 9.12a, 9.12b and 9.13
Note: *The following procedure applies to either cylinder head.*
1 Remove the engine (see Section 7) and place it on a heavy-duty engine stand.
2 Remove the valve cover (see Chapter 2B).
3 Remove the rocker arms and pushrods (see Chapter 2B). On 6.0L engines, the high pressure oil rail must be removed. Remove the fuel injection wiring connector from the rocker arm support and also the crankcase tube. The 6.0L four-valve motor also has valve bridges that can be removed at this time.
4 Remove the fuel injectors (see Chapter 4B). **Caution:** *Make sure that you drain the residual fuel from the cylinder head and oil from the high-pressure oil system before removing the fuel injectors. Failure to do so could allow fuel and/or oil to drain into the combustion chambers, onto the pistons, past the rings, down the cylinder walls and into the crankcase. It could also cause a piston to "hydraulic" when the engine is started. Fluid is not compressible, so if a combustion chamber fills with oil and the engine is cranked, the*

piston could be damaged when it comes over TDC, or the connecting rod could be bent.
5 Remove the exhaust manifold if you haven't already done so prior to engine removal (see Chapter 2B).
6 Remove the cylinder head bolts in the reverse order of the tightening sequence **(see illustration 9.12).** Throw away the cylinder head bolts from the 6.0L diesel engine; they are not reusable. Also discard the dowel pins from the 6.0L engine after the head is removed.
7 Remove the cylinder head with an engine hoist, or have an assistant handy to help you remove the head. **Warning:** *The cylinder head is very heavy. Do NOT attempt to lift it off the engine by yourself or you could seriously injure your back.*
8 Remove and discard the old cylinder head gasket.
9 Remove all traces of old gasket material from the cylinder head and from the head mating surface on the engine block.
10 Chase the threads of the cylinder head bolt holes and then blow out the holes with compressed air.
11 Install a new gasket and then, using an engine hoist or at least one assistant, very carefully place the cylinder head in position. **Warning:** *The cylinder head is VERY heavy.*

Do NOT attempt to place it in position on the engine block by yourself or you could seriously injure your back. **Caution:** *Make SURE that you don't damage the cylinder head gasket when installing the head on the block. Even the slightest nick or scratch can cause the head gasket to leak very soon after installation.*
12 On 6.0L and 6.4L diesel engines, purchase new head bolts and dowels. Lightly oil the cylinder head bolts with clean engine oil, install the cylinder head bolts and then tighten, following the indicated sequences **(see illustration)**, to the torque listed in this Chapter's Specifications.
13 The remainder of installation is the reverse of removal. When installing the high pressure oil rail, follow the tightening sequence **(see illustration)**.
14 After the head is fully reassembled, install the engine.

10 Oil pan (diesel engines) - removal and installation

Removal

1 Remove the engine (see Section 7).
2 Put the engine on a heavy-duty engine

12.3a Position the number one piston at TDC on the compression stroke by rotating the crankshaft until the timing notch on the crankshaft pulley is aligned with the stationary pointer on the front cover; verify that number one's at TDC by looking at the pushrods for the number one cylinder, both of which should be parallel and at their lowest point of travel

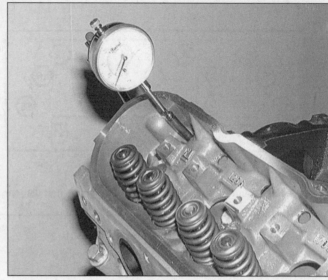

12.3b Mount a dial indicator on the cylinder head and position the plunger against the upper surface of the pushrod; it should be directly above and in line with the pushrod

stand and turn it upside down, so that the oil pan is facing up.

3 Remove the oil pan bolts.

4 On 7.3L engines, cut the oil pan sealant all the way around the circumference of the pan, then carefully pry the pan away from the block and remove it.

5 Remove the two bolts from the oil pump (front) end of the oil pump pick-up tube and the nut that secures the pick-up tube bracket (at the rear end of the tube), then remove the pick-up tube. Remove and discard the old pick-up tube gasket or O-ring.

Installation

6 Clean off all traces of old sealant from the oil pan flange and from the flange surface on the engine block. Also clean off all traces of old gasket material from the oil pump pick-up tube flange and from the mating surface for the pick-up-tube flange on the underside of the block. On 6.0L engines, install a new gasket.

7 Using a new gasket or O-ring, install the oil pump pick-up tube and tighten the fasteners to the torque listed in this Chapter's Specifications.

8 On 7.3L engines, apply a 1/8-inch bead of RTV sealant to the left and right flanges of the oil pan and a 1/4-inch wide strip to the front and rear flanges. **Caution:** *The pan must be installed within three minutes of applying the sealant.* On 6.0L engines, install a new gasket.

9 Align the pan with the pan mating surface of the block, carefully press the pan against the block and install the oil pan bolts. After all the bolts are installed, tighten them gradually and evenly until they're snug. Then tighten the oil pan bolts to the torque listed in this Chapter's Specifications.

10 Install the engine (see Section 7).

11 Engine front cover (diesel engines) - removal and installation

1 Remove the engine (see Section 7).

7.3L engines

2 Remove the fuel filter/water separator (see Chapter 4B).

3 Remove the high-pressure oil pump (see Chapter 4B).

4 Remove the thermostat and the water pump (see Chapter 3).

5 Remove the crankshaft pulley (see Chapter 2B).

6 Remove the oil pump (see Chapter 2B).

7 Remove the oil pan (see Section 10).

8 Remove any remaining engine front cover bolts (most of the cover bolts are the water pump bolts) and remove the front cover. Remove and discard the engine front cover gasket. Remove the engine front cover dowel pins and store them in a plastic bag.

9 Clean off any gasket material from the front cover and from the cover mating surface on the engine block.

10 Using a new gasket, install the front cover and tighten the cover bolts to the torque listed in this Chapter's Specifications.

11 The remainder of installation is the reverse of removal.

12 Install the engine when you're done (see Section 7).

6.0L and 6.4L engines

13 Remove the drivebelt tensioner assemblies.

14 Remove the water pump pulley. On 6.4L engines, drain and remove the vertical EGR coolant cooler in front of the engine.

15 Remove the cable bracket and any other interfering brackets.

16 Remove the oil pump (refer to Chapter 2B).

17 Use a sharp knife or razor blade to cut the RTV sealant where the upper and lower crankcases meet. Don't try to remove the cover without cutting this sealant as this could cause the seal to be pulled out when the cover is removed.

18 Remove the bolts and lift off the cover.

19 Installation is the reverse of removal. On 6.4L engines, use guide pins (made from bolts with the heads cut off and a screwdriver slot added with a hacksaw) in the corners of the cover for precise alignment until all other bolts can be started.

12 Camshaft and lifters (diesel engines) - inspection, removal and installation

Camshaft lobe lift check (camshaft installed)

Refer to illustrations 12.3a and 12.3b

1 Remove the valve covers (see Chapter 2B).

2 Remove the rocker arms (see Chapter 2B).

3 Position the number one piston (see the cylinder numbering diagram in the Chapter 2B Specifications) at TDC on the compression stroke by rotating the crankshaft until the timing notch on the crankshaft pulley is aligned with the stationary pointer on the front cover **(see illustration)**. Verify that the number one piston - and not the number four - is at TDC by looking at the pushrods for the number one cylinder, both of which should be parallel and at their lowest point of travel. If one of the pushrods is higher than the other when the timing notch in the pulley is aligned with the stationary pointer on the front cover, then the number *four* piston - *not* the number one - is at TDC. Rotate the crankshaft another 360

12.18a To calculate lobe lift after the camshaft has been removed from the engine, measure lobe height . . .

12.18b . . . then measure the camshaft base circle (diameter) and subtract the base circle from the lobe height

degrees, realign the timing marks and verify that the pushrods for the number one cylinder are now at their lowest point and are both at the same height. The number one piston is now at TDC. Beginning with the number one cylinder, mount a dial indicator on the cylinder head and position the plunger against the upper surface of the pushrod (or, if the heads are removed, the upper surface of the lifter). The plunger should be directly above and in line with the pushrod **(see illustration)**. **Note:** *This method can also be used even after the cylinder heads have already been removed by simply mounting the dial indicator on the deck surface of the engine block and placing the plunger against the top surface of the lifter at the cylinder you're checking.*

4   Zero the dial indicator, then very slowly turn the crankshaft in the normal direction of rotation (clockwise) until the indicator needle stops and begins to move in the opposite direction. The point at which it stops indicates maximum cam lobe lift.

5   Jot down this figure for future reference, then reposition the piston at TDC on the compression stroke again.

6   Move the dial indicator to the other number one cylinder pushrod or lifter and repeat the check. Be sure to record the results.

7   Repeat this procedure for each of the remaining pairs of pushrods. Since each piston must be at TDC on the compression stroke for this procedure, work from cylinder-to-cylinder in the *firing order sequence* (see the engine firing order and cylinder numbering diagram at the beginning of Chapter 2B). On an eight-cylinder engine, a cylinder fires every 90 degrees, so you'll have to rotate the crankshaft another 90 degrees (1/4-turn) to bring the next piston up to TDC, and the pushrods for that cylinder down to their low point.

8   When you're all done with your measurements, compare them with each other. If any of the indicated lobe lift figures are significantly less than the others, replace the camshaft (see below).

9   Install the rocker arms (see Chapter 2B).

10   Install the valve covers (see Chapter 2B).

Removal

Note: *Removing the camshaft on this engine is a big job; bigger perhaps than you might want to tackle at home. Read through the following procedure carefully and make sure that you know whvat you're getting yourself into before proceeding.*

11   Remove the engine (see Section 7).

12   Remove the cylinder heads (see Section 9).

13   Remove the engine front cover (see Section 11).

14   Remove the bolt from each lifter retainer and remove the retainer. Clearly mark each lifter with respect to its lifter bore and its orientation, then remove each lifter with a magnet. **Caution:** *If you are planning to reuse the old lifters, each lifter must be installed in the same lifter bore from which it was removed and it must face in the same direction. Failure to do so will result in premature lifter wear and a shortened service life. It might also cause excessive wear to the lifter bores.*

15   The camshaft is retained by a thrust plate which is bolted to the front of the engine block. To detach the camshaft from the block, remove the two camshaft thrust plate retaining bolts, which can be accessed through the holes in the camshaft drive gear **(see illustration 12.27)**.

16   Remove the camshaft and the drive gear.

Inspection

17   Wipe off the camshaft with a clean shop rag. Inspect the cam lobes for score marks, pitting, galling and evidence of overheating (blue, discolored areas). Look for flaking of the hardened surface of each lobe. If the camshaft shows any signs of excessive wear, replace it.

Camshaft lobe lift check (camshaft removed)

Refer to illustrations 12.18a and 12.18b

18   Measure the camshaft lobe height and the diameter of the circular part of the camshaft, or "base circle" **(see illustrations)**. The difference between the two measurements is the lobe lift (lobe height - base circle = lobe lift). Record

this figure for future reference and repeat the check on the remaining camshaft lobes.

19   After all of the lobe lifts have been measured, compare your measurements. If the lobe lift is significantly lower for some lobes than for others, replace the camshaft.

Bearing journals, lobes and bearings

Refer to illustration 12.21

20   Inspect the bearing journals for uneven wear, pitting and signs of seizure. If the journals are damaged, the bearing inserts in the block are probably damaged as well. Both the camshaft and bearings will have to be replaced. **Note:** *Camshaft bearing replacement requires special tools and expertise that place it beyond the scope of the average home mechanic. The tools for bearing removal and installation are available at stores that carry automotive tools, possibly even found at a tool rental business. But this is not a job for beginners. If the bearings are bad, we recommend that you take the engine to an automotive machine shop to ensure that the job is done correctly.*

21   Measure the bearing journals with a micrometer to determine if they are excessively worn or out-of-round **(see illustration)**.

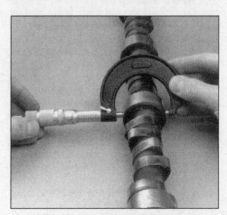

12.21 Measure the diameter of the camshaft bearing journals with a micrometer to determine whether they are excessively worn or out-of-round

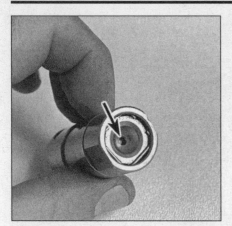

12.24 Inspect the pushrod seat in the top of each lifter for excessive wear

12.25 The roller on each lifter must turn freely; also inspect each roller for excessive wear and freeplay

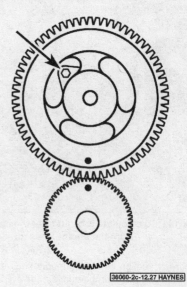

12.27 When installing the camshaft, make sure that the timing marks on the crankshaft drive gear and on the cam driven gear are aligned; the camshaft is retained by a thrust plate, which is secured to the block by two bolts, one of which (arrow) is visible here (to remove or install the thrust plate bolts, rotate the cam driven gear until you can see each bolt)

22   Inspect the camshaft lobes for heat dis-coloration, score marks, chipped areas, pitting and uneven wear.
23   If the lobes are in good condition and if the lobe lift measurements recorded earlier are uniform, the camshaft can be reused.

Lifters

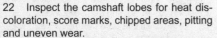

Refer to illustrations 12.24 and 12.25
24   Clean the lifters with solvent and dry them thoroughly without mixing them up. Check each lifter wall and pushrod seat and for score marks and uneven wear **(see illustration)**. If the lifter walls are damaged or worn (which is not very likely), inspect the lifter bores in the engine block as well. If the pushrod seats are worn, check the pushrod ends.
25   Check the rollers carefully for wear and damage and make sure they turn freely with-out excessive play **(see illustration)**.
26   The old camshaft can be reused with new lifters, but used roller lifters must NOT be reinstalled with a new camshaft. Always use new lifters when installing a new camshaft.

Installation

Refer to illustration 12.27
27   Before installing the camshaft, coat the bearing journals and the lobes with camshaft installation lube, then insert the camshaft into the block. When installing the camshaft, rotate the crankshaft drive gear until the timing mark is at the 12 o'clock position and align the tim-ing mark on the camshaft driven gear with the timing mark on the crank gear **(see illustra-tion)**. Align the thrust plate bolt holes with the holes in the block, install the thrust plate bolts and tighten them to the torque listed in this Chapter's Specifications.
28   Before installing the lifters, coat them with white grease or with engine assembly lube and then insert the lifters into their respective bores. If you're installing the old lifters, make sure that they're installed into the same bores from which they were removed and that they are oriented so that they facing in the same direction as before. Install the lifter retainers, and tighten the bolts to the torque listed in this

Chapter's Specifications.
29   The remainder of installation is otherwise the reverse of removal.
30   When you're done, install the engine (see Section 7).

---

13   Pistons and connecting rods - removal and installation

Removal

Refer to illustrations 13.1, 13.3, 13.4 and 13.6
Note: *Prior to removing the piston/connect-ing rod assemblies, remove the cylinder head and oil pan.*
1   Use your fingernail to feel if a ridge has formed at the upper limit of ring travel (about 1/4-inch down from the top of each cylinder). If carbon deposits or cylinder wear have produced ridges, they must be completely removed with a special tool **(see illustra-tion)**. Follow the manufacturer's instructions provided with the tool. Failure to remove the ridges before attempting to remove the piston/connecting rod assemblies may result in pis-ton breakage.

13.1 Before you try to remove the pistons, use a ridge reamer to remove the raised material (ridge) from the top of the cylinders

2   After the cylinder ridges have been removed, turn the engine so the crankshaft is facing up.
3   Before the main bearing cap assembly and connecting rods are removed, check the connecting rod endplay with feeler gauges. Slide them between the first connecting rod and the crankshaft throw until the play is removed **(see illustration)**. Repeat this pro-cedure for each connecting rod. The endplay is equal to the thickness of the feeler gauge(s). Check with an automotive machine shop for the endplay service limit. If the play exceeds the service limit, new connecting rods will be

13.3 Checking the connecting rod endplay (side clearance)

13.4 If the connecting rods and caps are not marked, use a center punch or numbered impression stamps to mark the caps to the rods by cylinder number (for example, this would be the No. 4 connecting rod)

13.6 On diesel engines, push a short section of plastic or rubber hose over the connecting rod bolts to prevent damage to the crankshaft journals during piston/rod removal

required. If new rods (or a new crankshaft) are installed, the endplay may fall under the minimum listed in this Chapter's Specifications. If it does, the rods will have to be machined to restore it. If necessary, consult an automotive machine shop for advice.

4   Check the connecting rods and caps for identification marks **(see illustration)**. If they aren't plainly marked, use a small center-punch to make the appropriate number of indentations on each rod and cap (1, 2, 3, etc., depending on the cylinder they're associated with).

5   Loosen each of the connecting rod cap nuts or bolts 1/2-turn at a time until they can be removed by hand. Remove the number one connecting rod cap and bearing insert. Don't drop the bearing insert out of the cap.

6   If you're removing the rods from a diesel engine, slip a short length of plastic or rubber hose over each connecting rod bolt to protect the crankshaft journal and cylinder wall as the rod is removed **(see illustration)**.

7   Remove the bearing insert and push the connecting rod/piston assembly out through the top of the engine. Use a wooden or plastic hammer handle to push on the upper bearing surface in the connecting rod. If resistance is felt, double-check to make sure that all of the ridge was removed from the cylinder.

8   Repeat the procedure for the remaining cylinders. **Note:** *On all except the 6.0L and 6.4L diesel engine, if the connecting rod caps are secured by bolts (instead of nuts), discard the old rod cap bolts. Use new bolts when reassembling the engine.*

9   After removal, reassemble the connecting rod caps and bearing inserts in their respective connecting rods and install the cap bolts finger tight. Leaving the old bearing inserts in place until reassembly will help prevent the connecting rod bearing surfaces from being accidentally nicked or gouged.

10   The pistons and connecting rods are now ready for inspection and overhaul at an automotive machine shop.

Piston ring installation

Refer to illustrations 13.13, 13.14, 13.15, 13.19a, 13.19b, 13.21 and 13.22

11   Before installing the new piston rings, the ring end gaps must be checked. It's assumed that the piston ring side clearance has been checked and verified correct.

12   Lay out the piston/connecting rod assemblies and the new ring sets so the ring sets will be matched with the same piston and cylinder during the end gap measurement and engine assembly.

13   Insert the top (number one) ring into the first cylinder and square it up with the cylinder walls by pushing it in with the top of the piston **(see illustration)**. The ring should be near the bottom of the cylinder, at the lower limit of ring travel.

14   To measure the end gap, slip feeler gauges between the ends of the ring until a gauge equal to the gap width is found **(see illustration)**. The feeler gauge should slide between the ring ends with a slight amount

13.13 Install the piston ring into the cylinder then push it down into position using a piston so the ring will be square in the cylinder

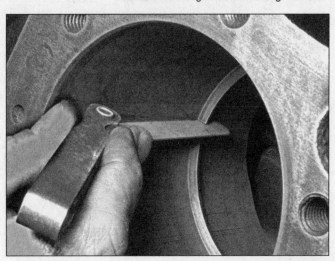

13.14 With the ring square in the cylinder, measure the ring end gap with a feeler gauge

13.15 If the ring end gap is too small, clamp a file in a vise as shown and file the piston ring ends - be sure to remove all raised material

13.19a Installing the spacer/expander in the oil ring groove

of drag. Check with an automotive machine shop for the correct end gap for your engine. If the gap is larger or smaller than specified, double-check to make sure you have the correct rings before proceeding.

15   If the gap is too small, it must be enlarged or the ring ends may come in contact with each other during engine operation, which can cause serious damage to the engine. The end gap can be increased by filing the ring ends very carefully with a fine file. Mount the file in a vise equipped with soft jaws, slip the ring over the file with the ends contacting the file face and slowly move the ring to remove material from the ends. When performing this operation, file only by pushing the ring from the outside end of the file towards the vise **(see illustration)**.

16   Repeat the procedure for each ring that will be installed in the first cylinder and for each ring in the remaining cylinders.

17   Remember to keep rings, pistons and cylinders matched up.

18   Once the ring end gaps have been checked/corrected, the rings can be installed on the pistons.

19   The oil control ring (lowest one on the piston) is usually installed first. It's composed of three separate components. Slip the spacer/expander into the groove **(see illustration)**. If an anti-rotation tang is used, make sure it's inserted into the drilled hole in the ring groove. Next, install the upper side rail in the same manner **(see illustration)**. Don't use a piston ring installation tool on the oil ring side rails, as they may be damaged. Instead, place one end of the side rail into the groove between the spacer/expander and the ring land, hold it firmly in place and slide a finger around the piston while pushing the rail into the groove. Finally, install the lower side rail.

20   After the three oil ring components have been installed, check to make sure that both the upper and lower side rails can be rotated smoothly inside the ring grooves.

21   The number two (middle) ring is installed next. It's usually stamped with a mark which must face up, toward the top of the piston. Do not mix up the top and middle rings, as they have different cross-sections **(see illustration)**. **Note:** *Always follow the instructions printed on the ring package or box - different manufacturers may require different approaches.*

13.19b DO NOT use a piston ring installation tool when installing the oil control side rails

22   Use a piston ring installation tool and make sure the identification mark is facing the top of the piston, then slip the ring into the middle groove on the piston **(see illustration)**. Don't expand the ring any more than necessary to slide it over the piston.

23   Install the number one (top) ring in the same manner. Make sure the mark is facing

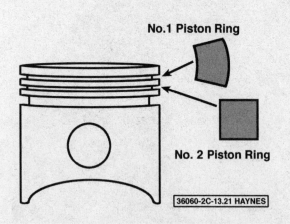

No.1 Piston Ring

No. 2 Piston Ring

36060-2C-13.21 HAYNES

13.21 Top and middle piston ring details

13.22 Use a piston ring installation tool to install the 2nd and top rings - be sure the mark on the piston ring(s) is facing toward the top of the piston (the appearance of the marks may vary)

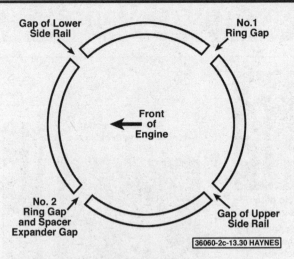

13.30 Position the piston ring end gaps as shown

13.35 Use a plastic or wooden hammer handle to push the piston into the cylinder

up. Be careful not to confuse the number one and number two rings **(see illustration 13.21)**.
24   Repeat the procedure for the remaining pistons and rings.

Installation

25   Before installing the piston/connecting rod assemblies, the cylinder walls must be perfectly clean, the top edge of each cylinder bore must be chamfered, and the crankshaft must be in place.
26   Remove the cap from the end of the number one connecting rod (refer to the marks made during removal). Remove the original bearing inserts and wipe the bearing surfaces of the connecting rod and cap with a clean, lint-free cloth. They must be kept spotlessly clean.

Connecting rod bearing oil clearance check

Refer to illustrations 13.30, 13.35, 13.37 and 13.41

27   Clean the back side of the new upper bearing insert, then lay it in place in the connecting rod. Make sure the tab on the bearing fits into the recess in the rod. Don't hammer the bearing insert into place and be very careful not to nick or gouge the bearing face. Don't lubricate the bearing at this time.
28   Clean the back side of the other bearing insert and install it in the rod cap. Again, make sure the tab on the bearing fits into the recess in the cap, and don't apply any lubricant. It's critically important that the mating surfaces of the bearing and connecting rod are perfectly clean and oil free when they're assembled.
29   On diesel engines, install a short section of plastic or rubber hose over the connecting rod bolts to avoid damaging the cylinder wall or crankshaft journal **(see illustration 13.6)**.
30   Position the piston ring gaps at 90-degree intervals around the piston as shown **(see illustration)**.
31   Lubricate the piston and rings with clean engine oil and attach a piston ring compressor to the piston. Leave the skirt protruding about

1/4-inch to guide the piston into the cylinder. The rings must be compressed until they're flush with the piston.
32   Rotate the crankshaft until the number one connecting rod journal is at BDC (bottom dead center) and apply a liberal coat of engine oil to the cylinder walls.
33   With the weight designation mark, or arrow, on top of the piston facing the front of the engine, gently insert the piston/connecting rod assembly into the number one cylinder bore and rest the bottom edge of the ring compressor on the engine block.
34   Tap the top edge of the ring compressor to make sure it's contacting the block around its entire circumference.
35   Gently tap on the top of the piston with the end of a wooden or plastic hammer handle **(see illustration)** while guiding the end of the connecting rod into place on the crankshaft journal. The piston rings may try to pop out of the ring compressor just before entering the cylinder bore, so keep some downward pressure on the ring compressor. Work slowly, and if any resistance is felt as the piston enters the cylinder, stop immediately. Find out what's hanging up and fix it before proceeding. Do not, for any reason, force the piston into the cylinder - you might break a ring and/or the piston.

36   Once the piston/connecting rod assembly is installed, the connecting rod bearing oil clearance must be checked before the rod cap is permanently installed.
37   Cut a piece of the appropriate size Plastigage slightly shorter than the width of the connecting rod bearing and lay it in place on the number one connecting rod journal, parallel with the journal axis **(see illustration)**.
38   Clean the connecting rod cap bearing face and install the rod cap. Make sure the mating mark on the cap is on the same side as the mark on the connecting rod **(see illustration 13.4)**.
39   Install the old rod bolts or nuts, at this time, and tighten them to the torque listed in this Chapter's Specifications, working up to it in three steps. **Note:** *Use a thin-wall socket to avoid erroneous torque readings that can result if the socket is wedged between the rod cap and the bolt or nut. If the socket tends to wedge itself between the fastener and the cap, lift up on it slightly until it no longer contacts the cap. DO NOT rotate the crankshaft at any time during this operation.*
40   Remove the fasteners and detach the rod cap, being very careful not to disturb the Plastigage. Discard the cap bolts at this time as they cannot be reused. **Note:** *You MUST use new connecting rod bolts.*

13.37 Place Plastigage on each connecting rod bearing journal parallel to the crankshaft centerline

ENGINE BEARING ANALYSIS

Debris

Babbitt bearing embedded with debris from machinings

Microscopic detail of debris

Microscopic detail of gouges

Overplated copper alloy bearing gouged by cast iron debris

Aluminum bearing embedded with glass beads

Microscopic detail of glass beads

Damaged lining caused by dirt left on the bearing back

Misassembly

Result of a lower half assembled as an upper - blocking the oil flow

Excessive oil clearance is indicated by a short contact arc

Polished and oil-stained backs are a result of a poor fit in the housing bore

Result of a wrong, reversed, or shifted cap

Overloading

Damage from excessive idling which resulted in an oil film unable to support the load imposed

Damaged upper connecting rod bearings caused by engine lugging; the lower main bearings (not shown) were similarly affected

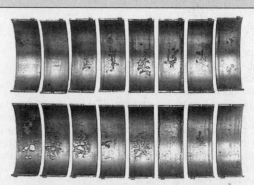

The damage shown in these upper and lower connecting rod bearings was caused by engine operation at a higher-than-rated speed under load

Misalignment

A poorly finished crankshaft caused the equally spaced scoring shown

A tapered housing bore caused the damage along one edge of this pair

A warped crankshaft caused this pattern of severe wear in the center, diminishing toward the ends

A bent connecting rod led to the damage in the "V" pattern

Lubrication

Result of dry start: The bearings on the left, farthest from the oil pump, show more damage

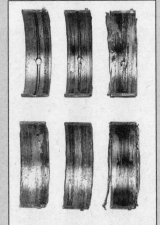

Result of a low oil supply or oil starvation

Severe wear as a result of inadequate oil clearance

Corrosion

Microscopic detail of corrosion

Corrosion is an acid attack on the bearing lining generally caused by inadequate maintenance, extremely hot or cold operation, or inferior oils or fuels

Microscopic detail of cavitation

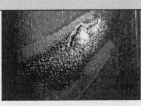

Example of cavitation - a surface erosion caused by pressure changes in the oil film

Damage from excessive thrust or insufficient axial clearance

Bearing affected by oil dilution caused by excessive blow-by or a rich mixture

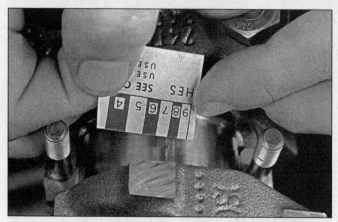

13.41 Use the scale on the Plastigage package to determine the bearing oil clearance - be sure to measure the widest part of the Plastigage and use the correct scale; it comes with both standard and metric scales

14.1 Checking crankshaft endplay with a dial indicator

41   Compare the width of the crushed Plastigage to the scale printed on the Plastigage envelope to obtain the oil clearance **(see illustration)**. The connecting rod oil clearance is usually about 0.001 to 0.002 inch. Consult an automotive machine shop for the clearance specified for the rod bearings on your engine.

42   If the clearance is not as specified, the bearing inserts may be the wrong size (which means different ones will be required). Before deciding that different inserts are needed, make sure that no dirt or oil was between the bearing inserts and the connecting rod or cap when the clearance was measured. Also, recheck the journal diameter. If the Plastigage was wider at one end than the other, the journal may be tapered. If the clearance still exceeds the limit specified, the bearing will have to be replaced with an undersize bearing. **Caution:** *When installing a new crankshaft always use a standard size bearing.*

Final installation

43   Carefully scrape all traces of the Plastigage material off the rod journal and/or bearing face. Be very careful not to scratch the bearing - use your fingernail or the edge of a plastic card.

44   Make sure the bearing faces are perfectly clean, then apply a uniform layer of clean moly-base grease or engine assembly lube to both of them. You'll have to push the piston into the cylinder to expose the face of the bearing insert in the connecting rod.

45   **Caution:** *If the connecting rod caps are secured to the rods with bolts (instead of nuts), install new connecting rod cap bolts. Do NOT reuse old bolts - they have stretched and cannot be reused.* Slide the connecting rod back into place on the journal, install the rod cap, install the nuts or new bolts and tighten them to the torque listed in this Chapter's Specifications. Again, work up to the torque in three steps.

46   Repeat the entire procedure for the remaining pistons/connecting rods.

47   The important points to remember are:

a) *Keep the back sides of the bearing*

inserts and the insides of the connecting rods and caps perfectly clean when assembling them.

b) *Make sure you have the correct piston/rod assembly for each cylinder.*

c) *The mark on the piston must face the front of the engine.*

d) *Lubricate the cylinder walls liberally with clean oil.*

e) *Lubricate the bearing faces when installing the rod caps after the oil clearance has been checked.*

48   After all the piston/connecting rod assemblies have been correctly installed, rotate the crankshaft a number of times by hand to check for any obvious binding.

49   As a final step, check the connecting rod endplay again (see Step 3). If it was correct before disassembly and the original crankshaft and rods were reinstalled, it should still be correct. If new rods or a new crankshaft were installed, the endplay may be inadequate. If so, the rods will have to be removed and taken to an automotive machine shop for resizing.

14 Crankshaft - removal and installation

Removal

Refer to illustrations 14.1 and 14.3

Note: *The crankshaft can be removed only after the engine has been removed from the vehicle. It's assumed that the flywheel or driveplate, crankshaft pulley, timing chain(s), oil pan, oil pump body, oil filter and piston/connecting rod assemblies have already been removed. The rear main oil seal retainer must be unbolted and separated from the block before proceeding with crankshaft removal.*

1   Before the crankshaft is removed, measure the endplay. Mount a dial indicator with the indicator in line with the crankshaft and touching the end of the crankshaft as shown **(see illustration)**.

2   Pry the crankshaft all the way to the

rear and zero the dial indicator. Next, pry the crankshaft to the front as far as possible and check the reading on the dial indicator. The distance traveled is the endplay. A typical crankshaft endplay will fall between 0.003 and 0.010-inch. If it's greater than that, check the crankshaft thrust surfaces for wear after its removed. If no wear is evident, new main bearings should correct the endplay.

3   If a dial indicator isn't available, feeler gauges can be used. Gently pry the crankshaft all the way to the front of the engine. Slip feeler gauges between the crankshaft and the front face of the thrust bearing or washer to determine the clearance **(see illustration)**.

4   Loosen the main bearing bolts 1/4-turn at a time each, until they can be removed by hand. On 6.0L and 6.4L diesel engines, remove all 28 bolts that retain the lower crankcase to the main engine block. Remove the lower crankcase.

5   On all engines except the 6.0L and 6.4L diesel, gently tap the main bearing caps with a soft-face hammer. Pull the main bearing caps straight up and off the cylinder block. Try not to drop the bearing inserts if they come out with the caps.

14.3 Checking crankshaft endplay with feeler gauges at the thrust bearing journal

14.17 Place the Plastigage onto the crankshaft bearing journal as shown

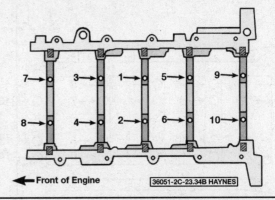

14.19a Main bearing cap bolt tightening sequence (V8 gasoline engine)

6   Carefully lift the crankshaft out of the engine. Have an assistant available, since the crankshaft is quite heavy and awkward to handle. With the bearing inserts in place inside the engine block and main bearing caps, reinstall the main bearing caps onto the engine block and tighten the bolts finger tight. Make sure you install the main bearing caps with the arrows facing the front end of the engine.

Installation

7   Crankshaft installation is the first step in engine reassembly. It's assumed at this point that the engine block and crankshaft have been cleaned, inspected and repaired or reconditioned.

8   Position the engine block with the bottom facing up.

9   Remove the mounting bolts and lift off the main bearing caps. **Note:** *The main bearing caps on V8 and V10 gasoline engines also use side bolts to secure the caps.*

10   If they're still in place, remove the original bearing inserts from the block and from the main bearing caps. Wipe the bearing surfaces of the block and main bearing caps with a clean, lint-free cloth. They must be kept

spotlessly clean. This is critical for determining the correct bearing oil clearance.

Main bearing oil clearance check

Refer to illustrations 14.17, 14.19a, 14.19b, 14.19c and 14.26

11   Without mixing them up, clean the back sides of the new upper main bearing inserts (with grooves and oil holes) and lay one in each main bearing saddle in the block. Each upper bearing has an oil groove and oil hole in it. **Caution:** *The oil holes in the block must line up with the oil holes in the upper bearing inserts.* The V8 and V10 gasoline engines have a two-piece thrust washer installed on the last (closest to the flywheel/driveplate) main bearing saddle in the block, and a single thrust washer on the rear side of the last main bearing cap. The grooves in the thrust washers must face the crankshaft (the plain sides against the main bearing saddle or cap). On the diesel engine the thrust washers are incorporated into the number five (closest to the flywheel/driveplate) main bearings and are not separable. Clean the back sides of the lower main bearing inserts (without grooves) and lay them in the caps. Make sure the tab on the bearing insert fits into the recess in the block or main bearing caps. **Caution:** *Do not hammer the bearing insert into place and*

don't nick or gouge the bearing faces. DO NOT apply any lubrication at this time.

12   Clean the faces of the bearing inserts in the block and the crankshaft main bearing journals with a clean, lint-free cloth.

13   Check or clean the oil holes in the crankshaft, as any dirt here can go only one way - straight through the new bearings.

14   Once you're certain the crankshaft is clean, carefully lay it in position in the cylinder block.

15   Before the crankshaft can be permanently installed, the main bearing oil clearance must be checked.

16   Cut several strips of the appropriate size of Plastigage (they must be slightly shorter than the width of the main bearing journal).

17   Place one piece on each crankshaft main bearing journal, parallel with the journal axis as shown **(see illustration)**.

All engines except 6.0L and 6.4L diesel

18   Clean the faces of the bearing inserts in the main bearing caps. Hold the bearing inserts in place and install the assembly onto the crankshaft and cylinder block. DO NOT disturb the Plastigage. Make sure you install the main bearing caps with the arrows facing the front (timing chain end) of the engine.

19   Apply clean engine oil to all bolt threads prior to installation, then install all bolts finger-tight. Tighten the main bearing cap bolts in

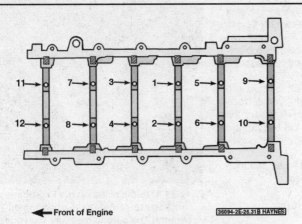

14.19b Main bearing cap bolt tightening sequence (V10 gasoline engine)

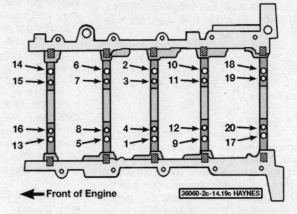

14.19c Main bearing cap bolt tightening sequence (7.3L diesel engine)

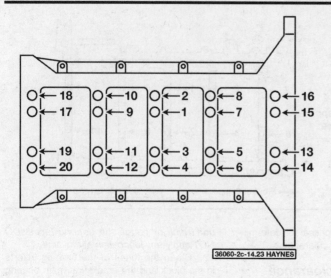

14.23 6.0L and 6.4L diesel main bearing carrier bolt tightening sequence

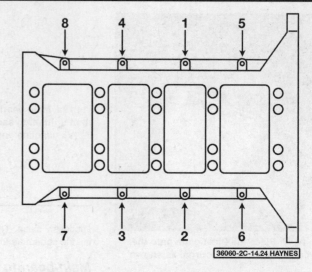

14.24 Diesel outer main bearing bolt tightening sequence - 6.0L engines only

the sequence shown **(see illustrations)** progressing in two steps, to the torque listed in this Chapter's Specifications. DO NOT rotate the crankshaft at any time during this operation.

20   Remove the bolts in the *reverse* order of the tightening sequence and carefully lift the main bearing caps straight up and off the block. Do not disturb the Plastigage or rotate the crankshaft. If a main bearing cap is difficult to remove, tap it gently from side-to-side with a soft-face hammer to loosen it.

6.0L and 6.4L diesel engines

21   Install the lower main bearings into the lower crankcase.

22   Install the lower crankcase over the crankshaft and engine block. Install the 28 fasteners finger tight. **Caution:** *Make sure that the longer main bolts are installed closest to the crankshaft to avoid damage.*

23   Tighten the 20 inner bolts in three steps to the torques listed in this Chapter's Specifications and in the proper sequence **(see illustration)**.

24   Tighten the 8 outer bolts (6.0L only) to the torque listed in this Chapter's Specifications and in the proper sequence **(see illustration)**.

25   Remove the bolts in the reverse order of the tightening sequence and carefully lift the lower crankcase straight up and off the block. Do not disturb the Plastigage or rotate the crankshaft.

All engines

26   Compare the width of the crushed Plastigage on each journal to the scale printed on the Plastigage envelope to determine the main bearing oil clearance **(see illustration)**. A typical main bearing oil clearance should fall between 0.0015 to 0.0023-inch on gasoline engines or 0.0015 to 0.0045-inch on diesel engines. Check with an automotive machine shop for the oil clearance for your engine.

27   If the clearance is not acceptable, the

bearing inserts may be the wrong size (which means different ones will be required). Before deciding if different inserts are needed, make sure that no dirt or oil was between the bearing inserts and the cap assembly or block when the clearance was measured. If the Plastigage was wider at one end than the other, the crankshaft journal may be tapered. If the clearance still exceeds the limit specified, the bearing insert(s) will have to be replaced with an undersize bearing insert(s). **Caution:** *When installing a new crankshaft always install a standard bearing insert set.*

28   Carefully scrape all traces of the Plastigage material off the main bearing journals and/or the bearing insert faces. Be sure to remove all residue from the oil holes. Use your fingernail or the edge of a plastic card - don't nick or scratch the bearing faces.

Final installation

Refer to illustrations 14.38a and 14.38b

29   Carefully lift the crankshaft out of the cylinder block.

30   Clean the bearing insert faces in the cylinder block, then apply a thin, uniform layer of moly-base grease or engine assembly lube to each of the bearing surfaces. Be sure to coat the thrust faces of the thrust washers/bearings as well. See Step 11 for thrust washer/bearing locations.

31   Make sure the crankshaft journals are clean, then lay the crankshaft back in place in the cylinder block. On diesel engines, if the camshaft is still installed in the engine, the timing marks must be aligned as the crankshaft is set in place.

32   Clean the bearing insert faces and then apply the same lubricant to them.

All engines except 6.0L and 6.4L diesel

33   Hold the bearing inserts in place and install the main bearing caps on the crankshaft and cylinder block. Tap the bearing caps

into place with a brass or a soft-face hammer.

34   Using NEW main bearing cap bolts, apply clean engine oil to the bolt threads, wipe off any excess oil and then install the bolts finger-tight. On V8 and V10 gasoline engines, install the dowel pins in the outboard holes of the caps with their flat sides toward the center of the engine.

35   Tighten the main bearing cap bolts in the indicated sequence to 120 to 144 inch-pounds.

36   Push the crankshaft forward using a screwdriver or prybar to seat the thrust bearing. Once the crankshaft is pushed fully forward to seat the thrust bearing, leave the screwdriver in position so that pressure stays on the crankshaft until after all main bearing cap bolts have been tightened.

37   Tighten the main bearing cap bolts in two steps in the indicated sequence and to the torque and angle listed in this Chapter's Specifications.

38   On V8 and V10 gasoline engines, tighten all side bolts, in two steps, to the torque listed

14.26 Use the scale on the Plastigage package to determine the bearing oil clearance - be sure to measure the widest part of the Plastigage and use the correct scale; it comes with both standard and metric scales

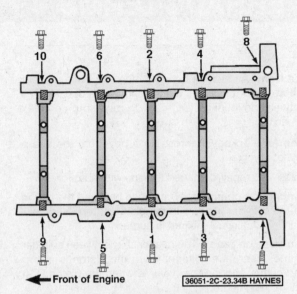

14.38a On V8 gasoline engines, tighten the side bolts in this sequence in two steps

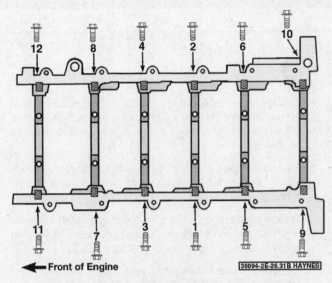

14.38b On V10 gasoline engines, tighten the side bolts in this sequence in two steps

in this Chapter's Specifications **(see illustrations)**.

6.0L and 6.4L diesel engines

39   Install the lower main bearings into the lower crankcase.

40   Install new lower crankcase seals.

41   Install the lower crankcase over the crankshaft and engine block. Install 28 fasteners finger tight. **Caution:** *Make sure that the longer main bolts are installed closest to the crankshaft to avoid damage.*

42   Tighten the 20 inner bolts in three steps to the torques listed in this Chapter's Specifications and in the proper sequence **(see illustration)**.

43   Tighten the 8 outer bolts to the torque listed in this Chapter's Specifications and in the proper sequence **(see illustration)**.

All engines

44   Recheck crankshaft endplay with a feeler gauge or a dial indicator. The endplay should be correct if the crankshaft thrust faces aren't worn or damaged and if new bearings have been installed.

45   Rotate the crankshaft a number of times by hand to check for any obvious binding.

46   Install the new rear main oil seal (see Chapter 2A or 2B).

15   Engine overhaul - reassembly sequence

Note: *Diesel engines have several components in addition to the standard ones covered here. These include the high pressure oil system, the internal engine oil cooler, etc. Make sure to get additional information or assis-*
tance regarding these components before attempting to assemble a diesel engine.

1   Before beginning engine reassembly, make sure you have all the necessary new parts, gaskets and seals as well as the following items on hand:

> *Common hand tools*
> *A 1/2-inch drive torque wrench*
> *New engine oil*
> *Gasket sealant*
> *Thread locking compound*

2   If you obtained a short block it will be necessary to install the cylinder head, the oil pump and pick-up tube, the oil pan, the water pump, the timing belt and timing cover, and the valve cover (see Chapter 2A or 2B). In order to save time and avoid problems, the external components must be installed in the following general order:

> *Thermostat and housing cover*
> *Water pump*
> *Intake and exhaust manifolds*
> *Carburetor or fuel injection components*
> *Emission control components*
> *Spark plug wires and spark plugs*
> *Ignition coils*
> *Oil filter*
> *Engine mounts and mount brackets*
> *Clutch and flywheel (manual transmission)*
> *Driveplate (automatic transmission)*

16   Initial start-up and break-in after overhaul

Warning: *Have a fire extinguisher handy when starting the engine for the first time.*

1   Once the engine has been installed in
the vehicle, double-check the engine oil and coolant levels.

2   With the spark plugs out of the engine and the ignition system and fuel pump disabled, crank the engine until oil pressure registers on the gauge or the light goes out.

3   Install the spark plugs, hook up the plug wires and restore the ignition system and fuel pump functions.

4   Start the engine. It may take a few moments for the fuel system to build up pressure, but the engine should start without a great deal of effort.

5   After the engine starts, it should be allowed to warm up to normal operating temperature. While the engine is warming up, make a thorough check for fuel, oil and coolant leaks.

6   Shut the engine off and recheck the engine oil and coolant levels.

7   Drive the vehicle to an area with minimum traffic, accelerate from 30 to 50 mph, then allow the vehicle to slow to 30 mph with the throttle closed. Repeat the procedure 10 or 12 times. This will load the piston rings and cause them to seat properly against the cylinder walls. Check again for oil and coolant leaks.

8   Drive the vehicle gently for the first 500 miles (no sustained high speeds) and keep a constant check on the oil level. It is not unusual for an engine to use oil during the break-in period.

9   At approximately 500 to 600 miles, change the oil and filter.

10   For the next few hundred miles, drive the vehicle normally. Do not pamper it or abuse it.

11   After 2000 miles, change the oil and filter again and consider the engine broken in.

COMMON ENGINE OVERHAUL TERMS

B

Backlash - The amount of play between two parts. Usually refers to how much one gear can be moved back and forth without moving gear with which it's meshed.

Bearing Caps - The caps held in place by nuts or bolts which, in turn, hold the bearing surface. This space is for lubricating oil to enter.

Bearing clearance - The amount of space left between shaft and bearing surface. This space is for lubricating oil to enter.

Bearing crush - The additional height which is purposely manufactured into each bearing half to ensure complete contact of the bearing back with the housing bore when the engine is assembled.

Bearing knock - The noise created by movement of a part in a loose or worn bearing.

Blueprinting - Dismantling an engine and reassembling it to EXACT specifications.

Bore - An engine cylinder, or any cylindrical hole; also used to describe the process of enlarging or accurately refinishing a hole with a cutting tool, as to bore an engine cylinder. The bore size is the diameter of the hole.

Boring - Renewing the cylinders by cutting them out to a specified size. A boring bar is used to make the cut.

Bottom end - A term which refers collectively to the engine block, crankshaft, main bearings and the big ends of the connecting rods.

Break-in - The period of operation between installation of new or rebuilt parts and time in which parts are worn to the correct fit. Driving at reduced and varying speed for a specified mileage to permit parts to wear to the correct fit.

Bushing - A one-piece sleeve placed in a bore to serve as a bearing surface for shaft, piston pin, etc. Usually replaceable.

C

Camshaft - The shaft in the engine, on which a series of lobes are located for operating the valve mechanisms. The camshaft is driven by gears or sprockets and a timing chain. Usually referred to simply as the cam.

Carbon - Hard, or soft, black deposits found in combustion chamber, on plugs, under rings, on and under valve heads.

Cast iron - An alloy of iron and more than two percent carbon, used for engine blocks and heads because it's relatively inexpensive and easy to mold into complex shapes.

Chamfer - To bevel across (or a bevel on) the sharp edge of an object.

Chase - To repair damaged threads with a tap or die.

Combustion chamber - The space between the piston and the cylinder head, with the piston at top dead center, in which air-fuel mixture is burned.

Compression ratio - The relationship between cylinder volume (clearance volume) when the piston is at top dead center and cylinder volume when the piston is at bottom dead center.

Connecting rod - The rod that connects the crank on the crankshaft with the piston. Sometimes called a con rod.

Connecting rod cap - The part of the connecting rod assembly that attaches the rod to the crankpin.

Core plug - Soft metal plug used to plug the casting holes for the coolant passages in the block.

Crankcase - The lower part of the engine in which the crankshaft rotates; includes the lower section of the cylinder block and the oil pan.

Crank kit - A reground or reconditioned crankshaft and new main and connecting rod bearings.

Crankpin - The part of a crankshaft to which a connecting rod is attached.

Crankshaft - The main rotating member, or shaft, running the length of the crankcase, with offset throws to which the connecting rods are attached; changes the reciprocating motion of the pistons into rotating motion.

Cylinder sleeve - A replaceable sleeve, or liner, pressed into the cylinder block to form the cylinder bore.

D

Deburring - Removing the burrs (rough edges or areas) from a bearing.

Deglazer - A tool, rotated by an electric motor, used to remove glaze from cylinder walls so a new set of rings will seat.

E

Endplay - The amount of lengthwise movement

between two parts. As applied to a crankshaft, the distance that the crankshaft can move forward and back in the cylinder block.

F

Face - A machinist's term that refers to removing metal from the end of a shaft or the face of a larger part, such as a flywheel.

Fatigue - A breakdown of material through a large number of loading and unloading cycles. The first signs are cracks followed shortly by breaks.

Feeler gauge - A thin strip of hardened steel, ground to an exact thickness, used to check clearances between parts.

Free height - The unloaded length or height of a spring.

Freeplay - The looseness in a linkage, or an assembly of parts, between the initial application of force and actual movement. Usually perceived as slop or slight delay.

Freeze plug - See Core plug.

G

Gallery - A large passage in the block that forms a reservoir for engine oil pressure.

Glaze - The very smooth, glassy finish that develops on cylinder walls while an engine is in service.

H

Heli-Coil - A rethreading device used when threads are worn or damaged. The device is installed in a retapped hole to reduce the thread size to the original size.

I

Installed height - The spring's measured length or height, as installed on the cylinder head. Installed height is measured from the spring seat to the underside of the spring retainer.

J

Journal - The surface of a rotating shaft which turns in a bearing.

K

Keeper - The split lock that holds the valve spring retainer in position on the valve stem.

Key - A small piece of metal inserted into matching grooves machined into two parts fitted together - such as a gear pressed onto a shaft - which prevents slippage between the two parts.

Knock - The heavy metallic engine sound, produced in the combustion chamber as a result of abnormal combustion - usually detonation. Knock is usually caused by a loose or worn bearing. Also referred to as detonation, pinging and spark knock. Connecting rod or main bearing knocks are created by too much oil clearance or insufficient lubrication.

L

Lands - The portions of metal between the piston ring grooves.

Lapping the valves - Grinding a valve face and its seat together with lapping compound.

Lash - The amount of free motion in a gear train, between gears, or in a mechanical assembly, that occurs before movement can begin. Usually refers to the lash in a valve train.

Lifter - The part that rides against the cam to transfer motion to the rest of the valve train.

M

Machining - The process of using a machine to remove metal from a metal part.

Main bearings - The plain, or babbit, bearings that support the crankshaft.

Main bearing caps - The cast iron caps, bolted to the bottom of the block, that support the main bearings.

O

O.D. - Outside diameter.

Oil gallery - A pipe or drilled passageway in the engine used to carry engine oil from one area to another.

Oil ring - The lower ring, or rings, of a piston; designed to prevent excessive amounts of oil from working up the cylinder walls and into the combustion chamber. Also called an oil-control ring.

Notes

Chapter 3
Cooling, heating and air conditioning systems

Contents

	Section
Air conditioning accumulator - removal and installation	14
Air conditioning and heater blower motor and resistor - replacement	10
Air conditioning and heater control assembly - removal and installation	12
Air conditioning and heating system - check and maintenance	13
Air conditioning compressor - removal and installation	15
Air conditioning condenser - removal and installation	16
Air conditioning evaporator - removal and installation	17
Air conditioning pressure cycling switch - replacement	18
Antifreeze - general information	2
Auxiliary climate control assembly (Excursion models) - removal and installation	19
Auxiliary climate control blower motor and resistor (Excursion models) - removal and installation	20

	Section
Coolant temperature sending unit - check and replacement	9
Cooling fan assembly - check, removal and installation	5
Cooling system - draining, flushing and refilling	See Chapter 1
Cooling system - inspection	See Chapter 1
Expansion tank - removal and installation	4
General information	1
Heater core - removal and installation	11
Oil cooler - removal and installation	21
Radiator - removal and installation	6
Thermostat - check and replacement	3
Water pump - check	7
Water pump - removal and installation	8

Specifications

Refrigerant type	R-134a

Torque specifications

Ft-lbs (unless otherwise indicated)

Note: *One foot-pound (ft-lb) of torque is equivalent to 12 inch-pounds (in-lbs) of torque. Torque values below approximately 15 foot-pounds are expressed in inch-pounds, because most foot-pound torque wrenches are not accurate at these smaller values.*

Air conditioning pressure cycling switch	12 to 33 in-lbs
Condenser inlet and outlet nuts	62 to 79 in-lbs
Engine oil cooler insert (V8 gasoline engine)	41 to 44
Engine oil cooler (diesel engine)	
Rear header mounting bolts	18
Front header bolts	18
Fan-to-clutch bolts	
1999 through 2003	15
2004 and later	13
Cooling fan stator fasteners (6.4L diesel engine)	18
Thermostat housing bolts	
Gasoline models	
1999 through 2004	20
2005 and later	89 in-lbs
Diesel models	
6.0L and 7.3L	20
6.4L	115 in-lbs
Water pump bolts	
All except 6.4L diesel	18
6.4L diesel	23

1   General information

Engine cooling system

The cooling system consists of a radiator, an expansion tank, a pressure cap (located on the expansion tank), a thermostat, a cooling fan and clutch, and a belt-driven water pump.

The cooling fan and clutch are mounted on the front of the water pump pulley. On all models except the 6.0L diesel, the fan incorporates a fluid-drive fan clutch, which saves horsepower and reduces noise. When the engine is cold, the fluid in the clutch offers little resistance and allows the fan to freewheel. As the engine heats up and reaches a predetermined temperature, the fluid in the clutch thickens and drives the fan. The system used on the 6.0L diesel engine is similar, however the fan is driven electrically.

The expansion tank (referred to by the manufacturer as a "degas bottle") functions somewhat differently than a conventional recovery tank. Designed to separate any trapped air in the coolant, it is pressurized by the radiator and has a pressure cap on top. The radiator on these models does not have a pressure cap. When the thermostat is closed, no coolant flows in the expansion tank, but when the engine is fully warmed up, coolant flows from the top of the radiator through a small hose that enters the top of the expansion tank, where the air separates and the coolant falls into a coolant reservoir in the bottom of the tank, which is fed to the cooling system through a larger hose connected to the lower radiator hose. **Warning:** *Unlike a conventional coolant recovery tank, the pressure cap on the expansion tank should never be opened after the engine has warmed up, because of the danger of severe burns caused by steam or scalding coolant.*

Coolant in the left side of the radiator circulates through the lower radiator hose to the water pump, where it is forced through coolant passages in the cylinder block. The coolant then travels up into the cylinder head, circulates around the combustion chambers and valve seats, travels out of the cylinder head past the open thermostat into the upper radiator hose and back into the radiator.

When the engine is cold, the thermostat restricts the circulation of coolant to the engine. When the minimum operating temperature is reached, the thermostat begins to open, allowing coolant to return to the radiator.

Transmission cooling systems

Vehicles with an automatic transmission are equipped with a transmission cooler, located inside the radiator, which cools the transmission fluid. The transmission is connected to the cooler by a pair of hoses: one delivers hot transmission fluid to the radiator and the other brings the cooled fluid back to the transmission. Some automatics are also equipped with an auxiliary external cooler, located between the air conditioning condenser and the radiator (just below the intercooler on diesel models).

Manual transmissions are also equipped with an oil cooler inside the radiator. Manual transmission lubricant is circulated through the hoses and the cooler by an internal pump driven by the countershaft.

For more information on transmission oil coolers, refer to Chapter 7.

Engine oil cooling system

Besides the engine and transmission cooling systems described above, engine heat is also dissipated through an external oil cooler that's integrated into the lubrication system on gasoline and diesel models. The oil cooler helps keep engine and oil temperatures within design limits under extreme load conditions.

The oil cooling system on gasoline engines consists of a housing mounted inline between the oil filter and the filter adapter, a heat exchanger inside the radiator and a pair of hoses that deliver hot oil from the housing to the radiator and bring the cooled oil back to the housing.

The oil cooling system on the 7.3L diesel engine consists of a cylindrical heat exchanger housed inside a tube located on the left side of the engine block. The forward end of the tube is connected to a front header that's bolted to the front cover; an oil passage inside the front cover connects the oil pump to the front header. The rear end of the tube is connected to the oil filter adapter. The oil cooling system on the 6.0L diesel engine uses a water-cooled heat exchanger mounted at the oil filter adapter on the top of the engine.

Heating system

The heating system consists of the heater controls, the heater core, the heater blower assembly (which houses the blower motor and the blower motor resistor), and the hoses connecting the heater core to the engine cooling system. Hot engine coolant is circulated through the heater core. When the heater mode is activated, a flap door opens to expose the heater box to the passenger compartment. A fan switch on the heater controls activates the blower motor, which forces air through the core, heating the air.

Air conditioning system

The air conditioning system consists of the condenser, which is mounted in front of the radiator, the evaporator case assembly under the dash, a compressor mounted on the engine, and the plumbing connecting all of the above components.

A blower fan forces the warmer air of the passenger compartment through the evaporator core (sort of a radiator-in-reverse), transferring the heat from the air to the refrigerant. The liquid refrigerant boils off into low pressure vapor, taking the heat with it when it leaves the evaporator.

An optional rear-mounted, one-piece, auxiliary heating and air conditioning system (for Excursion models) is located on the right side of the vehicle cargo area, behind the right rear wheelwell, between the window and the floorpan. The auxiliary heating and air conditioning system includes its own blower motor, resistor, heater core and evaporator. There are two sets of controls for the auxiliary climate control system, one for the driver and another for the passengers in the rear seating area.

2   Antifreeze - general information

Refer to illustration 2.5

Warning: *Do not allow antifreeze to come in contact with your skin or painted surfaces of the vehicle. Rinse off spills immediately with plenty of water. Antifreeze is highly toxic if ingested. Never leave antifreeze lying around in an open container or in puddles on the floor; children and pets are attracted by its sweet smell and may drink it. Check with local authorities about disposing of used antifreeze. Many communities have collection centers which will see that antifreeze is disposed of safely. Never dump used antifreeze on the ground or pour it into drains.*

Caution: *Do not mix coolants of different colors. Doing so might damage the cooling system and/or the engine. Read the warning label in the engine compartment for additional information.*

Note: *Non-toxic antifreeze is now manufactured and available at local auto parts stores, but even this type must be disposed of properly.*

The cooling system should be filled with a water/ethylene glycol based antifreeze solution, which will prevent freezing down to at least -20-degrees F (even lower in cold climates). It also provides protection against corrosion and increases the coolant boiling point. The engines in these vehicles have either cast iron or aluminum heads. Depending on the engine and model year, the specified coolant varies (see the Chapter 1 Specifications). The manufacturer recommends that the correct type of coolant be used and strongly urges that coolant types not be mixed.

Drain, flush and refill the cooling system at least every other year (see Chapter 1). The use of antifreeze solutions for periods of longer than two years is likely to cause damage and encourage the formation of rust and scale in the system.

Before adding antifreeze to the system, inspect all hose connections. Antifreeze can leak through very minute openings.

The exact mixture of antifreeze to water, which you should use, depends on the relative weather conditions. The mixture should contain at least 50-percent antifreeze, but should never contain more than 70-percent antifreeze. Consult the mixture ratio chart on the container before adding coolant.

Hydrometers are available at most auto parts stores to test the coolant **(see illustration)**. Use antifreeze that meets Ford specifications for engines with aluminum heads.

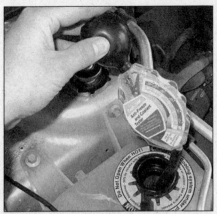

2.5 Use a hydrometer (available at auto parts stores) to test the condition of your coolant

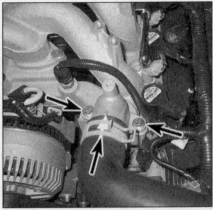

3.14a To disconnect the radiator hose from the thermostat housing on a gasoline engine, loosen this clamp (lower arrow) and pull off the hose; to remove the thermostat housing, remove these two bolts (upper arrows) (V10 engine shown, V8 engine similar)

3.14b To disconnect the radiator hose from the thermostat housing on a diesel engine, loosen this clamp and pull off the hose

3 Thermostat - check and replacement

Warning: *The engine must be completely cool when this procedure is performed.*
Note: *Don't drive the vehicle without a thermostat! The computer may stay in open loop and emissions and fuel economy will suffer.*

Check

1   Before proceeding, check the coolant level and the drivebelt tension (see Chapter 1) and then check the operation of the temperature gauge or temperature warning light circuit (see Chapter 12).
2   If the engine takes a long time to warm up, the thermostat is probably stuck open. Replace the thermostat.
3   If the engine runs hot, check the temperature of the upper radiator hose. If the hose isn't hot, the thermostat is probably stuck shut. Replace the thermostat.
4   If the upper radiator hose is hot, then the coolant is circulating and the thermostat is open. Refer to the *Troubleshooting* Section at the front of this manual for the cause of overheating.
5   If the engine has overheated, it might have leaking cylinder head gaskets, scuffed pistons and/or warped or cracked cylinder heads.

Replacement

Refer to illustrations 3.14a, 3.14b, 3.15 and 3.16

6   Drain the radiator so the coolant level is below the thermostat (see Chapter 1).
7   On 6.0L engines, remove the air filter housing and the charge air cooler duct (see Chapter 4B).

6.4L engines

8   Remove the upper cooling fan shroud (see Section 5).
9   Remove the expansion tank (see Section 6).

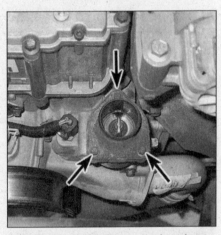

3.15 To detach the thermostat housing on a diesel engine, remove these three bolts

10   Use a small screwdriver to remove the spring clip from the upper radiator hose at the thermostat.
11   Remove the lower clamp from the vertical EGR cooler lower bracket (see Chapter 6).
12   Remove the vertical EGR cooler lower bracket.
13   Remove the left side heater return tube.

All models

14   Disconnect the upper radiator hose from the thermostat housing **(see illustrations)**.
15   Remove the thermostat housing bolts **(gasoline engine, see illustration 3.14a; diesel engine, see illustration)** and lift off the housing.
16   Note the orientation of the thermostat **(see illustration)**, then remove it along with the O-ring. Discard the old O-ring. Make sure that nothing falls into the thermostat opening; it's a good idea to stuff a rag into the opening until you're ready to install the thermostat.
17   Be sure to use a replacement thermostat

3.16 Before removing the thermostat, note the position of the bleed hole; when the thermostat is installed, the bleed hole must be in this position (thermostat on 7.3L diesel engine shown, thermostats on gasoline engines similar)

that's identical to the old thermostat. Compare the old and new thermostats carefully before installing the new unit. **Note:** *On 6.4L diesel engines, there are two thermostats within the one housing. The one without a bypass should be installed in the upper of the two thermostat holes.*

18   Install the thermostat. Make sure that the spring end faces down, toward the engine. And make sure that the bleed hole is correctly positioned **(see illustration 3.16)**.
19   Install the new O-ring in the recess in the thermostat housing **(see illustration 3.16)**.
20   Carefully position the thermostat housing, install the bolts and tighten them to the torque listed in this Chapter's Specifications. Do NOT overtighten the thermostat housing bolts; doing so will crack or distort the housing.
21   Inspect the hose and the clamp (see Chapter 1). Replace the hose and/or clamp if damaged.
22   Reattach the radiator hose to the housing and tighten the clamp

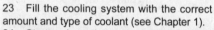

4.2   To remove the lug wrench, unscrew this wing bolt

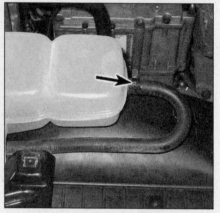

4.3   Loosen this hose clamp and disconnect the overflow hose

4.4   To detach the expansion tank, remove these three bolts

23   Fill the cooling system with the correct amount and type of coolant (see Chapter 1).
24   Start and run the engine until it reaches normal operating temperature, then check the coolant level and look for leaks.

4   Expansion tank - removal and installation

Refer to illustrations 4.2, 4.3, 4.4 and 4.5
Warning: *The engine must be completely cool before beginning this procedure.*
1   Drain the cooling system (see Chapter 1).
2   On early models with interfering jack components, remove the wing bolt **(see illustration)** and remove the lug wrench.
3   Loosen the hose clamp **(see illustration)** and disconnect the overflow hose.
4   Remove the expansion tank bolts **(see illustration)**, then lift up the tank far enough to access the supply hose.
5   Loosen the hose clamp and disconnect the supply hose **(see illustration)**. Remove the expansion tank.
6   Installation is the reverse of removal.
7   Refill the cooling system (see Chapter 1).

4.5   Lift up the expansion tank, loosen this hose clamp, disconnect the supply hose and remove the tank

5   Cooling fan assembly - check, removal and installation

All except 6.0L and 6.4L diesel engines

Check

Warning 1: *While checking the fan, make sure that the engine is NOT started. If it is, you could be severely injured.*
Warning 2: *Before the fan clutch operation can be checked in Step 5, the engine must be warmed up to its normal operating temperature and then turned off. Even though the engine won't be running during this check, it's HOT! Make sure that you don't touch the engine itself during this check, or you could be burned.*
Warning 3: *Keep hands, tools and clothing away from the fan when the engine is running. To avoid injury or damage DO NOT operate the engine with a damaged fan. Do not attempt to repair fan blades - replace a damaged fan with a new one.*
Note: *The following procedure applies only to gasoline engines and 7.3L diesel engines. 6.0L and 6.4L diesel engines use an electrically powered fan that is controlled by the PCM. If your fan is not operating properly,*

have a dealer or other qualified service center diagnose it.
1   Symptoms of fan clutch failure are continuous noisy operation, looseness, vibration and/or silicone fluid leaking from the clutch.

Cold engine checks

2   Rock the fan back and forth by hand to check for excessive bearing play.
3   With the engine cold, turn the blades by hand. The fan should turn freely.
4   Visually inspect for substantial fluid leakage from the fan clutch assembly, a deformed bi-metal spring or grease leakage from the cooling fan bearing. If any of these conditions exist, replace the fan clutch.

Hot engine check

5   Start the engine and allow it to warm up to its normal operating temperature. When the engine is fully warmed up, turn off the ignition switch. Turn the fan by hand. Some resistance should be felt. If the fan turns easily, replace the fan clutch.

Fan clutch removal and installation

Refer to illustrations 5.10a, 5.10b, 5.11, 5.12 and 5.13
6   Disconnect the cable(s) from the negative battery terminals.
7   Drain the cooling system (see Chapter 1).

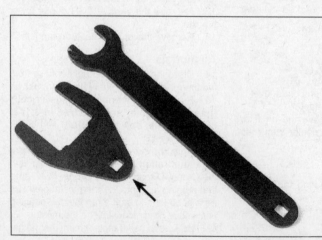

5.10a   Typical fan wrench set; on the vehicles covered in this manual, the big wrench (arrow) fits the nut that attaches the fan clutch to the drive hub

5.10b Holding the water pump pulley with a chain wrench, loosen the fan clutch nut with the special fan wrench and a breaker bar

5.11 To detach the fan shroud from the radiator, remove these two bolts

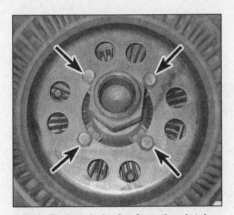

5.12 To detach the fan from the clutch, remove these four bolts

6.0L and 6.4L diesel engines
Check

14   6.0L and 6.4L diesel engines use an electrically powered fan that is controlled by the PCM. If your fan is not operating properly, have a dealer or other qualified service center diagnose it.

Fan removal and installation

15   Remove the radiator (refer to Section 6). **Note:** *On some 6.0L models, it may be necessary to cut the shroud for removal. Carefully slice the upper and lower sections along the molded-in line on each side, at the indentations, using a sharp razor knife. After the upper and lower shrouds have been separated, drill two small holes on each side (four total) and install self-tapping screws to secure the shroud together during installation.*
16   Disconnect the wiring from the fan.
17   Secure the fan hub from turning using the hole in it. The fan is on very tight.
18   Using a special wrench, unscrew the fan blade assembly from the hub.
19   Lift the fan blade assembly out, taking care to avoid damage to the radiator.
20   To remove the fan stator, remove the bolts that secure it to the engine front cover and carefully lift it out.
21   Installation is the reverse of removal.

6   Radiator - removal and installation

Refer to illustrations 6.3, 6.6, 6.7, 6.8, 6.9a, 6.9b, 6.10, 6.11 and 6.13
Warning: *The engine must be completely cool when this procedure is performed.*
1   Drain the cooling system (see Chapter 1).
2   Remove the coolant expansion tank (see Section 4).
3   Disconnect the upper radiator hose from the radiator **(see illustration)**.
4   Remove the cooling fan and clutch assembly (see Section 5).
5   Raise the vehicle and place it securely on jackstands.

5.13 When installing the fan shroud, make sure that the tab at each end of the shroud fits into its slot

6.3 To disconnect the upper radiator hose from the radiator, loosen this hose clamp, slide it back down the hose and pull off the hose; if the hose is stuck, carefully work a thin, tapered and *blunt* tool between the hose and the radiator pipe to break the seal (there are tools designed for this job, or you can fabricate your own)

8   Remove the coolant expansion tank (see Section 4).
9   Remove the upper radiator hose **(see illustration 6.3)**.
10   Special fan wrenches **(see illustration)** and a chain wrench, available at most auto parts stores, are needed to remove the cooling fan assembly. The fan clutch is attached to the drive hub with a large nut. Hold the water pump pulley with the chain wrench while loosening the clutch nut with the right size fan wrench and, if necessary, an extension **(see illustration)**. **Note:** *The fan clutch hub nut is right-hand thread (turn counterclockwise to loosen).*
11   Position the fan and fan clutch assembly inside the fan shroud, then unbolt the fan shroud **(see illustration)** and lift the fan assembly and the shroud up and out of the engine compartment together.
12   If you're going to replace the fan or the clutch, unbolt the two components **(see illustration)**. **Caution:** *To prevent silicone fluid from draining from the clutch assembly into the fan drive bearing and ruining the lubricant, place the drive unit so that the shaft points UP.*
13   Installation is the reverse of removal. When installing the fan and fan shroud assembly, make sure that the locator tabs on the bottom edge of the shroud fit into their respective slots **(see illustration)**.

6   On vehicles with an automatic transmission, disconnect the two transmission cooler lines from the lower rear side of the radiator

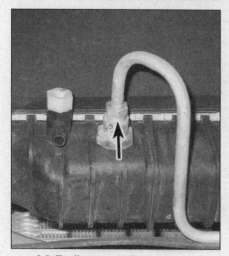

6.6 To disconnect the automatic transmission oil cooler lines from the radiator, unscrew this fitting and the other fitting (not shown) from the bottom of the radiator

6.7 Loosen these two hose clamps (arrows) and disconnect the lower radiator hose (left arrow) and the expansion tank supply hose (right arrow) if so equipped

(see illustration). (Diesel models with an automatic transmission have a separate transmission oil cooler that's located outside the radiator.)

7　　Disconnect the lower hose(s) **(see illustration)** from the radiator.

8　　Remove the plastic pin-type retainers **(see illustration)** and remove the radiator cover. On 6.0L diesel engines, remove the three plastic retainers from the cable at the top front of the radiator. Pull the cable aside so that the radiator can be moved forward in the vehicle.

9　　Remove the upper radiator support bolts **(see illustrations)** and remove the upper radiator supports.

10　　Remove the upper insulators from the radiator support brackets **(see illustration)** and inspect them for cracks, tears and deterioration. If the upper insulators are damaged or worn, replace them.

11　　Disconnect the vent hose from the radiator **(see illustration)**.

12　　Remove the radiator.

13　　Remove the lower insulators **(see illustration)** from the lower crossmember and

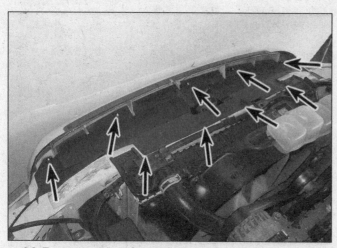

6.8 To remove this plastic radiator cover, remove these nine plastic pin-type retainers (diesel-powered model shown, other models similar)

6.9a To detach the left side of the radiator from the crossmember, remove these two bolts

6.9b To detach the right side of the radiator from the crossmember, remove these three bolts

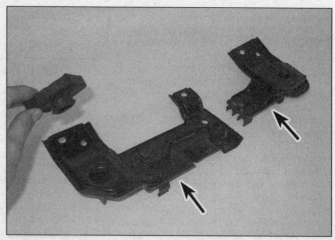

6.10 Inspect the upper right insulator (lower arrow) and the upper left insulator (upper arrow); if the insulators are cracked, torn or deteriorated, replace them

6.11 Loosen this hose clamp and disconnect the vent hose from the radiator

6.13 Be sure to remove each lower insulator and inspect it for cracks, tears and deterioration; if the lower insulators are damaged or worn, replace them

inspect them for cracks, tears and deterioration. If the lower insulators are damaged or worn, replace them.

14 Installation is the reverse of removal. When installing the radiator, make sure that both of the positioning pins on the bottom of the radiator seat correctly in the lower insulators.

15 After installation, fill the system with the proper mixture of antifreeze, and also check the automatic transmission fluid level.

16 Start the engine and allow it to reach normal operating temperature, then check for leaks.

7 Water pump - check

Refer to illustration 7.2

1 Water pump failure can cause overheating and serious damage to the engine. There are three ways to check the operation of the water pump while it's installed on the engine. If any one of the following quick checks indicates water pump problems, it should be replaced immediately.

2 A seal protects the water pump impeller shaft bearing from contamination by engine coolant. If this seal fails, a weep hole in the water pump snout will leak coolant. Use an inspection mirror to look at the hole **(see illustration)**, which is located on the underside of the pump. If the weep hole is leaking, the water pump impeller shaft bearing will soon fail. Replace the water pump immediately. **Note:** *A small amount of gray discoloration is normal. A wet area or heavy brown deposits indicate pump seal failure.*

3 Besides contamination by coolant after a seal failure, the water pump impeller shaft bearing can also prematurely wear out. If the pump is emitting a screeching sound, the shaft bearing has failed. Replace the water pump immediately. **Note:** *Do not confuse drivebelt noise with bearing noise. Loose or glazed drivebelts may also emit a high-pitched squealing noise.*

4 To diagnose excessive bearing wear before the bearing actually fails, grasp the water pump pulley (with the drivebelt removed) and try to force it up-and-down or from side-to-side. If the pulley can be moved up-and-down or side-to-side, the bearing is nearing the end of its service life. Replace the water pump.

8 Water pump - removal and installation

All engines

Refer to illustration 8.4

Warning: *Wait until the engine is completely cold before beginning this procedure.*

1 Disconnect the cable(s) from the negative battery terminal(s).

2 With the engine cold, drain the cooling system (see Chapter 1).

3 Remove the fan and the fan shroud (see Section 5). On 6.0L and 6.4L diesel engines, remove the fan stator (refer to Section 5).

4 If the water pump pulley bolts aren't too tight, you might be able to loosen them now, using the drivebelt to the hold the pulley **(see illustration)**. If that doesn't work, you'll have to hold the pulley with a chain wrench or a strap wrench after you remove the drivebelt.

5 Remove the drivebelt (see Chapter 1).

6 Remove the pulley bolts and remove the pulley. If you were unable to loosen the water pump pulley bolts with the drivebelt installed, use a chain wrench or a strap wrench to hold the pulley as you loosen the bolts.

7.2 Check for leakage at the water pump drain hole

8.4 While the drivebelt is still in place, try to loosen the four water pump pulley bolts

Gasoline engines and 6.0L diesel engine

Refer to illustrations 8.7, 8.9 and 8.10

7   Remove the water pump retaining bolts **(see illustration)** and remove the water pump. Take note of the installed positions of the various length bolts and studs. **Note:** *If the water pump sticks, dislodge it with a soft-face hammer or a hammer and a block of wood.*

8   Before installation, remove and clean all gasket or sealant material from the water pump and cylinder block.

9   Inspect the O-ring and sealing surface of water pump housing in the block for dirt and/or debris **(see illustration)**. Clean them thoroughly before reassembly.

10   Lubricate a new O-ring seal with clean antifreeze and install it to the water pump **(see illustration)**.

7.3L diesel engines

Refer to illustrations 8.12 and 8.14

11   Remove the thermostat (see Section 3).

12   Disconnect the heater hose from the water pump **(see illustration)**.

13   If the water pump is equipped with an Engine Coolant Temperature (ECT) sensor, disconnect the electrical connector **(see illustration 8.12)** and remove the ECT sensor (see Chapter 6).

14   Remove the two bolts that attach the coolant outlet tube flange to the water pump **(see illustration)** and disconnect the coolant outlet tube from the water pump.

15   Remove the bolt that attaches the harness for the Camshaft Position (CMP) sensor **(see illustration 8.12)**, detach the pin-type retainer and push the harness aside so it's clear of the water pump.

16   Remove the water pump pulley bolts and remove the pulley.

17   Before installation, clean off the gasket mating surfaces.

18   Install a new gasket.

All engines

19   Install the water pump and tighten the bolts to the torque listed in this Chapter's Specifications.

20   The remainder of installation is the

8.7 To remove the water pump, remove these bolts (gasoline engines)

reverse of removal.

21   Fill the cooling system with the correct coolant mixture (see Chapter 1).

22   Start the engine and make sure there are no leaks. Check the level frequently during the first few weeks of operation to ensure there are no leaks and that the coolant level is stable.

9   Coolant temperature sending unit - check and replacement

Check

Refer to illustrations 9.2 and 9.3

1   The coolant temperature indicator system consists of a temperature gauge mounted in the dash and a coolant temperature sending unit mounted on the engine.

2   On gasoline engines, the engine coolant temperature sending unit for the temperature gauge is located on the front of the intake manifold **(see illustration)**. On these models, another unit, known as a Cylinder Head Temperature (CHT) sensor, is used to monitor engine temperature for the Powertrain Control Module (PCM) (see Chapter 6 for information on the CHT sensor).

3   Diesel engines have an Engine Cool-

8.9 Inspect the sealing surface in the pump cavity for dirt or signs of pitting (gasoline engines)

8.10 Install a new O-ring seal on the water pump (gasoline engines)

ant Temperature (ECT) sensor **(see illustration)** that also serves as the sensor for the Powertrain Control Module (PCM) and as the temperature sending unit for the temperature gauge. On 6.4L diesel engines, the ECT sensor is located on the front cover just above the water pump.

4   If an overheating indication occurs, check

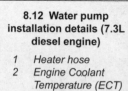

8.12 Water pump installation details (7.3L diesel engine)

1   *Heater hose*
2   *Engine Coolant Temperature (ECT) sensor electrical connector*
3   *Camshaft Position (CMP) sensor harness retainer (pull off to detach)*
4   *Water pump bolts (two lower middle bolts not visible in this photo)*

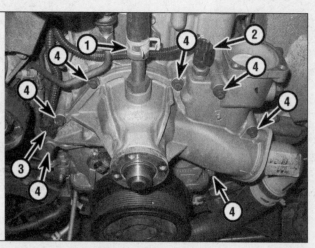

8.14 To detach the coolant outlet tube from the water pump housing, remove these two bolts

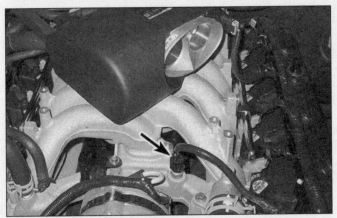

9.2 On gasoline engines, the coolant temperature sending unit is located on the front of the intake manifold (V10 shown, V8 similar)

9.3 On 7.3L diesel engines, the Engine Coolant Temperature (ECT) sensor/coolant temperature sending unit is located on the front cover, next to the thermostat

the coolant level in the system. Make sure that the wiring between the gauge and the sending unit is secure and all fuses are intact.

5   To test the coolant temperature circuit, verify that the temperature gauge reads in the COLD range when the engine is cold, then proceed as follows.

6   On gasoline engines, disconnect the electrical connector from the sender and attach a jumper wire between the two pins of the connector. With the key ON, the gauge needle should swing to full HOT. If it doesn't, the problem is in the circuit between the sending unit and the temperature gauge. If the gauge does swing to full HOT when the connector is jumped, but doesn't do so when the connector is plugged in and the engine is hot, then the coolant temperature sending unit is defective.

7   On diesel engines, DO NOT try to test the ECT sensor as described in the previous step. Checking this sensor is beyond the scope of the home mechanic. If you're having problems with the temperature gauge on a diesel model, have the ECT sensor and circuit checked by a dealer service department. You can, however, replace the ECT sensor yourself (see Chapter 6).

Replacement

Warning: *Wait until the engine is completely cool before beginning this procedure.*

8   Prepare the new coolant temperature sending unit by wrapping its threads with Teflon tape or applying thread sealant to the threads.

9   Remove the pressure cap from the expansion tank to release any pressure that may remain in the system, then reinstall the cap.

10   Disconnect the electrical connector from the coolant temperature sending unit.

11   Unscrew the sending unit from the engine. Install the replacement as quickly as possible to minimize coolant loss. There will be some coolant loss as the unit is removed, so be prepared to catch it. **Caution:** *The sending unit is made of metal and plastic and*

10.1 The blower motor resistor is located in the engine compartment firewall, next to the blower motor

is fragile. Use care not to crack the unit when removing it.

12   Check the coolant level after the replacement unit has been installed (see Chapter 1).

---

10   Air conditioning and heater blower motor and resistor - replacement

Blower motor resistor

2007 and earlier models

Refer to illustration 10.1

1   In the engine compartment, locate the resistor near the blower motor **(see illustration)**.

2   Disconnect the cable(s) from the negative battery terminal(s).

3   Disconnect the resistor electrical connector.

2008 and later models

4   Lower the glove compartment door completely for access to the air conditioning and heating housing (air box).

5   Disconnect and remove the two electrical connectors that are mounted on the upper

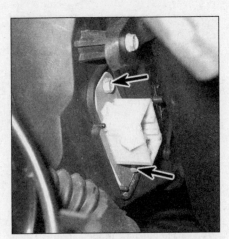

10.8 To replace the blower motor resistor, remove these two bolts

and lower right side of the housing then move them aside.

6   Locate the blower motor resistor (or speed control) and electrical connector by following the middle seam of the housing (where the two halves of the housing come together) towards the right side of the housing. Disconnect the electrical connector. **Note:** *Removal can be difficult because access is limited on the right side of the housing.*

7   The blower motor resistor mounting bolts are located on each side of the resistor **(see illustration 10.8)**.

All model years

Refer to illllustration 10.8

8   Remove the resistor mounting bolts **(see illustration)** and remove the resistor.

9   Installation is the reverse of removal.

Blower motor

2007 and earlier models

Refer to illustrations 10.11a, 10.11b, 10.11c, 10.17a, 10.17b, 10.18, 10.20, 10.21a and 10.21b

10   Disconnect the cable(s) from the negative battery terminal(s).

10.11a On 7.3L diesel models, remove the vacuum pump: unplug the electrical connector from the vacuum pump . . .

10.11b . . . disconnect the vacuum line from the pump . . .

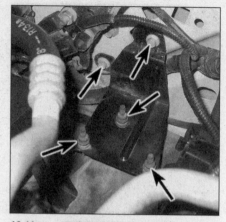

10.11c . . . pull the pump assembly straight up to disengage it from these three rubber insulators (three lower arrows), then remove the pump mounting bracket bolts (two upper arrows) and remove the bracket

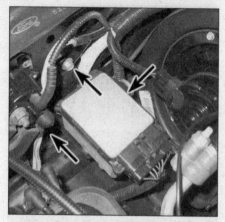
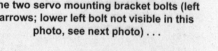

10.17a On gasoline models, remove the cruise control servo (right arrow): remove the two servo mounting bracket bolts (left arrows; lower left bolt not visible in this photo, see next photo) . . .

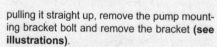

10.17b . . . then remove the servo and bracket as a single assembly (arrow indicates lower left bracket bolt hole that's not visible in previous photo)

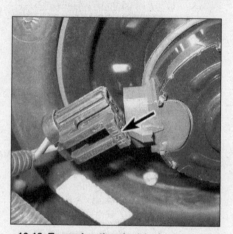

10.18 To unplug the electrical connector from the blower motor, release the locking tang on the side of the connector. When reattaching the connector, make sure that the end of the tang, labeled PUSH, snaps down firmly; if it doesn't, the connector is not fully plugged in

10.19 Remove the blower motor cooling tube by simply pulling it off

11   On diesel models, the vacuum pump is right in front of the blower motor assembly. Disconnect the electrical connector and the vacuum line from the vacuum pump, remove the pump from the three rubber insulators by

pulling it straight up, remove the pump mounting bracket bolt and remove the bracket **(see illustrations)**.

2008 and later models
12   Remove the fasteners for the lower insulator panel, located below the glove compartment, then remove the panel. **Note:** *The carpet will need to be moved away from the panel for removal.*
13   Remove the kick-panel trim on the lower right side and underneath the instrument panel.
14   Remove the vent tube that's attached to the blower motor by removing all retaining clips.
15   Disconnect the electrical connector from the blower motor.
16   Rotate the blower motor counterclockwise (when looking from the bottom) from the air conditioning and heating housing to remove it. **Note:** *There are no mounting bolts to remove.*
17   On gasoline models, remove the cruise control servo mounting bracket bolts. Remove the servo and bracket assembly **(see illustra-**

tions) and set it aside (it's not necessary to unplug the electrical connector from the servo).
18   Disconnect the electrical connector from the blower motor **(see illustration)**.
19   Remove the blower motor cooling tube **(see illustration)**.
20   Remove the blower motor mounting screws **(see illustration)** and remove the blower motor.

All model years
21   To separate the blower fan from the motor, remove any corrosion from the end of the shaft. Grasp the retaining washer with pliers and pull it off or pry it off with a small screwdriver, being careful not to crack it or the fan **(see illustrations)**. To reinstall the retaining washer, simply push it on to the shaft, but make sure that it's still snug. If the retainer washer is loose, replace it.
22   Installation is the reverse of removal.

10.20 To separate the blower motor assembly from the blower motor housing, remove these three screws

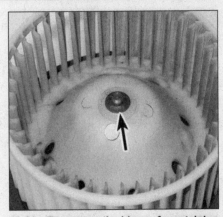

10.21a To remove the blower fan retaining washer, pinch it together with a pair of pliers and pull it straight off the shaft . . .

10.21b . . . then remove the blower fan from the blower motor shaft; you can reuse the retaining washer as long as it's still snug when pushed back onto the motor shaft

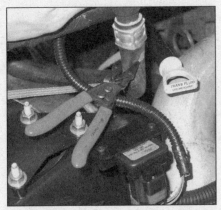

11.2a Clamp off the heater hoses to prevent them from leaking coolant

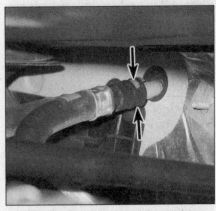

11.2b To disconnect each heater hose from its heater core pipe, squeeze the retainer locking tabs together with a pair of pliers . . .

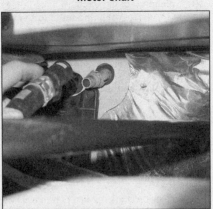

11.2c . . . then pull on the hose, twisting it back and forth at the same time, until it comes off the heater core pipe

11 Heater core - removal and installation

Note: *On 2008 and later models, the heater and evaporator cores are mounted in a large housing under the instrument panel. The instrument panel must be removed for access to the housing, and this is a difficult procedure for the home mechanic, involving many hard-to find/reach fasteners and electrical connectors. It is recommended that heater core replacement for these models be performed at a dealership.*

Removal

Refer to illustrations 11.2a, 11.2b, 11.2c, 11.2d, 11.3, 11.4a, 11.4b, 11.5, 11.6a and 11.6b

1   Drain the cooling system (see Chapter 1).

2   Disconnect the heater hoses from the heater core pipes at the firewall. Clamp off the hoses to prevent coolant from leaking out **(see illustration)**. To disconnect each hose, push it toward the heater core pipe to fully expose the locking tabs, compress the retainer locking tabs, and then, using a slight twisting motion while simultaneously pulling on the heater hose, pull

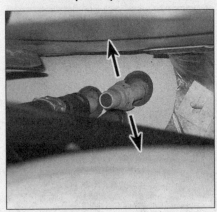

11.2d The old retainers must be discarded; to remove a retainer, spread the locking tabs apart and pull the retainer off the heater core pipe

the hose off the heater core pipe **(see illustrations)**. After disconnecting both hoses, remove and discard the coupling retainers. To remove a coupling retainer from the heater core pipe, spread the retainer tabs apart and then slide the retainer off the pipe **(see illustration)**. Always

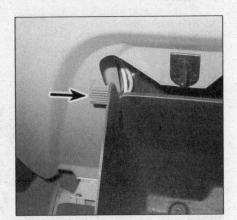

11.3 To release the glove compartment door, push in the stops at the left and right sides, then pull out the door (left stop shown, right stop at same location on right side)

use new retainers when reconnecting the hoses to the heater core pipes.

3   Push in the stops at the left and right sides of the glove compartment door, then lower the door **(see illustration)**.

11.4a To remove the panel/floor vacuum control motor, disconnect the vacuum lines (left arrow), remove the motor retaining bolts (other two arrows) . . .

11.4b . . . swing the motor assembly down and disengage the actuator rod

4   Remove the panel/floor door vacuum control motor (**see illustrations**).
5   Remove the electronic blend door actuator mounting screw (**see illustration**).
6   Remove the heater core cover screws (**see illustrations**), raise the heater core cover, then remove it.
7   Remove the heater core from the heater core housing.

Installation

8   Installation is the reverse of removal noting for the following:

a) *Before installing the heater core cover, add a gasket between the housing and the cover.)*
b) *Fill the cooling system with the correct type and amount of coolant (see Chapter 1).*
c) *Start the engine and check for leaks.*

12   Air conditioning and heater control assembly - removal and installation

Refer to illustrations 12.3 and 12.4
Warning: *The vehicles covered by this manual are equipped with Supplemental Restraint Systems (SRS), more commonly known as airbags. Always disable the airbag system before working in the vicinity of any airbag system components to avoid the possibility of accidental deployment of the airbag, which could cause personal injury (see Chapter 12).*
1   Disconnect the cable(s) from the negative battery terminal(s).
2   Remove the instrument cluster trim panel or center trim panel (see Chapter 12).
3   Remove the heater and air conditioning control assembly retaining screws (**see illustration**).
4   Pull the control assembly out far enough to disconnect the electrical connectors and the

vacuum harness connector (**see illustration**).
5   Remove the control assembly.
6   Installation is the reverse of removal.
7   Verify that all controls operate correctly.

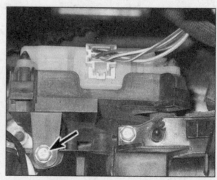

11.5 To detach the electronic blend door actuator, remove this retaining screw and then position the blend door actuator assembly out of the way

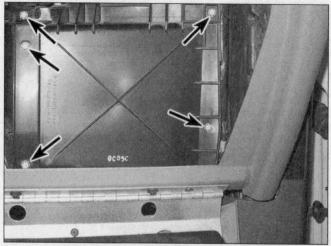

11.6a To remove the heater core cover, remove these screws . . .

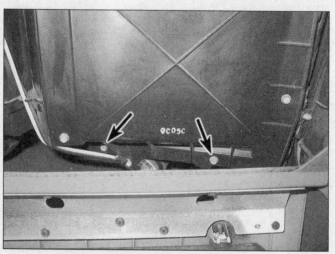

11.6b . . . and these two lower screws, then slide the cover up and remove it

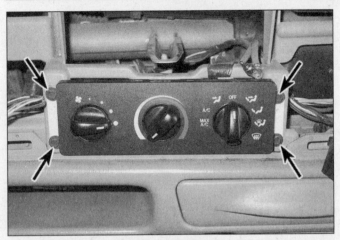

12.3 To detach the heater and air conditioning control assembly, remove these four screws

12.4 Pull out the heater and air conditioning control assembly far enough to disconnect the four electrical connectors and the vacuum harness connector

13 Air conditioning and heating system - check and maintenance

Refer to illustration 13.1

Warning: *The air conditioning system is under high pressure. Do not loosen any hose fittings or remove any components until after the system has been discharged by a dealer service department or service station. Always wear eye protection when disconnecting air conditioning system fittings.*

1   The following maintenance checks should be performed on a regular basis to ensure the air conditioner continues to operate at peak efficiency.

a) *Check the compressor drivebelt. If it's worn or deteriorated, replace it (see Chapter 1).*
b) *Check the drivebelt tension and, if necessary, adjust it (see Chapter 1).*
c) *Check the system hoses. Look for cracks, bubbles, hard spots and deterioration. Inspect the hoses and all fittings for oil bubbles and seepage. If there's any evidence of wear, damage or leaks, replace the hose(s).*

d) *Inspect the condenser fins for leaves, bugs and other debris. Use a "fin comb" or compressed air to clean the condenser.*
e) *Make sure the system has the correct refrigerant charge.*
f) *Check the evaporator housing drain tube (see illustration) for blockage.*

2   It's a good idea to operate the system for about 10 minutes at least once a month, particularly during the winter. Long term non-use can cause hardening, and subsequent failure, of the seals.

3   Because of the complexity of the air conditioning system and the special equipment necessary to service it, in-depth troubleshooting and repairs are not included in this manual (refer to the *Haynes Automotive Heating and Air Conditioning Repair Manual*). However, simple checks and component replacement procedures are provided in this Chapter.

4   The most common cause of poor cooling is simply a low system refrigerant charge. If a noticeable drop in cool air output occurs, the following quick check will help you determine if the refrigerant level is low.

Checking the refrigerant charge

Refer to illustration 13.8

5   Warm the engine up to normal operating temperature.

6   Place the air conditioning temperature selector at the coldest setting and the blower at the highest setting. Open the doors (to make sure the air conditioning system doesn't cycle off as soon as it cools the passenger compartment).

7   With the compressor engaged - the clutch will make an audible click and the center of the clutch will rotate. If the compressor discharge line feels warm and the compressor inlet pipe feels cool, the system is properly charged.

8   Place a thermometer in the dashboard vent nearest the evaporator **(see illustration)** and then operate the system until the indicated temperature is around 40 to 45 degrees F. If the ambient (outside) air temperature is very high, say 110 degrees F, the duct air temperature may be as high as 60 degrees F, but generally the air conditioning is 30 to 40 degrees F cooler than the ambient air.

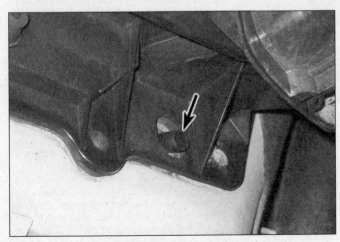

13.1 Evaporator drain tube (arrow)

13.8 To measure the output temperature of the air conditioning system, insert an accurate thermometer in the center vent

13.9 A basic charging kit for R-134a systems is available at most auto parts stores - it must say R-134a (not R-12) and so must the can of refrigerant

13.12 Always add refrigerant to the *low* side of the air conditioning system

Note: *Humidity of the ambient air also affects the cooling capacity of the system. Higher ambient humidity lowers the effectiveness of the air conditioning system.*

Adding refrigerant

Refer to illustrations 13.9 and 13.12

9   Buy an automotive charging kit **(see illustration)** at an auto parts store. A charging kit includes a 14-ounce can of refrigerant, a tap valve and a short section of hose that can be attached between the tap valve and the system low side service valve. Because one can of refrigerant may not be sufficient to bring the system charge up to the proper level, it's a good idea to buy an additional can. Make sure that one of the cans contains red refrigerant dye. If the system is leaking, the red dye will leak out with the refrigerant and help you pinpoint the location of the leak.

Caution: *There are two types of refrigerant used in automotive systems; R-12 - which has been widely used on earlier models - and the more environmentally-friendly R-134a used in all models covered by this manual. These two refrigerants (and their appropriate refrigerant oils) are not compatible and must never be mixed or components will be damaged. Use only R-134a refrigerant in the models covered by this manual.*

10   Hook up the charging kit by following the manufacturer's instructions. **Warning:** *DO NOT hook the charging kit hose to the system high side! The fittings on the charging kit are designed to fit **only** on the low side of the system.*

11   Back off the valve handle on the charging kit and screw the kit onto the refrigerant can, making sure first that the O-ring or rubber seal inside the threaded portion of the kit is in place. **Warning:** *Wear protective eyewear when dealing with pressurized refrigerant cans.*

12   Remove the dust cap from the low-side charging connection and attach the quick-connect fitting on the kit hose **(see illustration)**.

13   Warm up the engine and turn on the air con-

ditioner. Keep the charging kit hose away from the fan and other moving parts. **Note:** *The charging process requires the compressor to be running. Your compressor may cycle off if the pressure is low due to a low charge. If the clutch cycles off, you can pull the low-pressure cycling switch plug and attach a jumper wire. This will keep the compressor ON.*

14   Turn the valve handle on the kit until the stem pierces the can, then back the handle out to release the refrigerant. You should be able to hear the rush of gas. Add refrigerant to the low side of the system until both the receiver-drier surface and the evaporator inlet pipe feel about the same temperature. Allow stabilization time between each addition.

15   If you have an accurate thermometer, place it in the center air conditioning vent **(see illustration 13.8)** and then note the temperature of the air coming out of the vent. A fully-charged system which is working correctly should cool down to about 40 degrees F. Generally, an air conditioning system will put out air that is 30 to 40 degrees F cooler than the ambient air. For example, if the ambient (outside) air temperature is very high (over 100 degrees F), the temperature of air coming out of the registers should be 60 to 70 degrees F.

16   When the can is empty, turn the valve handle to the closed position and release the connection from the low-side port. Replace the dust cap. **Warning:** *Never add more than two cans of refrigerant to the system.*

17   Remove the charging kit from the can and store the kit for future use with the piercing valve in the UP position, to prevent inadvertently piercing the can on the next use.

Heating systems

18   If the carpet under the heater core is damp, or if antifreeze vapor or steam is coming through the vents, the heater core is leaking. Remove it (see Section 11) and install a new unit (most radiator shops will not repair a leaking heater core).

19   If the air coming out of the heater vents isn't hot, the problem could stem from any of the following causes:

a)   *The thermostat is stuck open, preventing the engine coolant from warming up enough to carry heat to the heater core. Replace the thermostat (see Section 3).*

b)   *There is a blockage in the system, preventing the flow of coolant through the heater core. Feel both heater hoses at the firewall. They should be hot. If one of them is cold, there is an obstruction in one of the hoses or in the heater core, or the heater control valve is shut. Detach the hoses and back flush the heater core with a water hose. If the heater core is clear but circulation is impeded, remove the two hoses and flush them out with a water hose.*

c)   *If flushing fails to remove the blockage from the heater core, the core must be replaced (see Section 11).*

Eliminating air conditioning odors

Refer to illustration 13.23

20   Unpleasant odors that often develop in air conditioning systems are caused by the growth of a fungus, usually on the surface of the evaporator core. The warm, humid environment there is a perfect breeding ground for mildew to develop.

21   The evaporator core on most vehicles is difficult to access, and factory dealerships have a lengthy, expensive process for eliminating the fungus by opening up the evaporator case and using a powerful disinfectant and rinse on the core until the fungus is gone. You can service your own system at home, but it takes something much stronger than basic household germ-killers or deodorizers.

22   Aerosol disinfectants for automotive air conditioning systems are available in most auto parts stores, but remember when shopping for them that the most effective treatments are also the most expensive. The basic procedure for using these sprays is to start by running the system in the RECIRC mode for ten minutes with the blower on its highest speed. Use the highest heat mode to dry out

13.23 To disinfect the evaporator housing, insert the nozzle of the disinfectant can through the insulating foam surrounding the outlet pipe of the evaporator

14.2 To disconnect the evaporator discharge line, put a wrench on the fixed nut (left arrow) and loosen and unscrew the other nut (right arrow) with another wrench

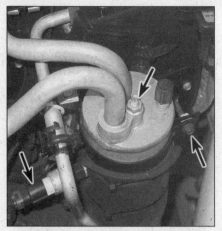

14.4 Remove this nut (upper arrow) and disconnect the manifold and tube assembly, unplug the electrical connector (left arrow) from the pressure cycling switch, loosen the accumulator mounting bracket bolt (right arrow) and then remove the accumulator

the system and keep the compressor from engaging by disconnecting the wiring connector at the compressor (see Section 15).

23   Make sure that the disinfectant can comes with a long spray hose. Work the nozzle through the insulating foam surrounding the evaporator outlet pipe so that it protrudes inside the evaporator housing **(see illustration)**, and then spray according to the manufacturer's recommendations. Try to cover the whole surface of the evaporator core, by aiming the spray up, down and sideways. Follow the manufacturer's recommendations for the length of spray and waiting time between applications.

24   Once the evaporator has been cleaned, the best way to prevent the mildew from coming back again is to make sure your evaporator housing drain tube is clear **(see illustration 13.1)**.

14   Air conditioning accumulator - removal and installation

Refer to illustration 14.2 and 14.4
Warning: *The air conditioning system is under high pressure. DO NOT loosen any fittings or remove any components until after the system has been discharged. Air conditioning refrigerant should be properly discharged into an EPA-approved container at a dealer service department or an automotive air conditioning repair facility. Always wear eye protection when disconnecting air conditioning system fittings.*

1   Have the air conditioning system discharged (see **Warning** above).
2   Disconnect the evaporator discharge line **(see illustration)**. Use a back-up wrench to prevent the line from twisting. Cap the line to prevent contamination. Remove and discard the old O-ring.
3   On vehicles equipped with an auxiliary air conditioning system, disconnect the auxiliary evaporator line. Remove and discard the

old O-ring.
4   Disconnect the manifold and tube assembly **(see illustration)**. Cap the line to prevent contamination. Remove and discard the old O-ring.
5   Disconnect the air conditioning pressure cycling switch electrical connector **(see illustration 14.4)**.
6   Remove the accumulator mounting bracket bolt **(see illustration 14.4)** and then remove the accumulator.
7   Replace all old O-rings. Before installing the new O-rings, coat them with refrigerant oil.
8   Installation is otherwise the reverse of removal.
9   Take the vehicle to the shop that discharged it and have the system evacuated and recharged.

15   Air conditioning compressor - removal and installation

Removal
Warning: *The air conditioning system is under high pressure. DO NOT loosen any fittings or remove any components until after the system*

has been discharged. Air conditioning refrigerant should be properly discharged into an EPA-approved container at a dealer service department or an automotive air conditioning repair facility. Always wear eye protection when disconnecting air conditioning system fittings.*
Note: *If you are replacing the compressor due to compressor failure, you must also replace the accumulator (see Section 14) and the evaporator orifice tube (see Step 16).*
1   Have the air conditioning system discharged (see **Warning** above).
2   Remove the drivebelt (see Chapter 1).

Gasoline models
Refer to illustration 15.4, 15.5, 15.6, 15.7 and 15.8
3   Raise the vehicle and secure it on jackstands. Remove the right front wheel. On 2008 and later models, release the clips at the bottom of the lower fan shroud and push the lower shroud upward as far as it goes.
4   Remove the right front fender splash shield **(see illustration)** if necessary for access.

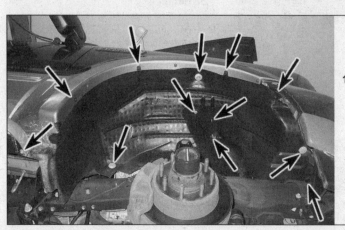

15.4 To detach the right front fender splash shield, remove these fasteners

15.5 To disconnect the inlet and outlet lines from the compressor, remove this manifold bolt; be sure to replace the manifold O-rings before reattaching it (gasoline models)

15.6 Unplug the electrical connector from the Crankshaft Position (CKP) sensor and then set it aside (gasoline models)

15.7 Unplug the electrical connector from the compressor clutch field coil (gasoline models)

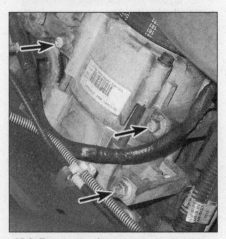

15.8 To remove the compressor, remove these three bolts (gasoline models)

15.9 Unplug the electrical connector from the compressor clutch field coil (diesel models)

15.10 To disconnect the inlet and outlet lines from the compressor, remove this manifold bolt; be sure to replace the manifold O-rings before reattaching it (diesel models)

15.11 To remove the compressor, remove these four bolts (diesel models)

5   Disconnect the compressor inlet and outlet lines from the compressor (see illustration). On models with automatic transmission, disconnect and set aside the transmission fluid cooler lines.
6   Disconnect the electrical connector from the Crankshaft Position (CKP) sensor and set

it aside (see illustration).
7   Disconnect the electrical connector from the compressor clutch field coil (see illustration).
8   Remove the compressor mounting bolts (see illustration) and remove the compressor.

Diesel models

7.3L engines

Refer to illustrations 15.9, 15.10 and 15.11
9   Disconnect the electrical connector from the compressor clutch field coil (see illustration).
10   Disconnect the compressor inlet and outlet lines from the compressor (see illustration). Remove and discard the old O-rings.
11   Remove the compressor mounting bolts (see illustration) and remove the compressor.

6.0L and 6.4L engines

12   Remove the transmission cooler (not necessary on 6.4L engines).
13   Raise the vehicle and support it securely on jackstands.
14   Remove the right fender inner splash shield.

15   Disconnect the refrigerant manifold from the compressor.
16   Disconnect the wiring at the compressor.
17   Remove the compressor mounting bolts and remove the compressor.

Installation

Refer to illustration 15.22
18   If a new compressor is being installed, follow the directions with the compressor regarding the draining of excess oil prior to installation.
19   The clutch may have to be transferred from the original to the new compressor.
20   Before reconnecting the inlet and outlet lines to the compressor, replace all manifold O-rings and lubricate them with refrigerant oil.
21   Installation is otherwise the reverse of removal.
22   Replace the orifice tube. The orifice is a plastic tube with a filter inside. It is located in the evaporator inlet line (see illustration). Recessed inside the refrigerant pipe slightly, it is difficult to remove without a small tool that is

15.22 When the air conditioning compressor is replaced, the orifice tube must be replaced, too

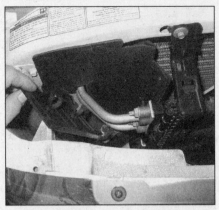

16.3a Remove this plastic shield to access the refrigerant line fittings at the condenser

16.3b To disconnect the refrigerant inlet and outlet lines from the condenser, remove these nuts

inserted and tightened until it grabs the orifice tube so that it can be pulled out. **Note:** *While it is sometimes possible to remove an orifice tube with a pair of pliers, this practice is not recommended since it can result in a broken orifice tube stuck inside the pipe. The same tool, available at auto parts stores, can be used to insert a new orifice tube. Make sure the tube is inserted in the same direction as the old one. If the orifice tube breaks, another tool is available that will extract the portion of the tube stuck inside the evaporator pipe.*

23   Have the system evacuated, recharged and leak tested by the shop that discharged it.

16 Air conditioning condenser - removal and installation

Refer to illustration 16.3a, 16.3b, 16.5a and 16.5b

Warning: *The air conditioning system is under high pressure. DO NOT loosen any fittings or remove any components until after the system has been discharged. Air conditioning refrigerant should be properly discharged into an EPA-approved container at a dealer service department or an automotive air conditioning repair facility. Always wear eye protection when dis-*

connecting air conditioning system fittings.

1   Have the air conditioning system discharged (see **Warning** above).

2   Remove the radiator cover **(see illustration 6.8)**. On diesel models, disconnect and set aside the horn (see Chapter 12).

3   Disconnect the refrigerant inlet and outlet lines from the condenser **(see illustrations)**. Remove and discard the old O-rings.

4   Remove the hood latch from the crossmember (see Chapter 11). On later models, disconnect the hood release cable from the power steering fluid cooler, then unbolt and set aside the power steering fluid cooler.

5   Remove the left and right condenser mounting bracket bolts **(see illustrations)**.

6   Remove the condenser. If you're going to reinstall the same condenser, store it with the line fittings facing up to prevent oil from draining out.

7   If you're going to install a new condenser, pour one ounce of refrigerant oil of the correct type into it prior to installation.

8   Before reconnecting the refrigerant lines to the condenser, be sure to coat a pair of new O-rings with refrigerant oil, install them in the refrigerant line fittings and then tighten the condenser inlet and outlet nuts to the torque listed in this Chapter's Specifications.

9   Installation is otherwise the reverse of removal.

10   Have the system evacuated, recharged and leak tested by the shop that discharged it.

17 Air conditioning evaporator - removal and installation

Warning: *The air conditioning system is under high pressure. DO NOT loosen any fittings or remove any components until after the system has been discharged. Air conditioning refrigerant should be properly discharged into an EPA-approved container at a dealer service department or an automotive air conditioning repair facility. Always wear eye protection when disconnecting air conditioning system fittings.*

Removal

Refer to illustrations 17.3, 17.4, 17.5a, 17.5b, 17.5c, 17.5d, 17.5e, 17.5f, 17.5g, 17.5h, 17.6, 17.8 and 17.9

1   Have the air conditioning system discharged (see **Warning** above).

2   Remove the accumulator (see Section 14).

3   On diesel models, remove the nuts that secure the Manifold Absolute Pressure (MAP) sensor bracket **(see illustration)** and set the MAP sensor and bracket aside.

16.5a To detach the left condenser mounting bracket from the crossmember, remove this bolt

16.5b To detach the right condenser mounting bracket from the crossmember, remove this bolt

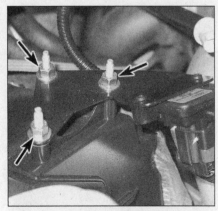

17.3 To detach the Manifold Absolute Pressure (MAP) sensor bracket on diesel models, remove these three nuts

17.4 To detach the vapor management
valve bracket on gasoline models,
remove these three nuts

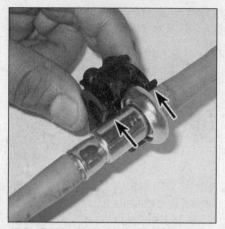

17.5a To remove the air conditioning tube
lock coupling clip, push back the two
locking arms to release the clip . . .

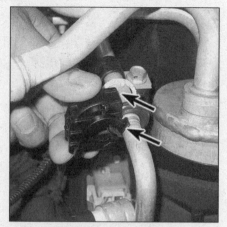

17.5b . . . then pull the clip
off the coupling

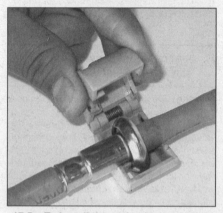

17.5c To install the spring lock coupling
disconnect tool on the spring lock
coupling, open it up and position the
lower half of the tool so that it cradles the
lower half of the coupling as shown . . .

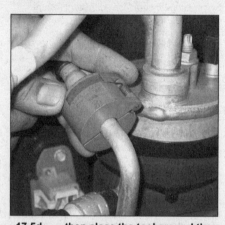

17.5d . . . then close the tool around the
upper half of the coupling like this

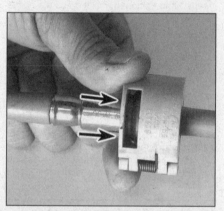

17.5e To disengage the female fitting
from the tube lock coupling spring, push
the tool to the right until you can see the
coupling through the "window" in the tool

4   On gasoline models, remove the nuts
that secure the vapor management valve
bracket **(see illustration)** and set the vapor
management valve and bracket aside.
5   Disconnect the condenser-to-evap-
orator tube from the A/C evaporator tube
as follows:

a) *Remove the tube lock coupling clip* **(see
    illustrations)**.
b) *Install the spring lock coupling discon-
    nect tool over the spring lock coupling*
    (see illustrations).
c) *Push the tool to the right to disengage
    the female fitting from the tube lock cou-
    pling spring* **(see illustration)**.

d) *Pull the spring lock coupling fittings apart*
    (see illustration).
e) *Remove the old O-rings and install new
    ones* **(see illustration)**.
f) *Remove the old tube lock coupling spring
    and install a new one* **(see illustration)**.
6   Remove the accumulator bracket bolts

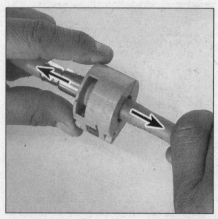

17.5f Pull the spring lock couplings apart

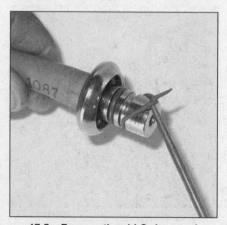

17.5g Remove the old O-rings and
install new ones

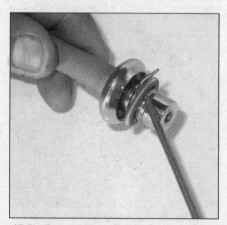

17.5h Remove the old tube lock coupling
spring and install a new one

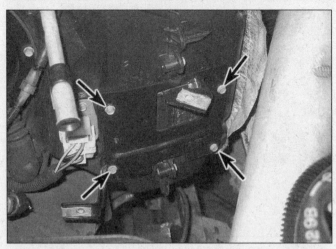

17.6 To detach the accumulator bracket, remove these bolts

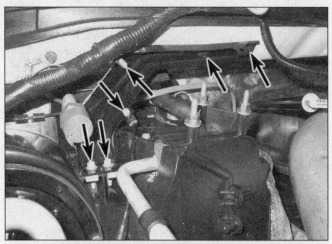

17.8 Detach the two harness clips from the evaporator housing support bracket, remove the bracket retaining bolts and remove the bracket

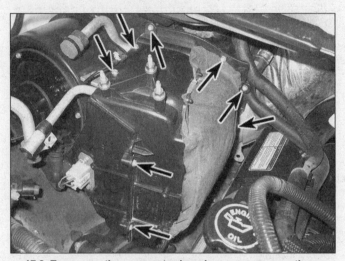

17.9 To remove the evaporator housing cover, remove these screws (two more screws, not visible in this photo, on underside of housing)

18.1 To remove the air conditioning pressure cycling switch, unplug the electrical connector and unscrew the switch from the accumulator

19.1a Remove the retaining screw . . .

(see illustration) and remove the bracket.
7   On diesel models, remove the intercooler duct (see Chapter 4B).
8   Detach the harness clips from the evaporator housing support bracket, remove the

bracket bolts (see illustration) and remove the bracket.
9   Remove the evaporator cover screws (see illustration) and remove the evaporator cover.
10   Remove the evaporator.
11   Installation is the reverse of removal.
12   When you're done, have the system evacuated, recharged and leak tested by the shop that discharged it.

18 Air conditioning pressure cycling switch - replacement

Refer to illustration 18.1
Note: A Schrader valve in the accumulator prevents refrigerant loss during pressure cycling switch replacement.
1   Unplug the electrical connector from the pressure cycling switch (see illustration).
2   Unscrew the pressure cycling switch

from the accumulator.
3   Lubricate the switch O-ring with clean refrigerant oil of the correct type.
4   Screw the new switch onto the accumulator threads until hand tight, then tighten it to the torque listed in this Chapter's Specifications.
5   Reconnect the electrical connector.

19 Auxiliary climate control assembly (Excursion models) - removal and installation

Front climate control assembly

Refer to illustrations 19.1a, 19.1b, 19.1c and 19.2
1   Remove the screw, disengage the clips and then lower the overhead console (see illustrations).

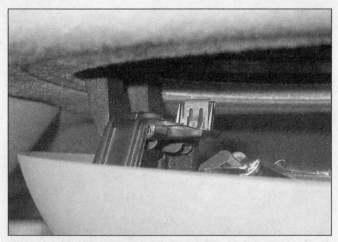

19.1b . . . disengage the clips (other clip not visible in this photo) . . .

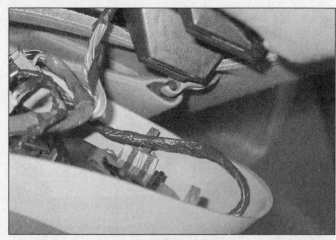

19.1c . . . and pull down the front climate control assembly

2   Disconnect the electrical connectors from the auxiliary climate control assembly **(see illustration)**.
3   Remove the two climate control assem-bly retaining screws **(see illustration 19.2)** and remove the auxiliary climate control assembly.
4   Installation is the reverse of removal.

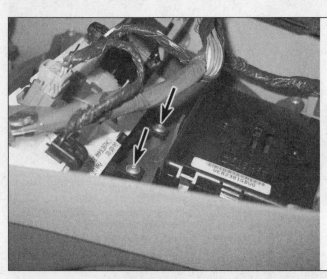

19.2 Disconnect the electrical connectors from the front climate control assembly, remove the control assembly retaining screws, then remove the control assembly

Rear climate control assembly

Refer to illustrations 19.5a, 19.5b and 19.6

5   Pull down on the front of the climate con-trol assembly to pop loose the two retaining clips, then slide it forward and downward to disengage the two retaining tabs from their engagement slots **(see illustrations)**.
6   Disconnect the electrical connectors from the climate control assembly **(see illus-tration)**.
7   Remove the climate control assembly retaining screws **(see illustration 19.6)** and remove the control assembly.
8   Installation is the reverse of removal.

20   Auxiliary climate control blower motor and resistor (Excursion models) - removal and installation

Blower motor resistor

Refer to illustrations 20.1 and 20.2

1   Remove the access panel from the right

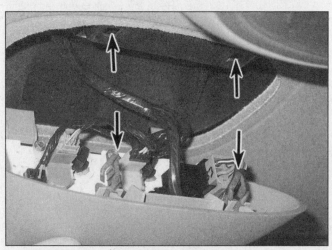

19.5a Pull down on the front edge of the rear climate control assembly housing to disengage the retaining clips (lower arrows) from the holes (upper arrows) in the overhead console . . .

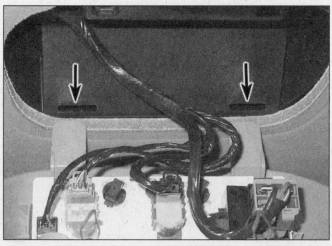

19.5b . . . then slide the assembly forward and down to disengage the two retaining tabs from their engagement slots

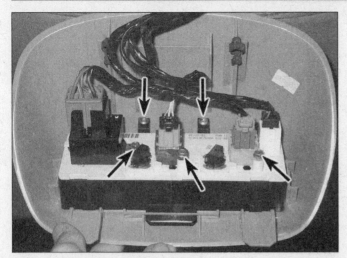

19.6 To remove the rear climate control assembly, disconnect the electrical connectors, remove the two retaining screws (upper arrows), then disengage the assembly retaining tab from its corresponding engagement slot; to replace one of the three individual components, remove the appropriate retaining bolt (lower arrows)

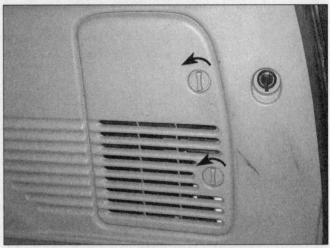

20.1 To remove the auxiliary climate control access panel from the right rear quarter trim panel, rotate these locking knobs one-quarter-turn counterclockwise

rear quarter trim panel (see illustration).

2   Disconnect the electrical connector from the resistor (see illustration).

3   Remove the blower motor resistor mounting bolts (see illustration 20.2) and remove the resistor.

4   Installation is the reverse of removal.

Blower motor

Refer to illustrations 20.6

5   Remove the access panel from the right rear quarter trim panel (see illustration 20.1).

6   Disconnect the electrical connector from the blower motor (see illustration).

7   Remove the blower motor cooling tube (see illustration 20.6).

8   Remove the blower motor retaining screws (see illustration 20.6).

9   Installation is the reverse of removal.

21 Oil cooler - removal and installation

Warning: *Wait until the engine is completely cool before beginning this procedure.*

1   Raise the vehicle and place it securely on jackstands.

2   Drain the engine coolant and the engine oil (see Chapter 1).

Gasoline engines

Refer to illustration 21.3

3   Remove the oil filter (see illustration).

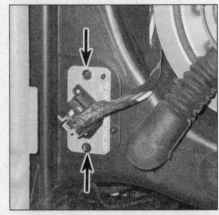

20.2 To replace the blower motor resistor for the auxiliary climate control, unplug the electrical connector and remove the retaining screws

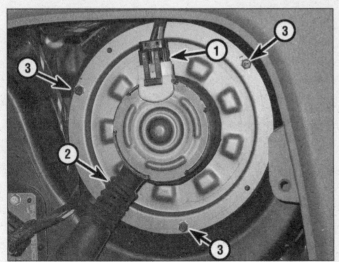

20.6 To remove the blower motor, unplug the electrical connector (1), remove the cooling tube (2) and remove the retaining screws (3)

21.3 To remove the oil cooler, remove the oil filter, loosen the two hose clamps) and disconnect the two coolant hoses, then unscrew the threaded insert (the same one that the oil filter screws onto) (V8 shown, V10 similar)

21.8 To detach the front oil cooler header, remove these two bolts

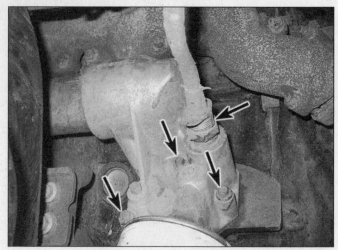

21.9 To detach the rear oil cooler header, disconnect the block heater electrical connector, then remove these three bolts

4   Disconnect the two coolant hoses **(see illustration 21.3)** from the oil cooler.

5   The oil cooler is attached to the engine by the same large threaded insert that the oil filter is screwed onto. Remove the oil cooler insert and remove the oil cooler assembly.

6   Installation is the reverse of removal.

Diesel engine

7.3L engines
Refer to illustrations 21.8 and 21.9

7   Remove the oil filter (see Chapter 1).

8   Remove the front oil cooler header **(see illustration)**.

9   Disconnect the block heater electrical connector and remove the rear oil cooler header **(see illustration)**.

10   Remove the oil cooler and headers as a single assembly.

11   Pull off the headers and remove and discard the old O-rings.

12   Be sure to use new O-rings and tighten all header bolts to the torque listed in this Chapter's Specifications.

13   Installation is otherwise the reverse of removal.

6.0L and 6.4L engines

14   Remove the intake manifold (refer to Chapter 2B).

15   Unbolt and remove the cover from the EGR cooler port.

16   Unbolt and remove the oil filter adapter.

17   Remove the bolts from the oil cooler and lift it off the engine.

18   Remove the oil strainer screen, inspect it for damage and clean it.

19   Installation is the reverse of removal. Always use a new gasket for the oil cooler.

Chapter 4 Part A
Fuel and exhaust systems - gasoline engines

Contents

	Section		Section
Accelerator cable - replacement and adjustment	11	Fuel pump/fuel pressure - check	3
Air filter housing - removal and installation	10	Fuel pressure regulator - removal and installation	8
Air filter replacement	See Chapter 1	Fuel pump/fuel pump module - removal and installation	7
SERVICE ENGINE SOON light	See Chapter 6	Fuel rail and injectors - removal and installation	15
Exhaust system check	See Chapter 1	Fuel system check	See Chapter 1
Exhaust system servicing - general information	17	Fuel tank - cleaning and repair	6
Fuel filter replacement	See Chapter 1	Fuel tank - removal and installation	5
Fuel injection system - general information	12	General information	1
Fuel injection system - check	13	Intake Manifold Tuning system (1999 V8 models) -	
Fuel level sending unit - replacement	9	general information and replacement	16
Fuel lines and fittings - general information	4	Throttle body - check, removal and installation	14
Fuel pressure relief procedure	2	Underhood hose check and replacement	See Chapter 1

Specifications

Fuel system

Fuel system pressure
1999 through 2001 models	30 to 45 psi

2002 through 2004 models
5.4L engines	30 to 55 psi
6.8L engines	30 to 45 psi
2005 through 2007 models	30 to 70 psi
2008 and later models	25 to 45 psi
Fuel system hold pressure (after 5 minutes)	Less than 5 psi loss

Injector resistance (approximate)
1999 through 2001 models	30 to 55 psi

2002 through 2004 models
V8 engines	13.8 to 15.2 ohms
V10 engines	11 to 18 ohms
2005 and later models	Unspecified*

Although unspecified, testing should still be done for comparison purposes and to check for an open or shorted coil.

Torque specifications
Ft-lbs (unless otherwise indicated)

Throttle body mounting fasteners
1999 through 2004 models	80 in-lbs

2005 and later models
Step 1	80 in-lbs
Step 2	Tighten an additional 90 degrees
Fuel rail mounting bolts	71 to 97 in-lbs

1.1 Fuel system components - 6.8L V10 gasoline model

1 Fuel injector	3 Accelerator cable (intake air duct)	5 Air filter housing
2 Fuel pressure test port	4 Fuse/relay box	

1   General information

Refer to illustration 1.1

The fuel system consists of a fuel tank, an electric fuel pump (located in the fuel tank), a fuel pump relay, a fuel pressure regulator (located on the fuel rail), the fuel rail and fuel injectors, an air filter housing and a throttle body unit **(see illustration)**. All models are equipped with an Electronic Fuel Injection (EFI) system.

Sequential Electronic Fuel Injection system - 1999 through 2004 models

The Sequential Electronic Fuel Injection uses timed impulses to inject the fuel directly into the intake port of each cylinder according to its firing order. The injectors are controlled by the Powertrain Control Module (PCM) or On-Board computer. The PCM monitors various engine parameters and delivers the exact amount of fuel required into the intake ports. The throttle body serves only to control the amount of air passing into the system. Because each cylinder is equipped with its own injector, much better control of the fuel/air mixture ratio is possible.

Sequential Multiport Fuel Injection (SFI) system - 2005 and later models

The fuel system consists of the Powertrain Control Module (PCM), the fuel pump relay, the Inertia Fuel Shutoff (IFS) switch, the Fuel Pump Driver Module (FPDM), the fuel tank, the electric in-tank fuel pump/fuel level sensor, the fuel rail pressure sensor, the fuel rail and fuel injectors, the air filter housing and the electronic throttle body. For a more detailed description of the SFI system, refer to Section 10.

Fuel pump and lines - 1999 through 2004 models

Fuel is circulated from the fuel tank to the fuel injection system, and back to the fuel tank, through a pair of metal lines running along the underside of the vehicle. An electric fuel pump and fuel level sending unit are located inside the fuel tank. A vapor return system routes all vapors back to the fuel tank through a separate return line.

The fuel pump relay is equipped with a primary and secondary voltage circuit. The primary circuit is controlled by the PCM and the secondary circuit is linked directly to battery voltage from the ignition switch. With the ignition switch ON (engine not running), the PCM will ground the relay for one second. During cranking, the PCM grounds the fuel pump relay as long as the ignition signal is present (see Chapter 5). If there are no reference pulses from the ignition system, the fuel pump will shut off after two or three seconds.

Fuel pump circuit - 2005 and later models

Fuel pump relay

The fuel pump relay is equipped with a primary and secondary voltage circuit. The primary circuit is controlled by the PCM and the secondary circuit is linked directly to battery voltage from the ignition switch. With the ignition switch ON (engine not running), the PCM will ground the relay for one second. During cranking, the PCM grounds the fuel pump relay as long as the Camshaft Position (CMP) sensor sends its position signal (see Chapter 6). If there are no reference pulses, the fuel pump will shut off after two or three seconds.

Inertia Fuel Shutoff (IFS) switch

The Inertia Fuel Shutoff (IFS) switch disables the fuel pump circuit in the event of a collision. The IFS switch is located behind the right (passenger side) kick panel, ahead of the fuse and relay box. Here's how it works: A cylindrical magnet inside the switch has a steel ball sitting on top of it. Under normal driving conditions, the magnetic attraction between the magnet and the ball holds the ball in position on top of the magnet. When a collision occurs, the steel ball breaks away from the magnet, rolls up a conical ramp and strikes a target plate, which opens the switch electrical contacts and the fuel pump circuit. Once the IFS switch is open, you must manually reset it (see Section 3).

Fuel pump

Fuel is circulated from the fuel tank to the fuel injection system through a metal line running along the underside of the vehicle. An electric fuel pump/fuel level sensor is located inside the fuel tank. The fuel pump/fuel level

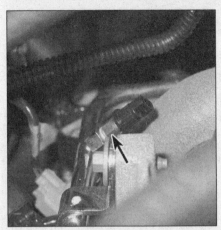

2.3 The fuel pressure test port is located at the right rear of the engine, on the fuel rail (V10 engine shown, V8 engine similar)

2.4 Connect the fuel pressure gauge to the test port and direct the bleed-off fuel into an approved container using the valve

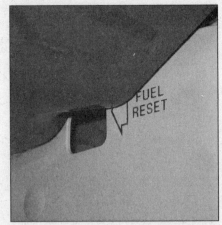

2.7 The inertia switch is located behind the passenger's side kick panel

sensor assembly consists of the pump, the fuel level sensor, an inlet filter (sometimes referred to as a *sock* or *strainer*), a check valve to maintain pressure after the pump is shut off and a pressure relief valve to protect the pump from overpressurization in the event of a blocked fuel line. But what sets this pump apart from conventional in-tank pumps is its variable speed capability. The PCM controls fuel pressure by controlling the speed (rpm) of the pump. The PCM alters the fuel pressure by controlling the duty cycle of the Fuel Pump Driver Module (FPDM), which in turn controls the speed of the fuel pump by modulating the voltage to the fuel pump.

Exhaust system

The exhaust system includes an exhaust manifold, diverter pipes fitted with upstream (before catalytic converter) and downstream (after catalytic converter) oxygen sensors, a catalytic converter and a muffler.

The catalytic converter is an emission control device added to the exhaust system to reduce pollutants. A single-bed converter is used in combination with a three-way (reduction) catalyst. Refer to Chapter 6 for more information regarding the catalytic converter.

2   Fuel pressure relief procedure

Warning: *Gasoline is extremely flammable, so take extra precautions when you work on any part of the fuel system. Don't smoke or allow open flames or bare light bulbs near the work area, and don't work in a garage where a gas-type appliance (such as a water heater or a clothes dryer) is present. Since gasoline is carcinogenic, wear fuel-resistant gloves when there's a possibility of being exposed to fuel, and, if you spill any fuel on your skin, rinse it off immediately with soap and water. Mop up any spills immediately and do not store fuel-soaked rags where they could ignite. The fuel system is under constant pressure, so, if any fuel lines are to be disconnected, the fuel*

pressure in the system must be relieved first. When you perform any kind of work on the fuel system, wear safety glasses and have a Class B type fire extinguisher on hand.
Note: *After the fuel pressure has been relieved, it's a good idea to lay a shop towel over any fuel connection to be disassembled, to absorb the residual fuel that may leak out when servicing the fuel system.*
1   There are two methods for relieving the fuel system pressure; the easiest and most accessible is using a special fuel pressure gauge with a bleed-off valve. This special tool can be purchased at most auto parts stores or from specialty tool dealers. In the event the tool is not available, locate the inertia switch and disable the fuel pump.

Fuel pressure gauge bleeding method

Refer to illustrations 2.3 and 2.4
2   Remove the fuel filler cap - this will relieve any pressure built up in the fuel tank.
3   Locate the fuel pressure test port on the fuel rail **(see illustration)** and connect the fuel pressure gauge to the Schrader valve.
4   Direct the bleed-off hose into a metal cup or suitable container for gasoline storage **(see illustration)**.

5   Turn the valve and allow the pressurized fuel to bleed into the container.
6   Close the valve, remove the fuel pressure gauge and cap the test port. Disconnect the cable from the negative terminal of the battery before performing any work on the fuel system.

Inertia switch method

Refer to illustrations 2.7 and 2.8
7   The fuel pump switch - sometimes called the "inertia switch" - which shuts off fuel to the engine in the event of a collision, affords a simple and convenient means by which fuel pressure can be relieved before servicing fuel injection components. The switch is located behind the passenger's side kick panel **(see illustration)**.
8   Unplug the inertia switch electrical connector **(see illustration)**.
9   Start the engine and allow it to run until it stops. This should take only a few seconds.
10   The fuel system pressure is now relieved. Disconnect the cable from the negative terminal of the battery before performing any work on the fuel system.
11   When you're finished working on the fuel system, simply plug the electrical connector back into the switch. If the inertia switch was "popped" (activated) during this procedure, push the reset button on the top of the switch.

2.8 Disconnect the electrical connector to disable the fuel pump

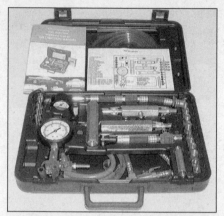

3.6 This fuel pressure testing kit contains all the necessary fittings and adapters, along with the fuel pressure gauge, to test most automotive fuel systems

3　Fuel pump/fuel pressure - check

Warning: *Gasoline is extremely flammable, so take extra precautions when you work on any part of the fuel system. See the **Warning** in Section 2.*
Note: *After the fuel pressure has been relieved, it's a good idea to lay a shop towel over any fuel connection to be disassembled, to absorb the residual fuel that may leak out when servicing the fuel system.*

General checks

Note 1: *The inertia switch is an electrical device wired into the fuel pump circuit that will shut down power to the fuel pump in an accident (see Section 2). Be sure to check that the inertia switch is activated and in working order if the fuel pump is not receiving the proper voltage.*
Note 2: *The fuel pump relay is equipped with a primary and secondary voltage circuit. The primary circuit is controlled by the PCM and the secondary circuit is linked directly to battery voltage from the ignition switch. With the ignition switch ON (engine not running), the PCM will ground the relay for one second. During cranking, the PCM grounds the fuel pump relay as long as the reference signal from the ignition system is received. If there are no reference pulses, the fuel pump will shut off after two or three seconds.*
1　If you suspect insufficient fuel delivery, check the following items first:
 a) *Check the battery and make sure it's fully charged (see Chapter 5).*
 b) *Check the fuel pump fuse.*
 c) *Check the fuel filter for restriction.*
 d) *Inspect all fuel lines to ensure that the problem is not simply a leak in a line.*
2　Verify the fuel pump actually runs. Place the transmission in Park (automatic) or Neutral (manual) and apply the parking brake. Have an assistant turn the ignition switch to ON - you should hear a brief whirring noise as the pump comes on and pressurizes the system. **Note:** *The fuel pump is easily heard*

through the gas tank filler neck. If there is no response from the fuel pump (makes no sound), check the fuel pump electrical circuit. If the fuel pump runs, but a fuel system problem is suspected, continue with the fuel pump pressure check.
3　If the pump does not turn on (makes no sound) with the ignition switch in the ON position, check the ignition fuse located in the engine compartment fuse center. Also, check the fuel pump relay. Refer to Chapter 12 for testing relays. **Note:** *The fuel pump relay is located either in the fuse/relay center in the engine compartment (Excursion models) or behind the radio in the center of the instrument panel (pick-up models).*
4　If the relays are good and the fuel pump does not operate, check the fuel pump circuit. If the wiring and the connectors are good, replace the fuel pump (see Section 7). **Note:** *On 2005 and later models the PCM commands the fuel pump driver module, which in turn operates the fuel pump. If you suspect that the fuel pump driver module is faulty, have the system diagnosed at a dealer or a qualified repair shop. Refer to Chapter 6 for information on replacement of this component.*

Pressure check

Refer to illustrations 3.6 and 3.9
Note: *In order to perform the fuel pressure test, you will need a fuel pressure gauge capable of measuring high fuel pressure. The fuel gauge must be equipped with the proper fitting required to attach it to the test port. To test the fuel pressure regulator, a fuel shut off valve must be installed in the fuel return line with the necessary adapters.*
5　Relieve the fuel system pressure (see Section 2).
6　Remove the cap from the fuel pressure test port **(see illustration 2.3)** and attach a fuel pressure gauge **(see illustration)**. If you don't have the correct adapter for the test port, remove the Schrader valve and connect the gauge hose to the fitting, using a hose clamp.
7　Turn all the accessories Off and switch the ignition key On (engine not running). The fuel pump should run for approximately one or two seconds. Note the reading on the gauge. If the fuel pressure is lower than specified, install a shut-off valve in the fuel return line, then turn the key Off and back On again.
Caution: *Do not allow the fuel pressure to rise above 85 psi or damage to the fuel pressure regulator may occur.* If the fuel pressure is now above the specified pressure, replace the fuel pressure regulator (see Section 8). If the fuel pressure is still lower than specified, check the fuel lines and the fuel filter for restrictions. If no restriction is found, remove the fuel pump (see Section 7) and check the strainer for restrictions. If no problems are found, replace the fuel pump.
8　If the fuel pressure recorded in Step 7 is higher than specified, check the fuel return line for restrictions. If no restrictions are found, replace the fuel pressure regulator (see Section 8).

3.9 Detach the vacuum line from the fuel pressure regulator and verify vacuum is present when the engine is running

9　Remove the shut-off valve (if you installed one). Start the engine and let it idle at normal operating temperature. With the engine running, the fuel pressure should be 5 to 10 psi below the pressure recorded in Step 7. If it isn't, verify there is 12 to 14 in-Hg of vacuum present at the fuel pressure regulator vacuum hose **(see illustration)**. If vacuum is not present at the hose, check the hose for a restriction or a break. If vacuum is present, reconnect the hose to the fuel pressure regulator. If the fuel pressure regulator does not decrease the fuel pressure with engine vacuum applied, replace the fuel pressure regulator.

4　Fuel lines and fittings - general information

Refer to illustrations 4.3a and 4.3b
Warning: *Gasoline is extremely flammable, so take extra precautions when you work on any part of the fuel system. See the **Warning** in Section 2.*
1　Always relieve the system fuel pressure before servicing fuel lines or fittings (see Section 2).
2　The fuel supply line extends from the fuel tank to the engine compartment. The EVAP purge line extends from the EVAP canister, which is located behind the fuel tank, up to the purge valve, which is located on the firewall in the engine compartment. Anytime you raise the vehicle for underbody service, inspect the lines underneath the vehicle for leaks, kinks and dents.
3　The fuel and EVAP lines are secured to the underbody with plastic and metal clips **(see illustrations)**. To disengage the fuel or EVAP lines from either type of clip, simply pull the line(s) straight out of the clip. To replace a damaged plastic clip, simply disengage the fuel and/or EVAP lines, then pull the clip out of its mounting bracket. To replace a damaged metal clip, disengage the fuel and/or EVAP lines, then unbolt the clip.

4.3a A typical plastic clip for the fuel delivery line. To replace this type of clip, simply disengage the fuel line from the clip by pushing it out of the clip, then push the clip out of its mounting bracket

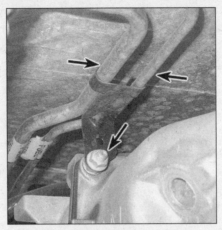

4.3b A typical metal clip for the fuel delivery line and EVAP purge line. To replace this type of clip, simply pinch the two lines together and pull them up and out of the clip, then remove the nut or bolt securing the mounting bracket for the clip and remove the clip

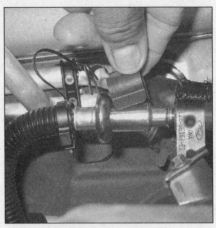

4.17 Remove the safety clamp from the spring lock coupling

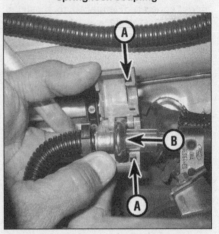

4.19a Place the spring-lock coupling tool around the coupling and close it so the lip (A) of the tool is flush against the garter spring housing (B) . . .

Steel tubing

4   If it's necessary to replace a fuel line or EVAP line, use steel tubing that complies with the manufacturer's specifications, or its equivalent.

5   Don't use copper or aluminum tubing to replace steel tubing. These materials cannot withstand normal vehicle vibration.

6   Because steel fuel lines are under high pressure when the engine is running, they require special consideration:

a) *Inspect all O-rings for cuts, cracks and deterioration. If an O-ring is torn, cracked, hardened or otherwise damaged, replace it.*

b) *If the lines are replaced, always use original equipment parts, or parts that meet the original equipment standards specified in this Section.*

c) *Never allow metal lines to chafe against the frame. Maintain a minimum of 1/4-inch clearance around a line to prevent contact with the frame.*

7   If you find dirt in the system during disassembly, disconnect the fuel supply line and then blow it out with compressed air. And be sure to inspect the fuel filter (see Chapter 1) and the fuel pump inlet strainer for contamination (see Section 7).

Flexible hoses

Caution: *Use only original equipment replacement hoses or their equivalent. Unapproved hose material might fail when subjected to the fuel pressure at which this system operates.*

8   Don't route fuel hose within four inches of any part of the exhaust system or within ten inches of the catalytic converter. Never allow rubber hoses to chafe against the frame. Maintain a minimum of 1/4-inch clearance around a hose to prevent contact with the frame.

9   If a hose is equipped with quick-connect fittings, the quick-connect fittings cannot be

serviced separately. If the fitting or hose is damaged, replace the entire fuel hose assembly. Do not attempt to repair fuel hoses.

Replacing fuel lines and hoses and EVAP lines

10   If a fuel line or hose or an EVAP line is damaged, replace it with factory replacement parts. Do not substitute fuel lines or hoses or EVAP lines of inferior quality. They might not be suitable for, and might fail when subjected to, the operating pressure of this system.

11   Always relieve the fuel system pressure before replacing fuel or EVAP lines (see Section 2).

12   Always disconnect the cable from the negative terminal of the battery (see Chapter 5, Section 1) before replacing fuel or EVAP lines.

13   Remove all clips that secure the fuel or EVAP line to the vehicle body. Pay close attention to all clips; they not only secure the fuel line and hoses, they also route them correctly. The hoses and line must be reattached to their respective clips when reassembled.

14   Be sure to use the correct tool and the correct procedure when disconnecting any fuel or EVAP couplings or fittings.

Disconnecting and connecting fuel line and EVAP line fittings

Spring-lock couplings

Refer to illustrations 4.17, 4.19a, 4.19b, 4.19c and 4.19d

15   The fuel supply line utilizes spring lock couplings at some connections such as the fuel rail and the fuel filter. The male side of the coupling, which is sealed by two O-rings, is simply the end of a fuel line with a flared end. The male side of the coupling is inserted into the female side of the coupling, which is secured by a garter spring that prevents unintentional disconnection by gripping the flared

end of the male side of the coupling. On some of these fittings on some models, a safety clamp provides additional security. These clamps are often tethered to the female side of the coupling so that you don't lose them while the coupling is disconnected.

16   BEFORE DISCONNECTING SPRING-LOCK COUPLINGS, ALWAYS RELIEVE SYSTEM FUEL PRESSURE (see Section 2), then DISCONNECT THE CABLE FROM THE NEGATIVE BATTERY TERMINAL (see Chapter 5, Section 1).

17   Remove the safety clamp **(see illustration)**.

18   If you're using a clamshell-type tool, install the tool over the coupling. Other types of release tools simply fit over the fuel line. **Note:** *These tools are available at most auto parts stores. They come in a variety of sizes, so it's a good idea to purchase a set of them to be sure you'll have the right size.*

19   Push the coupling tool firmly toward the garter spring housing to disengage the garter spring from the flared end of the female side of the connection **(see illustrations)**. Then pull the two fuel lines apart to disengage the tool from the garter spring, open and remove

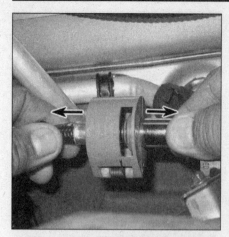

4.19b . . . push the spring-lock coupling tool toward the garter housing until the garter spring is disengaged, then pull the fuel lines apart

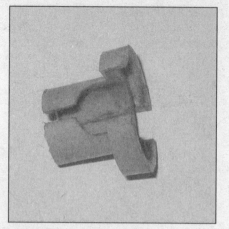

4.19c This type of spring-lock coupling tool can be used in places where access to the fitting is limited. To use it . . .

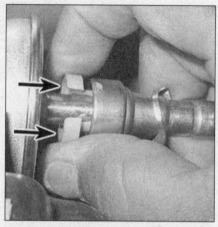

4.19d . . . slip it over the line, press it into the coupling and pull the lines apart

the tool and disconnect the lines.

20   Before reconnecting the coupling, wipe off the ends of both fuel lines with a clean cloth. Inspect the condition of the O-rings and the garter spring. If either O-ring or the garter spring is damaged or worn, replace it. Also inspect the inside of the female side of the fitting and make sure it's clean.

21   Lubricate the O-rings with some clean engine oil, then press the two sides of the connection together until the flared end of the male side of the fitting is locked into place by the garter spring. Pull on the coupling to verify that it's fully engaged.

22   When you have verified that the coupling is reconnected, install the safety clamp.

23   Reconnect the cable to the negative battery terminal (see Chapter 5, Section 1).

24   Turn the ignition key to ON (*not* START) and re-pressurize the fuel system (see Section 2), which will take a moment, then check for fuel leakage around the coupling. If there are no signs of leaks, start the engine and check again.

Quick-connect couplings

25   Besides spring-lock couplings, the vehicles covered by this manual also use various types of quick-connect couplings to connect fuel lines, EVAP lines and PCV lines. After you locate the coupling, determine which type it is, then use whichever of the following procedures that applies to that particular style of coupling.

26   There are several types of quick-connect couplings in use on these vehicles. If you're in need of a replacement, take it with you to the auto parts store or dealer parts department. If you show the counterperson the coupling, retainer and/or O-ring and tell them the location of the coupling, they will be able to determine which part you need.

27   Also, at the time of publication, the O-rings inside the following quick-connect couplings were not available separately from the coupling themselves. So if an O-ring is damaged, you must *replace the coupling* (which also includes the fuel hose or line to which it's permanently attached). And if one of these couplings is damaged, you can-

not repair it. So, whether you're replacing a coupling because the O-ring is damaged or because the coupling itself is damaged, you must replace the coupling, and the fuel line to which it's permanently connected, as a single assembly.

28   Always relieve the system fuel pressure before disconnecting fuel line couplings (see Section 2).

29   Always disconnect the cable from the negative battery terminal before disconnecting fuel lines (see Chapter 5, Section 1).

Type 1

Refer to illustrations 4.30. 4.31, 4.32 and 4.33

Note: *The retainer clip for a Type 1 quick-connect coupling can be replaced separately, but the rest of the assembly (the coupling, O-ring and fuel hose or line to which the coupling is attached, must be replaced as a single assembly).*

30   Pull up the locking tab to the RELEASE position (**see illustration**).

31   Press down the corners of the locking tab to release it, push the fuel or EVAP line into the coupling to disengage it from the retainer, then pull the fuel line out of the coupling (**see illustration**).

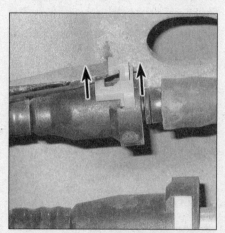

4.30 Using a screwdriver, carefully lever the locking tab up to its RELEASED position

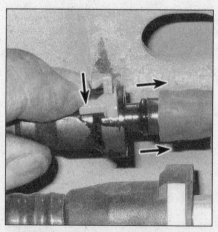

4.31 Press down on the corners of the locking tab to release it, push the fuel line into the coupling to release it from the retainer, then pull the fuel line out of the coupling

4.32 Inspect the condition of the O-ring inside the coupling. If the O-ring is cracked, torn or deteriorated, replace the coupling

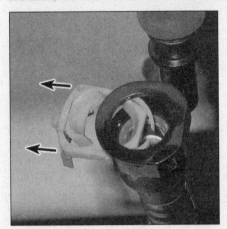

4.33 Inspect the condition of the retainer. If it's damaged, pull it out of the coupling, discard it and install a new retainer

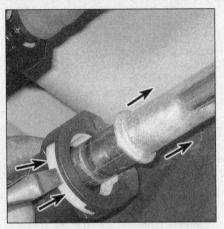

4.37 To disconnect a fuel line from this type of quick-connect coupling, depress the release button, then pull the fuel line out of the coupling

4.42a To disconnect this type of coupling, locate the brightly-colored locking tab on the side of the coupling . . .

32   Inspect the condition of the coupling and the O-ring inside **(see illustration)**. If the coupling is damaged or if the O-ring inside the coupling is cracked, torn or deteriorated, replace the coupling.

33   Inspect the condition of the retainer **(see illustration)**. If the retainer is damaged, remove it from the coupling and install a new retainer. (It's not a bad idea to replace the retainer anytime that you disconnect this type of coupling because retainers are inexpensive but critical parts.)

34   Before reconnecting the coupling to the fuel or EVAP line, apply a dab or two of clean engine oil to the end of the fuel line.

35   To connect the coupling, insert the fuel or EVAP line into the coupling until the fuel line clicks into place.

36   Verify that the coupling is fully connected by trying to pull the fuel or EVAP line and the coupling apart. If the coupling is fully connected, press down the locking tab to its LOCKED position.

Type II

Refer to illustration 4.37

Note: *This type of coupling has a brightly-colored, slender release button running along one side of the coupling body. You'll find this type of coupling used on both fuel and EVAP line connections anywhere from the fuel tank to the fuel and EVAP lines running under the vehicle. It's mainly used to connect EVAP lines together and to connect them to components such as the EVAP canister. If the coupling, the O-rings inside the coupling or the fuel hose or line to which the coupling is attached is damaged, they must be replaced as a single assembly.*

37   Press the button on the coupling and pull the fuel or EVAP line out of the coupling **(see illustration)**.

38   Inspect the condition of the quick-connect coupling and the O-rings inside the coupling. If the coupling is damaged or if the O-rings are cracked, torn or deteriorated, replace the coupling and the EVAP line to which it's attached.

39   Apply a dab or two of clean engine oil to

the fuel or EVAP line and to the O-rings inside the coupling.

40   To reconnect this type of coupling, simply insert the fuel or EVAP line into the coupling until it clicks into place.

41   Verify that the coupling is properly connected by trying to pull the coupling and the fuel or EVAP line apart.

Type III

Refer to illustrations 4.42a and 4.42b

Note: *This type of coupling has a brightly-colored locking tab on the side of the coupling body. It's used on some models to connect the PCV fresh air inlet and crankcase ventilation lines to the valve covers, the PCV valve and the intake manifold. If the coupling, the O-rings inside the coupling or the PCV line to which the coupling is attached is damaged, they must be replaced as a single assembly.*

42   Depress the locking tab on the side of the coupling body and disconnect the coupling **(see illustrations)**.

43   Inspect the condition of the quick-connect coupling and the O-rings inside the coupling. If the coupling is damaged or if the O-rings are cracked, torn or deteriorated, replace the coupling and the EVAP line to

which it's attached.

44   Apply a dab or two of clean engine oil to the O-rings inside the coupling.

45   To reconnect this type of coupling, release the locking tab by pushing it down again, then push the coupling onto the PCV pipe until the coupling clicks into place.

46   Verify that the coupling is properly connected by trying to pull the coupling and the EVAP line apart.

Type IV

Refer to illustration 4.47

Note: *This is another type of EVAP line quick-connect coupling that you'll find on some models. It's used to connect the EVAP purge line to the EVAP canister purge valve and to some other EVAP components. If the coupling, the O-rings inside the coupling or the fuel hose or line to which the coupling is attached is damaged, they must be replaced as a single assembly.*

47   To disconnect this type of quick-connect coupling, depress the two release tabs on the top and bottom of the fitting and pull it off the purge valve pipe (shown) or EVAP line **(see illustration)**.

4.42b . . . press it down firmly with the tip of a screwdriver and pull off the coupling

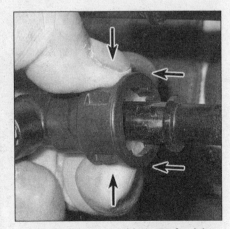

4.47 To disconnect this type of quick-connect coupling, depress the two release tabs on the top and bottom of the coupling and pull it off the pipe

5.8 Remove the bolts and separate the splash panel from the fenderwell

48 Inspect the condition of the quick-connect coupling and the O-rings inside the coupling. If the coupling is damaged or if the O-rings are cracked, torn or deteriorated, replace the coupling and the EVAP line to which it's attached.
49 Apply a dab or two of clean engine oil to the EVAP line and to the O-rings inside the coupling.
50 To reconnect this type of coupling, simply insert the EVAP line into the coupling, or push the coupling onto the EVAP line, until the line clicks into place.
51 Verify that the coupling is properly connected by trying to pull the coupling and the EVAP line apart.

5 Fuel tank - removal and installation

Refer to illustrations 5.8, 5.12a and 5.12b
Warning: *Gasoline is extremely flammable, so take extra precautions when you work on any part of the fuel system. See the* **Warning** *in Section 2.*
Note: *Don't begin this procedure until the gauge indicates that the tank is empty or nearly empty. If the tank must be removed when it's full (for example, if the fuel pump malfunctions), siphon any remaining fuel from the tank prior to removal.*

1 Relieve the fuel system pressure:
   a) On gasoline models, see Section 2.
   b) On diesel models, see Chapter 4B.
2 Remove the fuel filler cap to relieve fuel tank pressure.
3 Disconnect the cable from the negative terminal of the battery (see Chapter 5, Section 1).
4 If the tank is full or nearly full, siphon the fuel into an approved container using a siphoning kit available at most auto parts stores. **Warning:** *DO NOT start the siphoning action by mouth! Use a siphoning kit.*
5 Raise the vehicle and support it securely on jackstands.
6 Depending on the model and optional equipment, the fuel tank may be located either forward of the rear axle (midship) or behind the rear axle (aft).
7 Remove the fuel tank skid plate mounting bolts and lower the assembly.
8 Remove the fuel tank filler hose and vapor hose from the fuel filler neck and the fuel tank **(see illustration)**.
9 Place a floor jack under the tank. Raise the jack until it's supporting the tank.
10 Disconnect the fuel lines (see Section 4) and EVAP vapor lines. **Note:** *Disconnect the fuel tank pressure sensor, if equipped.*
11 Disconnect the electric fuel pump and sending unit electrical connector with a screwdriver (see Section 7). It may be necessary to lower the fuel tank slightly to access the components located directly on top of the fuel tank.
12 Remove the bolts that retain the fuel tank straps **(see illustrations)**. **Note:** *On diesel auxiliary fuel tanks, it will be necessary to remove the fuel tank cover strap bolts and the fuel tank straps and then carefully drop the fuel tank and the tank straps as a complete assembly.*

13 Lower the tank far enough to unplug any vapor lines or wire harness brackets that may be difficult to reach when the fuel tank is in the vehicle.
14 Slowly lower the jack while steadying the tank. Remove the tank from the vehicle.
15 If you're replacing the tank, or having it cleaned or repaired, refer to Section 6.
16 Refer to Section 7 to remove and install the fuel pump or sending unit.
17 Installation is the reverse of removal. Clean engine oil can be used as an assembly aid when pushing the fuel filler neck back into the tank.
18 Make sure the fuel tank heat shields, if equipped, are assembled correctly onto the fuel tank before reinstalling the tank in the vehicle.
19 Carefully angle the fuel tank filler neck into the filler pipe assembly and lift the tank into place.

6 Fuel tank - cleaning and repair

1 There are two different types of fuel tanks on these models: steel and plastic.
2 Fuel tanks may be steam-cleaned to remove sediment or rust in the bottom of the tank. Remove the fuel tank sending unit/fuel pump and vapor valve prior to cleaning. Allow plenty of time for the tank to air dry before returning it to service.
3 Repairs to the steel fuel tank or filler pipe should be performed by a professional with the proper training to carry out this critical and potentially dangerous job. Even after cleaning and flushing, explosive fumes can remain and could explode during repair of the tank.
4 The plastic (polyethylene) fuel tank cannot be repaired. No reliable repair procedures are available to correct leaks or damage. Fuel tank replacement is the only approved service.
5 If the fuel tank is removed from the vehicle, it should not be placed in an area where sparks or open flames could ignite the fumes coming out of the tank. Be especially careful inside garages where a gas-type appliance is

5.12a Remove the bolts from the rear of the tank . . .

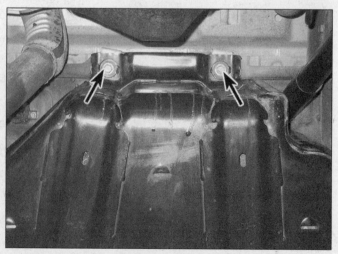

5.12b . . . and the bolts from the front of the tank - Excursion shown

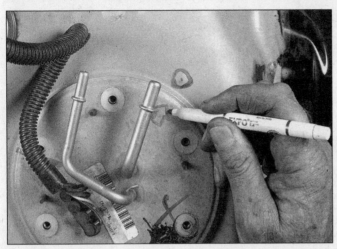

7.6 Using paint or a marker, highlight the alignment marks on the fuel pump assembly (metal tank shown)

7.7a On plastic fuel tanks, if a special tool is not available, use a pair of channel locks to remove the retaining ring

located, because the appliance could cause an explosion.

6 Whenever the fuel tank is steam-cleaned or otherwise serviced, the vapor valve assembly should be replaced. All grommets and seals must be replaced to prevent possible leakage.

7 Fuel pump/fuel pump module - removal and installation

Refer to illustrations 7.6, 7.7a and 7.7b

Warning: *Gasoline is extremely flammable, so take extra precautions when you work on any part of the fuel system. See the* **Warning** *in Section 2.*

1 Relieve the fuel pressure (refer to Section 2).

2 Disconnect the cable(s) from the negative terminal of the battery (see Chapter 5, Section 1).

3 Unless the vehicle has been driven far enough to completely empty the tank, it's a good idea to siphon out the residual fuel before removing the fuel pump from the vehicle. **Warning:** *DO NOT start the siphoning action by mouth! Use a siphoning kit (available at most auto parts stores).*

4 Raise the vehicle and support it securely on jackstands.

5 Remove the fuel tank from the vehicle (see Section 5). **Note:** *A special fuel line removal tool, available at most auto parts stores, may be required to disconnect the fuel lines from the fuel pump (see Section 4).*

6 Use paint or a marking pen to highlight the alignment marks that are scribed into the fuel pump assembly and the fuel tank **(see illustration)**.

7 Remove the fuel pump assembly from the fuel tank.

a) *On plastic fuel tanks, turn the retaining ring counterclockwise, until it's loose, using a special tool designed for fuel pump removal. Remove the retaining ring* **(see illustration)**. **Note:** *The spe-*

cial fuel pump lock ring tool is available at automotive tool suppliers and some auto parts retailers. If the special tool is not available, use a pair of channel lock pliers.

b) *On steel fuel tanks, remove the mounting bolts* **(see illustration)** *from the fuel pump assembly.*

8 Reach into the fuel tank and disconnect the fuel pump latches by squeezing them in, toward the fuel pump body. First, push down on the assembly to release it and then carefully lift the fuel pump assembly from the tank. Note the position of the fuel pump and latches when removing the assembly from the fuel tank.

9 Remove the old seal ring, if equipped and discard it.

10 Separate the fuel pump from the assembly.

11 Clean the fuel pump mounting flange, the tank mounting surface and seal ring groove.

12 Installation is the reverse of removal. Apply a thin coat of heavy grease to the new seal ring to hold it in place during assembly.

13 Be sure the fuel pump is aligned properly with the latches on the module inside the fuel tank. The fuel pump should snap fit into place when properly installed.

8 Fuel pressure regulator - removal and installation

Refer to illustrations 8.8a and 8.8b

Warning: *Gasoline is extremely flammable, so take extra precautions when you work on any part of the fuel system. See the* **Warning** *in Section 2.*

Note: *This procedure applies only to 1999 through 2004 models with conventional return-type fuel systems. 2005 and later models use returnless fuel systems. Refer to Section 12 for more information.*

1 Relieve the fuel system pressure (refer to Section 2).

2 Disconnect the cable from the negative

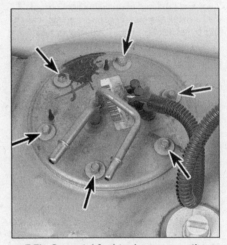

7.7b On metal fuel tanks, remove the mounting bolts from the fuel pump assembly

terminal of the battery (see Chapter 5, Section 1).

3 Remove the air filter housing (see Section 10).

4 Remove the accelerator cable and the splash shield (see Section 11).

5 On V10 engines, remove the throttle body (see Section 14). **Note:** *Depending on the model year, the throttle body spacer may have to be removed to gain access to the fuel pressure regulator.*

6 Disconnect the EGR vacuum regulator (see Chapter 6) and remove the EGR vacuum regulator bracket, if necessary.

7 Remove the vacuum hose from the pressure regulator.

8 Remove the fuel pressure regulator from the fuel rail;

a) *On 1999 models, remove the two pressure regulator mounting bolts* **(see illustration)**.

b) *On 2000 and later models, remove the snap-ring and separate the pressure regulator from the fuel rail* **(see illustration)**.

8.8a On 1999 models, remove the fuel pressure regulator mounting bolts

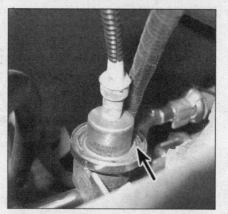

8.8b On 2000 and later models, remove the fuel pressure regulator retaining clip

10.5 Lift the air filter housing from the bracket

9   Installation is the reverse of removal.
10   Install new O-rings on the pressure regulator and lubricate them with a light coat of oil.
11   Install the fuel pressure regulator mounting bolts (1999 models) securely or install the snap-ring (2000 and later models).

---

9   Fuel level sending unit - replacement

Warning: *Gasoline is extremely flammable, so take extra precautions when you work on any part of the fuel system. See the* **Warning** *in Section 2.*
Note 1: *Diesel models are equipped with a separate fuel level sensor mounted in the fuel tank and an externally mounted fuel pump. The fuel tank must be removed to access the fuel level sending unit assembly.*
Note 2: *Later models have a fuel level sender that is part of the fuel pump module. The sender is not replaceable by itself*
1   Remove the fuel tank (see Section 5).
2   Remove the fuel pump/fuel level sending unit assembly (see Section 7). Carefully angle the assembly out of the opening without damaging the fuel level float located at the bottom of the assembly.
3   Remove the electrical connectors for the fuel level sending unit.

10.6 Air filter housing bracket bolt locations (arrows)

4   Disassemble the fuel level sending unit from the fuel pump.
5   Installation is the reverse of removal.
6   Be sure to install a new rubber gasket.

---

10   Air filter housing - removal and installation

---

1   Disconnect the cable(s) from the negative battery terminal(s) (see Chapter 5, Section 1).
2   Refer to Chapter 1 and remove the air filter.

Gasoline models

1999 through 2004 models
Refer to illustrations 10.5 and 10.6
3   Disconnect the IAT sensor, the MAF sensor, the PCV hose and the IAC valve connector.
4   Remove the air filter housing inlet and outlet ducts from the air filter housing.
5   Separate the air filter housing from the bracket **(see illustration)**.
6   Remove the air filter housing bracket mounting bolts **(see illustration)** and lift the bracket from the engine compartment, if necessary.
7   Installation is the reverse of removal.

10.18 Loosen the air duct clamp and detach the duct from the air filter housing

2005 and later models

5.4L engines
8   Remove the air filter (refer to Chapter 1). Inside the housing is the release tab for the intake duct. Remove the air cleaner intake duct.
9   Disconnect the vent hose and the wiring to the MAF sensor.
10   Remove the four mounting bolts and lift off the air cleaner.
11   Installation is the reverse of removal.

6.8L engines
12   Disconnect the vent hose and the wiring to the MAF sensor.
13   Remove the outlet duct from the air cleaner.
14   Disconnect the auxiliary inlet hose.
15   Remove the air cleaner.
16   Installation is the reverse of removal.

Diesel models

7.3L engines
Refer to illustration 10.18
17   Remove the left-side battery (see Chapter 5).
18   Remove the air filter housing outlet duct **(see illustration)** and the upper cover from the air filter housing.
19   Remove the mounting bolts from the air filter housing and lift the housing slightly to gain access to the IAT sensor connector.
20   Disconnect the IAT sensor connector from the rear of the battery tray.
21   Lift the air filter housing from the engine compartment.
22   Installation is the reverse of removal.

6.0L engines
23   Remove the air filter element/duct (refer to Chapter 1).
24   Disconnect the extra air intake tube and remove the front cover.
25   Disconnect the air filter condition monitor.
26   Disconnect the MAF sensor wiring connector.
27   Loosen the retaining clamp and then lift out the air cleaner housing.

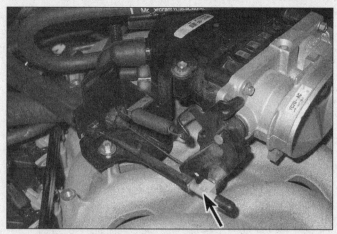

11.2 Use a screwdriver and gently pry the cruise control cable end off of the throttle body ballstud

11.3 Rotate the cable end and remove the accelerator cable from the slotted portion of the throttle valve

11 Accelerator cable - replacement and adjustment

Note: *This procedure applies only to 1999 through 2004 models with conventional throttle bodies. 2005 and later models have electronic throttle bodies and accelerator pedal position sensors instead of a cable.*

Replacement

Refer to illustrations 11.2, 11.3 and 11.5

1   Remove the accelerator cable protection shield.
2   Detach the cruise control cable end from the throttle lever **(see illustration)**.
3   Remove the accelerator cable from the throttle lever **(see illustration)**.
4   Separate the accelerator cable from the cable bracket.
5   Disconnect the accelerator cable from the pedal **(see illustration)**.
6   Pull the cable end out from the accelerator pedal recess in the driver's compartment.
7   Disconnect any cable clips or brackets securing the accelerator cable.
8   Remove the cable through the firewall

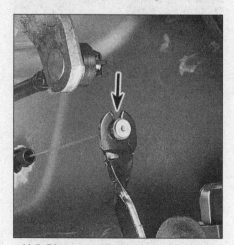

11.5 Disconnect the cable end from the accelerator pedal assembly

from the engine compartment.
9   Installation is the reverse of removal. Be sure the cable is routed correctly and the grommet seats completely in the firewall.
10   If necessary, at the engine compartment side of the firewall, apply sealant around the accelerator cable to prevent water from entering the passenger compartment.

Adjustment

11   Measure the freeplay by firmly gripping the cable and pressing it down from the cable housing. There should be a slight amount of cable freeplay.
12   If there is no cable freeplay or the cable is binding and not allowing the throttle lever to completely close, or if there's an excessive amount of freeplay, replace the cable.

12 Fuel injection system - general information

Sequential Electronic Fuel Injection (SEFI) system

The Sequential Electronic Fuel Injection (SEFI) system is a multi-point fuel injection system. On the SEFI system, fuel is metered into each intake port in sequence with the engine firing order in accordance with engine demand through one injector per cylinder mounted on an intake manifold. The intake manifold incorporates an air intake plenum to aid in air flow and distribution. Each engine uses a slightly different plenum design and fuel rail arrangement.

1999 5.4L engines are equipped with the Intake Manifold Tuning (IMT) system. The IMT system controls the air intake charge by opening or closing the Intake Manifold Tuning Valve located in the center of the air intake manifold, directly below the air intake plenum. By closing the IMTV, the dual plenum design sends the air intake charge through a single corridor into the intake system of the engine. Above 3,000 rpm, the IMTV is opened, allowing the

intake pulses to blend together at the intake manifold thereby creating a more efficient air/fuel intake charge for the additional rpm and engine load.

The Sequential Electronic Fuel Injection system accepts inputs from various engine sensors to compute the required fuel flow rate necessary to maintain a prescribed air/fuel ratio throughout the entire engine operational range. The computer then outputs a command to the fuel injectors to meter the required quantity of fuel. The system automatically senses and compensates for changes in altitude, load and speed.

Fuel delivery system - 1999 through 2004 models

The fuel delivery systems include an electric in-tank fuel pump which forces pressurized fuel through a series of metal and plastic lines and an inline fuel filter/reservoir to the fuel charging manifold assembly. The SEFI system uses a single high-pressure pump mounted inside the tank.

The fuel rail assembly incorporates an electrically actuated fuel injector directly above each intake port. When energized, the injectors spray a metered quantity of fuel into the intake air stream.

A constant fuel pressure drop is maintained across the injector nozzles by a pressure regulator. The regulator is positioned downstream from the fuel injectors. Excess fuel passes through the regulator and returns to the fuel tank through a fuel return line.

On the SEFI system, each injector is energized once every other crankshaft revolution in sequence with engine firing order. The period of time that the injectors are energized (known as "on time" or "pulse width") is controlled by the PCM. Air entering the engine is sensed by speed, pressure and temperature sensors. The signals of these sensors are processed by the PCM. The computer determines the needed injector pulse width and outputs a command to the injector to meter the exact quantity of fuel.

SEFI system - 2005 and later models

Torque based Electronic Throttle Control (ETC) system

In a conventional induction system with an accelerator cable, the position of the throttle plate inside the throttle body is determined by the position of the accelerator pedal, which is determined by your foot, isn't always appropriate to the prevailing operating conditions. For example, if you mash the accelerator pedal when the transmission is in high gear and the vehicle is cruising down the freeway under no load, it takes a moment for the PCM to downshift the transmission and spin up the engine speed so that it can respond to your new demand. The manufacturer claims that its Generation II (Gen II) Torque Based Electronic Throttle Control (ETC) system produces the ideal transmission output shaft torque because the position of the throttle plate inside the throttle body is no longer based solely on driver demand (the position of the accelerator pedal).

Electronic throttle body and Throttle Position (TP) sensors

The PCM-controlled electronic throttle body regulates the amount of air entering the intake manifold in response to driver demand *and* in response to the operating conditions. There is no accelerator cable or cruise control cable connected to the throttle body. Both of these functions are handled by the PCM. There is also no Idle Air Control (IAC) motor on the electronic throttle body. This function is also handled by the PCM, which opens the throttle plate slightly in response to any load imposed on the engine during idle or low-speed maneuvers.

The electronic throttle body uses two Throttle Position (TP) sensors (TP1 and TP2) because the monitor for this system requires a redundant TP sensor. TP1 has a negative slope (increasing angle, decreasing voltage) and TP2 has a positive slope (increasing angle, increasing voltage). When the engine is running, the negatively-sloped TP1 is used by the ETC system as the actual TP sensor and TP2 is used as a reference sensor by the monitor. The replacement procedure for the electronic throttle body is in this Chapter.

Electronic Throttle Control (ETC) module and Accelerator Pedal Position Sensors (APPS)

The accelerator pedal is equipped with three Accelerator Pedal Position Sensors (APPS), all three of which are housed inside a small plastic housing, known as the Electronic Throttle Control (ETC) module, at the top of the pedal. APP1 has a negative slop (increasing angle, decreasing voltage) and APP2 and APP3 have a positive slop (increasing angle, decreasing voltage). When the engine is running, APP1 is the actual APP sensor. The PCM uses APP2 and APP3 as reference sensors to calculate where a signal

should be so that it can infer whether a sensor signal makes sense or not. If any *one* signal is irrational (doesn't match the other two signals), the PCM is still able to compute the correct outcome. If *two* of the three input signals are bad, the PCM substitutes a default value and turns on the Malfunction Indicator Lamp (MIL). The ETC module and the accelerator pedal are integrated into a single assembly. Neither component can be serviced separately. If one of the APP sensors is defective, you must replace the "pedal and sensor assembly," which is the manufacturer's term for this assembly (see Chapter 6 for the replacement procedure).

Besides eliminating the accelerator and cruise control cables and the IAC motor, the torque based ETC system also results in, according to the manufacturer, an improved airflow range, a more responsive powertrain at altitude and improved shift quality.

Electronically controlled returnless fuel system

In a conventional fuel system with a return line, a fuel pressure regulator maintains the pressure within the correct operating range. When the vehicle decelerates, intake manifold goes up and a vacuum hose between the intake manifold and the pressure regulator lifts the spring-loaded diaphragm inside the regulator, allowing excess fuel pressure to bleed off and the unused fuel to return to the fuel tank. When the vehicle accelerates again, intake manifold vacuum goes down and the spring inside the regulator closes the diaphragm, shutting off the return line and allowing fuel pressure to rise again. The 2005 through 2006 models covered by this manual use a *returnless* fuel system, i.e. there is no fuel pressure regulator and no fuel return line.

Fuel Pump Driver Module (FPDM)

In the type of returnless fuel system used by the vehicles covered by this manual, the PCM controls the fuel pressure by controlling the duty cycle of the Fuel Pump Driver Module (FPDM), which in turn controls the speed of the fuel pump by modulating the voltage to the fuel pump. The FPDM is located underneath the vehicle. To replace the FPDM, refer to Chapter 6.

Fuel Rail Pressure Temperature (FRPT) sensor

The FRPT sensor measures the pressure *and the temperature* of the fuel in the fuel rail. The FRPT sensor uses intake manifold vacuum as a reference to determine the pressure difference between the fuel rail and the intake manifold. The relationship between fuel pressure and fuel temperature is used to determine the likelihood of the presence of fuel vapor in the fuel rail. Both the pressure and temperature signals are used to control the speed of the fuel pump. The speed of the fuel pump controls the pressure inside the fuel rail in order to keep the fuel in a liquid state. Keeping the fuel in a liquid state increases the efficiency of the injectors because the higher

fuel rail pressure allows a decrease in the injector pulse width (the interval of time during which the injector is open). The FRPT sensor is located on the left fuel rail, just ahead of the fuel supply line pipe. To replace the FRPT sensor, refer to Chapter 6.

---

13   Fuel injection system - check

Refer to illustrations 13.7 and 13.8
Warning: *Gasoline is extremely flammable, so take extra precautions when you work on any part of the fuel system. See the* **Warning** *in Section 2.*
Note: *The following procedure is based on the assumption that the fuel pump is working and the fuel pressure is adequate (see Section 3).*
1   Check all electrical connectors that are related to the system. Check the ground wire connections for tightness. Loose connectors and poor grounds can cause many problems that resemble more serious malfunctions.
2   Check to see that the battery is fully charged, as the control unit and sensors depend on an accurate supply voltage in order to properly meter the fuel.
3   Check the air filter element. A dirty or partially blocked filter will severely impede performance and economy (see Chapter 1).
4   Check the fuel pump operation (see Section 3). If the fuel pump fuse is blown, replace it and see if it is blown again. If it does, search for a wire shorted to ground in the harness.
5   Check the air intake duct to the intake manifold for leaks, which will result in an excessively lean mixture. Also check the condition of all vacuum hoses connected to the intake manifold and/or throttle body.
6   Remove the air intake duct from the throttle body and check for dirt, carbon, varnish, or other residue in the throttle body, particularly around the throttle plate. If it's dirty, refer to Chapter 6 and troubleshoot the PCV and EGR systems. Clean it with carburetor cleaner spray, a toothbrush and shop towel (see Section 14).

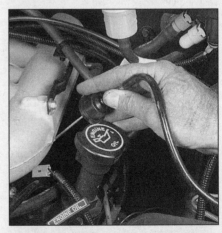

13.7 Use a stethoscope or screwdriver to determine if the injectors are working properly - they should make a steady clicking sound that rises and falls as engine speed changes

13.8 Measure the resistance of each injector. It should be within Specifications

14.2a The area inside the throttle body near the throttle plate (arrow) suffers from sludge build-up because the PCV hose vents vapor from the crankcase

14.2b With the engine off, use aerosol carburetor cleaner (make sure it is safe for use with catalytic converters and oxygen sensors), a toothbrush and a rag to clean the throttle body - open the throttle plate so you can clean behind it

7   With the engine running, place an automotive stethoscope against each injector, one at a time, and listen for a clicking sound that indicates operation **(see illustration)**. If you don't have a stethoscope, you can place the tip of a long screwdriver against the injector and listen through the handle. If you hear the injectors operating but there is a misfire condition present, the electrical circuits are functioning, but the injectors may be dirty or fouled from carbon deposits - commercial cleaning products may help, or the injectors may require replacement.

8   If you can't hear the injector operating, disconnect the injector electrical connector and measure the resistance of each injector with an ohmmeter **(see illustration)**. Compare the measurement with the resistance value listed in this Chapter's Specifications. Replace any injector whose resistance value does not fall within the specifications.

9   If the injector was not operating but the resistance reading was within specifications, the PCM or the circuit to the injector may be faulty.

10   Any further diagnosis of the fuel injection system should be left to a professional service technician.

14 Throttle body - check, removal and installation

Check

Refer to illustrations 14.2a and 14.2b
Note: *This procedure applies only to 1999 through 2004 models. These vehicles have conventional cable-operated throttle bodies.*
1   Verify that the throttle linkage operates smoothly.
2   Remove the air intake duct from the throttle body and check for carbon and residue build-up. If it is dirty, clean it with aerosol carburetor cleaner and a tooth brush. Make sure the can specifically states that it is safe with oxygen sensor systems and catalytic converters **(see illustrations)**. **Caution:** *Do not clean the throttle position sensor (TPS) or Idle Air Control (IAC) valve with the solvent.*

Removal

Refer to illustrations 14.7a and 14.7b
Note: *This procedure applies only to 1999 through 2004 models. These vehicles have conventional cable-operated throttle bodies.*
3   Disconnect the cable from the negative terminal of the battery (see Chapter 5, Section 1).
4   Remove the air filter housing (see Section 10).
5   Detach the throttle position sensor (TPS) and Idle Air Control (IAC) valve electrical connectors.
6   Disconnect the accelerator cable (see Section 11) and the cruise control cable, if equipped, from the throttle body.
7   Remove the throttle body mounting nuts **(see illustrations)**.
8   Remove and discard the throttle body gasket.

Installation

9   Clean the gasket mating surfaces. If scraping is necessary, be careful not to damage the gasket surfaces or allow material

to drop into the manifold. Installation is the reverse of removal. Be sure to tighten the throttle body mounting nuts to the torque listed in this Chapter's Specifications.

15 Fuel rail and injectors - removal and installation

Warning: *Gasoline is extremely flammable, so take extra precautions when you work on any part of the fuel system. See the* **Warning** *in Section 2.*

Removal

Refer to illustrations 15.4a, 15.4b, 15.4c, 15.5 and 15.10
1   Relieve the fuel pressure (see Section 2).
2   Disconnect the cable from the negative terminal of the battery (see Chapter 5, Section 1).
3   Remove the air filter housing (see Section 10).
4   Using the special spring lock coupling tool, disconnect the fuel line(s) from the fuel

14.7a Throttle body mounting bolts - 5.4L V8 engine

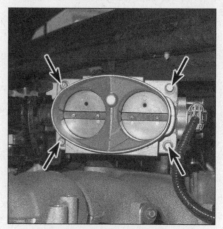

14.7b Throttle body mounting bolts - 6.8L V10 engine

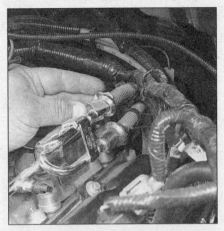

15.4a Press down to release the safety clamp from the fuel line connectors

15.4b Install the correct diameter spring lock coupling tool and push away from the fuel rail to release the internal locking mechanism

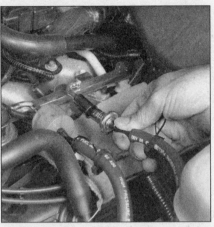

15.4c Detach the fuel line from the fuel rail

15.5 Injector electrical connector locations - 6.8L V10 engine

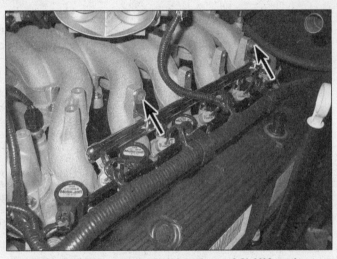

15.10 Fuel rail mounting bolt locations - 6.8L V10 engine

rail (see illustrations). **Note:** *Refer to Section 4 for additional information on disconnecting fuel lines.*

5   Disconnect the injector connectors **(see illustration)**.

6   Remove the vacuum hose from the fuel pressure regulator (see Section 6).

7   Remove the EGR pipe from the intake manifold and the exhaust manifold (see Chapter 6). Disconnect any other interfering EGR system components.

8   Disconnect the PCV hose from the engine (see Chapter 6). Check that all interfering hoses are disconnected. On 2005 and

later models with a 5.4L engine, also remove the FRPT sensor (refer to Chapter 6).

9   On 2005 and later models with a 6.8L engine, disconnect the wiring from the throttle body connectors and the FRPT sensor. Disconnect the wiring harness retainer and move it aside for access.

10   Remove the fuel rail mounting bolts **(see illustration)**.

11   Carefully remove the fuel rail with the fuel injectors attached as an assembly.

12   Use a rocking, side-to-side motion while lifting to remove the injectors from the fuel rail.

Installation

Refer to illustrations 15.13a and 15.13b

13   Inspect the injector O-rings (two per injector) for signs of deterioration **(see illustrations)**. Replace as required. **Note:** *As long as you have the fuel rail off, it's a good idea to replace all of the O-rings.*

14   Inspect the injector plastic "hat" (covering the injector pintle) and washer for signs of deterioration. Replace as required. If the hat

15.13a Remove the O-ring from the top of the fuel injector . . .

15.13b . . . then remove the lower O-ring from the injector

Notes

16.4 Remove the IMTV actuator mounting bolts

17.1a Be sure to apply penetrating fluid to the exhaust flange nuts before attempting to remove them

is missing, look for it in the intake manifold.

15 Ensure that the injector caps are clean and free of contamination.

16 Place the fuel rail over each of the injectors and seat the injectors into the fuel rail. Ensure that the injectors are well seated in the fuel rail assembly. **Note:** *It may be easier to seat the injectors in the fuel rail and then seat the entire assembly in the lower intake manifold.*

17 Secure the fuel rail assembly with the retaining bolts and tighten them to the torque listed in this Chapter's Specifications.

18 The remainder of installation is the reverse of removal.

16 Intake Manifold Tuning system (1999 V8 models) - general information and replacement

General information

1 The IMT system controls the air intake charge by opening or closing the Intake Manifold Tuning Valve located in the center of the air intake manifold, directly below the air intake plenum. By closing the IMTV, the dual plenum design sends the air intake charge through a single corridor into the intake system of the engine. Above 3,000 rpm, the IMTV is opened, allowing the intake pulses to blend together at the intake manifold thereby creating a more efficient air/fuel intake charge for the additional rpm and engine load. A later version of this system, called the Intake Manifold Runner Control (IMRC), is used on 2008 and later 6.8L V10 engines.

2 The IMT system is difficult to check and requires a special scan tool to access the PCM for information and operating conditions. Have the system diagnosed by a dealer service department or other qualified repair shop.

Replacement

Refer to illustration 16.4

3 Remove the intake manifold from the engine (see Chapter 2A), then remove the

lower section from the intake manifold.

4 Remove the bolts that retain the IMT valve to the lower air intake plenum **(see illustration)**.

5 Installation is the reverse of removal.

17 Exhaust system servicing - general information

Refer to illustrations 17.1a and 17.1b

Warning: *Inspection and repair of exhaust system components should be done only after enough time has elapsed after driving the vehicle to allow the system components to cool completely. Also, when working under the vehicle, make sure it is securely supported on jackstands.*

1 The exhaust system consists of the exhaust manifold, the catalytic converter, the resonator, exhaust pipe, muffler and all brackets, hangers and clamps. The exhaust system is attached to the body with mounting brackets and rubber hangers **(see illustrations)**. If any of the parts are damaged or deteriorated, excessive noise and vibration will be transmitted to the body.

2 Conducting regular inspections of the exhaust system will keep it safe and quiet. Look for any damaged or bent parts, open seams, holes, loose connections, excessive corrosion or other defects which could allow exhaust fumes to enter the vehicle. Also check the catalytic converter when you inspect the exhaust system (see Chapter 6). Deteriorated exhaust system components should not be repaired; they should be replaced with new parts.

3 If the exhaust system components are extremely corroded or rusted together, they will probably have to be cut from the exhaust system. The convenient way to accomplish this is to have a muffler repair shop remove the corroded sections with a cutting torch. If, however, you want to save money by doing it yourself (and you don't have a welding outfit with a cutting torch), simply cut off the old

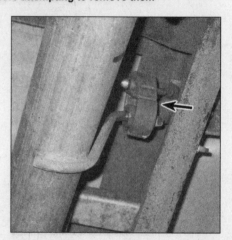

17.1b Check the condition of the rubber hangers (arrows) that support the exhaust system

components with a hacksaw. If you have compressed air, special pneumatic cutting chisels can also be used. If you decide to tackle the job at home, be sure to wear safety goggles to protect your eyes from metal chips and work gloves to protect your hands.

4 Here are some simple guidelines to follow when repairing the exhaust system:

a) *Work from the back to the front when removing exhaust system components.*

b) *Apply penetrating oil to the exhaust system component fasteners to make them easier to remove.*

c) *Use new gaskets, hangers and clamps when installing exhaust systems components.*

d) *Apply anti-seize compound to the threads of all exhaust system fasteners at reassembly.*

e) *Be sure to allow sufficient clearance between newly installed parts and all points on the underbody to avoid overheating the floor pan and possibly damaging the interior carpet and insulation. Pay particularly close attention to the catalytic converter and heat shield.*

Chapter 4 Part B
Fuel and exhaust systems - diesel engines

Contents

Section

Accelerator pedal position sensor ....See Chapter 6
Air filter - check and replacement.................................... See Chapter 1
Air filter housing - removal and installation....................See Chapter 4A
Engine oil temperature sensor...See Chapter 6
Exhaust system check.. See Chapter 1
Exhaust system servicing - general information........... See Chapter 4A
Fuel filter replacement.. See Chapter 1
Fuel filter/water separator housing and
   fuel pressure regulator - replacement 4
Fuel heater - general information and replacement.......................6
Fuel injectors - removal and installation 8
Fuel level sending unit - check and replacement .... See Chapter 4A
Fuel pressure check and fuel pump/fuel conditioning
   module replacement 3
Fuel pressure relief procedure...2
Fuel tank - removal and installation............................. See Chapter 4A

Section

Fuel tank cleaning and repair - general information ...... See Chapter 4A
General information..1
Glow plugs - general information and replacement.......................9
High-pressure oil pump/high-pressure fuel injection pump -
   removal and installation 7
Intercooler - replacement...12
Manifold air heater - general information
   and replacement 5
MAP sensor - replacement...See Chapter 6
Oil temperature sensor - replacement............................See Chapter 6
SERVICE ENGINE SOON light...................................... See Chapter 6
Turbocharger - general information and inspection.....................10
Turbocharger - removal, installation and
   wastegate adjustment 11
WATER IN FUEL light...See Chapter 1

Specifications

Fuel pressure
Fuel system pressure (at idle)

1999 models..	47 to 55 psi
2000 through 2003 7.3L engines	40 to 60 psi
6.4L engines (low pressure side only).............................	4 to 7 psi
6.0L engines,	
Running	45 to 55 psi
Key on, engine off..	0 to 55 psi

Torque specifications

Ft-lbs (unless otherwise noted)

Note: *One foot-pound (ft-lb) of torque is equivalent to 12 inch-pounds (in-lbs) of torque. Torque values below approximately 15 foot-pounds are expressed in inch-pounds, because most foot-pound torque wrenches are not accurate at these smaller values.*

Fuel filter /water separator housing bolts, 7.3L engine	23
Fuel conditioning module bolts, 6.0L engine	11
Fuel pressure regulator assembly	
7.3L engine	35
6.0L engine	37
High pressure oil pump	
Drive gear bolt	
7.3L	95
6.4L	58
Pump bolts	
7.3L engine	18
6.4L engine	46
6.0L engine	23
High-pressure fuel injection pump (6.4L engine)	
Drive gear bolt	57
Mounting bolts	45
High pressure threaded fittings-to-pump	33
Low pressure fitting threaded fittings-to-pump	35
Supply and return lines-to-threaded fittings on pump	
With copper sealing washers	28
With Viton sealing washers	18
Return tube fitting-to-pump	28
Fuel rail supply tube fittings	
Step 1	106 in-lbs
Step 2	Tighten an additional 60-degrees
Pump cover bolts	115 in-lbs
Fuel injectors	
7.3L engines	
Oil deflector shield bolts	108 in-lbs
Outboard bolts	120 in-lbs
6.4L (Injector hold-down clamp bolts)	28
6.0L engines	24
Fuel injector oil rail bolts, 6.0L engines	10
Glow plugs	
7.3L engines	15
6.4L engines	16
6.0L engines	168 in-lbs
Intercooler fasteners	
7.3L engines	19
6.4L engines	16
6.0L engines	132 in-lbs
Turbocharger-to-pedestal bolts	
7.3L engines	18
6.4L engines (hold-down bolts)	148 in-lbs
6.0L engines	23
Turbocharger pedestal-to-block bolts	
7.3L engines	18
6.4L engines	46
6.0L engines	23

1.1 Location of the fuel system components on the 7.3L turbo diesel model

1	Intercooler ducts	3	Turbocharger manifold
2	Manifold air heater	4	Turbocharger

5 High pressure oil system reservoir
6 Air intake duct

1   General information

General information

Refer to illustration 1.2

The fuel system is what most sets apart diesel engines from their gasoline powered cousins. Simply stated, fuel is injected directly into the combustion chambers; the more fuel injected, the more power the engine produces. Unlike gasoline engines, diesels have no throttle plate to limit the entry of air into the intake manifold. The only control is the amount of fuel injected; an unrestricted supply of air is always available through the intake.

There are two major sub-systems in the fuel injection system; the low pressure (also known as the supply) portion and the high pressure injection (delivery) portion **(see illustration)**.

The low pressure system moves fuel from the fuel tank to the cylinder heads. Fuel is drawn from the fuel tank by an externally mounted fuel pump adjacent to the fuel tank then pumped through a fuel filter/water separator located above the engine and then into the cylinder heads where it is routed through passageways to the fuel injectors. A fuel pressure regulator mounted on the fuel filter/water separator, relieves the fuel pressure and sends excess fuel back to the fuel tank acting as a bypass switching valve for fuel pressure control.

The 7.3L diesel engines use a high-pressure oil pump (Rexroth pump) to pressurize the fuel injectors. The pump is mounted directly behind the front cover on top of the engine. The pump reservoir is mounted on top of the front cover. The 6.0L diesel engines use a high pressure oil pump mounted in the engine valley at the rear of the block. Oil pressure is controlled by a solenoid operated poppet valve mounted on top of the amplifier piston on 7.3L engines. On 6.0L engines, oil pressure is controlled by the Injection Pressure Regulator (IPR) solenoid mounted on the high pressure oil pump. The PCM detects oil pressure within the system by the injection control oil pressure sensor mounted on the external oil rail. The PCM controls the fuel pressure within the high pressure oil pump system by way of the amplifier piston.

The 6.4L diesel engine is equipped with a high-pressure fuel injection pump mounted in the engine valley at the rear of the block. This pump provides pressurized diesel fuel to the common rail for each cylinder head without using a high pressure oil system for assist.

The PCM controls the injector timing and the injector output depending on information relayed to the PCM from the various sensors. The oil temperature sensor sends data to the PCM allowing the PCM to control the amount of fuel necessary for the particular driving condition (warm-up, cold start-up, operating mode, etc.). The MAP sensor and the BARO sensor send data to the PCM allowing the PCM to control the correct turbo boost for the exact driving condition (uphill, cruising, high altitude, hauling, etc.). These corrections are necessary to optimize the vehicle emissions and power.

Fuel system problems are by far the most frequent cause of breakdowns and loss of power in diesel-powered vehicles. Whenever a diesel engine quits running or loses power for no apparent reason, check the fuel system first. Begin with the most obvious items, such as the fuel filter and damaged fuel lines.

The fuel system on diesel engines is extremely sensitive to contamination. Because of the very minute orifices in the injection nozzles, fuel contamination can be a serious problem. The injection pump and the injectors can be damaged or ruined by contamination. Water-contaminated diesel fuel is a major problem. If it remains in the fuel system too long, water will cause serious and expensive damage. The fuel lines and the fuel filter can also become plugged with rust particles, or clogged with ice in cold weather.

Diesel fuel contamination

Before you replace an injector or some other expensive component, find out what caused the failure. If water contamination is present, buying a new or rebuilt injector or other component won't do much good. The following procedure will help you determine if water contamination is present:

a) Remove the engine fuel filter and inspect the contents for the presence of water or gasoline (see Chapter 1).

b) If the vehicle has been stalling, performance has been poor or the engine has been knocking loudly, suspect fuel contamination. Gasoline or water must be removed by flushing (see below).

c) If you find a lot of water in the fuel filter, remove the fuel return line and check for water there. If the pump has water in it, flush the system.

d) Small quantities of surface rust won't create a problem. If contamination is excessive, the vehicle will probably stall.

e) Sometimes contamination in the system becomes severe enough to cause damage to the system. If the damage reaches this stage, have the damaged parts replaced by an authorized diesel truck repair facility.

Storage

Good quality diesel fuel contains inhibitors to stop the formation of rust in the fuel lines and the injectors, so as long as there are no leaks in the fuel system, it's generally safe from water contamination. Diesel fuel is usually contaminated by water as a result of careless storage. There's not much you can do about the storage practices of service stations where you buy diesel fuel, but if you keep a small supply of diesel fuel on hand at home, as many diesel owners do, follow these simple rules:

a) Diesel fuel "ages" and goes stale. Don't store containers of diesel fuel for long periods of time. Use it up regularly and replace it with fresh fuel.

b) Keep fuel storage containers out of direct sunlight. Variations in heat and humidity promote condensation inside fuel containers.

c) Don't store diesel fuel in galvanized containers. It may cause the galvanizing to flake off, contaminating the fuel and clogging filters when the fuel is used.

d) Label containers properly, as containing diesel fuel.

Fighting fungi and bacteria with biocides

If there's water in the fuel, fungi and/or bacteria can form in warm or humid weather. Fungi and bacteria plug fuel lines, fuel filters and injection nozzles; they can also cause corrosion in the fuel system.

If you've had problems with water in the fuel system and you live in a warm or humid climate, have your dealer correct the problem. Then, use a diesel fuel biocide to sterilize the fuel system in accordance with the manufacturer's instructions. Biocides are available from your dealer, service stations and auto parts stores. Consult your dealer for advice on using biocides in your area and for recommendations on which ones to use.

Cleaning the fuel system

Warning: *Diesel fuel is flammable, so take extra precautions when you work on any part of the fuel system. Don't smoke or allow open flames or bare light bulbs near the work area, and don't work in a garage where a gas-type appliance (such as a water heater or a clothes dryer) is present. Since diesel fuel is carcinogenic, wear latex gloves when there's a possibility of being exposed to fuel, and, if you spill any fuel on your skin, rinse it off immediately with soap and water. Mop up any spills immediately and do not store diesel fuel-soaked rags where they could ignite. When you perform any kind of work on the fuel system, wear safety glasses and have a Class B type fire extinguisher on hand.*

Note: *If gasoline has been accidentally pumped into the fuel tank, it should be drained immediately. Gasoline in the fuel in small amounts - up to 30 percent - isn't usually noticeable. At higher ratios, the engine may make a knocking noise, which will get louder as the ratio of gasoline increases.*

Water in the fuel system

1   Disconnect the cable(s) from the negative battery terminal(s) (see Chapter 5, Section 1).

2   Drain the diesel fuel from the fuel tank into an approved container and dispose of it properly.

3   Remove the fuel tank gauge sending unit (see Chapter 4A).

4   Thoroughly clean the fuel tank. If it's rusted inside, send it to a repair shop or replace it.

5   Reinstall the fuel tank but don't connect the fuel lines to the fuel tank.

6   Disconnect the main fuel line from the fuel pump. Disconnect the supply line from the fuel filter/water separator (see Section 4) Using low air pressure, blow out the line toward the rear of the vehicle. **Warning:** *Wear eye protection when using compressed air.*

7   Temporarily disconnect the fuel return line at the fuel filter/water separator and at the fuel tank, using low air pressure, blow out the line toward the rear of the vehicle.

8   Reconnect the main fuel and return lines at the tank. Fill the tank to a fourth of its capacity with clean diesel fuel. Install the cap on the fuel filler neck.

9   Discard the fuel filter (see Chapter 1).

10   Connect the fuel line to the fuel pump.

11   Reconnect the battery cables.

12   Purge the fuel pump by cranking the engine until clean fuel is pumped out. Catch the fuel in a closed metal container.

13   Install a new fuel filter (see Chapter 1).

14   Install a hose from the fuel return line (at the fuel filter/water separator) to a metal container with a capacity of at least two gallons.

15   Crank the engine until clean fuel appears at the return line. Don't crank the engine for more than 30 seconds at a time. If it's necessary to crank it again, allow a three-minute interval before resuming.

16   Drain the fuel tank into an approved container and fill the tank with clean, fresh diesel fuel (see Chapter 4A).

17   Remove the fuel lines from the fuel filter/water separator at the cylinder heads.

18   Connect a short pipe and hose from the ends of the fuel lines to a metal container.

19   Crank the engine to purge the fuel pump and fuel filter. Don't crank the engine more than 30 seconds. Allow two or three minutes between cranking intervals for the starter to cool.

20   Remove the short pipe and hose and connect the fuel lines to the cylinder heads.

21   Remove the fuel drain plugs from the rear of the cylinder heads (refer to Section 8) and allow the diesel fuel and air to drain.

22   Install the fuel drain plugs on the back of the cylinder heads (see Section 8).

23   Try to start the engine. If it doesn't start, purge the air from the system again by removing the drain plugs at the back of the cylinder heads (see Section 8). **Warning:** *Avoid sources of ignition and have a fire extinguisher handy. Clean all the diesel fuel that may have spilled during the bleeding procedure.*

24   Start the engine and run it at idle for 15 minutes.

"Water-In-Fuel" (WIF) warning system

25   The system detects the presence of water in the fuel filter/water separator when it reaches excessive amounts. Water is detected by a probe located in the fuel filter that completes a circuit through a wire to a light in the instrument cluster that reads "Water In Fuel."

26   This system includes a bulb-check feature - when the ignition is turned on, the bulb glows momentarily, then fades away.

27   If the light comes on immediately after you've filled the tank or let the vehicle sit for an extended period of time, drain the water from the system immediately. Do not start the engine. There might be enough water in the system to shut the engine down before you've driven even a short distance. If, however, the light comes on during a cornering or braking maneuver, there's less water in the system; the engine probably won't shut down immediately, but you still should drain the water soon.

28   Water is heavier than diesel fuel, so it sinks to the bottom of the fuel tank. A bleed-off pipe on the fuel filter/water separator, which deposits the excess water onto the street enables you to siphon most of the water from the fuel filter/water separator without having to remove the tank. However, if the fuel tank is full of excessive amounts of water, siphoning won't remove all of the water; you'll still need to remove the tank and thoroughly clean it. **Warning:** *Do not start a siphon by mouth - use a siphoning kit (available at most auto parts stores).*

---

2   Fuel pressure relief procedure

Refer to illustration 2.2
Warning: *Diesel fuel is flammable, so take extra precautions when you work on any part of the fuel system. See the **Warning** in Section 1.*
Note: *After the fuel pressure has been relieved, it's a good idea to lay a shop towel over any fuel connection to be disassembled,*

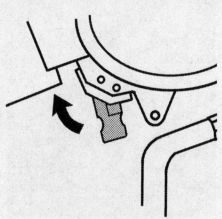

2.2 The drain valve lever is located on the right side of the fuel filter/water separator - 7.3L engine

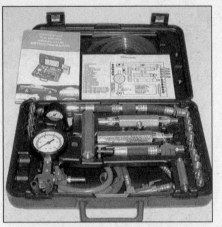

3.6a This fuel pressure testing kit contains all the necessary fittings and adapters, along with the fuel pressure gauge, to test most automotive fuel systems

3.6b Install the fuel pressure gauge between the fuel pump and the fuel supply line to the engine

to absorb the residual fuel that may leak out when servicing the fuel system.

7.3L engines

1   Remove the fuel filler cap - this will relieve any pressure built up in the fuel tank.

2   Locate the drain valve on the right side of the fuel filter/water separator **(see illustration)**.

3   Position a suitable container under the drain hose on the shop floor.

4   Open the fuel filter water drain valve by turning the lever clockwise and allow the fuel to bleed into the container.

5   After the residual fuel has drained from the valve, close the fuel filter water drain valve and wipe off any fuel that may have dripped along the fuel lines or the vehicle frame.

6.0L engines

6   Raise the vehicle and support it securely on jackstands. If you have a 4X4 vehicle, there is probably enough clearance to simply crawl under it after first setting the parking brake and making sure it's in Park.

7   Disconnect the cable from the negative battery terminal(s).

8   Locate the fuel conditioning module attached near the rear of the vehicle to the frame rail **(see illustration 3.12b)**. Place a drain pan under it.

9   Open the fuel and water drain valve on the side near the bottom of it and allow it to drain into the pan.

10   After draining it, close the valve and clean any spilled water and fuel.

6.4L engines

11   On 6.4L engines, the fuel passes through a small radiator (near the throttle body) that cools incoming fuel.

12   Attach a fuel pressure test kit to the Schrader valve on the fuel cooler.

13   With the drain tube in a suitable container, release the valve and drain until the fuel pressure is relieved.

3   Fuel pressure check and fuel pump/fuel conditioning module replacement

Warning: *Diesel fuel is flammable, so take extra precautions when you work on any part of the fuel system. See the* **Warning** *in Section 1.*

Note: *After the fuel pressure has been relieved, it's a good idea to lay a shop towel over any fuel connection to be disassembled, to absorb the residual fuel that may leak out when servicing the fuel system.*

General checks

Note 1: *The inertia switch is an electrical device wired into the fuel pump circuit that will shut down power to the fuel pump in an accident (see Chapter 4A, Section 2). Be sure to check that the inertia switch is activated and in working order if the fuel pump is not receiving the proper voltage.*

Note 2: *The fuel pump relay is equipped with a primary and secondary voltage circuit. The primary circuit is controlled by the PCM and the secondary circuit is linked directly to battery voltage from the ignition switch. With the ignition switch ON (engine not running), the PCM will ground the relay for one second. During cranking, the PCM grounds the fuel pump relay as long as the reference signal from the camshaft position sensor is received (see Chapter 6). If there are no reference pulses, the fuel pump will shut off after two or three seconds.*

1   If you suspect insufficient fuel delivery, check the following items first:

a) *Check the battery and make sure it's fully charged (see Chapter 5).*

b) *Check the fuel pump fuse.*

c) *Check the fuel filter for restriction.*

d) *Inspect all fuel lines to ensure that the problem is not simply a leak in a line.*

2   Verify the fuel pump actually runs. Place

the transmission in Park (automatic) or Neutral (manual) and apply the parking brake. Have an assistant turn the ignition switch to ON - you should hear a brief whirring noise (for approximately two seconds) as the pump comes on and pressurizes the system. If there is no response from the fuel pump (makes no sound), check the fuel pump electrical circuit. If the fuel pump runs, but a fuel system problem is suspected, continue with the fuel pump pressure check.

3   If the pump does not turn on (makes no sound) with the ignition switch in the ON position, check the ignition fuse located in the engine compartment fuse center. Also, check the fuel pump relay. Refer to Chapter 12 for testing relays. **Note:** *The fuel pump relay is located either in the fuse/relay center in the engine compartment or behind the radio in the center of the instrument panel.*

4   If the relays are good and the fuel pump does not operate, check the fuel pump circuit. If the wiring and the connectors are good, replace the fuel pump.

Pressure check

Refer to illustrations 3.6a and 3.6b

Note: *In order to perform the fuel pressure test, you will need a fuel pressure gauge capable of measuring high fuel pressure. The fuel gauge must be equipped with the proper fitting required to attach it to the fuel pump and the inlet line.*

5   Relieve the fuel system pressure (see Section 2).

6   Remove the fuel line from the fuel pump and attach a fuel pressure gauge **(see illustrations)**.

7   Turn all the accessories Off and switch the ignition key On (engine not running). The fuel pump should run for approximately two seconds. Note the reading on the gauge. If the fuel pressure is lower than specified, check the fuel line from the tank for restrictions. If no restriction is found, check the fuel pump wiring for high resistance. If no problems are found, replace the fuel pump.

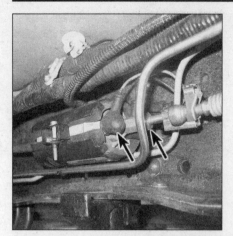

3.12a Disconnect the fuel pump electrical connectors - 7.3L engine

3.12b The fuel conditioning module on 6.0L engines is located on the left frame rail in front of the fuel tank

3.16 Loosen the fuel pump mounting bracket bolt - 7.3L engine

8   If the fuel pressure recorded in Step 7 is higher than specified, check the fuel line to the fuel filter/water separator for restrictions. If no restrictions are found, have the fuel pump and lines diagnosed by a dealer service department or other qualified truck repair facility. **Note:** *High fuel pump pressure is more difficult to diagnose. The fuel return lines, the pressure regulator, the fuel pump or the fuel filter/water separator assembly may be damaged, clogged or the fuel lines may be bent. Have the system checked by a qualified technician.*

Fuel pump/fuel conditioning module replacement

Refer to illustrations 3.12a, 3.12b and 3.16
Note: *On 6.0L and 6.4L models, the fuel pump is part of the fuel conditioning module. This module also contains a fuel filter, a water separator, a fuel heater (and recirculation), a pressure relief valve, a drain valve and a pressure regulator.*
9   Relieve the fuel system pressure (see Section 2).
10   Disconnect the cable(s) from the negative battery terminal(s) (see Chapter 5, Section 1).
11   Raise the vehicle and support it on jackstands.

12   Disconnect the fuel pump electrical connector **(see illustrations)**.
13   Remove the fuel lines from the fuel pump. Use special fuel line tools to release the spring locks on the fuel line connectors (see Chapter 4A).
14   Unclip the brake lines from the fuel pump bracket if they interfere.
15   Remove the fuel pump/fuel conditioning module nuts. On 6.0L and 6.4L models, remove the fuel conditioning module. **Caution:** *On 6.4L engines, use only a Fuel Conditioning Module with a brown cover on the fuel pump. Use of a module with a black cover could cause fuel system damage.*
16   On 7.3L models, loosen the pinch bolt and slide the fuel pump out of the bracket.
17   Installation is the reverse of removal.

---

4   Fuel filter/water separator housing and fuel pressure regulator - replacement

Warning: *Diesel fuel is flammable, so take extra precautions when you work on any part of the fuel system. See the* **Warning** *in Section 1.*
Note: *This procedure applies only to vehicles*

with 7.3L engines. On 6.0L and 6.4L engines, the fuel pressure regulator is an integral part of the fuel filter housing.

Fuel filter/water separator housing
Refer to illustrations 4.5 and 4.7
1   Disconnect the cable(s) from the negative battery terminal(s) (see Chapter 5, Section 1).
2   Relieve the fuel system pressure (see Section 2).
3   Remove the fuel filter (see Chapter 1).
4   Use a siphon or a suction pump to remove all the diesel fuel from the fuel filter/water separator housing.
5   Disconnect the fuel supply line and the fuel return line from the fuel filter/water separator housing **(see illustration)**.
6   Disconnect both fuel lines from the cylinder heads.
7   Disconnect the electrical connector from the fuel pressure regulator **(see illustration)** and the fuel heater.
8   Disconnect the exhaust backpressure sensor electrical connector (see Chapter 6) and remove the sensor.
9   Remove the fuel filter/water separator mounting bolts **(see illustration 7.2)**.
10   Lift the assembly from the engine compartment.

4.5 Location of the fuel return line (1) and the fuel supply line (2) on the fuel filter/water separator - 7.3L engine

4.7 Location of the fuel pressure regulator (1) and the fuel heater (2) on the fuel filter/water separator - 7.3L engine

4.18 The secondary fuel filter is adjacent to the oil filter housing on 6.0L diesel engines

5.4 Location of the intake air heater element electrical connector - 7.3L engine

11   Installation is the reverse of removal. Tighten the fuel filter/water separator housing bolts to the torque listed in this Chapter's Specifications.

Fuel pressure regulator

7.3L engines

12   Remove the fuel filter/water separator housing (see Steps 1 through 10).
13   Remove the fuel pressure regulator by turning it counterclockwise.
14   Separate the fuel pressure regulator from the housing. Remove the cap, the O-rings, the spring, the poppet valve and the valve seat.
15   Installation is the reverse of removal. Be sure to clean the fuel pressure regulator bore and replace the O-rings with new parts before reassembly.
16   Tighten the fuel pressure regulator to the torque listed in this Chapter's Specifications.

6.0L engines

Refer to illustration 4.18

17   Remove the engine-mounted fuel filter, then suction the fuel from the canister (refer to Chapter 1). Dispose of the fuel in an approved manner.
18   Disconnect the fuel line from the regulator cover on the side of the fuel filter housing **(see illustration)**.
19   Remove the four screws from the fuel pressure regulator cover and lift off the cover.
20   Remove the small restrictor from the top of the regulator
21   Remove the spring and the poppet from the lower area of the regulator.
22   Thoroughly and carefully clean the regulator bore.
23   Installation is the reverse of removal.

5   Manifold air heater - general information and replacement

Note: *This procedure applies only to 7.3L engines. Later models do not have a manifold air heater.*

General information

1   The manifold air heater provides heated air to the combustion chambers to enhance cold starting and reduce white smoke caused by low engine oil temperatures and low ambient air temperatures. The system is only activated after the glow plug system has shut down after start-up and the vehicle transmission is in Park or Neutral and the parking brake is applied. Depending upon the condition of the engine, the relays are energized by the PCM according to the information detected by the engine sensors (see Chapter 6).
2   The PCM operates the two heating elements within the air heater assembly through the two intake manifold air heater relays. Make sure the "WAIT-TO-START" light on the dash has canceled before starting the engine.

Replacement

Manifold air heater

Refer to illustration 5.4

3   Disconnect the cable(s) from the negative battery terminal(s) (see Chapter 5, Section 1).
4   Remove the nut from the intake air heater element connector **(see illustration)**.
5   Remove the insulator cables from the stud.
6   Disconnect the intake air heater connector.
7   Remove the insulator from the assembly.
8   Remove the intake air heater element and the copper washer.
9   Installation is the reverse of removal. Be sure to use new copper washers.

Relay

Refer to illustration 5.11

10   Disconnect the cable(s) from the negative battery terminal(s) (see Chapter 5, Section 1).
11   Disconnect the wires from the relay **(see illustration)**.
12   Unscrew the bolt(s) and remove the relay(s).
13   Installation is the reverse of removal.

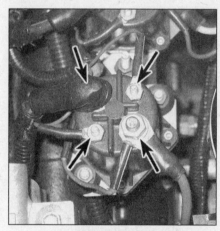

5.11 Location of the intake air heater relay connections - 7.3L engine

6   Fuel heater - general information and replacement

Warning: *Diesel fuel is flammable, so take extra precautions when you work on any part of the fuel system. See the* **Warning** *in Section 1.*
Note: *This procedure applies only to models with 7.3L engines. Models with 6.0L and 6.4L engines have a fuel conditioning module that incorporates a fuel heater as well as other components (refer to Section 3).*

General information

1   The fuel heater prevents diesel fuel from waxing during cold weather operation. A defective fuel heater can cause wax build-up in the fuel filter/water separator. This clogging effect can make the engine difficult to start and prevent the engine from revving up. This condition can also cause a blue or white exhaust. If the heater doesn't operate in a cold climate, the engine might not operate at all because of fuel waxing.
2   The fuel heater is located at the bottom of the fuel filter/water separator assembly.

6.7 Location of the fuel heater element mounting screws - 7.3L engine

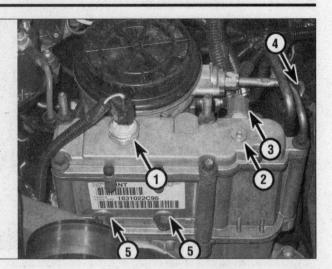

7.3 High pressure oil pump system details - 7.3L engine

1   Oil pressure switch
2   High pressure oil reservoir plug
3   High pressure oil temperature sensor
4   High pressure oil system pressure sensor
5   Fuel filter/water separator housing mounting bolts

Replacement

Refer to illustration 6.7

3   Remove the fuel filter/water separator assembly (see Section 4).

4   Remove the fuel heater thermostat mounting screws.

5   Remove the thermostat from the fuel filter/water separator housing.

6   Disconnect the electrical connector from the fuel heater.

7   Remove the mounting screws **(see illustration)** and lift the fuel heater from the fuel filter/water separator housing.

8   Installation is the reverse of removal.

7   High-pressure oil pump/high-pressure fuel injection pump - removal and installation

Removal

High-pressure oil pump

7.3L engines

Refer to illustrations 7.3, 7.5 and 7.7

1   Remove the turbocharger and the turbocharger inlet manifold (see Section 11).

2   Remove the fuel filter/water separator assembly (see Section 4).

3   Remove the plug from the high pressure oil pump reservoir **(see illustration)**.

4   Suction the oil from the reservoir using a special suction tool or pump.

5   Use a special tool designed for high pressure oil lines and remove the two high pressure oil lines from the pump **(see illustration)**.

6   Disconnect the electrical connector from the high pressure oil pump pressure regulator.

7   Working on the front of the engine, remove the bolts **(see illustration)** from the drive gear bolt cover. Remove the cover.

8   Remove the drive gear bolt and washer.

9   Working on the back of the front cover, remove the high pressure oil pump mounting bolts.

10   Remove the high pressure oil pump from the engine.

6.0L engines

11   Remove the turbocharger and the turbocharger inlet Y-pipe (see Section 11).

12   Remove the heat shield mounting nuts/bolts, the electrical connectors and separate the heat shield from the engine.

13   Pull back the heat insulating wrap and disconnect the fuel injection pressure regulator (IPR) valve connector.

14   Remove the heat wrap and the IPR valve.

15   Remove the eight bolts from the high pressure oil pump cover. Use a thin blade tool to carefully separate the cover from the block, starting at the rear seam.

16   Remove the two bolts on the high pressure oil branch tube adapter.

17   Remove the 3 high pressure oil pump bolts and separate the assembly from the engine valley.

18   Remove the two small seals and the large pump O-ring seal.

High-pressure fuel injection pump (6.4L engines)

19   Wait at least ten minutes for the high pressure fuel pump to cool down and the fuel pressure to bleed down before proceeding.

20   Remove the turbocharger and the Exhaust Gas Recirculation (EGR) inlet pipes (see Section 10).

21   Remove the glow plug module heat shield.

7.5 Location of the high pressure oil pump lines at the high pressure oil pump - 7.3L engine

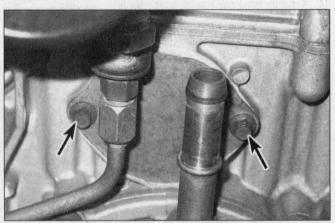

7.7 Location of the drive gear bolt cover mounting fasteners - 7.3L engine

8.2 Disconnect the injector electrical connector - 7.3L engine

8.3 Location of the left internal oil rail drain plug - two drain plugs in each cylinder head - 7.3L engine

1. *Left internal oil rail drain plug*
2. *Oil deflector retaining screws*
3. *Outboard injector retaining bolt (hidden from view)*

22 Remove the bolts/nuts/brackets and the left and right side high pressure fuel injection pump heat shields.

23 Remove the fuel rail supply line brackets.

24 Remove the fuel rail supply lines from the main pump and the cylinder heads. Use a back-up wrench on the high pressure fuel injection pump fittings while the supply lines are being loosened.

25 Remove the mounting bolts and the high pressure fuel injection pump cover.

26 Disconnect the electrical connectors and remove the high pressure fuel injection pump mounting bolts.

27 Lift the high pressure fuel injection pump and gear assembly from the engine valley.

Installation

High-pressure oil pump

7.3L engines

28 Replace the oil pump pressure regulator if the pump is being replaced with a new one. Remove the mounting nut and the pressure regulator solenoid from the high pressure oil pump.

29 Install a new gasket onto the high pressure oil pump flange.

30 Position the oil pump onto the front cover. Make sure the drive gear is fully seated on the high pressure oil pump before installing the bolt and washer.

31 Tighten the drive gear bolt to the torque listed in this Chapter's Specifications.

32 Install the high pressure oil pump mounting bolts and torque them to the Specifications listed in this Chapter.

33 Install the drive gear bolt cover and tighten the cover bolts securely.

6.0L engines

34 Install new O-ring seals.

35 Tighten the oil pump bolts to the torque listed in this Chapter's Specifications.

36 Use a new gasket when installing the pump cover. Also thoroughly clean the mounting surface and apply a small amount of RTV sealant to the seams.

37 The remainder of installation is the reverse of removal.

High-pressure fuel injection pump (6.4L engines)

38 Install new O-ring seals.

39 If a new high pressure fuel injection pump will be installed, remove the original drive gear and install it onto the pump, tightening the bolt to the torque listed in this Chapter's Specifications. **Caution:** *The drive gear bolt is a REVERSE (left handed) thread.*

40 Install the pump and tighten the mounting bolts to the torque listed in this Chapter's Specifications.

41 Reconnect the electrical connectors.

42 Install the pump cover and tighten the bolts to the torque listed in this Chapter's Specifications.

43 Install the fuel rail supply lines. Be sure to use a back-up wrench on the high pressure fuel injection pump fittings while the supply lines are being tightened.

44 Use a deep socket and tighten the high and low pressure fittings on the pump to this Chapter's Specifications. Using new sealing washers, connect the lines to the threaded fittings, then tighten the fitting nuts to the torque listed in this Chapter's Specifications.

45 Install the high pressure fuel injection pump heat shield and the glow plug module heat shield.

46 The remainder of installation is the reverse of removal.

8 Fuel injectors - removal and installation

Warning: *Diesel fuel is flammable, so take extra precautions when you work on any part of the fuel system. See the* **Warning** *in Section 1.*
Note: *Several special tools are needed to remove and install the fuel injectors. Read through the procedure and obtain the special tools (or their equivalents) before beginning.*

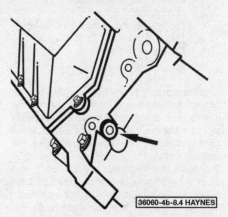

8.4 Remove the drain plug from the rear of each cylinder head - 7.3L engine

Removal

7.3L engines

Refer to illustrations 8.2, 8.3, 8.4, 8.7 and 8.10

1 Remove the valve cover (see Chapter 2B). **Warning:** *Allow the engine to cool for ten minutes before beginning the procedure. This will allow the fuel pressure to decrease.*

2 Disconnect the electrical connector from the fuel injector **(see illustration)**.

3 Remove all the internal oil rail drain plugs and allow the oil to drain from the oil galleries **(see illustration)**. **Caution:** *If the plugs are not removed prior to removing the injectors, oil will enter the combustion chamber and could cause hydrostatic lock and severe engine damage.* **Note:** *There are two oil rail drain plugs in each cylinder head.*

4 Drain the diesel fuel from the cylinder heads by removing the drain plugs located at the rear of the cylinder heads **(see illustration)**.

5 Remove the retaining screws and oil deflectors **(see illustration 8.3)** from each fuel injector hold-down plate.

6 Remove the outboard injector retaining bolt.

7 Remove the injector. Retrieve the copper washer and any O-ring material from the bore

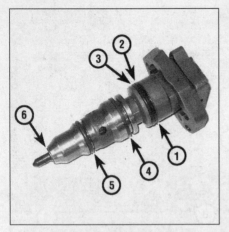

8.7 Diesel injector details

1　Steel back-up ring
2　Cushion ring - square section (black)
3　O-ring (black)
4　O-ring - square section (blue/black)
5　O-ring (black)
6　Copper gasket

8.10 Be sure to seal the injector bores with a soft cloth to prevent debris from falling inside

(see illustration). Note: *The manufacturer recommends using a special tool to remove the injector from the cylinder head and a special tool to install the injector. Check with a dealer parts department or a special automotive tool manufacturer.*

8　Mark the injectors, cap the ends and store them in a holder so they can be kept clean and returned to their original locations.

9　Normally the injector sleeves do not require removal. There are several special tools required to extract the injector sleeves from the cylinder heads.

10　Be sure to seal the injector bores in the cylinder head to prevent debris from entering **(see illustration)**.

6.0L and 6.4L engines

11　Remove the valve covers (refer to Chapter 2B).

12　Unbolt and remove the high pressure fuel rail. **Caution:** *Don't try to remove components on the fuel rail such as the end plugs.*

13　Remove the block-to-head tubes from the oil rail assemblies or the branch tube assemblies by prying on their rings.

14　Use manufacturer special tool #303-1115 or an equivalent to push the injector wiring out of the rocker arm carrier.

15　Carefully put clean rags in all of the oil drain holes near the injectors. **Caution:** *There are small snap-rings in the injector assemblies. Be extremely careful to avoid dropping or losing one. Severe engine damage will result if a snap-ring is dropped into the oil system.*

16　Using Snap-On tool #SDMT440 or an equivalent, remove the bolts securing the fuel injector clamps. Remove the bolts, clamps and injectors.

17　Verify that all snap-rings and other small components are accounted for and then remove the rags from the oil holes.

Installation
7.3L engine

18　Make sure the oil drain plugs and the fuel drain plugs are installed and tightened securely.

19　Carefully clean the injector sleeve with a bottle brush and wipe it with a clean cloth to ensure a good O-ring seal.

20　Install new O-rings, cushion ring and a new copper gasket as shown **(see illustration 8.7)**. Apply engine oil to the O-rings and insert the injector into the cylinder head. Press the injector in by hand until the injector hold-down plate is under the head of the shoulder bolt. Do not strike the top of the injector to seat the injector in the bore. **Caution:** *Make sure all deposits of oil and fuel are removed from the cylinder. Oil and fuel will cause hydrostatic lock and severe engine damage. It is possible to expel excess fuel and/or oil by removing the glow plug(s) and rotating the engine using a breaker bar and socket on the crankshaft pulley bolt. After the glow plug(s) are installed, double-check the procedure by turning the engine over three complete revolutions using a breaker bar and socket on the crankshaft pulley bolt. If the engine locks or exhibits any resistance, repeat the clean-out procedure. If the engine locks again or exhibits any resistance, have the fuel system, the high pressure oil system and the cylinders tested by a dealer service department or other qualified repair facility. Make sure the excess fuel and oil deposits are thoroughly cleaned from the engine and surrounding area before proceeding.*

21　Install the outboard injector retaining bolt(s) and the oil deflector bolt(s). Tighten the bolts to the torque listed in this Chapter's Specifications.

22　The remainder of installation is the reverse of removal.

6.0L and 6.4L engines

23　Before beginning the reassembly procedure, install new D-ring seals on each block-to-head tube. The tubes will have to sit for several hours afterwards in order for the seals to relax back to their original shape. If you try to install the tubes before the seals have relaxed, they may tear.

24　Install new O-rings and a new copper washer on each injector. On 6.4L engines, the injector combustion gaskets are soft steel. **Note:** *Check the oil inlet D-rings for damage. If they are damaged in any way, the injector must be replaced.*

25　Install the injectors along with the clamps and bolts. On 6.4L engines, install new tubes between the injectors and the fuel rail.

26　Install the wiring into the rocker carrier. **Note:** *Make certain that the wiring is not interfering with any mechanical components.*

27　Oil both of the block-to-head tube seals and install them into the branch tube assemblies, making sure that they are completely bottomed out.

28　Carefully set the oil rail on the injectors. Make sure that the four single ball tubes are properly mating with the injector lead angle.

29　Start a bolt at each end of the manifold and one in the center of the side with the wavy edge for use as guide studs. Tighten the guide studs six or seven turns.

30　Push the oil rail down onto the fuel injectors. Verify that its feet are flat against the mounting surface.

31　Start the six remaining bolts.

32　Remove the guide studs and replace them with the original bolts.

33　Tighten all nine bolts to the torque listed in this Chapter's Specificatons and in the correct sequence **(see illustration)**.

34　Connect the injector wiring and install the valve covers. The remainder of installation is the reverse of removal.

9　Glow plug system - general information and replacement

Warning 1: *Diesel fuel is flammable, so take extra precautions when you work on any part of the fuel system. See the* **Warning** *in Section 1.*
Warning 2: *The glow plugs operate on 115-volts DC. Do not pierce the wiring insulation or use a conventional test light on the glow plug wiring, as you could receive a severe shock.*

General information

1　The glow plugs are designed to heat up extremely fast. When voltage is applied to the glow plug, rapid heating of the glow plug tip occurs, which in turn heats up the air inside the pre-chamber. As the fuel is injected into the pre-chamber, it is ignited. The rapid burning of the fuel forces it through the small opening in the pre-chamber into the cylinder where it mixes with more hot air and a second combustion takes place. To prevent overheating of the glow plug, a cycling device is used in the circuit. **Note:** *If the tip is missing from a glow plug or is damaged, the fuel quality is probably incorrect. If the tip is distorted, the glow plugs are probably staying on too long. Glow plugs are not interchangeable between the early and later model systems.*

9.7 Location of the glow plug electrical connector - 7.3L engine

9.8 Location of the glow plug - 7.3L engine

2   The PCM controls the glow plug relay on-off time. The system consists of eight glow plugs, a glow plug relay, the PCM, an engine oil temperature sensor and a barometric pressure sensor. The PCM decreases the glow plug on-time as oil temperature and barometric pressure increase. The glow plugs are located in the cylinder heads and are accessible only by removing the valve covers.

3   The WAIT TO START lamp is located in the instrument cluster. This lamp informs the driver when the glow plugs are hot enough for the engine to be started. The wait lamp will come on when the ignition switch is in the On position, only when the engine is below 165 degrees F. For a bulb check, the bulb will come on when the ignition switch is in the Start position.

4   The glow plug relay switches power to the glow plugs when signaled by the PCM. The glow plug relay system varies depending upon vehicle destination; Federal or California standards. The Federal models use a single relay mounted in the engine compartment near the fuel filter/water separator. On time varies between 1 and 120 seconds. California models are equipped with a glow plug module. The glow plug module monitors and detects individual glow plug functions. This information is relayed to the PCM where it is accessible by scan tool. Glow plug system diagnostics are part of the On Board II (OBD-II) diagnostic system (see Chapter 6).

5   The wiring harness to the glow plug circuit incorporates two replaceable fusible links, one for each glow plug bank.

Replacement
Glow plugs

7.3L engine
Refer to illustrations 9.7 and 9.8

6   Remove the valve cover (see Chapter 2B).
7   Disconnect the electrical connector from the glow plug(s) **(see illustration)**.
8   Remove the glow plug using a deep socket **(see illustration)**.

9   Be sure to inspect the tip of the glow plug for damage. Replace the glow plug with a new part, if necessary.
10   Installation is the reverse of removal.

6.0L and 6.4L engines
11   Use Ford special tool #303-1114 or an equivalent to remove the wiring from each glow plug. **Note:** *This tool simply hooks under the bottom of the wiring connector so that the wiring can be pushed off from the bottom rather than pulled off. Pulling the wiring off can easily damage the assembly.*
12   Unscrew the glow plugs.
13   Installation is the reverse of removal.

Glow plug relay

6.0L and 6.4L engines
Refer to illustration 9.18
14   Disconnect the cable from the negative battery terminal(s).
15   Disconnect the electrical connectors from the glow plug relay. On 6.0L engines, also disconnect the injection control presure (ICP) wiring connector.
16   Remove the relay mounting nuts and remove the relay.
17   Installation is the reverse of removal.

7.3L engines
18   Disconnect the electrical connectors from the glow plug relay **(see illustration)**.
19   Remove the glow plug relay mounting nuts.
20   Replace the glow plug relay with a new part, if necessary.
21   Installation is the reverse of removal.

10   Turbocharger - general information and inspection

General information
Refer to illustration 10.3
1   The turbocharger pressurizes the air entering the combustion chamber by using

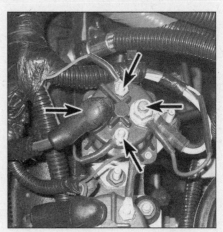

9.18 Location of the glow plug relay electrical connectors - Federal 7.3L models

an exhaust gas-driven turbine. Compressing more air into the combustion chamber increases power output, improves fuel efficiency and performance at high altitudes. The turbocharger identification number is located on an ID plate riveted to the housing. This number should be referred to if replacement is required. **Note:** *The turbocharger is normally covered by the Federally mandated emissions warranty. Check with a dealer service department concerning coverage.*

2   A turbocharger improves engine performance, lowers the density of exhaust smoke, improves fuel economy, reduces engine noise and mitigates the effects of lower density air at higher altitude.

7.3L engine
3   The amount of "boost" (intake manifold pressure) is controlled by a "wastegate" (exhaust bypass valve). The wastegate is operated by a spring-loaded actuator assembly which controls the maximum boost level by allowing a certain amount of exhaust gas to bypass the turbine in accordance with the

10.3 The exhaust backpressure sensor is located in the front of the high-pressure oil system reservoir - 7.3L engine

10.12 Location of the wastegate actuator control rod - 7.3L engine

intake manifold pressure. An exhaust back-pressure sensor is used to detect exhaust system backpressure information for the PCM **(see illustration)**.

6.0L and 6.4L engines

4   6.0L and 6.4L engines don't have a conventional wastegate; a Variable Geometry Turbocharger (VGT) design is used instead. In this system, boost is controlled by variable vanes in the exhaust turbine section of the turbocharger. The vanes are connected to a unison ring that moves all the vanes together. The unison ring in turn is moved by the actuator and the control valve. The control valve uses engine oil pressure to supply sufficient force to move the unison ring. All of these components are part of the turbocharger assembly itself. The operation of this system is done by the powertrain control module (PCM) responding to inputs from various sensors including the exhaust pressure (EP) sensor.

5   Turbocharged models are equipped with an "intercooler," a heat exchanger through which the compressed air intake charge is routed to lower the temperature of the intake charge. Cooler air is denser, which promotes combustion efficiency, increasing power and reducing emissions.

Inspection

Turbocharger

6   Though it's a relatively simple device, the turbocharger is a precision component. Special tools are needed to disassemble and overhaul a turbocharger, so servicing should be left to a specialist. However, you can inspect some things yourself, such as a cracked turbo mounting flange, a worn out or overheated turbine/compressor shaft bearing or a defective wastegate actuator.

7   On 6.4L engines, the turbocharger assembly utilizes two turbochargers. One is optimized for low-pressure output, and one for high-pressure output resulting in higher engine power and efficiency. The two variable-vane turbochargers are controlled by the

PCM through the turbocharger actuator.

8   A turbocharger has its own distinctive sound, so a change in the quality or the quantity of noise can be a sign of potential problems. Before assuming that a funny sound is caused by a defective turbocharger, inspect the exhaust manifold for cracks and loose connections. For example, a high-pitched or whistling sound might indicate an intake air or exhaust gas leak. Inspect the turbocharger mounting flange at the exhaust manifold and make sure that the hose clamp that attaches the air intake duct to the turbocharger is tight.

9   If an unusual sound is coming from the turbocharger, remove the intake duct between the air cleaner housing and the turbocharger. Reach inside the housing and turn the compressor wheel to make sure it spins freely. If it doesn't, it's possible the turbo lubricating oil has sludged or coked up from overheating. Push in on the turbine wheel and check for binding. The turbine should rotate freely with no binding or rubbing on the housing. If it does, the turbine or compressor shaft bearing is worn out. **Warning:** *Inspect the turbocharger with the engine off and cool to the touch. Touching or reaching inside a hot and/or operating turbocharger can cause serious injury.*

10   The turbocharger is lubricated by engine oil that has been pressurized, cooled and filtered. Oil is delivered to the turbocharger entering through a channel directly under the turbocharger from the engine block. Oil travels to the turbocharger's bearing housing, where it lubricates the shaft and bearings. A return channel at the bottom of the turbocharger routes the engine oil back to the crankcase. Because the turbine and compressor wheels spin at speeds up to 140,000 rpm, severe damage can result from the interruption or contamination of the oil supply to the turbocharger bearings. Burned oil on the turbine housing is a sign of a blocked return line. **Caution:** *Whenever a major engine bearing such as a main, connecting rod or camshaft bearing is replaced, flush the turbocharger oil passages with clean oil.*

Wastegate actuator

Refer to illustration 10.12

11   The turbocharger wastegate regulates intake manifold air pressure and prevents over-boosting at high engine speeds. When the wastegate valve is closed, all exhaust gas flows through the turbine wheel. As the intake manifold pressure increases, the wastegate actuator opens the exhaust bypass valve, diverting some exhaust gas around the turbine wheel, limiting turbine shaft speed and, therefore, air output from the turbocharger.

12   To test the wastegate actuator, disconnect the pressure hose from the actuator, connect a hand-held pressure pump in its place and apply approximately 5 psi pressure to the actuator. The control rod **(see illustration)** should move slightly and hold its position. If the rod doesn't move, replace the wastegate actuator.

---

11   Turbocharger - removal, installation and wastegate adjustment

Caution: *The turbocharger is a precision component which has been assembled and balanced to very fine tolerances. Do not disassemble it or try to repair it. Turbochargers should only be overhauled or repaired by authorized turbocharger repair facilities. An incorrectly assembled turbocharger could result in damage to the turbocharger and/or the engine.*

Removal

7.3L engine

Refer to illustrations 11.2a, 11.2b, 11.3, 11.4a, 11.4b, 11.5, 11.6, 11.7, 11.8, 11.11, 11.12 and 11.14

1   Disconnect the cable(s) from the negative battery terminal(s) (see Chapter 5, Section 1).

2   Remove the air filter housing (see Chapter 4A) and the inlet and outlet intercooler ducts from the turbocharger manifold **(see illustrations)**.

11.2a Location of the clamps for the inlet and outlet intercooler ducts at the turbocharger manifold - 7.3L engine

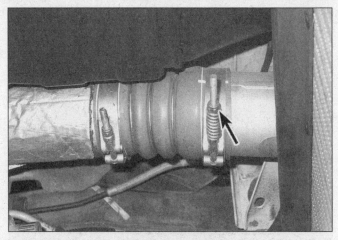

11.2b Location of the intercooler duct clamp at the intercooler - 7.3L engine

11.3 Disconnect the manifold air heater connector (1), the MAP sensor vacuum hoses (2) and the IAT sensor connector (3) - 7.3L engine

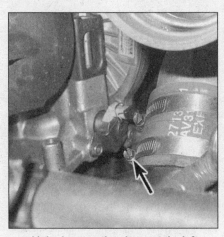

11.4a Loosen the clamp at the left manifold intake hose and . . .

11.4b . . . the right manifold intake hose and lift the turbocharger manifold from the 7.3L engine

3   Label and disconnect the manifold air heater connector, the MAP sensor vacuum lines and electrical connector and the IAT sensor connector (see illustration).

4   Loosen the clamps and remove the turbocharger manifold (see illustrations).
5   Remove the turbocharger O-ring seal (see illustration).

6   Remove the exhaust outlet pipe clamp from the turbocharger (see illustration).
7   On vehicles equipped with an exhaust backpressure valve, slide the retaining clip from

11.5 Remove the turbocharger O-ring - 7.3L engine

11.6 Remove the pipe clamp from the turbocharger exhaust outlet - 7.3L engine

11.7 Disconnect the actuator lever arm from the actuator rod -7.3L engine

11.8 Location of the wastegate solenoid (1) and the inlet duct (2) on the turbocharger - 7.3L engine

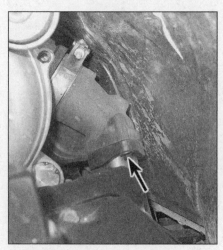

11.11 Disconnect the exhaust pipe at the catalytic converter and the transmission brace - 7.3L engine

the actuator lever arm and disconnect the actuator rod from the turbocharger **(see illustration)**.

8   Label and disconnect the wastegate solenoid vacuum hose **(see illustration)**.

9   Loosen the clamps and remove the inlet ducts from the turbocharger **(see illustration 11.8)**.

10   Raise the vehicle and support it securely on jackstands.

11   Disconnect the exhaust outlet pipe **(see illustration)** from the catalytic converter and the transmission brace.

12   Loosen the clamp from the turbocharger and remove the turbocharger mounting bolts **(see illustration)**.

13   Lift the turbocharger from the pedestal.

14   If necessary, remove the turbocharger pedestal **(see illustration)**. Replace the engine block/pedestal O-ring seals with new ones.

15   Use soft cloths to cap the open passages in the engine block while the turbocharger and/or the turbocharger pedestal is removed.

6.0L and 6.4L engines
Refer to illustration 11.23

16   Disconnect the cable from the negative battery terminal(s).

17   Wait for the engine to cool completely, and then disconnect the hoses from the coolant reservoir (degas bottle). Refer to Chapter 1 for more information and safety precautions.

18   Unbolt the degas bottle and set it aside for access to the turbocharger intake duct.

19   Remove the turbocharger intake duct.

20   Disconnect the intercooler intake pipe.

21   Remove the three pushpin retainers from the plastic cover at the center of the cowl. Lift off the plastic cover.

22   Release the two retainers from the wiring harness under the cover and push the harness aside.

23   Disconnect the electrical wiring from the turbocharger **(see illustration)**.

24   Unbolt the oil supply line from the turbo-

11.12 Remove the turbocharger mounting bolts - 7.3L engine

11.14 Remove the turbocharger pedestal mounting bolts and lift the pedestal from the engine block (two bolts hidden from view) - 7.3L engine

11.23 The variable-vane system on the 6.0L engine has electrical wiring (arrow) that must be disconnected

11.30 Location of the oil supply drain passage O-rings on the turbocharger pedestal - 7.3L engine

charger and from the engine. Remove the oil line.

25   Remove the large clamps from the intake and discharge ends of the turbocharger.

26   Remove the interfering wiring retainer that is bolted to the assembly.

27   Remove the turbocharger mounting bolts.

28   Lift the turbocharger up and disconnect the oil drain tube. Remove the turbocharger.

Caution: *On 6.4L engines, the dual-turbocharger assembly is both very heavy and somewhat delicate. Care must be taken not to drop or hit the assembly against solid objects during removal or installation. It is suggested that the assembly be lifted/lowered only by using a heavy-duty engine hoist.*

Installation

Refer to illustration 11.30

29   Use a die to clean the studs on the turbocharger mounting portion for the exhaust manifold and coat them with anti-seize compound.

30   Replace the oil supply and drain passage O-rings **(see illustration)** on the turbocharger pedestal. Install a new gasket on the oil supply line where it meets the engine on 6.0L engines.

31   Install the turbocharger onto the turbocharger pedestal.

32   The remainder of installation is the reverse of removal.

33   Torque the bolts to the Specifications listed in this Chapter.

Wastegate control rod adjustment

Note: *This procedure applies only to 7.3L engines. 6.0L and 6.4L engines use a variable turbine vane method for controlling boost (refer to Section 10).*

34   Adjustment of the wastegate control rod length is critical. The wastegate is precisely adjusted at the factory. It does not need to be readjusted unless it is damaged or replaced.

Caution: *Do not adjust the wastegate to increase the operating pressure (boost) or*

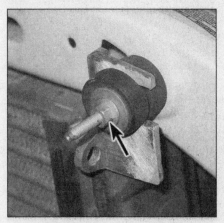

12.4a Location of the intercooler mounting stud on the right side of the vehicle - 7.3L engine

12.4b Location of the intercooler mounting stud on the left side of the vehicle - 7.3L engine

damage to the turbocharger and engine may result.

35   Disconnect the vacuum line from the wastegate control solenoid.

36   Disconnect the actuator rod from the lever.

37   Using a hand-held vacuum pump, apply 5 psi (34.5 kPa) to the wastegate control solenoid.

38   Using hand pressure, press the wastegate control lever toward the wastegate control solenoid until it stops. Hold it in this position. The actuator rod should be perfectly aligned with the wastegate control lever. The eye of the actuator rod should slide over the pin on the lever without resistance. If it does not align exactly, adjust the rod length.

39   Loosen the jam nut and turn the clevis either in or out as necessary to acquire the correct amount of actuator rod length with the precise amount of vacuum. Install the eye of the actuator rod onto the lever. Retest the actuator control rod travel.

40   Once the adjustment is correct, tighten the jam nut on the clevis.

12 Intercooler - replacement

Refer to illustrations 12.4a and 12.4b

1   Remove the radiator from the engine compartment (see Chapter 3).

2   On 6.0L engines, remove the air filter (refer to Chapter 1). Also remove the air filter assembly front cover for clearance.

3   Remove the intercooler inlet and outlet ducts (see Section 11).

4   Remove the stud bolts from the radiator support **(see illustrations)**.

5   Remove the intercooler from the engine compartment.

6   Inspect the intercooler for cracks and damage to the flanges, tubes and fins. Replace it or have it repaired if necessary.

7   Installation is the reverse of removal.

8   Tighten the intercooler mounting nuts to the torque listed in this Chapter's Specifications.

Notes

Chapter 5
Engine electrical systems

Contents

	Section		Section
Alternator - removal and installation	10	Ignition coils - replacement	7
Battery cables - check and replacement	4	Ignition system - check	6
Battery check, maintenance and charging	See Chapter 1	Ignition system - general information and precautions	5
Battery - emergency jump starting	2	SERVICE ENGINE SOON light	See Chapter 6
Battery - check and replacement	3	Spark plug replacement	See Chapter 1
Charging system - check	9	Starter motor and circuit - in-vehicle check	12
Charging system - general information and precautions	8	Starter motor - removal and installation	13
Drivebelt check, adjustment and replacement	See Chapter 1	Starting system - general information and precautions	11
General information, precautions and battery disconnection	1		

Specifications

Charging system

Charging voltage	13.5 to 15.0 volts
Standard amperage	
No load	30 amps or less
With load	87 amps or more

Torque specifications

Ft-lbs (unless otherwise indicated)

Note: *One foot-pound (ft-lb) of torque is equivalent to 12 inch-pounds (in-lbs) of torque. Torque values below approximately 15 foot-pounds are expressed in inch-pounds, because most foot-pound torque wrenches are not accurate at these smaller values.*

Starter motor mounting bolts	18
Alternator mounting bolts	
Gasoline engines	
Upper bracket bolts	89 in-lbs
Lower mounting bolts	18
Diesel engines	35

1.1a Typical engine electrical system components - 2001 6.8L V10 engine

| 1 | Battery | 2 | Alternator | 3 | Ignition coil | 4 | Fuse/relay box |

1   General information, precautions and battery disconnection

Refer to illustrations 1.1a and 1.1b

The engine electrical systems include all ignition, charging and starting components **(see illustrations)**. Because of their engine-related functions, these components are discussed separately from body electrical devices such as the lights, the instruments, etc. (which are included in Chapter 12).

Most turbo diesel models are equipped with a dual alternator system. The alternators have different ratio pulleys and are not interchangable. The PCM monitors and controls the charging system. If one alternator fails, the other alternator will maintain the voltage for the entire system under light operating conditions. The PCM controls the charging system warning indicator. If the dual alternator system fails and sets a diagnostic trouble code, the PCM will set the warning light on the dash.

1.1b Typical engine electrical system components - 1999 7.3L V8 diesel engine

| 1 | Main battery | 2 | Alternator | 3 | Auxiliary battery | 4 | Fuse/relay box |

The dual alternator system is also equipped with a dual battery package. Each battery is independently charged by a single alternator but monitored as a complete system by the PCM. However, there are diesel options that include dual batteries with a single alternator.

Precautions

Always observe the following precautions when working on the electrical system:

a) *Be extremely careful when servicing engine electrical components. They are easily damaged if checked, connected or handled improperly.*

b) *Never leave the ignition switched on for long periods of time when the engine is not running.*

c) *Never disconnect the battery cables while the engine is running.*

d) *Maintain correct polarity when connecting battery cables from another vehicle during jump starting - see the "Booster battery (jump) starting" section at the front of this manual.*

e) *Always disconnect the negative battery cable(s) from the battery(ies) before working on the electrical system, but read the following battery disconnection procedure first.*

It's also a good idea to review the safety-related information regarding the engine electrical systems located in the *"Safety first!"* section at the front of this manual, before beginning any operation included in this Chapter.

Battery disconnection

Several systems on the vehicle require battery power to be available at all times, either to ensure their continued operation (such as the radio, alarm system, power door locks, windows, etc.) or to maintain control unit memories (such as that in the engine management system's Powertrain Control Module [PCM]) which would be lost if the battery were to be disconnected. Therefore, whenever the battery is to be disconnected, first note the following to ensure that there are no unforeseen consequences of this action:

a) *The engine management system's PCM will lose the information stored in its memory when the battery is disconnected. This includes idling and operating values, any fault codes detected and system monitors required for emissions testing. Whenever the battery is disconnected, the computer will require a certain period of time to "re-learn" the operating values (see Chapter 6).*

b) *On any vehicle with power door locks, it is a wise precaution to remove the key from the ignition and to keep it with you, so that it does not get locked inside if the power door locks should engage accidentally when the battery is reconnected!*

Devices known as "memory-savers" can be used to avoid some of the above problems. Precise details vary according to the device used. Typically, it is plugged into the cigarette lighter and is connected by its own wires to a spare battery; the vehicle's own battery is then disconnected from the electrical system, leaving the "memory-saver" to pass sufficient current to maintain audio unit security codes and ECM memory values, and also to run permanently live circuits such as the clock and radio memory, all the while isolating the battery in the event of a short-circuit occurring while work is carried out.

Warning 1: *Some of these devices allow a considerable amount of current to pass, which can mean that many of the vehicle's systems are still operational when the main battery is disconnected. If a "memory-saver" is used, ensure that the circuit concerned is actually "dead" before carrying out any work on it!*

Warning 2: *If work is to be performed around any of the airbag system components, the battery must be disconnected. If a memory-saver device is used, power will be supplied to the airbag and personal injury may result if the airbag is accidentally deployed.*

Single battery system

To disconnect the battery for service procedures requiring power to be cut from the vehicle, peel back the insulator (if equipped), loosen the negative cable clamp nut and detach the cable from the negative battery post (see Section 3). Isolate the cable end to prevent it from coming into accidental contact with the battery post.

Dual battery system

To disconnect the battery for service procedures requiring power to be cut from the vehicle, working on the auxiliary battery (left side of engine compartment), peel back the insulator (if equipped), loosen the negative cable clamp nut and detach the cable from the negative battery post (see Section 3).

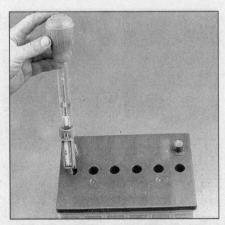

3.1a Use a battery hydrometer to draw electrolyte from the battery cell - this hydrometer is equipped with a thermometer to make temperature corrections

Next, working on the main battery (right side of engine compartment), peel back the insulator (if equipped), loosen the negative cable clamp nut and detach the cable from the negative battery post (see Section 3). Isolate the cable ends to prevent them from coming into accidental contact with the battery posts.

2 Battery - emergency jump starting

Refer to the *Booster battery (jump) starting* procedure at the front of this manual.

3 Battery - check and replacement

Warning: *Hydrogen gas is produced by the battery, so keep open flames and lighted cigarettes away from it at all times. Always wear eye protection when working around a battery. Rinse off spilled electrolyte immediately with large amounts of water.*

Check

Refer to illustrations 3.1a, 3.1b and 3.1c

1   A battery cannot be accurately tested until it is at or near a fully charged state. Disconnect the negative battery cable from the battery and perform the following tests:

a) ***Battery state of charge test*** *- Visually inspect the indicator eye (if equipped) on the top of the battery. If the indicator eye is dark in color, charge the battery as described in Chapter 1. If the battery is equipped with removable caps, check the battery electrolyte. The electrolyte level should be above the upper edge of the plates. If the level is low, add distilled water. DO NOT OVERFILL. The excess electrolyte may spill over during periods of heavy charging. Test the specific gravity of the electrolyte using a hydrometer* **(see illustration)**. *Remove the caps and extract a sample of the electrolyte and observe the float inside the barrel of the hydrometer. Follow the instructions from the tool manufacturer and determine the specific gravity of the electrolyte for each cell. A fully charged battery will indicate approximately 1.270 (green zone) at 68-degrees F (20-degrees C). If the specific gravity of the electrolyte is low (red zone), charge the battery as described in Chapter 1.*

b) ***Open circuit voltage test*** *- Using a digital voltmeter, perform an open circuit voltage test* **(see illustration)**. *Connect the negative probe of the voltmeter to the negative battery post and the positive probe to the positive battery post. The battery voltage should be greater than 12.5 volts. If the battery is less than the specified voltage, charge the battery before proceeding to the next test. Do not proceed with the battery load test until the battery is fully charged.*

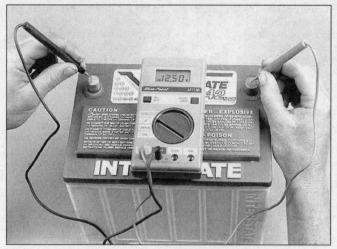

3.1b To test the open circuit voltage of the battery, connect the black probe of the voltmeter to the negative terminal and the red probe to the positive terminal of the battery - a fully charged battery should indicate approximately 12.5 volts depending on the outside air temperature

3.1c Some battery load testers are equipped with an ammeter which enables the battery load to be precisely dialed in, as shown - less expensive testers have a load switch and a voltmeter only

c) **Battery load test** - *An accurate check of the battery condition can only be performed with a load tester (available at most auto parts stores). This test evaluates the ability of the battery to operate the starter and other accessories during periods of heavy amperage draw (load). Install a special battery load testing tool onto the battery terminals* **(see illustration)**. *Load test the battery according to the tool manufacturer's instructions. This tool utilizes a carbon pile to increase the load demand (amperage draw) on the battery. Maintain the load on the battery for 15 seconds and observe that the battery voltage does not drop below 9.6 volts. If the battery condition is weak or defective, the tool will indicate this condition immediately.* **Note:** *Cold temperatures will cause the minimum voltage requirements to drop slightly. Follow the*

chart given in the tool manufacturer's instructions to compensate for cold climates. Minimum load voltage for freezing temperatures (32 degrees F/0-degrees C) should be approximately 9.1 volts.

d) **Battery drain test** - *This test will indicate whether there's a constant drain on the vehicle's electrical system that can cause the battery to discharge. Make sure all accessories are turned Off. If the vehicle has an underhood light, verify it's working properly, then disconnect it. Connect one lead of a digital ammeter to the disconnected negative battery cable clamp and the other lead to the negative battery post. A drain of approximately 100 milliamps or less is considered normal (due to the engine control compudigital clocks, digital radios and other components which normally cause a key-off battery drain). An excessive drain*

(approximately 500 milliamps or more) will cause the battery to discharge. The problem circuit or component can be located by removing the fuses, one at a time, until the excessive drain stops and normal drain is indicated on the meter.

Replacement
Refer to illustrations 3.2a, 3.2b, 3.4a and 3.4b
Caution: *Always disconnect the negative cable first and hook it up last or the battery may be shorted by the tool being used to loosen the cable clamps.*

2   Disconnect the cable(s) from the negative battery terminal(s).

a) *On single battery systems, loosen the cable clamp nut and remove the negative battery cable from the negative battery post* **(see illustration)**. *Isolate the cable end to prevent it from accidentally coming into contact with the battery post.*

3.2a Location of the negative battery cable and negative terminal (arrow) - gasoline models

3.2b On diesel batteries with the dual battery system, be sure to disconnect the auxiliary battery negative cable (arrow) and then the main battery negative cable

3.4a Location of the battery hold-down clamp bolt - gasoline models

3.4b Location of the battery hold-down clamp bolt - diesel models

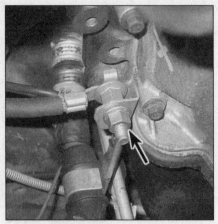

4.4a Location of the negative battery cable at the engine block - gasoline models

b) *On dual battery systems, working on the auxiliary battery (left side of the engine compartment), peel back the insulator (if equipped), loosen the negative cable clamp nut and detach the cable from the negative battery post* **(see illustration)**. *Next, working on the main battery (right side of engine compartment), peel back the insulator (if equipped), loosen the negative cable clamp nut and detach the cable from the negative battery post. Isolate the cable ends to prevent them from coming into accidental contact with the battery posts.*

3   Loosen the cable clamp nut and remove the positive battery cable from the positive battery post.

4   Remove the battery hold-down clamp bolts **(see illustrations)**.

5   Lift out the battery. Be careful - it's heavy. **Note:** *Battery straps and handlers are available at most auto parts stores for a reasonable price. They make it easier to remove and carry the battery.*

6   While the battery is out, inspect the battery tray for corrosion. If corrosion exists, clean the deposits with a mixture of baking soda and water to prevent further corrosion. Flush the area with plenty of clean water and dry thoroughly.

7   If you are replacing the battery, make sure you replace it with a battery with the identical dimensions, amperage rating, cold cranking rating, etc.

8   When installing the battery, make sure the center notch in the battery foot is aligned with the cut-out in the battery tray. Install the hold-down clamp nuts and tighten them securely. Do not over-tighten the bolt.

9   The remainder of installation is the reverse of removal.

10   After connecting the cables to the battery, apply a light coating of petroleum jelly or grease to the connections to help prevent corrosion.

4   Battery cables - check and replacement

Refer to illustrations 4.4a, 4.4b, 4.4c and 4.4d

1   Periodically inspect the entire length of each battery cable for damage, cracked or burned insulation and corrosion. Poor battery cable connections can cause starting problems and decreased engine performance.

2   Check the cable-to-terminal connections at the ends of the cables for cracks, loose wire strands and corrosion. The presence of white, fluffy deposits under the insulation at the cable terminal connection is a sign that the cable is corroded and should be replaced. Check the terminals for distortion, missing mounting bolts and corrosion.

3   When removing the cables, always disconnect the negative cable from the negative battery post first and hook it up last or the battery may be shorted by the tool used to loosen the cable clamps. Even if only the positive cable is being replaced, be sure to disconnect the negative cable from the negative battery post first (see Chapter 1 for further information regarding battery cable maintenance).

4   Disconnect the old cables from the battery, then disconnect them from the opposite end. Detach the cables from the starter solenoid, the relay and fuse box and ground terminals, as necessary **(see illustrations)**. Note the routing of each cable to ensure correct installation.

4.4b Location of the negative battery cable at the engine block - diesel models

4.4c Location of the battery cable terminal connectors at the starter solenoid relay - gasoline models

4.4d Location of the battery cable terminal connectors at the starter solenoid relay - diesel models

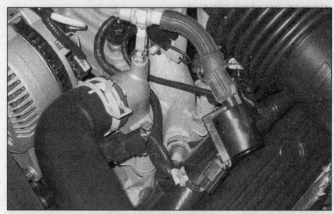

6.3   To use a calibrated ignition tester, simply remove a spark plug/coil assembly, clip the tester to a convenient ground (like a thermostat housing bolt) and operate the starter - if there is enough power to fire the test plug, sparks will be visible between the electrode tip and the tester body

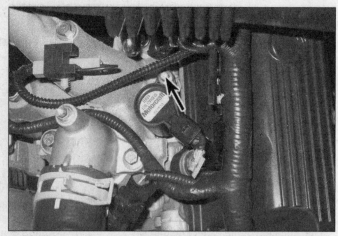

7.3   Remove the coil mounting bolt and pull the assembly up while twisting it

5   If you are replacing either or both of the battery cables, take them with you when buying new cables. It is vitally important that you replace the cables with identical parts. Cables have characteristics that make them easy to identify: Positive cables are usually red and larger in cross-section; ground cables are usually black and smaller in cross-section.

6   Clean the threads of the starter solenoid or ground connection with a wire brush to remove rust and corrosion. Apply a light coat of battery terminal corrosion inhibitor or petroleum jelly to the threads to prevent future corrosion.

7   Attach the cable to the terminal and tighten the mounting nut/bolt securely.

8   Before connecting a new cable to the battery, make sure that it reaches the battery post without having to be stretched.

9   After installing the cables, connect the negative cable to the negative battery post.

5   Ignition system - general information and precautions

General information

1   5.4L and 6.8L models are equipped with a distributorless ignition system with individual coils for each cylinder. The ignition system consists of the ignition switch, the battery, the coil assemblies, the spark plugs, the camshaft position sensor, the crankshaft position sensor, the primary (low tension) and secondary (high tension) circuits and the PCM (powertrain control module).

2   Each cylinder is fired sequentially on its compression stroke. The crankshaft and camshaft sensors generate cylinder identification signals which allow the PCM to trigger the correct coil and spark plug assembly.

Precautions

3   When working on the ignition system, take the following precautions:

a)   *Do not keep the ignition switch on for more than 10 seconds if the engine will not start.*

b)   *Always connect a tachometer in accordance with the manufacturer's instructions. Some tachometers may be incompatible with this ignition system. Consult an auto parts counterperson before buying a tachometer for use with this vehicle.*

c)   *Never allow the ignition coil terminals to touch ground. Grounding the coil could result in damage to the PCM and/or the ignition coil.*

d)   *Do not disconnect the battery when the engine is running.*

6   Ignition system - check

Refer to illustration 6.3

Warning: *Because of the very high voltage generated by the ignition system, extreme care should be taken whenever an operation is performed involving ignition components. This not only includes the coil and spark plugs, but related items connected to the system as well, such as the electrical connectors, tachometer and any test equipment.*

Note: *The ignition system components on these models are expensive and difficult to diagnose. In the event of ignition system failure, if the checks do not clearly indicate the source of the ignition system problem, have the vehicle tested by a dealer service department or other qualified repair facility.*

1   If a malfunction occurs and the vehicle won't start, do not immediately assume that the ignition system is causing the problem. First, check the following items:

a)   *Make sure the battery cable clamps, where they connect to the battery, are clean and tight.*

b)   *Test the condition of the battery (see Section 3). If it does not pass all the tests, replace it with a new battery.*

c)   *Check the ignition coil wiring and connections.*

d)   *Check the related fuses inside the fuse box (see Chapter 12). If they're burned, determine the cause and repair the circuit.*

2   If the engine turns over but won't start, make sure there is sufficient secondary ignition voltage to fire the spark plug.

3   Remove an ignition coil (see Section 7) and attach a calibrated ignition tester (available at most auto parts stores). Connect the clip on the tester to a bolt or metal bracket on the engine **(see illustration)**.

4   Relieve the fuel pressure (see Chapter 4A). Keep the fuel system disabled while performing the ignition system checks.

5   Crank the engine and watch the end of the tester to see if bright blue, well-defined sparks occur (weak spark or intermittent spark is the same as no spark).

6   If sparks occur, sufficient voltage is reaching the spark plug to fire it (repeat the check at the remaining ignition coils to verify that all coils are functioning). However, the plugs themselves may be fouled, so remove and check them as described in Chapter 1 or install new ones.

7   If no sparks or intermittent sparks occur, check for battery voltage to the ignition coils. If battery voltage is not present, check the ignition fuse (see Chapter 12).

8   If the checks are all correct, there may be a defective camshaft position sensor and/or crankshaft position sensor (see Chapter 6).

7   Ignition coils - replacement

Refer to illustration 7.3

1   Disconnect the cable(s) from the negative battery terminal(s) (see Section 1).

2   Disconnect the ignition coil electrical connector(s) from each individual coil. Use tape and mark each electrical connector with the correct cylinder number to prevent mixups during reassembly, if necessary.

3   Remove the bolt securing the ignition coil **(see illustration)**, then pull the coil from the cylinder head. **Note:** *2006 and later models have individual coils for each spark plug. The coils are mounted to the top of the valve covers.*

4   Installation is the reverse of the removal procedure with the following additions:

   a) *Prior to installing the coil, coat the entire interior of the rubber boot with silicone dielectric compound.*

   b) *Connect each coil electrical connector to its correct coil and make sure they are tight and secure.*

8   Charging system - general information and precautions

The charging system includes the alternator, a voltage regulator, a charge indicator or warning light, the battery, a large fuse (called a mega fuse) and the wiring between all the components. The charging system supplies electrical power for the ignition system, the lights, the radio, etc. The alternator is driven by a drivebelt at the front of the engine.

The purpose of the voltage regulator is to limit the alternator's voltage to a preset value. This prevents power surges, circuit overloads, etc., during peak voltage output. On integral voltage regulator systems, a solid state regulator is housed inside a plastic module mounted on the alternator itself.

There are two different types of alternators equipped on these models. Gasoline engines are equipped with alternators with integrally mounted voltage regulators. The voltage regulator can be removed from the backside of the alternator but the alternator must be removed from the engine first. Diesel engines are equipped with internally mounted voltage regulators. The voltage regulator is not accessible and the alternator must be replaced as a complete unit. Some 2008 and later 6.4L diesel models have an optional arrangement that includes two batteries and two alternators. One alternator is located low on the engine (standard location for diesel) with another alternator mounted on top of the engine.

The charging system is protected by a series of large fusible links. In the event of charging system problems, check these fusible links for damage or broken contacts.

The charging system doesn't ordinarily require periodic maintenance. However, the drivebelt, battery and harness connections should be inspected at the intervals outlined in Chapter 1.

Be very careful when making electrical circuit connections to a vehicle equipped with an alternator and note the following:

   a) *When reconnecting wires to the alternator from the battery, be sure to note the polarity.*

   b) *Before using arc welding equipment to repair any part of the vehicle, disconnect the wiring from the alternator and the cables from the battery.*

   c) *Never start the engine with a battery charger connected.*

   d) *Always disconnect both battery cables before using a battery charger.*

   e) *The alternator is turned by an engine drivebelt which could cause serious injury if your hands, hair or clothes become entangled in it with the engine running.*

   f) *Because the alternator is connected directly to the battery, it could arc or cause a fire if overloaded or shorted out.*

9   Charging system - check

Refer to illustration 9.3

Note: *Some diesel models are equipped with a self-diagnostic charging system included with the On Board Diagnostic (OBD-II) system (see Chapter 6). This system is useful for detecting charging system problems. Due to the special equipment necessary to diagnose the charging system on these models, it is recommended that the vehicle be tested by a dealer service department or other qualified automotive repair facility.*

1   If a malfunction occurs in the charging circuit, do not immediately assume that the alternator is causing the problem. First, check the following items:

   a) *Make sure the battery cable clamps, where they connect to the battery, are clean and tight.*

   b) *Test the condition of the battery (see Section 3). If it does not pass all the tests, replace it with a new battery.*

   c) *Check the external alternator wiring and connections.*

   d) *Check the drivebelt condition and tension (see Chapter 1).*

   e) *Check the alternator mounting bolts for tightness.*

   f) *Run the engine and check the alternator for abnormal noise.*

   g) *Check the fusible links (if equipped) in the engine compartment fuse box (see Chapter 12). If they're burned, determine the cause and repair the circuit.*

   h) *Check the charge light on the dash. It should illuminate when the ignition key is turned ON (engine not running). If it does not, check the circuit from the alternator to the charge light on the dash.*

   i) *Check all the fuses that are in series with the charging system circuit. The location of these fuses and fusible links may vary from year and model but the designations are generally the same. Refer to the wiring schematics at the end of Chapter 12 for additional information.*

2   With the ignition key off, check the battery voltage with no accessories operating. It should be approximately 12.5 volts. It may be slightly higher if the engine had been operating within the last hour.

3   Start the engine and check the battery voltage again **(see illustration)**. It should now be greater than the voltage recorded in Step 2, but not more than 14.5 volts. Turn On all the vehicle accessories (air conditioning, rear window defogger, blower motor, etc.) and increase the engine speed to 2,000 rpm - the voltage should not drop below the voltage recorded in Step 2.

4   If the indicated voltage is greater than the specified charging voltage, replace the voltage regulator. **Note:** *On these models, it is recommended that the alternator and voltage regulator be replaced as a complete unit, using either a rebuilt or new alternator.*

5   If the indicated voltage reading is less than the specified charging voltage, the alternator is probably defective. Have the charging system checked at a dealer service department or other properly equipped repair facility. **Note:** *Many auto parts stores will bench test an alternator off the vehicle. Refer to your local auto parts store regarding their policy, many will perform this service free of charge.*

9.3 To measure charging voltage, attach the voltmeter leads to the battery terminals - check the battery voltage with the engine OFF, then start the engine and record the voltage reading at idle

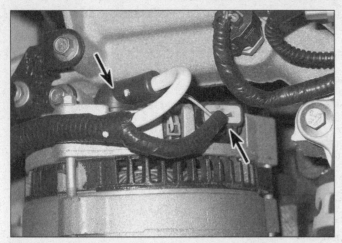

10.4 Disconnect the alternator electrical connectors from the rear of the alternator (arrows) - 6.8L V10 engine

10.5 Remove the mounting bolts (arrows) and separate the alternator bracket from the intake manifold - 5.4L V8 engine

10   Alternator - removal and installation

Gasoline engines

Refer to illustrations 10.4, 10.5 and 10.6

1   Disconnect the cable from the negative terminal of the battery (see Section 1).
2   Remove the drivebelt (see Chapter 1).
3   Remove the alternator harness clamp from the alternator stud.
4   Disconnect the electrical connectors from the alternator **(see illustration)**.
5   Remove the bolts from the alternator bracket if so equipped **(see illustration)**.
6   Remove the lower mounting bolts and separate the alternator from the engine **(see illustration)**.
7   Installation is the reverse of removal.
8   Install the drivebelt and reconnect the cable to the negative terminal of the battery.

Diesel engines

Refer to illustration 10.13

9   Disconnect the cable from the negative battery terminal(s).

10   Remove the drivebelt (see Chapter 1).
11   On 2003 6.0L diesel models, remove the upper fan shroud. On 2004 and later diesel models, remove the cooling fan (refer to Chapter 3).
12   Disconnect the wiring from the alternator.
13   Remove the bolts and separate the alternator from the engine **(see illustration)**. If you are working on the auxiliary alternator, it may be necessary to raise the vehicle and support it securely on jackstands for access.

All models

14   Installation is the reverse of removal.
15   Install the drivebelt and reconnect the cable(s) to the negative battery terminal(s).

11   Starting system - general information and precautions

There are two different gear reduction starter motor assemblies used on these models; a gasoline engine gear reduction type or a diesel engine gear reduction type starter

motor assembly. The starter solenoid relay is mounted in the engine compartment on the right side. The starter solenoid is mounted on the starter assembly. Early models are equipped with only a starter solenoid relay while later models are equipped with a starter relay (fuse/relay box) and a starter solenoid relay (engine compartment fenderwell).

The starting system consists of the battery, the starter motor/solenoid assembly, the starter solenoid relay, the clutch start switch (manual transmissions), the transmission range sensor (automatic transmissions), ignition switch and the wires that connect the components. The starter solenoid relay is located in the engine compartment towards the right side of the vehicle.

When the ignition key is turned to the Start position, the starter solenoid is actuated through the starter control circuit which includes a starter solenoid relay. The starter solenoid relay then connects the battery to the starter. The battery supplies the electrical energy to the starter motor, which does the actual work of cranking the engine.

The starter motor on a vehicle equipped with a manual transmission can be operated

10.6 Location of the lower mounting bolts (arrows) - 5.4L V8 engine

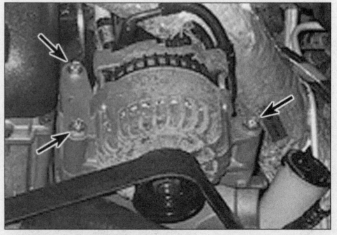

10.13 Location of the alternator mounting bolts (arrows)

12.1 The starter solenoid relay is mounted on the engine compartment fenderwell (on early models)

A *Signal wire from ignition switch*

B *B+ terminal*
C *Ignition enable terminal*

12.3 To use an inductive ammeter, simply hold the ammeter over the positive or negative cable (whichever cable has better clearance)

only when the clutch pedal is depressed. The starter on a vehicle equipped with an automatic transmission can be operated only when the transmission selector lever is in Park or Neutral.

Always observe the following precautions when working on the starting system:

a) *Excessive cranking of the starter motor can overheat it and cause serious damage. Never operate the starter motor for more than 15 seconds at a time without pausing for at least two minutes to allow it to cool.*

b) *The starter is connected directly to the battery and could arc or cause a fire if mishandled, overloaded or short circuited.*

c) *Always detach the negative battery cable(s) from the negative battery terminal(s) before working on the starting system.*

12 Starter motor and circuit - in-vehicle check

Refer to illustrations 12.1 and 12.3

1   If a malfunction occurs in the starting circuit, do not immediately assume that the starter is causing the problem. First, check the following items:

a) *Make sure the battery cable clamps, where they connect to the battery, are clean and tight.*

b) *Check the condition of the battery cables (see Section 4). Replace any defective battery cables with new ones.*

c) *Test the condition of the battery (see Section 3). If it does not pass all the tests, replace it with a new battery.*

d) *Check the starter solenoid wiring and connections. Refer to the wiring diagrams at the end of Chapter 12.*

e) *Check the starter mounting bolts for tightness.*

f) *Check the fusible links (if equipped) exiting the engine compartment fuse box (see Chapter 12). If they're burned, determine the cause and repair the circuit. Also, check the ignition switch circuit for correct operation (see Chapter 12).*

g) *Check the operation of the transmission range sensor (automatic transmission) or clutch start switch (manual transmission). Make sure the shift lever is in PARK or NEUTRAL (automatic transmission), or the clutch pedal is pressed (manual transmission). Refer to Chapter 7B for the transmission range sensor and adjustment procedure. Refer to Chapter 12 wiring diagrams, if necessary, when performing circuit checks. These systems must operate correctly to provide battery voltage to the ignition switch.*

h) *Check the operation of the starter solenoid relay. The starter solenoid relay is located on the engine compartment fenderwell (see illustration). The starter relay on late models is located in the fuse/relay box inside the engine compartment. Refer to Chapter 12 for the testing procedure.*

2   If the starter does not actuate when the ignition switch is turned to the start position, check for battery voltage to the solenoid. This will determine if the solenoid is receiving the correct voltage signal from the ignition switch. Connect a test light or voltmeter to the starter solenoid positive terminal and while an assistant turns the ignition switch to the start position. If voltage is not available, refer to the wiring diagrams in Chapter 12 and check all the fuses and relays in series with the starting system. If voltage is available but the starter motor does not operate, remove the starter (see Section 13) and bench test it (see

Step 4).

3   If the starter turns over slowly, check the starter cranking voltage and the current draw from the battery. This test must be performed with the starter assembly on the engine. Crank the engine over (for 10 seconds or less) and observe the battery voltage. It should not drop below 8.0 volts on manual transmission models or 8.5 volts on automatic transmission models. Also, observe the current draw using an ammeter **(see illustration)**. It should not exceed 400 amps or drop below 250 amps. **Caution:** *The battery cables may be excessively heated because of the large amount of amperage being drawn from the battery. Discontinue the testing until the starting system has cooled down. If the starter motor cranking amp values are not within the correct range, replace it with a new unit. There are several conditions that may affect the starter cranking potential. The battery must be in good condition and the battery cold-cranking rating must not be under-rated for the particular application. Be sure to check the battery specifications carefully. The battery terminals and cables must be clean and not corroded. Also, in cases of extreme cold temperatures, make sure the battery and/or engine block is warmed before performing the tests.*

4   If the starter is receiving voltage but does not activate, remove and check the starter/solenoid assembly on the bench. Most likely the solenoid is defective. In some rare cases, the engine may be seized so be sure to try and rotate the crankshaft pulley (see Chapter 2A or 2B) before proceeding. With the starter/solenoid assembly mounted in a vise on the bench, install one jumper cable from the negative battery terminal to the body of the starter. Install the other jumper cable from the positive battery terminal to the B+ terminal on the starter. Install a starter switch and apply battery voltage to the solenoid S terminal (for 10 seconds or less) and

13.4a Location of the lower starter motor mounting bolt - gasoline engines (upper bolts hidden from view)

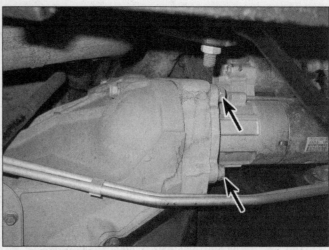

13.4b Location of the starter motor mounting bolts - diesel engine (one bolt hidden from view)

see if the solenoid plunger, shift lever and overrunning clutch extends and rotates the pinion drive. If the pinion drive extends but does not rotate, the solenoid is operating but the starter motor is defective. If there is no movement but the solenoid clicks, the solenoid and/or the starter motor is defective. If the solenoid plunger extends and rotates the pinion drive, the starter/solenoid assembly is working properly.

---

13   Starter motor - removal and installation

Refer to illustrations 13.4a and 13.4b

1   Disconnect the cable(s) from the negative battery terminal(s) (see Section 1).
2   Raise the vehicle and support it securely on jackstands.
3   If the starter has a heat shield, remove it. Remove the protective plastic cap and disconnect the wiring from the terminals on the starter solenoid.
4   Remove the starter motor mounting bolts **(see illustration)** and detach the starter from the engine.
5   Installation is the reverse of removal. Torque the starter bolts to the Specifications listed in this Chapter.

Chapter 6
Emissions and engine control systems

Contents

	Section		Section
Accelerator pedal position sensor - replacement	18	Fuel tank pressure sensor - replacement	17
Barometric pressure (BARO) sensor		General information	1
(6.0L and 6.4L diesel models) - replacement	19	Idle Air Control (IAC) valve (gasoline models) - replacement	16
Camshaft position (CMP) sensor - replacement	12	Intake Air Temperature (IAT) sensor (diesel models) -	
Catalytic converter	24	replacement	7
CHECK ENGINE light	2	Knock sensor (gasoline models) - replacement	14
Crankshaft position (CKP) sensor - replacement	11	Manifold Absolute Pressure (MAP) sensor	
Cylinder head temperature sensor (gasoline models) -		(diesel models) - replacement	5
replacement	10	Mass Airflow (MAF) sensor - replacement	6
Engine Coolant Temperature (ECT) sensor		On-Board Diagnostic (OBD) system and trouble codes	2
(diesel models) - replacement	8	Oxygen sensor (gasoline models) -	
Engine oil temperature sensor (diesel models) -		general information and replacement	13
replacement	9	Positive Crankcase Ventilation (PCV) system	21
Exhaust Gas Recirculation (EGR) system	22	Powertrain Control Module (PCM) - removal and installation	3
Exhaust pressure sensor (6.0L and 6.4L diesel models) -		Throttle Position Sensor (TPS) - replacement	4
replacement	20	Transmission range sensor	See Chapter 7B
Evaporative emissions control (EVAP) system	23	Vehicle Speed Sensor (VSS) - replacement	15

Specifications

Torque specifications

Ft-lbs (unless otherwise indicated)

Note: *One foot-pound (ft-lb) of torque is equivalent to 12 inch-pounds (in-lbs) of torque. Torque values below approximately 15 foot-pounds are expressed in inch-pounds, because most foot-pound torque wrenches are not accurate at these smaller values.*

IAC valve mounting bolts
    Step 1 .... 89 in-lbs
    Step 2 .... Tighten additional 90 degrees
EGR mounting bolts
    Step 1 15
    Step 2 .... Tighten additional 90 degrees

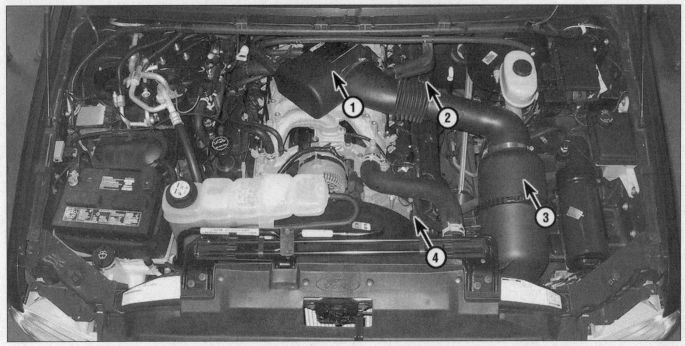

1.1a Typical engine emission control system components - 2001 6.8L V10 engine

1	*TPS (located on side of throttle body)*		*3*	*MAF sensor (located inside air filter housing)*
2	*PCV valve*		*4*	*Camshaft position sensor*

1   General information

Refer to illustrations 1.1a, 1.1b and 1.6

To prevent pollution of the atmosphere from incompletely burned and evaporating gases, and to maintain good driveability and fuel economy, a number of emission control systems are incorporated **(see illustrations).** They include the:

On-Board Diagnostic (OBD) II system (gasoline and diesel models)

Electronic Fuel Injection (EFI) system (gasoline and diesel models)

Exhaust Gas Recirculation (EGR) system (gasoline models)

Evaporative Emissions Control (EVAP) system (gasoline and diesel models)

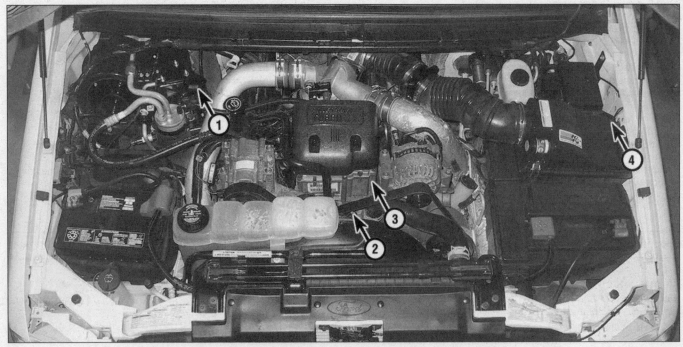

1.1b Typical engine emission control system components - 1999 7.3L V8 diesel engine

1	*MAP sensor*	*3*	*Oil temperature sensor (behind high pressure oil system reservoir)*	*4*	*IAT sensor*
2	*ECT sensor*				

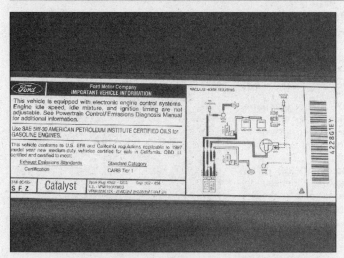

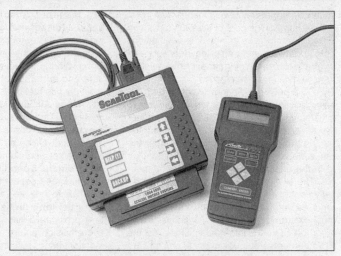

1.6 The Vehicle Emission Control Information (VECI) label contains such essential information as the types of emission control systems installed on the engine and a vacuum diagram

2.1 Hand-held scan tools like these can extract computer codes and also perform diagnostics

Positive Crankcase Ventilation (PCV) system (gasoline and diesel models)
Catalytic converter (gasoline models and manual transmission diesels)

The Sections in this Chapter include general descriptions, checking procedures within the scope of the home mechanic and component replacement procedures (when possible) for each of the systems listed above.

Before assuming that an emissions control system is malfunctioning, check the fuel and ignition systems carefully. The diagnosis of some emission control devices requires specialized tools, equipment and training. If checking and servicing become too difficult or if a procedure is beyond your ability, consult a dealer service department or other repair shop. Remember, the most frequent cause of emissions problems is simply a loose or broken wire or vacuum hose, so always check the hose and wiring connections first.

This doesn't mean, however, that emissions control systems are particularly difficult to maintain and repair. You can quickly and easily perform many checks and do most of the regular maintenance at home with common tune-up and hand tools. **Note:** *Because of a Federally mandated warranty which covers the emissions control system components, check with your dealer about warranty coverage before working on any emissions-related systems. Once the warranty has expired, you may wish to perform some of the component checks and/or replacement procedures in this Chapter to save money.*

Pay close attention to any special precautions outlined in this Chapter. It should be noted that the illustrations of the various systems may not exactly match the system installed on your vehicle because of changes made by the manufacturer during production or from year-to-year.

A Vehicle Emissions Control Information (VECI) label is attached to the underside of the hood **(see illustration)**. This label contains important emissions specifications and adjustment information. Part of this label, the Vacuum Hose Routing Diagram, provides a vacuum hose schematic with emissions components identified. When servicing the engine or emissions systems, the VECI label and the vacuum hose routing diagram in your particular vehicle should always be checked for up-to-date information.

2 On-Board Diagnostic (OBD) system and trouble codes

Scan tool information

Refer to illustrations 2.1 and 2.2

1 Hand-held scanners are the most powerful and versatile tools for analyzing engine management systems used on later model vehicles **(see illustration)**. Early model scanners handle codes and some diagnostics for many systems. Each brand scan tool must be examined carefully to match the year, make and model of the vehicle you are working on. Often, interchangeable cartridges are available to access the particular manufacturer (Ford, GM, Chrysler, Toyota etc.). Some manufacturers will specify by continent (Asia, Europe, USA, etc.). **Note:** *An aftermarket generic scanner should work with any model covered by this manual. However, some early OBD-II models, although technically classified as OBD-II compliant by the manufacturer and by the federal government, might not be fully compliant with all SAE standards for OBD-II. Some generic scanners are unable to extract all the codes from these early OBD-II models. Before purchasing a generic scan tool, contact the manufacturer of the scanner you're planning to buy and verify that it will work properly with the OBD-II system you want to scan. If necessary, of course, you can always have the codes extracted by a dealer service department or an independent repair shop*

with a professional scan tool.

2 With the arrival of the Federally mandated emission control system (OBD-II), a specially designed scanner has been developed. Several tool manufacturers have released OBD-II scan tools for the home mechanic **(see illustration)**. Ask the parts salesman at a local auto parts store for additional information concerning dates and costs.

OBD system general description

Note: *8500 GVW and larger trucks are equipped with OBD-II.*

3 All models are equipped with the second generation OBD-II system. This system consists of an on-board computer known as the Powertrain Control Module (PCM), and information sensors, which monitor various functions of the engine and send data to the PCM. This system incorporates a series of diagnos-

2.2 Simple code readers are an economical way to extract trouble codes when the CHECK ENGINE light comes on

tic monitors that detect and identify fuel injection and emissions control systems faults and store the information in the computer memory. This updated system also tests sensors and output actuators, diagnoses drive cycles, freezes data and clears codes.

4   This powerful diagnostic computer must be accessed using an OBD-II scan tool and 16 pin Data Link Connector (DLC) located under the driver's dash area. The PCM is mounted behind the driver's side kick panel near the brake pedal on 1999 through 2001 models or in the engine compartment on 2002 models. The PCM is the "brain" of the electronically controlled fuel and emissions system. It receives data from a number of sensors and other electronic components (switches, relays, etc.). Based on the information it receives, the PCM generates output signals to control various relays, solenoids (i.e. fuel injectors) and other actuators. The PCM is specifically calibrated to optimize the emissions, fuel economy and driveability of the vehicle.

5   It isn't a good idea to attempt diagnosis or replacement of the PCM or emission control components at home while the vehicle is under warranty. Because of a Federally mandated warranty which covers the emissions system components and because any owner-induced damage to the PCM, the sensors and/or the control devices may void this warranty, take the vehicle to a dealer service department if the PCM or a system component malfunctions.

Information sensors

6   **Oxygen sensors (O2S) -** The O2S generates a voltage signal that varies with the difference between the oxygen content of the exhaust and the oxygen in the surrounding air.

7   **Crankshaft Position (CKP) sensor (gasoline models) -** The crankshaft sensor provides information on crankshaft position and the engine speed signal to the PCM.

8   **Camshaft Position (CMP) sensor -** The camshaft position sensor produces a signal in which the PCM uses to identify number 1 cylinder and to time the sequential fuel injection.

9   **Engine Coolant Temperature (ECT) sensor (diesel models) -** The coolant temperature (ECT) sensor monitors engine coolant temperature and sends the PCM a voltage signal that affects PCM control of the fuel mixture, ignition timing, and EGR operation.

10   **Intake Air Temperature (IAT) sensor (diesel models) -** The IAT sensor provides the PCM with intake air temperature information. The PCM uses this information to control fuel flow, ignition timing, and EGR system operation. Gasoline models are equipped with an IAT sensor built into the MAF sensor.

11   **Throttle Position Sensor (TPS) (gasoline models) -** The TPS senses throttle movement and position, then transmits a voltage signal to the PCM. This signal enables the PCM to determine when the throttle is closed, in a cruise position, or wide open.

12   **Manifold Absolute Pressure (MAP) sensor (diesel models) -** The MAP sensor measures the amount (volume) of the intake airflow entering the engine. The MAP sensor along with the IAT sensor, provide airflow volume and air temperature information for the most precise fuel metering.

13   **Mass Airflow (MAF) sensor (gasoline models) -** The mass airflow sensor measures the mass of the intake air by detecting volume and weight of the air from samples passing over the hot wire element.

14   **Vehicle Speed Sensor (VSS) -** The vehicle speed sensor provides information to the PCM to indicate vehicle speed.

15   **Fuel tank pressure sensor -** The fuel tank pressure sensor is part of the evaporative emission control system and is used to monitor vapor pressure in the fuel tank.

16   **Power Steering Pressure (PSP) switch -** The PSP sensor is used to increase engine idle speed during low-speed vehicle maneuvers.

17   **Transmission sensors -** In addition to the vehicle speed sensor, the PCM receives input signals from the following sensors:

a) *the input speed sensor*
b) *the output speed sensor*

Output actuators

18   **PCM power relay -** The PCM power relay activates power to the fuel injectors, the ignition coils and the heating elements in the O2 sensors. The PCM will deactivate power to the relay if it does not receive signals from the crankshaft sensor and the camshaft sensor. Refer to Chapter 4 or your owner's manual for more information on relay location.

19   **Fuel injectors -** The PCM opens the fuel injectors individually in firing order sequence. The PCM also controls the time the injector is open, called the "pulse width." The pulse width of the injector (measured in milliseconds) determines the amount of fuel delivered. For more information on the fuel delivery system and the fuel injectors, including injector replacement, refer to Chapter 4A or 4B.

20   **Power transistor -** The power transistor triggers the ignition coil and determines proper spark advance based on inputs from the PCM. The power transistor is mounted inside the PCM.

21   **Idle air control (IAC) valve (gasoline models) -** The IAC valve controls the amount of air to bypass the throttle plate when the throttle valve is closed or at idle position. The IAC valve opening and the resulting airflow is controlled by the PCM. Refer to Chapter 4A for more information on the IAC valve.

22   **EVAP purge control solenoid -** The EVAP vacuum switching valve is a solenoid valve, operated by the PCM to purge the fuel vapor canister and route fuel vapor to the intake manifold for combustion. This valve is also called the purge control solenoid.

23   **Intake manifold tuning valve (1999 5.4L models) -** The intake manifold tuning

2.25 Location of the 16-pin Data Link Connector (DLC)

valve operates a valve which opens a crossover passage inside the intake manifold providing acoustical tuning for improved intake charges.

Obtaining OBD-II system trouble codes

Refer to illustration 2.25

Note: *All models covered by this manual are equipped with the OBD-II system. It is necessary to use a SCAN tool to read trouble codes on all models. Before outputting the trouble codes, thoroughly inspect ALL electrical connectors and hoses. Make sure all electrical connections are tight, clean and free of corrosion; make sure all hoses are properly connected, fit tightly and are in good condition (no cracks or tears).*

24   The PCM will illuminate the SERVICE ENGINE SOON light (also called the Check Engine light) on the dash if it recognizes a component fault for two consecutive drive cycles. It will continue to set the light until the PCM does not detect any malfunction for three or more consecutive drive cycles.

25   The self-diagnosis information contained in the PCM can be accessed by using a scan tool. This tool is attached to the diagnostic connector **(see illustration)** located under the left (driver's) side of the instrument panel in the passenger compartment and reads the codes and parameters on the digital display screen. If the information cannot be obtained readily, have the vehicle's self-diagnosis system analyzed by a dealer service department or other qualified repair shop.

26   The diagnostic codes for the OBD-II system can be extracted from the PCM by plugging a generic OBD-II scan tool **(see illustrations 2.1 and 2.2)** into the PCM's data link connector **(see illustration 2.25)**, which is located under the left side of the dash.

27   Plug the scan tool into the 16-pin data link connector (DLC), and then follow the instructions included with the scan tool to extract any stored diagnostic codes.

Trouble codes - gasoline engines

Code	Probable cause
P0010	Intake camshaft position actuator, circuit open
P0011	Intake camshaft position actuator, over advanced
P0012	Intake camshaft position timing, over retarded
P0016	Crankshaft position correlation, bank 1, sensor A
P0020	Intake camshaft position actuator, circuit open, Bank 2
P0021	Intake camshaft position actuator, over advanced, Bank 2
P0022	Intake camshaft position actuator, over retarded, Bank 2
P0030	Upstream oxygen sensor, bank 1, heater circuit
P0040	Upstream oxygen sensors swapped (crossed wiring harnesses)
P0041	Downstream oxygen sensors swapped (crossed wiring harnesses)
P0050	Oxygen sensor heater control circuit open or short, Bank 2, sensor 1
P0054	Oxygen sensor heater control circuit resistance, Bank 1, sensor 2
P0055	Oxygen sensor heater control circuit resistance, Bank 1, sensor 3
P0059	Oxygen sensor heater control circuit resistance, Bank 2, sensor 1
P0060	Downstream oxygen sensor heater circuit open or short, Bank 2, sensor 2
P060A	Internal Powertrain Control Module (PCM) error
P060B	Internal Powertrain Control Module (PCM) analog to digital processing error
P060C	Internal Powertrain Control Module (PCM) main processor error
P061B	Internal Powertrain Control Module (PCM) torque calculation error
P061C	Internal Powertrain Control Module (PCM) engine rpm calculation error
P061D	Internal Powertrain Control Module (PCM) air mass error
P061F	Internal Powertrain Control Module (PCM) Throttle Actuator Controller (TAC) error
P0068	Throttle Position (TP) sensor inconsistent with Mass Air Flow sensor
P0097	Intake Air Temperature sensor circuit, sensor 2, circuit low
P0098	Intake Air Temperature sensor circuit, open or short
P0102	Mass Air Flow (MAF) sensor circuit, low input

Trouble codes - gasoline engines (continued)

Code	Probable cause
P0103	Mass Air Flow (MAF) sensor circuit, high input
P0104	Mass Air Flow (MAF) sensor circuit, intermittent failure
P0106	Barometric (BARO) pressure sensor circuit, performance problem
P0107	Barometric (BARO) pressure sensor/MAP sensor circuit, low voltage
P0108	Barometric (BARO) pressure sensor/MAP sensor circuit, high voltage
P0109	BARO/MAP sensor circuit intermittent
P0111	Intake Air Temperature (IAT) sensor 1 circuit, range/performance problem
P0112	Intake Air Temperature (IAT) sensor 1 circuit, low input
P0113	Intake Air Temperature (IAT) sensor circuit, high input
P0114	Intake Air Temperature (IAT) sensor circuit, intermittent failure
P0117	Engine Coolant Temperature (ECT) sensor circuit, low input
P0118	Engine Coolant Temperature (ECT) sensor circuit, high input
P0119	Engine Coolant Temperature (ECT) sensor circuit, intermittent failure (4.0L V6)
P0121	Throttle Position (TP) circuit out of range or performance problem
P0122	Throttle pedal position sensor, A circuit low
P0123	Throttle Position (TP) sensor circuit, A high input
P0125	Insufficient coolant temperature for closed loop fuel control (4.0L V6)
P0127	IAT2 sensor, problem with Charge Air Cooler
P0128	Coolant temperature below thermostat regulated temperature (4.0L V6)
P012B	Turbocharger inlet pressure sensor, circuit range/performance problem
P012C	Turbocharger inlet pressure sensor, circuit low
P012D	Turbocharger inlet pressure sensor, circuit high
P012E	Turbocharger inlet pressure sensor, circuit erratic
P0130	Oxygen sensor heater control circuit resistance, Bank 1, sensor 1
P0131	Upstream oxygen sensor circuit problem (right cylinder bank)
P0132	Upstream oxygen sensor circuit, high voltage (right cylinder bank)

Code	Probable cause
P0134	Oxygen sensor circuit, open or damaged sensor
P0136	Downstream oxygen sensor circuit problem (right cylinder bank)
P0138	Downstream oxygen sensor circuit, high voltage (right cylinder bank)
P0139	Upstream oxygen sensor heater circuit, slow response, Bank 1, sensor 2
P0141	Downstream oxygen sensor heater circuit problem, Bank 1, sensor 2
P0144	Oxygen sensor, Bank 1, sensor 3, high voltage
P0147	Oxygen sensor, Bank 1, sensor 3, circuit open or short
P0148	Fuel delivery error
P0150	Oxygen sensor heater control circuit resistance, Bank 2, sensor 1
P0151	Upstream oxygen sensor circuit, low voltage (left cylinder bank)
P0152	Upstream oxygen sensor circuit, high voltage (left cylinder bank)
P0153	Heated oxygen sensor circuit, slow response (left cylinder bank)
P0154	Upstream oxygen sensor heater circuit problem, Bank 2, sensor 1
P0155	Oxygen sensor, Bank 2, sensor 2, circuit open or short
P0156	Downstream oxygen sensor circuit problem (left cylinder bank)
P0158	Downstream oxygen sensor circuit, high voltage (left cylinder bank)
P0159	Downstream oxygen sensor circuit, slow response, Bank 2, sensor 2
P0161	Downstream oxygen sensor heater circuit problem, Bank 2, sensor 2
P0171	System too lean (right cylinder bank)
P0172	System too rich (right cylinder bank)
P0174	System too lean (left cylinder bank)
P0175	System too rich (left cylinder bank)
P0176	Flexible Fuel (FF) sensor circuit malfunction
P0180	Fuel Rail Temperature (FRT) sensor A circuit, open or short
P0181	Fuel Rail Temperature (FRT) sensor A circuit, range/performance problem
P0182	Fuel Rail Temperature (FRT) sensor circuit, low input
P0183	Fuel Rail Temperature (FRT) sensor circuit, high input

Trouble codes - gasoline engines (continued)

Code	Probable cause
P0190	Fuel Rail Pressure (FRP) sensor A circuit, reference voltage
P0191	Fuel Rail Pressure (FRP) sensor circuit, range/performance problem
P0192	Fuel Rail Pressure (FRP) sensor circuit, low input
P0193	Fuel Rail Pressure (FRP) sensor circuit, high input
P0196	Engine Oil Temperature sensor circuit range/performance problem
P0197	Engine Oil Temperature sensor circuit, low input
P0198	Engine Oil Temperature sensor circuit, high input
P020X	Injector circuit, open, cylinders 1 through 9 (V10 engines)
P0201	Injector no. 1 circuit malfunction
P0202	Injector no. 2 circuit malfunction
P0203	Injector no. 3 circuit malfunction
P0204	Injector no. 4 circuit malfunction
P0205	Injector no. 5 circuit malfunction
P0206	Injector no. 6 circuit malfunction
P0207	Injector no. 7 circuit malfunction
P0208	Injector no. 8 circuit malfunction
P0209	Injector no. 9 circuit malfunction
P0210	Injector no. 10 circuit malfunction
P0217	Engine coolant over-temperature
P0218	Transmission fluid over-temperature
P0219	Engine over speed condition
P0221	Throttle Position (TP) sensor B circuit range/performance problem
P0222	Throttle Position (TP) sensor B circuit, low input
P0223	Throttle Position (TP) sensor B circuit, high input
P0230	Fuel pump primary circuit malfunction
P0231	Fuel pump secondary circuit low

Code	Probable cause
P0232	Fuel pump secondary circuit high
P0261	Cylinder 1 injector circuit low
P0262	Cylinder 1 injector circuit high
P0264	Cylinder 2 injector circuit low
P0265	Cylinder 2 injector circuit high
P0267	Cylinder 3 injector circuit low
P0268	Cylinder 3 injector circuit high
P0270	Cylinder 4 injector circuit low
P0271	Cylinder 4 injector circuit high
P0273	Cylinder 5 injector circuit low
P0274	Cylinder 5 injector circuit high
P0276	Cylinder 6 injector circuit low
P0277	Cylinder 6 injector circuit high
P0297	Vehicle overspeed condition
P0298	Engine oil over temperature condition
P0300	Random misfire detected
P0301	Cylinder no. 1 misfire detected
P0302	Cylinder no. 2 misfire detected
P0303	Cylinder no. 3 misfire detected
P0304	Cylinder no. 4 misfire detected
P0305	Cylinder no. 5 misfire detected
P0306	Cylinder no. 6 misfire detected
P0307	Cylinder no. 7 misfire detected
P0308	Cylinder no. 8 misfire detected
P0309	Cylinder no. 9 misfire detected
P0310	Cylinder no. 10 misfire detected
P0315	PCM unable to learn crankshaft pulse wheel tooth spacing

Trouble codes - gasoline engines (continued)

Code	Probable cause
P0316	Misfire occurred during first 1000 engine revolutions
P0320	Ignition engine speed input circuit malfunction
P0325	Knock sensor 1 circuit malfunction (right cylinder head)
P0326	Knock sensor 1 circuit range/performance problem (right cylinder bank)
P0330	Knock sensor 2 circuit malfunction (left cylinder bank)
P0331	Knock sensor 2 circuit range/performance problem (left cylinder bank)
P0340	Camshaft Position (CMP) sensor circuit malfunction (right cylinder head)
P0341	Camshaft Position (CMP) sensor, A circuit, Bank 1, range or performance problem
P0344	Camshaft Position (CMP) sensor, A circuit, intermittent
P0345	Camshaft Position (CMP) sensor circuit malfunction (left cylinder head)
P0346	Camshaft Position (CMP) sensor, A circuit, range or performance problem
P0349	Camshaft Position (CMP) sensor, A circuit, Bank 2, intermittent
P0350	Ignition coil primary or secondary circuit malfunction
P0351 - P0360	Ignition coil primary or secondary circuit malfunction, coils 1 through 10
P0400	EGR flow failure (outside the minimum or maximum limits)
P0401	Exhaust Gas Recirculation (EGR) valve, insufficient flow detected
P0402	Exhaust Gas Recirculation (EGR) valve, excessive flow detected
P0403	EEGR electric motor windings or circuits to PCM shorted or open (6.8L engine)
P0405	EGR sensor, A circuit, low
P0406	EGR sensor, A circuit, high
P0410	Secondary Air Injection (AIR) system, low flow
P0411	Secondary Air Injection (AIR) system, upstream flow
P0412	Secondary Air Injection (AIR) system, circuit malfunction
P0420	Catalyst system efficiency below threshold (right cylinder bank)
P0430	Catalyst system efficiency below threshold (left cylinder bank)

Code	Probable cause
P0442	EVAP control system, small leak detected
P0443	EVAP control system, canister purge valve circuit malfunction
P0446	EVAP control system canister vent solenoid circuit malfunction
P0451	Fuel tank pressure sensor circuit out of range or performance problem
P0452	Fuel tank pressure sensor circuit, low input
P0453	Fuel tank pressure sensor circuit, high input
P0454	Fuel tank pressure sensor circuit, noisy
P0455	EVAP control system, big leak detected
P0456	EVAP control system, very small leak detected
P0457	EVAP control system, leak detected (fuel filler neck cap loose or off)
P0460	Fuel level sensor circuit malfunction
P0461	Fuel level sensor circuit range or performance problem
P0462	Fuel level sensor circuit, low input
P0463	Fuel level sensor circuit, high input
P0480	Fan 1, control primary circuit malfunction
P0481	Fan 2, control circuit, open or short
P0482	Medium Fan Control (MFC) primary circuit failure
P0483	Cooling fan, binding or mechanical failure
P0491	Secondary Air Injection (AIR) system, Bank 1, low flow
P0500	Vehicle Speed Sensor (VSS), circuit malfunction
P0501	Vehicle Speed Sensor (VSS) range/performance problem
P0503	Vehicle Speed Sensor (VSS), intermittent malfunction
P0504	Brake switch circuit, correlation to brake position switch
P0505 - P0507	Idle Air Control (IAC) system malfunction - on models w/o IAC, code indicates restricted air intake or damaged throttle body preventing proper idle
P0511	Idle Air Control (IAC) circuit malfunction
P0512	Starter relay circuit, short
P0528	Visctronic Drive Fan (VDF) speed sensor circuit malfunction

Trouble codes - gasoline engines (continued)

Code	Probable cause
P052A	Cold start cam position timing, Bank 1, over-advanced
P052B	Cold start cam position timing, Bank 1, over-retarded
P052C	Cold start cam position timing, Bank 2, over-advanced
P052D	Cold start cam position timing, Bank 2, over-retarded
P0532	Air conditioning pressure sensor circuit, low voltage
P0533	Air conditioning pressure sensor circuit, high voltage
P0534	Low air conditioning cycling period
P0537	Air conditioning evaporator temperature circuit, low input
P0538	Air conditioning evaporator temperature circuit, high input
P053A	PCV heater system, Bank 1, control circuit open
P0552	Power Steering Pressure (PSP) sensor circuit malfunction
P0553	Power Steering Pressure (PSP) sensor circuit malfunction
P0562	System voltage low
P0563	System voltage high
P0571	Brake switch, A circuit
P0572	Brake switch, A circuit, low voltage
P0573	Brake switch, A circuit, high voltage
P0579	Cruise control multifunction input A circuit range or performance problem
P0581	Cruise control multifunction input A circuit, high
P0600	Serial communication link (PCM) error
P0602	Control module programming error
P0603	Powertrain Control Module (PCM) Keep-Alive-Memory (KAM) test error
P0604	Powertrain Control Module (PCM) Random (RAM) memory corrupted
P0605	Powertrain Control Module (PCM) Read-Only-Memory (ROM) error
P0606	Powertrain Control Module (PCM), internal communication error
P0607	Powertrain Control Module (PCM), PCM needs reprogramming

Code	Probable cause
P060A to P060D	Powertrain Control Module (PCM), processor performance problem
P0610	Powertrain Control Module (PCM), vehicle options error
P0611	Fuel injector control module performance problem
P0620	Generator control circuit failure
P0622	Generator field terminal, circuit failure
P0625	Generator field terminal, circuit low
P0626	Generator field terminal, circuit high
P0627	Fuel pump, A circuit, control/open
P062F	Powertrain Control Module (PCM) EEPROM error
P0634	PCM/ECM/TCM internal temperature too high
P0641	Sensor reference voltage A circuit or open
P0642	Reference voltage circuit, low voltage
P0643	Reference voltage circuit, high voltage
P0645	Air conditioning clutch relay (wide open throttle a/c cutoff) primary circuit malfunction
P0657	Transmission solenoid actuator, supply voltage circuit open
P0660	Intake manifold tuning valve control circuit open (right cylinder bank) V6
P0663	Intake manifold tuning valve control circuit open (left cylinder bank) V6
P0685	Powertrain control module, power relay control circuit open
P0689	Ignition switch or PATS circuits, open or short
P0690	Powertrain control module, power relay control circuit, high
P0703	Brake Pedal Position (BPP) switch circuit input malfunction
P0704	Clutch pedal position switch malfunction
P0705	Transmission range sensor, A circuit input
P0707	Transmission range sensor, A circuit, low
P0708	Transmission range sensor, A circuit, high
P0720	Insufficient input from Output Shaft Speed (OSS) sensor
P0721	Noise interference on Output Shaft Speed (OSS) sensor signal

Trouble codes - gasoline engines (continued)

Code	Probable cause
P0722	No signal from Output Shaft Speed (OSS) sensor
P0723	Output Shaft Speed (OSS) sensor circuit, intermittent failure
P0812	Reverse Switch (RS) input circuit malfunction
P0815	Automatic transmission, upshift switch circuit
P0830	Clutch pedal switch A circuit
P0833	Clutch pedal switch, B circuit
P0840	Transmission fluid temp/pressure sensor, switch A circuit

Trouble Codes - diesel engines

Code	Probable cause
P0AXX	DC - AC converter malfunction
P00B7	Engine coolant flow/temperature performance problem
P0001	Fuel Volume Regulator Control Valve (FVCV)
P0003	Fuel Volume Regulator Control Valve (FVCV) driver circuit - low voltage
P0004	Fuel Volume Regulator Control Valve (FVCV) driver circuit - high voltage
P000E	Fuel Volume Regulator Control Valve (FVCV) driver circuit - exceeding learn values
P0046	Turbocharger boost control solenoid - performance problem
P0069	Manifold Absolute Pressure (MAP) sensor correlation problem
P006B	Manifold Absolute Pressure (MAP) sensor/Exhaust Pressure correlation problem
P0087	Fuel rail system pressure - low
P0088	Fuel rail system pressure - high
P008C	Fuel cooling pump circuit - open
P008D	Fuel cooling pump circuit - low voltage
P008E	Fuel cooling pump circuit - high voltage
P008F	Engine Coolant Temperature (ECT)/Fuel temperature correlation problem

Code	Probable cause
P0090	Fuel Pressure Control Valve (FPCV)
P0091	Fuel Pressure Control Valve (FPCV) circuit - low voltage
P0092	Fuel Pressure Control Valve (FPCV) circuit - high voltage
P0096	Intake Air Temperature (IAT) sensor circuit number 2 - performance problem
P0097	Intake Air Temperature (IAT) sensor circuit number 2 - low voltage
P0098	Intake Air Temperature (IAT) sensor circuit number 2 - high voltage
P0101	Mass Airflow (MAF) sensor circuit - performance problem
P0102	Mass Airflow (MAF) sensor circuit - low voltage
P0103	Mass Airflow (MAF) sensor circuit - high voltage
P0104	Mass Airflow (MAF) sensor circuit - intermittent, erratic
P0106	Barometric Pressure (BARO) sensor circuit - performance problem
P0107	Barometric Pressure (BARO) sensor circuit - low voltage
P0108	Barometric Pressure (BARO) sensor circuit - high voltage
P0112	Intake Air Temperature (IAT) sensor circuit - low voltage
P0113	Intake Air Temperature (IAT) sensor circuit - high voltage
P0114	Intake Air Temperature (IAT) sensor circuit - voltage erratic
P0117	Engine Coolant Temperature (ECT) sensor circuit - low voltage
P0118	Engine Coolant Temperature (ECT) sensor circuit - high voltage
P0122	Accelerator Pedal Position (APP) sensor circuit - low voltage
P0123	Accelerator Pedal Position (APP) sensor circuit - high voltage
P0128	Coolant below regulating temperature for thermostat - possible stuck open
P012F	Engine coolant temperature/fuel temperature - correlation problem
P0148	Fuel delivery error
P0149	Fuel timing error
P0168	Fuel temperature excessive - high
P0181	Fuel temperature sensor circuit - performance problem
P0182	Fuel temperature sensor circuit - low voltage

Trouble Codes - diesel engines (continued)

Code	Probable cause
P0183	Fuel temperature sensor circuit - high voltage
P0191	Fuel rail pressure sensor circuit - performance
P0192	Fuel rail pressure sensor circuit - low voltage
P0193	Fuel rail pressure sensor circuit - high voltage
P0194	Fuel rail pressure sensor circuit - erratic
P0196	Engine Oil Temperature (EOT) sensor circuit performance problem
P0197	Engine Oil Temperature (EOT) sensor circuit - low voltage
P0198	Engine Oil Temperature (EOT) sensor circuit - high voltage
P0201 - 208	Cylinder X (X = cylinder no.) - injector circuit open
P0216	Injection/injector timing control circuit
P0219	Engine overspeed condition
P0220	Throttle Switch B circuit malfunction
P0221	Throttle Switch B circuit performance problem
P0230	Fuel pump relay driver circuit
P0231	Fuel pump relay secondary circuit - low voltage
P0232	Fuel pump relay secondary circuit - high voltage
P0234	Turbocharger overboost condition
P0236	Turbocharger boost sensor A - performance problem
P0237	Turbocharger boost sensor A - low voltage
P0238	Turbocharger boost sensor A - high voltage
P0261	Cylinder 1 - injector circuit low voltage
P0262	Cylinder 1 - injector circuit high voltage
P0263	Cylinder 1 balance system - possible rough idle detected
P0264	Cylinder 2 - injector circuit low voltage
P0265	Cylinder 2 - injector circuit high voltage
P0266	Cylinder 2 balance system - possible rough idle detected

Code	Probable cause
P0267	Cylinder 3 - injector circuit low voltage
P0268	Cylinder 3 - injector circuit high voltage
P0269	Cylinder 3 balance system - possible rough idle detected
P0270	Cylinder 4 - injector circuit low voltage
P0271	Cylinder 4 - injector circuit high voltage
P0272	Cylinder 4 balance system - possible rough idle detected
P0273	Cylinder 5 - injector circuit low voltage
P0274	Cylinder 5 - injector circuit high voltage
P0275	Cylinder 5 balance system - possible rough idle detected
P0276	Cylinder 6 - injector circuit low voltage
P0277	Cylinder 6 - injector circuit high voltage
P0278	Cylinder 6 balance system - possible rough idle detected
P0279	Cylinder 7 - injector circuit low voltage
P0280	Cylinder 7 - injector circuit high voltage
P0281	Cylinder 7 balance system - possible rough idle detected
P0282	Cylinder 8 - injector circuit low voltage
P0283	Cylinder 8 - injector circuit high voltage
P0284	Cylinder 8 balance system - possible rough idle detected
P0297	Vehicle overspeed condition
P0298	Engine oil over-temperature condition
P0299	Turbocharger underboost condition
P02CC	Fuel injector number 1 offset learning at minimal limit
P02CD	Fuel injector number 1 offset learning at maximum limit
P02CE	Fuel injector number 2 offset learning at minimal limit
P02CF	Fuel injector number 2 offset learning at maximum limit
P02D0	Fuel injector number 3 offset learning at minimal limit
P02D1	Fuel injector number 3 offset learning at maximum limit

Trouble Codes - diesel engines (continued)

Code	Probable cause
P02D2	Fuel injector number 4 offset learning at minimal limit
P02D3	Fuel injector number 4 offset learning at maximum limit
P02D4	Fuel injector number 5 offset learning at minimal limit
P02D5	Fuel injector number 5 offset learning at maximum limit
P02D6	Fuel injector number 6 offset learning at minimal limit
P02D7	Fuel injector number 6 offset learning at maximum limit
P02D8	Fuel injector number 7 offset learning at minimal limit
P02D9	Fuel injector number 7 offset learning at maximum limit
P02DA	Fuel injector number 8 offset learning at minimal limit
P02DB	Fuel injector number 8 offset learning at maximum limit
P0300	Random misfire detected
P030X	Cylinder misfire detected (X = cylinder number)
P0335	Crankshaft Position (CKP) sensor circuit - malfunction
P0336	Crankshaft Position (CKP) sensor circuit - performance problem
P0337	Crankshaft Position (CKP) sensor circuit - low voltage
P0340	Camshaft Position (CMP) sensor circuit - malfunction
P0341	Camshaft Position (CMP) sensor circuit - performance problem
P0344	Camshaft Position (CMP) sensor circuit - intermittent failure
P0380	Glow plug circuit - performance problem
P0381	Glow plug light indicator circuit - malfunction
P0401	Exhaust Gas Recirculation (EGR) flow - insufficient
P0402	Exhaust Gas Recirculation (EGR) flow - excessive
P0403	Exhaust Gas Recirculation (EGR) circuit - malfunction
P0404	Exhaust Gas Recirculation (EGR) circuit - performance problem
P0405	Exhaust Gas Recirculation (EGR) circuit - low voltage
P0406	Exhaust Gas Recirculation (EGR) circuit - high voltage

Code	Probable cause
P040B	Exhaust Gas Recirculation Temperature (EGRT) sensor A circuit - performance problem
P040C	Exhaust Gas Recirculation Temperature (EGRT) sensor A circuit - low voltage
P040D	Exhaust Gas Recirculation Temperature (EGRT) sensor A circuit - high voltage
P041B	Exhaust Gas Recirculation Temperature (EGRT) sensor B circuit - performance problem
P041C	Exhaust Gas Recirculation Temperature (EGRT) sensor B circuit - low voltage
P041D	Exhaust Gas Recirculation Temperature (EGRT) sensor B circuit - high voltage
P0420	Catalytic converter efficiency - below threshold (Bank 1)
P042E	Exhaust Gas Recirculation (EGR) control - stuck open
P042F	Exhaust Gas Recirculation (EGR) control - stuck closed
P0460	Fuel tank level sensor circuit - performance problem
P0462	Fuel tank level sensor circuit - low voltage
P0463	Fuel tank level sensor circuit - high voltage
P0470	Exhaust backpressure sensor circuit - malfunction
P0471	Exhaust backpressure sensor circuit - performance problem
P0472	Exhaust backpressure sensor circuit - low voltage
P0473	Exhaust backpressure sensor circuit - high voltage
P0475	Exhaust pressure control valve - malfunction
P0476	Exhaust pressure control valve - performance problem
P0478	Exhaust pressure control valve - high voltage
P0480	Cooling fan control circuit
P0488	Throttle control circuit - performance problem
P0494	Cooling fan speed - low
P0495	Cooling fan speed - high
P0500	Vehicle Speed Sensor (VSS) circuit
P0503	Vehicle Speed Sensor (VSS) circuit - interference
P0512	Starter request circuit - shorted
P0528	Cooling fan sensor circuit - no signal

Trouble Codes - diesel engines (continued)

Code	Probable cause
P0529	Cooling fan sensor circuit - intermittent fault
P0541	Manifold intake air heater - voltage high
P0542	Manifold intake air heater - connection
P0544	Exhaust gas temperature sensor circuit (Bank 1 Sensor 1) - malfunction
P0545	Exhaust gas temperature sensor circuit (Bank 1 Sensor 1) - low voltage
P0546	Exhaust gas temperature sensor circuit (Bank 1 Sensor 1) - high voltage
P0560	System voltage - diagnostic monitor system problem
P0562	System voltage low
P0563	System voltage high
P0565	Cruise control ON circuit - not detecting
P0566	Cruise control OFF circuit - not detecting
P0567	Cruise control RESUME circuit - not detecting
P0568	Cruise control SET circuit - not detecting
P0569	Cruise control COAST circuit - not detecting
P0571	Cruise control Brake Switch circuit - not detecting
P0600	PCM communication link
P0602	PCM programming error
P0603	PCM long-term memory reset
P0604	PCM Random Access Memory (RAM) problem
P0605	PCM Read-Only Memory (ROM)
P0606	PCM malfunction
P06XX	PCM internal control module - malfunction(s)
P0611	Fuel Injector Control Module (FICM) - performance problem
P0620	Alternator control circuit - malfunction
P0623	Alternator light control circuit - malfunction
P0625	Alternator field circuit - low

Code	Probable cause
P0626	Alternator field circuit - high
P0627	Fuel pump control circuit - open
P0628	Fuel pump control circuit - low voltage
P0629	Fuel pump control circuit - high voltage
P062X	Fuel injector driver circuit (X = cylinder number) - performance problem
P0640	Manifold intake air heater - voltage low
P0642	Sensor reference A voltage - low voltage
P0643	Sensor reference A voltage - high voltage
P0645	A/C clutch relay control circuit - malfunction
P0646	A/C clutch relay control circuit - low voltage
P0647	A/C clutch relay control circuit - high voltage
P0649	Cruise control light circuit - malfunction
P0652	Sensor reference B voltage - low voltage
P0653	Sensor reference B voltage - high voltage
P0657	Transmission actuator supply voltage circuit - open
P0670	Glow plug module control circuit malfunction
P067X	Glow plug circuit failure (X = cylinder number)
P0683	Glow plug diagnostic signal communication fault
P0684	Glow plug control module-to-PCM communication fault
P0691	Cooling fan control circuit - low voltage
P0692	Cooling fan control circuit - high voltage
P0700	Transmission control system - malfunction
P0703	Brake On Off (BOO) switch - malfunction
P0704	Transmission clutch switch circuit
P0705*	Transmission Range (TR) sensor circuit - malfunction
P0707*	Transmission Range (TR) sensor circuit - low voltage
P0708*	Transmission Range (TR) sensor circuit - high voltage

Trouble Codes - diesel engines (continued)

Code	Probable cause
P0712*	Transmission Fluid Temperature (TFT) sensor - low voltage
P0713*	Transmission Fluid Temperature (TFT) sensor - high voltage
P0715*	Transmission Shift Solenoid (TSS) sensor circuit - malfunction
P0717*	Transmission Shift Solenoid (TSS) sensor circuit - intermittent failure
P0718*	Transmission Shift Solenoid (TSS) - noisy
P0720*	Shift Solenoid (OSS) sensor circuit - malfunction
P0721*	Shift Solenoid (OSS) sensor circuit - noisy
P0732	Transmission gear 2 ratio error
P0733	Transmission gear 3 ratio error
P0741	Torque Converter Clutch (TCC) circuit - performance problem
P0743*	Torque Converter Clutch (TCC) system - electrical failure
P0750	Shift solenoid 1 - malfunction
P0755*	Shift solenoid 2 - malfunction
P0781*	1 - 2 shift malfunction
P0782*	2 - 3 shift malfunction
P0783*	3 - 4 shift malfunction
P0830	Clutch pedal switch A circuit - malfunction
P0833	Clutch pedal switch B circuit - malfunction
P1000	OBD-II monitor checks incomplete, require another drive cycle
P1001	Key On Engine Running (KOER) test aborted
P1102	Mass Airflow (MAF) sensor circuit - low voltage
P1103	Mass Airflow (MAF) sensor values - higher than normal
P1105	Dual alternator monitor circuit - fault
P1106	Dual alternator control circuit - fault
P1107	Dual alternator control circuit - malfunction
P1108	Dual alternator BATT light circuit - malfunction

Code	Probable cause
P1118	Manifold Air Temperature sensor circuit - low voltage
P1119	Manifold Air Temperature sensor circuit - high voltage
P1139	Water In Fuel indicator circuit - malfunction
P1140	Water In Fuel condition
P1148	Alternator number 2 control circuit - malfunction
P1149	Alternator number 2 control circuit - high voltage
P115A	Low fuel level indication - limited power
P117B	Exhaust gas temperature sensor - correlation problem
P1184	Engine oil temperature sensor circuit - performance problem
P120F	Fuel pressure regulator - excessive variation
P1209	Injection control system pressure peak fault
P1210	Injection control pressure above expected level
P1211*	Injection control pressure not controllable - pressure above/below normal
P1212*	Injection control pressure voltage - not at normal values
P1218	Cylinder Identification (CID) values - stuck high
P1219	Cylinder Identification (CID) values - stuck low
P123C	Cold start turbocharger protection - block heater inoperative
P1247	Turbocharger boost pressure - low
P1248	Turbocharger boost pressure - not detected
P1249	Turbocharger wastegate Fail Steady State test
P1250	Electronic passive anti theft system failure
P1260	Electronic anti-theft system - vehicle immobilized
P126X	Injector high to low side circuit short (X = cylinder no.)
P127X	Injector high to low side circuit open (X = cylinder no.)
P127A	Fuel pressure failure - aborted KOER test
P1280	Injection control pressure out of range - low
P1281	Injection control pressure out of range - high

Trouble Codes - diesel engines (continued)

Code	Probable cause
P1282	Injection control pressure not controllable - excessive
P1283	Injection Pressure Regulator (IPR) circuit - failure
P1284	Injection control pressure circuit - testing failure
P1291	Injector high side (number 1) circuit - short to ground or battery
P1292	Injector high side (number 2) circuit - short to ground or battery
P1293	Injector high side (Bank 1) circuit - open
P1294	Injector high side (Bank 2) circuit - open
P1295*	Injector Bank 1 circuit - multiple faults
P1296*	Injector Bank 2 circuit - multiple faults
P1297	Injector high side circuits - shorted together
P1298	Injector Driver Module (IDM) - failure
P1316	Injector circuit - Injector Driver Module (IDM) codes detected
P132X	Turbocharger boost control - malfunction
P1335	Exhaust Gas Recirculation (EGR) sensor - performance problem
P1336	Crankshaft (CKP)/Camshaft (CMP) sensor information - erratic
P1378	Fuel Injector Control Module (FICM) supply voltage circuit - low voltage
P1379	Fuel Injector Control Module (FICM) supply voltage circuit - high voltage
P138D	Turbocharger boost control - high
P1397	Glow plug system voltage - out of self-test range
P1408	Exhaust Gas Recirculation (EGR) flow - out of self test range
P1464	A/C on during KOER test procedure
P1501	Vehicle moved during testing procedure
P1502	Invalid testing procedure - APCM functioning
P1531	Invalid test - accelerator pedal movement during test procedure
P1536	Parking brake applied during testing - circuit failure
P1551 - 1558	Cylinder injector circuit - performance problem

Code	Probable cause
P1561	Brake line pressure sensor circuit - malfunction
P1586	Electronic throttle control error
P1610	Interactive reprogramming code - diagnose PCM
P1611	Interactive reprogramming code - diagnose PCM
P1615	Interactive reprogramming code - erase flash error
P1616	Interactive reprogramming code - flash error, low voltage
P1617	Interactive reprogramming code - block programming error
P1618	Interactive reprogramming code - block programming error
P162E	PTO internal control module malfunction
P1633	Keep Alive power voltage - low
P1635	Tire/axle out of acceptable range
P1639	Vehicle ID block corrupted
P1662	Injector Driver Module (IDM) EN circuit - failure
P1663	Fuel Demand Command Signal (FDCS) circuit - failure
P1667	Cylinder Identification (CID) circuit failure
P1668	Injector Driver Module (IDM)/PCM circuit - failure
P1670	Electronic Feedback signal not detected
P1690	Turbocharger wastegate control valve malfunction
P1702*	Digital Transmission Range (TR) sensor - intermittent circuit failure
P1703	Brake switch out of self test range
P1704	Digital Transmission Range (TR) sensor - failed to transition state
P1705	Digital Transmission Range (TR) sensor - out of self test range
P1711	Transmission Fluid Temperature (TFT) sensor - out of self test range
P1713*	Transmission Fluid Temperature (TFT) sensor - failure below 50 degrees F
P1714	Shift solenoid A inductive signature malfunction
P1715	Shift solenoid B inductive signature malfunction
P1718*	Transmission Fluid Temperature (TFT) sensor - failure above 250 degrees F

Trouble Codes - diesel engines (continued)

Code	Probable cause
P1725	Insufficient engine speed during self test
P1726	Excessive engine speed during self test
P1728*	Torque Converter Clutch (TCC) transmission slip error
P1729*	4WD Low switch error
P1744	Torque Converter Clutch (TCC) system performance
P1746	Exhaust Pressure Control (EPC) solenoid - open circuit
P1747	Exhaust Pressure Control (EPC) solenoid - short circuit
P1754	Coast Clutch Solenoid (CCS) circuit - malfunction
P1760*	Exhaust Pressure Control (EPC) circuit - intermittent failure
P1780	TCS circuit out of self test range
P1781	4WD Low circuit out of self test range
P1783*	Transmission over-temperature condition
P179A	Controller Area Network (CAN)/PCM/turbocharger communication error

* Transmission Control Indicator Light (TCIL) will flash when fault code present

3.5 The PCM harness connector is accessible outside the fenderwell on 2001 and earlier models

3.7 Location of the PCM mounting nuts - 1999 model

3   Powertrain Control Module (PCM) - removal and installation

Warning: *The models covered by this manual are equipped with Supplemental Restraint systems (SRS), more commonly known as airbags. Always disable the airbag system before working in the vicinity of any airbag system components to avoid the possibility of accidental deployment of the airbag, which could cause personal injury (see Chapter 12).*
Caution: *To avoid electrostatic discharge damage to the PCM, handle the PCM only by its case. Do not touch the electrical terminals during removal and installation. If available, ground yourself to the vehicle with an anti-static ground strap, available at computer supply stores.*
Note: *On 2008 and later models, the replacement of the PCM requires the original programming to be retrieved via a scan tool before PCM removal. The programming would then be downloaded to the new PCM and the original instrument cluster. This is a procedure best performed at a dealership.*

1   The Powertrain Control Module (PCM) is located behind the driver's side kick panel on 1999 through 2001 models or in the engine compartment on 2002 models. On 2003 through 2004 gasoline models, it's mounted on the passenger-side lower dash panel. On 2005 and later gasoline models it's in the cowl, accessible from the engine compartment. On 2003 and later diesel models it's mounted on the left side of the engine compartment.
2   Disconnect the cable(s) from the negative battery terminal(s) (see Chapter 5, Section 1).

1999 through 2001 models
Refer to illustrations 3.1a and 3.1b
3   Loosen the left front wheel lug nuts. Raise the vehicle and secure it on jackstands.
4   Remove the left front wheel and remove the fender apron from the wheelwell (see Chapter 11).

5   Unscrew the bolt and unplug the electrical connector for the PCM **(see illustration)**.
6   Working inside the driver's compartment, remove the driver's side kick panel (see Chapter 11).
7   Remove the retaining bolts from the PCM bracket **(see illustration)**.
8   Carefully remove the PCM. **Note:** *Avoid any static electricity damage to the computer by grounding yourself to the body before touching the PCM and using a special anti-static pad to store the PCM on once it is removed.*
9   Installation is the reverse of removal.

2002 models
10   Remove the air filter housing (see Chapter 4A).
11   Unplug the electrical connectors from the PCM.
12   Remove the retaining bolts from the PCM bracket.
13   Carefully remove the PCM. **Note:** *Avoid any static electricity damage to the computer by grounding yourself to the body before touching the PCM and using a special anti-static pad to store the PCM on once it is removed.*
14   Installation is the reverse of removal.

2003 and 2004 gasoline models
15   Unbolt and disconnect the wiring harness from the PCM.
16   Unlatch the two wiring harness retainers.
17   Remove the two screws and slip the PCM and its bracket out. Pull the PCM from the bracket.
18   Installation is the reverse of removal.

2005 and later gasoline models
19   Disconnect the wiring harnesses from the PCM.
20   Remove the two bolts and pull the PCM from the cowl on the engine side.
21   Installation is the reverse of removal.

2003 and later diesel models
22   On 2003 models, remove the left-side battery (refer to Chapter 1). On 2004 and later models, remove only the left-side battery cover.
23   Disconnect the wiring harnesses from the PCM.
24   Remove the two bolts and pull the PCM out.
25   Installation is the reverse of removal.

4   Throttle Position Sensor (TPS) (gasoline models) - replacement

Refer to illustration 4.1
Note: *Diesel engines are not equipped with a throttle position sensor. Idle is detected by the idle validation switch while acceleration is detected by the accelerator position sensor. Both components are mounted on the accelerator pedal (see Section 18).*
1   The Throttle Position Sensor (TPS) is located on the end of the throttle shaft on the throttle body **(see illustration)**. By monitoring the output voltage from the TPS, the PCM can determine fuel delivery based on throttle valve

4.1 Location of the TPS on a 6.8L V10 model

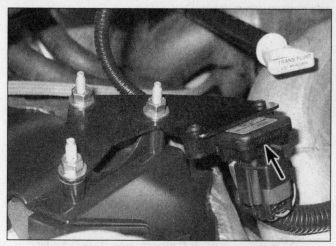

5.1 The MAP sensor is located on a bracket attached to the air conditioning evaporator housing (7.3L diesel models)

6.1 The MAF sensor is located inside the air filter housing on 1999 through 2004 models

angle (driver demand). A broken or loose TPS can cause intermittent bursts of fuel from the injectors and an unstable idle because the PCM thinks the throttle is moving. A problem with the TPS circuits will set a diagnostic trouble code (see Section 2).

2   Make sure the ignition key is in the OFF position.

2005 and earlier models

3   Remove the air filter housing duct at the throttle body (see Chapter 4A). On 2005 models with 5.4L models, the entire air cleaner must be removed.

4   Remove the accelerator shield if it interferes (see Chapter 4A).

5   Disconnect the electrical connector from the TPS.

6   Remove the screws that retain the TPS to the throttle body and remove the TPS.

7   Installation is the reverse of removal.

8   Tighten the TPS mounting screws securely.

2006 and later models

Removal

9   Disconnect the crankcase vent tube from the air cleaner.

10   Remove the air cleaner.

11   Remove the four bolts and the pedestal that locates the air cleaner outlet pipe over the throttle body.

12   Disconnect the connector at the TPS.

13   The TPS on these models is attached to the throttle body with adhesive on the screws. Use a heat gun (no more than 1,100 watts) for three minutes at a distance of 1 inch from the sensor. If you have access to a hand-held infrared temperature reader, stop using the heat gun when the screw area reaches 130 degrees F. Use hand tools to remove the screws. **Caution:** *Direct the heat at the area of screws only, not the TPS itself or other plastic parts near it.*

Installation

14   On later models with adhesive screws, the TPS and the screws cannot be reused. They must be replaced.

15   Align the plastic tab on the new TPS with the notch or hole at the throttle body, then install the screws to 27 in-lbs.

16   The remainder of installation is the reverse of removal.

---

5   Manifold Absolute Pressure (MAP) sensor (diesel models) - replacement

Refer to illustration 5.1

1   The MAP sensor is mounted on a bracket in the engine compartment **(see illustration)**. On 6.4L engines, the MAP sensor is threaded into the top of the intake manifold. The Manifold Absolute Pressure (MAP) sensor monitors the intake manifold pressure changes resulting from changes in engine load and speed and converts the information into a voltage output. The PCM uses the MAP sensor to control fuel delivery and ignition timing. The PCM will receive information as a voltage signal that will vary from 1.9 to 2.1 volts at closed throttle (high vacuum) and 0.3 to 0.5 volt at wide open throttle (low vacuum). The voltage range values will vary slightly according to changes in altitude. A problem in any of the MAP sensor circuits will set a diagnostic trouble code (see Section 2).

2   Make sure the ignition key is in the OFF position.

3   Disconnect the electrical connector and the vacuum hose from the MAP sensor.

4   Remove the screws that retain the MAP sensor to the bracket. Remove the MAP sensor.

5   Installation is the reverse of removal.

---

6   Mass Airflow (MAF) sensor - replacement

Gasoline models

1999 through 2004

Refer to illustrations 6.1 and 6.6

1   The mass airflow sensor is located inside the air filter housing **(see illustration)**. The MAF system circuit consists of a platinum hot wire, a thermistor and a control circuit inside a plastic housing. The sensor uses a hot wire sensing element to measure the molecular mass (weight) of air entering the engine. As the throttle opens, increasing volume of air passes over the hot wire, which cools the wire. The MAF sensor circuit is designed to maintain the hot wire at a constant preset temperature by controlling the current flow through the hot wire. So, as the wire cools, the PCM increases the flow of current through the hot wire in order to maintain the wire at a constant temperature. The output voltage signal of the MAF sensor varies in accordance with this current flow. This voltage signal is measured by the PCM, which converts this signal into a digital wave form, calculates the fuel injector pulse width (duration) and turns the injectors on and off accordingly. A problem in the MAF sensor circuit will set a diagnostic trouble code (see Section 2).

2   Make sure the ignition key is in the OFF position.

3   Disconnect the electrical connector from the MAF sensor near the air filter housing.

4   Remove the air filter housing (see Chapter 4A).

5   Remove the MAF sensor assembly from inside the air filter housing and disconnect the MAF sensor connector directly at the sensor.

6   Remove the bolts from the MAF sensor base **(see illustration)** and separate the MAF sensor.

7   Installation is the reverse of removal.

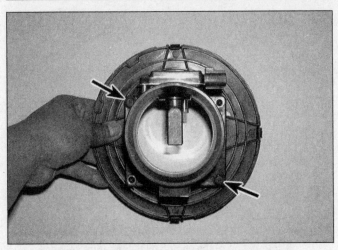

6.6 The location of the MAF sensor mounting bolts on a 6.8L V10 engine

7.1 Location of the IAT sensor on a 7.3L V8 engine

2005 and later models

Note: *2005 and later models use a drop-in style MAF sensor. It is located in the air inlet duct.*

8   Disconnect the cable from the negative battery terminal.

9   Disconnect the electrical connector from the MAF sensor **(see illustration)**.

10   Remove the MAF sensor mounting screws **(see illustration)** and remove the MAF sensor from the air inlet duct.

11   If you're planning to install the old MAF sensor, inspect the condition of the rubber sealing ring at the mounting flange **(see illustration)**. If the seal is cracked, torn or deteriorated, replace the MAF sensor (or make your own sealing ring). The ring is only available as part of a new MAF sensor.

12   Installation is the reverse of removal.

Diesel engines

13   6.4L diesel engines are equipped with a drop-in style MAP sensor similar to those used on gasoline engines. The sensor is mounted to the top of the air intake tube.

14   Turn the ignition Off.

15   Disconnect the electrical connector at the MAF and remove the two screws securing the MAF sensor.

16   When reinstalling, make sure the electrical harness retainer is reattached to the air cleaner assembly.

7   Intake Air Temperature (IAT) sensor (diesel models) - replacement

Refer to illustration 7.1

1   The intake air temperature sensor is mounted in the air inlet system. Its exact location varies from year to year, but it always has two wires in its harness **(see illustration)**. The intake air temperature (IAT) sensor is a thermistor (a resistor which varies the value of its resistance in accordance with tempera-

ture changes). The change in the resistance values will directly affect the voltage signal from the sensor to the PCM. As the sensor temperature DECREASES, the resistance values will INCREASE. As the sensor temperature INCREASES, the resistance values will DECREASE. A problem in any of the IAT sensor circuits will set a diagnostic trouble code.

2   Make sure the ignition key is in the OFF position.

3   Disconnect the electrical connector from the IAT sensor.

4   Rotate the IAT sensor counterclockwise 1/4 turn and pull the IAT sensor from the air filter housing.

5   Installation is the reverse of removal.

8   Engine Coolant Temperature (ECT) sensor (diesel models) - replacement

Refer to illustrations 8.1 and 8.5

Warning: *Wait until the engine has cooled completely before beginning this procedure.*

Note: *On later 7.3L and 6.4L models, the ECT*

sensor is located in the engine front cover.

1   The engine coolant temperature sensor is mounted near the thermostat housing **(see illustration)**. The engine coolant temperature (ECT) sensor is a thermistor. The thermistor is a resistor which varies the value of its resistance in accordance with temperature changes. The change in the resistance values will directly affect the voltage signal from the sensor to the PCM. As the sensor temperature DECREASES, the resistance values will INCREASE. As the sensor temperature INCREASES, the resistance values will DECREASE. A problem in any of the ECT sensor circuits will set a diagnostic trouble code.

2   Make sure the ignition key is in the OFF position.

3   Drain approximately one gallon from the cooling system.

4   On 6.0L models, disconnect the wiring connector for the cooling fan. Disconnect the electrical connector and carefully unscrew the sensor. On 6.4L engines, remove the air cleaner housing to access the sensor, which is located near the base of the oil filter housing.

5   Wrap the threads of the new sensor with

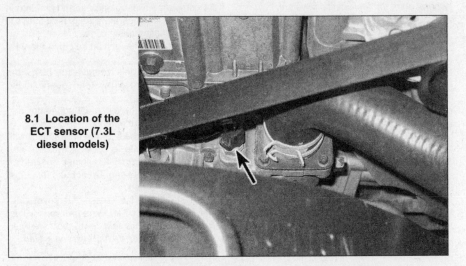

8.1 Location of the ECT sensor (7.3L diesel models)

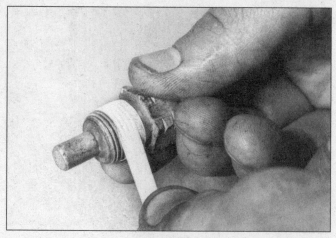

8.5 Wrap the threads of the ECT sensor with Teflon tape to prevent leakage

9.1 Location of the engine oil temperature sensor on a 7.3L V8 engine

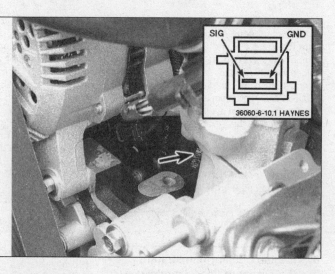

10.1 Location of the cylinder head temperature sensor

Teflon sealing tape to prevent leakage and thread corrosion **(see illustration)**. On 6.4L engines, the sensor is sealed with an O-ring. Do not use tape, just install a new O-ring.

6   Installation is the reverse of removal. **Caution:** *Handle the coolant sensor with care. Damage to this sensor will affect the operation of the fuel injection system.*

9 Engine oil temperature sensor (diesel models) - replacement

Refer to illustration 9.1
Warning: *Wait until the engine has cooled completely before beginning this procedure.*

1   The engine oil temperature sensor is located on the high-pressure oil pump reservoir on 7.3L models **(see illustration)**. On 6.0L models it is located at the top front of the engine. On 6.4L engines, the oil temperature sensor is located just below the base of the oil filter housing, just forward of the ECT sensor. The engine oil temperature sensor is a thermistor which varies the value of its resistance

in accordance with temperature changes. The change in the resistance values will directly affect the voltage signal from the sensor to the PCM. The PCM uses this signal to calculate the fuel quantity, injection timing, glow plug operation and exhaust back pressure. Low oil temperatures signal the PCM to increase idle for complete warm-up operation. A problem in any of the oil temperature sensor circuits will set a diagnostic trouble code.

2   Make sure the ignition key is in the OFF position.

3   On 7.3L models, remove the plug from the high pressure oil system reservoir and suction out the oil.

4   Disconnect the electrical connector and carefully unscrew the sensor.

5   Wrap the threads of the new sensor with Teflon sealing tape to prevent leakage and thread corrosion. On 6.4L engines, the sensor is sealed with an O-ring. Do not use tape, just install a new O-ring.

6   Installation is the reverse of removal. **Caution:** *Handle the oil temperature sensor with care. Damage to this sensor will affect the operation of the entire diesel fuel injection system.*

10 Cylinder head temperature sensor (gasoline models) - replacement

Refer to illustration 10.1

1   The cylinder head temperature sensor is a major component of the Fail Safe Cooling system. This sensor varies the value of its voltage output in accordance with temperature changes **(see illustration)**. The change in the resistance values will directly affect the voltage signal from the CHT sensor. As the sensor temperature DECREASES, the resistance values will INCREASE (voltage increases). If the cylinder head temperature exceeds 265-degrees F, the PCM disables four (V8) or 5 (V10) fuel injectors at a time. The cylinders that do not receive fuel act as cooling air pumps for the other cylinders. If the temperature exceeds 330-degrees F, the PCM disables all the fuel injectors.

2   To remove the cylinder head temperature sensor, the intake manifold must be removed from the engine (see Chapter 2A).

3   Unplug the electrical connector, then carefully unscrew the CHT sensor. **Caution:** *Handle the CHT sensor with care. Damage to this sensor will affect the operation of the entire fuel injection system.* Install the sensor and tighten it securely.

4   Installation is the reverse of removal.

11 Crankshaft position (CKP) sensor - replacement

1   The crankshaft position sensor (CKP) determines the timing on each cylinder for the fuel injectors and ignition system. The crankshaft sensor is mounted near the crankshaft pulley. A problem in the crankshaft sensor circuit will set a diagnostic trouble code (see Section 2).

2   Make sure the ignition key is in the OFF position.

12.1a The location of the camshaft sensor on a 7.3L diesel engine

12.1b The location of the camshaft sensor on a gasoline engine

3   Remove the air conditioning compressor (see Chapter 3). On 2004 models it is not necessary to remove the compressor. It is possible to simply lower the compressor about an inch for access to the sensor.
4   Raise the vehicle and support it securely on jackstands.
5   Working under the vehicle, disconnect the crankshaft position sensor electrical connector.
6   Remove the bolt and detach the sensor.
7   Installation is the reverse of removal.

12 Camshaft position (CMP) sensor - replacement

Refer to illustrations 12.1a and 12.1b
1   The camshaft position (CMP) sensor determines the position of the cylinder for ignition start-up signals and for sequential fuel injection signals to each cylinder. The camshaft position sensor is mounted near the crankshaft pulley on 7.3L diesel models **(see illustration)** or on the cylinder head near the camshaft sprocket **(see illustration)** on gasoline models. On 6.0L and 6.4L

13.7 Use a slotted socket to remove the oxygen sensor

diesel models it is behind the power steering pump.
2   Make sure the ignition key is in the OFF position.

Gasoline models
3   Disconnect the electrical connector from the camshaft position sensor.
4   Remove the bolt and detach the sensor.
5   Installation is the reverse of removal.

Diesel models
6   On 7.3L models, raise the vehicle and support it on jackstands.
7   Remove the bolt and detach the sensor.
8   Installation is the reverse of removal.

13 Oxygen sensor (gasoline models) - general information and replacement

General information
1   All gasoline models covered by this manual have On-Board Diagnostics II (OBD-II) engine management systems, which means, that they have the ability to verify the accuracy of the basic feedback loop between the oxygen sensor and the PCM. They accomplish this by using an oxygen sensor in front of the catalytic converter and an oxygen sensor behind the catalytic converter. By sampling the exhaust gas before and after the catalytic converter, the PCM can determine the efficiency of the converter and can even predict when it will fail.
2   The primary (upstream) oxygen sensor is located in the exhaust manifold and the secondary (downstream) oxygen sensor is located behind the catalytic converter. The upstream and downstream oxygen sensors on all models is a heated oxygen sensor. The PCM uses a supply wire and ground wire to control the power to the O2 sensor heater during warm-up.
3   Special care must be taken whenever a

sensor is serviced.
a) *Oxygen sensors have a permanently attached pigtail and an electrical connector which should not be removed from the sensor. Damage or removal of the pigtail or electrical connector can adversely affect operation of the sensor.*
b) *Grease, dirt and other contaminants should be kept away from the electrical connector and the louvered end of the sensor.*
c) *Do not use cleaning solvents of any kind on an oxygen sensor.*
d) *Do not drop or roughly handle an oxygen sensor.*
e) *The silicone boot must be installed in the correct position to prevent the boot from being melted and to allow the sensor to operate properly.*

Replacement
Refer to illustration 13.7
Note: *Because it is installed in the exhaust manifold or pipe, which contracts when cool, the oxygen sensor may be very difficult to loosen when the engine is cold. Rather than risk damage to the sensor, assuming you are planning to reuse it in another manifold or pipe, start and run the engine for a minute or two, then shut it off. Be careful not to burn yourself during the following procedure.*
4   Make sure the ignition key is in the OFF position.
5   If you're replacing the oxygen sensor on a V10 model, raise the vehicle and secure it on jackstands. Access the oxygen sensor harness and then unplug the electrical connector.
6   The oxygen sensors on V8 models can be replaced without raising the vehicle. Unplug the sensor electrical connector.
7   Unscrew the sensor from the exhaust manifold or exhaust pipe **(see illustration)**.
Note: *The best tool for removing an oxygen sensor is a special slotted socket, especially if you're planning to reuse a sensor. If you don't have this tool, and you plan to reuse the sensor, be extremely careful when unscrewing the sensor.*

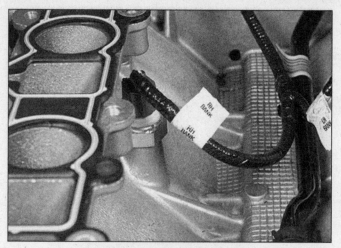

14.1 Location of the knock sensor on 5.4L V8 models

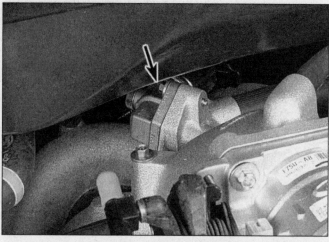

16.1 Location of the IAC valve on a 5.4L V8 model

8   Apply anti-seize compound to the threads of the sensor to facilitate future removal. The threads of new sensors should already be coated with this compound, but if you're planning to reuse an old sensor, recoat the threads. Install the sensor and tighten it securely.
9   Reconnect the electrical connector of the pigtail lead to the main wiring harness.
10   Lower the vehicle (if it was raised), test drive the car and verify that no trouble codes have been set.

---

14   Knock sensor (gasoline models) - replacement

Refer to illustration 14.1
Note: *2005 and 2006 models use two knock sensors. The service procedure is the same.*
1   The knock sensor is located under the intake manifold **(see illustration)**. The knock control system is designed to reduce spark knock during periods of heavy detonation. This allows the engine to use optimal spark advance to improve driveability. The knock sensor detects abnormal vibration in the engine and produces a voltage output which increases with the severity of the knock. The voltage signal is monitored by the PCM, which retards ignition timing until the detonation ceases. A problem in the knock sensor circuit will set a diagnostic trouble code (see Section 2).
2   Make sure the ignition key is in the OFF position.
3   Drain the cooling system (see Chapter 1).
4   Remove the intake manifold (see Chapter 2A).
5   Disconnect the electrical connector and remove the knock sensor.
6   If you're going to reuse the old sensor, coat the threads with thread sealant. New sensors are pre-coated with thread sealant; do not apply any additional sealant or the operation of the sensor may be affected.
7   Install the knock sensor and tighten it securely. Don't overtighten the sensor or damage may occur.

8   Plug in the electrical connector, refill the cooling system and check for leaks.
9   Installation is the reverse of removal.

---

15   Vehicle Speed Sensor (VSS) - replacement

Check

1   The Vehicle Speed Sensor (VSS) is located on top of the rear differential. The VSS sensor is an electronic component that produces a pulsing voltage signal whenever the sensor shaft is rotated. These voltage pulses are monitored by the PCM, which uses this information to help control the fuel and ignition systems and transmission shifting. The VSS is also used for the ABS system and the cruise control system. A problem in the VSS sensor circuit will set a diagnostic trouble code (see Section 2).
2   Make sure the ignition key is in the OFF position.
3   Disconnect the electrical connector from the VSS.
4   Remove the bolt and remove the VSS from the rear differential.
5   Replace the O-ring, if equipped.
6   Installation is the reverse of removal.

---

16   Idle Air Control (IAC) valve (1999 through 2004 gasoline models) - replacement

Refer to illustration 16.1
Note: *The minimum idle speed is pre-set at the factory and should not require adjustment under normal operating conditions. However, if the throttle body has been replaced or you suspect the minimum idle speed has been tampered with (for example, if the idle speed screw was removed from the throttle body), have the vehicle checked by a dealer service department or other qualified automotive repair shop.*

Note: *2005 and later models do not use idle air control valves. The idle is adjusted by movement of the throttle by the PCM.*
1   The Idle Air Control Valve (IAC) controls the engine idle speed **(see illustration)**. The IAC valve controls the amount of air that bypasses the throttle plate into the intake manifold. The IAC valve is controlled by the PCM in accordance with the demands on the engine (air conditioning, power steering) and the operating conditions (cold or warm up). A problem in the IAC valve circuit will set a diagnostic trouble code (see Section 2).
2   Make sure the ignition key is in the OFF position.
3   Disconnect the IAC valve connector.
4   Remove the throttle bypass hose from the valve.
5   Remove the mounting bolts and detach the IAC valve and gasket.
6   Installation is the reverse of removal.
7   Be sure to use a new gasket when installing the IAC valve.
8   Tighten the IAC valve mounting bolts to the torque listed in this Chapter's Specifications.

---

17   Fuel tank pressure (FTP) sensor - replacement

Refer to illustration 17.1
Warning: *Gasoline is extremely flammable, so take extra precautions when you work on any part of the fuel system. Don't smoke or allow open flames or bare light bulbs near the work area, and don't work in a garage where a gas-type appliance (such as a water heater or clothes dryer) is present. Since gasoline is carcinogenic, wear fuel-resistant gloves when there's a possibility of being exposed to fuel, and, if you spill any fuel on your skin, rinse it off immediately with soap and water. Mop up any spills immediately and do not store fuel-soaked rags where they could ignite. When you perform any kind of work on the fuel system, wear safety glasses and have a Class B*

17.1 Location of the fuel tank pressure sensor

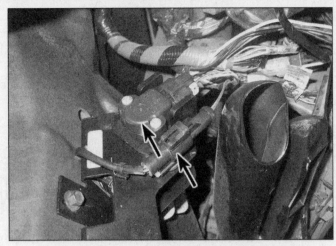

18.1 The location of the idle validation switch and the accelerator pedal position sensor

type fire extinguisher on hand. The fuel system is under pressure, so if any lines must be disconnected, the pressure in the system must be relieved first (see Chapter 4 for more information).

1   The fuel tank pressure (FTP) sensor is used to monitor the fuel tank pressure or vacuum during the OBD-II test portion for emissions integrity. This test scans various sensors and output actuators to detect abnormal amounts of fuel vapors that may not be purging into the canister or the intake system for recycling. The FTP sensor helps the PCM monitor this pressure differential (pressure vs. vacuum) inside the fuel tank. A problem in the fuel tank pressure sensor circuit will set a diagnostic trouble code (see Section 2).

2   Make sure the ignition key is in the OFF position.

3   Remove the fuel tank (see Chapter 4A).

4   Push down and rotate the fuel tank pressure sensor counterclockwise. Remove the sensor from the fuel tank.

5   Installation is the reverse of removal.

6   Be sure to install a new gasket.

18 Accelerator pedal position sensor - replacement

Refer to illustration 18.1

Note: *The idle validation switch, the accelerator pedal position sensor and accelerator pedal are replaced as a single unit.*

1   The accelerator pedal position sensor is used to monitor the driver's demand for power **(see illustration)**. The idle validation switch and the accelerator pedal position sensor are combined into a single unit. The PCM adjusts the amount of fuel injected into the cylinders according to the position of the pedal. The idle validation switch protects the engine from in-range acceleration problems. A problem in the accelerator pedal position sensor circuit will

set a diagnostic trouble code (see Section 2).

2   Make sure the ignition key is in the OFF position.

3   Access the accelerator pedal assembly under the dash.

4   If the vehicle is equipped with adjustable pedals, move the pedal as far to the rear as possible. Disconnect the cable from the pedal assembly.

5   Disconnect all of the wiring from the pedal assembly.

6   Remove the accelerator pedal mounting bolts and separate the assembly from the vehicle. The pedal assembly cannot be serviced. If there is a problem with any component, the entire unit must be replaced.

7   Installation is the reverse of removal.

19 Barometric pressure (BARO) sensor (6.0L and 6.4L diesel models) - replacement

1   The barometric pressure sensor monitors the pressure of the ambient atmosphere around the vehicle. It provides a reference point for the operation of other pressure sensors that is based on altitude and weather conditions. A problem in the barometric pressure sensor will set a trouble code (see Section 2). On 6.4L engines, the BARO function is internal to the PCM. If there is a problem with the BARO sensor function (setting a code), the PCM must be replaced.

2   The BARO sensor is located directly below the steering column and behind the plastic column cover.

3   Release the retainers that secure the lower steering column cover (refer to Chapter 11).

4   Disconnect the wiring from the sensor and unclip it from the instrument panel.

5   Installation is the reverse of removal.

20 Exhaust pressure sensor (6.0L and 6.4L diesel models) - replacement

1   The exhaust pressure sensor is connected to the left exhaust manifold by a tube. It provides information to the PCM especially for the proper operation of the variable-vane turbocharger. A problem with the exhaust pressure sensor circuit will set a trouble code (see Section 2).

2   Disconnect the wiring from the sensor.

3   Unscrew the sensor from its mount.

Note: *On late 2005 and 2006 models, it is necessary to use a back-up wrench when loosening the sensor to avoid damaging the fitting.*

4   Installation is the reverse of removal.

21 Positive Crankcase Ventilation (PCV) system

Refer to illustration 21.5

1   The Positive Crankcase Ventilation (PCV) system reduces hydrocarbon emissions by scavenging crankcase vapors. It does this by circulating fresh air from the air cleaner through the crankcase, where it mixes with blow-by gases and is then rerouted through a PCV valve to the intake manifold (on gasoline engines) or through a breather housing on the left valve cover (on diesel engines).

Gasoline engines

2   The main components of the PCV system are the PCV valve, a blow-by filter and the vacuum hoses connecting these two components with the engine.

3   To maintain idle quality, the PCV valve restricts the flow when the intake manifold vacuum is high. If abnormal operating conditions (such as piston ring problems) arise, the sys-

21.5 The 7.3L diesel engines are equipped with a crankcase ventilation breather housing located on top of the valve cover

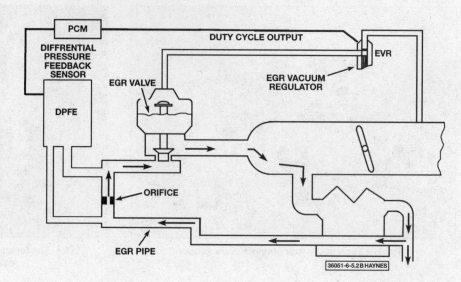

22.2 Typical EGR system and components on the DPFE system

tem is designed to allow excessive amounts of blow-by gases to flow back through the crankcase vent tube into the air cleaner to be consumed by normal combustion.

4   Checking and replacement of the PCV valve is covered in Chapter 1.

7.3L Diesel engine

5   To replace the breather housing, remove the air intake duct, unscrew the two mounting bolts and detach the breather from the valve cover **(see illustration)**. Installation is the reverse of removal.

22   Exhaust Gas Recirculation (EGR) system

General description

Refer to illustration 22.2

1   The EGR system reduces oxides of nitrogen (NOx) by recirculating exhaust gases from the exhaust ports through the EGR valve and back into the intake manifold for recirculation into the engine which lowers the peak flame temperature during combustion.

2   These models are equipped with the Electronic Exhaust Gas Recirculation (EEGR) system. This system relies upon the PCM for EGR control. The EGR flow rate is determined by monitoring the pressure across a fixed metering orifice as exhaust gasses pass through it. This system is called the Differential Pressure Feedback (DPFE) system **(see illustration)**. The pressure sensor monitors upstream (before) and downstream (after) exhaust backpressure. This backpressure coefficient is relayed to the PCM and the correct amount of EGR (duty cycle) is applied to the EGR vacuum regulator control (EVR). By calculating the difference between the two pressures, the PCM determines exactly the EGR flow rate at all driving conditions. The DPFE is more accurate than early systems in that the computer does not have to guess at the upstream pressure coefficient to

determine EGR flow rate as the engine drives through various road conditions such as hard acceleration, downshifting, engine misfire, poor fuel combustion, etc. All these conditions will cause the exhaust backpressure to vary and requires more strict and responsive EGR control to limit NOx emission levels.

3   The DPFE EGR system consists of the EGR valve, the EGR vacuum regulator (EVR), the Powertrain Control Module (PCM), the differential feedback pressure sensor, the EGR pipe and the various vacuum hoses.

Replacement

EGR valve

4   When buying a new EGR valve, make sure that you get the correct EGR valve. Use the stamped code located on the top of the EGR valve when purchasing an EGR valve.

5   Make sure the ignition key is in the OFF position.

6   Remove the air filter housing (see Chapter 4A).

7   Disconnect the EGR valve electrical connector and vacuum hose.

8   Remove the EGR pipe from the exhaust manifold and the EGR valve.

9   On 6.8L V10 models, remove the EGR differential pressure feedback sensor and position it out of the way.

10   Remove the EGR valve retainer bolts and EGR valve from the intake manifold.

11   Remove the EGR gasket, clean the manifold of any remaining gasket material and clean the EGR valve gasket surface if valve is to be reused.

12   Installation is the reverse of removal. Torque the EGR valve mounting bolts to the Specifications listed in this Chapter.

EGR pipe

13   Remove the air filter housing (see Chapter 4A).

14   Disconnect the vacuum lines from the differential pressure feedback sensor.

15   Disconnect the EGR pipe at the manifold and at the EGR valve.

16   Installation is the reverse of removal.

EGR vacuum regulator (EVR)

Refer to illustration 22.18

17   Make sure the ignition key is in the OFF position.

18   Unplug the electrical connector from the EGR vacuum regulator **(see illustration)**.

19   Clearly label and detach both vacuum hoses.

20   Remove the EGR vacuum regulator mounting bolts and remove the regulator.

21   Installation is the reverse of removal.

Differential pressure (DPFE) sensor

Refer to illustration 22.25

22   Make sure the ignition key is in the OFF position.

23   Unplug the electrical connector from the sensor.

24   Clearly label and detach both vacuum hoses.

25   Remove the sensor mounting nuts **(see illustration)** and remove the assembly.

26   Installation is the reverse of removal.

6.4L diesel EGR

27   An EGR system is used on the 6.4L diesel engine. It uses two coolers, one vertical and one horizontal, to reduce the temperature of exhaust gasses routed to the EGR valve, which is located on the top of the engine. The EGR valve itself is cooled by engine coolant circulated through the valve by two hoses.

28   The EGR valve fits into a precise-fit hole in the intake tract and is sealed by an O-ring.

29   The EGR valve is mounted to the intake with three bolts. Since the EGR valve is such a tight fit, it requires a special tool to remove

22.18 Location of the EVR valve on the 5.4L V8 engine

22.25 Location of the DPFE valve on the 5.4L V8 engine

it (manufacturer tool #303-1267). The tool is expensive to buy, and fabricating a copy of it would not be worth it for a one-time use. It is suggested that EGR replacement on these engines be performed at a dealership.

23 Evaporative emissions control (EVAP) system

Warning: *Gasoline is extremely flammable, so take extra precautions when you work on any part of the fuel system. Don't smoke or allow open flames or bare light bulbs near the work area, and don't work in a garage where a gas-type appliance (such as a water heater or clothes dryer) is present. Since gasoline is carcinogenic, wear fuel-resistant gloves when there's a possibility of being exposed to fuel, and, if you spill any fuel on your skin, rinse it off immediately with soap and water. Mop up any spills immediately and do not store fuel-soaked rags where they could ignite. When you perform any kind of work on the fuel system, wear safety glasses and have a Class B type fire extinguisher on hand. The fuel system is under pressure, so if any lines must be disconnected, the pressure in the system must be relieved first (see Chapter 4 for more information).*

General description

1   This system is designed to trap and store fuel vapors that evaporate from the fuel tank, throttle body and intake manifold during non-operation or idling, store them in the charcoal canister and then route them into the combustion chamber to be burned during engine operation.
2   The Evaporative Emission Control System (EVAP) consists of a charcoal-filled canister and the lines connecting the canister to the fuel tank, a fuel vapor management valve (VMV), a fuel tank pressure sensor, fuel filler cap, a canister vent solenoid, a fuel vapor vent valve, ported vacuum and intake manifold vacuum.

3   Fuel vapors are transferred from the fuel tank, throttle body and intake manifold to a canister where they are stored when the engine is not operating. When the engine is running, the fuel vapors are purged from the canister by a vapor management valve (VMV), which is PCM controlled and consumed in the normal combustion process. The fuel tank pressure sensor detects internal fuel tank pressure and relays the information to the PCM which in turn regulates the EVAP system purge controls.

Replacement
Charcoal canister
4   Remove the fuel filler cap to relieve the pressure inside the fuel tank.
5   Make sure the ignition key is in the OFF position.
6   Disconnect the purge control solenoid electrical connector.
7   Remove the charcoal canister outlet hose.
8   Remove the charcoal canister mounting bolt.
9   Withdraw the charcoal canister from the vehicle.
10   Installation is the reverse of removal.

Vapor management valve (VMV)
11   Make sure the ignition key is in the OFF position.
12   Disconnect the electrical connector from the vapor management valve.
13   Clearly label and disconnect the vacuum hoses.
14   Remove the vapor management valve mounting bolts.
15   Installation is the reverse of removal.

24 Catalytic converter

Note: *Because of a Federally mandated extended warranty which covers emissions-related components such as the catalytic con-* *verter, check with a dealer service department before replacing the converter at your own expense.*

General description

1   The catalytic converter is an emission control device added to the exhaust system to reduce pollutants from the exhaust gas stream. There are two types of converters. The conventional oxidation catalyst reduces the levels of hydrocarbon (HC) and carbon monoxide (CO). The three-way catalyst lowers the levels of oxides of nitrogen (NOx) as well as hydrocarbons (HC) and carbon monoxide (CO). Gasoline models are equipped only with three-way catalytic converters. **Note:** *2001 and earlier diesel models are not equipped with catalytic converters.*

Check

2   The test equipment for a catalytic converter is expensive and highly sophisticated. If you suspect that the converter on your vehicle is malfunctioning, take it to a dealer or authorized emissions inspection facility for diagnosis and repair.
3   Whenever the vehicle is raised for servicing of underbody components, check the converter for leaks, corrosion, dents and other damage. Check the welds/flange bolts that attach the front and rear ends of the converter to the exhaust system. If damage is discovered, the converter should be replaced.
4   Although catalytic converters don't break too often, they can become plugged. The easiest way to check for a restricted converter is to use a vacuum gauge to diagnose the effect of a blocked exhaust on intake vacuum.

a) *Connect a vacuum gauge to an intake manifold vacuum source (see Chapter 2C).*
b) *Warm the engine to operating temperature, place the transmission in Park (automatic) or Neutral (manual) and apply the parking brake.*

c) Note and record the vacuum reading at idle.

d) Quickly open the throttle to near full throttle and release it shut. Note and record the vacuum reading.

e) Perform the test three more times, recording the reading after each test.

f) If the reading after the fourth test is more than one in-Hg lower than the reading recorded at idle, the exhaust system may be restricted (the catalytic converter could be plugged or an exhaust pipe or muffler could be restricted).

Replacement

5   Be sure to spray the nuts on the exhaust flange studs before removing them from the catalytic converter.

6   Remove the nuts and separate the catalytic converter from the exhaust system.

7   Installation is the reverse of removal.

Chapter 7 Part A
Manual transmission

Contents

	Section		Section
Extension housing oil seal - replacement	3	Manual transmission overhaul - general information	6
General information	1	Shift lever - removal and installation	2
Manual transmission - removal and installation	5	Transmission mount - check and replacement	4

Specifications

General

Transmission type
5-speed
    Models through 2007 .... ZF S5-47
    2008 and 2009 .... Tremec TR4050
6-speed
    Gasoline engines .... ZF S6-650
    Diesel engines .... ZF M6HD-W
Fluid type and capacity.. See Chapter 1

Torque specifications   **Ft-lbs** (unless otherwise indicated)

Transmission crossmember-to-frame support.. See Chapter 7B
Transmission-to-engine bolts 46
Transmission flange locknut
    ZF 247
    Tremec 118

1   General information

Vehicles covered by this manual are equipped with either a five or six-speed manual, or a four-speed or five-speed automatic transmission. 2010 models do not have a manual-transmission option. Information on the manual transmission is included in this Part of Chapter 7. Information on the automatic transmission can be found in Part B of this Chapter. You'll also find certain procedures common to both transmissions - such as oil seal replacement - in Part A. Information on the transfer case used on 4WD models can be found in Part C.

If you're planning to replace the transmission, look for the service identification tag on the side of the transmission. If the tag is missing or indecipherable, go to the Vehicle Safety Compliance Label on the left (driver's) side door pillar; it has the correct transmission identification codes.

Depending on the expense involved in having a transmission overhauled, it might be a better idea to consider replacing it with either a new or rebuilt unit. Your local dealer or transmission shop should be able to supply information concerning cost, availability and exchange policy. Regardless of how you decide to remedy a transmission problem, you can still save a lot of money by removing and installing the unit yourself.

3.9 Install the extension housing oil seal with a large socket or section of pipe with the proper diameter

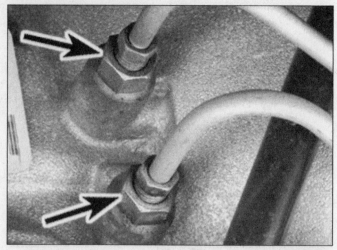

5.10 Use a flare-nut wrench, if available, to disconnect the transmission cooler lines at the transmission - hold the stationary fitting nuts (arrows) with another wrench to prevent the lines from twisting

2   Shift lever - removal and installation

1   Remove the fasteners that attach the trim bezel and boot to the floor and slide the boot up the shifter.
2   Remove the shifter retaining bolts.
3   Remove the shifter.
4   Installation is the reverse of removal.

3   Extension housing oil seal - replacement

Note: *This procedure applies to automatic transmission equipped models, with the exception of Steps 4, 5 and 10.*
1   Oil leaks frequently occur due to wear of the extension housing seal. Replacement of this seal is relatively easy, since the repair can be performed without removing the transmission from the vehicle.
2   If you suspect a leak at the extension housing seal, raise the vehicle and support it securely on jackstands. The extension housing seal is located at the rear end of the transmission, where the driveshaft is attached. If the extension housing seal is leaking, transmission lubricant will be evident on the front of the drive shaft and may be dripping from the rear of the transmission.
3   Remove the driveshaft (see Chapter 8).

2WD models

4   Remove the transmission flange lock nut using a flange holding tool or a chain wrench to hold the flange.
5   Remove the transmission flange; a small puller may be required for removal.

All models
Refer to illustration 3.9
6   Using a screwdriver, pry bar or seal

removal tool, carefully pry out the seal.
7   Inspect the extension housing bore for burrs. If found, remove them with emery cloth or medium grit wet-and-dry sandpaper. Use a clean cloth dipped in solvent and remove any oil or sanding residue from the bore.
8   Apply a small amount of silicone sealant to the outside diameter of the oil seal and apply multi-purpose grease to the seal lip.
9   Using a seal driver, large socket or section of pipe, install the new oil seal. Drive it into the bore squarely and make sure it's completely seated **(see illustration)**.
10   On 2WD models, install the flange and locknut. Tighten the locknut to the torque listed in this Chapter's Specifications.
11   Connect the driveshaft (see Chapter 8).

4   Transmission mount - check and replacement

1   Insert a large screwdriver or pry bar into the space between the transmission extension housing and the frame crossmember and pry up.
2   The transmission should not move significantly away from the mount. If the mount does, the mount should be replaced.
3   Place a jack under the transmission with a wood block on top of it to protect the transmission case. Apply a slight amount of jack pressure to support the weight of the transmission.
4   Remove the two nuts securing the mount to the frame crossmember and the two bolts securing the mount to the transmission extension housing.
5   Raise the transmission with the jack until the studs on the bottom of the transmission mount clear the crossmember. Remove the mount and install a new one.
6   Installation is the reverse of the removal.

5   Manual transmission - removal and installation

Refer to illustrations 5.10 and 5.15
1   Disconnect the cable(s) from the negative battery terminals(s) (see Chapter 5, Section 1).
2   From inside the vehicle, remove the shifter (see Section 2). Where equipped, also remove the lower shifter boot on the floor.
3   Raise the vehicle and support it securely on jackstands. Remove the exhaust Y-pipe (see Chapter 4).
4   Remove the starter motor (see Chapter 5).
5   Drain the transmission lubricant (see Chapter 1).
6   Remove the driveshaft(s) (see Chapter 8). On some models, engine fuel lines pass over or next to the transmission. Unbolt any clips that secure the lines to the transmission.
7   On 4WD models, remove the transfer case (see Chapter 7C).
8   If equipped, remove any Power Take Off (PTO) equipment.
9   Disconnect the clutch release cylinder (see Chapter 8).
10   Disconnect the transmission cooler lines, if equipped **(see illustration)**.
11   Disconnect the electrical connector from the backup light switch. Detach the wiring harness from the transmission and position it aside.
12   Place a jack under the engine and protect the oil pan with a wood block. Apply a slight amount of jack pressure to support the rear of the engine.
13   Place a transmission jack under the transmission. Apply a slight amount of jack pressure to support the transmission, using a strap or chain to secure the transmission to the jack.

5.15 Remove the crossmember bolts (left side shown)

14 Remove the nuts securing the transmission mount to the frame crossmember and transmission.

15 Remove the nuts/bolts securing the crossmember to the frame side rails and remove the crossmember and the mount **(see illustration)**.

16 Remove the inspection plate bolts and cover.

17 Remove the transmission-to-engine bolts.

18 Slowly lower the jacks until you can remove the upper bolts securing the transmission to the engine. Several long extensions may have to be used to reach the upper bolts.

19 Carefully pull the transmission toward the rear, straight back until the input shaft clears the clutch assembly.

20 Lower the transmission jack and remove the transmission.

Installation

21 Lubricate the input shaft with a light coat of high-temperature grease. With the transmission secured to the jack, raise it into position behind the engine and carefully slide it forward, engaging the input shaft with the clutch. Do not use excessive force to install the transmission - if the input shaft won't slide into place, readjust the angle of the transmission or turn the input shaft so the splines engage properly with the clutch.

22 Once the transmission is flush with the engine, install the transmission-to-engine bolts. Tighten the bolts to the torque listed in this Chapter's Specifications. **Caution:** *Don't use the bolts to force the transmission and engine together.*

23 Install the transmission mount and crossmember and tighten all nuts and bolts securely.

24 Remove the jacks supporting the transmission and the engine.

25 Attach the two oil cooler lines.

26 Install the clutch release cylinder.

27 Install the transmission inspection cover and tighten the bolts securely.

28 Install the starter motor (see Chapter 5).

29 If the vehicle is equipped with 4WD, install the transfer case (see Chapter 7C).

30 Install the driveshaft(s) (see Chapter 8).

31 Plug in the electrical connectors for the transmission.

32 Lower the vehicle and install the shifter (see Section 2),

33 Attach the negative battery cable(s).

34 Fill the transmission with the specified fluid (see Chapter 1), run the engine and check for fluid leaks.

6 Manual transmission overhaul - general information

Overhauling a manual transmission is a difficult job for the do-it-yourselfer. It involves the disassembly and reassembly of many small parts. Numerous clearances must be precisely measured and, if necessary, changed with select fit spacers and snap-rings. As a result, if transmission problems arise, it can be removed and installed by a competent do-it-yourselfer, but overhaul should be left to a transmission repair shop. Rebuilt transmissions may be available - check with your dealer parts department and auto parts stores. At any rate, the time and money involved in an overhaul is almost sure to exceed the cost of a rebuilt unit.

Nevertheless, it's not impossible for an inexperienced mechanic to rebuild a transmission if the special tools are available and the job is done in a deliberate step-by-step manner so nothing is overlooked.

The tools necessary for an overhaul include internal and external snap-ring pliers, a bearing puller, a slide hammer, a set of pin punches, feeler gauges, a dial indicator and possibly a hydraulic press. In addition, a large, sturdy workbench and a vise or transmission stand will be required.

During disassembly of the transmission, make careful notes of how each piece comes off, where it fits in relation to other pieces and what holds it in place. If you note how each part is installed before removing it, getting the transmission back together again will be much easier.

Before taking the transmission apart for repair, it will help if you have some idea what area of the transmission is malfunctioning. Certain problems can be closely tied to specific areas in the transmission, which can make component examination and replacement easier. Refer to the *Troubleshooting* Section at the front of this manual for information regarding possible sources of trouble.

Notes

Chapter 7 Part B
Automatic transmission

Contents

	Section
Automatic transmission - removal and installation	10
Automatic transmission fluid change	See Chapter 1
Automatic transmission fluid level check	See Chapter 1
Automatic transmission overhaul - general information	11
Auxiliary cooler - removal and installation	9
Diagnosis - general	2
Extension housing oil seal - replacement	See Chapter 7A
General information	1
Shift cable - removal, installation and adjustment	6

	Section
Shift indicator cable adjustment	3
Shift interlock system - description, check and actuator replacement	8
Shift lever - removal and installation	4
Transmission control switch - check and replacement	5
Transmission mount - check and replacement	See Chapter 7A
Transmission Range (TR) sensor - description, adjustment and replacement	7

Specifications

Torque specifications
Ft-lbs (Unless otherwise indicated)

Note: *One foot-pound (ft-lb) of torque is equivalent to 12 inch-pounds (in-lbs) of torque. Torque values below approximately 15 foot-pounds are expressed in inch-pounds, because most foot-pound torque wrenches are not accurate at these smaller values.*

Torque converter-to-driveplate nuts	
Models through 2005	26
2006 and later	35
Transmission-to-engine bolts	
1999 through 2002 diesel models	45
2003 and later diesel and all gasoline models	35
Transmission Range (TR) sensor mounting bolts	80 in-lbs
Transmission crossmember-to-frame support	60

1 General information

1999 through 2004 models equipped with an automatic transmission use the 4R100. This transmission is a fully automatic, electronic-shift four-speed with a lock-up torque converter, known as a torque converter clutch, or TCC (the TCC provides a direct connection between the engine and the drive wheels for improved efficiency and fuel economy).

Later models use the TorqShift automatic transmission. The basic features of this transmission are similar to the 4R100, however the TorqShift uses five speeds rather than four and has a selectable Tow/Haul feature.

Because of the complexity of the clutches and the electronic and hydraulic control systems, and because of the special tools and expertise needed to overhaul an automatic transmission, diagnosis and repair of this transmission must be handled by a dealer service department or a transmission repair shop. The procedures in this Chapter are limited to general diagnosis, routine maintenance and adjustment: replacing the shift lever, replacing and adjusting the shift cable, and similar jobs. Serious repair work, however, must be done by a transmission specialist. But if the transmission must be rebuilt or replaced, you can save money by removing and installing it yourself, so instructions for that procedure are included as well.

2 Diagnosis - general

Note 1: *Automatic transmission malfunctions may be caused by five general conditions: poor engine performance, improper adjustments, hydraulic malfunctions, mechanical malfunctions or malfunctions in the computer or its signal network. Diagnosis of these prob-*

lems should always begin with a check of the easily repaired items: fluid level and condition (see Chapter 1), and shift cable adjustment. Next, perform a road test to determine if the problem has been corrected or if more diagnosis is necessary. If the problem persists after the preliminary tests and corrections are completed, additional diagnosis should be done by a dealer service department or transmission repair shop. Refer to the Troubleshooting Section at the front of this manual for information on symptoms of transmission problems.

Note 2: All of the vehicles covered in this manual require battery power to be available at all times to maintain strategy parameters which are stored in the keep alive memory (KAM). Therefore, whenever the battery is to be disconnected, first note the following to ensure that there are no unforeseen consequences of this action:

a) The KAM will lose the information stored in its memory when the battery is disconnected. This is a temporary condition. Whenever the battery is disconnected, the information relating to operating values will have to be re-programmed into the unit's memory.

b) The PCM does this by itself, but until then, there may be a generally inferior level of performance. Once the PCM relearns these values it will return to normal operating condition.

Preliminary checks

1   Drive the vehicle to warm the transmission to normal operating temperature.
2   Check the fluid level as described in Chapter 1:

a) If the fluid level is unusually low, add enough fluid to bring the level within the designated area of the dipstick, then check for external leaks (see below).

b) If the fluid level is abnormally high, drain off the excess, then check the drained fluid for contamination by coolant. The presence of engine coolant in the automatic transmission fluid indicates that a failure has occurred in the internal radiator walls that separate the coolant from the transmission fluid (see Chapter 3).

c) If the fluid is foaming, drain it and refill the transmission, then check for coolant in the fluid or a high fluid level.

3   Check the engine idle speed. **Note:** If the engine is malfunctioning, do not proceed with the preliminary checks until it has been repaired and runs normally.
4   Inspect the shift cable (see Section 6). Make sure it's properly adjusted and operates smoothly.

Fluid leak diagnosis

5   Most fluid leaks are easy to locate visually. Repair usually consists of replacing a seal or gasket. If a leak is difficult to find, the following procedure may help.
6   Identify the fluid. Make sure it's transmission fluid and not engine oil or brake fluid

3.3 Turn this thumbwheel to adjust the shift indicator cable

(automatic transmission fluid is a deep red color).
7   Try to pinpoint the source of the leak. Drive the vehicle several miles, then park it over a large sheet of cardboard. After a minute or two, you should be able to locate the leak by determining the source of the fluid dripping onto the cardboard.
8   Make a careful visual inspection of the suspected component and the area immediately around it. Pay particular attention to gasket mating surfaces. A mirror is often helpful for finding leaks in areas that are hard to see.
9   If the leak still cannot be found, clean the suspected area thoroughly with a degreaser or solvent, then dry it.
10   Drive the vehicle for several miles at normal operating temperature and varying speeds. After driving the vehicle, visually inspect the suspected component again.
11   Once the leak has been located, the cause must be determined before it can be properly repaired. If a gasket is replaced but the sealing flange is bent, the new gasket will not stop the leak. The bent flange must be straightened.
12   Before attempting to repair a leak, check to make sure the following conditions are corrected or they may cause another leak. **Note:** Some of the following conditions cannot be fixed without highly specialized tools and expertise. Such problems must be referred to a transmission repair shop or a dealer service department.

Gasket leaks

13   Check the pan periodically. Make sure the bolts are tight, no bolts are missing, the gasket is in good condition and the pan is flat (dents in the pan may indicate damage to the valve body inside).
14   If the pan gasket is leaking, the fluid level or the fluid pressure may be too high, the vent may be plugged, the pan bolts may be too tight, the pan sealing flange may be warped, the sealing surface of the transmission housing may be damaged, the gasket may be damaged or the transmission casting may be cracked or porous. If sealant instead

of gasket material has been used to form a seal between the pan and the transmission housing, it may be the wrong sealant.

Seal leaks

15   If a transmission seal is leaking, the fluid level or pressure may be too high, the vent may be plugged, the seal bore may be damaged, the seal itself may be damaged or improperly installed, the surface of the shaft protruding through the seal may be damaged or a loose bearing may be causing excessive shaft movement.
16   Make sure the dipstick tube seal is in good condition and the tube is properly seated. Periodically check the area around the speedometer gear or sensor for leakage. If transmission fluid is evident, check the O-ring for damage.

Case leaks

17   If the case itself appears to be leaking, the casting is porous and will have to be repaired or replaced.
18   Make sure the oil cooler hose fittings are tight and in good condition.

Fluid comes out vent pipe or fill tube

19   If this condition occurs, the transmission is overfilled, there is coolant in the fluid, the case is porous, the dipstick is incorrect, the vent is plugged or the drain back holes are plugged.

---

3   Shift indicator cable adjustment

Refer to illustration 3.3

1   Remove the steering column covers (see Chapter 11).
2   Move the shift lever clockwise until it stops (all the way to the 1st gear position), then move it back to the Drive position.
3   Rotate the thumbwheel under the steering column to center the indicator needle (the pointer) in the middle of the Drive position. **(see illustration)**.

5.2a Pry the cover off the end of the shift lever top to expose the transmission control switch

5.2b The transmission control switch simply pulls out of the shift lever - check the pins for continuity when the button is depressed

4   Move the shift lever through all gear positions and verify that the indicated positions correspond with the actual gear positions at the manual lever. If necessary, readjust the cable until these conditions are met.

5   Install the steering column covers.

4   Shift lever - removal and installation

1   Remove the ignition key lock cylinder (see Chapter 12).
2   Remove the steering column covers (see Chapter 11).
3   Unplug the electrical connector for the transmission control switch (TCS).
4   Use a punch to drive out the shift lever pin.
5   Remove the shift lever.
6   Installation is the reverse of removal. Be sure to replace the shift lever pin; do NOT use the old pin.

5   Transmission control switch - check and replacement

Refer to illustrations 5.2a and 5.2b

1   The Transmission Control Switch located on the shift lever allows the driver to turn the Overdrive capability On or Off. In normal driving the Overdrive is always turned On.
2   Pry off the cover on the end of the shift lever and pull out the transmission control switch **(see illustrations)**.
3   Using a ohmmeter, check for continuity across the pins when the switch is depressed. If continuity is not indicated, replace the switch.
4   Press the new switch into the lever, making sure the pins are aligned with the sockets. Press the cover back on.

6   Shift cable - removal, installation and adjustment

Refer to illustrations 6.5 and 6.6

Removal and installation

1   Detach the shift cable from the steering column shift tube lever.
2   Detach the shift cable from the steering column bracket.

3   Push the rubber grommet and shift cable through the firewall.
4   Raise the vehicle and place it securely on jackstands.
5   Detach the shift cable from the manual lever **(see illustration)**.
6   Detach the shift cable from the cable bracket **(see illustration)**.
7   Installation is the reverse of removal. Be sure to adjust the cable before reattaching it to the manual lever (see below).

Adjustment

8   Working inside the vehicle, put the shift lever in the Drive position.
9   Raise the vehicle and support it securely on jackstands.
10   With the shift cable detached from the manual lever, unlock the lock tab on the shift cable.
11   Move the manual lever to the First gear position, then move it back two detent positions to the Drive position.
12   Reattach the shift cable to the manual lever.
13   Lock the shift cable locking tab.
14   Remove the jackstands and lower the vehicle.
15   Move the shift lever through all gear positions and verify that the indicated positions correspond with the actual gear positions at the manual lever. Also verify that the engine will start only in Park and Neutral, and that the back-up lights come on when the shift lever is placed in Reverse. If necessary, readjust the cable until these conditions are met. It may also be necessary to adjust the transmission range sensor (see Section 7).

7   Transmission Range (TR) sensor - description, adjustment and replacement

Note: *This procedure applies only to the 4R100 transmission. The TorqShift transmission uses a transmission range sensor that is inside the transmission and requires a special tool for service.*

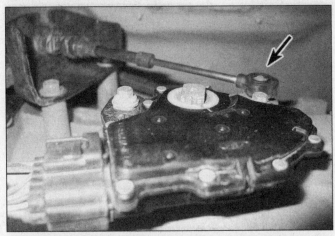

6.5 Detach the shift cable from the shift lever at the transmission

6.6 Detach the shift cable from the cable bracket

7.6 Unplug the connector

7.8 Remove the mounting bolts

Description

1   The Transmission Range (TR) sensor, which is located at the manual lever on the transmission, is an information sensor for the powertrain control module (PCM). Among its functions are those normally handled by a conventional Park/Neutral switch: it prevents the engine from starting in any gear other than Park or Neutral, and closes the circuit for the back-up lights when the shift lever is moved to Reverse.

Adjustment

2   If the engine starts in any position other than Park or Neutral, the TR sensor is either out of adjustment or defective. First, perform a quick functional check to verify that the sensor is operating properly.

3   Raise the vehicle and support it securely on jackstands.

4   The manufacturer recommends the use of a special transmission range (TR) sensor alignment tool, but there's a quick and easy method to verify whether the sensor is adjusted, and to adjust it if it isn't:

a) *Turn the ignition switch to On, put the shift lever in Reverse and verify that the back-up lights come on:*

b) *If they do, but the engine can't be started in Park or Neutral, or it can be started in any gear other than Park or Neutral, then the sensor is probably defective.*

c) *If they don't, detach the shift cable from the manual lever (see Section 6), loosen the sensor retaining bolts and move the sensor slightly until the back-up lights come on. Tighten the sensor retaining bolts to the torque listed in this Chapter's Specifications and reattach the shift cable.*

d) *If you can't get the back-up lights to come on by moving the sensor slightly, verify that the back-up lights and the back-up light circuit are okay. If the back-up lights and circuit are okay, the sensor is probably bad.*

Replacement

Refer to illustrations 7.6 and 7.8

5   Raise the vehicle and place it securely on jackstands.

6   Unplug the electrical connector from the TR sensor **(see illustration)**.

7   Detach the shift cable from the manual lever (see Section 6).

8   Remove the TR sensor retaining bolts **(see illustration)**.

9   Remove the TR sensor.

10   Installation is the reverse of removal. Be sure to tighten the sensor retaining bolts to the torque listed in this Chapter's Specifications and adjust the sensor (see Step 4). Remove the jackstands and lower the vehicle.

---

8   Shift interlock system - description, check and actuator replacement

Description

1   The shift interlock system prevents the shift lever from being moved out of the Park position unless the brake pedal is depressed. The system consists of a shift lock actuator mounted on the steering column. When the ignition key is turned to the Run position, the actuator is energized unless the brake pedal is depressed.

Check

2   The shift lock actuator receives voltage when the ignition key is in the Run position. This circuit energizes the actuator and it prevents you from moving the shift lever out of the Park position. The actuator also receives voltage from another circuit, through the brake light switch, that is closed only when the brake pedal is depressed. It's this second circuit that de-energizes the solid state actuator when the brake pedal is depressed. So first, try to verify that the actuator is working.

3   Get inside the vehicle, close the doors

and windows, start the engine, put your head under the dash so that your ear is close to the actuator (it's mounted on the steering column), then depress the brake pedal and listen carefully for the sound of the actuator clicking.

4   If you don't hear the actuator click when you depress the brake pedal, check the 5A fuse for the actuator and the 15A fuse for the brake light switch (see Chapter 12). Replace either fuse if it's bad and recheck the actuator.

5   If the actuator and brake light switch fuses are good but the actuator still doesn't click when the brake pedal is depressed, verify that the actuator is getting battery voltage through both circuits (one is hot in the Run position, one is hot only when the brake light switch is closed).

6   If the actuator isn't getting voltage through the first "hot-in-Run-only" circuit, repair that circuit and retest.

7   If the actuator isn't getting voltage through the brake light switch circuit, apply the brake pedal and verify that the brake lights come on.

a) *If the brake lights don't come on, troubleshoot the brake light circuit and determine whether the circuit itself or the brake light switch is defective (see Chapter 9), make the necessary repairs or component replacement, then retest the actuator.*

b) *If the brake lights come on, the brake light switch and circuit are okay. Repair the circuit between the brake light switch and the actuator and retest.*

c) *If the actuator still doesn't work, replace it.*

Actuator replacement

8   Remove the steering column (see Chapter 10).

9   Remove the three shift lock actuator bolts.

10   Remove the insert plate and shift lock actuator.

9.6a Use a flare-nut wrench with the help of a back-up wrench while disconnecting the cooler lines (2001 and earlier models)

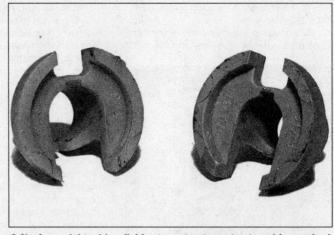

9.6b A special tool (available at most auto parts stores) is required to disconnect the quick-connect fitting (2002 and later models)

11 Remove and discard the shift lock actuator clip. (The shift lock actuator clip is an assembly aid and doesn't need to be replaced). Separate the insert plate from the shift lock actuator.

12 Installation is the reverse of removal.

9 Auxiliary cooler - removal and installation

1999 through 2002 models

Refer to illustrations 9.6a and 9.6b

1 Disconnect the cable(s) from the negative battery terminal(s) (see Chapter 5, Section 1).

2 Working through the front grille, remove the cooler upper mounting bolts. Use a long extension and socket to reach the bolts.

3 Raise the vehicle and support it securely on jackstands.

4 On 4WD models, if equipped, remove the skid plate.

5 Remove the air deflector.

6 On 2001 and earlier models, use a flare-nut wrench to disconnect the fluid lines **(see illustration)**. 2002 models have quick-connect fittings that require a special tool to disconnect the lines **(see illustration)**.

7 Remove the two lower mounting bolts and remove the cooler.

8 Installation is the reverse of removal. Be sure to tighten all cooler fasteners and cooler lines securely.

2003 and later models with 4R100 transmission

9 Remove the grille (refer to Chapter 11).

10 Remove the four plastic pins from the upper radiator cover and lift it off.

11 Remove the plastic left and right lower air deflector retainers.

12 Remove the bolts from the top brackets of the air conditioning condenser. Pull the condenser forward as far as possible for access

to the transmission cooler.

13 Disconnect the two transmission cooler hoses.

14 Move the two lower air deflectors aside and then remove the bolts from the transmission cooler upper brackets

15 Working under the front of the vehicle, remove the lower bumper filler by first removing the six retainers.

16 Remove the four lower splash shield retainers and pull the shield forward.

17 Remove the remaining cooler mount bolts and lift out the cooler.

18 Installation is the reverse of removal.

2003 and later models with TorqShift transmission

19 Remove the grille (refer to Chapter 11).

20 Remove the upper cooler mounting bolts.

21 Remove the plastic push-style retainers from the lower splash shields.

22 Remove the four lower splash shield retainers

23 Working under the front of the vehicle, remove the lower bumper filler by first remov-

10.7 Disconnect the transmission oil cooler lines (other line, not visible in this photo)

ing the six retainers.

24 Unbolt the power steering cooler (if so equipped) and secure it out of the way.

25 Remove the two lower splash shield push-style retainers for access to the condenser bracket.

26 Disconnect the transmission cooler hoses.

27 Remove both lower air conditioning condenser mounting brackets.

28 Remove the transmission cooler bolts. Pull the air conditioning condenser forward for clearance and then lift the transmission cooler up and forward as you remove it.

29 Installation is the reverse of removal.

10 Automatic transmission - removal and installation

Removal

Refer to illustrations 10.7, 10.12a, 10.12b, 10.13, 10.14 and 10.19

1 Disconnect the cable(s) from the negative battery terminal(s) (see Chapter 5, Section 1).

2 Put the shift lever in the Neutral position

3 Raise the vehicle and support it securely on jackstands. Remove the exhaust Y-pipe (see Chapter 4).

4 Remove the driveshaft(s) (see Chapter 8).

5 On 4WD models, remove the skid plate, if equipped, and transfer case (see Chapter 7C).

6 Remove the oil filler tube mounting nut and remove the tube.

7 Disconnect the transmission oil cooler lines **(see illustration)**.

8 Disconnect the shift cable from the manual lever and from the cable bracket (see Section 6).

9 Unplug the electrical connectors from the vehicle speed sensor, the output shaft sensor, the transmission range sensor and the solenoid body assembly.

10 Remove the starter motor (see Chapter 5).

11   If the vehicle is equipped with Power Take Off, remove the PTO.

12   On gasoline engines remove the plastic plug from the access hole and the metal

10.12a On gasoline engines, remove both the plastic plug from the access hole on the left rear part of the block . . .

inspection cover **(see illustrations)**.

13   On diesel engines, remove the inspection cover **(see illustration)**.

14   Mark the relationship of the torque converter to the driveplate, then remove the four torque converter retaining nuts **(see illustration)**. Rotate the crankshaft to bring each nut within reach through the inspection cover hole.

15   On models with a transmission-mounted parking brake, remove the parking brake lever return spring, then remove the adjuster clevis from the parking brake lever. Remove the parking brake cable from its bracket by pinching the cable end retainer tangs while pulling the cable away.

16   Some models require the starter to be removed. Refer to Chapter 5 if necessary.

17   Place a floor jack under the engine. Place a wood block between the jack head and the engine oil pan.

18   Place a transmission jack or a floor jack under the transmission and secure the transmission to the jack with safety chains.

19   Raise the transmission slightly to take the weight off the crossmember, then remove the crossmember bolts and remove the crossmember **(see illustration)**.

20   Remove the nuts or bolts that attach the transmission mount to the transmission, then remove the mount.

21   Release the electrical harnesses clipped to brackets on the transmission. Squeeze the clips with pliers and pull them through the brackets. Tie the harnesses out of the way.

22   Remove the transmission-to-engine bolts.

23   Make a final check that all wires have been disconnected from the transmission, then move the transmission and jack toward the rear of the vehicle until the torque converter is separated from the driveplate. Secure the torque converter to the transmission so it won't fall out during removal.

Installation

24   Prior to installation, make sure the torque

10.12b . . . and remove the metal inspection cover

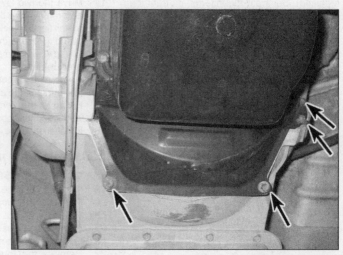

10.13 On diesel engines, remove the inspection cover for access to the torque converter retaining nuts

10.14 Mark the relationship of the torque converter to the flexplate

10.19 Remove the bolts on each side of the crossmember

converter hub is securely engaged with the pump gear.

25   With the transmission secured to the jack, raise it into position. Be sure to keep it level so the torque converter doesn't fall out and disengage itself from the pump gear.

26   Turn the torque converter until the marks on the converter and driveplate are aligned.

27   Move the transmission forward carefully until the dowel pins engage with the holes in the bellhousing.

28   Install the transmission-to-engine bolts and tighten them to the torque listed in this Chapter's Specifications.

29   Attach the exhaust pipes to the exhaust manifolds (see Chapter 4).

30   Install the transmission mount and crossmember and tighten all nuts and bolts securely.

31   Remove the jacks supporting the transmission and the engine.

32   Attach the two oil cooler lines.

33   Attach the shift cable to the manual lever (see Section 6).

34   Install four *new* torque converter nuts and tighten them to the torque listed in this Chapter's Specifications.

35   Install the transmission inspection cover and tighten the bolts securely. Install the rubber access plug (if equipped).

36   Install the starter motor (see Chapter 5).

37   Install the dipstick tube.

38   If the vehicle is equipped with 4WD, install the transfer case (see Chapter 7C).

39   Install the driveshaft(s) (see Chapter 8).

40   Plug in the electrical connectors for the transmission.

41   Attach the negative battery cable(s).

42   Fill the transmission with the specified fluid (Chapter 1), then run the engine and check for fluid leaks.

11   Automatic transmission overhaul - general information

In the event of a fault occurring, it will be necessary to establish whether the fault is electrical, mechanical or hydraulic in nature, before repair work can be contemplated. Diagnosis requires detailed knowledge of the transmission's operation and construction, as well as access to specialized test equipment, and so is deemed to be beyond the scope of this manual. It is therefore essential that problems with the automatic transmission are referred to a dealer service department or other qualified repair facility for assessment.

Note that a faulty transmission should not be removed before the vehicle has been assessed by a knowledgeable technician equipped with the proper tools, as troubleshooting must be performed with the transmission installed in the vehicle.

Notes

Chapter 7 Part C
Transfer case

Contents

	Section			Section
Electric shift motor - replacement	2		Transfer case - fluid change	See Chapter 1
General information	1		Transfer case - removal and installation	6
Manual shift lever - removal and installation	4		Transfer case overhaul - general information	7
Oil seal - replacement	5			
Shift range selector switch (electric-shift models) - replacement	3			

Specifications

Torque Specifications
Ft-lbs (unless otherwise indicated)

Transfer case-to-transmission bolts	37
Rear output shaft-to-flange nut	186
Front output shaft-to-flange nut	164
Drain plug	20
Fill plug	20

1 General information

Mechanical shift

The mechanical shift system on 4WD vehicles allows the driver to manually select one of three ranges: 2WD High, 4WD Low or 4WD High. The hub locks are engaged manually. The driver can shift from 4WD High to 2WD High at speeds up to 55 mph. 4WD Low can only be engaged or disengaged with the brake pedal depressed, the transmission in Neutral, and the vehicle at a complete stop.

Electronic shift-on-the-fly (ESOF) system

The electronic shift-on-the-fly (ESOF) system on 4WD vehicles allows the driver to engage 4WD High while the vehicle is moving. The hub locks are engaged automatically, and an electronic shift is initiated. A switch on the dash allows a selection of 2WD, 4WD High or 4WD Low. The vehicle must be at a complete stop, with the transmission in Neutral and the brake applied before 4WD Low can be engaged.

2 Electric shift motor - replacement

Refer to illustrations 2.3 and 2.4
Note: *The electric shift motor must be replaced as an assembly.*

1   Place the shift range selector switch into the 4X4 High position.
2   Raise the vehicle and place it securely on jackstands.
3   Unplug the shift motor electrical connectors **(see illustration)**.
4   Remove the three electric shift motor bolts **(see illustration)**.

2.3 Shift motor electrical connectors

2.4 Shift motor mounting bolts

3.3 Carefully pry the switch plate off with a small screwdriver

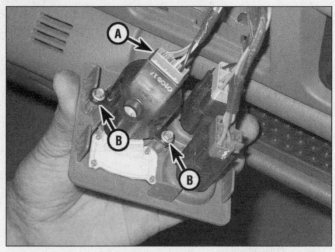

3.4 Remove the connector and mounting screws

A   Connector   *B   Mounting screws*

5   Remove the electric shift motor.
6   Clean the grease from the motor adapter and apply a new coat of multi-purpose grease.
7   The remainder of installation is the reverse of removal.

3   Shift range selector switch (electric-shift models) - replacement

Refer to illustrations 3.3 and 3.4

1   Disconnect the cable(s) from the negative battery terminal(s) (see Chapter 5, Section 1).
2   Pull the switch knob straight off.
3   Using a small screwdriver, carefully pry out the switch plate **(see illustration)**.
4   Unplug the electrical connector from the backside of the switch, and remove the

mounting screws and switch **(see illustration)**.
5   Installation is the reverse of removal.

4   Manual shift lever - removal and installation

1   Remove the fasteners that attach the trim bezel and boot to the floor and slide the boot up the shifter.
2   If the shifter is attached with two bolts, place the transfer case shift lever in the 4H position and remove the shifter retaining bolts.
3   If the shifter is attached with one bolt, place the transfer case shift lever in the 2H position to remove the shifter retaining bolt.
4   Remove the shifter.
5   Installation is the reverse of removal.

5   Oil seal - replacement

Refer to illustrations 5.3 and 5.7

1   Raise the vehicle and support it securely on jackstands.
2   Remove the driveshaft(s) depending on which seal is being replaced (see Chapter 8).
3   Remove the flange mounting nut **(see illustration)**.
4   Remove the companion flange; a small puller may be required for removal.
5   Pry out the seal with a screwdriver or a seal removal tool. Don't damage the seal bore.
6   Lubricate the new seal lips with petroleum jelly.
7   Drive the seal into place with a large socket or section of tubing **(see illustration)**. The outside diameter of the socket should be slightly smaller than the outside diameter of the seal.
8   Install the flange, slinger and retaining

5.3 Use a chain wrench to hold the pinion flange while loosening the lock nut

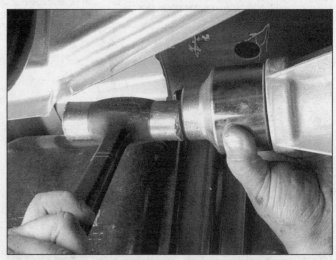

5.7 Use a large socket to drive in the new seal

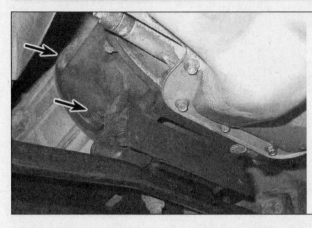

6.13 Remove the six transfer case-to-extension housing bolts

nut onto the output shaft. Tighten the nut to the torque listed in this Chapter's Specifications.

9   Install the driveshaft (see Chapter 8).

10   The remainder of installation is the reverse of removal.

6   Transfer case - removal and installation

Removal

Refer to illustration 6.11

1   Make sure the transfer case is shifted to 2WD High.

2   Disconnect the cable(s) from the negative battery terminal(s) (see Chapter 5, Section 1).

3   Raise the vehicle and support it securely on jackstands.

4   If equipped, remove the transfercase skid plate bolts, then remove the skid plate.

5   Drain the transfer case lubricant (see Chapter 1).

6   Remove the front and rear driveshafts (see Chapter 8).

7   On manual-shift vehicles, remove the shifter (see Section 4).

8   On manual-shift vehicles, unplug the position switch electrical connector on the top of the transfer case.

9   On electric-shift vehicles, unplug the electric shift motor connectors.

10   Support the transfer case with a jack - preferably a special jack made for this purpose. Safety chains or tie-downs will help steady the transfer case on the jack.

11   Remove the transfer case crossmember from the vehicle.

12   Disconnect the transfer case vent hose.

13   Remove the transfer case bolts that connect to the transmission extension housing **(see illustration).**

14   Make a final check that all wires and hoses have been disconnected from the transfer case, then move the transfer case and jack toward the rear of the vehicle until the transfer case is clear of the transmission. Keep the transfer case level as this is done. Once the input shaft is clear, lower the transfer case and remove it from under the vehicle.

Installation

15   Installation is the reverse of removal. Be sure to install a new mounting gasket and tighten the transmission-to-transfer case bolts to the torque listed in this Chapter's Specifications.

16   Fill the transfer case with the specified fluid (see Chapter 1), run the engine and check for fluid leaks.

7   Transfer case overhaul - general information

1   Overhauling a transfer case is a difficult job for the do-it-yourselfer. It involves the disassembly and reassembly of many small parts. Numerous clearances must be precisely measured and, if necessary, changed with select-fit spacers and snap-rings. As a result, if transfer case problems arise, it can be removed and installed by a competent do-it-yourselfer, but overhaul should be left to a transmission repair shop. Rebuilt transfer cases may be available - check with your dealer parts department and auto parts stores. At any rate, the time and money involved in an overhaul is almost sure to exceed the cost of a rebuilt unit.

2   Nevertheless, it's not impossible for an inexperienced mechanic to rebuild a transfer case if the special tools are available and the job is done in a deliberate step-by-step manner so nothing is overlooked.

3   The tools necessary for an overhaul include internal and external snap-ring pliers, a bearing puller, a slide hammer, a set of pin punches, a dial indicator and possibly a hydraulic press. In addition, a large, sturdy workbench and a vise or transfer case stand will be required.

4   During disassembly of the transfer case, make careful notes of how each piece comes off, where it fits in relation to other pieces and what holds it in place. Noting how they are installed when you remove the parts will make it much easier to get the transfer case back together.

5   Before taking the transfer case apart for repair, it will help if you have some idea what area of the transfer case is malfunctioning. Certain problems can be closely tied to specific areas in the transfer case, which can make component examination and replacement easier. Refer to the Troubleshooting section at the front of this manual for information regarding possible sources of trouble.

Notes

Chapter 8
Clutch and driveline

Contents

	Section
Clutch - description and check	2
Clutch components - removal, inspection,	
adjustment and installation	5
Clutch hydraulic system - removal and installation	3
Clutch release bearing - removal, inspection and installation	4
Clutch start switch - removal and installation	8
Differential lubricant level change	See Chapter 1
Differential lubricant level check	See Chapter 1
Differential pinion seal - replacement	20
Driveshaft center bearing - check and replacement	11
Driveshaft(s) - general information	9
Driveshaft(s) - removal and installation	10
Flywheel - inspection	7
Front axle assembly (4WD models) - removal and installation	19

	Section
General information	1
Hub bearing assembly and front axleshaft (4WD models) -	
removal and installation	18
Hub lock - removal and installation	21
Pilot bearing - inspection and replacement	6
Pulse vacuum hub lock solenoid - replacement	22
Rear axle - general information	14
Rear axle assembly - removal and installation	15
Rear axleshaft - removal and installation	16
Rear wheel hub bearings and grease seal - removal,	
inspection and installation	17
Universal joints - general information,	
lubrication and check	12
Universal joints - replacement	13

Specifications

Torque specifications

	Ft-lbs
ABS sensor-to-rear differential bolt	30
Clutch pressure plate-to-flywheel bolts	
Gasoline engines	33
Diesel engine	21
Driveshaft center bearing mounting bolts	46
Driveshaft-to-manual transmission flange	76
Driveshaft-to-transfer case (4WD)	
Front driveshaft	82
Rear driveshaft	76
Driveshaft-to-front axle (4WD)	26
Driveshaft-to-rear axle	
Round flange	82
Split pin yoke	26
Driveshaft flange-to-driveshaft nut	300
Hub bearing-to-steering knuckle nuts	133
Pinion nut	
Front	160 (minimum; see Section 20)
Rear	
Dana 80	470
Ford 10.50 inch	See Section 20
Rear axleshaft flange bolts	
Dana	98
Ford 10.50 inch	80

3.8 To remove the clutch master cylinder reservoir from the firewall, remove these two "push pins"

3.10 To detach the master cylinder, rotate it clockwise 45-degrees and pull it out

3.14 Secure the master cylinder reservoir in a bench vise as shown

1   General information

The Sections in this Chapter deal with the components from the rear of the engine to the rear wheels (except for the transmission and transfer case, which are dealt with in Chapter 7), and to the front wheels on four-wheel drive models. In this Chapter, the components are grouped into three categories: clutch, driveshaft(s) and axle(s). Separate Sections within this Chapter cover checks and repair procedures for components in each of these three groups.

Since nearly all these procedures involve working under the vehicle, make sure it's safely supported on sturdy jackstands or a hoist where the vehicle can be safely raised and lowered.

2   Clutch - description and check

1   All vehicles with a manual transmission have a single dry plate, diaphragm spring-type clutch. The clutch disc has a splined hub which allows it to slide along the splines of the transmission input shaft. The clutch and pressure plate are held in contact by spring pressure exerted by the diaphragm in the pressure plate.

2   The clutch release system is operated by hydraulic pressure. The hydraulic release system consists of the clutch pedal, a master cylinder and fluid reservoir, a release (or slave) cylinder and the hydraulic line connecting the two components.

3   When the clutch pedal is depressed, a pushrod pushes against brake fluid inside the master cylinder, applying hydraulic pressure to the release cylinder, which pushes the release bearing against the diaphragm fingers of the clutch pressure plate.

4   Terminology can be a problem when discussing the clutch components because common names are in some cases different from those used by the manufacturer. For example, the driven plate is also called the clutch plate or

disc, the clutch release bearing is sometimes called a throwout bearing, the release cylinder is sometimes called the slave cylinder.

5   Unless you're replacing components with obvious damage, do these preliminary checks to diagnose clutch problems:

  a) *The first check should be of the fluid level in the clutch master cylinder. If the fluid level is low, add fluid as necessary and inspect the hydraulic system for leaks. If the master cylinder reservoir is dry, bleed the system as described in Section 8 and recheck the clutch operation.*

  b) *To check "clutch spin-down time," run the engine at normal idle speed with the transmission in Neutral (clutch pedal up - engaged). Disengage the clutch (pedal down), wait several seconds and shift the transmission into Reverse. No grinding noise should be heard. A grinding noise would most likely indicate a bad pressure plate or clutch disc.*

  c) *To check for complete clutch release, run the engine (with the parking brake applied to prevent vehicle movement) and hold the clutch pedal approximately 1/2-inch from the floor. Shift the transmission between 1st gear and Reverse several times. If the shift is rough, component failure is indicated.*

  d) *Visually inspect the pivot bushing at the top of the clutch pedal to make sure there's no binding or excessive play.*

3   Clutch hydraulic system - removal and installation

Removal
Refer to illustrations 3.8 and 3.10

1   Raise the vehicle and place it securely on jackstands.

2   Push in the release cylinder at the bellhousing, then twist it one-quarter turn counterclockwise to remove it from the transmission.

3   Disconnect the hydraulic line from the clip on the floor pan.

4   Lower the vehicle.

5   Working under the dash, disconnect the clutch master cylinder pushrod from the clutch pedal.

6   Remove the cover from the clutch pedal position switch and remove the switch from the pedal push rod.

7   Working in the engine compartment, separate the power distribution box from its bracket and place it out of the way, to gain access to the clutch master cylinder.

8   Remove the two clutch master cylinder reservoir push pins **(see illustration)**.

9   Disconnect the hydraulic line from the clip on the firewall.

10   To detach the clutch master cylinder from the firewall, rotate the master cylinder clockwise 45-degrees **(see illustration)**.

11   Remove the clutch hydraulic assembly from the vehicle.

12   Disconnect the hydraulic line from the master cylinder or release cylinder by driving out the roll pin with a hammer and a punch.

Installation
Refer to illustration 3.14

13   Connect the hydraulic line to the master or release cylinder, and install a new roll pin.

14   Before installing the clutch hydraulic system, bleed it as follows:

  a) *Secure the master cylinder reservoir in a bench vise **(see illustration)**.*

  b) *Place the hydraulic system components vertically with the master cylinder reservoir at the highest position.*

  c) *Fill the clutch master cylinder to the "Full" line. Fill any disconnected component with the specified brake fluid to make sure no trapped air is in the hydraulic system.*

  d) *Depress and hold the release cylinder pushrod slowly, long enough to let the trapped air escape the system.*

  e) *Very slowly release the pushrod so that air is not drawn back into the system.*

  f) *Wait about ten seconds for the air bubbles to rise.*

4.6 To check the clutch release bearing, hold the hub (the center) of the bearing and rotate the outer portion while applying pressure; if the bearing doesn't turn smoothly or if it's noisy or rough, replace it

5.4 Use the clutch alignment tool to hold the clutch plate prior to loosening or to center it before tightening the pressure plate bolts

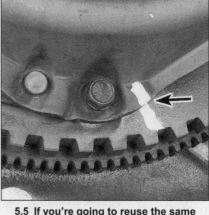

5.5 If you're going to reuse the same pressure plate, mark its relationship to the flywheel

g) *Repeat this procedure until the air bubbles are purged from the system.*

h) *Check that the fluid reservoir is free of air bubbles.*

15 Installation is the reverse of removal. Make sure the hydraulic tube routing is correct.

16 Check and refill the fluid reservoir, as necessary.

---

4 Clutch release bearing - removal, inspection and installation

---

Warning: *Dust produced by clutch wear is hazardous to your health. DO NOT blow it out with compressed air and DO NOT inhale it. DO NOT use gasoline or petroleum-based solvents to remove the dust. Brake system cleaner should be used to flush the dust into a drain pan. After the clutch components are wiped clean with a rag, dispose of the contaminated rags and cleaner in a covered, marked container.*

Removal

1 Disconnect the cable(s) from the negative battery terminal(s) (see Chapter 5, Section 1).

2 Raise the vehicle and support it securely on jackstands.

3 Remove the transmission (see Chapter 7A).

4 Detach the clutch release lever from the ball stud and remove the bearing and lever from the input shaft.

Inspection

Refer to illustration 4.6

5 Wipe off the bearing with a clean rag and inspect it for damage, wear and cracks. Don't immerse the bearing in solvent - it's sealed for life and immersion in solvent will ruin it.

6 Hold the center of the bearing and rotate the outer portion while applying pressure

(see illustration). If the bearing doesn't turn smoothly or if it's noisy or rough, replace it.

Note: *Considering the difficulty involved with replacing the release bearing, we recommend replacing the release bearing whenever the clutch components are replaced.*

Installation

7 Lightly lubricate the friction surfaces of the release bearing, ball stud and the input shaft with high-temperature grease.

8 Install the release lever and bearing onto the input shaft.

9 The remainder of installation is the reverse of removal.

---

5 Clutch components - removal, inspection, adjustment and installation

---

Warning: *Dust produced by clutch wear and deposited on clutch components is hazardous to your health. DO NOT blow it out with compressed air and DO NOT inhale it. DO NOT use gasoline or petroleum-based solvents to remove the dust. Brake system cleaner should be used to flush the dust into a drain pan. After the clutch components are wiped clean with a rag, dispose of the contaminated rags and cleaner in a covered, marked container.*

Caution: *Wear gloves when working on clutch components to avoid cuts from sharp ring gear teeth, and when handling the pressure plate and disc. To protect against dust, put on latex gloves first, then cloth or leather gloves.*

Removal

Refer to illustrations 5.4, 5.5 and 5.6

Note: *The clutch components are normally accessed by removing the transmission. However, any time the engine is removed, check the clutch for wear and replace worn components as necessary. The relatively low cost of the clutch components compared to the time and trouble spent gaining access to them war-*

rants their replacement anytime the engine or transmission is removed, unless they are new or in near-perfect condition. The following procedures are based on the assumption the engine will stay in place.

1 Disconnect the cable(s) from the negative battery terminal(s) (see Chapter 5, Section 1).

2 Raise the vehicle and support it securely on jackstands.

3 Remove the transmission (see Chapter 7A).

4 To support the clutch disc during removal, install an alignment tool through the clutch disc hub **(see illustration).**

5 Paint a mark so the pressure plate and the flywheel will be in the same alignment during installation **(see illustration).**

6 Loosen the pressure plate-to-flywheel bolts **(see illustration)** in 1/4-turn increments until they can be removed by hand. Work in a criss-cross pattern until all spring pressure is

5.6 Loosen the pressure plate-to-flywheel bolts in 1/4-turn increments until they can be removed by hand. Work in a criss-cross pattern until all spring pressure is relieved, then hold the pressure plate securely and completely remove the bolts, followed by the pressure plate and clutch disc

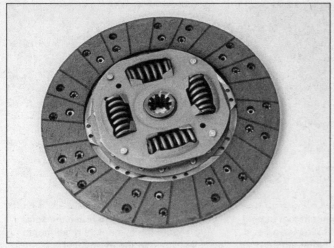

5.10 Inspect the clutch plate lining, springs and splines for wear

5.12a Inspect the surface of the pressure plate for cracks, dark-colored areas (signs of overheating) and other obvious defects

NORMAL FINGER WEAR   **EXCESSIVE FINGER WEAR**   **BROKEN OR BENT FINGERS**

5.12b Replace the pressure plate if excessive wear or damage is noted

relieved, then hold the pressure plate securely and completely remove the bolts, followed by the pressure plate and clutch disc.

Inspection

Refer to illustrations 5.10, 5.12a and 5.12b

7   Ordinarily, when a problem occurs in the clutch, it can be attributed to wear of the clutch driven plate assembly (clutch disc). However, all components should be inspected at this time. **Note:** *If the clutch components are contaminated with oil, there will be shiny, black glazed spots on the clutch disc lining, which will cause the clutch to slip. Replacing clutch components won't completely solve the problem - be sure to check the crankshaft rear oil seal and the transmission input shaft seal for leaks. If it looks like a seal is leaking, be sure to install a new one to avoid the same problem with the new clutch.*

8   Check the flywheel for cracks, heat checking, grooves and other obvious defects. If the imperfections are slight, a machine shop can machine the surface flat and smooth, which is highly recommended regardless of the surface appearance. Refer to Chapter 2 for the flywheel removal and installation procedure.

9   Inspect the pilot bearing (see Section 6).

10   Check the lining on the clutch disc. There

should be at least 1/16-inch of lining above the rivet heads. Check for loose rivets, distortion, cracks, broken springs and other obvious damage **(see illustration)**. As mentioned above, ordinarily the clutch disc is routinely replaced, so if you're in doubt about its condition, replace it.

11   The release bearing should also be replaced along with the clutch disc (see Section 4).

12   Check the machined surfaces and the diaphragm spring fingers of the pressure plate **(see illustrations)**. If the surface is grooved or otherwise damaged, replace the pressure plate. Also check for obvious damage, distortion, cracks, etc. Light glazing can be removed with medium-grit emery cloth. If a new pressure plate is required, new and factory-rebuilt units are available.

Adjustment

Refer to illustrations 5.14 and 5.15

Note: *If installing the original pressure plate on gasoline engines, before installation, the self-adjusting pressure plate must be pre-adjusted, and to do so requires a hydraulic press. If you don't have a press, take the flywheel and pressure plate to an automotive machine shop for adjustment. Disregard Steps 13 through 17 if you're replacing the*

pressure plate with a new one.

13   Remove the flywheel (see Chapter 2), if you haven't already done so.

14   Position the pressure plate on the flywheel, place both of them in a hydraulic press, then depress the clutch diaphragm fin-

5.14 Position the pressure plate on the flywheel and place both components in a hydraulic press as shown, then, using a suitable adapter, depress the clutch diaphragm fingers until the adjusting ring moves freely

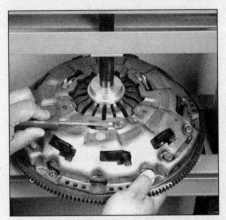

5.15 Using a screwdriver, move the adjusting ring counterclockwise

6.5 To remove the pilot bearing use a special puller designed for the job

6.6 Tap the bearing into place with a bushing driver or a socket slightly smaller than the outside diameter of the bearing

gers until the adjusting ring moves freely **(see illustration)**.

15   Using a screwdriver, move the adjusting ring counterclockwise until the tension springs are compressed **(see illustration)**.

16   Holding the adjusting ring in place, release pressure on the diaphragm fingers.

17   Remove the flywheel and pressure plate from the press.

Installation

18   Clean the machined surfaces with lacquer thinner or acetone. It's important that no oil or grease is on these surfaces or the lining of the clutch disc. Handle the parts only with clean hands. Install the flywheel (see Chapter 2).

19   Position the clutch disc and pressure plate against the flywheel, engaging the pressure plate on the dowels. If installing the original pressure plate, align the index marks. Hold the clutch in place with an alignment tool **(see illustration 5.4)**. Make sure it's installed properly (most replacement clutch plates will be marked "flywheel side" or something similar - if it's not marked, install the clutch disc with the damper springs toward the transmission).

20   Tighten the pressure plate-to-flywheel bolts only finger-tight, working around the pressure plate.

21   Center the clutch disc by ensuring the alignment tool extends through the splined hub and into the pilot bearing in the crankshaft. Wiggle the tool up, down or from side-to-side as needed to bottom the tool in the pilot bearing. Tighten the pressure plate-to-flywheel bolts a little at a time, working in a criss-cross pattern, to prevent distorting the cover. After all the bolts are snug, tighten them to the torque listed in this Chapter's Specifications. Remove the alignment tool.

22   Using high-temperature grease, lubricate the inner groove of the release bearing (see Section 4). Also place grease on the release lever contact areas and the transmission input shaft bearing retainer.

23   Install the clutch release bearing, if removed (see Section 4).

24   Install the transmission (see Chapter 7A) and all components removed previously.

25   Remove the jackstands and lower the vehicle.

6   Pilot bearing - inspection and replacement

Refer to illustrations 6.5 and 6.6

1   The clutch pilot bearing is a needle roller type bearing which is pressed into the rear of the crankshaft. It's greased at the factory and does not require additional lubrication. Its primary purpose is to support the front of the transmission input shaft. The pilot bearing should be inspected whenever the clutch components are removed from the engine. Because of its inaccessibility, replace it with a new one if you have any doubt about its condition. **Note:** *If the engine has been removed from the vehicle, disregard the following Steps which don't apply.*

2   Remove the transmission (see Chapter 7A).

3   Remove the clutch components (see Section 5).

4   Using a flashlight, inspect the bearing for excessive wear, scoring, dryness, roughness and any other obvious damage. If any of these conditions are noted, replace the bearing.

5   Removal can be accomplished with a special puller available at most auto parts stores **(see illustration)**.

6   To install the new bearing, lightly lubricate the outside surface with grease, then drive it into the recess with a soft-face hammer **(see illustration)**.

7   Install the clutch components, transmission and all other components removed previously. Tighten all fasteners to the recommended torque.

7   Flywheel - inspection

1   Inspect the flywheel when the vehicle suffers from excessive transmission gear wear, transmission jumping out of gear, driveline vibration, clutch pedal vibration, clutch slippage, pilot bearing noise or release bearing noise.

2   Visually inspect the flywheel for signs of

cracking, warpage, scoring or heat checking. If any of these conditions exist, the flywheel must be removed and resurfaced at an automotive machine shop (see Chapter 2).

8   Clutch start switch - removal and installation

1   Disconnect the cable(s) from the negative battery terminal(s) (see Chapter 5, Section 1).

2   Disconnect the electrical connector from the clutch start interlock switch, also called a clutch pedal position switch.

3   Rotate the switch so the plastic retainer is visible. Squeeze the retainer tabs together and slide the retainer rearward off the switch.

4   Detach the switch from the master cylinder pushrod and take it out.

5   Installation is the reverse of the removal Steps. Be sure the switch is securely seated on the master cylinder pushrod.

9   Driveshaft(s) - general information

The driveshaft is of tubular construction and may be of a one or two-section type according to the wheelbase of the vehicle. The front driveshaft on 4WD models is connected by two strap-type clamps at the front axle pinion and bolted to a flange at the transfer case. The attachment of the rear driveshaft to the rear axle pinion flange may be connected by bolted flange or two strap-type clamps, while attachment to the transmission or transfer case may include strap-type clamps, a bolted flange or a splined sliding sleeve connecting it to the output shaft. The type of connection used depends on the wheelbase and transmission type. Where a two-section shaft is used, the shaft is supported near its forward end on a ball bearing which is flexibly mounted in a bracket attached to the frame crossmember.

The driveshaft is finely balanced during manufacture and it is recommended that care be used when universal joints are replaced to help maintain this balance. It is sometimes better to have the universal joints replaced by a dealership or shop specializing in this type of work. If you replace the joints yourself, mark each individual yoke in relation to the one opposite in order to maintain the balance. Do not drop the assembly during servicing operations.

10.2 Mark the relationship of the driveshaft U-joint to the differential pinion flange

10   Driveshaft(s) - removal and installation

Note: *The manufacturer recommends replacing driveshaft fasteners with new ones when installing the driveshaft.*

Removal

Rear

Refer to illustrations 10.2, 10.3 and 10.4
Note: *Where a two-piece driveshaft is involved, the rear shaft must be removed before the front shaft.*
1   Raise the vehicle and support it securely on jackstands.
2   Use chalk or a scribe to "index" the relationship of the driveshaft to the differential axle assembly mating flange. This ensures correct alignment when the driveshaft is reinstalled **(see illustration)**.
3   Remove the bolts securing the driveshaft flange or universal joint clamps to the differential pinion flange **(see illustration)**.
4   If the vehicle is equipped with a two-piece driveshaft, remove the center support bearing mounting bolts **(see illustration)**.
5   For vehicles with 4WD, or vehicles equipped with manual transmissions, "index" the relationship of the driveshaft to the transmission or transfer case flange. Remove the mounting bolts.

6   Some automatic transmissions have a splined slip yoke. Mark the relationship of the output shaft to slip yoke and simply slide the yoke out of the transmission.
7   Pry the universal joint away from its mating flange and remove the shaft from the flange. Be careful not to let the caps fall off of the universal joint (which would cause contamination and loss of the needle bearings).

Front (4WD)

8   Using a scribe, white paint or a hammer and punch, place marks on the driveshaft and differential flanges in line with each other. This is to make sure the driveshaft is reinstalled in the same position to preserve the balance.
9   Make alignment marks on the driveshaft and transfer case flanges.
10   Unbolt the flange that secures the driveshaft double-cardan joint to the transfer case.
11   Remove the bolts and straps that secure the front end of the driveshaft to the differential yoke.
12   Wrap tape around the universal joint bearings at the axle end of the driveshaft so they won't fall off.

Installation

13   Installation is the reverse of removal. If the shaft cannot be lined up due to the components of the differential or transmission having been rotated, put the vehicle in Neutral or rotate one wheel to allow the original alignment to be achieved. Make sure the universal joint caps are properly placed in the flange seat. Tighten the fasteners to the torque listed in this Chapter's Specifications.

11   Driveshaft center bearing - check and replacement

Note: *Driveshaft center bearing replacement requires the use of a hydraulic press. Remove the driveshaft and have a repair shop or automotive machine shop remove the bearing.*

Check

1   The center bearing can be checked in a similar manner as the universal joints are examined (see Section 12). Check for looseness or deterioration of the flexible rubber mounting.

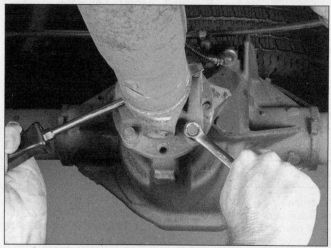

10.3   Insert a screwdriver through the U-joint to prevent the driveshaft from turning as you break loose the four U-joint-to-pinion flange bolts

10.4   Remove the two bolts for the center support bearing

13.2 A pair of needle-nose pliers can be used to remove the universal joint snap-rings

13.4 To press the universal joint out of the driveshaft yoke, set it up in a vise with the small socket pushing the joint and bearing cap into the large socket

2   Further examination of the center bearing can be made by running the vehicle in gear with the rear wheels raised in the air. However, this should be done with the vehicle supported on a lift and by a dealer service department or other qualified repair facility who can perform the tests safely.

Replacement

3   Raise the vehicle and support it securely on jackstands.

4   Remove the driveshaft assembly (see Section 10).

5   With the driveshaft removed from the vehicle and the shaft sections placed on a suitable work bench, hold the driveshaft flange with a chain wrench to prevent the driveshaft from rotating, then remove the flange retaining nut.

6   Remove the strap which retains the rubber cushion to the bearing support bracket.

7   Separate the cushion, bracket and remove the rubber insulator.

8   Have the old bearing and dust slinger pressed off.

9   Install a new slinger and bearing.

10   Pack the space between the inner dust slinger and the bearing with lithium-base grease.

11   Carefully tap the bearing and slinger assembly onto the driveshaft journal until the components are tight against the shoulder on the shaft. Use a suitable piece of tubing to do this, taking care not to damage the shaft splines.

12   Lubricate the shaft splines with lithium-base grease.

13   Install the bearing rubber cushion, bracket and strap. The center bearing bracket should be installed with the deep flange rearward.

14   Install the flange and retaining nut. Tighten the nut to the torque listed in this Chapter's Specifications.

15   The remainder of installation is the reverse of removal.

12 Universal joints - general information, lubrication and check

1   Universal joints are mechanical couplings which connect two rotating components that meet each other at different angles.

2   These joints are composed of a yoke on each side connected by a crosspiece called a trunnion. Cups at each end of the trunnion contain needle bearings which provide smooth transfer of the torque load. Snap-rings, either inside or outside of the bearing cups, hold the assembly together.

3   Refer to Chapter 1 for details on universal joint lubrication. Also see the routine maintenance schedule at the beginning of Chapter 1.

4   Wear in the needle roller bearings is characterized by vibration in the driveline, noise during acceleration, and in extreme cases of lack of lubrication, metallic squeaking and ultimately grating and shrieking sounds as the bearings disintegrate.

5   It is easy to check if the needle bearings are worn with the driveshaft in position, by trying to turn the shaft with one hand, the other hand holding the rear axle flange when the rear universal joint is being checked, and the front half coupling when the front universal joint is being checked. Any movement between the driveshaft and the front half couplings, and around the rear half couplings, is indicative of considerable wear. Another method of checking for universal joint wear is to use a pry bar inserted into the gap between the universal joint and the driveshaft or flange. Leave the vehicle in gear and try to pry the joint both radially and axially. Any looseness should be apparent with this method. A final test for wear is to attempt to lift the shaft and note any movement between the yokes of the joints.

6   If any of the above conditions exist, replace the universal joints with new ones.

13 Universal joints - replacement

Single-cardan U-joints

Refer to illustrations 13.2, 13.4 and 13.9

Note: *A press or large vise will be required for this procedure. It may be advisable to take the driveshaft to a local dealer service department, service station or machine shop where the universal joints can be replaced for you, normally at a reasonable charge.*

1   Remove the driveshaft as outlined in Section 10.

2   On U-joints with external snap-rings, use a small pair of pliers to remove the snap-rings from the spider **(see illustration)**.

3   Supporting the driveshaft, place it in position on a workbench equipped with a vise.

4   Place a piece of pipe or a large socket, having an inside diameter slightly larger than the outside diameter of the bearing caps, over one of the bearing caps. Position a socket with an outside diameter slightly smaller than that of the opposite bearing cap against the cap **(see illustration)** and use the vise or press to force the bearing cap out (inside the pipe or large socket). Use the vise or large pliers to work the bearing cap the rest of the way out.

5   Transfer the sockets to the other side and press the opposite bearing cap out in the same manner.

6   Pack the new universal joint bearings with grease. Ordinarily, specific instructions for lubrication will be included with the universal joint servicing kit and should be followed carefully.

7   Position the spider in the yoke and partially install one bearing cap in the yoke.

8   Start the spider into the bearing cap and then partially install the other cap. Align the spider and press the bearing caps into position, being careful not to damage the dust seals.

9   Install the snap-rings. If difficulty is encountered in seating the snap-rings, strike

13.9 If the snap-ring will not seat in the groove, strike the yoke with a brass hammer - this will relieve the tension that has set up in the yoke and slightly spring the yoke ears (this should also be done if the joint feels tight when assembled)

15.11 Remove the U-bolts and spring plates

the driveshaft yoke sharply with a hammer. This will spring the yoke ears slightly and allow the snap-rings to seat in the groove **(see illustration)**.

10   Install the grease fitting and fill the joint with grease. Be careful not to overfill the joint, as this could blow out the grease seals.

11   Install the driveshaft (see Section 10).

Double-cardan U-joints

12   Use the above procedure, but note that it will have to be repeated because the double-cardan joint is made up of two single-cardan joints. Also pay attention to how the spring, centering ball and bearing are arranged. **Note:** *Both U-joints in the double-cardan assembly must be replaced at the same time, even if only half of it is worn out.*

14   Rear axle - general information

The rear axle assembly consists of a straight, hollow housing enclosing a differential assembly and axleshafts. These assemblies support the vehicle's 'sprung' weight components through leaf springs attached between the axle housings and the vehicle's frame rails.

The rear axle assemblies employed on vehicles covered by this manual are heavy duty full-floating axleshafts. Full-floating axleshafts do not themselves bear any of the vehicle's weight, can be removed independent of the tapered roller wheel bearings and are designed only to transfer power to the rear wheels.

Due to the need for special tools and equipment, it is recommended that operations on these models be limited to those described in this Chapter. Where repair or overhaul is required, remove the axle assembly and take it to a rebuilder, or exchange it for a new or reconditioned unit. Always make sure that an

axle unit is exchanged for one of identical type and gear ratio.

15   Rear axle assembly - removal and installation

Removal

Refer to illustration 15.11

1   Raise the rear of the vehicle and support it with jackstands placed under the frame rails.

2   Remove the rear wheels.

3   Disconnect the driveshaft from the rear axle yoke (see Section 10).

4   Disconnect the ABS sensor.

5   Disconnect the parking brake cable from the parking brake lever (see Chapter 9).

6   Disconnect the axle vent hose and remove the brake hose junction block.

7   Detach the stabilizer bar from the axle housing.

16.1 Remove the axleshaft flange bolts

8   Disconnect the brake lines from the axle housing. Remove the rear brake calipers (see Chapter 9). **Caution:** *Tie the calipers up with wire to keep any strain off the flexible brake lines.*

9   Support the rear axle with a jack or other suitable device. It may take two jacks to do this safely as the offset of the rear differential causes this assembly to be heavily weighted to one side.

10   Remove the lower mounting bolts securing the rear shocks to the axle (see Chapter 10).

11   With the jack(s) supporting the axle, remove the U-bolts and spring plates securing the axle to the springs.

12   Lower the axle assembly and remove it from under the vehicle.

Installation

13   Installation is the reverse of the removal procedure.

14   Tighten the U-bolt nuts to the torque listed in the Chapter 10 Specifications. If necessary, check and fill the axle with the specified lubricant (see Chapter 1).

16   Rear axleshaft - removal and installation

Removal

Refer to illustrations 16.1 and 16.2

1   Remove the bolts which attach the axleshaft flange to the hub **(see illustration)**. There is no need to remove the wheel or jack up the vehicle.

2   Tap the flange with a soft-faced hammer to loosen the shaft, then grip the rib of the face of the flange with a pair of locking pliers; twist the shaft slightly in both directions and withdraw it from the axle tube **(see illustration)**.

16.2 Pull the axleshaft straight out of the axle housing

16.3 Inspect this O-ring seal for cracks or wear

Installation

Refer to illustration 16.3

3   Inspect the O-ring seal for cracks or wear and if necessary, replace it with a new one, coated with clean differential lubricant **(see illustration)**. Installation is the reverse of removal, but hold the axleshaft level in order to engage the splines at its inner end with those in the differential side gear. Use new bolts, lock washers and/or a thread locking compound and tighten the bolts to the torque listed in this Chapter's Specifications. **Note:** *Final tightening of the axleshaft retaining bolts should be done after the wheel lug nuts have been tightened (if the wheel was removed).*

4   If a loss of fluid is observed, check the differential lubricant level and re-fill if required (see Chapter 1).

5   Test drive the vehicle and check for leaks.

17 Rear wheel hub bearings and grease seal - removal, inspection and installation

Removal

1   Remove the axleshafts (see Section 16).

2   Raise the rear of the vehicle and place it securely on jackstands.

3   Remove the rear wheels.

Dana axle

Refer to illustration 17.5

4   Remove the disc brake caliper (see Chapter 9).

5   Install a special hub wrench so that the drive tangs of the tool engage the four slots in the hub nut and remove the nut **(see illustration)**.

6   Remove the outer bearing from the hub and pull the hub and brake disc straight off the spindle.

7   Separate the hub from the disc by removing the bolts on the inside of the disc.

8   Use a large screwdriver or pry bar to pry the seal from the back of the wheel hub. Remove the inner bearing.

Ford 10.50-inch axle

Refer to illustration 17.11

9   Remove the disc brake caliper (see Chapter 9).

10   Install a special hub wrench so that the drive tangs of the tool engage the four slots in the hub nut and remove the nut **(see illustra-**

tion 17.5). **Note:** *The left side nut has a left-hand thread.*

11   Using a step plate installed in the axle tube and a 3-jaw puller, loosen the rear hub to the point of removal **(see illustration)**.

12   Remove the rear hub. Take care not to drop the outer hub bearing while removing the hub.

13   Use a large screwdriver or pry bar to pry the seal from the back of the wheel hub. Remove the inner bearing.

Inspection

14   Clean the hub nut and bearings with cleaning solvent; allow the parts to air dry.

15   Clean the inside of the wheel hub to remove all axle lubricant and grease. Clean the axle spindle.

16   Inspect the bearing assemblies for signs of wear, pitting, galling and other damage. Replace the bearings if any of these conditions exist. Inspect the bearing races for signs of erratic wear, galling and other damage.

17   If the bearing races need replacement, drive out the bearing races from the wheel hub with a brass drift. Install the new races with a bearing cup replacement tool or other suitable tool designed for this purpose. Never

17.5 The drive tangs of the tool engage with the four slots in the hub nut

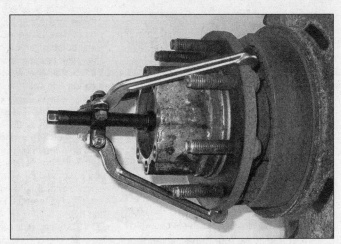

17.11 Use a puller to loosen the hub

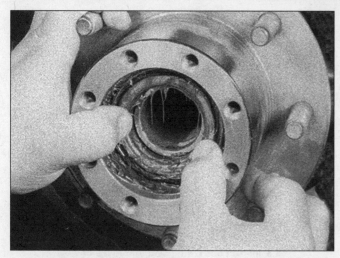

17.23 Slide the hub onto the axle tube and install the outer bearing

18.4 Use a pair of snap-ring pliers to remove this snap-ring

use a drift or punch for this operation as these races must be driven squarely, seated correctly and can be damaged easily.

Installation

Dana axle

Refer to illustration 17.23

18   Prior to installation, pack the inner and outer wheel bearings with high temperature grease (see Chapter 1) or equivalent. If you do not have access to a bearing packer, pack each bearing carefully by hand and make sure the entire bearing is filled with grease.

19   Install the newly packed inner wheel bearing into the hub. Install a new hub inner seal with a suitable drive tool (tubular drift, large socket or special tool) being careful not to damage the seal.

20   Install the rear disc onto the hub (see Chapter 9).

21   Prior to installing the wheel hub, coat the inner seal lip with grease. Also, cover the spindle with a light coat of grease. Pour one ounce of differential lubricant in the center of the hub.

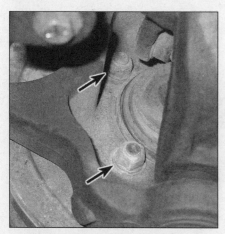

18.6 Remove the four hub-to-steering knuckle fasteners (two not shown in picture)

22   Carefully slide the hub and disc assembly over the spindle, being very careful to keep it straight so as not to contact the spindle with the seal (which would damage it).

23   Install the newly packed outer wheel bearing over the spindle and into the wheel hub **(see illustration)**.

24   Install the hub nut, making sure the tab is aligned in the keyway slot.

25   Start the nut while applying inward pressure to the socket, then tighten the nut to 70 ft-lbs. Rotate the hub occasionally while tightening the locknut.

26   Back the locknut off 90-degrees (1/4 turn counterclockwise), then tighten it to 15 to 20 ft-lbs.

27   After the final torque, the endplay should be zero and the maximum torque to rotate the hub should be no greater than 20 in-lbs.

28   The remainder of installation is the reverse of removal. Be sure to tighten the fasteners securely. Check the axle lubricant level and adjust if necessary (see Chapter 1).

Ford 10.50-inch axle

29   Prior to installation, pack the inner and outer wheel bearings with high temperature grease (see Chapter 1) or equivalent. If you do not have access to a bearing packer, pack each bearing carefully by hand and make sure the entire bearing is penetrated with grease.

30   Install the newly packed inner wheel bearing into the hub. Install a new hub inner seal with a suitable drive tool (tubular drift, large socket or special tool) being careful not to damage the seal.

31   On dual rear wheel axles, install the rear disc onto the hub (see Chapter 9).

32   Prior to installing the wheel hub, coat the inner seal lip with grease. Also, cover the spindle with a light coat of grease. Pour one ounce of differential lubricant in the center of the hub.

33   Carefully slide the hub assembly over the spindle, being very careful to keep it straight so as not to contact the spindle with the seal (which would damage it).

34   Install the newly packed outer wheel bearing over the spindle and into the wheel hub **(see illustration 17.23)**.

35   Install the hub nut, make sure the tab is aligned in the keyway. Using the locknut wrench, tighten the locknut clockwise for right-hand threads and counter clockwise for left-hand threads. Rotate the hub occasionally while tightening the locknut. The hub nut should ratchet as torque is applied.

36   Tighten the hub nut to 60 ft-lbs.

37   Adjust the hub nut as follows:

a) *Ratchet back 5 notches for new bearings*

b) *Ratchet back 7 notches for used bearings*

38   The remainder of installation is the reverse of removal. Be sure to tighten all fasteners securely. Check the axle lubricant level and adjust if necessary (see Chapter 1).

18 Hub bearing assembly and front axleshaft (4WD models) - removal and installation

Removal

Refer to illustrations 18.4 and 18.6

1   Loosen the wheel lug nuts. Raise the vehicle and support it securely on jackstands. Remove the wheel.

2   Remove the brake caliper and support it out of the way with wire. Remove the caliper mounting bracket and the brake disc (see Chapter 9).

3   Remove the hub lock (see Section 21).

4   Remove the axleshaft snap-ring and thrust washers **(see illustration)**.

5   Disconnect the ABS wheel sensor harness connector and routing clips.

6   Remove the hub-to-knuckle nuts **(see illustration)**.

7   Remove the hub bearing from the steering knuckle and axleshaft. **Note:** *The hub*

19.13 Unbolt the lower ends of the shock absorbers from the axle

19.15 The radius arms on 2005 and later 4x4 vehicles are mounted to the front axle with two bolts

bearing assembly may become rusted and seized to the steering knuckle depending on the severity of driving conditions (snow, rain, salt, etc.). In this event, have the hub bearing assembly removed by an automotive repair shop.

8   Remove the brake dust shield and ABS sensor from the hub bearing.

9   On the back side of the knuckle, use a hammer and brass drift to drive the axle shaft main seal out of the knuckle.

10   Carefully pull the axleshaft and seal from the axle housing. If the U-joint is worn out, it can be replaced using the procedure described in Section 13.

Installation

11   Clean the axleshaft of all dirt and grease.

12   Place the axleshaft in a padded vise so the vise grips the shaft's second step.

13   Place the new main seal onto the axle shaft. Using a hammer and seal installer, seat the main seal onto the axle shaft.

14   Apply a thin film of wheel bearing grease to the shaft splines, seal contact surface and hub bore. Install the axleshaft, engaging the splines with the differential side gears. Be very careful not to damage the axleshaft oil seals.

15   Using a hammer and seal installer, seat the main seal into the steering knuckle.

16   Install the ABS sensor and dust shield.

17   Install a new O-ring seal onto the wheel hub. Apply a small coat of high-temperature grease to the O-ring and wheel hub contact area.

18   Install the wheel hub bearing. Install the hub bearing-to-steering knuckle nuts and tighten them to the torque listed in this Chapter's Specifications.

19   Install the three thrust washers and snap-ring. **Caution:** *Be sure to place the non-metallic washer between the two metallic washers. Incorrect installation will lead to severe wear to the washer, resulting in damage to the wheel hub, bearing, the*

axle shaft and end seal.

20   Install the brake disc and caliper (see Chapter 9).

21   The remainder of installation is the reverse of removal.

---

19   Front axle assembly (4WD models) - removal and installation

Refer to illustrations 19.13 and 19.15

Removal

1   Raise the front of the vehicle and support it on jackstands placed under the frame rails.

2   Remove the wheels.

3   Disconnect the driveshaft from the front axle yoke (see Section 10).

4   Remove the front brake calipers (see Chapter 9). **Caution:** *Tie the calipers up with wire to keep any strain off the flexible brake lines.*

5   Disconnect the ABS sensor and the vacuum hose for the hub locks.

6   If the vehicle is equipped with a steering damper, disconnect it at the axle.

7   Detach the tie-rod ends from the steering knuckles and position them aside (see Chapter 10).

8   Unbolt the stabilizer bar clamps from the axle and the stabilizer bar link nuts (see Chapter 10).

9   Disconnect the vent tube and be sure to plug the fitting to prevent anything from falling into the vent.

10   Support the front axle with a pair of floor jacks. Two jacks should be used, as the offset of the front differential causes this assembly to be heavily weighted to one side.

11   Raise the axle enough to relieve tension on the trackbar. Unbolt the trackbar at the axle. Disconnect the trackbar and relieve the load on the suspension.

12   Move the hub-lock vacuum hoses aside.

13   Unbolt the shocks from the axle assembly on coil spring-equipped vehicles **(see illustration)**.

14   On early models with leaf-spring front suspension, remove the U-bolts securing the axle to the leaf springs while the jacks are supporting the axle.

15   On 2005 and later models with coil-spring front suspension, carefully lower the axle assembly and then remove the coil springs (see Chapter 10). Unbolt the radius arms from the front axle **(see illustration)**.

16   Lower the axle assembly completely and remove it from the vehicle.

Installation

17   Installation is the reverse of the removal procedure.

18   Tighten all fasteners securely. If necessary, check and fill the axle with the specified lubricant (see Chapter 1).

---

20   Differential pinion seal - replacement

1   Raise the vehicle and place it securely on jackstands.

2   Remove the driveshaft (see Section 10).

Ford 10.50 inch rear axle and Dana model 50/60 front axles

Refer to illustrations 20.4, 20.6, 20.7 and 20.11

Caution: *This procedure disturbs the pinion bearing preload adjustment. Follow the procedure very carefully to reset the pinion bearing preload during reassembly.*

3   Depending on which axle pinion seal is being replaced, remove the rear or front wheels and brake calipers. **Note:** *The removal of the wheels and brake calipers is advisable to eliminate the added pinion shaft rotation resistance that otherwise might contribute to a false pinion shaft rotation preload torque value.*

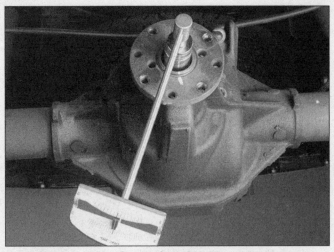

20.4 Use an inch-pound torque wrench to check the torque necessary to rotate the pinion shaft

20.6 Mark the relative positions of the pinion and flange before removing the nut

4   Using an inch-pound torque wrench (scale from approximately 0 to 40 inch-pounds) on the drive pinion nut, measure and record the torque necessary to rotate the drive pinion in a load-free state **(see illustration)**.

5   Count the number of threads visible between the end of the nut and the end of the pinion shaft and record it for use later.

6   Mark the drive pinion-to-companion flange orientation for proper location of flange to pinion upon reassembly **(see illustration).**

7   Using a flange holding tool (available at most auto parts stores), or a chain wrench to prevent the flange from turning while removing the nut, unscrew the pinion flange locknut **(see illustration)**. Discard the nut - a new one must be used when reassembling.

8   Using a two-jaw puller, remove the companion flange from the drive pinion shaft. **Note:** *Some fluid loss may occur.*

9   Avoiding contact with the pinion shaft/threads, tap out an edge of the seal using a dull screwdriver. Using vise-grips or other similar clamping pliers, grip the exposed edge

and strike the side of the pliers until the seal is removed.

10   Prior to installing the new seal, clean the seal mating surfaces.

11   Lubricate the lips of the new seal with high-temperature grease and tap it evenly into position with a seal installation tool or a large socket. Make sure it enters the housing squarely and is tapped in to its full depth **(see illustration)**.

12   Align the mating marks made before disassembly and install the companion flange and a new nut. If necessary, tighten the pinion nut to draw the flange into place. Do not try to hammer the flange into position.

13   Using a suitable holding tool, secure the companion flange while tightening the nut carefully until the original number of threads are exposed and the marks are aligned.

14   Measure the torque required to rotate the pinion and tighten the nut in small increments until it matches the figure recorded in Step 4. In order to compensate for the drag of the new oil seal, the nut should be tightened more until

the rotational torque of the pinion exceeds earlier recording by no more than 5 in-lbs. Check the final torque of the pinion nut; be sure that it meets the minimum torque specification at the beginning of the Chapter (front differential only - no specification available for the rear).

15   The remainder of installation is the reverse of removal. Be sure to check the differential lubricant level and add if required (see Chapter 1).

Dana model 80 rear axle

16   Mark the relationship of the companion flange to the pinion shaft.

17   Remove the pinion nut. A special flange holding tool, available at most auto parts stores, or a chain wrench can be used to keep the companion flange from moving while the self-locking pinion nut is loosened **(see illustration 20.7)**.

18   Withdraw the companion flange. It may be necessary to use a two or three-jaw puller engaged behind the flange to draw it out. Do

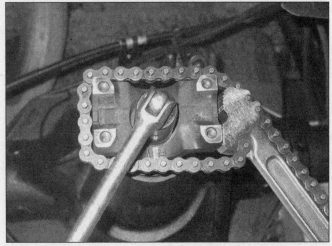

20.7 Use a chain wrench to hold the flange while loosening the pinion flange locknut

20.11 Lubricate the lips of the new pinion seal and seat it squarely in the bore, then drive it into the carrier with a seal driver or a large socket

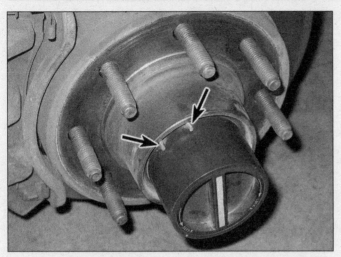

21.1 Squeeze the retaining ring with a pair of pliers and pull the hub lock from the hub

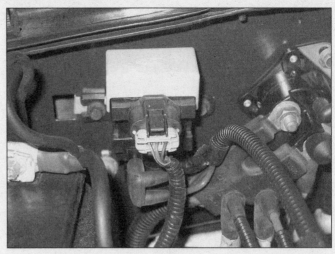

22.1 The pulse vacuum hub lock solenoid is located on the firewall

not attempt to pry behind the flange or hammer on the end of the pinion shaft.

19   Pry out the old seal and discard it.

20   Lubricate the lips of the new seal with high-temperature grease and tap it evenly into position with a seal installation tool or a large socket. Make sure it enters the housing squarely and is tapped in to its full depth **(see illustration 20.11)**.

21   Align the mating marks made before disassembly and install the companion flange. If necessary, tighten the pinion nut to draw the flange into place. Do not try to hammer the flange into position.

22   Tighten the nut to the torque listed in this Chapter's Specifications.

23   Install the driveshaft (see Section 10).

24   The remainder of installation is the reverse of removal.

25   Check the differential lubricant level and add if required (see Chapter 1).

21   Hub lock - removal and installation

Removal

Refer to illustration 21.1

1   Using a pair of pliers squeeze the retaining ring and pull outward on the hub lock **(see illustration)**. **Note:** *To prevent damage to the hub lock while removing it, use your hands to remove the lock. Do not use tools to grip the lock.*

Installation

2   Install a new O-ring. Clean the contact areas for the O-ring and apply a light coat of high temperature grease to the O-ring before installing it. **Note:** *Some models also have a gasket at the flange. Replace the gasket.*

3   While pushing the hub lock in firmly by

hand, be sure to seat the O-ring seal completely.

4   Install the retainer ring. Verify the retainer ring is completely expanded into the wheel hub groove.

22   Pulse vacuum hub lock solenoid - replacement

Refer to illustration 22.1

1   Disconnect the vacuum hose and harness connector **(see illustration)**.

2   Remove the mounting bolts.

3   Installation is the reverse of the removal steps.

Notes

Chapter 9
Brakes

Contents

	Section			Section
Anti-lock brake system (ABS) - general information	2		Disc brake pads - replacement	3
Brake check	See Chapter 1		Front wheel bearing check, repack and adjustment	
Brake disc - inspection, removal and installation	5		(2WD models only)	See Chapter 1
Brake fluid level check	See Chapter 1		General information	1
Brake hoses and lines - check and replacement	7		Master cylinder - removal and installation	6
Brake hydraulic system - bleeding	8		Parking brake shoes - replacement	11
Brake light switch - check and replacement	9		Power brake booster - check, removal and installation	10
Disc brake caliper - removal and installation	4			

Specifications

General

Brake fluid type	See Chapter 1
Power brake booster pushrod protrusion (vacuum boosters only)	0.980 to 0.995 inch
Brake pad minimum thickness	See Chapter 1
Disc lateral runout limit (1999 through 2002 models)	
Front	
2WD	
With single rear wheels	0.0020 inch
With dual rear wheels	0.0028 inch
4WD	0.0015 inch
Rear	0.0015 inch
Disc minimum (discard) thickness	Cast into disc

Torque specifications

Ft-lbs (unless otherwise indicated)

Note: *One foot-pound (ft-lb) of torque is equivalent to 12 inch-pounds (in-lbs) of torque. Torque values below approximately 15 foot-pounds are expressed in inch-pounds, because most foot-pound torque wrenches are not accurate at these smaller values.*

ABS wheel speed sensor bolt	
Front	
1999	156 to 204 in-lbs
2000	132 to 168 in-lbs
2001	63 to 80 in-lbs
2002	108 in-lbs
2003	108 in-lbs
2004	
2WD	108 in-lbs
4WD	71 in-lbs
2005 and later	13
Rear	
1999 through 2000	25 to 29
2001 through 2003	20
2004	27
2005 and later	15

Torque specifications (continued)   Ft-lbs (unless otherwise indicated)

Brake disc-to-hub nuts
   Front (hub extender nuts, 4WD with dual rear wheels)...................... 130
   Rear
      1999 through 2004... 94
      2005 and later.. 89
Brake hose-to-caliper fitting bolt
   Front.. 26
   Rear
      1999 through 2004... 37
      2005 and later.. 26
Caliper mounting bolts
   Front
      1999 through 2004... 42
      2005 and later.. 56
   Rear 27
Caliper mounting bracket bolts
   Front.. 166
   Rear
      1999 through 2004... 128
      2005 and later.. 203
Master cylinder mounting nuts
   With vacuum brake booster 20
   With hydraulic brake booster... 28
Power brake booster mounting nuts... 18
Wheel lug nuts... See Chapter 1

1   General information

General

All models covered by this manual are equipped with hydraulically operated, power-assisted brake systems. Brakes are disc type front and rear, and are self-adjusting.

The hydraulic system has separate circuits for the front and rear brakes. If one circuit fails, the other circuit will remain functional and a warning indicator will light up on the dashboard when a substantial amount of brake fluid is lost, showing that a failure has occurred.

Master cylinder

The master cylinder is mounted on the front of the power brake booster, and can be identified by the large fluid reservoir on top. The master cylinder has separate primary and secondary piston assemblies for the front and rear circuits.

Power brake booster

On models with gasoline engines, the power brake booster uses engine manifold vacuum to provide assistance to the brakes. It is mounted on the firewall in the engine compartment, directly behind the master cylinder. On models with diesel engines, a hydraulic brake booster, pressurized by the power steering pump, is used. It is also mounted on the firewall.

Anti-lock Brake System (ABS)

All models are equipped with an Anti-lock Braking System to improve directional stability and control during hard braking. On 2000 and earlier models a rear wheel anti-lock brake system (RABS) was standard equipment, with a four-wheel Anti-lock Braking system available as an option. All 2001 and later models are equipped with four-wheel ABS.

Parking brake

The parking brake mechanically operates the rear brakes only. The parking brake cables actuate a pair of parking brake shoes mounted inside the drum (hub) portion of each rear brake disc.

Precautions

There are some general precautions and warnings related to the brake system:

a) *Use only brake fluid conforming to DOT 3 specifications.*

b) *The brake pads and linings contain fibers which are hazardous to your health if inhaled. Whenever you work on brake system components, clean all parts with brake system cleaner and wear an approved filtering mask. Do not allow the fine dust to become airborne.*

c) *Safety should be paramount whenever any servicing of the brake components is performed. Do not use parts or fasteners which are not in perfect condition, and be sure all clearances and torque specifications are adhered to. If you are at all unsure about a certain procedure, seek professional advice. Upon completion of any brake system work, test the brakes carefully in a controlled area before driving the vehicle in traffic. If a problem is suspected in the brake system, don't drive the vehicle until it's fixed.*

2   Anti-lock Brake System (ABS) - general information

Refer to illustrations 2.3, 2.6a and 2.6b

Description

The Anti-lock brake system is designed to maintain vehicle maneuverability, directional stability and optimum deceleration under severe braking conditions on most road surfaces. It does so by monitoring the rotational speed of the wheels and controlling the brake line pressure during braking. This prevents the wheels from locking up prematurely.

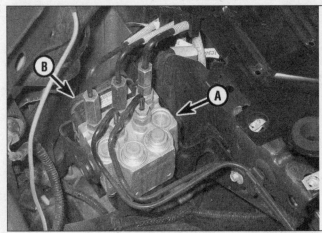

2.3 The ABS hydraulic control unit (A) is located in the left front corner of the engine compartment. (B) is the control module

erly diagnose the system, the home mechanic can perform a few preliminary checks before taking the vehicle to a dealer service department.

a) *Make sure the brake, pads and calipers are in good condition.*
b) *Check the electrical connectors at the control unit.*
c) *Check the fuses.*
d) *Follow the wiring harness to the speed sensors and brake light on-off (BOO) switch and make sure all connections are secure and the wiring isn't damaged.*

If the above preliminary checks don't rectify the problem, the vehicle should be diagnosed by a dealer service department or other qualified repair shop.

Two types of systems are used: Rear Wheel Anti-lock Brake System (RABS) and 4-Wheel Anti-lock Brake System (4WABS). RABS only controls lockup on the rear wheels, whereas 4WABS prevents lockup on all four wheels.

Hydraulic control unit

The hydraulic control unit is located in the left front corner of the engine compartment **(see illustration)**.

Control module

The control module for either system is mated to the hydraulic control unit and is the "brain" for the system. The function of the control module is to accept analog voltage inputs from the speed sensors, process that data, and control hydraulic line pressure to avoid wheel lockup.

The control modules for both systems constantly monitor the system, even under normal driving conditions, to detect malfunctions. If a problem develops within the system, the control module illuminates an ABS warning light on the instrument cluster, and may even shut down the anti-lock system if it's a serious malfunction. A diagnostic trouble code will also be stored, which, when retrieved by a service technician, will indicate the problem area or component.

Speed sensor

A speed sensor produces an "analog" (continuously variable) voltage output, which is transmitted to the control module, where it's converted to digital information, compared to the control unit's program, and interpreted as wheel rotation speed **(see illustrations)**. On both systems, a single rear wheel speed sensor is located in the top of the differential housing. 4WABS systems also use a front wheel speed sensor in each front steering knuckle.

Brake light switch

The brake light switch, known as the brake on-off (or BOO) switch on these models, signals the control unit when the driver steps on the brake pedal. Without this signal the anti-lock system won't activate. The system is de-activated when the brake pedal is released.

Diagnosis and repair

If the ABS warning light on the instrument cluster comes on and stays on, make sure the parking brake is released and there's no problem with the brake hydraulic system. If neither of these is the cause, the anti-lock system is probably malfunctioning. Although special test procedures are necessary to prop-

3 Disc brake pads - replacement

Refer to illustrations 3.2 and 3.3a through 3.3o

Warning: *Disc brake pads must be replaced on both wheels at the same time - never replace the pads on only one wheel. Also, brake system dust is hazardous to your health. DO NOT blow it out with compressed air and DO NOT inhale it. An approved filtering mask should be worn when working on the brakes. DO NOT use gasoline or petroleum-based solvents to remove the dust. Use brake system cleaner only!*

Note: *This procedure applies to the front and rear brake pads.*

1   Loosen the wheel lug nuts, raise the vehicle and support it securely on jackstands. Block the wheels at the opposite end. Remove the wheels.

2   Remove about two-thirds of the fluid from the master cylinder reservoir and discard it; as the pistons are pushed in for clearance to allow the new pads to be installed, the fluid will be forced back into the reservoir. Position a drain pan under the brake assembly and clean the caliper and surrounding area with brake system cleaner **(see illustration)**.

2.6a The ABS front wheel speed sensors are located on the steering knuckles

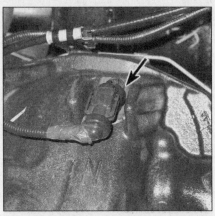

2.6b The ABS rear wheel speed sensor is mounted on the top of the differential

3.2 Wash the disc and caliper with brake system cleaner to remove brake dust; DO NOT blow off brake dust with compressed air

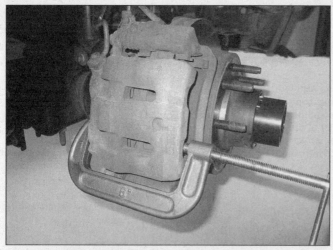

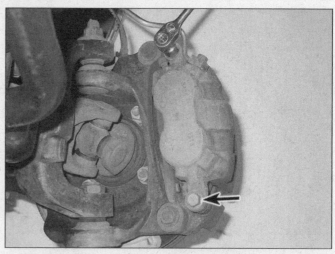

3.3a Push the pistons back into their bores with a C-clamp to provide room for the new brake pads

3.3b Remove the two caliper mounting bolts, check them for thread damage and replace as necessary

3.3c Pull off the caliper . . .

3.3d . . . and hang it with a piece of wire; DON'T allow the caliper to hang by the brake hose!

3   To replace the brake pads, follow the accompanying photos, beginning with **illustration 3.3a.** Be sure to stay in order and read the caption under each illustration. Work on one brake assembly at a time so that you'll have something to refer to if necessary.

4   While the pads are removed, inspect the caliper for brake fluid leaks and ruptures in the piston boots. If necessary, replace the caliper (see Section 4). Also inspect the brake disc carefully (see Section 5). If machining is necessary, follow the information in that Section to remove the disc.

5   Before installing the caliper mounting bolts, clean them and check them for corrosion and damage. If they're significantly corroded or damaged, replace them. Be sure to tighten the caliper mounting bolts to the torque listed in this Chapter's Specifications.

6   Install the brake pads on the opposite wheel, then install the wheels and lower the

3.3e Remove the V-springs - older models

3.3f Remove the outer brake pad

3.3g Remove the inner brake pad

3.3h Pry off the anti-rattle clips with a small screwdriver (check them for cracks and make sure they fit tightly)

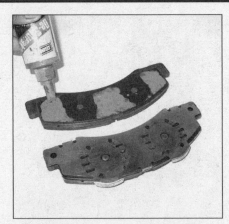

3.3i Apply some anti-squeal compound to the backing plates of the new pads (follow the instructions on the product)

3.3j Install the anti-rattle clips; make sure they're fully seated on the caliper mounting bracket

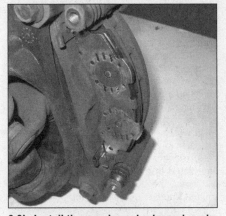

3.3k Install the new inner brake pad; make sure both ends of the pad are properly seated in the mounting bracket and anti-rattle clips

3.3l Install the new outer brake pad; make sure both ends of the pad are properly seated in the mounting bracket and anti-rattle clips

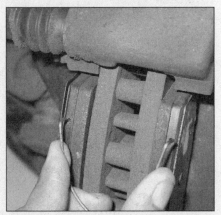

3.3m Install the ends of the V-springs into the holes in the pad backing plates

vehicle. Tighten the lug nuts to the torque listed in the Chapter 1 Specifications.

7   Add brake fluid to the reservoir until it's full (see Chapter 1). Pump the brakes several times to seat the pads against the disc, then check the fluid level again.

8   Check the operation of the brakes before driving the vehicle in traffic. Try to avoid heavy brake applications until the brakes have been applied lightly several times to seat the pads.

3.3n Apply high temperature grease to the caliper slide pins - install both bolts, tighten the lower bolt first

3.3o Install the caliper over the pads, install the bolts and tighten them to the torque listed in this Chapter's Specifications. Be sure to pump the pedal a few times to bring the pads into contact with the disc, and also check the brake fluid level

4   Disc brake caliper - removal and installation

Refer to illustration 4.2

Warning: *The dust created by the brake system is harmful to your health. Never blow it out with compressed air and don't inhale any of it. An approved filtering mask should be worn when working on the brakes. Do not, under any circumstances, use petroleum-based solvents to clean brake parts. Use brake system cleaner only!*

Note: *If replacement is indicated (usually because of fluid leakage), it is recommended that the calipers be replaced, not overhauled. New and factory rebuilt units are available on an exchange basis. Always replace the calipers in pairs - never replace just one of them.*

Removal

1   Loosen the wheel lug nuts, raise the vehicle and place it securely on jackstands. Block the wheels at the opposite end. Remove the wheel.
2   Remove the inlet fitting bolt and disconnect the brake hose from the caliper **(see illustration)**. Discard the old sealing washers. Plug the brake hose immediately to keep contaminants and air out of the brake system and to prevent losing any more brake fluid than is necessary. **Note:** *If you are simply removing the caliper for access to other components, leave the brake hose connected and suspend the caliper with a length of wire - don't let it hang by the hose* **(see illustration 3.3d)**.
3   Remove the caliper mounting bolts **(see illustration 3.3b)** and detach the caliper from the mounting bracket.

Installation

4   Installation is the reverse of removal. Don't forget to use new sealing washers on each side of the brake hose inlet fitting and be sure to tighten the fitting bolt and the caliper mounting bolts to the torque values listed in this Chapter's Specifications.
5   Bleed the brake system (see Section 8). **Note:** *If the brake hose was not disconnected, bleeding won't be required.* **Warning:** *If air*

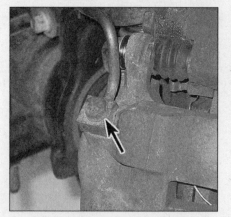

4.2   Remove the brake hose inlet fitting bolt

has found its way into the hydraulic control unit, the system must be bled with the use of a scan tool. If the brake pedal feels "spongy" even after bleeding the brakes, or the ABS light on the instrument panel does not go off, or if you have any doubts whatsoever about the effectiveness of the brake system, have the vehicle towed to a dealer service department or other repair shop equipped with the necessary tools for bleeding the system.
6   Make sure there are no leaks from the hose connections. Test the brakes carefully before returning the vehicle to normal service.

5   Brake disc - inspection, removal and installation

Inspection

Refer to illustrations 5.2, 5.3, 5.4a and 5.4b

1   Loosen the wheel lug nuts, raise the vehicle and support it securely on jackstands. Apply the parking brake. Remove the wheels.
2   Visually inspect the disc surface for score marks and other damage **(see illustration)**. Light scratches and shallow grooves are normal after use and won't affect brake operation. Deep grooves require disc removal and refinishing by an automotive machine shop. Be

5.2   The brake pads on this vehicle were obviously neglected - they wore down to the rivets and cut deep grooves into the disc (wear this severe means the disc must be replaced)

sure to check both sides of the disc.
3   To check disc runout, place a dial indicator at a point about 1/2-inch from the outer edge of the disc **(see illustration)**. If you're checking a front or rear disc on a 4WD model with single rear wheels, install the lug nuts, with the flat sides facing in, and tighten them securely to hold the disc in place. Set the indicator to zero and turn the disc. The indicator reading should not exceed the runout limit listed in this Chapter's Specifications. If it does, the disc should be refinished by an automotive machine shop. **Note:** *The manufacturer recommends resurfacing the brake discs only in the event of pedal pulsations or hard (overheated) spots on the disc. If you elect not to have the discs resurfaced, deglaze them with sandpaper or emery cloth.*
4   The disc must not be machined to a thickness less than the specified minimum thickness, which is cast into the disc **(see illustration)**. The disc thickness can be checked with a micrometer **(see illustration)**.

Removal and installation

Refer to illustration 5.6

5   Remove the brake calipers (don't dis-

5.3   Measure the brake disc runout with a dial indicator

5.4a   The minimum (discard) thickness of the brake disc is cast into the disc

5.4b Measure the brake disc thickness at several points with a micrometer

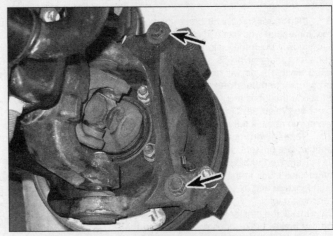

5.6 The caliper mounting bracket is retained by two bolts (front shown, rear similar)

connect the brake hoses) and hang them out of the way (see Section 4).

6   Remove the caliper mounting bracket **(see illustration)**.

7   On 2WD model front discs, remove the grease cap, wheel bearing retainer nut, spindle nut, outer bearing retainer washer and outer wheel bearing, then remove the disc/hub (see *Front wheel bearing check, repack and adjustment* in Chapter 1).

8   If you're removing a front disc on a 4WD model with single rear wheels, simply remove the lug nuts installed in Step 3 and pull the disc off the hub. If you're removing a front disc on a truck with dual rear wheels, remove the hub extender bolts and detach the hub extender, then remove the disc.

9   If you're removing a rear disc on a dual rear wheel axle, remove the hub assembly from the rear axle (see Chapter 8), then unbolt the disc from the hub. On single rear wheel axles the disc can simply be slid off the wheel studs.

10   Installation is the reverse of removal. On models so equipped, tighten the disc-to-hub bolts to the torque listed in this Chapter's Specifications.

11   Lower the vehicle and tighten the wheel lug nuts to the torque listed in the Chapter 1 Specifications.

6   Master cylinder - removal and installation

Removal

Refer to illustration 6.2

1   Place rags under the brake line fittings and prepare caps or plastic bags to cover the ends of the lines once they're disconnected. **Caution:** *Brake fluid will damage paint. Cover all painted surfaces and avoid spilling fluid during this procedure.*

2   If equipped, unplug the electrical connector from the brake pressure switch **(see illustration)**. Also unplug the electrical connector from the fluid level warning switch. On later models, remove the air cleaner housing and also set aside the cooling system degas bottle (see Chapter 3). On diesel models,

remove the left-side battery (see Chapter 5).

3   Loosen the tube nuts at the ends of the brake lines where they enter the master cylinder. To prevent rounding off the flats on these nuts, a flare-nut wrench, which wraps around the nut, should be used. Pull the brake lines away from the master cylinder slightly and plug the ends to prevent contamination. Disconnect the electrical connectors on the master cylinder. On models with Hydro-Boost, disconnect the power steering hose.

4   Remove the mounting nuts and pull the master cylinder off the power brake booster.

5   Remove the reservoir cap, then discard any fluid remaining in the reservoir.

Installation

Refer to illustration 6.7

6   Bench bleed the master cylinder before installing it. Mount the master cylinder in a vise, with the jaws of the vise clamping on the mounting flange.

7   Attach a pair of master cylinder bleeder tubes to the outlet ports of the master cylinder **(see illustration)**.

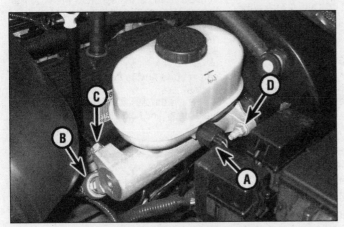

6.2 Master cylinder mounting details

A   *Fluid level warning switch connector*
B   *Brake pressure switch connector*
C   *Brake line fitting*
D   *Mounting nut*

6.7 The best way to bleed air from the master cylinder before installing it on the vehicle is with a pair of bleeder tubes that direct brake fluid into the reservoir during bleeding

8   Fill the reservoir with brake fluid of the recommended type (see Chapter 1).

9   Slowly push the pistons into the master cylinder (a large Phillips screwdriver can be used for this) - air will be expelled from the pressure chambers and into the reservoir. Because the tubes are submerged in fluid, air can't be drawn back into the master cylinder when you release the pistons.

10   Repeat the procedure until no more air bubbles are present.

11   Remove the bleed tubes, one at a time, and install plugs in the open ports to prevent fluid leakage and air from entering. Install the reservoir cap.

12   Install the master cylinder over the studs on the power brake booster and tighten the nuts only finger-tight at this time.

13   Thread the brake line fittings into the master cylinder. Since the master cylinder is still a bit loose, it can be moved slightly so the fittings thread in easily. Don't strip the threads as the fittings are tightened.

14   Tighten the mounting nuts to the torque listed in this Chapter's Specifications. Tighten the brake line fittings securely.

15   Fill the master cylinder reservoir with fluid, then bleed the master cylinder and the rest of the brake system (see Section 8). To bleed the master cylinder on the vehicle, have an assistant depress the brake pedal and hold it down. Loosen the rear fitting to allow air and fluid to escape. Tighten the fitting, then allow your assistant to return the pedal to its rest position. Repeat this procedure on the other fitting until the fluid is free of air bubbles.

16   Reinstall any components that were removed for access to the master cylinder.

Warning: *If air has found its way into the hydraulic control unit, the system must be bled with the use of a scan tool. If the brake pedal feels "spongy" even after bleeding the brakes, or the ABS light on the instrument panel does not go off, or if you have any doubts whatsoever about the effectiveness of the brake system, have the vehicle towed to a dealer service department or other repair shop equipped with the necessary tools for bleeding the system.*

17   Re-check the brake fluid level, then check the operation of the brake system carefully before driving the vehicle in traffic.

7   Brake hoses and lines - check and replacement

Warning: *If air has found its way into the hydraulic control unit, the system must be bled with the use of a scan tool. If the brake pedal feels "spongy" even after bleeding the brakes, or the ABS light on the instrument panel does not go off, or if you have any doubts whatsoever about the effectiveness of the brake system, have the vehicle towed to a dealer service department or other repair shop equipped with the necessary tools for bleeding the system.*

1   About every six months, with the vehicle raised and placed securely on jackstands, the flexible hoses which connect the steel brake lines with the front and rear brake assemblies should be inspected for cracks, chafing of the outer cover, leaks, blisters and other damage. These are important and vulnerable parts of the brake system and inspection should be complete. A light and mirror will be needed for a thorough check. If a hose exhibits any of the above defects, replace it with a new one.

Flexible hoses

2   Clean all dirt away from the ends of the hose. To disconnect a front brake hose from the brake lines, unscrew the brake line fittings from the hose junction block. Be careful not to bend the junction bracket or kink the lines. If necessary, soak the connections with penetrating oil.

3   To disconnect a rear brake hose from the brake line, unscrew the metal tube nut with a flare nut wrench, then remove the U-clip from the female fitting at the bracket and remove the hose from the bracket.

4   Disconnect the hose from the caliper, discarding the sealing washers on either side of the fitting.

5   Using new sealing washers, attach the new brake hose to the caliper or wheel cylinder.

6   To reattach a front brake hose to the metal lines, bolt the hose junction bracket to the frame, tighten the bolt securely, and screw in the tube nuts.

7   To reattach a rear brake hose to the metal line, insert the end of the hose through the frame bracket, make sure the hose isn't twisted, then attach the metal line by tightening the tube nut fitting securely. Install the U-clip at the frame bracket. **Note:** *The weight of the vehicle must be on the suspension, so the vehicle should not be raised while positioning the hose.*

8   Carefully check to make sure the suspension or steering components don't make contact with the hose. Have an assistant push down on the vehicle and also turn the steering wheel lock-to-lock during inspection.

9   Bleed the brake system (see Section 8).

Metal brake lines

10   When replacing brake lines, be sure to use the correct parts. Don't use copper tubing for any brake system components. Purchase steel brake lines from a dealer parts department or auto parts store.

11   Prefabricated brake line, with the tube ends already flared and fittings installed, is available at auto parts stores and dealer parts departments. These lines can be bent to the proper shapes using a tubing bender.

12   When installing the new line make sure it's well supported in the brackets and has plenty of clearance between moving or hot components.

13   After installation, check the master cylinder fluid level and add fluid as necessary. Bleed the brake system as outlined in Section 8 and test the brakes carefully before placing the vehicle into normal operation.

8   Brake hydraulic system - bleeding

Refer to illustration 8.8

Warning: *Wear eye protection when bleeding the brake system. If the fluid comes in contact with your eyes, immediately rinse them with water and seek medical attention.*

Note: *Bleeding the brake system is necessary to remove any air that's trapped in the system when it's opened during removal and installation of a hose, line, caliper, wheel cylinder or master cylinder.*

1   It will probably be necessary to bleed the system at all four brakes if air has entered the system due to low fluid level, or if the brake lines have been disconnected at the master cylinder.

2   If a brake line was disconnected only at a wheel, then only that caliper or wheel cylinder must be bled.

3   If a brake line is disconnected at a fitting located between the master cylinder and any of the brakes, that part of the system served by the disconnected line must be bled.

4   Remove any residual vacuum (or hydraulic pressure) from the brake power booster by applying the brake several times with the engine off.

5   Remove the master cylinder reservoir cap and fill the reservoir with brake fluid. Reinstall the cap. **Note:** *Check the fluid level often during the bleeding operation and add fluid as necessary to prevent the fluid level from falling low enough to allow air bubbles into the master cylinder.*

6   Have an assistant on hand, as well as a supply of new brake fluid, an empty clear plastic container, a length of plastic, rubber or vinyl tubing to fit over the bleeder valve and a wrench to open and close the bleeder valve.

7   Beginning at the right rear wheel, loosen the bleeder screw slightly, then tighten it to a point where it's snug but can still be loosened quickly and easily.

8   Place one end of the tubing over the bleeder screw fitting and submerge the other end in brake fluid in the container **(see illustration)**.

9   Have the assistant slowly depress the brake pedal and hold it in the depressed position.

10   While the pedal is held depressed, open the bleeder screw just enough to allow a flow of fluid to leave the valve. Watch for air bubbles to exit the submerged end of the tube. When the fluid flow slows after a couple of seconds, tighten the screw and have your assistant release the pedal.

11   Repeat Steps 9 and 10 until no more air is seen leaving the tube, then tighten the bleeder screw and proceed to the left rear wheel, the right front wheel and the left front wheel, in that order, and perform the same

8.8 When bleeding the brakes, a hose is connected to the bleed screw at the caliper and submerged in brake fluid - air will be seen as bubbles in the tube and container (all air must be expelled before moving to the next wheel)

procedure. Be sure to check the fluid in the master cylinder reservoir frequently.

12   Never use old brake fluid. It contains moisture which can boil, rendering the brake system inoperative.

13   Refill the master cylinder with fluid at the end of the operation.

14   Check the operation of the brakes. The pedal should feel solid when depressed,

9.1 The brake light switch is located near the upper end of the brake pedal, where it's attached to the pedal pin and to the power brake booster pushrod

10.7 Detach the intake manifold vacuum hose from the booster (vacuum booster units only)

with no sponginess. If necessary, repeat the entire process. **Warning:** *Do not operate the vehicle if you are in doubt about the effectiveness of the brake system. It is possible for air to become trapped in the anti-lock brake system hydraulic control unit, so, if the pedal continues to feel spongy after repeated bleedings or the BRAKE or ANTI-LOCK light stays on, have the vehicle towed to a dealer service department or other qualified shop to be bled with the aid of a scan tool.*

9   Brake light switch - check and replacement

Refer to illustration 9.1

Check

1   The brake light switch (**see illustration**) illuminates the rear brake lights when the brake pedal is applied. Ford refers to the brake light switch as the brake on-off (or BOO) switch because it also functions as a digital information switch for the powertrain control module. The switch is located at the upper end of the brake pedal, at the connection between the pedal pin and the power brake booster pushrod. You'll need to remove the trim panel beneath the steering column to get to the switch and connector.

2   If the brake lights are inoperative, check the fuse first (see Chapter 12).

3   If the fuse is good, check for voltage to the switch on the feed wire (refer to the wiring diagrams at the end of this manual for the proper color wire to check). If no voltage is present, repair the wire between the switch and the fuse box.

4   If voltage is present, depress the brake pedal and check for voltage at the output wire terminal (again, refer to the wiring diagrams). If no voltage is present, replace the switch.

5   If voltage is present, check for power on the brake light wires at the tail light housings (with the brake pedal depressed). If voltage is not present, repair the circuit between the switch and the brake lights.

6   If voltage is present, check for a bad ground; using a jumper wire connected to a

good ground, probe the ground wire terminal at the tail light connector. If the brake lights go on, repair the ground circuit (follow the ground wire from the tail light housing).

7   Keep in mind that the brake light bulbs *could* be burned out, but the likelihood of all the bulbs being burned out is very slim.

Replacement

8   Remove the trim panel below the steering column.

9   Unplug the electrical connector from the switch.

10   Remove the retaining pin.

11   Disengage the brake light switch from the master cylinder pushrod and from the pin on the brake pedal. Note how the nylon washers are installed; be sure to install them the same way.

12   Installation is the reverse of removal.

10   Power brake booster - check, removal and installation

Refer to illustration 10.7, 10.9, 10.12a and 10.12b

Operating check

1   Depress the brake pedal several times with the engine off and make sure that there is no change in the pedal reserve distance.

2   Depress the pedal and start the engine. If the pedal goes down slightly, operation is normal.

Airtightness check (vacuum booster only)

3   Start the engine and turn it off after one or two minutes. Depress the brake pedal several times slowly. If the pedal goes down farther the first time but gradually rises after the second or third depression, the booster is airtight.

4   Depress the brake pedal while the engine is running, then stop the engine with the pedal depressed. If there is no change in the pedal reserve travel after holding the pedal for 30 seconds, the booster is airtight.

Removal and installation

5   Disassembly of the power unit requires special tools and is not ordinarily performed by the home mechanic. If a problem develops, it's recommended that a new or factory rebuilt unit be installed.

6   In the engine compartment, remove the nuts attaching the master cylinder to the booster and carefully pull the master cylinder forward until it clears the mounting studs. Be careful not to bend or kink the brake lines.

7   If you're working on a model with a vacuum booster, disconnect the vacuum hose where it attaches to the power brake booster (**see illustration**). If you're working on a model with a hydraulic booster, detach the fluid pressure and return lines from the booster.

10.9 To detach the power brake booster from the firewall, remove these four nuts

10.12a Measure the length of the booster pushrod with vacuum applied

8   In the passenger compartment, remove the retaining pin and the brake light switch, then disconnect the pushrod from the top of the brake pedal (see Section 9).

9   Remove the nuts attaching the booster to the firewall **(see illustration)**.

10   Carefully lift the booster unit away from the firewall and out of the engine compartment.

11   To install the booster, place it into position and tighten the retaining nuts. Connect the pushrod to the brake pedal and install the brake light switch (see Section 9).

12   If you're installing a new vacuum booster, apply a vacuum of approximately 18 to 20 in-Hg to the booster with a hand-held vacuum pump, then measure the protrusion of the pushrod from the face of the booster **(see illustration)**. Compare your measurement with the value listed in this Chapter's Specifications; if it is not as specified, adjust the length of the pushrod by turning the screw at the end of the pushrod **(see illustration)**.

13   Install the master cylinder. Reconnect the vacuum hose or pressure and return lines, as applicable.

14   If you're working on a model with a hydraulic booster, bleed the air from the booster unit as follows:

a) *Remove the PCM fuse from the engine compartment fuse block (fuse no. 24).*

b) *Crank the engine over for a few seconds, then check the power steering fluid level (see Chapter 1). Add fluid as necessary, then reinstall the PCM fuse.*

c) *Start the engine and allow it to idle. Turn the steering wheel from stop-to-stop two times, then turn off the engine.*

d) *Depress the brake pedal several times to discharge the accumulator (the pedal will become harder to push).*

e) *Repeat this procedure until the fluid in the power steering fluid reservoir is free of air bubbles.*

15   Carefully test the operation of the brakes before placing the vehicle in normal service.

11 Parking brake shoes - replacement

1999 through 2004 models

Refer to illustration 11.5

1   Release the parking brake. Loosen the rear wheel lug nuts. Raise the vehicle and support it securely on jackstands. Remove the wheels.

2   Remove the brake calipers (see Section 4) and the brake discs (see Section 5). Disconnect both of the parking brake rear cables from the middle cable connector. Disconnect the cables from the levers at the rear wheels.

3   Remove the rear axleshafts and hub bearings (see Chapter 8).

4   Clean the parking brake assembly with brake system cleaner before beginning work.

5   Remove the upper, outer shoe retracting spring and the adjusting screw spring **(see illustrations)**. Remove the adjusting screw.

10.12b If necessary, adjust the length of the pushrod by turning the adjusting screw in or out

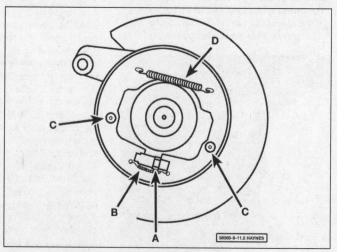

11.5 Remove the hold-down spring from each shoe

a) *Adjusting screw*   c) *Hold-down spring*
b) *Adjusting screw spring*   d) *Outer retracting spring*

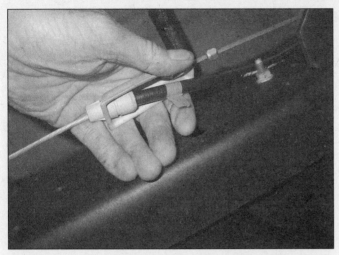

11.10a Have an assistant pull down on the parking brake cable . . .

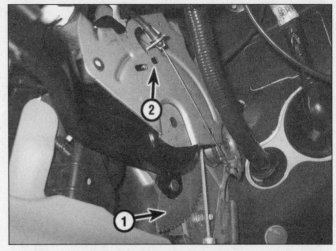

11.10b . . . while you lock the pedal in place by inserting a small pin through the hole in the bracket

1	Sector	2	Hole for retaining pin

6   Remove the hold-down springs from the shoes **(see illustration)**.

7   Spread the bottoms of the shoes apart and lift them up off the actuator (the upper inner retracting spring will still be attached). Once the shoe assembly is free, remove the inner retracting spring.

2005 and later models
Refer to illustrations 11.10a and 11.10b

8   Remove the disc (refer to Section 5).

9   Remove the left lower interior trim panel to expose the parking brake mechanism near the driver's left knee.

10   Have an assistant pull down on the middle parking brake cable **(see illustration)**. The parking brake sector will rotate until it stops **(see illustration)**. When it stops, insert a small steel pin through the hole in the parking brake mechanism bracket to hold the sector in place. This will allow tension to be relieved in the cable so it can be disconnected.

11   Disconnect the parking brake cables at the equalizer. Squeeze the clips to disconnect the cables at the brackets at each rear wheel.

12   The cables can now be rotated a quarter turn (upright) to disconnect them from the parking brake levers.

13   Remove the two clips and the pins that retain the parking brake shoes.

14   Remove the lower spring and the adjusting screw.

15   Remove the brake shoes along with the retracting spring.

All models

16   Clean the brake disc/parking brake drum and check it for score marks, deep grooves, hard spots (which will appear as small discolored areas) and cracks. If the disc/drum is worn, scored or out-of-round, it can be resurfaced by an automotive machine shop.

17   Install the shoes by reversing the removal procedure. Turn the adjusting screw so the disc just fits over the new shoes. When the disc is installed, the shoes should not rub as the disc is turned. If you have a brake shoe adjusting gauge, adjust the diameter of the shoes 0.030-inch less than that of the drum surface of the rear brake disc.

18   Repeat this procedure for the other parking brake assembly.

19   Install the brake discs (see Section 5) and the brake calipers (see Section 4). Reconnect the parking brake cable to the actuator arm.

20   Remove the rubber plug from the brake backing plate and, using a screwdriver or brake adjusting tool, turn the adjusting screw star wheel until the parking brake shoes start to drag as the disc is turned, then back off the star wheel until the shoes don't drag.

21   Install the rear wheels and lug nuts, lower the vehicle and tighten the lug nuts to the torque listed in the Chapter 1 Specifications.

Notes

Chapter 10
Suspension and steering systems

Contents

	Section
Balljoints - replacement	7
Coil spring - removal and installation	4
Front axle I-beam and radius arm (2WD models) - removal and installation	8
Front wheel bearing check, repack and adjustment (2WD models)	See Chapter 1
General information	1
Hub and bearing assembly (front, 4WD models) - removal and installation	See Chapter 8
Leaf spring (front, 4WD models) - removal and installation	5
Leaf spring (rear) - removal and installation	12
Power steering fluid level check	See Chapter 1
Power steering pump - removal and installation	17
Power steering system - bleeding	18
Shock absorbers (front) - removal and installation	2
Shock absorbers (rear) - removal and installation	10

	Section
Stabilizer bar (front) - removal and installation	3
Stabilizer bar (rear) - removal and installation	11
Steering column - removal and installation	14
Steering gear - removal and installation	15
Steering knuckle - removal and installation	6
Steering linkage - removal and installation	16
Steering wheel and airbag clockspring - removal and installation	13
Suspension and steering check	See Chapter 1
Tire and tire pressure checks	See Chapter 1
Tire rotation	See Chapter 1
Track bar (4WD models) - removal and installation	9
Wheel alignment - general information	21
Wheel studs - replacement	19
Wheels and tires - general information	20

Specifications

General

Power steering fluid type	See Chapter 1

Torque specifications

Ft-lbs (unless otherwise indicated)

Front suspension (2WD models)

Lower balljoint nut	99
Upper balljoint nut	60
Coil spring retainer bolt-to-spring/shock tower	26
Coil spring retainer nut-to-lower spring seat	
Models through 2008	99
2009 and later	148
Radius arm-to-I-beam axle bolt/nut	295
Radius arm pivot bolt retainer nut-to-radius arm bracket	
1999 through 2004	185
2005 and later	221
Radius arm bracket-to-frame bolts/nuts	60
I-beam axle-to-bracket pivot bolt/nut	130
I-beam axle bracket-to-frame bolt/nut	60
Shock absorber upper mounting nut	
Models through 2008	60
2009 and later	52
Upper balljoint pinch bolt	60
Lower shock absorber retainer nut	60
Stabilizer bar link nut-to-lower spring seat	
1999 through 2002	60
2003 through 2004	80
2005 and later	85
Stabilizer bar link nut-to-stabilizer bar	
1999 through 2002	60
2003 through 2004	80
2005 and later	85
Stabilizer bar retainer bracket-to-frame bolts	36

Torque specifications (continued)

Ft-lbs (unless otherwise indicated)

Note: One foot-pound (ft-lb) of torque is equivalent to 12 inch-pounds (in-lbs) of torque. Torque values below approximately 15 foot-pounds are expressed in inch-pounds, because most foot-pound torque wrenches are not accurate at these smaller values.

Front suspension (1999 through 2004 4WD models)

Leaf spring-to-axle U-bolt nuts	99
Leaf spring-to-spring hanger nut	203
Leaf spring-to-shackle nut	185
Leaf spring hanger-to-frame bolts	76
Leaf spring shackle-to-frame nut	185
Stabilizer bar-to-spring spacer bolts (left side)	
1999 through 2002	35
2003 through 2004	41
Stabilizer bar-to-axle bracket bolts (right side)	
1999 through 2002	35
2003 through 2004	41
Stabilizer bar-to-link nut	
1999 models	60
2000 through 2002 models	85
2003 through 2004 models	80
Stabilizer bar link-to-axle nut	
1999 models	60
200 through 2002 models	85
2003 through 2004 models	80
Stabilizer bar bracket-to-frame bolts	35
Shock absorber upper mounting nut	76
Shock absorber lower mounting nut	76
Jounce bumper-to-frame bolts	30
Shock absorber upper mounting bracket-to-frame bolts	76
Track bar-to-upper and lower mounting bracket nut	
1999 models	129
2000 through 2002 models	369
2003 through 2004 models	406
Shackle bracket assembly-to-frame bolts	66
Front hub and bearing-to-knuckle nuts	133
Upper ball-joint nut	
2001 and earlier models	101
2002 models	69
Lower ball-joint nut	
2001 and earlier models	101
2002 models	150

Front suspension (2005 and later 4WD models)

Track bar bracket-to-frame bolts	129
Track bar-to-track bar bracket bolt	406
Track bar-to-axle nut	185
Track bar balljoint nut	184
Radius arm-to-bracket nut	222
Radius arm-to-axle bolts	
Models through 2007	222
2008 and later	295
Jounce bumper-to-frame nut	26
Stabilizer bar link-to-stabilizer bar nut	111
Stabilizer bar-to-axle nut	59
Stabilizer bar-to-frame bolts	35
Shock absorber-to-bracket bolt	111
Shock absorber-to-frame nut	46
Lower balljoint nut	150
Upper balljoint nut	68

Rear suspension

Leaf spring-to-axle U-bolts (at ride height)	
1999 through 2004	185
2005	148
2006 and later	
Step 1	37
Step 2	74
Step 3	111
Step 4	148

Leaf spring-to-front spring hanger bolt
    1999 through 2004 185
    2005 through 2007 277
    2008 and later 340
Leaf spring-to-rear shackle bolt
    1999 through 2004 F-250/F-350 wide frame and Excursion 185
    1999 through 2004 F-250/F-350 narrow frame 166
    2005 through 2007 184
    2008 and later 166
Rear shackle-to-frame bracket bolt
    1999 through 2004 F-250/F-350 wide frame and Excursion 185
    1999 through 2004 F-250/F-350 narrow frame 166
    2005 through 2007 184
    2008 and later 166
Shock absorber upper mounting nut
    1999 through 2002 Excursion 17
    All except 1999 through 2002 Excursion.............................. 46
Shock absorber lower mounting bolt
    1999 through 2004 models 46
    2005 and later models 66
Shock absorber bracket-to-axle U-bolt (Ford axle)
    1999 through 2002 35
    2003 through 2004 41
    2005 and later wide frame.. 35
    2005 and later narrow frame... 30
Stabilizer bar bracket-to-axle bolt (Dana axle) 30
Stabilizer bar bracket-to-axle U-bolt (Ford axle)
    1999 through 2002 35
    2003 and later 30

Steering

Airbag module-to-steering wheel screws
    1999 and 2000 models... 98 in-lbs
    2001 and later models... 108 in-lbs
Steering wheel bolt.. 28
Steering column nuts
    Models through 2007 .... 144 in-lbs
    2008 and later 22
Intermediate shaft pinch bolts
    Upper (to steering column shaft).. 19
    Lower (to steering gear)
        Models through 2007 36
        2008 and later... 26
Steering gear-to-frame bolts
    1999 models... 45
    2000 and later models... 59
Pitman arm nut
    1999 through 2004 199
    2005 and later 350
Drag link-to-Pitman arm nut
    1999 models... 60
    2000 through 2004 models 66
    2005 and later models... 148
Drag link-to-tie-rod nut (1999 through 2004 4WD models)...................... 67
Tie-rod end nuts
    1999 through 2004 2WD models 67
    1999 through 2004 4WD models 52
    2005 85
    2006 and later
        Inner.. 129
        Outer... 85
Tie-rod/drag link adjuster sleeve clamp bolt/nut 41
Steering damper-to-axle nut/bolt 67
Steering damper-to-tie-rod nut/bolt.. 67
Steering damper bracket-to-steering linkage............................. 21
Steering damper-to-frame bracket bolt....................................... 66
Steering damper bracket-to-frame nuts...................................... 59

1.1 Front suspension and steering components - 2WD model

1   Stabilizer bar
2   Pitman arm
3   Tie-rod
4   Coil spring
5   Tie-rod end
6   Drag link
7   Steering knuckle
8   Front axle I-beam
9   Radius arm

1.2 Front suspension and steering components (1999 - 2004 4WD models)

1   Pitman arm
2   Leaf spring
3   Drag link
4   Steering damper
5   Tie-rod
6   Track bar
7   Tie-rod end
8   Steering knuckle
9   Front axle assembly
10   Stabilizer bar link
11   Stabilizer bar

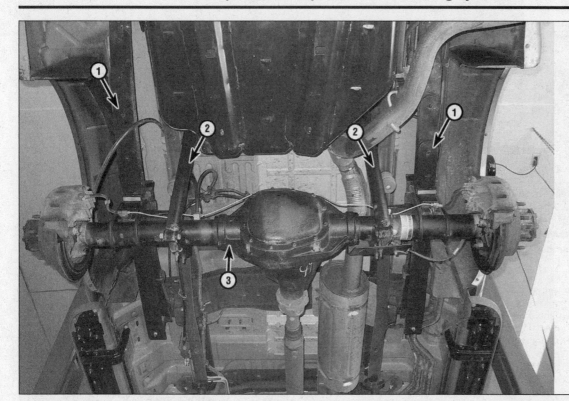

1.3 Rear suspension components

1   *Leaf spring*
2   *Shock absorber*
3   *Rear axle housing*

1   General information

Refer to illustrations 1.1, 1.2 and 1.3

The front suspension on 2WD models covered in this manual is a twin I-beam type, which is composed of coil springs, I-beam axle arms, radius arms, upper and lower balljoints and steering knuckles, tie-rods, shock absorbers and a stabilizer bar **(see illustration)**.

On 1999 through 2004 4WD models, the front suspension is a solid axle suspended by leaf springs, shock absorbers and a stabilizer bar **(see illustration)**. 2005 and later models use a similar solid axle, however it is suspended by coil springs rather than leaf springs and uses radius arms.

The rear suspension uses shock absorbers and leaf springs **(see illustration)**. The forward end of each spring is attached to the bracket on the side of the frame side rail. The rear of each spring is shackled to a bracket on the side of the frame rail.

The steering system consists of a steering column, intermediate shaft, steering gear, Pitman arm, drag link, tie-rod and tie-rod ends. The tie-rods are equipped with an adjusting sleeve for setting the toe-in. All models are equipped with power steering.

Frequently, when working on the suspension or steering system components, you may come across fasteners which seem impossible to loosen. These fasteners on the underside of the vehicle are continually subjected to water, road grime, mud, etc., and can become rusted or "frozen," making them extremely difficult to remove. In order to unscrew these stubborn fasteners without damaging them

(or other components), be sure to use lots of penetrating oil and allow it to soak in for a while. Using a wire brush to clean exposed threads will also ease removal of the nut or bolt and prevent damage to the threads. Sometimes a sharp blow with a hammer and punch will break the bond between a nut and bolt threads, but care must be taken to prevent the punch from slipping off the fastener and ruining the threads. Heating the stuck fastener and surrounding area with a torch sometimes helps too, but isn't recommended because of the obvious dangers associated with fire. Long breaker bars and extension, or "cheater," pipes will increase leverage, but never use an extension pipe on a ratchet - the ratcheting mechanism could be damaged. Sometimes tightening the nut or bolt first will help to break it loose. Fasteners that require drastic measures to remove should always be

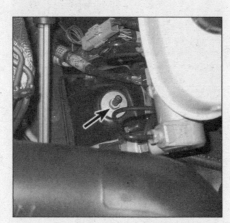

2.1 Shock absorber upper mounting nut (left side shown) - 2WD model

replaced with new ones.

Since most procedures that are dealt with in this chapter involve jacking up the vehicle and working underneath it, a good pair of jackstands will be needed. A hydraulic floor jack is the preferred type of jack to lift the vehicle, and it can also be used to support certain components during various operations. **Warning 1:** *Never, under any circumstances, rely on a jack to support the vehicle while working under it - always support the vehicle with jackstands.* **Warning 2:** *Whenever any of the suspension or steering fasteners are loosened or removed they must be inspected and, if necessary replaced with new ones of the same part number or of original equipment quality and design. Torque specifications must be followed for proper reassembly and component retention. Never attempt to heat or straighten suspension or steering components. Instead, replace bent or damaged parts with new ones.*

2   Shock absorbers (front) - removal and installation

Refer to illustrations 2.1, 2.3, 2.4a, 2.4b, 2.4c and 2.4d

Caution: *The shock absorbers are pressurized with nitrogen gas. Do not attempt to open, puncture or apply heat to the shock absorbers.*

1   If you're working on a 2WD model, open the hood and remove the shock absorber upper mounting nut, washer and bushing **(see illustration)**.

2   Loosen the front wheel lug nuts. Raise the front of the vehicle, support it securely on

2.3 Shock absorber upper mounting nut - 4WD model

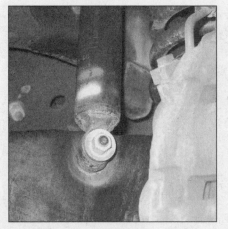

2.4a Shock absorber lower mounting nut - 2WD model

2.4b Shock absorber lower mounting nut/ bolt - 4WD model

jackstands, block the rear wheels and set the parking brake. Remove the front wheel.

3   Support the outer end of the axle with a floor jack. If you're working on a 4WD model, remove the shock absorber upper mounting nut **(see illustration)**.

4   Remove the shock absorber lower mounting nut and, on 4WD models, the bolt **(see illustrations)**, then remove the shock absorber.

5   Installation is the reverse of the removal steps with the following additions:

a) *Tighten the nuts and bolts to the torque listed in this Chapter's Specifications.*

b) *Install the wheel and lug nuts, lower the vehicle and tighten the lug nuts to the torque listed in Chapter 1.*

3   Stabilizer bar (front) - removal and installation

Refer to illustrations 3.2 and 3.3

1   Raise the front of the vehicle, support it securely on jackstands, block the rear wheels

and set the parking brake. Position the front wheels in the straight ahead position.

2   Remove the nuts, washers and bolts and detach the stabilizer bar links from the bar **(see illustration)**.

3   Remove the stabilizer bar retaining brackets and bushings **(see illustration)** and remove the stabilizer bar.

4   Installation is the reverse of the removal steps. Tighten the bolts and nuts to the torque listed in this Chapter's Specifications. **Note:** *The stabilizer bar-to-link bolts/nuts should be tightened with the vehicle sitting at normal ride height.*

4   Coil spring - removal and installation

Refer to illustrations 4.5 and 4.6

Removal

1   Loosen the front wheel lug nuts. Raise the front of the vehicle, support it securely on jackstands placed under the frame rails, block the rear wheels and set the parking brake.

2.4c Lower shock mount, 2005 and later 4X4 model

Remove the front wheel.

2   Place a floor jack under the outer end of the front axle I-beam.

3   Detach the lower end of the shock absorber from the radius arm **(see illustration 2.4a)**.

2.4d Upper shock mount, 2005 and later 4X4 model

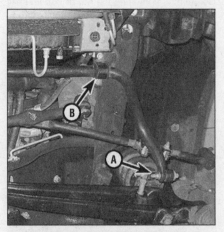

3.2 Front stabilizer bar details - 2WD models

A   *Stabilizer bar-to-link bolt/nut*
B   *Stabilizer bar retaining bracket*

3.3 Front stabilizer bar retaining bracket nuts/bolts- 4WD model

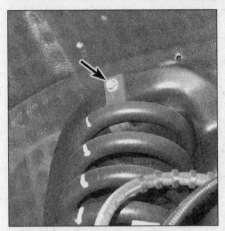

4.5 Remove the retainer bolt and retainer securing the spring to the frame - 2WD models

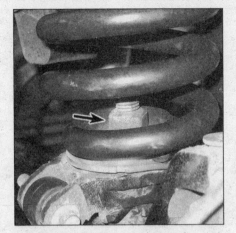

4.6 Remove the lower spring retainer nut (it's easier to reach this nut with a long extension from the top, rather than with a wrench from the side) - 2WD models

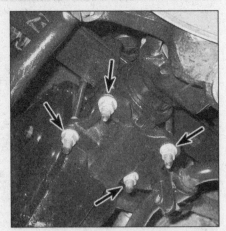

5.3 With the axle supported, remove the nuts from the U-bolts

2WD models

4   On early models, if required for access, remove the brake caliper and suspend it with a length of wire to relieve stress on the brake hose (see Chapter 9).

5   Remove the retainer bolt at the upper end of the spring **(see illustration)**. Remove the retainer.

6   Use a long extension through the center of the spring to remove the spring lower retainer nut **(see illustration).**

All models

7   Lower the floor jack slightly and remove the spring.

Installation

8   Make sure the lower retainer and insulator are in place on the front axle and radius arm.

9   Push the front axle down to allow installation of the spring. Install the lower end of the spring onto the spring seat, then install the retainer and nut. Make sure the upper end of the spring is oriented correctly. Tighten the lower retainer nut to the torque listed in this Chapter's Specifications.

10   Slowly raise the front axle and orient the spring's upper coil into the front spring tower helix in the frame. Raise the front axle until the spring is correctly seated.

2WD models

11   Install the upper spring retainer. Tighten the bolt to the torque listed in this Chapter's Specifications.

12   Install the brake caliper if it was removed (see Chapter 9).

All models

13   Install the brake caliper (see Chapter 9).

14   Connect the shock absorber to the radius arm. Tighten the nut to the torque listed in this Chapter's Specifications.

15   Install the wheel and lug nuts. Lower the vehicle and tighten the lug nuts to the torque listed in the Chapter 1 Specifications.

---

5   Leaf spring (front, 4WD models) - removal and installation

Refer to illustrations 5.3, 5.4 and 5.5

1   Loosen the wheel lug nuts, raise the front of the vehicle and support it securely on jackstands. Block the rear wheels to keep the vehicle from rolling off the stands. Remove the front wheels.

2   Support the axle with a floor jack placed under the axle tube and raise it slightly to take the weight of the axle. If you're removing the left side leaf spring, detach the lower end of the shock absorber from the spring plate (see Section 2).

3   Remove the four U-bolt nuts **(see illustration)**, the spring plate and the two U-bolts.

4   At the front end of the spring, remove the nut and bolt from the spring-to-front bracket **(see illustration)**. **Note:** *On some models it may be necessary to unbolt and remove the condenser mounting bracket to allow the spring mounting bolt to be removed.*

5   At the rear end of the spring, remove

the lower spring-to-shackle nut and bolt **(see illustration)**.

6   Remove the spring assembly. It may be necessary to pry the ends of the spring out of the shackle and front mounting bracket.

7   If the bushings at the ends of the spring are worn or deteriorated, an automotive machine shop or other repair facility can press the old ones out and press new ones in.

8   Installation is the reverse of removal. Gradually tighten the U-bolt nuts in a criss-cross pattern to the torque listed in this Chapter's Specifications. Don't tighten the spring-to-front bracket bolt/nut or the spring-to-shackle bolt/nut until the vehicle has been lowered.

9   If you're working on the left side, reconnect the lower end of the shock absorber to the spring plate.

10   Install the wheel and lug nuts. Lower the vehicle and tighten the lug nuts to the torque listed in the Chapter 1 Specifications.

11   Tighten the spring-to-front bracket bolt/nut and the spring-to-shackle bolt/nut to the torque listed in this Chapter's Specifications.

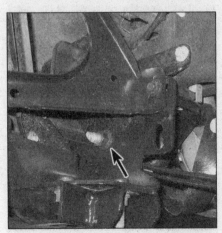

5.4 To detach the front end of the leaf spring from its bracket, remove this nut and bolt

5.5 To detach the rear end of the leaf spring from the spring shackle, remove the lower nut and bolt

6.4 Remove the cotter pin and lower balljoint nut

6.5 Upper balljoint clamp bolt (2WD models)

6   Steering knuckle - removal and installation

Refer to illustrations 6.4, 6.5 and 6.6

Removal

1   Remove the front wheel and brake disc (see Chapter 9). Remove the brake dust shield. If equipped with four-wheel ABS, remove the ABS wheel speed sensor from the steering knuckle.
2   If you're working on a 4WD model, remove the hub and bearing assembly and the front axleshaft (see Chapter 8).
3   Disconnect the tie-rod end from the steering knuckle (see Section 16).
4   Remove the cotter pin from the lower balljoint stud nut, then remove the nut **(see illustration)**.
5   If you're working on a 2WD model, remove the clamp bolt from the upper balljoint **(see illustration)**. If you're working on a 4WD model, remove the cotter pin and nut from the upper balljoint stud.
6   Mark the exact orientation of the camber adjuster to the steering knuckle **(see illustra-**

tion). Pry the camber adjuster from the steering knuckle. If necessary, use a two-jaw puller to remove the camber adjuster.
7   On 2WD models, strike the lower yoke of the axle to break the steering knuckle loose from the balljoint studs. On 4WD models, you'll have to strike both yokes. **Caution:** *Don't use a fork-type separator to detach the balljoint. This will damage the balljoint seal.*
8   Remove the steering knuckle together with the balljoints.

Installation

9   Before installation, check that the upper and lower balljoint seals were not damaged during steering knuckle removal and that they are positioned correctly. Replace if necessary.
10   Position the steering knuckle and balljoints in the axle arm.
11   On 2WD models, install the camber adjuster on the upper balljoint, making sure it's aligned correctly.
12   Tighten the balljoint nut(s) to the torque listed in this Chapter's Specifications, then tighten further until the cotter pin hole lines up. Install a new cotter pin and bend it to secure the nut.
13   If you're working on a 2WD model, install

and tighten the upper balljoint clamp bolt to the torque listed in this Chapter's Specifications.
14   The remainder of installation is the reverse of removal.
15   Install the wheel and lug nuts. Lower the vehicle and tighten the lug nuts to the torque listed in the Chapter 1 Specifications.
16   Have the front end alignment checked and, if necessary, adjusted.

7   Balljoints - replacement

The balljoints are a press fit in the steering knuckle, which necessitates the use of a special press tool and receiver cup to remove and install them. Since the tool is not normally available to the home mechanic, it is recommended that the vehicle be taken to an automotive machine shop or other qualified repair facility to have the balljoints replaced.

At the time of this writing, balljoints on 1999 through 2003 2WD models were not replaceable.

8   Front axle I-beam and radius arm (2WD models) - removal and installation

Refer to illustrations 8.4 and 8.5

Removal

1   Raise the front of the vehicle, support it securely on jackstands, block the rear wheels and set the parking brake. Position the front wheels in the straight ahead position.
2   Remove the front stabilizer bar (see Section 3).
3   Remove the shock absorber (see Section 2), coil spring (see Section 4) and steering knuckle (see Section 6). Unscrew the radius arm-to-I-beam axle nut, then, using a hammer and punch, drive out the radius arm-to-I-beam bolt.

6.6 Mark the position of the camber adjuster to the steering knuckle (2WD model shown)

8.4 I-beam axle-to-frame bracket bolt and nut

8.5 Radius arm-to-frame bracket bolt/nut

9.3 Upper track bar bolt location, 2005 and later 4X4 model

4   Remove the bolt and nut securing the I-beam axle arm to the frame pivot bracket **(see illustration)**. Remove the axle arm.

5   To remove the radius arm, remove the bolt and nut attaching the rear of the arm to the frame bracket, then detach the arm from the bracket **(see illustration)**.

Installation

6   Install the I-beam axle arm and the radius arm to their brackets on the frame and install the bolts and nuts. Don't fully tighten the nuts yet.

7   Connect the radius arm to the I-beam axle and install the bolt and nut. Tighten the nut to the torque listed in this Chapter's Specifications.

8   Install the steering knuckle (see Section 6) and the coil spring (see Section 4).

9   Install the stabilizer bar (see Section 3).

10   Install the wheel and lug nuts. Lower the vehicle and tighten the lug nuts to the torque listed in the Chapter 1 Specifications.

11   Tighten the I-beam axle and radius arm

pivot bolts/nuts to the torque listed in this Chapter's Specifications.

12   Have the front end alignment checked and, if necessary, adjusted.

9   Track bar (4WD models) - removal and installation

Refer to illustration 9.3

1   Raise the front of the vehicle and place jackstands under the front axle, not the frame. Block the rear wheels and set the parking brake.

2   Disconnect the lower end of the track bar from the axle bracket on the right end of the axle.

3   Disconnect the upper end of the track bar from the frame bracket **(see illustration)**.

4   Installation is the reverse of removal. Tighten all fasteners to the torques listed in this Chapter's Specifications.

10   Shock absorbers (rear) - removal and installation

Refer to illustrations 10.2 and 10.4

1   Raise the rear of the vehicle, support it securely on jackstands and block the front wheels. Place a floor jack under the axle adjacent to the shock absorber being removed. Raise the jack just enough to take the load off the shock absorber.

2   Remove the nut and bolt securing the lower end of the shock absorber to the rear axle **(see illustration)**.

3   If you're working on an F-250 or F-350, remove the nut securing the top of the shock absorber to the upper mounting bracket on the frame **(see illustration 10.2)**.

4   If you're working on an Excursion, remove the two shock absorber upper mounting bolts **(see illustration)**.

5   Installation is the reverse of the removal steps. Tighten the nuts and bolts to the torque listed in this Chapter's Specifications.

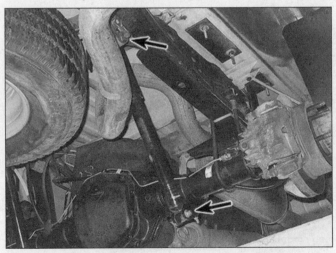

10.2 Shock absorber mounting details (F-250 shown, Excursion lower mount similar)

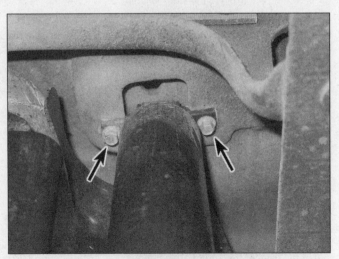

10.4 Shock absorber upper mounting bolts - Excursion models

12.3 With the axle supported, remove the nuts from the U-bolts

12.4 Remove the shackle-to-frame bracket bolt and nut at the rear of the spring . . .

11   Stabilizer bar (rear) - removal and installation

1   Raise the rear of the vehicle, support it securely on jackstands and block the front wheels.
2   Remove the nuts from each end of the stabilizer bar links and remove the links.
3   Remove the stabilizer bar retaining brackets and bushings and detach the stabilizer bar from the axle housing.
4   Installation is the reverse of the removal steps. Tighten the bolts and nuts to the torque listed in this Chapter's Specifications.

12   Leaf spring (rear) - removal and installation

Refer to illustrations 12.3, 12.4 and 12.5

Removal

1   Loosen the rear wheel lug nuts. Raise the rear of the vehicle, support it securely on jackstands and block the front wheels.

Remove the wheel.
2   Support the vehicle securely on jackstands placed under the frame rails. Support the axle with a floor jack placed under the axle tube and raise it slightly to take the weight off the axle.
3   Remove the nuts from the U-bolts, then remove the U-bolts and the spring plate from the spring **(see illustration)**. Now lower the jack far enough to relieve tension on the spring.
4   Remove the lower bolt and nut securing the shackle assembly to the frame bracket at the rear of the spring **(see illustration)**.
5   Remove the spring hanger bolt and nut at the front of the spring **(see illustration)**. Remove the spring.
6   Inspect the spring eye bushings for wear or distortion. If worn or damaged have them replaced by a dealer service department or properly equipped shop.

Installation

7   Install the spring in the front bracket. Tighten the bolt and nut finger-tight.
8   Place the spring shackle in the frame

bracket. Install the bolt and nut and tighten them finger-tight.
9   Raise the axle into contact with the spring and install the spring seat. Make sure the spring tie-bolt or pin is positioned in the hole in the seat, then install the U-bolts and nuts.
10   Install the wheel and lug nuts. Lower the vehicle to the ground and tighten the spring bracket bolt and nut, spring U-bolts and shackle-to-frame bracket bolt and nut to the torque values listed in this Chapter's Specifications. Tighten the lug nuts to the torque listed in the Chapter 1 Specifications.

13   Steering wheel and airbag clockspring - removal and installation

Warning: *These models are equipped with airbags. Always disable the airbag system whenever working in the vicinity of any airbag system components to avoid the possibility of accidental airbag deployment, which could cause personal injury (see Chapter 12).*

12.5 . . . then the spring hanger bolt and nut at the front of the spring, then remove the spring (it may be necessary to pry the spring out of the bracket)

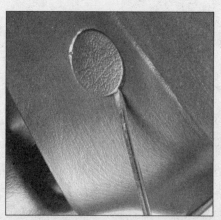

13.2a To detach the airbag module from the steering wheel, pry off the screw covers (left cover shown, right cover on other side of steering wheel) . . .

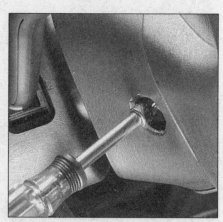

13.2b . . . and remove the airbag module retaining screws

13.3 Lift the airbag off the steering wheel and unplug the electrical connectors for the horn (upper arrow) and for the airbag (lower arrow)

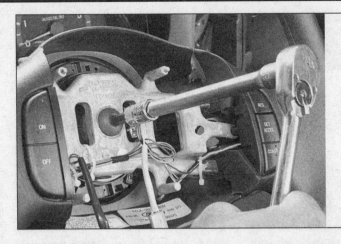

13.4 Remove the steering wheel retaining bolt

Steering wheel

Removal

Refer to illustrations 13.2a, 13.2b, 13.3, 13.4, 13.5, 13.6 and 13.7

1   **Warning:** *Disconnect the cable(s) from the negative battery terminal(s) and wait at least two minutes for the airbag system back-up power supply to be depleted (see Chapter 5).*

2   On 2007 and earlier models, remove the two airbag module retaining screws **(see illustrations)** and lift off the airbag module. On 2008 and later models, the airbag is retained by three spring clips. To access the clips, rotate the steering wheel counterclockwise until the top of the wheel is at the 9 o'clock position. Remove the screw and the tilt lever (if equipped), then remove the steering column covers (see Chapter 11). Position a mirror behind the steering wheel to see the three wire clips, then release them one at a time, using a screwdriver to move them inward. Return the steering wheel to the straight-ahead position. **Warning:** *Carry the airbag module with the trim cover (upholstered side) facing away from you, and set the airbag module in a safe location with the trim cover facing up.*

3   Unplug the electrical connectors for the airbag and horn **(see illustration)**.

4   Remove the steering wheel bolt **(see illustration)**.

5   Mark the relationship of the steering wheel to the steering shaft and unplug the electrical connector(s) from the steering wheel **(see illustration)**.

6   Using a two-jaw puller, remove the steering wheel **(see illustration)**. **Caution:** *Any attempt to remove the steering wheel without using a puller to do so can damage the column.*

7   The airbag clockspring has a locking mechanism which prevents it from rotating after the steering wheel has been removed. If this lock is missing, apply two strips of tape across it to prevent accidental rotation **(see illustration)**.

13.5 Mark the relationship of the steering wheel to the steering shaft before removing the wheel, and unplug these two electrical connectors

13.6 Remove the steering wheel with a two-jaw puller - do not try to hammer off the steering wheel or you will damage the column bearings

13.7 Apply two pieces of tape to secure the clockspring

13.16 Carefully pry the retaining clips out to release the clockspring

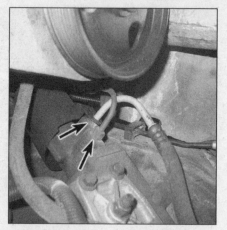

15.5 Using a flare-nut wrench, unscrew the pressure and return line fittings from the steering gear

Installation

8   Before installing the steering wheel, make sure the airbag clockspring is properly aligned. The dot on the end of the steering shaft must be in the 9 o'clock position and the electrical lead for the clockspring must be in the 3 o'clock position. Take note of any other alignment marks which may be present on the airbag clockspring, and of any other instructions which may be printed on the clockspring. If the clockspring is not aligned properly, rotate the hub of the clockspring clockwise until it stops (don't apply too much force), then turn it in the opposite direction 2-1/4 revolutions to center it. Proceed to Step 23.

Clockspring

Refer to illustration 13.16

Removal

9   Remove the steering wheel (see Steps 1 through 6). Remove the tilt-wheel handle by twisting it.
10   Remove the lower steering column cover (see Chapter 11).
11   Remove the ignition switch lock cylinder (see Chapter 12).
12   Remove the upper steering column cover by lifting up.
13   Stabilize the service lock on the clockspring by installing two pieces of tape across the airbag clockspring **(see illustration 13.7)**.
14   Remove the key-in-ignition warning switch. If the vehicle is equipped with a passive anti-theft system, remove the Torx-head retaining screw and lift off the transmitter.
15   Disconnect the clockspring connector from the bracket.
16   Pry the retaining clips out **(see illustration)** from the clockspring.
17   Separate the harness from any retaining clips securing it to the steering column.
18   Remove the clockspring from the steering column.

Installation

19   Install the clockspring onto the steering column and make sure the electrical harness

connector is positioned at 3 o'clock. **Note:** *If the clockspring has been become uncentered (or if you're not sure), center it as described in Step 8.*
20   Press the retaining clips back in to secure the clockspring.
21   Secure the harness wiring into the clips and install the electrical connectors.
22   The remaining steps are the reverse of the removal.
23   To install the wheel, align the mark on the steering wheel hub with the mark on the shaft and slip the wheel onto the shaft. Install a *new* bolt and tighten it to the torque listed in this Chapter's Specifications.
24   Plug in the horn connector and the cruise control connector, if equipped.
25   On models with a driver's side airbag, connect the airbag electrical connector and install the airbag module. Tighten the fasteners to the torque listed in this Chapter's Specifications.
26   Connect the cable(s) to the negative terminal(s) of the battery(ies).

14   Steering column - removal and installation

Warning: *These models are equipped with airbags. Always disable the airbag system whenever working in the vicinity of any airbag system components to avoid the possibility of accidental airbag deployment, which could cause personal injury (see Chapter 12).*

Removal

1   Park the vehicle with the wheels pointing straight ahead. Disconnect the cable(s) from the negative battery terminal(s). Wait at least two minutes before proceeding (to allow the backup power supply for the airbag system to become depleted).
2   Remove the knee bolster (see Chapter 11).
3   Remove the steering wheel and airbag clockspring (see Section 13).
4   On automatic transmission models,

detach the shift cable from the shift lever on the column. Also detach the shift indicator cable (see Chapter 7B).
5   If the vehicle is equipped with a tilt column, unscrew the tilt lever.
6   Remove the steering column covers (see Chapter 11).
7   Detach the electrical connector from the multi-function switch (see Chapter 12). Unplug any other electrical connectors that would interfere with column removal.
8   Remove the shaft coupler bolt (securing the steering column shaft to the intermediate shaft).
9   Remove the steering column mounting nuts, lower the column and pull it to the rear while separating the steering column shaft from the intermediate shaft. Make sure nothing is still connected.

Installation

10   Guide the steering column into position, connecting the steering column shaft to the intermediate shaft. Install the mounting nuts, but don't tighten them yet.
11   Install the coupler bolt, then tighten the nut to the torque listed in this Chapter's Specifications.
12   Tighten the column mounting nuts to the torque listed in this Chapter's Specifications.
13   The remainder of installation is the reverse of removal. On automatic transmission models, adjust the shift cable and the shift indicator cable following the procedures described in Chapter 7B.

15   Steering gear - removal and installation

Refer to illustrations 15.5 and 15.9
Warning: *These models are equipped with airbags. Always disable the airbag system before working in the vicinity of any airbag system components to avoid the possibility of accidental deployment of the airbag, which could cause personal injury (see Chapter 12).*

Removal

1   Set the front wheels to the straight-ahead position. Remove the air filter housing (see Chapter 4). On models with a diesel engine, remove the intercooler outlet duct (see Chapter 4) if it interferes.
2   On models with a diesel engine, pump the brake pedal several times (until it gets harder to depress) to discharge the accumulator.
3   Disconnect the cable(s) from the negative battery terminal(s).
4   Turn the ignition key to the Run position to unlock the steering wheel. **Warning:** *Make sure that the steering shaft is not rotated with the steering gear removed or damage to the airbag clockspring assembly could occur. One method of preventing the steering shaft from rotating is to run the seat belt through the steering wheel and clip the seat belt buckles together.*

15.9 To detach the steering gear from the frame, remove these three bolts

16.3a Disconnecting the drag link from the Pitman arm with a puller

16.3b Disconnecting the drag link from the tie-rod (4WD models)

5   Place a pan under the steering gear. Unscrew the power steering pressure and return line fittings and cap the ends and the ports to prevent excessive fluid loss and contamination **(see illustration)**.

6   Mark the relationship of the intermediate shaft to the steering gear input shaft, then remove the pinch bolt.

7   Loosen the left front wheel lug nuts. Raise the front of the vehicle, support it securely on jackstands, block the rear wheels and set the parking brake. Remove the front wheel.

8   Disconnect the drag link from the Pitman arm (see Section 16).

9   Loosen all three bolts securing the steering gear box to the frame **(see illustration)**. Support the steering gear and remove the bolts and washers and remove the steering gear from the lower steering column shaft. If necessary, unscrew the nut and detach the Pitman arm from the steering gear.

Installation

10   Make sure the steering gear is centered. Turn the input shaft to full lock in one direction, then count and record the number of turns required to rotate it to the opposite full lock position. Turn the shaft back through one-half of the number of turns just counted to center the unit.

11   Check that the front wheels are in the straight ahead position and that the steering wheel spokes is centered. Reposition if necessary.

12   Raise the steering gear into position, connecting the intermediate shaft to the steering gear input shaft (be sure to align the marks made earlier).

13   Install the three bolts securing the steering gear box to the frame. Tighten the bolts to the torque listed in this Chapter's Specifications.

14   Connect the drag link to the Pitman arm, tightening the nut to the torque listed in this Chapter's Specifications.

15   Install the bolt securing the flex coupling to the steering gear input shaft. Tighten the bolt to the torque listed in this Chapter's

Specifications.

16   Install the front wheel and lug nuts.

17   Lower the vehicle and tighten the lug nuts to the torque listed in the Chapter 1 Specifications.

18   Connect the pressure and return lines to the steering gear and tighten them securely.

19   The remainder of installation is the reverse of removal.

20   Turn the ignition key Off and connect the negative battery cable(s).

21   Fill the fluid reservoir with the specified fluid and refer to Section 18 for the power steering bleeding procedure.

---

16   Steering linkage - removal and installation

Drag link

Refer to illustrations 16.3a and 16.3b

Removal

1   Raise the front of the vehicle, support it securely on jackstands, block the rear wheels and set the parking brake. Position the front wheels in the straight ahead position.

2   Remove the cotter pins and loosen the nuts securing the drag link at each end.

3   Use a Pitman arm puller (or equivalent) and break loose the drag link from the Pitman arm and the tie-rod (4WD models) or steering knuckle (2WD models) **(see illustrations)**. Remove the nuts and detach the ball-studs.

4   If you're replacing the drag link end, loosen the clamp bolts on the tie-rod adjusting sleeve. Unscrew the drag link end from the adjusting sleeve. Count and record the number of turns it takes to turn the drag link off the sleeve.

Installation

5   Installation is the reverse of the removal procedure. Make sure the ballstuds are seated in the tapers to prevent them from rotating while tightening the nuts to the torque listed in this Chapter's Specifications. Be sure to

install new cotter pins and bend the ends over completely. **Warning:** *If necessary, tighten the nuts a little more to align the slots of the nut with the hole in the ballstud. Never loosen the nut to achieve this alignment.*

6   Tighten the clamp bolts on the tie-rod adjusting sleeve to the torque listed in this Chapter's Specifications, if removed.

7   Have the front end alignment checked and, if necessary, adjusted.

Tie-rod/tie-rod ends

Refer to illustration 16.10

Removal

8   Loosen the front wheel lug nuts on the side to be dismantled. Raise the front of the vehicle, support it securely on jackstands, block the rear wheels and set the parking brake. Remove the front wheel.

9   Remove the cotter pin and loosen the nut on the tie-rod end stud. Discard the cotter pin.

10   Disconnect the tie-rod end from the steering knuckle with a puller **(see illustration)**. If you're working on a 4WD model, detach the drag link from the tie-rod **(see illustration 16.3b)**. Repeat this at the other end of the rod.

16.10 Disconnecting a tie-rod end from the steering knuckle

17.3 A power steering pump pulley removal tool is needed to remove the power steering pump pulley - they're commonly available at most auto parts stores

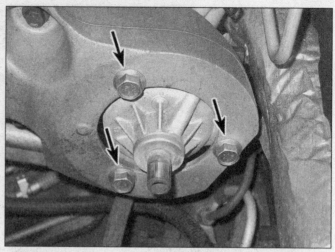

17.6 Power steering pump mounting bolts (diesel model shown, others similar)

11   If you're replacing a tie-rod end, loosen the clamp bolts on the tie-rod adjusting sleeve.

12   Unscrew the tie-rod end from the adjusting sleeve. Count and record the number of turns it takes to back the tie-rod end off the sleeve.

13   Remove the tie-rod end.

Installation

14   Installation is the reverse of the removal procedure. Make sure the ballstuds are seated in the tapers to prevent them from rotating while tightening the nuts to the torque listed in this Chapter's Specifications. Be sure to install new cotter pins and bend the ends over completely. **Warning:** *If necessary, tighten the nuts a little more to align the slots of the nut with the hole in the ballstud. Never loosen the nut to achieve this alignment.*

15   Install the wheel and lug nuts. Lower the vehicle and tighten the lug nuts to the torque listed in the Chapter 1 Specifications.

16   Have the front end alignment checked and, if necessary, adjusted.

17   Power steering pump - removal and installation

Refer to illustrations 17.3, 17.6 and 17.8

Warning: *The manufacturer states that it is necessary to replace the power steering pump pulley with a new one after it has been removed two times. Before removing the pulley, clean the face of the pulley and apply a paint mark to it (if there are two marks, you'll have to obtain a new one).*

Note: *On later models, the power steering pump is located low on the left side of the engine block.*

Removal

1   Disconnect the cable(s) from the negative battery terminal(s). If you're working on a model with a diesel engine, remove the intercooler outlet duct (see Chapter 4).

2   Remove the drivebelt from the power steering pump pulley (see Chapter 1). On later-model 6.0L and 6.4L diesel models remove the fan (refer to Chapter 3).

3   Remove the pulley as follows:

a) *Install a power steering pump pulley removal tool onto the pulley* **(see illustration).**

b) *Hold the large nut with a wrench and rotate the screw nut clockwise, pulling the pulley from the pump.* **Caution:** *Do not apply excessive force on the pulley shaft as it may damage the internal parts of the pump.*

4   Place a container or drip pan under the vehicle to catch the power steering fluid that will inevitably spill when the lines are detached.

5   Disconnect the fluid lines from the pump. Plug the lines and the pump fittings to prevent excessive fluid loss and the entry of contaminants.

6   Remove the bolts securing the pump to the mounting bracket **(see illustration)** and detach the pump from the bracket.

Installation

7   Place the pump in the bracket and install the mounting bolts. Tighten the bolts securely.

8   Install the pulley onto the pump using a special tool **(see illustration).**

9   Install the drivebelt (see Chapter 1).

10   Connect the pressure and return hoses to the proper fittings on the pump. New Teflon® seals should be installed anytime the hoses have been disconnected.

11   Fill the pump reservoir with the specified fluid (see Chapter 1) and bleed the system (see Section 18).

18   Power steering system - bleeding

1   The power steering system must be bled whenever a line is disconnected. Bubbles can be seen in power steering fluid that has air in it and the fluid will often have a milky appearance. Low fluid level can cause air to mix with the fluid, resulting in a noisy pump as well as foaming of the fluid.

17.8 This tool is used to install the power steering pump pulley (available at most auto parts stores)

19.3 Use a press tool such as this to push the
stud out of the flange

19.4 Install a spacer or washers and a lug nut on the stud, then
tighten the nut to draw the stud into place

1 Axle flange	2 Spacer

2   Open the hood and check the fluid level in the reservoir, adding the specified fluid necessary to bring it up to the proper level (see Chapter 1).

3   Start the engine and slowly turn the steering wheel several times from left-to-right and back again. Do not turn the wheel completely from lock-to-lock. Check the fluid level, topping it up as necessary until it remains steady and no more bubbles are visible.

19   Wheel studs - replacement

Refer to illustrations 19.3 and 19.4
Note: *This procedure applies to both the front and rear wheel studs.*
Note: *On some models, you may need to remove the rear axle for clearance.*

1   Loosen the wheel lug nuts, raise the vehicle and support it securely on jackstands. Remove the wheel.

2   Remove the brake disc (see Chapter 9).

3   Push the stud out of the hub flange or axle flange with a press tool **(see illustration)**.

4   Insert the new stud into the hub flange or axle flange from the back side and install some flat washers and a lug nut on the stud **(see illustration)**.

5   Tighten the lug nut until the stud is seated in the flange.

6   Reinstall the disc and caliper (see Chapter 9).

7   Install the wheel and lug nuts. Lower the vehicle and tighten the lug nuts to the torque listed in the Chapter 1 Specifications.

20   Wheels and tires - general information

Refer to illustration 20.1

Most models covered by this manual are equipped with radial tires **(see illustration)**.

Use of other size or type of tires may affect the ride and handling of the vehicle. Don't mix different types of tires, such as radials and bias belted tires, on the same vehicle - handling may be seriously affected. It's recommended that tires be replaced in pairs on the same axle, but if only one tire is being replaced, be sure it's the same size, structure and tread design as the other tire on the same axle.

Because tire pressure has a substantial effect on handling and wear, the pressure of all tires should be checked at least once a month or before any extended trips are taken (see Chapter 1).

Wheels must be replaced if they are bent, dented, leak air, have elongated bolt holes, are heavily rusted, out of vertical symmetry or if the lug nuts won't stay tight. Wheel repairs that use welding or peening are not recommended.

Tire and wheel balance are important to the overall handling, braking and performance of the vehicle. Unbalanced wheels can adversely affect handling and ride characteristics as well as tire life. Whenever a tire is installed on a wheel, the tire and wheel should be balanced by a shop with the proper equipment and expertise.

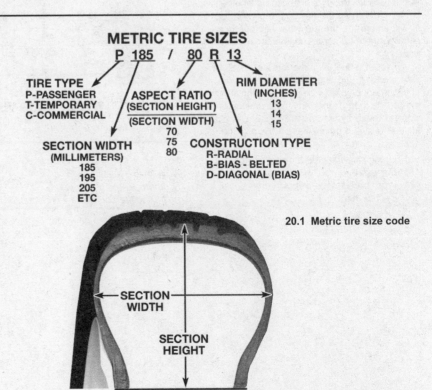

20.1 Metric tire size code

21   Wheel alignment - general information

Refer to illustration 21.1

Note: *Since wheel alignment requires special equipment and techniques it is beyond the scope of this manual. This section is intended only to familiarize the reader with the basic terms used and procedures followed during a typical wheel alignment.*

The three basic checks made when aligning a vehicle's front wheels are camber, caster and toe-in **(see illustration)**.

Camber and caster are the angles at which the wheels and suspension are inclined in relation to a vertical centerline. Camber is the angle of the wheel in the lateral, or side-to-side plane, while caster is the tilt between the steering axis and the vertical plane, as viewed from the side. Camber angle affects the amount of tire tread which contacts the road and compensates for changes in suspension geometry as the vehicle travels around curves and over bumps. Caster angle affects the self-centering action of the steering, which governs straight-line stability. Camber and caster are adjusted by changing or turning an adjuster sleeve in the top of the steering knuckle.

Toe-in is the amount the front wheels are angled in relationship to the center line of the vehicle. For example, in a vehicle with zero toe-in, the distance measured between the front edges of the wheels and the distance measured between the rear edges of the wheels are the same. In other words, the wheels are running parallel with the centerline of the vehicle. Toe-in is adjusted by lengthening or shortening the tie-rods. Incorrect toe-in will cause the tires to wear improperly by allowing them to "scrub" against the road surface.

Proper wheel alignment is essential for safe steering and even tire wear. Symptoms of alignment problems are pulling of the steering to one side or the other and uneven tire wear. If these symptoms are present, check for the following before having the alignment adjusted:

a) *Loose steering gear mounting bolts*
b) *Damaged or worn steering gear mounts*
c) *Worn or damaged wheel bearings*
d) *Bent tie-rods*
e) *Worn balljoints*
f) *Improper tire pressures*
g) *Mixing tires of different construction*

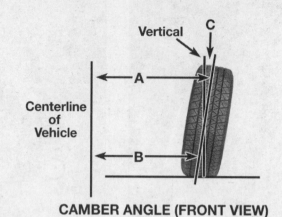

CAMBER ANGLE (FRONT VIEW)

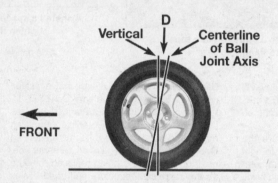

CASTER ANGLE (SIDE VIEW)

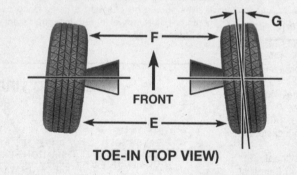

TOE-IN (TOP VIEW)

21.1 Front wheel alignment details

A minus B = C (degrees camber)
D = degrees caster
E minus F = toe-in (measured in inches)
G = toe-in (expressed in degrees)

Front wheel alignment should be left to an alignment shop with the proper equipment and experienced personnel.

Chapter 11
Body

Contents

	Section			Section
Body - maintenance	2	Hood and rear liftgate support struts -		
Body repair - major damage	6	removal and installation		9
Body repair - minor damage	5	Hood latch and release cable - removal and installation		11
Bumpers - removal and installation	13	Instrument cluster bezel - removal and installation		25
Center console - removal and installation	24	Liftgate and cargo doors (Excursion) - removal,		
Cowl cover - removal and installation	28	installation and adjustment		21
Dashboard trim panels - removal and installation	26	Radiator grille - removal and installation		12
Door latch, lock cylinder and handles -		Seats - removal and installation		29
removal and installation	17	Sideview mirrors - removal and installation		20
Door - removal, installation and adjustment	16	Steering column cover - removal and installation		27
Door trim panels - removal and installation	15	Tailgate latch, handle and lock cylinder -		
Door window glass regulator - removal and installation	19	removal and installation		23
Door window glass - removal and installation	18	Tailgate - removal, installation and adjustment		22
Front fender - removal and installation	14	Upholstery and carpets - maintenance		4
General information	1	Vinyl trim - maintenance		3
Hinges and locks - maintenance	7	Windshield and fixed glass - replacement		8
Hood - removal, installation and adjustment	10			

1   General information

These models feature a full-frame construction, using frame side rails which support the body components, front and rear suspension systems and other mechanical components. Certain components are particularly vulnerable to accident damage and can be unbolted and repaired or replaced. Among these parts are the body moldings, bumpers, hood, fenders, doors, tailgate and all glass.

Only general body maintenance practices and body panel repair procedures within the scope of the do-it-yourselfer are included in this Chapter.

2   Body - maintenance

1   The condition of your vehicle's body is very important, because the resale value depends a great deal on it. It's much more difficult to repair a neglected or damaged body than it is to repair mechanical components. The hidden areas of the body, such as the wheel wells, the frame and the engine compartment, are equally important, although they don't require as frequent attention as the rest of the body.

2   Once a year, or every 12,000 miles, it's a good idea to have the underside of the body steam cleaned. All traces of dirt and oil will be removed and the area can then be inspected carefully for rust, damaged brake lines, frayed electrical wires, damaged cables and other problems. The front suspension components should be greased after completion of this job.

3   At the same time, clean the engine and the engine compartment with a steam cleaner or water soluble degreaser.

4   The wheel wells should be given close attention, since undercoating can peel away and stones and dirt thrown up by the tires can cause the paint to chip and flake, allowing rust to set in. If rust is found, clean down to the bare metal and apply an anti-rust paint.

5   The body should be washed about once a week. Wet the vehicle thoroughly to soften the dirt, then wash it down with a soft sponge and plenty of clean soapy water. If the surplus dirt is not washed off very carefully, it can wear down the paint.

6   Spots of tar or asphalt thrown up from the road should be removed with a cloth soaked in solvent.

7   Once every six months, wax the body and chrome trim. If a chrome cleaner is used to remove rust from any of the vehicle's plated parts, remember that the cleaner also removes part of the chrome, so use it sparingly.

3   Vinyl trim - maintenance

Don't clean vinyl trim with detergents, caustic soap or petroleum-based cleaners. Plain soap and water works just fine, with a soft brush to clean dirt that may be ingrained. Wash the vinyl as frequently as the rest of the vehicle.

After cleaning, application of a high quality rubber and vinyl protectant will help prevent oxidation and cracks. The protectant can also be applied to weatherstripping, vacuum lines and rubber hoses (which often fail as a result of chemical degradation) and to the tires.

4   Upholstery and carpets - maintenance

1   Every three months remove the carpets or mats and clean the interior of the vehicle (more frequently if necessary). Vacuum the upholstery and carpets to remove loose dirt and dust.

2   Leather upholstery requires special care. Stains should be removed with warm water and a very mild soap solution. Use a clean, damp cloth to remove the soap, then wipe again with a dry cloth. Never use alcohol, gasoline, nail polish remover or thinner to clean leather upholstery.

3   After cleaning, regularly treat leather upholstery with a leather wax. Never use car wax on leather upholstery.

4   In areas where the interior of the vehicle is subject to bright sunlight, cover leather seats with a sheet if the vehicle is to be left out for any length of time.

5   Body repair - minor damage

See photo sequence

Repair of minor scratches

1   If the scratch is superficial and does not penetrate to the metal of the body, repair is very simple. Lightly rub the scratched area with a fine rubbing compound to remove loose paint and built-up wax. Rinse the area with clean water.

2   Apply touch-up paint to the scratch, using a small brush. Continue to apply thin layers of paint until the surface of the paint in the scratch is level with the surrounding paint. Allow the new paint at least two weeks to harden, then blend it into the surrounding paint by rubbing with a very fine rubbing compound. Finally, apply a coat of wax to the scratch area.

3   If the scratch has penetrated the paint and exposed the metal of the body, causing the metal to rust, a different repair technique is required. Remove all loose rust from the bottom of the scratch with a pocket knife, then apply rust inhibiting paint to prevent the formation of rust in the future. Using a rubber or nylon applicator, coat the scratched area with glaze-type filler. If required, the filler can be mixed with thinner to provide a very thin paste, which is ideal for filling narrow scratches. Before the glaze filler in the scratch hardens, wrap a piece of smooth cotton cloth around the tip of a finger. Dip the cloth in thinner and then quickly wipe it along the surface of the scratch. This will ensure that the surface of the filler is slightly hollow. The scratch can now be painted over as described earlier in this Section.

Repair of dents

4   When repairing dents, the first job is to pull the dent out until the affected area is as close as possible to its original shape. There is no point in trying to restore the original shape completely as the metal in the damaged area will have stretched on impact and cannot be restored to its original contours. It is better to bring the level of the dent up to a point which is about 1/8-inch below the level of the surrounding metal. In cases where the dent is very shallow, it is not worth trying to pull it out at all.

5   If the back side of the dent is accessible, it can be hammered out gently from behind using a soft-face hammer. While doing this, hold a block of wood firmly against the opposite side of the metal to absorb the hammer blows and prevent the metal from being stretched.

6   If the dent is in a section of the body which has double layers, or some other factor makes it inaccessible from behind, a different technique is required. Drill several small holes through the metal inside the damaged area, particularly in the deeper sections. Screw long, self-tapping screws into the holes just enough for them to get a good grip in the metal. Now the dent can be pulled out by pulling on the protruding heads of the screws with locking pliers.

7   The next stage of repair is the removal of paint from the damaged area and from an inch or so of the surrounding metal. This is done with a wire brush or sanding disk in a drill motor, although it can be done just as effectively by hand with sandpaper. To complete the preparation for filling, score the surface of the bare metal with a screwdriver or the tang of a file, or drill small holes in the affected area. This will provide a good grip for the filler material. To complete the repair, see the subsection on filling and painting later in this Section.

Repair of rust holes or gashes

8   Remove all paint from the affected area and from an inch or so of the surrounding metal using a sanding disk or wire brush mounted in a drill motor. If these are not available, a few sheets of sandpaper will do the job just as effectively.

9   With the paint removed, you will be able to determine the severity of the corrosion and decide whether to replace the whole panel, if possible, or repair the affected area. New body panels are not as expensive as most people think and it is often quicker to install a new panel than to repair large areas of rust.

10   Remove all trim pieces from the affected area except those which will act as a guide to the original shape of the damaged body, such as headlight shells, etc. Using metal snips or a hacksaw blade, remove all loose metal and any other metal that is badly affected by rust. Hammer the edges of the hole in to create a slight depression for the filler material.

11   Wire brush the affected area to remove the powdery rust from the surface of the metal. If the back of the rusted area is accessible, treat it with rust inhibiting paint.

12   Before filling is done, block the hole in some way. This can be done with sheet metal riveted or screwed into place, or by stuffing the hole with wire mesh.

13   Once the hole is blocked off, the affected area can be filled and painted. See the following subsection on filling and painting.

Filling and painting

14   Many types of body fillers are available, but generally speaking, body repair kits which contain filler paste and a tube of resin hardener are best for this type of repair work. A wide, flexible plastic or nylon applicator will be necessary for imparting a smooth and contoured finish to the surface of the filler material. Mix up a small amount of filler on a clean piece of wood or cardboard (use the hardener sparingly). Follow the manufacturer's instructions on the package, otherwise the filler will set incorrectly.

15   Using the applicator, apply the filler paste to the prepared area. Draw the applicator across the surface of the filler to achieve the desired contour and to level the filler surface. As soon as a contour that approximates the original one is achieved, stop working the paste. If you continue, the paste will begin to stick to the applicator. Continue to add thin layers of paste at 20-minute intervals until the level of the filler is just above the surrounding metal.

16   Once the filler has hardened, the excess can be removed with a body file. From then on, progressively finer grades of sandpaper should be used, starting with a 180-grit paper

9.2a Use a small screwdriver to pry the clip out of its locking groove, then detach the end of the strut from the locating stud

9.2b Have an assistant support the hood or liftgate before attempting to remove the support strut - pry the clip out, then detach the end of the strut from the locating stud

10.2 Before removing the hood, draw a mark around the hinge plate

and finishing with 600-grit wet-or-dry paper. Always wrap the sandpaper around a flat rubber or wooden block, otherwise the surface of the filler will not be completely flat. During the sanding of the filler surface, the wet-or-dry paper should be periodically rinsed in water. This will ensure that a very smooth finish is produced in the final stage.

17   At this point, the repair area should be surrounded by a ring of bare metal, which in turn should be encircled by the finely feathered edge of good paint. Rinse the repair area with clean water until all of the dust produced by the sanding operation is gone.

18   Spray the entire area with a light coat of primer. This will reveal any imperfections in the surface of the filler. Repair the imperfections with fresh filler paste or glaze filler and once more smooth the surface with sandpaper. Repeat this spray-and-repair procedure until you are satisfied that the surface of the filler and the feathered edge of the paint are perfect. Rinse the area with clean water and allow it to dry completely.

19   The repair area is now ready for painting. Spray painting must be carried out in a warm, dry, windless and dust free atmosphere. These conditions can be created if you have access to a large indoor work area, but if you are forced to work in the open, you will have to pick the day very carefully. If you are working indoors, dousing the floor in the work area with water will help settle the dust which would otherwise be in the air. If the repair area is confined to one body panel, mask off the surrounding panels. This will help minimize the effects of a slight mismatch in paint color. Trim pieces such as chrome strips, door handles, etc., will also need to be masked off or removed. Use masking tape and several thickness of newspaper for the masking operations.

20   Before spraying, shake the paint can thoroughly, then spray a test area until the spray painting technique is mastered. Cover the repair area with a thick coat of primer. The thickness should be built up using several thin layers of primer rather than one thick one. Using 600-grit wet-or-dry sandpaper,

rub down the surface of the primer until it is very smooth. While doing this, the work area should be thoroughly rinsed with water and the wet-or-dry sandpaper periodically rinsed as well. Allow the primer to dry before spraying additional coats.

21   Spray on the top coat, again building up the thickness by using several thin layers of paint. Begin spraying in the center of the repair area and then, using a circular motion, work out until the whole repair area and about two inches of the surrounding original paint is covered. Remove all masking material 10 to 15 minutes after spraying on the final coat of paint. Allow the new paint at least two weeks to harden, then use a very fine rubbing compound to blend the edges of the new paint into the existing paint. Finally, apply a coat of wax.

6   Body repair - major damage

1   Major damage must be repaired by an auto body shop specifically equipped to perform these repairs. Most shops have the specialized equipment required to do the job properly.

2   If the damage is extensive, the body must be checked for proper alignment or the vehicle's handling characteristics may be adversely affected and other components may wear at an accelerated rate.

3   Due to the fact that all of the major body components (hood, fenders, etc.) are separate and replaceable units, any seriously damaged components should be replaced rather than repaired. Sometimes the components can be found in a wrecking yard that specializes in used vehicle components, often at considerable savings over the cost of new parts.

7   Hinges and locks - maintenance

Once every 3000 miles, or every three months, the hinges and latch assemblies on the doors, hood and trunk should be given a

few drops of light oil or lock lubricant. The door latch strikers should also be lubricated with a thin coat of grease to reduce wear and ensure free movement. Lubricate the door and trunk locks with spray-on graphite lubricant.

8   Windshield and fixed glass - replacement

Replacement of the windshield and fixed glass requires the use of special fast-setting adhesive/caulk materials and some specialized tools. It is recommended that these operations be left to a dealer or a shop specializing in glass work.

9   Hood and rear liftgate support struts - removal and installation

Refer to illustrations 9.2a and 9.2b

Note: *The hood and rear liftgate are heavy and somewhat awkward to hold - at least two people should perform this procedure.*

1   Open the hood or rear liftgate (*Excursion only*) and support it securely.

2   Using a small screwdriver, detach the retaining clips at both ends of the support strut. Then pry or pull sharply to detach it from the vehicle **(see illustrations)**.

3   Installation is the reverse of removal.

10   Hood - removal, installation and adjustment

Note: *The hood is heavy and somewhat awkward to remove and install - at least two people should perform this procedure.*

Removal and installation

Refer to illustrations 10.2 and 10.4

1   Use blankets or pads to cover the cowl area of the body and fenders. This will protect the body and paint as the hood is lifted off.

2   Make marks or scribe a line around the hood hinge to ensure proper alignment during installation **(see illustration)**.

These photos illustrate a method of repairing simple dents. They are intended to supplement *Body repair - minor damage* in this Chapter and should not be used as the sole instructions for body repair on these vehicles.

1 If you can't access the backside of the body panel to hammer out the dent, pull it out with a slide-hammer-type dent puller. In the deepest portion of the dent or along the crease line, drill or punch hole(s) at least one inch apart . . .

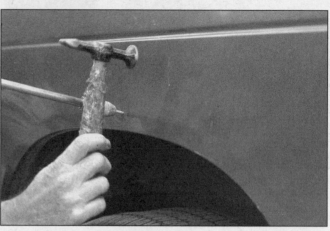

2 . . . then screw the slide-hammer into the hole and operate it. Tap with a hammer near the edge of the dent to help 'pop' the metal back to its original shape. When you're finished, the dent area should be close to its original contour and about 1/8-inch below the surface of the surrounding metal

3 Using coarse-grit sandpaper, remove the paint down to the bare metal. Hand sanding works fine, but the disc sander shown here makes the job faster. Use finer (about 320-grit) sandpaper to feather-edge the paint at least one inch around the dent area

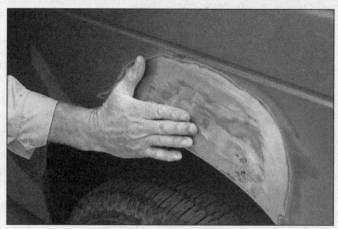

4 When the paint is removed, touch will probably be more helpful than sight for telling if the metal is straight. Hammer down the high spots or raise the low spots as necessary. Clean the repair area with wax/silicone remover

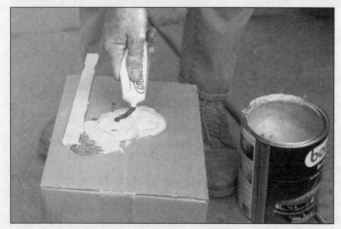

5 Following label instructions, mix up a batch of plastic filler and hardener. The ratio of filler to hardener is critical, and, if you mix it incorrectly, it will either not cure properly or cure too quickly (you won't have time to file and sand it into shape)

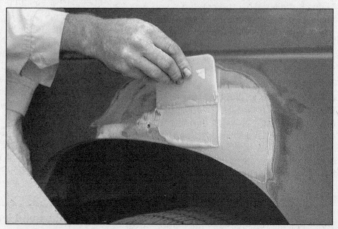

6 Working quickly so the filler doesn't harden, use a plastic applicator to press the body filler firmly into the metal, assuring it bonds completely. Work the filler until it matches the original contour and is slightly above the surrounding metal

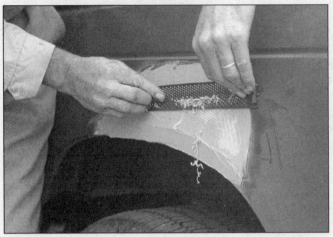

7 Let the filler harden until you can just dent it with your fingernail. Use a body file or Surform tool (shown here) to rough-shape the filler

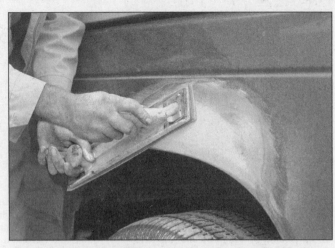

8 Use coarse-grit sandpaper and a sanding board or block to work the filler down until it's smooth and even. Work down to finer grits of sandpaper - always using a board or block - ending up with 360 or 400 grit

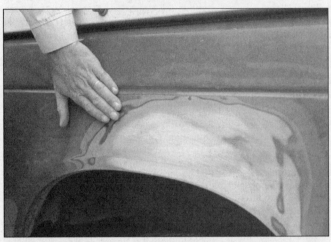

9 You shouldn't be able to feel any ridge at the transition from the filler to the bare metal or from the bare metal to the old paint. As soon as the repair is flat and uniform, remove the dust and mask off the adjacent panels or trim pieces

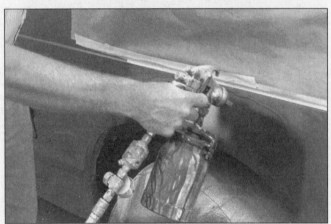

10 Apply several layers of primer to the area. Don't spray the primer on too heavy, so it sags or runs, and make sure each coat is dry before you spray on the next one. A professional-type spray gun is being used here, but aerosol spray primer is available inexpensively from auto parts stores

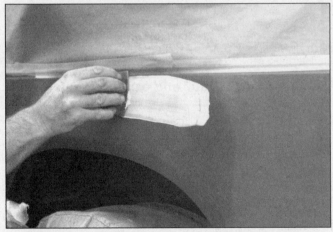

11 The primer will help reveal imperfections or scratches. Fill these with glazing compound. Follow the label instructions and sand it with 360 or 400-grit sandpaper until it's smooth. Repeat the glazing, sanding and respraying until the primer reveals a perfectly smooth surface

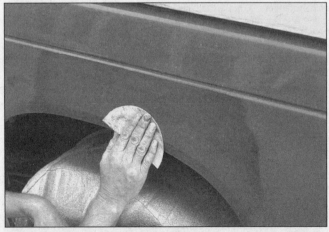

12 Finish sand the primer with very fine sandpaper (400 or 600-grit) to remove the primer overspray. Clean the area with water and allow it to dry. Use a tack rag to remove any dust, then apply the finish coat. Don't attempt to rub out or wax the repair area until the paint has dried completely (at least two weeks)

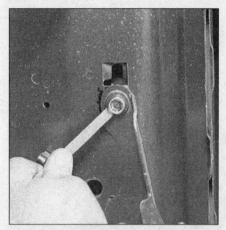

10.4 Remove the hinge-to-hood retaining bolts and lift off the hood with the help of an assistant

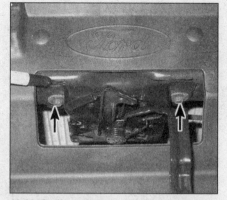

10.10 Scribe a line around the latch to use as a reference point. To adjust the hood latch, loosen the retaining bolts, move the latch and retighten bolts, then close the hood to check the fit

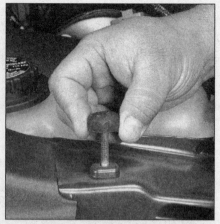

10.11 Adjust the hood closing height by turning the hood bumpers in or out

3 Disconnect any cables or wires that will interfere with removal.
4 Have an assistant support one side of the hood while you support the other. Simultaneously remove the hinge-to-hood bolts **(see illustration)**.
5 Lift off the hood.
6 Installation is the reverse of removal.

Adjustment

Refer to illustrations 10.10 and 10.11
7 Fore-and-aft and side-to-side adjustment of the hood is done by moving the hinge plate slot after loosening the bolts or nuts.
8 Scribe a line around the entire hinge plate so you can determine the amount of movement **(see illustration 10.2)**.
9 Loosen the bolts or nuts and move the hood into correct alignment. Move it only a little at a time. Tighten the hinge bolts and carefully lower the hood to check the position.
10 If necessary after installation, the entire hood latch assembly can be adjusted up-and-down as well as from side-to-side on the radiator support so the hood closes securely and flush with the fenders. To make the adjustment, scribe a line or mark around the hood latch mounting bolts to provide a reference point, then loosen them and reposition the latch assembly, as necessary **(see illustration)**. Following adjustment, retighten the mounting bolts.

11 Finally, adjust the hood bumpers on the radiator support so the hood, when closed, is flush with the fenders **(see illustration)**.
12 The hood latch assembly, as well as the hinges, should be periodically lubricated with white, lithium-base grease to prevent binding and wear.

11 Hood latch and release cable - removal and installation

Latch

1 Scribe a line around the latch to aid alignment when reinstalling the latch assembly.
2 Remove the latch retaining bolts securing the latch to the radiator support **(see illustration 10.10)** and remove the latch.
3 Disconnect the hood release cable by disengaging the cable from the back of the latch assembly.
4 Installation is the reverse of the removal procedure. **Note:** *Adjust the latch so the hood engages securely when closed and the hood bumpers are slightly compressed.*

Cable

5 Remove the hood latch as described earlier in this Section, then detach the cable

from the latch.
6 Working in the passenger compartment, remove the Powertrain Control Module (see Chapter 6) and unbolt the parking brake pedal assembly and pull it toward the center of the vehicle for access to the hood release cable. Detach the cable from the hood release handle.
7 Attach a length of wire to the end of the cable (in the passenger compartment). This will be used to pull the new cable back into the vehicle.
8 Working in the engine compartment, detach the cable from all of its retaining clips. It may be necessary to cut some of the clips to free the cable. Now pull the cable and grommet into the engine compartment, detach the wire from the old cable, then attach it to the handle end of the new cable. **Note:** *Make sure the new cable is equipped with a grommet.*
9 Working inside the vehicle, pull the new cable through the firewall. Move to the engine compartment and seat the grommet in the firewall.
10 The remainder of installation is the reverse of removal.

12 Radiator grille - removal and installation

2007 and earlier models

Refer to illustrations 12.1, 12.2 and 12.3
1 Open the hood and remove the plastic trim panel covering the top of the grille assembly **(see illustration)**.
2 Detach the screws securing the upper half of the radiator grille **(see illustration)**.
3 Remove the clips securing the lower half of the grille and remove the grille from the vehicle **(see illustration)**.
4 Installation is the reverse of removal.

2008 and later models

5 On these models, the radiator grille is actually mounted to the front of the hood, rather than the radiator support panel. When

12.1 Remove retainers (arrows) and detach the plastic trim panel attached between the radiator and the grille

12.2 Remove the upper grille screws (arrows)

12.3 Detach the lower grille clip (arrow)

the hood is opened, the grille comes up with it.

6   Remove the seven pushpins securing the grille at the top. Two are located at the top of the two side grille openings.

7   Open the hood and remove the two bolts on each side securing the grille mounting brackets to the underside of the hood.

8   Installation is the reverse of removal.

13 Bumpers - removal and installation

Caution: *The bumpers are heavy and awkward. Have an assistant help you with removal or installation.*

1   Apply the parking brake, raise the vehicle and support it securely on jackstands.

Front bumper

2   Working under the vehicle, disconnect the fog light electrical connections, if equipped.

3   Working from the backside of the bumper, remove the retaining bolts securing the bumper brackets to each frame rail. Then remove the bumper from the vehicle.

4   Installation is the reverse of removal.

Rear bumper

5   Unplug any electrical connectors which would interfere with bumper removal.

6   Working from the backside of the bumper, remove the retaining bolts securing the bumper brackets to each frame rail. Then remove the bumper from the vehicle.

7   Installation is the reverse of removal.

14 Front fender - removal and installation

Refer to illustration 14.9

1   Open the hood, support it securely with a prop and remove the support strut (see Section 9).

2   Remove the headlight and turn signal housings (see Chapter 12).

3   Remove the radiator grille (see Section 12).

4   Remove the screws retaining the fender inner splash shield.

5   If equipped, remove the running board.

6   Remove the fender-to-rocker panel bolts and retainers. On later models, remove the two pushpins securing the lower rear of the fender at the rocker panel.

7   Remove the bolts retaining the fender to the grille opening. Also remove the fender-to-

radiator support bolts.

8   Open the door and remove the fender-to-door pillar bolts.

9   Remove the remaining fender mounting bolts **(see illustration)**.

10   Detach the fender. It's a good idea to have an assistant support the fender while it's being moved away from the vehicle to prevent damage to the surrounding body panels.

11   Installation is the reverse of removal.

15 Door trim panels - removal and installation

Refer to illustrations 15.3a, 15.3b, 15.3c, 15.4a, 15.4b, 15.6a, 15.6b, and 15.7

1   Disconnect the cable(s) from the negative battery terminal(s) (see Chapter 5, Section 1).

2   On manual window equipped models, pull the window crank cover aside, remove the screw and detach the handle.

3   On the front door of power window equipped models, pry out the front edge of the armrest switch control plate and disconnect the electrical connections, then remove the retaining bolt from the opening **(see illustrations)**. On later models, remove the small

14.9 Remove the bolts (arrows) retaining the top edge of the fender

15.3a Pry up on the retaining clip at the front edge and lift the armrest switch control plate out

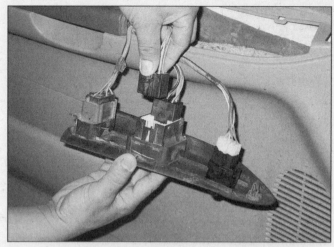

15.3b After detaching the front edge, lift the switch panel out and disconnect the electrical connectors

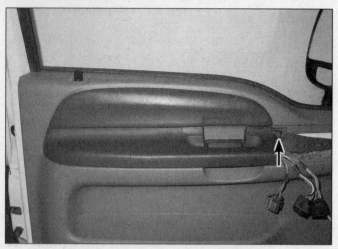

15.3c Remove the trim panel retaining bolt

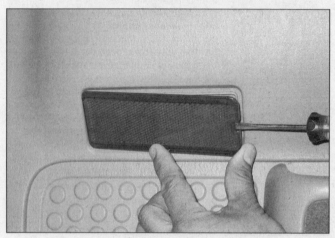

15.4a Using a small screwdriver, pry off the door courtesy light cover . . .

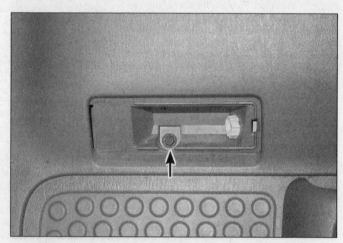

15.4b . . . then remove the door trim panel retaining bolt

cover just below the door pull, and remove the two door panel screws. There are also two screws located at the center/bottom of the door panel.

4 Use a small screwdriver to pry off the courtesy light cover for access to the trim panel retaining bolt (see illustrations).
5 Carefully pry off the mirror trim panel

from above the front edge of the door panel.
6 Once all of the bolts are removed, remove the trim panel by gently pulling it up and out (see illustration). Detach the cour-

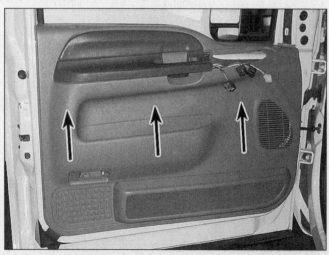

15.6a Lift the trim panel up to disengage the hooks at the top and bottom

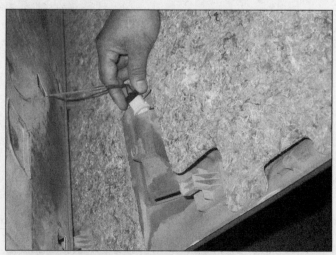

15.6b Lift the trim panel away from the door and remove the light bulb housing

15.7 Carefully peel the watershield from the door

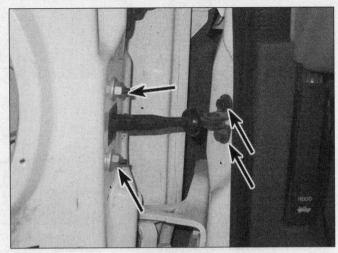

16.6a Remove the door stop retaining bolts and nuts (front doors)

tesy light bulb housing from the panel **(see illustration)**.

7   For access to the inner door components, remove the speaker (if it would interfere with watershield removal) and the screws from the trim piece at the lower trailing corner of the door, then carefully peel the watershield from the door **(see illustration)**.

8   Installation is the reverse of removal.

---

16   Door - removal, installation and adjustment

Note: *The door is heavy and somewhat awkward to remove and install - at least two people should perform this procedure.*

Removal and installation

Refer to illustrations 16.6a, 16.6b and 16.7

1   Raise the window completely in the door and disconnect the cable(s) from the negative battery terminal(s) (see Chapter 5, Section 1).

2   Open the door all the way and support it on jacks covered with rags to prevent damaging the paint.

3   Remove the door trim panel and watershield as described in Section 15.

4   Unplug all electrical connections, ground wires and harness retaining clips from the door. **Note:** *It is a good idea to label all connections to aid the reassembly process.*

5   Working through the door opening, detach the rubber conduit between the body and the door. Then pull the wiring harness through the conduit hole and remove it from the door.

6   On all front doors and Excursion/Crew Cab rear doors, mark around the door hinges with a marking pen or scribe to facilitate alignment during reassembly, then remove the bolts securing the door stop **(see illustration)**. With an assistant supporting the door, remove the hinge-to-door bolts and remove the door **(see illustration)**.

7   On Super Cab pick-up rear doors, mark around the door hinges with a pen or scribe to facilitate realignment during reassembly. With an assistant supporting the door, remove the hinge-to-body bolts and nuts **(see illustration)**.

8   Installation is the reverse of the removal.

Adjustment

Refer to illustrations 16.12a, 16.12b and 16.12c

9   Having proper door-to-body alignment is a critical part of a well functioning door assembly. First check the door hinge pins for excessive play. Fully open the door and lift up and down on the door without lifting the body. If a door has 1/16-inch or more excessive play, the hinges should be replaced.

10   Door-to-body alignment adjustments are made by loosening the hinge-to-body or hinge-to-door bolts and moving the door. Proper body alignment is achieved when the top of the door is aligned with the top of the front fender and rear door or quarter panel and the bottom of the door is aligned with the lower rocker panel. If these goals can't be reached by adjusting the hinge-to-body or hinge-to-door bolts, body alignment shims may have to be purchased and inserted behind the hinges to achieve correct alignment.

11   To adjust the door closed position, first check that the door latch is contacting the center of the latch striker. If not, remove the striker and add or subtract shims to achieve correct alignment.

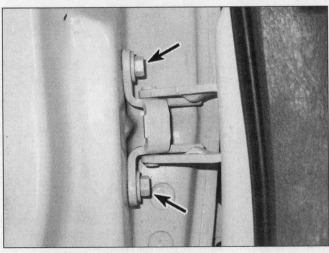

16.6b Front door hinge-to-door bolts (lower shown)

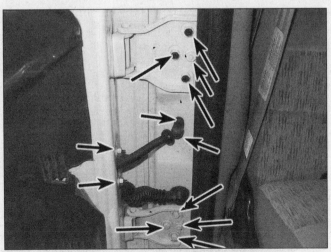

16.7 Super Cab rear door stop and hinge fasteners

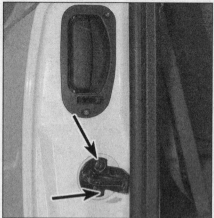

16.12a Adjust the door lock striker by loosening the mounting screws and gently tapping the striker in the desired direction

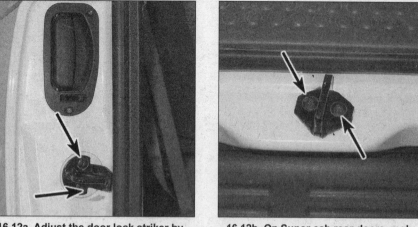

16.12b On Super cab rear doors, make adjustments by loosening the mounting screws and tapping in the desired direction gently on both the lower striker . . .

16.12c . . . and the upper striker

12   Finally adjust the latch striker as necessary to provide positive engagement with the latch mechanism **(see illustrations)** and so

the door panel is flush with the rear door or quarter panel.

17   Door latch, lock cylinder and handles - removal and installation

Door latch

Refer to illustration 17.2

1   Raise the window then remove the door trim panel and watershield as described in Section 15.
2   Remove the screws securing the latch to the door **(see illustration)**.
3   Working through the large access hole, position the latch as necessary to disconnect the electrical connector and disengage the outside door handle and outside lock cylinder to latch rods and the inside handle-to-latch cable.
4   Detach the locking rods by unsnapping the portion of the plastic clip engaging the connecting rod, then pulling the rod out of its

locating hole.
5   Position the latch as necessary to disengage the door lock actuator hook. Detach the cable cover and disconnect the cable from the latch. Remove the latch assembly from the door.
6   Installation is the reverse of removal.

Outside handle and door lock cylinder

Refer to illustrations 17.8a, 17.8b, 17.9 and 17.12

7   To remove the outside handle and door lock cylinder assembly, raise the window and remove the door trim panel and watershield as described in Section 15.
8   Remove the rubber plug in the end of the door and remove upper outside handle retaining nut **(see illustration)**. Working through the large access hole remove the upper retaining nut **(see illustration)**.
9   Pull the handle and lock cylinder assembly from the door and disengage the plastic clips that secure the lock cylinder to latch rod and door handle to latch rod **(see illustration)**.
10   Flip up the cover and disconnect the cable from the handle assembly.
11   Disconnect any electrical connectors

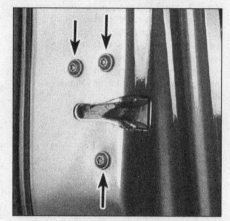

17.2 Remove the latch retaining screws from the end of the door, then detach the locking rods and cable and pull the latch assembly through the access hole

17.8a Remove the rubber plug for access to the outside handle upper retaining nut

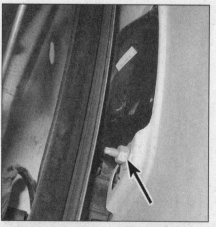

17.8b The remaining outside handle retaining nut can be reached through the access hole in the door frame

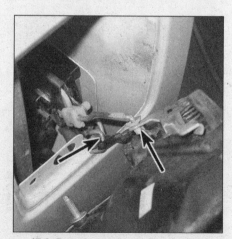

17.9 Detach the two outside handle latch rods

which would interfere with removal.

12   To remove the lock cylinder from the handle assembly, detach the clip and withdraw the cylinder **(see illustration)**.

13   Installation is the reverse of removal.

Inside handle and cable

Refer to illustration 17.15

14   Remove the door trim panel and watershield as described in Section 15.

15   Remove the nuts securing the inside handle **(see illustration)**. Pull rearward on the handle to disengage it from the inner door panel.

16   Detach the latch rod from the backside of the handle and remove it from the vehicle.

17   Installation is the reverse of removal.

18   Door window glass - removal and installation

Refer to illustrations 18.2 and 18.4

1   Remove the door trim panel and the watershield (see Section 15).

2   Lower the window glass for access to the glass retaining nuts and remove the nuts **(see illustration)**.

17.12 Remove the clips, detach the lock cylinder lever and withdraw the cylinder from the handle assembly

3   Carefully pry the inner and outer weatherstripping out of the door window opening.

4   Loosen the rear glass run bolt **(see illustration)**.

5   Slide the glass channel forward to detach it from the glass, then lower the glass to the bottom of the door.

6   Remove the glass by tilting it forward,

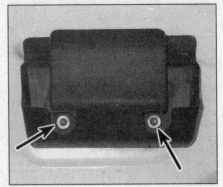

17.15 Remove the two inner door handle retaining nuts

then lifting it out of the door.

7   Installation is the reverse of removal.

19   Door window glass regulator - removal and installation

Refer to illustration 19.4

Warning: *The regulator arms are under extreme pressure and can cause serious injury if the motor is removed without locking the sector gear. This can be done by inserting a bolt and nut through the holes in the backing plate and sector gear to lock them together.*

1   Remove the door trim panel and the plastic watershield (see Section 15).

2   Detach the window glass from the regulator (see Section 18). Push it up all the way and tape it to the top of the door frame.

3   On power-operated windows, disconnect the electrical connector from the window regulator motor.

4   Remove the regulator retaining bolts **(see illustration)**.

5   Pull the regulator assembly through the service hole in the door frame to remove it.

6   Installation is the reverse of removal.

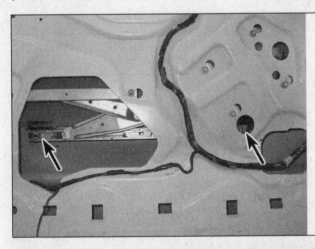

18.2 Raise the window just enough to access the glass retaining nuts through the holes in the door frame - remove the nuts securing the glass to the equalizer arm

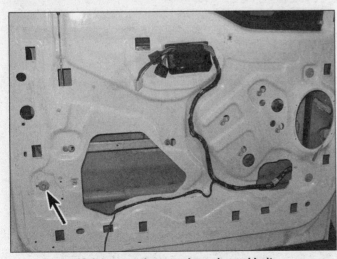

18.4 Loosen the rear glass channel bolt

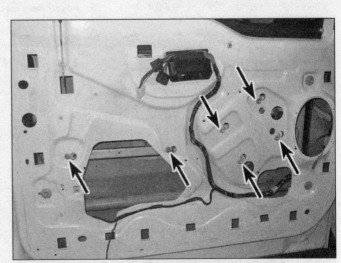

19.4 Remove the bolts securing the window regulator to the door frame

20   Sideview mirrors - removal and installation

1   Remove the mirror trim cover above the front of the door panel.
2   If you're working on a model with electric mirrors, remove the door trim panel and the watershield (see Section 15). Follow the harness and disconnect the electrical connector from the mirror.
3   Remove the dust shield and rubber plugs for access, then remove the mirror retaining nuts and detach the mirror from the vehicle.
4   Installation is the reverse of removal.

21   Liftgate and cargo doors (Excursion) - removal, installation and adjustment

Liftgate

Note: *The liftgate is heavy and somewhat awkward to hold - at least two people should perform this procedure.*

Removal and installation

Refer to illustration 21.4
1   Open the liftgate and support it securely.
2   Remove the liftgate trim panels and disconnect the washer hose and all wiring harness connectors leading to the liftgate. Pull the harness through the liftgate.
3   While an assistant supports the liftgate, remove the support struts (see Section 9).
4   Detach the hinge-to-liftgate bolts and remove the liftgate from the vehicle **(see illustration)**.
5   Installation is the reverse of removal.

Adjustment

Refer to illustration 21.7
6   Adjustments are made by loosening the hinge-to-liftgate bolts and moving the liftgate. Proper alignment is achieved when the edges

21.4 Remove the hinge bolts to remove the liftgate

of the liftgate are parallel with the rear quarter panel and the top of the cargo doors.
7   Finally, adjust the latch striker assembly as necessary (up and down) to provide positive engagement with the latch mechanism **(see illustration)**.

Cargo doors
Removal and installation

Refer to illustrations 21.10 and 21.11
8   Open the door all the way and support it on jacks or blocks covered with rags to prevent damaging the paint.
9   Remove the trim panel and disconnect all electrical connectors in the wiring harness to the cargo door, then pull the harness through the door.
10   Remove the bolts securing the door stop **(see illustration)**.
11   Mark around the door hinges with a pen or scribe to facilitate realignment during reassembly. With an assistant supporting the door, remove the bolts/nuts and detach the doors **(see illustration).**
12   Installation is the reverse of removal.

Adjustment

13   Adjustments are made by loosening the

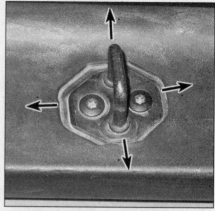

21.7 If the liftgate does not close properly, it will be necessary to loosen the screws to adjust the striker plate in the desired direction

hinge-to-cargo door bolts and moving the liftgate. Proper alignment is achieved when the edges of the cargo doors are parallel with the rear quarter panel and the bottom of the tailgate.
14   Finally, adjust the latch striker assembly as necessary (up and down) to provide positive engagement with the latch mechanism.

22   Tailgate - removal, installation and adjustment

Note: *The tailgate is heavy and somewhat awkward to remove and install - at least two people should perform this procedure.*

Removal and installation

Refer to illustration 22.3
1   Open the tailgate.
2   Cover the lower bumper area around the opening with pads or cloths to protect the painted surfaces when the tailgate is removed.
3   While an assistant supports the tailgate, detach the tailgate support cables **(see illustration)**.

21.10 Remove the two bolts and detach the door stop

21.11 Remove the hinge fasteners to remove the cargo door

22.3 Pry up the clip and detach the tailgate support cable from the striker

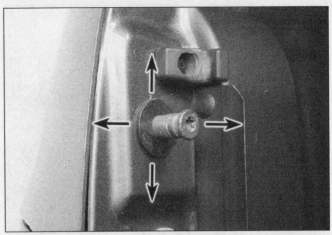

22.7 Loosen the striker and adjust as necessary to provide positive latch engagement

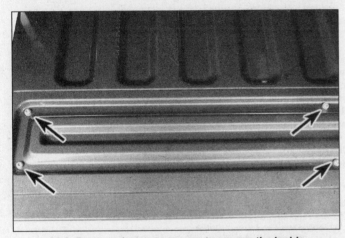

23.1 Remove the cover screws to access the inside of the tailgate (typical)

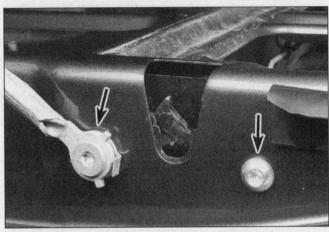

23.2 Remove the tailgate latch retaining screws (arrows)

4   With the help of your assistant, raise the tailgate half-way up, then pull the left side off its hinge, followed by the right side. Remove the tailgate.

5   Installation is the reverse of removal.

Adjustment

Refer to illustration 22.7

6   To adjust the tailgate closed position, first check that the latch is contacting the center of the latch striker. If not, remove the striker and add or subtract shims to achieve correct alignment.

7   Finally, adjust the latch striker assembly as necessary (up and down or sideways) to provide positive engagement with the latch mechanism and the outside of the tailgate is flush with rear or the bed **(see illustration)**.

23 Tailgate latch, handle and lock cylinder - removal and installation

Refer to illustrations 23.1, 23.2 and 23.5

1   Lower the tailgate and remove the tailgate access cover **(see illustration)**.

Latch

2   Remove the latch mounting screws **(see illustration)**. It may be necessary to use an impact-driver to loosen them.

3   Disconnect the control rods from the latch and remove the latch from the door.

4   Installation is the reverse of removal.

Handle and lock cylinder

5   Disconnect the control rods **(see illustration)**.

6   Detach the retaining nuts and remove the handle and lock cylinder assembly from the tailgate.

7   Installation is the reverse of removal.

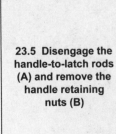

23.5 Disengage the handle-to-latch rods (A) and remove the handle retaining nuts (B)

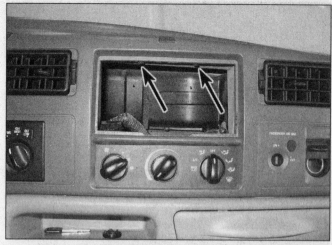

25.3 Loosen the two instrument cluster bezel screws

25.4 Detach the instrument cluster bezel from the instrument panel (clips engage with the slots around the perimeter of the instrument panel)

24 Center console - removal and installation

Warning 1: *These models are equipped with airbags. Always disable the airbag system before working in the vicinity of any airbag system component to avoid the possibility of accidental deployment of the airbag(s), which could cause personal injury (see Chapter 12).*
Warning 2: *Do not use a memory saving device to preserve the ECM's memory when working on or near airbag system components.*

1 Disconnect the cable(s) from the negative battery terminal(s) (see Chapter 5, Section 1).
2 Open the console glove box and remove the storage compartment for access to the retaining screws.
3 Remove the retaining screws securing the console to the floor and slide it rearward to detach it from the bracket.
4 Disconnect any electrical connections and remove the console from the vehicle.
5 Installation is the reverse of removal.

25 Instrument cluster bezel - removal and installation

2005 and earlier models

Refer to illustrations 25.3, 25.4 and 25.5

Warning 1: *These models are equipped with airbags. Always disable the airbag system before working in the vicinity of any airbag system component to avoid the possibility of accidental deployment of the airbag(s), which could cause personal injury (see Chapter 12).*
Warning 2: *Do not use a memory saving device to preserve the ECM's memory when working on or near airbag system components.*

1 Disconnect the cable(s) from the negative battery terminal(s) (see Chapter 5, Section 1).

2 Remove the radio (see Chapter 12).
3 Loosen the two screws in the radio opening **(see illustration)**.
4 Use a screwdriver to carefully detach the bezel retaining clips **(see illustration)**.
5 Pull the bezel back, disconnect the electrical connectors and remove the bezel from the vehicle **(see illustration)**.
6 Installation is the reverse of removal.

2006 and later models

7 If equipped with tilt steering, lower the steering wheel.
8 On 2006 and 2007 models, use a plastic trim tool around the top of the instrument cluster bezel until the clips are released, then remove the bezel.
9 On 2008 and later models, remove the two screw covers (on either side of the radio) and the two screws securing the upper/center instrument panel trim panel.
10 Carefully pull rearward on the upper/center panel to release the clips. Remove the upper/center panel.
11 Remove the driver's knee bolster to access the four cluster screws.
12 Pull the instrument cluster bezel out, dis-

connecting any electrical connectors behind it.
13 Installation is the reverse of removal.

26 Dashboard trim panels - removal and installation

Warning 1: *These models are equipped with airbags. Always disable the airbag system before working in the vicinity of any airbag system component to avoid the possibility of accidental deployment of the airbag(s), which could cause personal injury (see Chapter 12).*
Warning 2: *Do not use a memory saving device to preserve the ECM's memory when working on or near airbag system components.*

Center trim panel

1 Disconnect the cable(s) from the negative battery terminal(s) (see Chapter 5, Section 1).
2 Remove the instrument cluster bezel (see Section 25).
3 Remove the retaining screws and detach the utility hook.
4 Open the ashtray/cup holder for access,

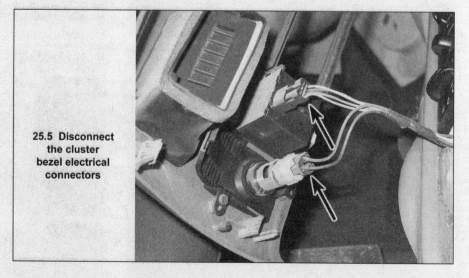

25.5 Disconnect the cluster bezel electrical connectors

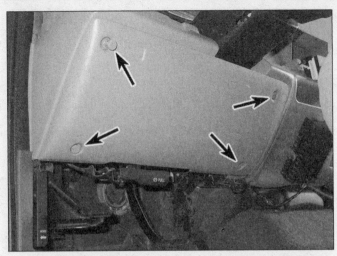

26.7 Loosen the plastic retainers securing the knee bolster

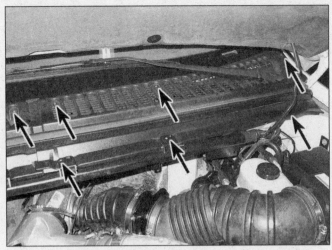

28.3 Remove the cowl cover retaining screws and pushpins - the pins at the outer ends are locating pins and aren't removable (left side shown, right side similar)

then remove the screws and remove the ash-tray/cup holder assembly.

5   Remove the four screws retaining the trim panel to the instrument panel and detach trim panel.

6   Installation is the reverse of removal.

Knee bolster

Refer to illustration 26.7

7   Use a screwdriver to release the four retainers by turning them 1/4-turn **(see illustration)**.

8   Detach the knee bolster.

9   Installation is the reverse of removal.

Glove box

10   Open the glove box door. Press inward on the door stops to release the upper half of the glove box.

11   Remove the door hinge screws and detach the glove box.

12   Installation is the reverse of removal.

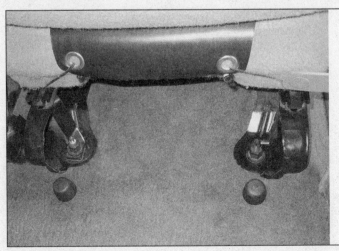

29.2 On some models you will have to detach the trim covers to access the seat retaining bolts

27   Steering column cover - removal and installation

1   Remove the knee bolster (see Section 26).

2   Remove the key lock cylinder (see Chapter 12).

3   Remove the screws from the lower steering column cover.

4   Separate the cover halves and detach them from the steering column.

5   Installation is the reverse of removal.

28   Cowl cover - removal and installation

Refer to illustrations 28.3

1   Remove the windshield wiper arms (see Chapter 12).

2   Remove the antenna (see Chapter 12).

3   Remove the screws and clips securing the left hand and right hand cowl covers and weatherstrips **(see illustration)**.

4   Disconnect the windshield washer hose.

5   Installation is the reverse of removal.

29   Seats - removal and installation

Warning 1: *Some models are equipped with seat belt pre-tensioners, which are pyrotechnic (explosive) devices that tighten the seat belts during an impact of sufficient force. Always disable the airbag system before working in the vicinity of any restraint system component to avoid the possibility of accidental deployment of the airbag(s) and seat belt pre-tensioners, which could cause personal injury* (see Chapter 12).

Warning 2: *Do not use a memory saving device to preserve the ECM's memory when working on or near restraint system components.*

Front seat

Refer to illustration 29.2

1   Position the seat all the way forward and all the way to the rear to access the front seat retaining bolts.

2   Detach any bolt trim covers and remove the retaining bolts **(see illustration)**.

3   Tilt the seat upward to access the underneath, then disconnect any electrical connectors and lift the seat from the vehicle.

4   Installation is the reverse of removal.

Rear seat

5   Remove the seat-to-floor mounting bolts, then detach the seat and lift it out of the vehicle.

6   Installation is the reverse of removal.

Notes

Chapter 12
Chassis electrical system

Contents

	Section		Section
Airbag system - general information	25	Ignition switch and key lock cylinder - replacement	8
Antenna and cable - replacement	13	Instrument cluster - removal and installation	10
Bulb replacement	19	Instrument panel switches - replacement	9
Circuit breakers - general information	4	Power door lock system - description	23
Cruise control system - description	21	Power window system - description	22
Daytime Running Lights (DRL) - general information	24	Radio and speakers - removal and installation	12
Electric side view mirrors - description	20	Rear window defogger - check and repair	14
Electrical troubleshooting - general information	2	Relays - general information and testing	5
Fuses and fusible links - general information	3	SERVICE ENGINE SOON light	See Chapter 6
General information	1	Steering column switches - replacement	7
Headlight housing (halogen bulb type) - replacement	17	Turn signal and hazard flasher - check and replacement	6
Headlights - adjustment	16	Wiper motor - check and replacement	11
Headlight bulb - replacement	15	Wiring diagrams - general information	26
Horn - replacement	18		

1   General information

The electrical system is a 12-volt, negative ground type. Power for the lights and all electrical accessories is supplied by a lead/acid-type battery which is charged by the alternator.

This Chapter covers repair and service procedures for the various electrical components not associated with the engine. Information on the battery, alternator, distributor and starter motor can be found in Chapter 5.

It should be noted that when portions of the electrical system are serviced, the negative battery cable(s) should be disconnected from the battery(ies) to prevent electrical shorts and/or fires.

2   Electrical troubleshooting - general information

Refer to illustrations 2.5a, 2.5b, 2.6 and 2.9

A typical electrical circuit consists of an electrical component, any switches, relays, motors, fuses, fusible links or circuit breakers related to that component and the wiring and connectors that link the component to both the battery and the chassis. To help you pinpoint an electrical circuit problem, wiring diagrams are included at the end of this Chapter.

Before tackling any troublesome electrical circuit, first study the appropriate wiring diagrams to get a complete understanding of what makes up that individual circuit. Trouble spots, for instance, can often be narrowed down by noting if other components related to the circuit are operating properly. If several components or circuits fail at one time, chances are the problem is in a fuse or ground connection, because several circuits are often routed through the same fuse and ground connections.

Electrical problems usually stem from simple causes, such as loose or corroded connections, a blown fuse, a melted fusible link or a failed relay. Visually inspect the condition of all fuses, wires and connections in a problem circuit before troubleshooting the circuit.

If test equipment and instruments are going to be utilized, use the diagrams to plan ahead of time where you will make the necessary connections in order to accurately pinpoint the trouble spot.

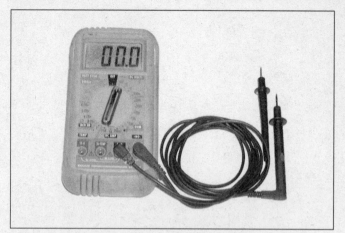

2.5a The most useful tool for electrical troubleshooting is a digital multimeter that can check volts, amps, and test continuity

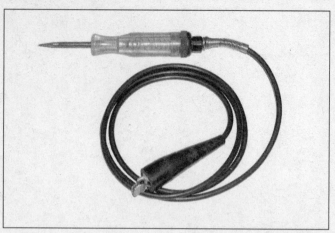

2.5b A simple test light is a very handy tool for testing voltage

The basic tools needed for electrical troubleshooting include a circuit tester or voltmeter (a 12-volt bulb with a set of test leads can also be used), a continuity tester, which includes a bulb, battery and set of test leads, and a jumper wire, preferably with a circuit breaker incorporated, which can be used to bypass electrical components **(see illustrations)**. Before attempting to locate a problem with test instruments, use the wiring diagram(s) to decide where to make the connections.

Voltage checks

Voltage checks should be performed if a circuit is not functioning properly. Connect one lead of a circuit tester to either the negative battery terminal or a known good ground. Connect the other lead to a connector in the circuit being tested, preferably nearest to the battery or fuse **(see illustration)**. If the bulb of the tester lights, voltage is present, which means that the part of the circuit between the connector and the battery is problem free. Continue checking the rest of the circuit in the same fashion. When you reach a point at

which no voltage is present, the problem lies between that point and the last test point with voltage. Most of the time the problem can be traced to a loose connection. **Note:** *Keep in mind that some circuits receive voltage only when the ignition key is in the Accessory or Run position.*

Finding a short

One method of finding shorts in a live circuit is to remove the fuse and connect a test light in place of the fuse terminals (fabricate two jumper wires with small spade terminals, plug the jumper wires into the fuse box and connect the test light). There should be voltage present in the circuit. Move the suspected wiring harness from side-to-side while watching the test light. If the bulb goes off, there is a short to ground somewhere in that area, probably where the insulation has rubbed through.

Ground check

Perform a ground test to check whether a component is properly grounded. Disconnect the battery and connect one lead of

a continuity tester or multimeter (set to the ohms scale), to a known good ground. Connect the other lead to the wire or ground connection being tested. If the resistance is low (less than 5 ohms), the ground is good. If the bulb on a self-powered test light does not go on, the ground is not good.

Continuity check

A continuity check is done to determine if there are any breaks in a circuit - if it is passing electricity properly. With the circuit off (no power in the circuit), a self-powered continuity tester or multimeter can be used to check the circuit. Connect the test leads to both ends of the circuit (or to the "power" end and a good ground), and if the test light comes on the circuit is passing current properly **(see illustration)**. If the resistance is low (less than 5 ohms), there is continuity; if the reading is 10,000 ohms or higher, there is a break somewhere in the circuit. The same procedure can be used to test a switch, by connecting the continuity tester to the switch terminals. With the switch turned On, the test light should

2.6 In use, a basic test light's lead is clipped to a known good ground, then the pointed probe can test connectors, wires or electrical sockets - if the bulb lights, the circuit being tested has battery voltage

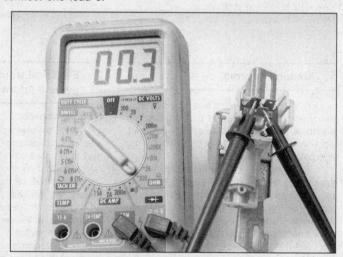

2.9 With a multimeter set to the ohms scale, resistance can be checked across two terminals - when checking for continuity, a low reading indicates continuity, a high reading or infinity indicates high resistance or lack of continuity

3.1a The fuse/relay box is mounted to the left inner fenderwell in the engine compartment - it contains miniaturized fuses, cartridge-type fusible links, relays and circuit breakers

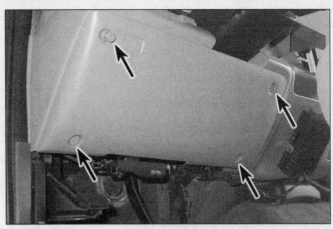

3.1b Remove the fuse panel cover below the steering column for access to the fuse block (turn the fasteners counterclockwise to release them)

come on (or low resistance should be indicated on a meter).

Finding an open circuit

When diagnosing for possible open circuits, it is often difficult to locate them by sight because the connectors hide oxidation or terminal misalignment. Merely wiggling a connector on a sensor or in the wiring harness may correct the open circuit condition. Remember this when an open circuit is indicated when troubleshooting a circuit. Intermittent problems may also be caused by oxidized or loose connections.

Electrical troubleshooting is simple if you keep in mind that all electrical circuits are basically electricity running from the battery, through the wires, switches, relays, fuses and fusible links to each electrical component (light bulb, motor, etc.) and to ground, from which it is passed back to the battery. Any electrical problem is an interruption in the flow of electricity to and from the battery.

Connectors

Most electrical connections on these vehicles are made with multiwire plastic con-nectors. The mating halves of many connectors are secured with locking clips molded into the plastic connector shells. The mating halves of large connectors, such as some of those under the instrument panel, are held together by a bolt through the center of the connector.

To separate a connector with locking clips, use a small screwdriver to pry the clips apart carefully, then separate the connector halves. Pull only on the shell, never pull on the wiring harness as you may damage the individual wires and terminals inside the connectors. Look at the connector closely before trying to separate the halves. Often the locking clips are engaged in a way that is not immediately clear. Additionally, many connectors have more than one set of clips.

Each pair of connector terminals has a male half and a female half. When you look at the end view of a connector in a diagram, be sure to understand whether the view shows the harness side or the component side of the connector. Connector halves are mirror images of each other, and a terminal shown on the right side end view of one half will be on the left side end view of the other half.

3 Fuses and fusible links - general information

Fuses

Refer to illustrations 3.1a, 3.1b, 3.1c and 3.3

The electrical circuits of the vehicle are protected by a combination of fuses, circuit breakers and fusible links. Fuse blocks are located under the instrument panel and in the engine compartment **(see illustrations)**. **Note:** *On 2002 models, the auxiliary fuse block is located behind the glovebox.*

Each of the fuses is designed to protect a specific circuit, and the various circuits are identified on the fuse panel cover.

Miniaturized fuses are employed in the fuse blocks. These compact fuses, with blade terminal design, allow fingertip removal and replacement. If an electrical component fails, always check the fuse first. The best way to check a fuse is with a test light. Check for power at the exposed terminal tips of each fuse. If power is present on one side of the fuse but not the other, the fuse is blown. A blown fuse can also be confirmed by visually inspecting it **(see illustration)**.

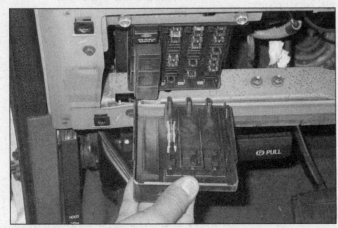

3.1c The passenger compartment fuse block is located under the drivers side of the instrument panel, behind the fuse panel cover

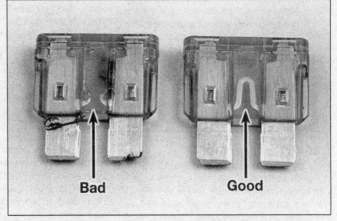

3.3 When a fuse blows, the element between the terminals melts - the fuse on the left is blown, the fuse on the right is good

Be sure to replace blown fuses with the correct type. Fuses of different ratings are physically interchangeable, but only fuses of the proper rating should be used. Replacing a fuse with one of a higher or lower value than specified is not recommended. Each electrical circuit needs a specific amount of protection. The amperage value of each fuse is molded into the fuse body.

If the replacement fuse immediately fails, don't replace it again until the cause of the problem is isolated and corrected. In most cases, this will be a short circuit in the wiring caused by a broken or deteriorated wire.

Fusible links

Some circuits are protected by fusible links. The links are used in circuits which are not ordinarily fused, or which carry high current.

Cartridge type fusible links are located in the engine compartment fusible link box and are similar to a large fuse. After disconnecting the negative battery cable(s), simply unplug and replace a fusible link with one of the same amperage.

4   Circuit breakers - general information

Circuit breakers protect certain circuits, such as the power windows or heated seats. Depending on the vehicle's accessories, there may be one or two circuit breakers, located in the fuse/relay box in the engine compartment **(see illustration 3.1a)**.

Because the circuit breakers reset automatically, an electrical overload in a circuit-breaker-protected system will cause the circuit to fail momentarily, then come back on. If the circuit does not come back on, check it immediately.

For a basic check, pull the circuit breaker up out of its socket on the fuse panel, but just far enough to probe with a voltmeter. The breaker should still contact the sockets.

With the voltmeter negative lead on a good chassis ground, touch each end prong of the circuit breaker with the positive meter probe. There should be battery voltage at each end. If there is battery voltage only at one end, the circuit breaker must be replaced.

Some circuit breakers must be reset manually.

5   Relays - general information and testing

General information

1   Several electrical accessories in the vehicle, such as the fuel injection system, horns, starter, and fog lamps use relays to transmit the electrical signal to the component. Relays use a low-current circuit (the control circuit) to open and close a high-current circuit (the

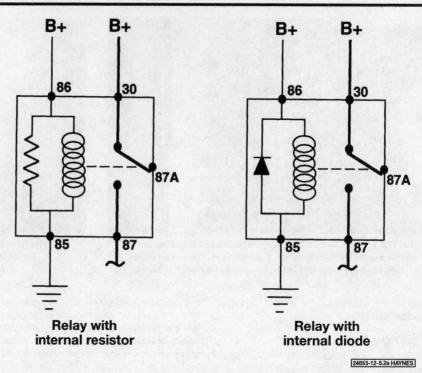

Relay with internal resistor   **Relay with internal diode**

`24053-12-5.2a HAYNES`

5.2a Typical ISO relay designs, terminal numbering and circuit connections

power circuit). If the relay is defective, that component will not operate properly. Most relays are mounted in the engine compartment fuse/relay box, with some specialized relays located above the interior fuse box in the dash **(see illustrations 3.1a and 3.1c)**. If a faulty relay is suspected, it can be removed and tested using the procedure below or by a dealer service department or a repair shop. Defective relays must be replaced as a unit.

Testing

Refer to illustrations 5.2a and 5.2b

2   Most of the relays used in these vehicles are of a type often called "ISO" relays, which refers to the International Standards Organization. The terminals of ISO relays are numbered to indicate their usual circuit connections and functions. There are two basic layouts of terminals on the relays used in these vehicles **(see illustrations)**.

3   Refer to the wiring diagram for the circuit to determine the proper connections for the relay you're testing. If you can't determine the correct connection from the wiring diagrams, however, you may be able to determine the test connections from the information that follows.

4   Two of the terminals are the relay control circuit and connect to the relay coil. The other relay terminals are the power circuit. When the relay is energized, the coil creates a magnetic field that closes the larger contacts of the power circuit to provide power to the circuit loads.

5   Terminals 85 and 86 are normally the control circuit. If the relay contains a diode,

5.2b Most relays are marked on the outside to easily identify the control circuits and the power circuits - four terminal type shown

terminal 86 must be connected to battery positive (B+) voltage and terminal 85 to ground. If the relay contains a resistor, terminals 85 and 86 can be connected in either direction with respect to B+ and ground.

6   Terminal 30 is normally connected to the battery voltage (B+) source for the circuit loads. Terminal 87 is connected to the ground side of the circuit, either directly or through a load. If the relay has several alternate terminals for load or ground connections, they usually are numbered 87A, 87B, 87C, and so on.

7   Use an ohmmeter to check continuity through the relay control coil.

a) Connect the meter according to the polarity shown in the illustration for one check; then reverse the ohmmeter leads and check continuity in the other direction.

6.1 The electronic flasher unit is mounted to the right of the steering column under the instrument panel

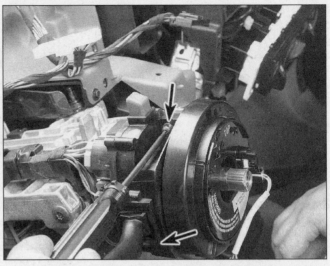

7.3a Remove the retaining screws (arrows) and . . .

b) *If the relay contains a resistor, resistance will be indicated on the meter, and should be the same value with the ohmmeter in either direction.*

c) *If the relay contains a diode, resistance should be higher with the ohmmeter in the forward polarity direction than with the meter leads reversed.*

d) *If the ohmmeter shows infinite resistance in both directions, replace the relay.*

8   Remove the relay from the vehicle and use the ohmmeter to check for continuity between the relay power circuit terminals. There should be no continuity between terminal 30 and 87 with the relay de-energized.

9   Connect a fused jumper wire to terminal 86 and the positive battery terminal. Connect another jumper wire between terminal 85 and ground. When the connections are made, the relay should click.

10   With the jumper wires connected, check for continuity between the power circuit terminals. Now, there should be continuity between terminals 30 and 87.

11   If the relay fails any of the above tests, replace it.

6   Turn signal and hazard flasher - check and replacement

Refer to illustration 6.1

Warning: *The models covered by this manual are equipped with Supplemental Restraint systems (SRS), more commonly known as airbags. Always disconnect the negative battery cable(s) and wait two minutes before working in the vicinity of any airbag system component to avoid the possibility of accidental deployment of the airbag, which could cause personal injury (see Section 25).*

1   The turn signal and hazard flashers are controlled from a single electronic flasher unit which is mounted to the right of the steering column under the instrument panel (**see illus-**

tration) on 2001 and earlier models or in the relay box number 1 behind the glovebox on 2002 models.

2   When the flasher unit is functioning properly, an audible click can be heard during its operation. If the turn signal indicator (on the instrument panel) on one side of the vehicle flashes much more rapidly than normal, a faulty turn signal bulb is indicated.

3   If both turn signals fail to blink, the problem may be due to a blown fuse, a faulty flasher unit, a broken switch or a loose or open connection. If a quick check of the fuse box indicates that the turn signal fuse has blown, check the wiring for a short before installing a new fuse. **Note:** *On 2006 and later models, there are two fuses related to the turn signal lighting, one for the hazard flasher circuit and one for the turn signal circuit.*

4   To replace the flasher, simply disconnect the electrical connectors, then remove the screw securing the flasher retaining bracket.

5   Make sure that the replacement unit is identical to the original. Compare the old one to the new one before installing it.

6   Installation is the reverse of removal.

7   Steering column switches - replacement

Warning: *The models covered by this manual are equipped with Supplemental Restraint systems (SRS), more commonly known as airbags. Always disconnect the negative battery cable(s) and wait two minutes before working in the vicinity of any airbag system component to avoid the possibility of accidental deployment of the airbag, which could cause personal injury (see Section 25).*

Multi-function switch

Refer to illustrations 7.3a and 7.3b

1   Disconnect the cable(s) from the negative battery terminal(s) (see Chapter 5, Section 1).

7.3b . . . unplug the electrical connectors, then remove the combination switch

2   Remove the steering column covers (see Chapter 11) and the ignition lock cylinder (see Section 8).

3   Remove the retaining screws, disconnect the electrical connectors, then detach the switch from the steering column (**see illustrations**).

4   Installation is the reverse of removal.

Cruise control switches

5   Disconnect the cable(s) from the negative battery terminal(s) (see Chapter 5, Section 1).

6   Remove the driver's side airbag from the steering wheel (see Chapter 10).

7   Release the cruise control switch retaining clips, disconnect the switch and remove it from the steering wheel. On 2006 and later models, there are two cruise control switches in the steering wheel, one on either side. On models that also have audio switches in the steering wheel, carefully cut the wire ties on the wiring bundle to separate out the cruise control switches.

8   Installation is the reverse of removal. When reinstalling 2006 and later cruise control switches, use the smallest size of plastic tie-wraps to rebundle the wiring.

8.5 Unplug the electrical connector and remove the ignition switch retaining screws

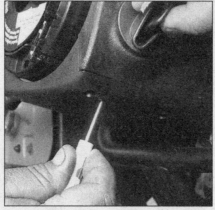

8.12 To remove the ignition lock cylinder, place the key in the "RUN" position, push in on the release tab with a screwdriver or a small punch and pull the cylinder straight out

9.2 Carefully pry the headlight switch assembly from the instrument panel

8   Ignition switch and key lock cylinder - replacement

Warning: *The models covered by this manual are equipped with Supplemental Restraint systems (SRS), more commonly known as airbags. Always disconnect the negative battery cable(s) and wait two minutes before working in the vicinity of any airbag system component to avoid the possibility of accidental deployment of the airbag, which could cause personal injury (see Section 25).*

Ignition switch
Refer to illustration 8.5

1   Disconnect the cable(s) from the negative battery terminal(s) (see Chapter 5, Section 1).
2   Remove the center trim panel (early models) and the driver side knee bolster (see Chapter 11).
3   Remove the steering column covers and the tilt-column handle, if equipped (see Chapter 11).
4   Position the ignition key in the Run position.
5   Unplug the ignition switch electrical con-

nector and remove the switch retaining screws **(see illustration)**.
6   Disengage the ignition switch from the actuator pin and remove the switch from the vehicle.
7   Make sure the actuator pin slot in the new ignition switch is in the Run position. **Note:** *A new replacement switch will be set in this position.*
8   Place the new switch in position on the actuator pin and install the retaining screws. It may be necessary to move the switch back and forth to line up the screw holes.
9   The remainder of the installation is the reverse of removal. Check for proper operation of the ignition switch in the lock, start and accessory positions.

Lock cylinder
Refer to illustration 8.12

10   Disconnect the cable(s) from the negative battery terminal(s) (see Chapter 5, Section 1).
11   Turn the ignition key lock cylinder to the Run position.

12   Insert a 1/8-inch punch into the hole at the bottom of the steering column cover surrounding the lock cylinder. Depress the punch while pulling out on the lock cylinder to remove it from the steering column housing **(see illustration)**.
13   To install the lock cylinder, depress the retaining pin on the side of the lock cylinder and rotate the ignition key/lock cylinder to the Run position.
14   Install the lock cylinder into the steering column housing, making sure it's fully seated and aligned in the interlocking washer.
15   Rotate the key back to the Off position. This will allow the retaining pin to extend itself back into the locating hole in the steering column housing.
16   Turn the lock to ensure that operation is correct in all positions.
17   The remainder of installation is the reverse of removal.

9   Instrument panel switches - replacement

Warning: *The models covered by this manual are equipped with Supplemental Restraint systems (SRS), more commonly known as airbags. Always disconnect the negative battery cable(s) and wait two minutes before working in the vicinity of any airbag system component to avoid the possibility of accidental deployment of the airbag, which could cause personal injury (see Section 25).*

Headlight switch and panel dimmer switch
Refer to illustrations 9.2 and 9.3

1   Disconnect the cable(s) from the negative battery terminal(s) (see Chapter 5, Section 1).
2   Carefully pry the switch assembly from the instrument panel **(see illustration)**.
3   Disconnect the electrical connector **(see illustration)** and remove the switch.
4   Installation is the reverse of the removal procedure.

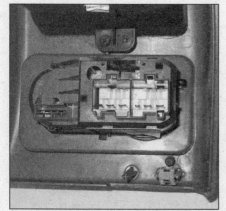

9.3 Working on the rear of the panel, disconnect the headlight switch electrical connector from the switch

9.6 Carefully pry the defogger switch/ 4WD selector switch assembly from the instrument panel

9.7 Disconnect the electrical connectors from the various switches

9.11 Disconnect the auxiliary power point electrical connector from the backside of the instrument cluster trim panel

10.3a Location of the instrument cluster screws on the left side

Rear window defogger switch and 4WD selector

Refer to illustrations 9.6 and 9.7

5   Disconnect the cable(s) from the negative battery terminal(s) (see Chapter 5, Section 1).
6   Carefully pry the switch assembly from the instrument panel **(see illustration)**.
7   Disconnect the electrical connector **(see illustration)** and remove the switch.
8   Installation is the reverse of the removal procedure.

Auxiliary power point

Refer to illustration 9.11

9   Disconnect the cable(s) from the negative battery terminal(s) (see Chapter 5, Section 1).
10   Remove the instrument cluster trim panel (see Chapter 11).
11   Disconnect the power point electrical connector **(see illustration)**.
12   Remove the mounting screws and lift the assembly from the instrument panel.
13   Installation is the reverse of the removal procedure.

10 Instrument cluster - removal and installation

Refer to illustrations 10.3a, 10.3b, 10.4 and 10.5
Warning: *The models covered by this manual are equipped with Supplemental Restraint systems (SRS), more commonly known as airbags. Always disconnect the negative battery cable(s) and wait two minutes before working in the vicinity of any airbag system component to avoid the possibility of accidental deployment of the airbag, which could cause personal injury (see Section 25).*
Note: *If you are installing a new instrument cluster, it will be necessary to first have the configuration information from the old cluster recorded onto a factory scan tool for installation onto the new cluster. Contact a dealer or qualified service facility for more information.*

1   Disconnect the cable(s) from the negative battery terminal(s) (see Chapter 5, Section 1).
2   Tilt the steering wheel to its lowest position and remove the instrument cluster finish panel (see Chapter 11).
3   Remove the instrument cluster retaining screws **(see illustrations)**.
4   Pull the instrument cluster out and unplug the electrical connectors from the backside **(see illustration)**, then remove the cluster from the instrument panel.
5   On models equipped with automatic transmissions, detach the transmission range indicator **(see illustration)**.
6   Installation is the reverse of removal.

11 Wiper motor - check and replacement

Wiper motor circuit check

Note: *Refer to the wiring diagrams for wire colors in the following checks. When checking for voltage, probe a grounded 12-volt test light to each terminal at a connector until it lights; this verifies voltage (power) at the terminal. If the following checks fail to locate the problem,*

10.3b Location of the instrument cluster screws on the right side

have the system diagnosed by a dealer service department or other properly equipped repair facility.
1   If the wipers work slowly, make sure the battery is in good condition and has a strong charge (see Chapter 5). If the battery is in good condition, remove the wiper motor (see below) and operate the wiper arms by hand. Check for binding linkage and pivots. Lubricate or repair the linkage or pivots as

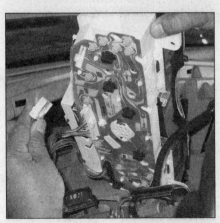

10.4 Disconnect the instrument cluster harness connectors

10.5 Push the clips and remove the transmission selector indicator from the instrument cluster

11.7a Release the wiper locking tab using a small screwdriver or pick and . . .

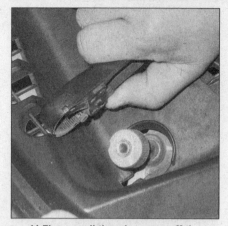

11.7b . . . pull the wiper arm off the wiper motor shaft

necessary. Reinstall the wiper motor. If the wipers still operate slowly, check for loose or corroded connections, especially the ground connection. If all connections look OK, replace the motor.

2   If the wipers fail to operate when activated, check the fuse (see Section 3). If the fuse is OK, connect a jumper wire between the wiper motor's ground terminal and ground, then retest. If the motor works now, repair the ground connection. If the motor still doesn't

work, turn the wiper switch to the HI position and check for voltage at the motor. **Note:** *The cowl cover will have to be removed* (see Chapter 11) *to access the electrical connector.*

3   If there's voltage at the connector, remove the motor and check it off the vehicle with fused jumper wires from the battery. If the motor now works, check for binding link-age (see Step 1). If the motor still doesn't work, replace it. If there's no voltage to the motor,

check for voltage at the wiper control relays. If there's voltage at the wiper control relays and no voltage at the wiper motor, have the switch tested. If the switch is OK, the wiper control relay is probably bad. See Section 5 for relay testing.

4   If the interval (delay) function is inoperative, check the continuity of all the wiring between the switch and wiper control module.

5   If the wipers stop at the position they're in when the switch is turned off (fail to park), check for voltage at the park feed wire of the wiper motor connector when the wiper switch is OFF but the ignition is ON. If no voltage is present, check for an open circuit between the wiper motor and the fuse panel.

Wiper motor replacement
Refer to illustrations 11.7a and 11.7b

6   Disconnect the cable(s) from the negative battery terminal(s) (see Chapter 5, Section 1).

7   Mark the positions of the wiper arm(s) on the windshield, then remove the wiper arm(s) **(see illustrations)**.

Front wiper motor
Refer to illustrations 11.9 and 11.11

8   Remove the windshield cowl cover (see Chapter 11).

11.9 Wiper assembly mounting bolts

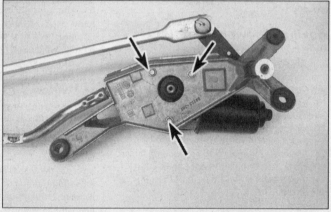

11.11 Front wiper motor mounting bolts

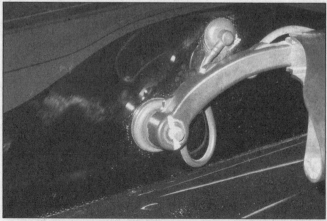

11.14 Use paint to mark the alignment of the rear wiper arm to the wiper motor shaft

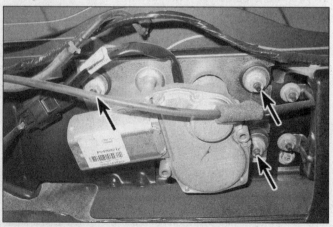

11.15 Rear wiper motor mounting bolts

12.3 Insert the radio removal tools until they seat, then push outward simultaneously on both tools to release the clips and withdraw the radio from the dash

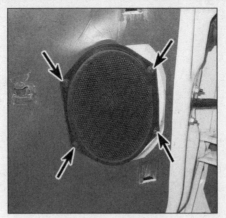

12.6a Remove the speaker mounting screws . . .

12.6b . . . disconnect the speaker connector and separate the speaker from the door

9   Disconnect the wiper motor harness connector and remove the windshield wiper motor/linkage assembly mounting nuts **(see illustration)**.
10   Lift the windshield wiper motor assembly from the cowl area.
11   Remove the wiper motor mounting nuts and separate the motor from the assembly **(see illustration)**.
12   Installation is the reverse of removal.
Note: *It will be necessary to pull the locking tab on the wiper arm to its full open position while assembling the wiper arm onto the motor shaft. Also, align the key on the wiper arm with the notch on the wiper motor shaft.*

Rear wiper motor (Excursion models)
Refer to illustrations 11.14 and 11.15
13   Remove the back door trim board from the hatch area (see Chapter 11).
14   Use paint to mark the position of the wiper blade to the wiper motor **(see illustration)**.
15   Disconnect the wiper motor harness connector and remove the windshield wiper motor mounting bolts **(see illustration)**.
16   Lift the windshield wiper motor assembly from the hatch area.
17   Installation is the reverse of removal.

12   Radio and speakers - removal and installation

Warning: *The models covered by this manual are equipped with Supplemental Restraint systems (SRS), more commonly known as airbags. Always disconnect the negative battery cable(s) and wait two minutes before working in the vicinity of any airbag system component to avoid the possibility of accidental deployment of the airbag, which could cause personal injury (see Section 25).*
1   Disconnect the cable(s) from the negative battery terminal(s) (see Chapter 5, Section 1).

Radio
Refer to illustration 12.3
2   For theft protection, the radio receiver is retained in the instrument panel by special clips on early models. Releasing these clips requires the use of a pair of special radio removal tools, available at most auto parts stores, or two short lengths of coat hanger wire bent into U-shapes. Insert the tools into the holes at the corners of the radio assembly until you feel the internal clips release.
3   With the clips released, push outward

simultaneously on both tools **(see illustration)** and pull the assembly out of the instrument panel, disconnect the antenna and electrical connectors and remove the unit from the vehicle. On later models, remove the center/upper instrument panel trim panel (see Chapter 11), then remove the four screws securing the radio.
4   Install by plugging in the electrical connectors, then sliding the radio along the track and into the instrument panel until the clips can be felt snapping in place.

Speakers
Refer to illustrations 12.6a and 12.6b
5   Remove the door trim panel (see Chapter 11).
6   Remove the mounting screws **(see illustration)**, withdraw the speaker, unplug the electrical connector **(see illustration)** and remove the speaker from the vehicle.
7   Installation is the reverse of removal.

13   Antenna and cable - removal and installation

Antenna
Refer to illustrations 13.2 and 13.3
1   Remove the vent panel cover from the right side cowl (see Chapter 11).
2   Remove the antenna mast **(see illustration)** and the rubber grommet.
3   Remove the antenna base mounting screws **(see illustration)**.
4   Lift the antenna and disconnect the antenna cable from the base.
5   Installation is the reverse of removal.

Antenna cable
Refer to illustration 13.11
Note: *These models are equipped with an antenna cable that is attached to the instrument panel reinforcement and the defroster air duct. The cable must be left inside the dash area when the new cable is installed.*
6   Loosen the right front wheel lug nuts. Raise the vehicle and secure it on jackstands.

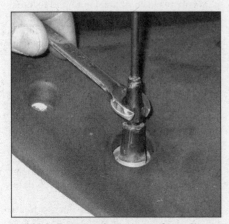

13.2 Remove the antenna from the antenna base

13.3 Antenna base mounting screws

13.11 Location of the antenna cable inside the dash area

14.4 When measuring the voltage at the rear window defogger grid, wrap a piece of aluminum foil around the positive probe of the voltmeter and press the foil against the wire with your finger

14.5 To determine if a heating element has broken, check the voltage at the center of each element - if the voltage is 5 or 6-volts, the element is unbroken - if the voltage is 10 or 12-volts, the element is broken between the center and the ground side - if there is no voltage, the element is broken between the center and the positive side

7   Remove the right front wheel and the right, front inner fenderwell (see Chapter 11).
8   Remove the right, front cowl side trim panel.
9   Working in the inner fenderwell opening, detach the antenna cable from the antenna base.
10   Remove the cable retaining clip securing the cable to the inner fender. Then push the cable and grommet assembly into the passenger compartment.
11   Remove the radio (see Section 12) and disconnect the antenna lead from the rear side of the radio.
12   Installation is the reverse of removal.

14 Rear window defogger - check and repair

1   The rear window defogger consists of a number of horizontal elements baked onto the glass surface.

14.7 To find the break, place the voltmeter negative lead against the defogger ground terminal, place the voltmeter positive lead with the foil strip against the heating element at the positive terminal end and slide it toward the negative terminal end - the point at which the voltmeter reading changes abruptly is the point at which the element is broken

2   Small breaks in the element can be repaired without removing the rear window.

Check

Refer to illustrations 14.4, 14.5 and 14.7
3   Turn the ignition switch and defogger system switches to the ON position. Using a voltmeter, place the positive probe against the defogger grid positive terminal and the negative probe against the ground terminal. If battery voltage is not indicated, check the fuse, defogger switch and related wiring. If voltage is indicated, but all or part of the defogger doesn't heat, proceed with the following tests.
4   When measuring voltage during the next two tests, wrap a piece of aluminum foil around the tip of the voltmeter positive probe and press the foil against the heating element with your finger **(see illustration)**. Place the negative probe on the defogger grid ground terminal.
5   Check the voltage at the center of each heating element **(see illustration)**. If the voltage is 5 or 6-volts, the element is okay (there is no break). If the voltage is 0-volts, the ele-

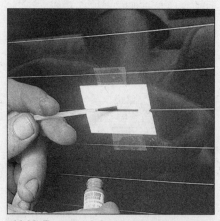

14.13 To use a defogger repair kit, apply masking tape to the inside of the window at the damaged area, then brush on the special conductive coating

ment is broken between the center of the element and the positive end. If the voltage is 10 to 12-volts the element is broken between the center of the element and ground. Check each heating element.
6   Connect the negative lead to a good body ground. The reading should stay the same. If it doesn't, the ground connection is bad.
7   To find the break, place the voltmeter negative probe against the defogger ground terminal. Place the voltmeter positive probe with the foil strip against the heating element at the positive terminal end and slide it toward the negative terminal end. The point at which the voltmeter deflects from several volts to zero is the point at which the heating element is broken **(see illustration)**.

Repair

Refer to illustration 14.13
8   Repair the break in the element using a repair kit specifically recommended for this purpose, available at most auto parts stores. Included in this kit is plastic conductive epoxy.
9   Prior to repairing a break, turn off the system and allow it to cool off for a few minutes.
10   Lightly buff the element area with fine steel wool, then clean it thoroughly with rubbing alcohol.
11   Use masking tape to mask off the area being repaired.
12   Thoroughly mix the epoxy, following the instructions provided with the repair kit.
13   Apply the epoxy material to the slit in the masking tape, overlapping the undamaged area about 3/4-inch on either end **(see illustration)**.
14   Allow the repair to cure for 24 hours before removing the tape and using the system.

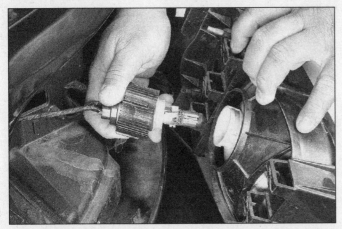

15.4 Rotate the headlight bulb retaining ring counterclockwise and pull the bulb socket out of the housing - when installing the new bulb, don't touch the surface; clean it with rubbing alcohol if you do

16.1 Location of the headlight adjustment screws (aerodynamic headlight)

15 Headlight bulb - replacement

Warning: *Halogen gas filled bulbs are under pressure and may shatter if the surface is scratched or the bulb is dropped. Wear eye protection and handle the bulbs carefully, grasping only the base whenever possible. Do not touch the surface of the bulb with your fingers because the oil from your skin could cause it to overheat and fail prematurely. If you do touch the bulb surface, clean it with rubbing alcohol.*

Halogen bulb (aerodynamic) type

Refer to illustration 15.4

1   Remove the headlight bulb cover from the back of the headlight housing.

2   Disconnect the electrical connector from the bulb holder.

3   Rotate the headlight bulb retaining ring one-eighth-turn counterclockwise as viewed from the rear.

4   Withdraw the bulb and retaining ring from the headlight housing **(see illustration)**.

5   Remove the bulb from the socket.

6   Without touching the glass with your bare fingers, insert the new bulb into the socket and then into the headlight housing, install and tighten the retaining ring by turning it clockwise.

7   Plug in the electrical connector, test the headlight operation, then close the hood.

Sealed beam type

8   Remove the parking light bulbs and the parking light assembly (see Section 19).

9   Remove the headlight bezel upper and lower mounting bolts and lift the bezel from the headlight.

10   Remove the headlight ring screws and remove the ring.

11   Disconnect the headlight electrical connector and remove the headlight.

12   Installation is the reverse of removal.

13   Reposition the headlight back into place and install the retaining ring. Test headlight operation, then close the hood.

16 Headlights - adjustment

Refer to illustrations 16.1 and 16.3
Note: *The headlights must be aimed correctly. If adjusted incorrectly they could blind the driver of an oncoming vehicle and cause a serious accident or seriously reduce your ability to see the road. The headlights should be checked for proper aim every 12 months and any time a new headlight is installed or front end body work is performed. It should be emphasized that the following procedure is only an interim step which will provide temporary adjustment until the headlights can be adjusted by a properly equipped shop.*

1   Identify the exact location of the adjustment screws:

a) *On halogen bulb style headlights, the adjustment screws are located on top of the housing* **(see illustration)**. **Note:** *On 2006 and later models, only the vertical aiming can be adjusted.*

b) *On sealed beam style headlights, the inboard (vertical) adjustment screw and the upper (horizontal) adjustment screw are accessible on the exterior of the vehicle.*

2   There are several methods of adjusting the headlights. The simplest method requires masking tape, a blank wall and a level floor.

3   Position masking tape vertically on the wall in reference to the vehicle centerline and the centerlines of both headlights **(see illustration)**.

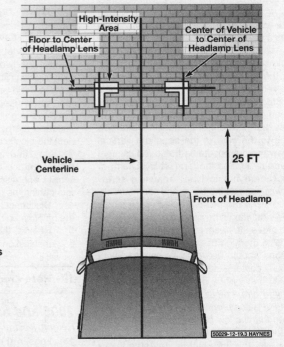

16.3 Headlight adjustment details

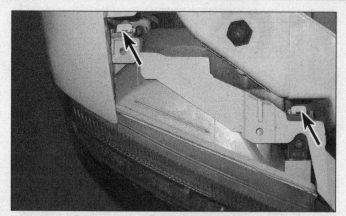

17.1 Pull the release clips and separate the headlight housing from the vehicle

18.4 Location of the horns

4   Position a horizontal tape line in reference to the centerline of all the headlights. **Note:** *It may be easier to position the tape on the wall with the vehicle parked only a few inches away.*

5   Adjustment should be made with the vehicle parked 25 feet from the wall, sitting level, the gas tank half-full and no heavy load in the vehicle.

6   Starting with the low beam adjustment, position the high intensity zone so it is two inches below the horizontal line and two inches to the side of the headlight vertical line, away from oncoming traffic. Adjustment is made by turning the top (sealed beam) or inner (aerodynamic type) adjusting screw clockwise to raise the beam and counterclockwise to lower the beam. The adjusting screw on the side should be used in the same manner to move the beam left or right.

7   With the high beams on, the high intensity zone should be vertically centered with the exact center just below the horizontal line. **Note:** *It may not be possible to position the headlight aim exactly for both high and low beams. If a compromise must be made, keep in mind that the low beams are the most used and have the greatest effect on safety.*

8   Have the headlights adjusted by a dealer service department or service station at the earliest opportunity.

17   Headlight housing (aerodynamic type) - replacement

Refer to illustration 17.1

1   On models through 2005, lift up and remove the two upper and two lower headlight housing clips **(see illustration)**.

2   On 2006 and 2007 models, remove the four screws securing the radiator grille and remove the grille. Remove the fours screws securing the headlight housing and disconnect the electrical connectors.

3   On 2008 and later models, open the hood, remove the four headlight mounting screws and disconnect the electrical connectors behind the headlight.

4   Disconnect the electrical connector from the halogen bulb (see Section 15).

5   Remove the headlight housing.

6   Installation is the reverse of removal.

18   Horn - replacement

2005 and earlier models

Refer to illustration 18.4

1   Loosen the right front wheel lug nuts. Raise the vehicle and secure it on jackstands.

2   Remove the front wheel.

3   Remove the right front fenderwell (see Chapter 11).

4   Disconnect the electrical connector(s) from the horn(s) **(see illustration)**.

5   Remove the horn mounting bolt(s) and separate the horn(s) from the body.

6   Installation is the reverse of removal.

2006 and later

7   On these models the horns are mounted below the battery.

8   Remove the battery and the battery tray (see Chapter 5).

9   Disconnect the electrical connector from the horn and remove the mounting bolt.

10   Installation is the reverse of removal.

19   Bulb replacement

Front turn signal and side marker lights

Refer to illustrations 19.1 and 19.2

1   Remove the front turn signal assembly mounting screws **(see illustration)** and slide the assembly forward, out of the vehicle body. On later models, the turn signal and side-marker lamps are part of the headlight housing. Remove the headlight housing (see Section 17) to access the bulbs.

19.1 Location of the front turn signal housing mounting screws (arrows)

19.2 Remove the housing and replace the defective bulbs

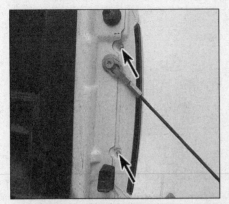

19.6 Remove the rear tail light housing mounting screws

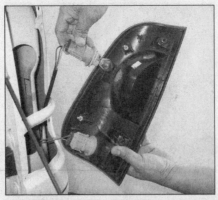

19.7 Remove the tail light housing and replace the defective bulbs

19.10 Remove the rear tail light housing mounting screws

19.11 Remove the tail light housing and replace the defective bulbs

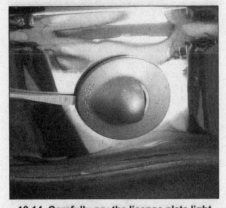

19.14 Carefully pry the license plate light housing out using a flat-bladed screwdriver

19.15 Remove the bulb holder from the light housing by twisting it 1/4-turn

2   Twist the bulb socket a quarter turn counterclockwise, then remove the bulb assembly from the housing **(see illustration)**.
3   The defective bulb can then be removed from the socket and replaced.
4   Installation of the front turn signal assembly is the reverse of removal.

Rear turn signal, brake, tail and back-up lights

Pick-up truck models
Refer to illustrations 19.6 and 19.7
5   Open the tailgate or liftgate.
6   Remove the retaining screws securing

the rear tail light housing, then pull the tail light assembly outward to access the tail light bulbs **(see illustration)**.
7   Twist the bulb socket a quarter turn counterclockwise, then remove the bulb assembly from the housing **(see illustration)**.
8   The defective bulb can then be removed from the socket and replaced.
9   Installation of the tail light housing is the reverse of removal.

Excursion models
Refer to illustrations 19.10 and 19.11
10   Remove the retaining screws securing the rear tail light housing, then pull the tail

light assembly outward to access the tail light bulbs **(see illustration)**.
11   Twist the bulb socket a quarter turn counterclockwise, then remove the bulb assembly from the housing **(see illustration)**.
12   The defective bulb can then be removed from the socket and replaced.
13   Installation of the tail light housing is the reverse of removal.

License plate light
Refer to illustrations 19.14 and 19.15
14   The license plate light bulbs can be accessed from the rear of the bumper **(see illustration)**. Carefully pry the light housing out using a flat-bladed screwdriver, then pull the bulb assembly from the bumper.
15   Twist the bulb holder 1/4-turn to remove it from the housing **(see illustration)**. The defective bulb can then be pulled straight out of the socket and replaced.
16   Installation is the reverse of removal.

High-mounted brake light
Refer to illustrations 19.17 and 19.18
17   Remove the lens retaining screws and pull the lamp assembly outward to access the bulbs **(see illustration)**.
18   Twist the bulb socket a quarter turn counterclockwise **(see illustration)**, then remove the bulb assembly from the housing.
19   The defective bulb can then be pulled straight out of the socket and replaced.

19.17 Location of the mounting screws on the high-mounted brake light assembly

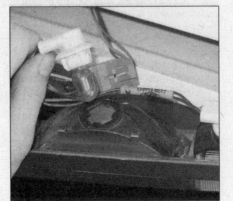

19.18 Remove the defective bulb from the high-mounted brake light assembly

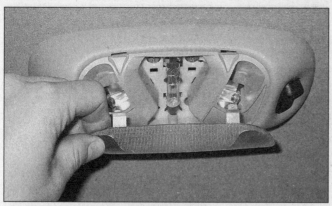

19.20a Carefully remove the dome light lens to access the bulbs

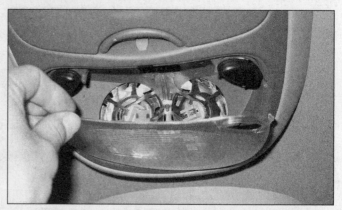

19.20b Remove the cargo light lens to access the bulbs

Dome and cargo lights

Refer to illustrations 19.20a and 19.20b

20   Using a small screwdriver, remove the lens and replace the bulb **(see illustrations)**.

Instrument cluster illumination

21   To gain access to the instrument cluster illumination lights, the instrument cluster will have to be removed (see Section 10). The bulbs can then be removed and replaced from the rear of the cluster.

20   Electric side view mirrors - description

1   Most electric rear view mirrors use two motors to move the glass; one for up and down adjustments and one for left-right adjustments.
2   The control switch has a selector portion which sends voltage to the left or right side mirror. With the ignition ON but the engine OFF, roll down the windows and operate the mirror control switch through all functions (left-right and up-down) for both the left and right side mirrors.
3   Listen carefully for the sound of the electric motors running in the mirrors.
4   If the motors can be heard but the mirror glass doesn't move, there's a problem with the drive mechanism inside the mirror.

21.1 Location of the cruise control module (arrow)

5   If the mirrors do not operate and no sound comes from the mirrors, check the fuse (see Chapter 1).
6   If the fuse is OK, remove the mirror control switch. Have the switch continuity checked by a dealership service department or other qualified automobile repair facility.
7   Test the ground connections. Refer to the wiring diagrams at the end of Chapter 12.
8   If the mirror still doesn't work, remove the mirror and check the wires at the mirror for voltage.
9   If there's not voltage in each switch position, check the circuit between the mirror and control switch for opens and shorts.
10   If there's voltage, remove the mirror and test it off the vehicle with jumper wires. Replace the mirror if it fails this test.

21   Cruise control system - description

Refer to illustration 21.1

1   The cruise control system maintains vehicle speed with an electrically-operated motor located in the engine compartment, which is connected to the accelerator pedal by a cable. The system consists of the cruise control module **(see illustration)**, the brake switch, control switches and vehicle speed sensor. Some features of the system require special testers and diagnostic procedures which are beyond the scope of this manual. Listed below are some general procedures that may be used to locate common problems.
2   Check the fuses (see Section 3).
3   Have an assistant operate the brake lights while you check their operation (voltage from the brake light switch deactivates the cruise control).
4   If the brake lights don't come on or stay on all the time, correct the problem and retest the cruise control.
5   Visually inspect the control cable between the cruise control motor and the throttle linkage for free movement. Replace it if necessary.
6   The cruise control system uses inputs from the Vehicle Speed Sensor (VSS). Refer to

Chapter 6 for more information on the VSS.
7   Test drive the vehicle to determine if the cruise control is now working. If it isn't, take it to a dealer service department or an automotive electrical specialist for further diagnosis.

22   Power window system - description

1   The power window system operates electric motors, mounted in the doors, which lower and raise the windows. The system consists of the control switches, the motors, regulators, glass mechanisms and associated wiring.
2   The power windows can be lowered and raised from the master control switch by the driver or by remote switches located at the individual windows. Each window has a separate motor which is reversible. The position of the control switch determines the polarity and therefore the direction of operation.
3   The circuit is protected by a fuse and a circuit breaker. Each motor is also equipped with an internal circuit breaker, this prevents one stuck window from disabling the whole system.
4   The power window system will only operate when the ignition switch is ON. In addition, many models have a window lockout switch at the master control switch which, when activated, disables the switches at the rear windows and, sometimes, the switch at the passenger's window also. Always check these items before troubleshooting a window problem.
5   These procedures are general in nature, so if you can't find the problem using them, take the vehicle to a dealer service department or other properly equipped repair facility.
6   If the power windows won't operate, always check the fuse and circuit breaker first.
7   If only the rear windows are inoperative, or if the windows only operate from the master control switch, check the rear window lockout switch for continuity in the unlocked position. Replace it if it doesn't have continuity.
8   Check the wiring between the switches and fuse panel for continuity. Repair the wiring, if necessary.
9   If only one window is inoperative from the master control switch, try the other con-

trol switch at the window. **Note:** *This doesn't apply to the driver's door window.*

10 If the same window works from one switch, but not the other, check the switch for continuity.

11 If the switch tests OK, check for a short or open in the circuit between the affected switch and the window motor.

12 If one window is inoperative from both switches, remove the trim panel from the affected door and check for voltage at the switch and at the motor while the switch is operated.

13 If voltage is reaching the motor, disconnect the glass from the regulator (see Chapter 11). Move the window up and down by hand while checking for binding and damage. Also check for binding and damage to the regulator. If the regulator is not damaged and the window moves up and down smoothly, replace the motor. If there's binding or damage, lubricate, repair or replace parts, as necessary.

14 If voltage isn't reaching the motor, check the wiring in the circuit for continuity between the switches and motors. You'll need to consult the wiring diagram for the vehicle. If the circuit is equipped with a relay, check that the relay is grounded properly and receiving voltage.

23 Power door lock system - description

1 A power door lock system operates the door lock actuators mounted in each door. The system consists of the switches, actuators, a control unit and associated wiring. Diagnosis can usually be limited to simple checks of the wiring connections and actuators for minor faults that can be easily repaired.

2 Power door lock systems are operated by bi-directional solenoids located in the doors. The lock switches have two operating positions: Lock and Unlock. When activated, the switch sends a ground signal to the door lock control unit to lock or unlock the doors. Depending on which way the switch is activated, the control unit reverses polarity to the solenoids, allowing the two sides of the circuit to be used alternately as the feed (positive) and ground side.

3 Some vehicles may have an anti-theft system incorporated into the power locks. If you are unable to locate the trouble using the following general Steps, consult a dealer service department or other qualified repair shop.

4 Always check the circuit protection first. Some vehicles use a combination of circuit breakers and fuses.

5 Operate the door lock switches in both directions (Lock and Unlock) with the engine off. Listen for the click of the solenoids operating.

6 Test the switches for continuity. Remove the switches and have them checked by a dealer service department or other qualified automobile repair facility.

7 Check the wiring between the switches, control unit and solenoids for continuity. Repair the wiring if there's no continuity.

8 Check for a bad ground at the switches or the control unit.

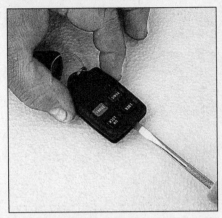

23.14 Use a small screwdriver to separate the transmitter halves

9 If all but one lock solenoids operate, remove the trim panel from the affected door (see Chapter 11) and check for voltage at the solenoid while the lock switch is operated. One of the wires should have voltage in the Lock position; the other should have voltage in the Unlock position.

10 If the inoperative solenoid is receiving voltage, replace the solenoid.

11 If the inoperative solenoid isn't receiving voltage, check the relay for an open or short in the wire between the lock solenoid and the control unit. **Note:** *It's common for wires to break in the portion of the harness between the body and door (opening and closing the door fatigues and eventually breaks the wires).*

Keyless entry system
Refer to illustration 23.14

12 The keyless entry system consists of a remote control transmitter that sends a coded infrared signal to a receiver which then operates the door lock system. On models so equipped, the transmitter may also engage the alarm system and provide a "panic" button which flashes the lights and blows the horn for emergencies.

13 Replace the transmitter batteries when the red LED light on the case doesn't light when the button is pushed. As the batteries deteriorate with age, the distance at which the remote transmitter operates will diminish.

14 Use a coin or small screwdriver to carefully separate the case halves for battery replacement **(see illustration)**.

15 Replace the two lithium batteries with the same type as originally installed, observing the polarity diagram on the case.

16 Snap the case halves together.

24 Daytime Running Lights (DRL) - general information

The Daytime Running Lights (DRL) system illuminates the headlights whenever the engine is running. The only exception is with the engine running and the parking brake engaged. Once the parking brake is released, the lights will remain on as long as the ignition switch is

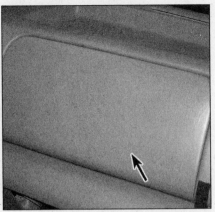

25.1 Location of the passenger's side airbag

on, even if the parking brake is later applied.

The DRL system supplies reduced power to the headlights so they won't be too bright for daytime use, while prolonging headlight life.

25 Airbag system - general information

General information
Refer to illustration 25.1

1 All models are equipped with a Supplemental Restraint System (SRS), more commonly known as an airbag. This system is designed to protect the driver, and the front seat passenger, from serious injury in the event of a head-on or frontal collision. It uses an electronic crash sensor (ESC) (also known as the Restraints Control Module [RCM] on later models) mounted on the center tunnel behind the instrument panel. The airbag assemblies are mounted on the steering wheel and the right side of the passenger's side dash **(see illustration)**. Beginning with the 2002 model year, seat belt pre-tensioners became available. These are pyrotechnic devices controlled by the Restraints Control Module (RCM) that reduce the slack in the seat belts during an impact of sufficient force to trigger the airbags.

Airbag module
Driver's side

2 The airbag inflator module contains a housing incorporating the cushion (airbag) and inflator unit, mounted in the center of the steering wheel. The inflator assembly is mounted on the back of the housing over a hole through which gas is expelled, inflating the bag almost instantaneously when an electrical signal is sent from the system. A "clockspring" on the steering column under the steering wheel carries this signal to the module.

3 This clockspring assembly can transmit an electrical signal regardless of steering wheel position. The igniter in the airbag converts the electrical signal to heat and ignites the powder, which inflates the bag.

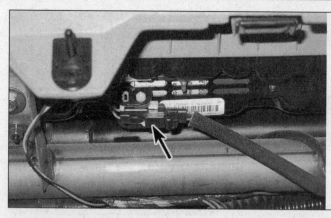

25.21 Location of the passenger's side airbag connector

Passenger's side

4   The airbag is mounted above the glove compartment and designated by the letters SRS (Supplemental Restraint System). It consists of an inflator containing an igniter, a reaction housing/airbag assembly and a trim cover.

5   The airbag is considerably larger than the steering wheel-mounted unit and is supported by the steel reaction housing. The trim cover is textured and painted to match the instrument panel and has a molded seam which splits when the bag inflates.

Electronic crash sensor (ESC)/ Restraints Control Module (RCM) diagnostic unit

6   This unit supplies the current to the airbag system (and seat belt pre-tensioners, on models so equipped) in the event of the collision, even if battery power is cut off. It checks this system every time the vehicle is started, causing the "SRS" light to go on then off, if the system is operating properly. If there is a fault in the system, the light will go on and stay on, flash, or the dash will make a beeping sound. If this happens, the vehicle should be taken to your dealer immediately for service.

Servicing components near the SRS system

7   There are times when you need to remove the steering wheel, the instrument cluster, the radio, the heater/air conditioning control assembly or other components that are near airbag components. At these times you'll be working around components and wire harnesses for the SRS system. Do not use electrical test equipment on airbag system wires; it could cause the airbag(s) to deploy. ALWAYS DISABLE THE SRS SYSTEM BEFORE WORKING NEAR THE SRS SYSTEM COMPONENTS OR RELATED WIRING.

Disarming the system and other precautions

Refer to illustration 25.21

Warning: *Failure to follow these precautions could result in accidental deployment of the airbag and personal injury.*

8   Whenever working in the vicinity of the steering wheel, instrument panel or any of the other SRS system components, the system must be disarmed. To disarm the system:

a) Point the wheels straight ahead and turn the key to the Lock position.

b) Disconnect the cable from the negative battery terminal(s). On dual battery systems, be sure to disconnect both negative battery terminals. Refer to Chapter 5, Section 1 for the disconnecting procedure.

c) Wait at least two minutes for the back-up power supply to be depleted.

2006 and later models
Disabling

9   Turn Off all accessories on the vehicle and disconnect any memory-saver devices. Turn Off the ignition switch.

10   At the interior fuse/relay box under the right side of the instrument panel, remove the fuse marked RCM. On later models the fuse is in the junction box behind the right kick-panel.

11   Turn the ignition switch to On. Observe the airbag warning light on the instrument panel for 30 seconds. If you have removed the correct fuse, the warning light should be steady (no blinking).

12   Turn the ignition switch Off.

13   Disconnect the negative battery cable and wait two minutes before doing any work around SRS components.

Enabling

14   Turn the ignition switch from Off to On.

15   Reinstall the RCM fuse.

16   Connect the battery cable. **Warning:** *When the battery cable is connected, no one should be in front of any airbag module, in case of accidental deployment.*

17   To test if the SRS system is working properly, turn the ignition switch from On to Off for ten seconds, then back to On. The warning light should illuminate for six seconds and go out.

18   The warning light indicates a problem with the SRS system if: the light blinks, stays illuminated continuously, or fails to illuminate in one minute. If one of these conditions exists, have your system checked with a scan tool at a dealership.

19   Whenever handling an airbag module, always keep the airbag opening (the trim side) pointed away from your body. Never place the airbag module on a bench or other surface with the airbag opening facing the surface. Always place the airbag module in a safe location with the airbag opening facing up.

20   Never measure the resistance of any SRS component or use any electrical test equipment on any of the wiring or components. An ohmmeter has a built-in battery supply that could accidentally deploy the airbag.

21   Never use electrical welding equipment on a vehicle equipped with an airbag without first disconnecting the airbag electrical connectors, located under the steering column near the combination switch connector (driver's airbag) (see Chapter 10) and behind the glove box (passenger's airbag) **(see illustration)**. On models with seat belt pre-tensioners, the pre-tensioner electrical connectors are located behind the B-pillar trim panels and/or under the seats, depending on the model.

22   Never dispose of a live airbag module or seat belt pre-tensioner. Return it to a dealer service department or other qualified repair shop for safe deployment and disposal.

Airbag module removal and installation
Driver's side airbag module and clockspring

23   Refer to Chapter 10, *Steering wheel - removal and installation*, for the driver's side airbag module and clockspring removal and installation procedures.

Passenger's side airbag module

24   Disarm the airbag system as described previously in this Section.

25   Lower the glovebox door fully to gain access to the airbag by pressing the glovebox door tabs and pushing down, then unplug the electrical connector **(see illustration 25.21)** and remove the airbag module mounting nuts and bolts. Be sure to heed the precautions outlined previously in this Section.

26   Carefully slide a flat-bladed screwdriver under the right bottom edge of the airbag panel and lift up. Separate the panel from the clips.

27   Installation is the reverse of the removal procedure. Tighten the airbag module mounting screws securely.

26   Wiring diagrams - general information

Since it isn't possible to include all wiring diagrams for every year covered by this manual, the following diagrams are those that are typical and most commonly needed.

Prior to troubleshooting any circuits, check the fuse and circuit breakers (if equipped) to make sure they're in good condition. Make sure the battery is properly charged and check the cable connections (see Chapter 1).

When checking a circuit, make sure that all connectors are clean, with no broken or loose terminals. When unplugging a connector, do not pull on the wires. Pull only on the connector housings themselves.

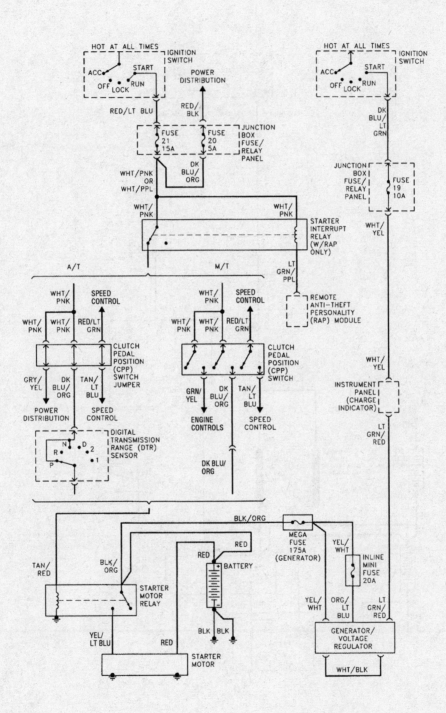

Starting and charging systems - 1999 through 2001 gasoline models

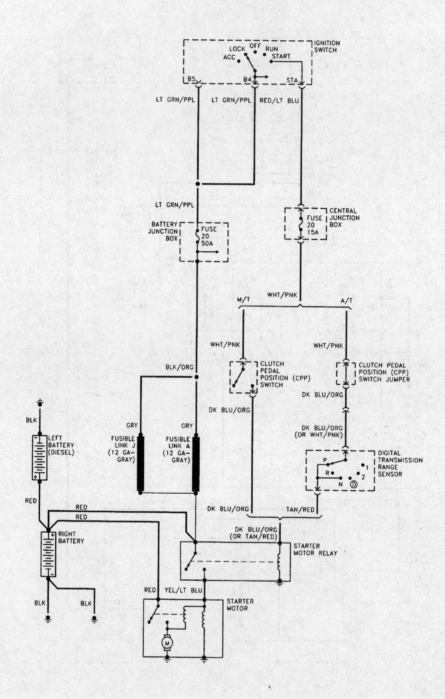

Starting system - 1999 through 2001 F-250, F-350 diesel models

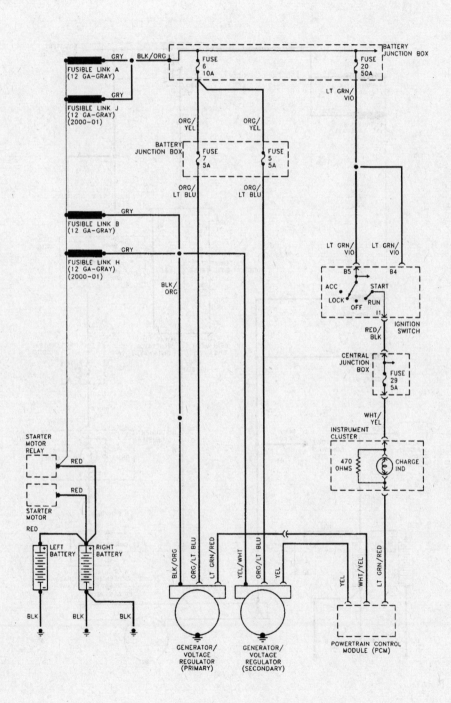

Charging system (with dual alternators) - 1999 through 2001 F-250, F-350 diesel models

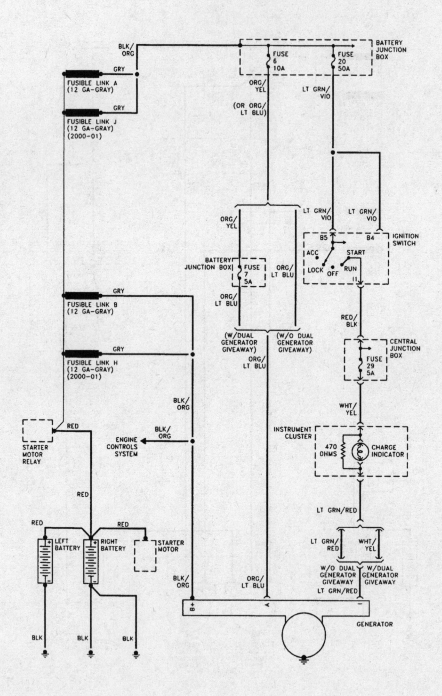

Charging system (without dual alternators) - 1999 through 2001 F-250, F-350 diesel models

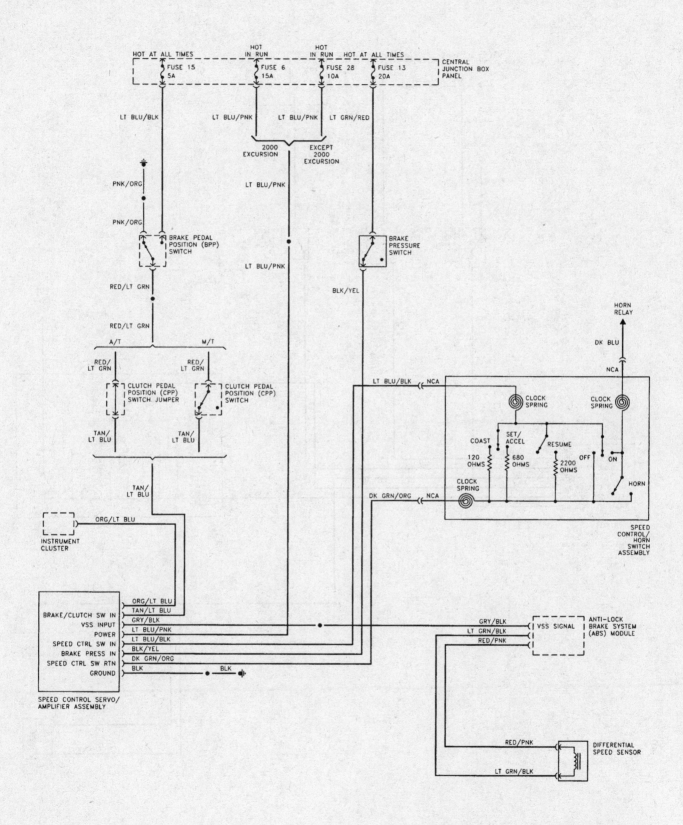

Cruise control system - 1999 through 2001 gasoline models

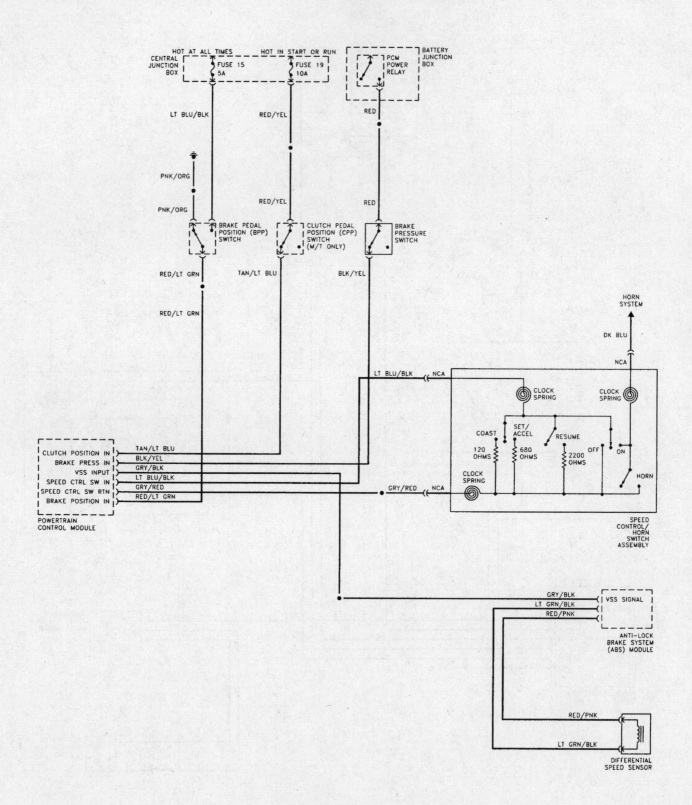

Cruise control system - 1999 through 2001 diesel models

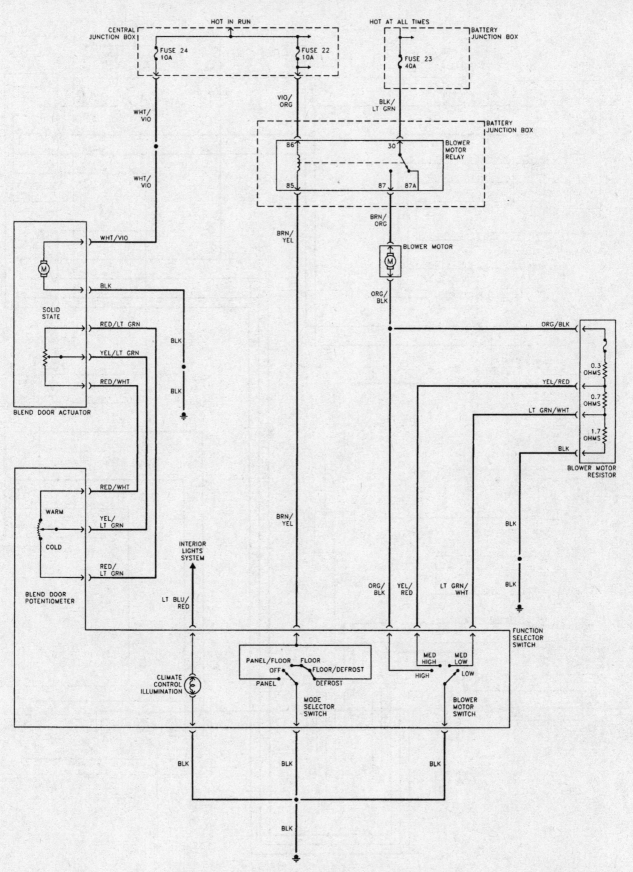

Heater blower motor system - 1999 through 2001 models

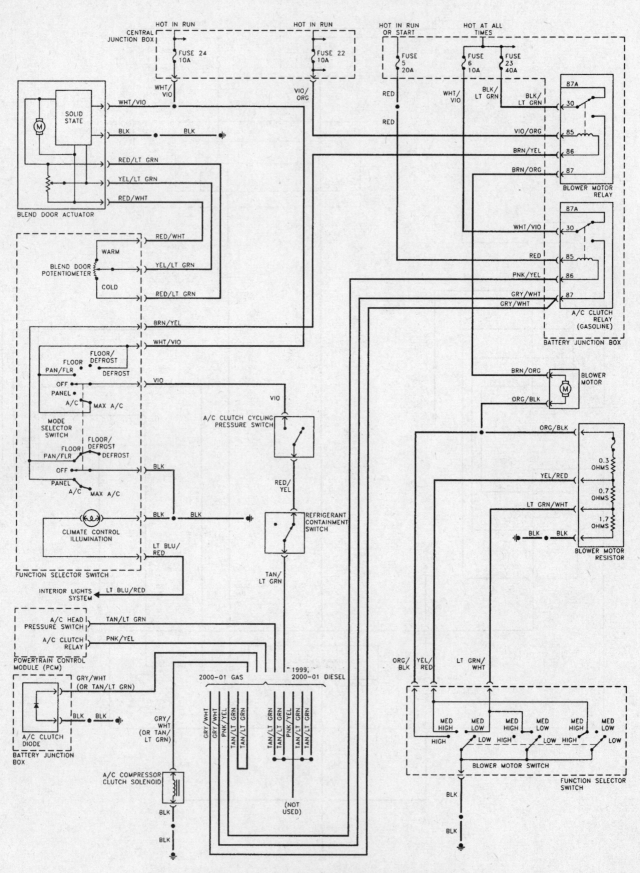

Air conditioning system - 1999 through 2001 F-250, F-350 models

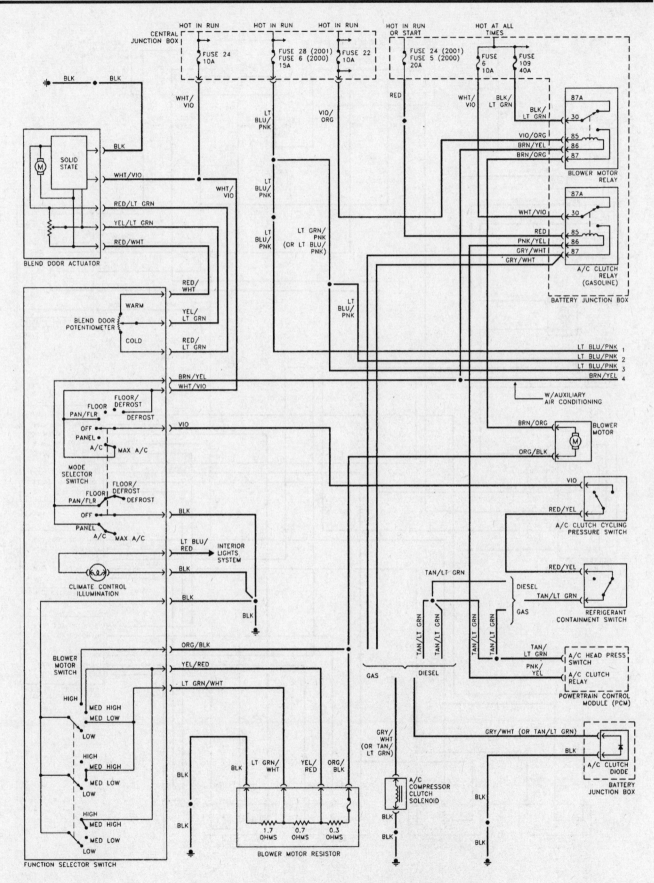

Air conditioning system - 2000 and 2001 Excursion models (1 of 2)

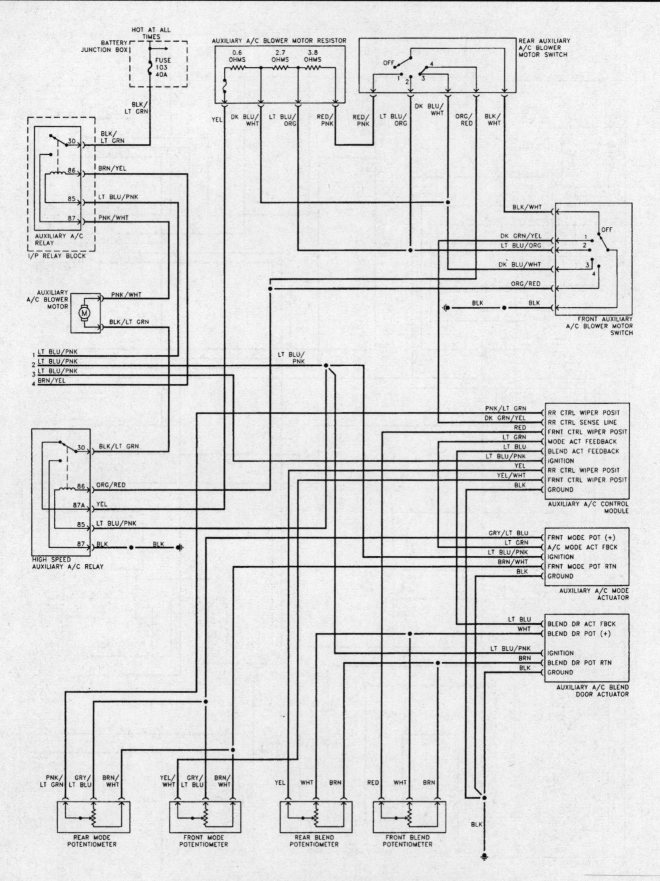

Air conditioning system - 2000 and 2001 Excursion models (2 of 2)

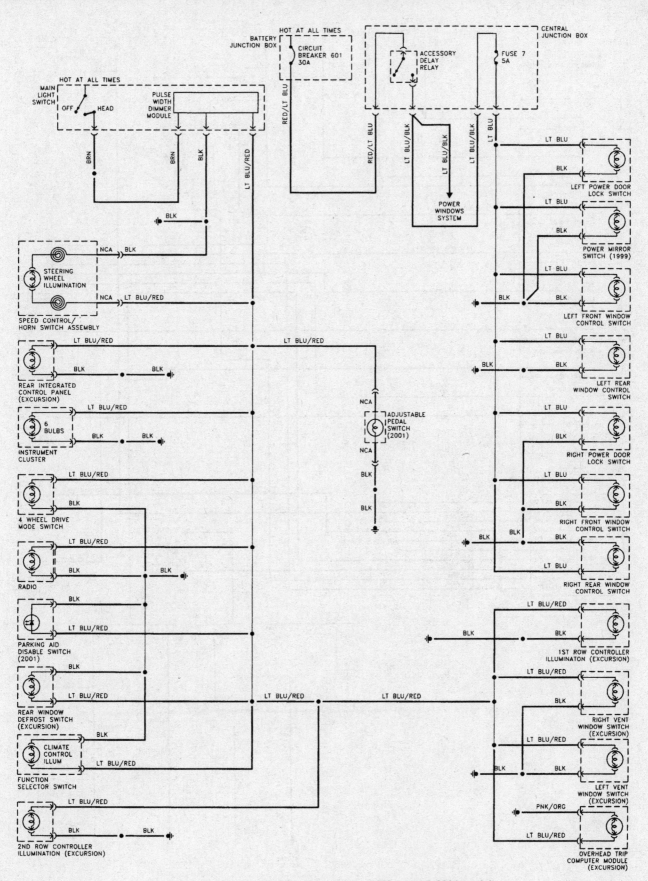

Instrument and switch illumination system - 1999 through 2001 models

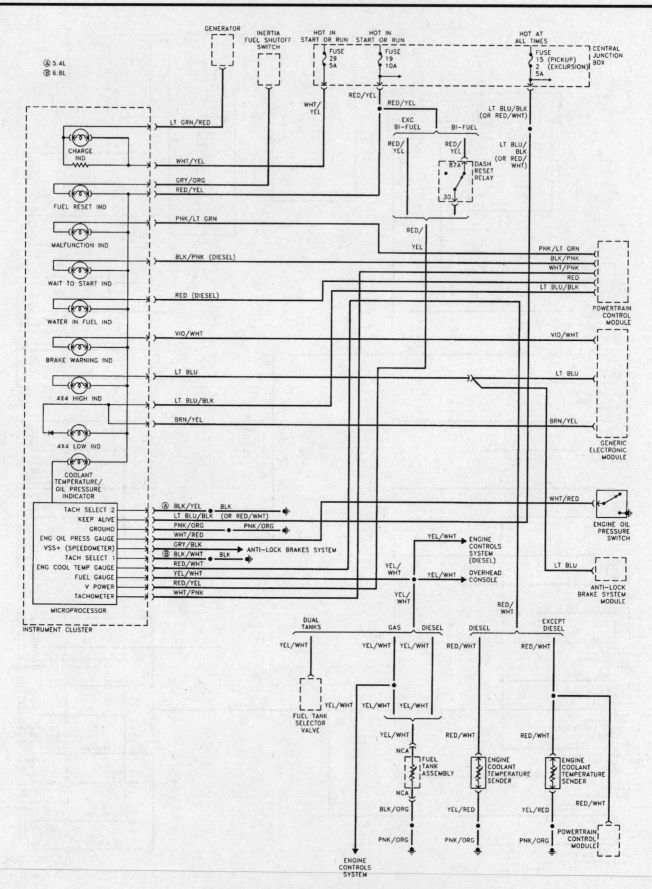

Warning light systems - 1999 through 2001 models

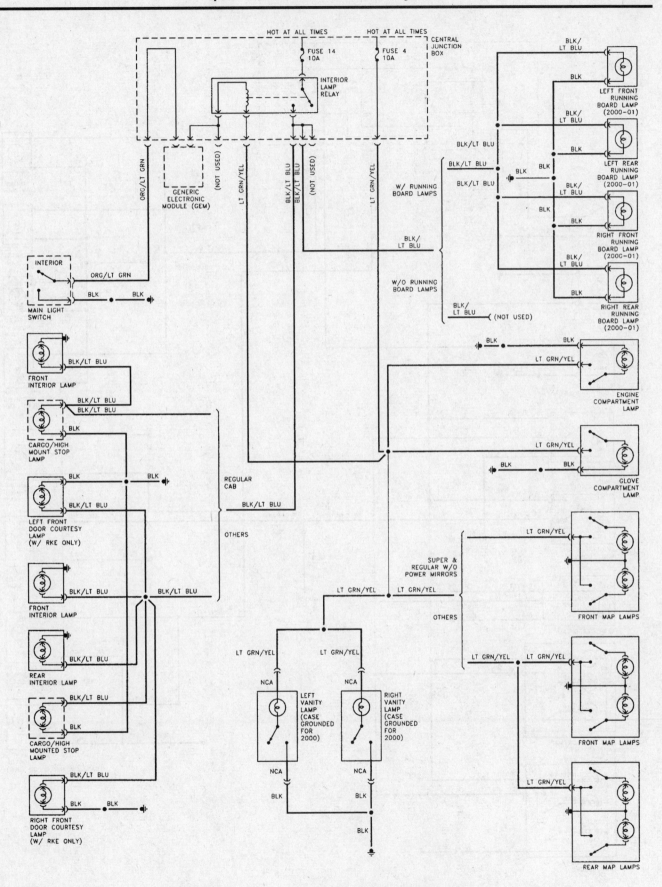

Interior lighting system - 1999 through 2001 F-250, F-350 models

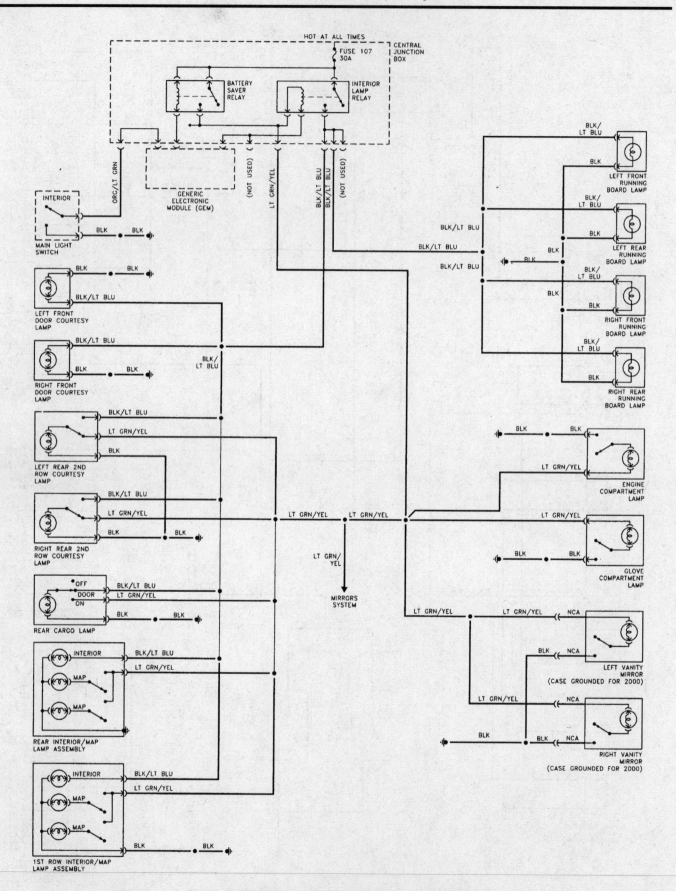

Interior lighting system - 2000 and 2001 Excursion models

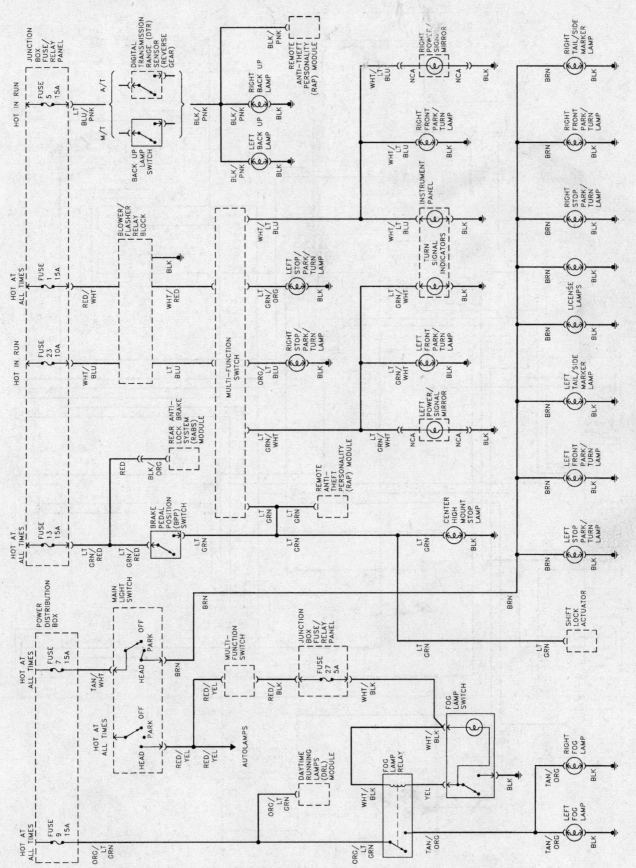

Typical exterior lighting system - F-250, F-350 models

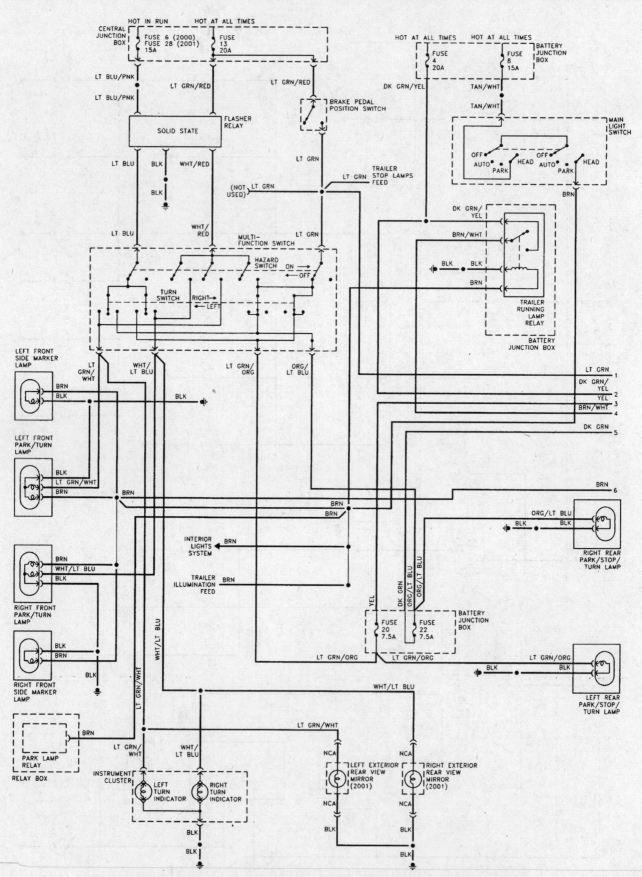

Exterior lighting system (except headlights) - 2000 and 2001 Excursion models (1 of 2)

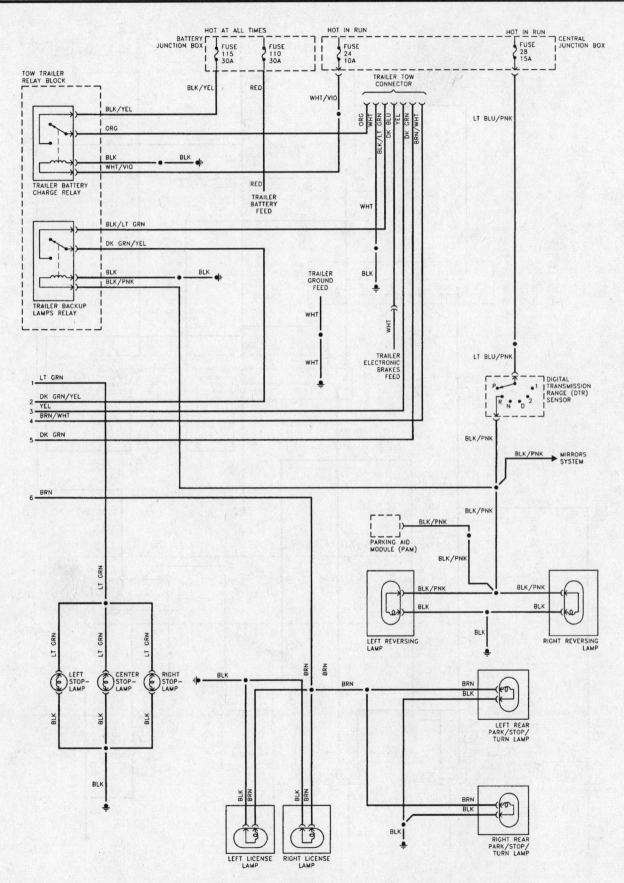

Exterior lighting system (except headlights) - 2000 and 2001 Excursion models (2 of 2)

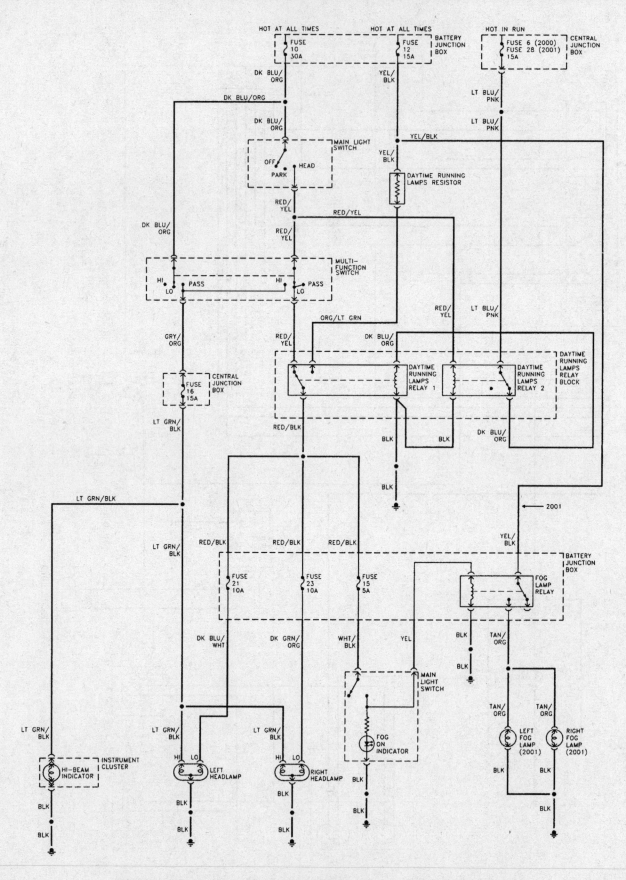

Headlight system (with Daytime Running Lights) - 2000 and 2001 Excursion models

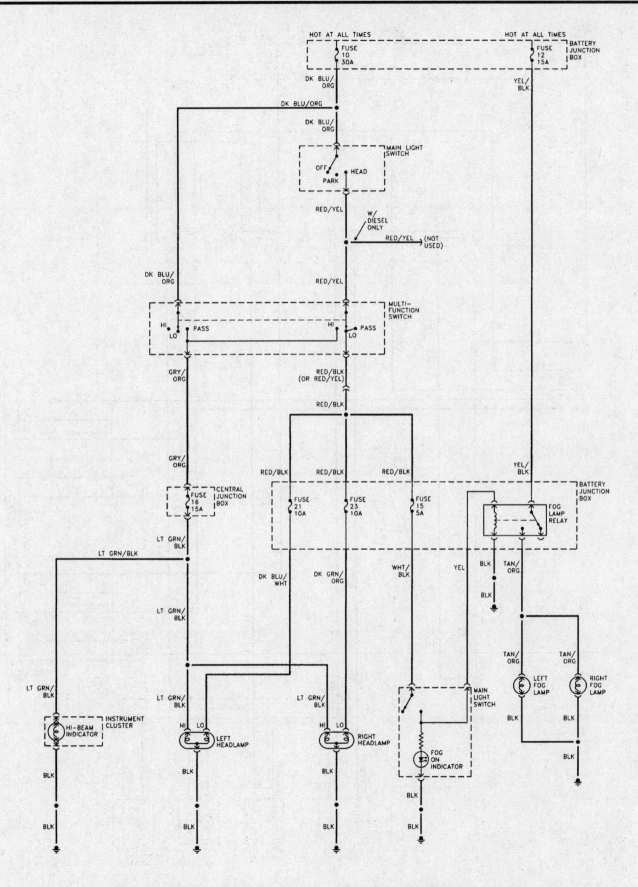

Headlight system (without Daytime Running Lights) - 2000 and 2001 Excursion models

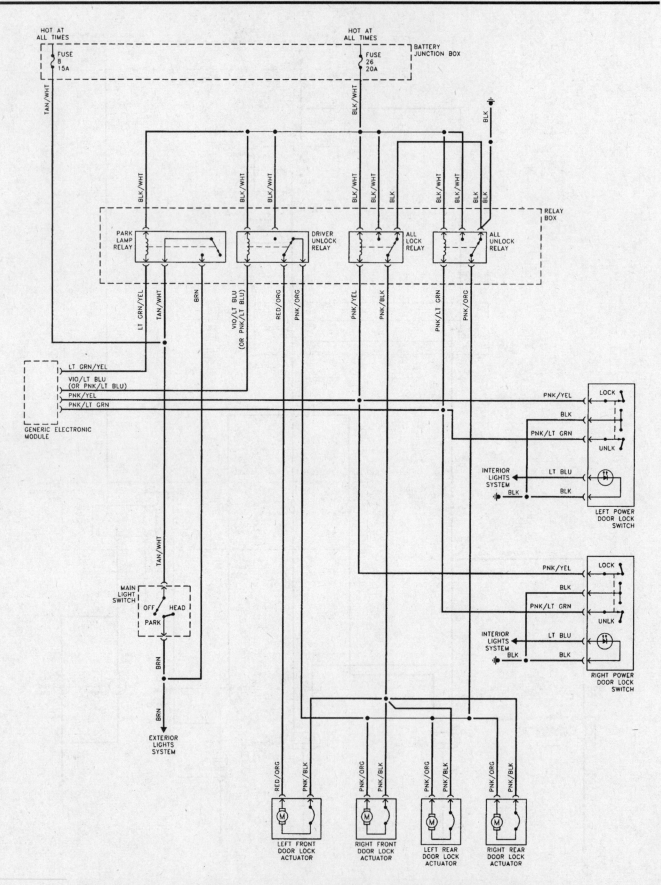

Power door lock system with keyless entry (crew cab pick-up models) - 1999 through 2001 models

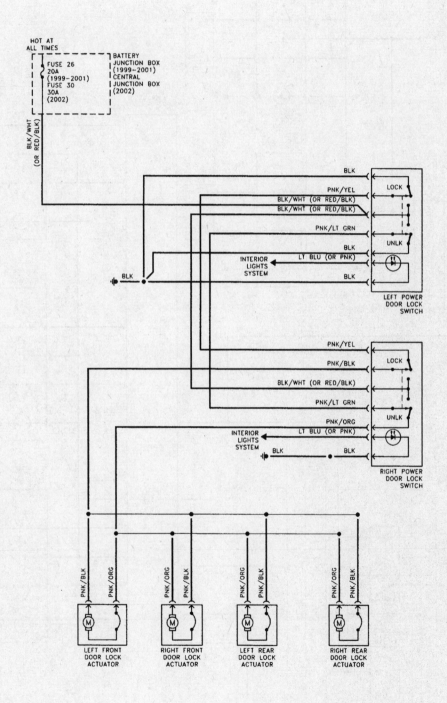

Power door lock system without keyless entry (crew cab pick-up models) - 1999 through 2001 models

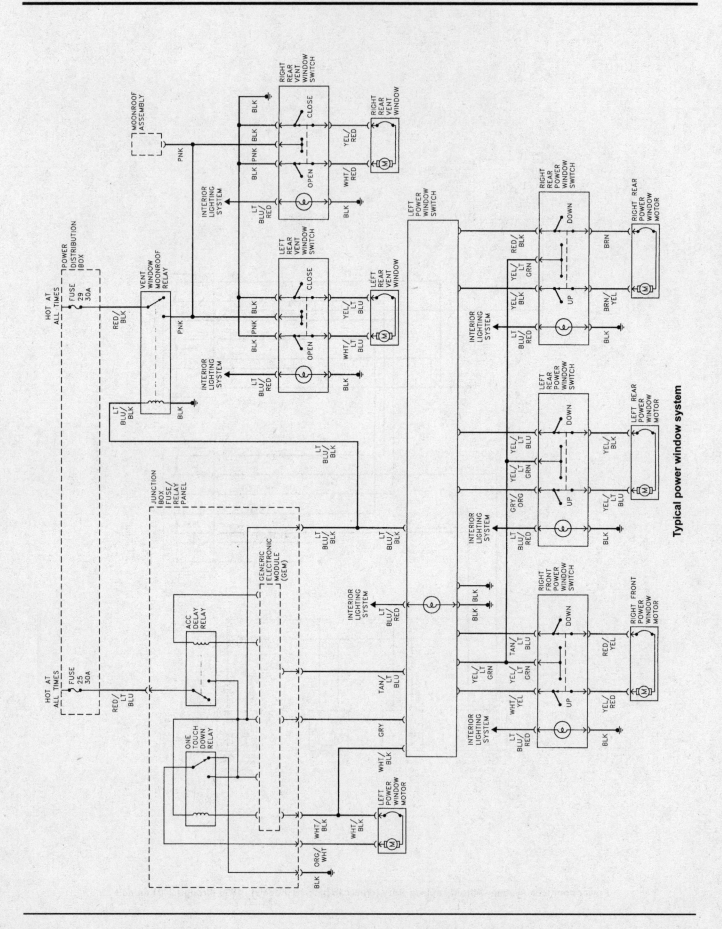

Typical power window system

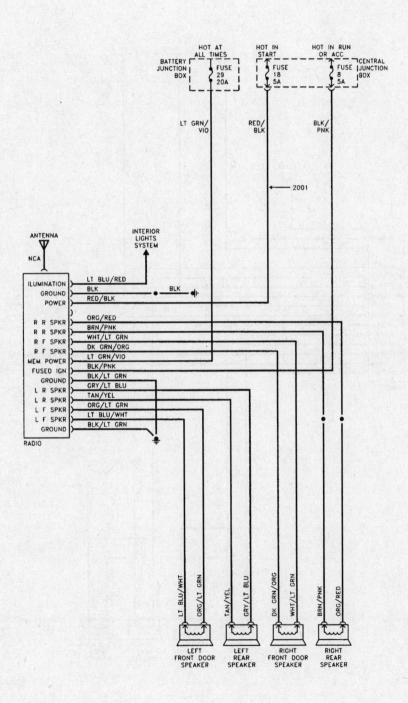

Radio system - 1999 through 2001 F-250, F-350 models

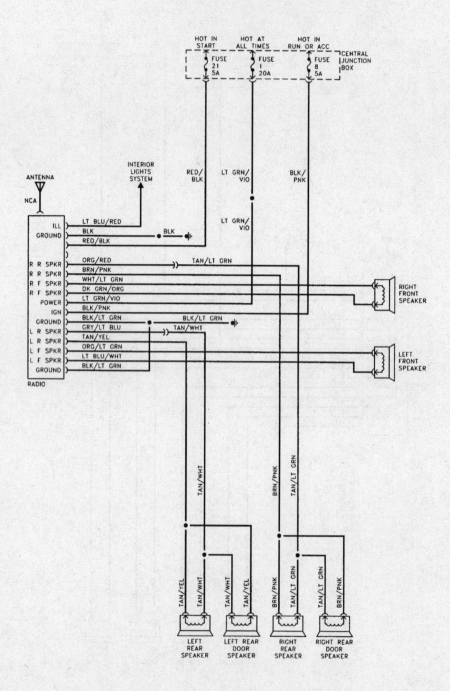

Radio system - 2000 and 2001 Excursion models

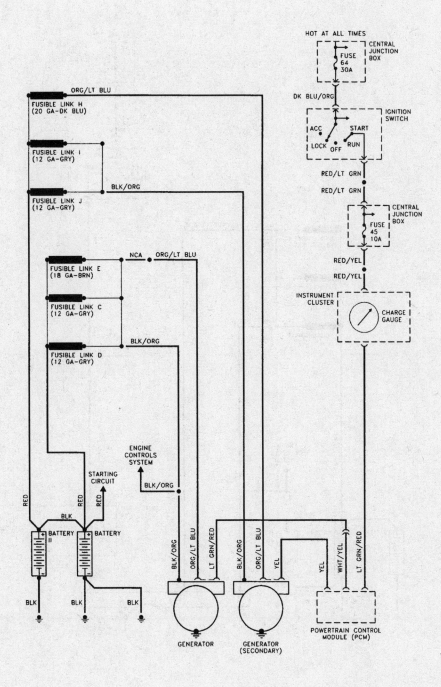

Charging system (with dual alternators) - 2002 and later F-250, F-350 diesel models

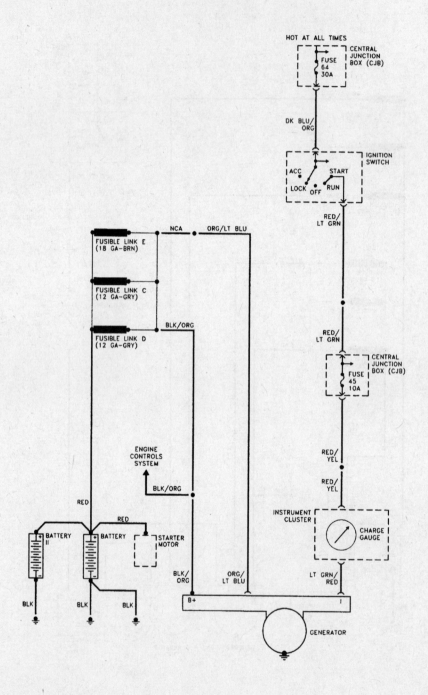

Charging system (without dual alternators) - 2002 and later F-250, F-350 diesel models

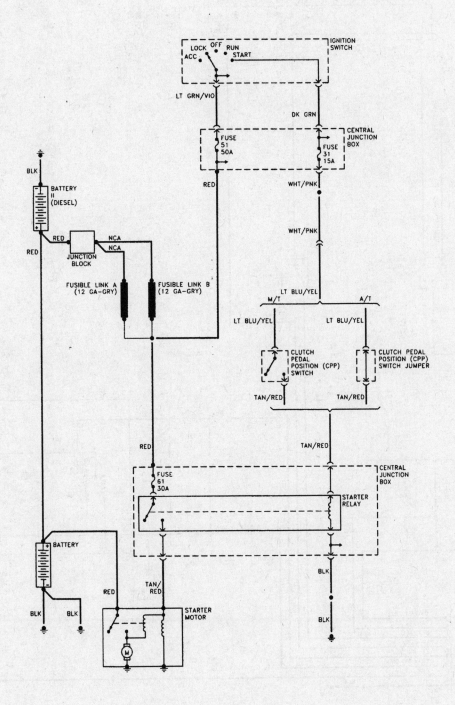

Starting system - 2002 and later F-250, F-350 diesel models

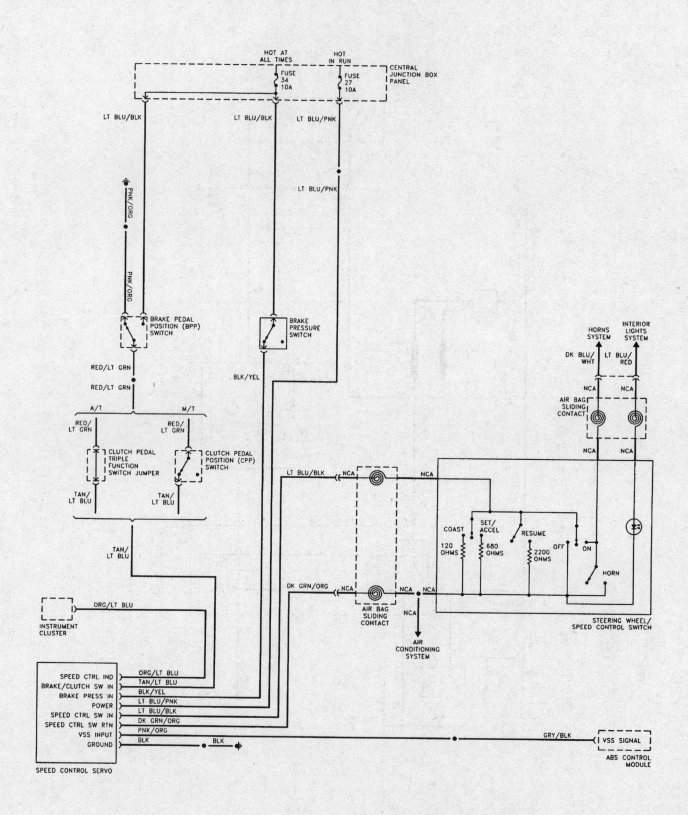

Cruise control system - 2002 and later gasoline models

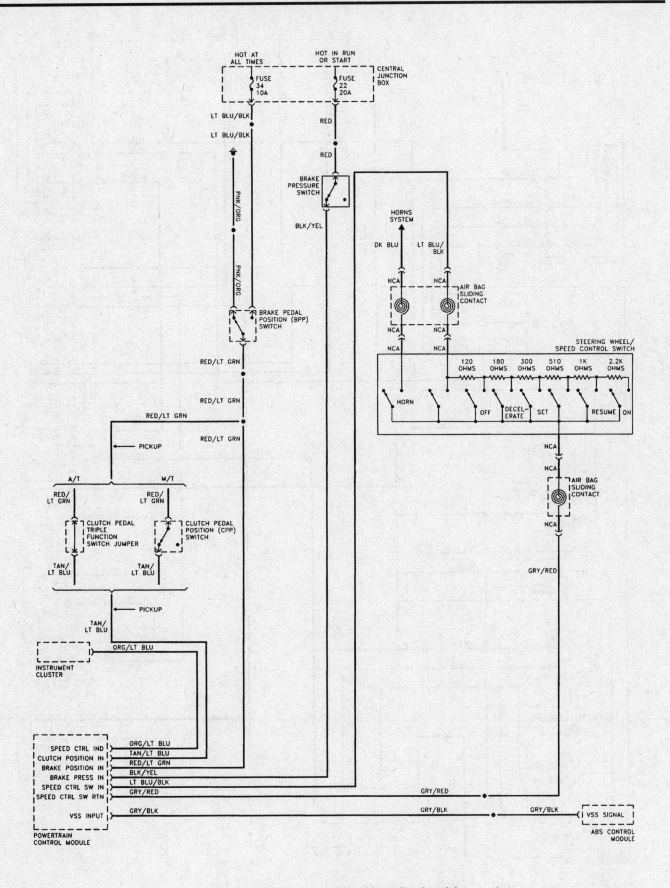

Cruise control system - 2002 and later diesel models

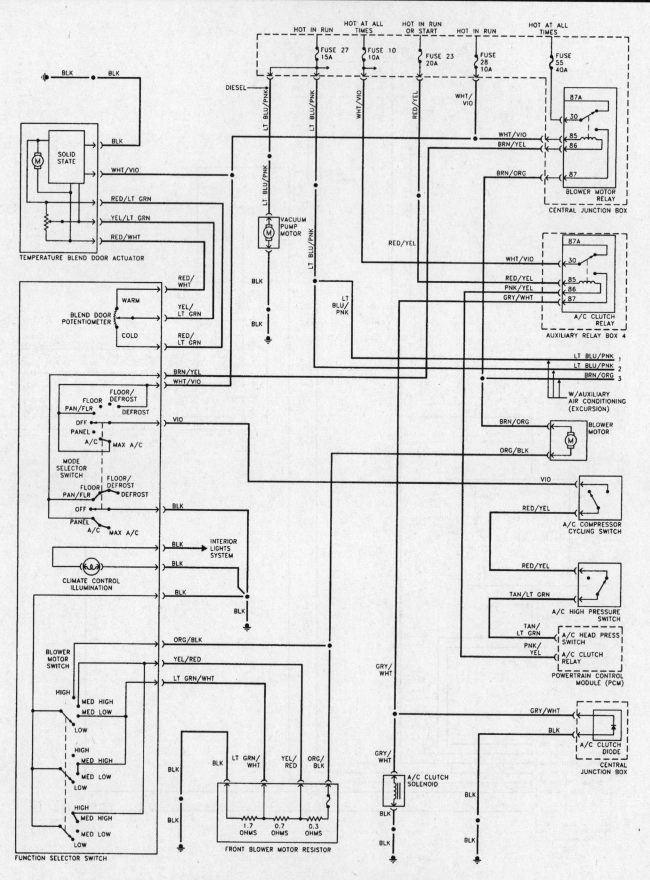

Manual air conditioning system - 2002 and later models (1 of 2)

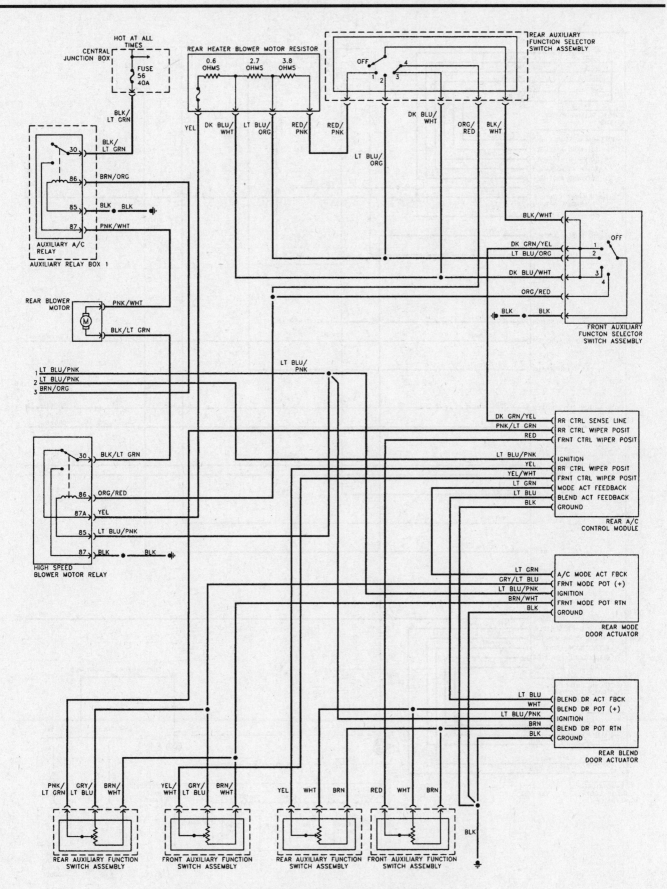

Manual air conditioning system - 2002 and later models (2 of 2)

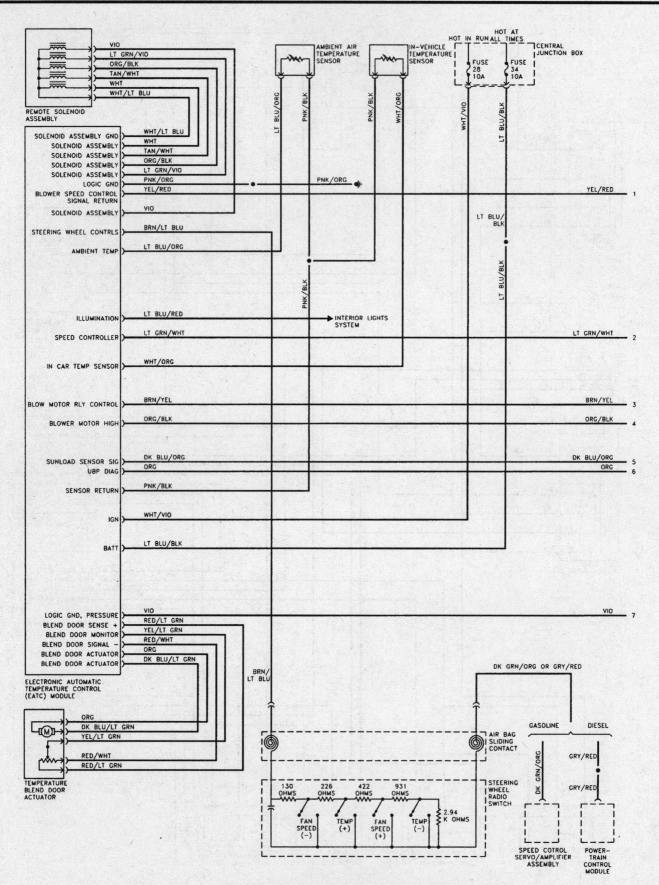

Automatic air conditioning system - 2002 and later Excursion models (1 of 2)

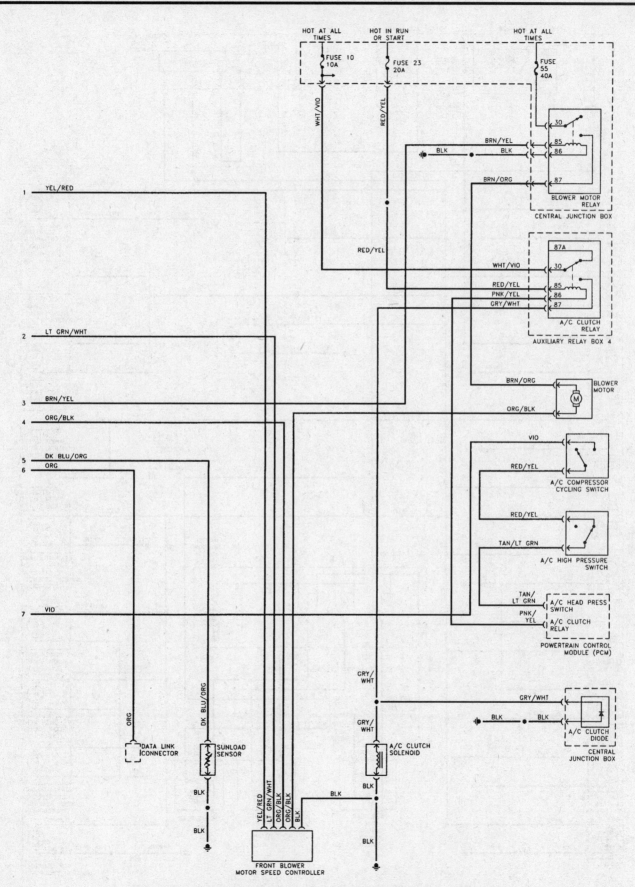

Automatic air conditioning system - 2002 and later Excursion models (2 of 2)

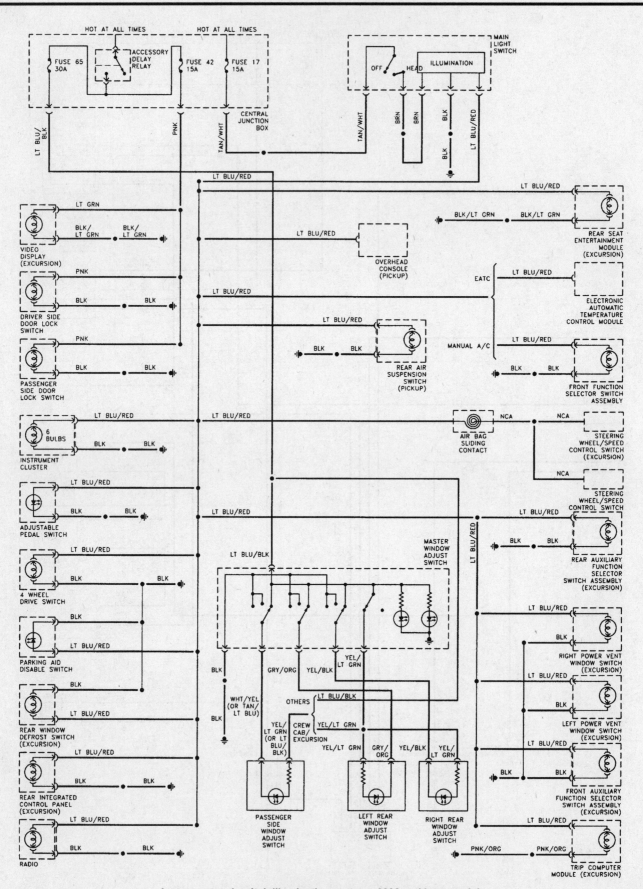

Instrument and switch illumination system - 2002 and later models

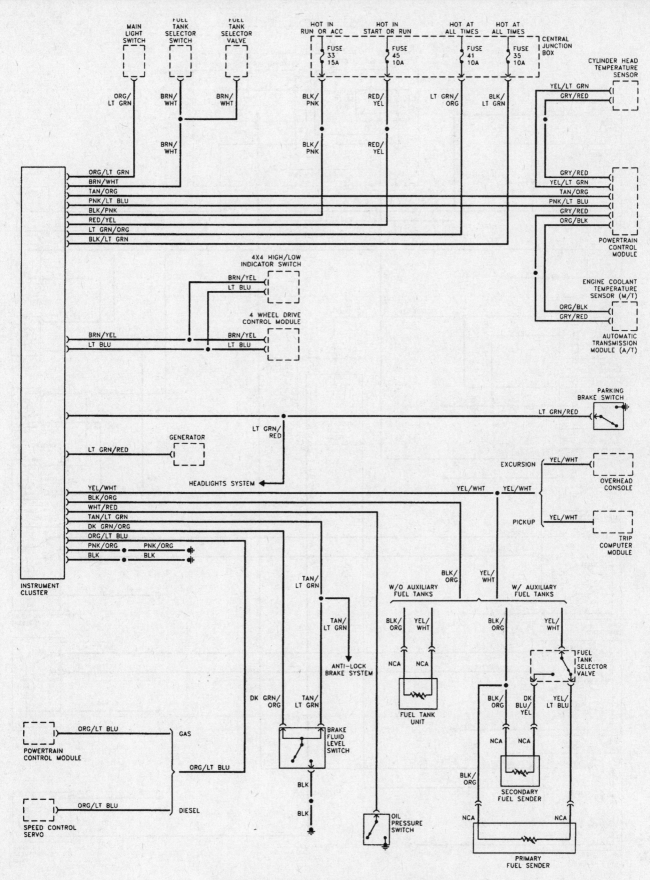

Warning light system - 2002 and later models

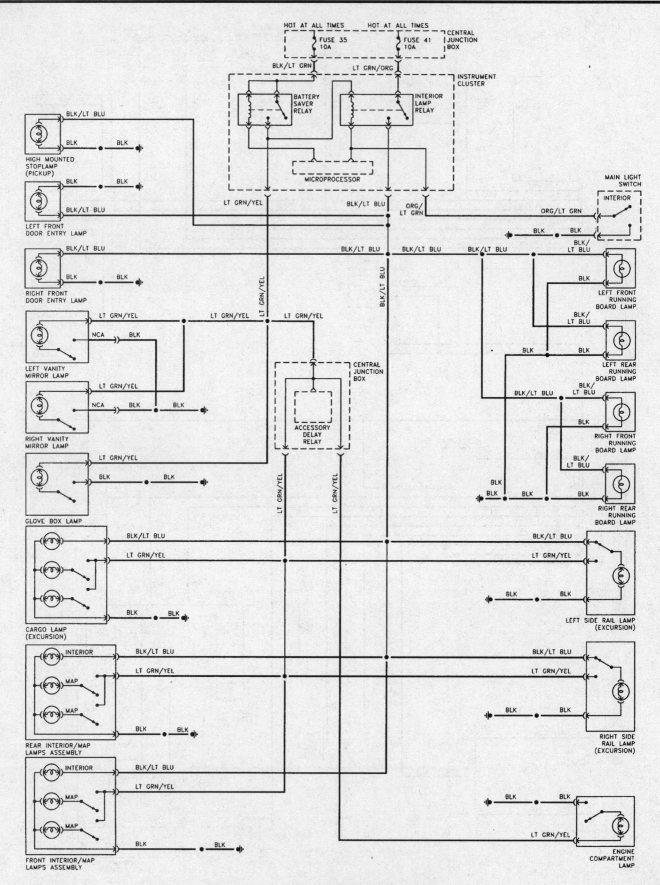

Interior lighting system - 2002 and later models

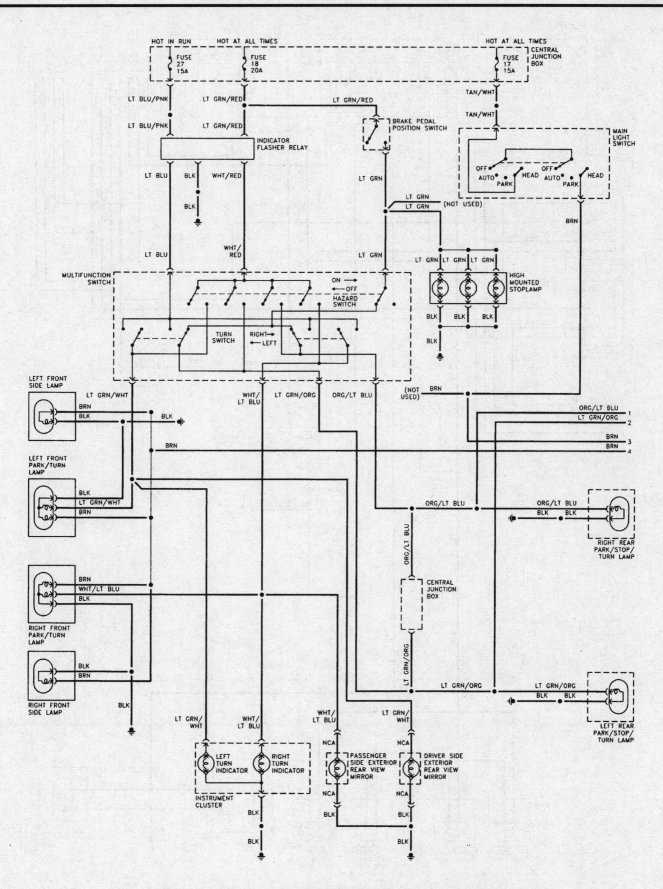

Exterior lighting system (except headlights) - 2002 and later Excursion models (1 of 2)

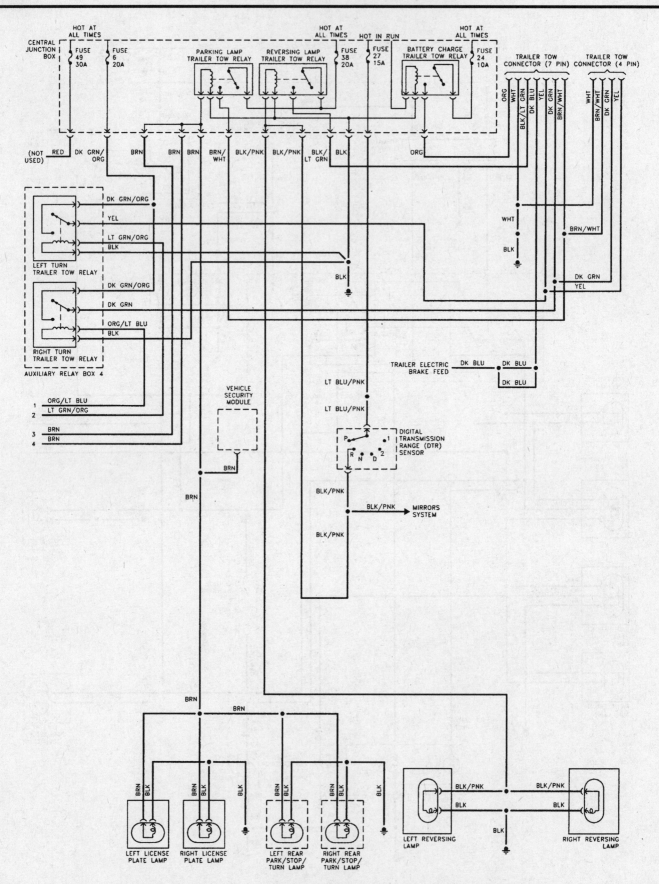

Exterior lighting system (except headlights) - 2002 and later Excursion models (2 of 2)

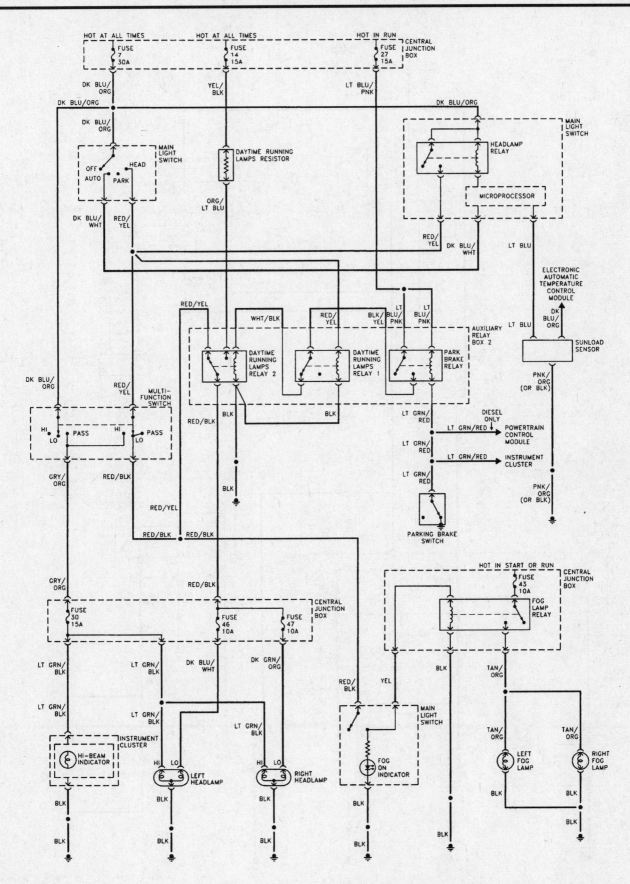

Headlight system (with Daytime Running Lights) - 2002 and later Excursion models

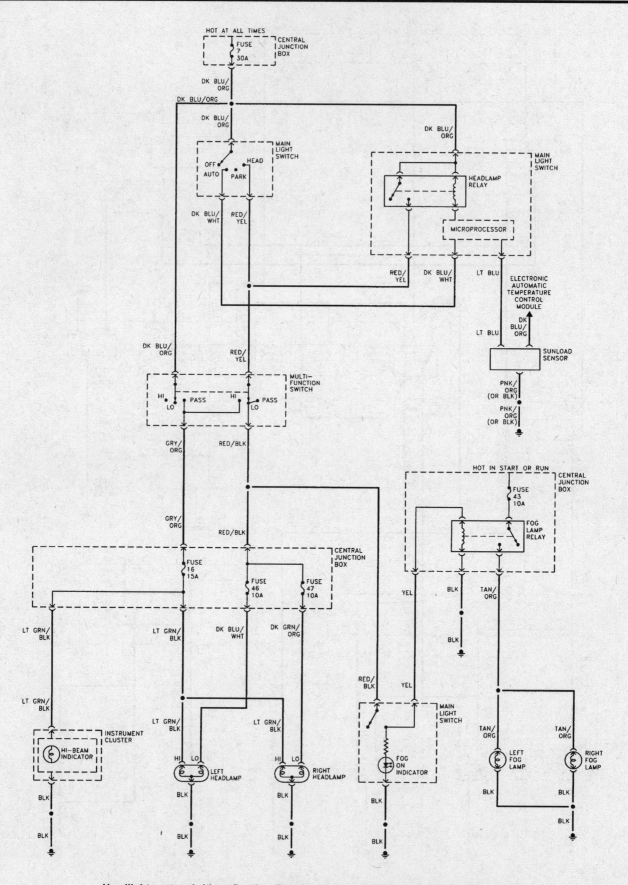

Headlight system (without Daytime Running Lights) - 2002 and later Excursion models

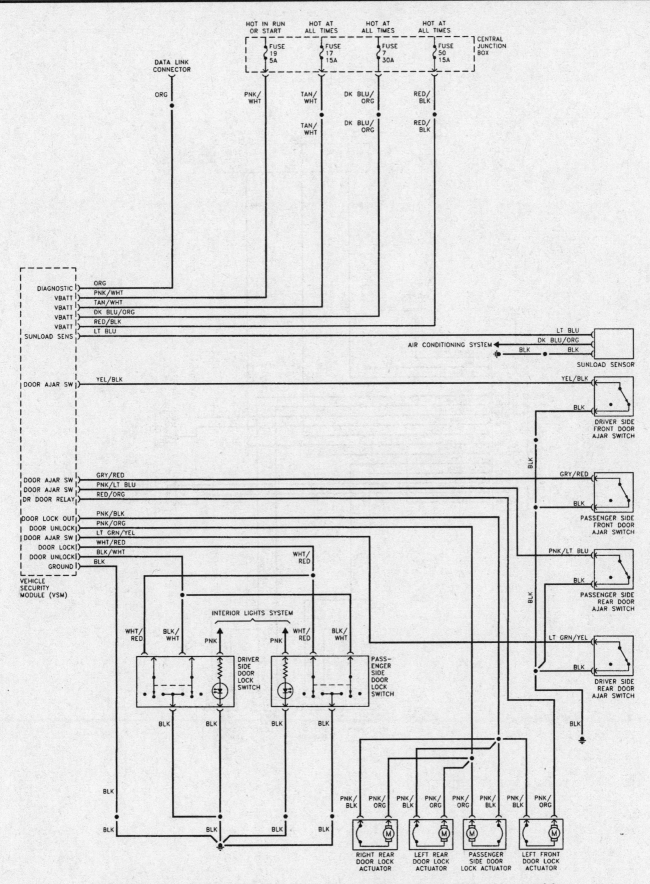

Power door lock system with keyless entry (crew cab pick-up models) - 2002 and later models

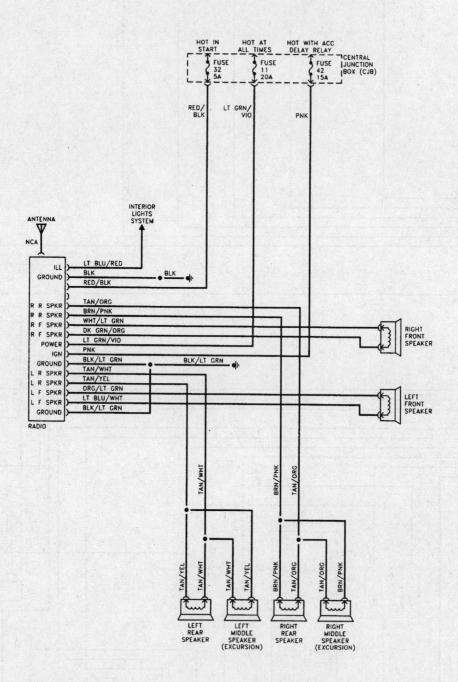

Radio system - 2002 and later models

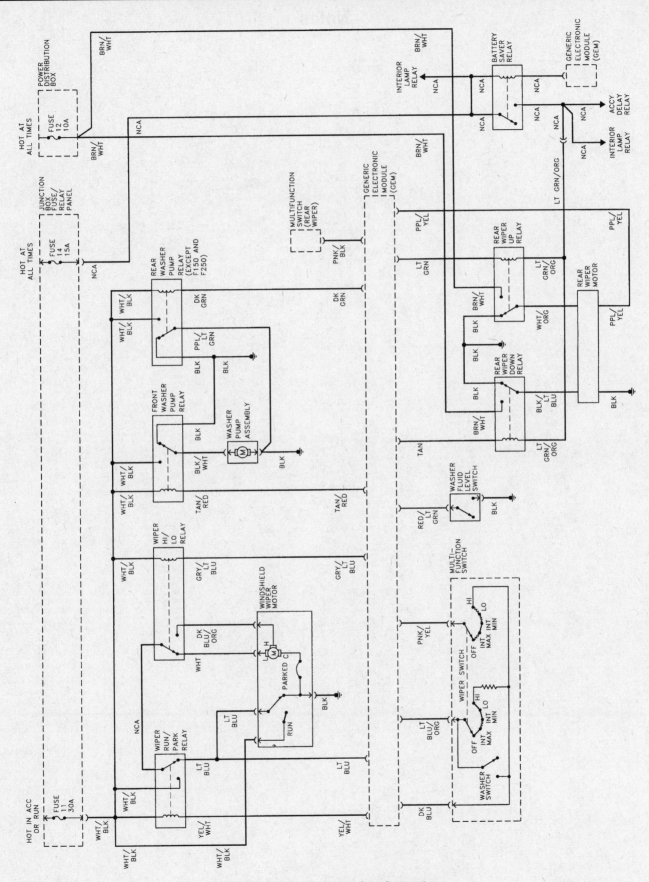

Typical windshield wiper and washer system

Notes

Index

A

About this manual, 0-5
Accelerator cable, replacement and adjustment, 4A-11
Accelerator pedal position sensor, replacement, 6-33
Air conditioning
    accumulator, removal and installation, 3-15
    and heater blower motor and resistor, replacement, 3-9
    and heater control assembly, removal and installation, 3-12
    and heating system, check and maintenance, 3-13
    auxiliary climate control assembly (Excursion models),
        removal and installation, 3-19
    auxiliary climate control blower motor and resistor
        (Excursion models), removal and installation, 3-20
    compressor, removal and installation, 3-15
    condenser, removal and installation, 3-17
    evaporator, removal and installation, 3-17
    pressure cycling switch, replacement, 3-19
Air filter
    check and replacement, 1-23
    housing, removal and installation, 4A-10
Airbag
    clockspring, removal and installation, 10-10
    system, general information, 12-15
Alternator, removal and installation, 5-8
Antenna and cable, replacement, 12-9
Antifreeze, general information, 3-2
Anti-lock brake system (ABS), general information, 9-2
Automatic transmission, 7B-1 through 7B-8
    auxiliary cooler, removal and installation, 7B-5
    diagnosis, general, 7B-1
    extension housing oil seal, replacement, 7A-2
    fluid
        and filter change, 1-26
        level check, 1-11
    overhaul, general information, 7B-7
    removal and installation, 7B-5
    shift
        cable, removal, installation and adjustment, 7B-3
        indicator cable, adjustment, 7B-2
        interlock system, description, check and actuator
          replacement, 7B-4

        lever, removal and installation, 7B-3
    transmission control switch, check and replacement, 7B-3
    transmission mount, check and replacement, 7A-2
    Transmission Range (TR) sensor, description, adjustment
        and replacement, 7B-3
Automotive chemicals and lubricants, 0-16
Auxiliary climate control
    assembly (Excursion models), removal and
        installation, 3-19
    blower motor and resistor (Excursion models), removal and
        installation, 3-20
Auxiliary cooler (automatic transmission), removal and
**   installation, 7B-5**
Axle assembly, removal and installation
    front, 8-11
    rear, 8-8
Axleshaft, removal and installation
    front, 8-10
    rear, 8-8

B

Balance shaft (V10 engine), removal and installation, 2A-13
Balljoints, replacement, 10-8
Barometric pressure (BARO) sensor (6.0L and 6.4L diesel
**   models), replacement, 6-33**
Battery
    cables, check and replacement, 5-5
    check and replacement, 5-3
    check, maintenance and charging, 1-14
    precautions and disconnection, 5-2
Blower motor and resistor, replacement
    auxiliary climate control, 3-20
    primary, 3-9
Body, 11-1
    maintenance, 11-1
    repair
        major damage, 11-3
        minor damage, 11-2
Booster battery (jump) starting, 0-15

Brakes, 9-1
Anti-lock Brake System (ABS), general information, 9-2
caliper, removal and installation, 9-6
disc, inspection, removal and installation, 9-6
fluid
    change, 1-28
    level check, 1-8
hoses and lines, check and replacement, 9-8
hydraulic system, bleeding, 9-8
light switch, check and replacement, 9-9
master cylinder, removal and installation, 9-7
pads, replacement, 9-3
parking brake shoes, replacement, 9-10
power brake booster, check, removal and installation, 9-9
system check, 1-21
Bulb replacement, 12-12
Bumpers, removal and installation, 11-7
Buying parts, 0-8

C

Cable replacement
accelerator, 4A-9
antenna, 12-9
battery, 5-5
hood release, 11-6
shift (automatic transmission), 7B-3
Caliper, disc brake, removal and installation, 9-6
Camshaft position (CMP) sensor, replacement, 6-31
Camshaft(s), removal, inspection and installation
diesel engine, 2C-12
gasoline engines, 2A-14
Capacities, lubricants and fluids, 1-2
Catalytic converter, 6-35
Center console, removal and installation, 11-14
Charging system
check, 5-7
general information and precautions, 5-7
Chassis electrical system, 12-1
Chassis lubrication, 1-14
Chemicals and lubricants, 0-16
Circuit breakers, general information, 12-4
Clutch
components, removal, inspection, adjustment and
    installation, 8-3
description and check, 8-2
hydraulic system, removal and installation, 8-2
release bearing, removal, inspection and installation, 8-3
start switch, removal and installation, 8-5
Clutch and driveline, 8-1
Coil spring (2WD models), removal and installation, 10-6
Coils, ignition, replacement, 1-31, 5-6
**Compressor, air conditioning, removal and
installation, 3-15**
Condenser, air conditioning, removal and installation, 3-17
Conversion factors, 0-17
Coolant level check, 1-8
Cooling, heating and air conditioning systems, 3-1
Cooling system
antifreeze, general information, 3-2

coolant temperature sending unit, check and
    replacement, 3-8
expansion tank, removal and installation, 3-4
fan and clutch, check, removal and installation, 3-4
radiator, removal and installation, 3-5
system
    check, 1-18
    servicing (draining, flushing and refilling), 1-25
thermostat, check and replacement, 3-3
water pump
    check, 3-7
Cowl cover, removal and installation, 11-15
Crankshaft oil seals, replacement
diesel engine, 2B-8
gasoline engines, 2A-26
**Crankshaft Position (CKP) sensor (gasoline models),
replacement, 6-30**
Crankshaft pulley, removal and installation
diesel engine, 2B-7
gasoline engines, 2A-7
Crankshaft, removal and installation, 2C-20
Cruise control system, description, 12-14
Cylinder compression check, 2C-5
**Cylinder head temperature sensor (gasoline models),
replacement, 6-30**
Cylinder heads, removal and installation
diesel engine, 2C-11
gasoline engines, 2A-22

D

Dashboard trim panels, removal and installation, 11-14
Daytime Running Lights (DRL), general information, 12-15
Diagnosis, 0-20
Diesel engine, in-vehicle repair procedures, 2B-1
Differential
lubricant
    change, 1-31
    level check, 1-23
pinion seal, replacement, 8-11
Disc brake
caliper, removal and installation, 9-6
disc, inspection, removal and installation, 9-6
pads, replacement, 9-3
Door
latch, lock cylinder and handles, removal and
    installation, 11-10
lock system, power, description, 12-15
removal, installation and adjustment, 11-9
trim panels, removal and installation, 11-7
window glass regulator, removal and installation, 11-11
window glass, removal and installation, 11-11
Drag link, removal and installation, 10-11
Drivebelt check and replacement, 1-28
Driveshaft
center bearing, check and replacement, 8-6
general information, 8-5
removal and installation, 8-6
universal joints
    general information, lubrication and check, 8-7
    replacement, 8-7

E

Electric shift motor (transfer case), replacement, 7C-1
Electric side view mirrors, description, 12-14
Electrical troubleshooting, general information, 12-1
Emissions and engine control systems, 6-1
Engine
    balance shaft (V10 engine), removal and installation, 2A-13
    camshaft(s), removal, inspection and installation
        diesel engine, 2C-12
        gasoline engines, 2A-14
    cooling fan and clutch, check, removal and installation, 3-4
    crankshaft oil seals, replacement
        diesel engine, 2B-8
        gasoline engines, 2A-26
    crankshaft pulley, removal and installation
        diesel engine, 2B-7
        gasoline engines, 2A-7
    crankshaft, removal and installation, 2C-20
    cylinder compression check, 2C-5
    cylinder heads, removal and installation
        diesel engine, 2C-11
        gasoline engines, 2A-22
    exhaust manifolds, removal and installation
        diesel engine, 2B-6
        gasoline engines, 2A-20
    firing order, 1-2
    flywheel/driveplate, removal and installation
        diesel engine, 2B-8
        gasoline engines, 2A-25
    front cover (diesel engine), removal and installation, 2C-12
    general overhaul procedures, 2C-1
    initial start-up and break-in after overhaul, 2C-23
    intake manifold (gasoline engines), removal and installation, 2A-18
    intake manifold covers (diesel engine), removal and installation, 2B-5
    mounts, check and replacement, 2A-27
    oil cooler, removal and installation, 3-21
    oil level check, 1-7
    oil pan, removal and installation
        diesel engine, 2C-11
        gasoline engines, 2A-23
    oil pressure check, 2C-4
    oil pump, removal and installation
        diesel engine, 2B-9
        gasoline engines, 2A-24
    overhaul
        disassembly sequence, 2C-10
        general information, 2C-3
        reassembly sequence, 2C-23
        terminology, 2C-24
    pistons and connecting rods, removal and installation, 2C-14
    rebuilding alternatives, 2C-7
    removal and installation, 2C-8
    removal, methods and precautions, 2C-7
    repair operations possible with the engine in the vehicle
        diesel engine, 2B-2
        gasoline engines, 2A-3
    rocker arms, removal, inspection and installation
        diesel engine, 2B-4
        gasoline engines, 2A-13
    timing chain cover, timing chains, tensioners and sprockets, removal, inspection and installation, gasoline engines, 2A-7
    Top Dead Center (TDC) for number one piston, locating (gasoline engines), 2A-4
    vacuum gauge diagnostic checks (gasoline engines), 2C-5
    valve covers, removal and installation
        diesel engine, 2B-3
        gasoline engines, 2A-4
    valve lash adjusters (gasoline engines), removal, inspection and installation, 2A-13
    valve springs, retainers and seals, removal and installation
        gasoline engines, 2A-17
    water pump
        check, 3-7
        removal and installation, 3-7
Engine Coolant Temperature (ECT) sensor (diesel models), replacement, 6-29
Engine electrical systems, 5-1
Engine electrical systems, general information, precautions and battery disconnection, 5-2
Engine oil and filter change, 1-12
Engine oil temperature sensor (diesel models), replacement, 6-30
Evaporative emissions control (EVAP) system, 6-35
Evaporator, air conditioning, removal and installation, 3-17
Exhaust Gas Recirculation (EGR) system, 6-34
Exhaust manifolds, removal and installation
    diesel engine, 2B-6
    gasoline engines, 2A-20
Exhaust pressure sensor (6.0L and 6.4L diesel models), replacement, 6-33
Exhaust system check, 1-17
Exhaust system servicing, general information, 4A-15
Expansion tank, removal and installation, 3-4
Extension housing oil seal, replacement, 7A-2

F

Fan and clutch, engine cooling, check, removal and installation, 3-4
Fault finding, 0-20
Filter replacement
    air, 1-23
    engine oil, 1-12
    fuel, 1-19
Firing order, engine, 1-2
Fluid level checks
    brake, 1-9
    clutch, 1-9
    differential, 1-23
    engine coolant, 1-9
    engine oil, 1-8
    manual transmission, 1-22
    power steering, 1-11
    transfer case, 1-22
    windshield washer, 1-10

Fluids and lubricants
    capacities, 1-2
    recommended, 1-1
Flywheel, inspection, 8-5
Flywheel/driveplate, removal and installation
    diesel engine, 2B-8
    gasoline engines, 2A-25
Fraction/decimal/millimeter equivalents, 0-19
Front axle assembly (4WD models), removal and installation, 8-11
Front axle I-beam and radius arm (2WD models), removal and installation, 10-8
Front cover (diesel engine), removal and installation, 2C-12
Front fender, removal and installation, 11-7
Front wheel bearing check, repack and adjustment, 1-27
Fuel
    filter replacement, 1-19
    glow plug system (diesel engine), general information and replacement, 4B-10
    system check, 1-18
Fuel and exhaust systems
    diesel engines, 4B-1
    gasoline engines, 4A-1
Fuel filter/water separator (diesel engine)
    draining, 1-12
    housing and fuel pressure regulator, replacement, 4B-6
Fuel heater (diesel engine), general information and replacement, 4B-7
Fuel injection system (gasoline engines), check, 4A-11
Fuel injectors, removal and installation
    diesel engine, 4B-9
    gasoline engines, 4A-11
Fuel level sending unit, replacement, 4A-10
Fuel lines and fittings, general information, 4A-4
Fuel pressure check (gasoline engines), 4A-4
Fuel pressure check and fuel pump/fuel conditioning module replacement, diesel engine, 4B-5
Fuel pressure regulator, replacement
    diesel engine, 4B-6
    gasoline engines, 4A-9
Fuel pressure relief procedure
    diesel engine, 4B-4
    gasoline engines, 4A-3
Fuel pump, removal and installation
    diesel engine, 4B-5
    gasoline engines, 4A-9
Fuel rail and injectors, removal and installation, 4A-13
Fuel system, general information
    diesel engine, 4B-3
    gasoline engines, 4A-2
Fuel tank
    cleaning and repair, 4A-8
    removal and installation, 4A-8
Fuel Tank Pressure (FTP) sensor, replacement, 6-32
Fuses and fusible links, general information, 12-3

G

Gasoline engines, in-vehicle repair procedures, 2A-1
General engine overhaul procedures, 2C-1

H

Hazard flasher and turn signal, check and replacement, 12-5
Headlight
    adjustment, 12-11
    bulb replacement, 12-11
    housing (aerodynamic type), replacement, 12-12
Heater and air conditioning control assembly, removal and installation, 3-12
Heater blower motor and resistor, replacement, 3-9
Heater core, removal and installation, 3-11
Heating and air conditioning system, check and maintenance, 3-13
High-pressure oil pump/high-pressure fuel injection pump (diesel engine), removal and installation, 4B-8
Hinges and locks, maintenance, 11-3
Hood
    and rear liftgate support struts, removal and installation, 11-3
    latch and release cable, removal and installation, 11-6
    removal, installation and adjustment, 11-3
Horn, replacement, 12-12
Hoses, underhood, check and replacement, 1-16
Hub bearing assembly and front axleshaft (4WD models), removal and installation, 8-10
Hub bearings and grease seal, rear, removal, inspection and installation, 8-9
Hub lock, removal and installation, 8-13
Hydraulic system, brake, bleeding, 9-8

I

Idle Air Control (IAC) valve (1999 through 2004 gasoline models), replacement, 6-32
Ignition
    coils, replacement, 5-6
    switch and key lock cylinder, replacement, 12-6
    system
        check, 5-6
        general information and precautions, 5-6
Initial start-up and break-in after overhaul, 2C-23
Instrument
    cluster bezel, removal and installation, 11-14
    cluster, removal and installation, 12-7
    panel switches, replacement, 12-6
Intake Air Temperature (IAT) sensor (diesel models), replacement, 6-29
Intake manifold (gasoline engines), removal and installation, 2A-18
Intake manifold covers (diesel engine), removal and installation, 2B-5
Intake Manifold Tuning system (1999 V8 gasoline models), general information and replacement, 4A-15
Intercooler (diesel engine), replacement, 4B-15
Introduction to the Ford Super Duty F-250, F-350 Pick-ups and Excursion, 0-5

Glow plug system (diesel engine), general information and replacement, 4B-10

J

Jacking and towing, 0-14
Jump starting the battery, 0-15

K

Key lock cylinder, replacement, 12-6
Knock sensor (gasoline models), replacement, 6-32

L

Leaf spring, removal and installation
    front, 10-7
    rear, 10-10
Liftgate and cargo doors (Excursion), removal, installation
    and adjustment, 11-12
Lubricants and chemicals, 0-16
Lubricants and fluids
    capacities, 1-2
    recommended, 1-1

M

Maintenance schedule, 1-7
Maintenance techniques, tools and working facilities, 0-8
Maintenance, routine, 1-1
Manifold Absolute Pressure (MAP) sensor (diesel models),
    replacement, 6-28
Manifold air heater (diesel engine), general information
    and replacement, 4B-7
Manual shift lever, transfer case, removal and
    installation, 7C-2
Manual transmission, 7A-1
    extension housing oil seal, replacement, 7A-2
    lubricant
        change, 1-31
        level check, 1-22
    overhaul, general information, 7A-4
    removal and installation, 7A-2
    shift lever, removal and installation, 7A-2
    transmission mount, check and replacement, 7A-2
Mass Airflow (MAF) sensor, replacement, 6-28
Master cylinder, brake, removal and installation, 9-7

O

Oil and filter, engine, change, 1-11
Oil cooler, removal and installation, 3-21
Oil pan, removal and installation
    diesel engine, 2C-11
    gasoline engines, 2A-23
Oil pressure check, 2C-4
Oil pump, removal and installation
    diesel engine, 2B-9
    gasoline engines, 2A-24

Oil temperature sensor (diesel models), replacement, 6-30
On Board Diagnostic (OBD) system and trouble codes, 6-3
Overhaul procedures, engine, 2C-1
Oxygen sensor (gasoline models), general information
    and replacement, 6-31

P

Pads, disc brake, replacement, 9-3
Parking brake shoes, replacement, 9-10
Parts, replacement, buying, 0-8
Pilot bearing, inspection and replacement, 8-5
Pinion seal, differential, replacement, 8-11
Pistons and connecting rods, removal and
    installation, 2C-14
Positive Crankcase Ventilation (PCV) system, 6-33
Positive Crankcase Ventilation (PCV) valve check, 1-30
Power brake booster, check, removal and installation, 9-9
Power door lock system, description, 12-15
Power steering
    fluid level check, 1-11
    pump, removal and installation, 10-14
    system, bleeding, 10-14
Power window system, description, 12-14
Powertrain Control Module (PCM), removal and
    installation, 6-27
Pressure cycling switch, air conditioning,
    replacement, 3-19
Pulse vacuum hub lock solenoid, replacement, 8-13

R

Radiator grille, removal and installation, 11-6
Radiator, removal and installation, 3-5
Radio and speakers, removal and installation, 12-9
Radius arm (2WD models), removal and installation, 10-8
Rear axle
    assembly, removal and installation, 8-8
    axleshaft, removal and installation, 8-8
    general information, 8-8
Rear wheel hub bearings and grease seal, removal,
    inspection and installation, 8-9
Rear window defogger, check and repair, 12-10
Rebuilding alternatives, engine, 2C-7
Recommended lubricants and fluids, 1-1
Relays, general information and testing, 12-4
Release bearing, clutch, removal, inspection and
    installation, 8-3
Repair operations possible with the engine in the
    vehicle, 2A-3
    diesel engine, 2B-2
    gasoline engines, 2A-3
Rocker arms, removal, inspection and installation
    diesel engine, 2B-4
    gasoline engines, 2A-13
Rotor, disc brake, inspection, removal and installation, 9-6
Routine maintenance schedule, 1-6
Routine maintenance, 1-1

S

Safety first!, 0-18
Scheduled maintenance, 1-6
Seat belt check, 1-17
Seats, removal and installation, 11-15
Shift
    cable (automatic transmission), removal, installation and
        adjustment, 7B-3
    indicator cable, adjustment, 7B-2
    interlock system, description, check and actuator
        replacement, 7B-4
    lever, removal and installation
        automatic transmission, 7B-3
        manual transmission, 7A-2
    range selector switch, transfer case (electric-shift models),
        replacement, 7C-2
Shock absorbers, removal and installation
    front, 10-5
    rear, 10-9
Side view mirrors
    electric, description, 12-14
    removal and installation, 11-12
Spark plug
    check and replacement, 1-30
    torque specifications, 1-3
    type and gap, 1-2
Speakers, removal and installation, 12-9
Stabilizer bar, removal and installation
    front, 10-6
    rear, 10-10
Starter motor
    and circuit, in-vehicle check, 5-9
    removal and installation, 5-10
Starting system, general information and precautions, 5-8
Steering
    and suspension check, 1-20
    column
        cover, removal and installation, 11-15
        removal and installation, 10-12
        switches, replacement, 12-5
    gear, removal and installation, 10-12
    knuckle, removal and installation, 10-8
    linkage, removal and installation, 10-13
    wheel and airbag clockspring, removal and
        installation, 10-10
Support struts (hood and rear liftgate), removal and
    installation, 11-3
Suspension and steering systems, 10-1

T

Tailgate latch, handle and lock cylinder, removal and
    installation, 11-13
Tailgate, removal, installation and adjustment, 11-12
Temperature sending unit, engine coolant, check and
    replacement, 3-8
Thermostat, check and replacement, 3-3
Throttle body, check, removal and installation, 4A-13

Throttle Position Sensor (TPS) (gasoline models),
    replacement, 6-27
Throw-out bearing, clutch, removal, inspection and
    installation, 8-3
Tie-rod ends, removal and installation, 10-12
Timing chains (gasoline engines), removal, inspection
    and installation, 2A-7
Tire and tire pressure checks, 1-10
Tire rotation, 1-15
Tools and working facilities, 0-8
Top Dead Center (TDC) for number one piston, locating
    (gasoline engines), 2A-4
Torque specifications
    brake caliper mounting bolts, 9-2
    connecting rod bearing cap bolts, 2C-1
    cylinder head bolts
        diesel engine, 2C-1
        gasoline engines, 2A-2
    main bearing cap bolts, 2C-2
    spark plugs, 1-3
    suspension and steering, 10-1
    thermostat housing bolts, 3-1
    water pump bolts, 3-1
    wheel lug nuts, 1-3
    *Other torque specifications can be found in the Chapter that
        deals with the particular component being serviced*
Towing the vehicle, 0-14
Track bar (4WD models), removal and installation, 10-9
Transfer case, 7C-1
    electric shift motor, replacement, 7C-1
    lubricant
        change, 1-31
        level check, 1-22
    manual shift lever, removal and installation, 7C-2
    oil seal, replacement, 7C-2
    overhaul, general information, 7C-3
    removal and installation, 7C-3
    shift range selector switch (electric-shift models),
        replacement, 7C-2
Transmission mount, check and replacement, 7A-2
Transmission Range (TR) sensor, description, adjustment
    and replacement, 7B-3
Transmission, automatic, 7B-1
    auxiliary cooler, removal and installation, 7B-5
    control switch, check and replacement, 7B-3
    diagnosis, general, 7B-1
    extension housing oil seal, replacement, 7A-2
    fluid
        and filter change, 1-24
        level check, 1-10
    overhaul, general information, 7B-7
    removal and installation, 7B-5
    shift
        cable, removal, installation and adjustment, 7B-3
        indicator cable, adjustment, 7B-2
        interlock system, description, check and actuator
            replacement, 7B-4
        lever, removal and installation, 7B-3
    transmission control switch, check and replacement, 7B-3
    transmission mount, check and replacement, 7A-2

Transmission Range (TR) sensor, description, adjustment
and replacement, 7B-3
Transmission, manual, 7A-1
extension housing oil seal, replacement, 7A-2
lubricant
change, 1-29
level check, 1-20
overhaul, general information, 7A-4
removal and installation, 7A-2
shift lever, removal and installation, 7A-2
transmission mount, check and replacement, 7A-2
Trouble code chart
diesel engines, 6-14
gasoline engines, 6-5
Trouble codes, accessing, 6-4
Troubleshooting, 0-20
Tune-up and routine maintenance, 1-1
Tune-up general information, 1-8
Turbocharger
general information and inspection, 4B-11
removal, installation and wastegate adjustment, 4B-12
**Turn signal and hazard flasher, check and
replacement, 12-5**

U

Underhood hose check and replacement, 1-17
**Universal joints, general information, lubrication and
check, 8-7**
Universal joints, replacement, 8-7
Upholstery and carpets, maintenance, 11-2

V

Vacuum gauge diagnostic checks (gasoline engines), 2C-5
Valve covers, removal and installation
diesel engine, 2B-3
gasoline engines, 2A-4
**Valve springs, retainers and seals, removal and
installation, gasoline engines, 2A-17**
Vehicle identification numbers, 0-6
Vehicle Speed Sensor (VSS), replacement, 6-32
Vinyl trim, maintenance, 11-2

W

Water pump
check, 3-7
removal and installation, 3-7
Water separator/fuel filter, draining, 1-12
Wheel
alignment, general information, 10-16
bearing assembly and front axleshaft (4WD models),
removal and installation, 8-10
bearings and grease seal, rear, removal, inspection and
installation, 8-9
bearings, front (2WD models), check, repack and
adjustment, 1-25
studs, replacement, 10-15
Wheels and tires, general information, 10-15
Window system, power, description, 12-14
Windshield and fixed glass, replacement, 11-3
Windshield wiper blade inspection and replacement, 1-16
Wiper motor, check and replacement, 12-7
Wiring diagrams, general information, 12-16
Working facilities, 0-8

Notes